Dramatic Romance

Dramatic Romance

PLAYS, THEORY, AND CRITICISM

EDITED BY

HOWARD FELPERIN
Yale University

Harcourt Brace Jovanovich, Inc.

NEW YORK   CHICAGO   SAN FRANCISCO   ATLANTA

Cover drawing by Ben Shahn, © Estate of Ben Shahn

ISBN: 0-15-518362-1

Library of Congress Catalog Card Number: 72-93697

Printed in the United States of America

ACKNOWLEDGMENTS

HARCOURT BRACE JOVANOVICH, INC. for *The Alcestis of Euripides* translated by Dudley Fitts and Robert Fitzgerald, copyright, 1936, by Harcourt Brace Jovanovich, Inc.; copyright, 1964, by Dudley Fitts and Robert Fitzgerald. Reprinted by permission of the publisher.
>   CAUTION: All rights, including professional, amateur, motion picture, recitation, lecturing, public reading, radio broadcasting, and television are strictly reserved. Inquiries on all rights should be addressed to Harcourt Brace Jovanovich, Inc., 757 Third Avenue, New York, N.Y. 10017.

For *The Cocktail Party,* copyright 1950, by T. S. Eliot. Reprinted by permission of Harcourt Brace Jovanovich, Inc.
>   CAUTION: This play is fully protected by copyright and is subject to royalty. No performance, professional or amateur, may be given without a license. Applications for licenses for stock and amateur performances in the United States and Canada should be made to Samuel French, Inc., 25 West 45th Street, New York, New York 10036 or Samuel French (Canada) Ltd., 27 Grenville Street, Toronto 5, Ontario, Canada. All other applications should be addressed to The League of Dramatists, 84 Drayton Gardens, London, S.W. 10.

For *The Tempest* from *Shakespeare: The Complete Works* edited by G. B. Harrison, copyright, 1948, 1952, by Harcourt Brace Jovanovich, Inc. and reprinted with their permission.

HOUGHTON MIFFLIN COMPANY for J. H. Wilson: John Gay's *Beggar's Opera,* from *Six Eighteenth-Century Plays*. Houghton Mifflin Company. Reprinted by permission.

THE UNIVERSITY OF MINNESOTA PRESS for *The Caucasian Chalk Circle,* Bentley, Eric, trans. *Parables for the Theatre*. University of Minnesota Press, Minneapolis. Copyright 1947, 1948, 1961, 1963 E. Bentley.

CONTENTS

Plays

Theory

Criticism

INTRODUCTION

Though tragedy, comedy, and satire have engaged students of literature from Aristotle and Horace onward, only recently has romance begun to be taken seriously as a literary genre. During the early part of this century, for example, it was usual for scholars to regard Shakespeare's final romances, including *The Tempest,* as "unexacting and agreeable dreams," the by-products of alleged boredom or fatigue or even senility on the part of the aging playwright. In the same era and spirit, William Archer, Ibsen's first English translator, dismissed *When We Dead Awaken* as "deserting the domain of reality [for] the wholly impossible, the inconceivable," and as "one of the premonitions of [Ibsen's] coming end." Ironically, Shakespeare and Ibsen had themselves supplied the touchstones, in the form of their "mature" social tragedies, that were used to disvalue their late plays. Yet the very fact that both great playwrights chose to write a very different kind of drama toward the end of their careers than they had previously should itself caution us against readily accepting these disparaging assessments of their final works. The critical principle on which these judgments are based—that the imaginative life of an author is subject to the same inexorable process of growth, maturity, and decline as the life of a natural organism—is by no means certain.

The statements quoted above were made in the spirit of "realism," theatrical and philosophical, that dominated the stage from the Renaissance until well into this century. There have since been attempts to redeem the final romances of Shakespeare and Ibsen (and to revive romance in general), but they have too often proceeded only by idealizing those plays into mystical intuitions of approaching death and transfiguration. To idealize romance on these grounds, just as much as to debunk it on realistic grounds, is misleadingly to isolate it from the rest of our literary experience and from the rest of an author's work. Ibsen himself exploded such mystifications when he remarked that he would write his last play in verse if only he knew which would be his last play. But if romance is not to be viewed as the by-product of either fanciful senescence or mystical revelation, then what did move not only Shakespeare and Ibsen but such diversely and distinctively "realistic" playwrights as Euripides and Brecht to turn, on occasion, to romance?

Allowing for historical differences in theatrical conditions—the Greek theater of Dionysus, for example, with its reliance on masks and music, could not be considered "realistic" or "naturalistic" by modern standards—romance has always been the mode in which the imagination enjoys its freest expression. Relatively uninhibited by psychological norms of causality and motivation or by neoclassical conventions of spatial and temporal unity—the *sine qua non* of naturalistic or illusionistic drama—romance offers the dramatist a unique opportunity to explore the imaginative resources of his art. This is not to suggest that the playwright turns to romance for a holiday or respite from the rigors of tragedy, comedy, or satire, for that would only support the prejudice that romance is somehow less "serious" than other modes. Rather, the mode enables him to examine overtly the imaginative function itself—that which underlies all fictional modes, even the most naturalistic.

It is not surprising, therefore, to find that artists or artist-figures often occupy a central place within romance—Prospero and Rubek are examples from the present collection; nor is it surprising that in the greatest romances such figures are not simply aggrandized. In each case, the dangers and perversities of imagination are revealed as much as its saving power. Through such figures the skilled naturalistic playwright, particularly as he nears the end of his career, can reflect upon the illusion-making powers he has exercised theretofore, albeit in more covert forms—the essence of naturalism being the concealment of art through the techniques of art. The last romances of Shakespeare and Ibsen, it has often been noted, have a recapitulatory relation to their previous work, but one that suggests not fatigue—the playwright repeating himself—but a new self-consciousness—the playwright revising himself and reviewing his past achievements.

Though romance has held a special challenge of self-reflection for the dramatist, its audience appeal has nonetheless been timeless and universal. Originating in myth, folktale, and balladry—what W. B. Yeats once termed "the book of the people"—romance has always retained a distinctly popular cast. This may help to account for its having been so long neglected by critics primarily concerned with "high" culture and "serious" art, with, in sum, the "classics." As the fictional mode closest to dream and fantasy, romance typically moves toward a happy, even "Hollywood," ending, illustrating the triumph of human will or desire over the determinisms that dominate other fictional modes, particularly tragedy and satire. It is true, as Harold Bloom points out (pp. 208–12), that romance in its Romantic and post-Romantic form often takes a downward or inward turn, muting the triumphs toward which it moves; among the playwrights represented here, this is most strikingly the case with Ibsen. But a more characteristic tendency of the mode is to defy all reality-principles, even death itself, as is well illustrated in the eleventh-hour reprieve of Macheath in *The Beggar's Opera:*

PLAYER. Why then, friend, this is a downright deep tragedy. The catastrophe is manifestly wrong, for an opera must end happily.

BEGGAR. Your objection, sir, is very just, and is easily removed; for you must allow that in this kind of drama, 'tis no matter how absurdly things are brought about. So—you rabble there! run and cry a reprieve!—let the prisoner be brought back to his wives in triumph.

PLAYER. All this we must do, to comply with the taste of the town.

The Beggar's Opera suggests through its title a further dimension of the "popularity" of romance: what Northrop Frye terms its "genuinely proletarian element." This is not simply a matter of the apparent social subversiveness of such plays as *The Beggar's Opera* and *The Caucasian Chalk Circle*—for each of them can also be seen as socially conservative—but of the aesthetic subversiveness of the mode itself. In its tendency to ally itself with music and spectacle, romance constantly threatens to break down the boundaries that high culture has established between the arts in order to ensure their purity. When opera was introduced in the seventeenth century, it was a decidedly popular form regarded with suspicion by many theorists of pure drama. Saint-Evremond's view of opera as a "bizarre mixture of poetry and music where the writer and the composer, equally embarrassed by one another, go to a lot of trouble to create an execrable work" is shared by such French neoclassicists as Boileau and Voltaire. The ease with which opera appropriates romance materials is evident in Gluck's *Alceste* and Dryden's *Tempest,* and Mozart, Wagner, and Richard Strauss have all adopted and transformed works of vernacular romance. In our own age the genre of Broadway musical comedy (along with its Hollywood counterpart) is perhaps the principal incarnation of romance at its most popular (or, as some would no doubt say, at its most vulgar) and illustrates how easily the spirited synesthesia of romance can collapse into anesthesia.

For all its freedom and flexibility, however, romance at its best is not a mode in which "anything goes" nor, Gay's Beggar to the contrary, one in which " 'tis no matter how absurdly things are brought about." It is precisely because of its tendency toward sweet anarchy that romance must and can find ways of guarding against charges of escapism or solipsism, dangers particularly acute for works that resort to magic or miracle in bringing off their resolutions: the "best-of-all-possible-worlds" is always vulnerable to being dismissed as the "best-of-all-*im*possible-worlds." Thus, romance calls upon its chief resource of imaginative freedom in order to counter that freedom, and does so by co-opting within itself the forces of other, less indulgent, fictional modes—tragedy, for example, or satire. By having his Beggar and Player call attention to the operatic "absurdity" of Macheath's reprieve, Gay ironizes the romance ending of his play and disarms our skepticism by giving voice to it himself. The heroic and romantic dimension of Gay's play, as William Empson shows, is not destroyed, but rather preserved, by self-mockery. Similarly, the experience Shakespeare and Ibsen gained in writing more naturalistic dramas was not left behind when each playwright turned to romance: it was retained as a positive asset. Indeed the naturalistic techniques of tight plotting and consistent characterization serve to ballast the potential extravagance of the romantic imagination. Romance may thus subsume tragedy, as in *Alcestis* and *When We Dead Awaken,* or satire, as in *The Beggar's Opera,* while still remaining—in fact, in order to remain —romance.

This raises the question of the usefulness of generic distinctions among works of literature and the rationale behind my selections for this volume. In choosing the plays I have tried to respect two antagonistic principles: that the selections represent the romance mode in its most typical and recurrent aspects—the common features that enable us to speak of a "mode" or a "genre" in the first place—and that each play have some claim to distinction, even to the status of masterpiece. These two principles are antagonistic because a "distinguished" work cannot, by definition, be "typical." Yet we must know the convention in order to apprehend and appreciate the masterpiece that transforms and transcends convention. This might be an argument for also including some conventional or bad romances (of which there is no scarcity) in order to highlight the excellence of the masterpieces. Yet each of these plays already casts and casts out, so to speak, its own pale shadow, the conventional potboiler or melodrama it might have been had its playwright been less of a master. The conventional motifs of romance—resurrection, rebirth, reunion—are present in each of these works, forming a tissue of parallels and interconnections among them and with other romances, good and bad. But they are present in each play in a distinctive form, a form that departs significantly from the facile formulas offered by lesser romancers. Consider that Alcestis, though resurrected, cannot speak; that Antonio and Caliban remain unredeemed; that the price of Rubek's awakening is death; that the ascendancy of Azdak is referred to as a brief and past golden age, *"almost* an age of justice." In each case, the conventional triumph of romance is so qualified as to defy reduction to mere conventionality, thereby ensuring the play's real triumph.

It might be objected that several of the plays contained here are not romances at all—*The Beggar's Opera* is usually discussed as a satire, *The Cocktail Party* as a comedy, *Alcestis* as a tragedy—and that to include them under the rubric of romance is willful or eccentric. But as I have tried to suggest, the genre of a work is not fixed and innate but exists only in relation to other works. In fact, insofar as a work defines itself by and against other works, it implies at any given point the possibility of other genres. Genre is not a fixed Platonic essence but a provisional set of guidelines calculated to aid in the creation and interpretation of the specific work, very different acts from mere imitation or pigeonholing. As one critic has recently written, "If the nexus between a genre and a single work is rather puzzling, we need not be reminded of the virtues, and even the necessity, of studious puzzlement. Genres . . . condition and incite the questioning of literary works. The dynamics of the history of genres shows that this basically fruitful questioning never ceases."* When William Empson,

---

* Claudio Guillén, *Literature as System* (Princeton: Princeton University Press, 1971), p. 122.

for example, discusses *The Beggar's Opera* as a version of pastoral, he brings aspects of it to light that are scarcely visible when the play is seen through the grid of eighteenth-century political satire. Far from being arbitrary or anachronistic, Empson's perception of the interaction in the play between high and low life, and between high and low art, develops the implications of the suggestion, by Jonathan Swift, that Gay write a "Newgate pastoral."

The other critical essays are chosen on the same principle: to reveal, through various approaches, the peculiarly romantic character of each play, while respecting its autonomy as a work of art. More intensive in focus than the theoretical essays that precede them, these later essays are intended to mediate between genre and work, to provide the student with a handhold on each of the plays and the instructor with a point of departure for discussion. The theoretical essays, in their turn, trace the large structural and historical contours of the mode. Northrop Frye, the foremost modern theorist of romance, ranges over its full length and breadth in verse, prose, and drama and distinguishes its recurrent patterns, motifs, and archetypes. Harold Bloom addresses himself to the burdens and dangers that beset the Romantic poet, particularly the English Romantic, in his attempt to revive the romantic forms of his Renaissance precursors. Though none of the English Romantics are represented here, Bloom's remarks bear directly on Ibsen and Eliot. The essay by Yeats—at once the plea of a man of letters, and the program of a practicing poet, for a return to romantic drama—well illustrates how that mode is not only timeless and universal in itself but in many ways fundamental to the study of all other modes.

HOWARD FELPERIN

I

PLAYS

Alcestis

BY EURIPIDES

TRANSLATED BY DUDLEY FITTS
AND ROBERT FITZGERALD

Alcestis, the earliest of Euripides' surviving plays, was first performed in
438 B.C. at the Great Dionysia, an annual festival in honor of the god
Dionysus. Like most of Euripides' plays, *Alcestis* is disturbing and provocative, in spite of, or perhaps because of, its happy ending. In an effort
to rationalize the action and justify the unexpected ending, many have
viewed the play as an illustration of wifely courage overcoming husbandly
cowardice or as a vindication of exemplary friendship and hospitality; but
Euripidean drama eludes such simple formulations. Its human protago-
nists are largely unaware of and unaccountable for the shape of their des-
tinies, and not even the gods seem wholly in control. In its surprising
outcome, *Alcestis* anticipates several of Euripides' later plays in which
catastrophe is miraculously avoided and tragedy redeemed: namely, *Helen,*
Ion, Iphigenia in Tauris, and *Iphigenia at Aulis.* Each moves toward the
celebration of the mystery and wonder of an action that finally defies rational explanation. It is no surprise that scholars have yet to decide on a
classification for these plays, particularly since in them Euripides departs
from Aristotle's prescriptions for tragedy—but they may not unjustly be
called the first dramatic romances.

Persons Represented

APOLLO

DEATH

CHORUS OF PHERAIAN CITIZENS

A MAIDSERVANT

ALCESTIS

ADMETOS

A CHILD [EUMELOS]

HERAKLES

PHERES

A SERVANT

SCENE: *Before the palace of* ADMETOS, *in Pherai* *

[*Enter from the palace* APOLLO, *clothed in white, masked, armed with golden bow. He faces the house, and apostrophizes it in a declamatory tone.*]

APOLLO. House of Admetos, where I brought myself to share the food of slaves—and I a god!

[*To the audience*]

Zeus's providence. He had stabbed my son, Asklêpios, with lightning, and I, raging, cut down his fire-forgers, the Wheeleyes;[1] and for penalty the Father of Heaven bound me servant to death-bound man.

So I came here to be a cowherd in a stranger's country. His house I have cared for to this day. Returning good for good, I saved him even from death when I tricked the three fatal Sisters, forcing their word for it that he need not go down into the dark land if he found a friend to take his place among the Dead.[2]

A friend?

Admetos went to all his friends in turn, to his father and his mother also; and he found none but his wife who dared to die for him, dared to give up the sweet sunlight for him! None but his wife: and now in the house they are comforting her, for she is fainting; this is the day appointed for her death; and I must leave the dear shelter of this place, not to be stained with it.

For see: already Thánatos, priest of the dying, has come to lead her down to the sad world under ground.[3]

[*Enter the figure of* DEATH, *shrouded in black, masked, holding a naked sword.*]

So you have come, Death. You have remembered her day.

DEATH. Prince of Light, have you come to quarrel with me in this house again? Will you assume again those rights that only Hell should use? That you charmed the Sisters, that your twisting slippery tricks delayed Admetos' death, I know; but why you stand armed at the door, bright guardian of Alcestis, I do not know. Has she not promised— to save her husband's life, Apollo— has she not promised to die? And on this day?

---

* The scene is Pherai, a town in Thessaly founded by Pherês, the father of Admetos. Here Apollo, exiled from Heaven for killing the Cyclopês, has spent nine years *incognito* as a common herdsman in the employ of the King. Within the last year Admetos has learned from an oracle that he is fated shortly to die. Apollo, grateful for the kindly treatment he has received as herdsman, has persuaded the Three Fates to alter their decree: Admetos need not die if he can find someone to die in his place.

1. Asklêpios, a physician, son of Apollo, was killed by Zeus for presuming to push his skill too far: he had succeeded in reviving patients from death. In revenge Apollo killed the Cyclopês, the one-eyed armorers of Zeus who had fashioned the thunderbolt that struck Asklêpios down.

2. We do not know how Apollo persuaded the Fates to change their decree, and the event itself seems almost without parallel. Not unnaturally, interested opponents of

the deal attributed the god's success to the trickery of eloquence, or of wine, or of both.

3. Thánatos, 'Death', is not to be confused with Hadês, the Infernal King, but is here a subsidiary god representing physical death itself. As such, his presence is especially hateful to Apollo, who represents the principle of life.

APOLLO. You need not fear. I have my own rights; and my reasons.

DEATH. Yet you go armed, Apollo.

APOLLO.   I go armed always.

DEATH. And are always over-kind to Admetos' house.

APOLLO. I only sympathize with a friend in trouble.

DEATH. And you would rob me of this second death?

APOLLO. Did I take Admetos from you by force?

DEATH.   He walks above ground: why is he not beneath it?

APOLLO. He has given you his wife—

DEATH.   And I have come for her.

APOLLO. Then take her, and go!
                    —Not that I imagine
that any words of mine could move you—

DEATH.   To what?
To take a life that is forfeit? I should say
that I know my office.

APOLLO.   No, no. I would have you postpone her death.

DEATH.   Your proposal is duly noted.

APOLLO. Allow Alcestis to reach her old age!

DEATH.   Never.
My honor is mine, Apollo, as yours is yours.

APOLLO. Honor?
What honor do you find in taking one life?

DEATH. A young life; more glory.

APOLLO.   Let her die old,
and her grave will bring you riches.

DEATH.   How like you!
You have the interests of the rich at heart.

APOLLO. Who would ever have thought Death had a sense of humor?

DEATH. Your rich men could all buy up length of days.

APOLLO. Then you will not grant me this?

DEATH.   I will not. You have measured me, you know what I am.

APOLLO.   I know you:
the hatred of men, the loathing of the gods!

DEATH. For once, you may not have what is not yours.

APOLLO. Death, Death, I swear to you,
cruel as you are, your cruelty is too weak!
Listen: a man is coming,[4]

here, to Pherês' house: a man is coming
on his way to the Thracian snowfields, sent
by Eurystheus to steal the famous horses.
In this very house
Admetos will receive him and honor him.
And it is he, Death, who will wrestle you and take
Alcestis from you. You will get no thanks from us
when you yield her, Death; and I will hate you
    still!
                              [*Exit* APOLLO.]

DEATH. This was a god of many words; but words
are not enough, Apollo.
    [DEATH *moves to the central door and touches
    it with the point of his sword. The door
    slowly opens while he addresses the audience
    directly.*]
Today this woman must go down to Death.
My sword is ready.
The lock of hair, the sign of sacrifice
to the dark gods under ground,
now it is mine to take.[5]
    [*Exit slowly into the house. The door closes.*]

[*The* CHORUS, *composed of fifteen men of Pherai,
enters the* orchêstra *during the opening speech
of the* CHORAGOS.]

CHORAGOS. I wonder what the silence means.
Why is the whole house so silent?
There is no one here to tell us
If we must mourn for our Queen,
Or if she is alive still—
Alcestis, Pelias' daughter,
surely the best of women, best
of wives to her husband.

CHORUS. Can anyone hear them weeping?
Is there any beating of hands, or lamentation,
Or any cry of death inside? No, nothing,
There is nothing. No sound.
No servant stands at the door.—O Paian,
God of Healing, come,
Use this lull in the storm!

A VOICE. Would they be so quiet if she were dead?

A VOICE. She is surely dead.

A VOICE. One thing is sure: she has not been taken away.

---

4. *a man is coming:* The outcome of the plot is stated in the Prologue. This is an admirable illustration of the unimportance, to the Greek mind, of the element of suspense in building a plot. The material is given (as usu-

ally in Shakespeare); the audience is interested not in the novelty of the dramatist's situations, but in his handling of them.

5. The cutting off of a lock of hair at the nape of a dying person's neck was supposed to expedite the passage of the soul from the body.

A VOICE. I would not say for sure. How do you
    know?

A VOICE. How could Admetos have given private
    burial

To a wife so loyal?

CHORUS. I can not see the urn at the door
With water in it, which is usual
When a person is dead; nor any lock of hair
Fallen, the sign of mourning, at the threshold.
There is no sound at all
Of young breasts beaten—
Grief of her maids about her.

A VOICE. And yet, this is her day—

A VOICE. What are you murmuring?

A VOICE. Today she must go under ground.

A VOICE. You have touched my heart, you have
    touched my soul.

A VOICE. It must be so: when goodness dies,
All good men suffer, too.

CHORUS. There is no power in the world
To whom we could send to save her,
Neither in Lykia, nor in the dry land
Where the temples of Ammon are.
Strong death comes down upon her.
I do not know what altars
We could make sacrifices on.
Only if Apollo's son were here,[6]
If his eyes opened on the light again,
He yet might save her from the night,
From Death's dark corridor. That god
Made men stand up whom death had overthrown.
But Heaven's thunder consumed him,
Him also. Where then is our hope?

CHORAGOS. The King has exhausted every ritual.
The black blood
Glows on the altars of the gods, a hopeless
Sacrifice against evil.

    [A MAIDSERVANT *enters from the palace.*]

CHORAGOS. But look: here is one of her servants
    from the house,

and in tears. What can she tell us?

                            —You grieve
for your lord and lady, girl; and that's reasonable.
But Alcestis? Tell us, is she alive, or dead?

MAIDSERVANT. She is alive. And dead.

CHORAGOS.   How can that be?

MAIDSERVANT. Her breath is failing. Her soul
    stands on the brink.

CHORAGOS. Oh lost, Admetos!

MAIDSERVANT.   Let the King be.

He will not understand, until she is gone.

CHORAGOS. Can nothing be done to save her?

MAIDSERVANT.   Nothing.
The fatal day takes her.

CHORAGOS.   And the arrangements of custom,
have they been made?

MAIDSERVANT.   Her fine things are set out
for her adornment at burial.

CHORAGOS. She is beyond praise in her death. No
    wife,

no other under the great sun is her equal!

MAIDSERVANT. Not in all the world. Who will
    deny it?

Is there a higher excellence
than this, that a wife should die her husband's
    death?
The entire city knows it, and affirms it.

But you will marvel when you hear what she has
    been doing.

This morning, when she knew her day had come,
she bathed her white body in fresh water from the
    stream,
took her prettiest things from the cedar rooms
and dressed herself becomingly; then stood
before the Flame upon the hearth[7] and prayed:
'Goddess, now I am going into earth.
'I shall not ever pray to you again.
'Watch over my children when I am dead.
'Give the boy a wife who will be dear to him,
'and give the girl a good husband.
'Do not let them die, like their mother, while
    they are young,
'but grant that they may be fortunate.
'Let them live happy lives in the land of their
    people.'

Then she went from altar to altar in the house,
praying, making wreaths for every shrine,
shearing off the leaves of young myrtle branches,
quietly, without a word, so still, so lovely,
you would have said no threat of evil had touched
    her.
But in her chamber,
then there were tears: 'Dear bed,'
she cried, 'dear bridal bed, where first I lay
'naked for him, and now I die for him . . .
'You are no longer mine. I do not hate you:
'you have destroyed me, only me. I would not

---

6. 'Apollo's son' is Asklêpios.

7. *the Flame:* The goddess is Hestía (*cf.* the Roman
Vesta), for whom a votive fire was kept burning on a
hearth in every house.

'betray you and my husband by denials,
'and so I die. Another wife
'will lie here, it may be, no more faithful than I—
'but oh, let her be more fortunate!'
                                        She knelt
and kissed the bed, weeping until
she could cry no more. Then rose
and left the chamber, slowly, returning often,
faltering.
            Her children
clung sobbing to her robe; she took them up
and embraced them in farewell; seeing her
        servants' tears,
she gave her right hand sweetly to each in turn:
even the meanest blessed her, and was blessed.

These are the sorrows of Admetos' house.

If he had died, why then he would have died;
but now his grief is so bitter that all his life
he never will escape it, never forget.
    CHORAGOS. He shows his grief, then? Knows
        what he must lose,
and the sorrows of his house?
    MAIDSERVANT   Weeping.
Holding her in his arms, his dearest wife,
begging her not to leave him now. All
        madness . . .
For she has only a little time to breathe,
and always her eyes are upon the moving sunlight,
as though she would never see the sun again
and now must say good-bye to it for ever . . .

Well. I will say to Admetos that you have come.
Not everyone is fond enough of princes
to have stood by in bitter times like these.
But you are a good friend, and have been always.
You are welcome here.
                            [*Exit.*]

    A VOICE. Is there no escape, O God?
Must this evil come upon us?
    A VOICE. Is there no help? Must my locks
Be shorn? Must I go in mourning?[8]
    CHORAGOS. Clearly we must. Even so,
Pray to the gods: they have great power.
    CHORUS. Lord Apollo, Lord of Healing,
Find a remedy for Admetos.
Grant it, oh grant it!
Save him, save him, as once before,[9]
From angry Death:

Beat back murderous Hadês!
    A VOICE. My tears are for you, Admetos.
How will you live, once she is gone?
    A VOICE. A man could cut his own throat
Or hang himself against heaven for this.
    CHORAGOS. She is not dear, but dearest of all,
This woman whose death you will see today.
    CHORUS. Ah, she is coming from her house,
And he is with her. Cry out,
Let all Pherai mourn,
Let earth itself cry out for her
Who passes now, fainting, sick,
To the house of Hadês.

Never say that marriage has more of joy than pain.
I have seen marriages. I have seen
The fortune of my king.
Lost is the loveliest, lost the dear wife.
What now can his days bring,
What pleasure to his life that is no life?
[*Enter* ALCESTIS *from the house, supported by*
ADMETOS, *leading the child* EUMELOS *by the hand.*
She speaks remotely, as if entranced, disregarding
at first the prosaic interruptions of her husband.]
    ALCESTIS. O Sun! O shining clear day,
And white clouds wheeling in the clear of heaven!
    ADMETOS. He looks down and sees that we are
        both unhappy.
How have we harmed him, or the other gods?
Why should you die?
    ALCESTIS. O Iôlkos,[10] and the dear roof
That sheltered me the day that I was married!
    ADMETOS. Try to stand up, poor darling. Do not
        fail me.
Only pray to the almighty gods; it may be
they will have mercy on us both.
    ALCESTIS. I see the dark lake,
The skiff in shore,
And Charôn holding the double oar, calling,
'Why are you waiting, Alcestis? Come,
'You are keeping us back . . .'
Can you not hear him? Listen!
He is angry.
    ADMETOS. To me it is a bitter voyage that you
        speak of . . .
What a terrible thing this is for both of us!
    ALCESTIS. Something is touching me—
Do you see *anyone?*—
Someone drawing me, drawing me down to
        death . . .

8. Cropping one's hair was a sign of mourning.
9. Apollo had 'saved' Admetos the first time when he
bargained with the Fates.

10. *O Iôlkos:* Alcestis was a daughter of King Pelias of
Iôlkos, a city in Magnesia.

Ah the great black brows of Death!
                              Frowning! Wings!
Let me alone!—Strange journey,
And I am afraid.
    ADMETOS. This is a terrible thing for those who
      love you,
terrible for your husband and your children.
    ALCESTIS. You need not hold me any more.
    Please,
let me lie down. I have no strength to stand,
so near to death, and the dark
creeps on my eyes like night.
                              Children,
no more. You have no mother any more.
Be happy in the sweet sunlight.
    ADMETOS. Oh God, I'd rather die than hear you
      say these things!
For my sake, for your children's sake, do not leave
    me now.
Come, make an effort, rise.
With you gone, how could I live? You, only you,
mean life or death to us, blest by your love.
    ALCESTIS. Admetos, Admetos . . .
You see what is happening to me now; but before
    I die,
I must tell you what I have in mind to ask you.

In deference to you, laying down my life
to let you see the sunlight in this country,
I come to die. Yet I need not have died.
I could have married any man in Thessaly,
lived with some great prince in his splendid house;
but without you, with my children fatherless,
I would not live. Yet I am young, and these years
have been pleasant.
                    Your father and mother failed
    you in their age,
When, death being near, they might have died
    with honor
and saved their son with honor. You were all
they had, nor had they hope of other children.
You and I could have lived out all our days,
and you would not be abandoned, left alone
with these poor children.
                              But I suppose some god
managed all this to turn out as it has,
and so let it be.
                    —But now, Admetos,
I ask a favor in return: not so great a thing
(for nothing is more precious than a life),
but a favor that I deserve, surely. You love
these children just as I do—oh, you must!

Make them the masters of this house, my house,
and do not set another wife above them.
Whoever she might be, sometimes she'd strike
    them—
and they are our children!

I beg you, never that!
                              A second wife
is hateful to the children of the first,
a viper is not more hateful.

                              The boy here
has a strong defending tower in his father.
But, dearest daughter! . . .
                              How will it be with you,
growing up, if your father marries again?
Will she be kind to you? If only
she will bring no scandal upon you in your
    girlhood
and spoil your wedding day!
Dearest, your mother will never see your wedding,
never hold your hand in childbirth, at that time
when there's no comfort greater than having her
    near you.
No. I must die, And it comes
not tomorrow, not the day after tomorrow, but
    now,
in only a moment: and I must take my place
with those who are not.
                              Good-bye. Be happy.

Admetos, you can be proud of a good wife.
Children, you can say that your mother was good.
    CHORAGOS. Be confident. I will speak for Ad-
    metos.
He is a man of sense, he will do this for you.
    ADMETOS. It shall be as you ask, believe me, it
    shall be so.
You only I have loved in life, love now you are
    dying.
You are my only Queen.
There is no other woman in all Thessaly
shall ever take your place beside me here;
no other woman, however beautiful, however
noble she may be. These are my life,
these children—and I pray the gods I may
live in them, since I am denied you.

Oh, grief for me to bear as long as I live!

But I shall hate my father and my mother:
friends in words, but enemies in deed,
while you gave up your dear life for my life.

Mourning?
I'll have mourning! I'll stop the dancing.
There will be no more feasts in my house, no
     garlands,
no laughter, no music.
I'll never touch the strings of a lyre again
or bring myself to sing the Libyan flute.
You take my happiness away with you.

And listen:
I'll have wise carvers make your body's image
in ivory, for our own bed; and I'll lie against it,
dreaming
that when I clasp it and whisper your name
you are with me there . . .
                              Cold comfort, surely! Yet
it may relieve the weight around my heart.
And often, I think, in sleep you'll come to me:
a sweet thing, for whatever time,
to revisit in dreams the dear dead we have lost.

Oh, if I had Orpheus' voice and poetry
with which to move the Dark Maid and her Lord,
I'd call you back, dear love, from the world below.
I'd go down there for you. Charôn or the grim
King's dog[11] could not prevent me then
from carrying you up into the fields of light.

But you, down there, be patient: I am coming.
Make a place for me, that we may be together.
In the same cedar boards with you I shall command
that these bones of mine be laid down with your
     own:
for not in death would I be far from you,
my dearest, my only faithful friend!
     CHORAGOS. Your grief is my grief, Admetos, bitter
          and strong,
as a friend to friend. She is worthy of it.
     ALCESTIS. Children, you have heard your father
          promise.
He will not marry another woman to rule you.
He will not dishonor my memory.
     ADMETOS.   I swear it.
     ALCESTIS. Then I leave you my children. Take
          them, love them.
     ADMETOS. A dear gift, from a dear hand!
     ALCESTIS. You must be their mother, too, now I
          am gone.
     ADMETOS. No question, since they have lost you.
     ALCESTIS.   Oh, my children,
to die so, with you needing me!

11. The 'grim King's dog' is Cerberus, a three-headed
beast of inordinate savagery.

     ADMETOS.   Tell me, tell me,
what shall I do, alone?
     ALCESTIS.   Why, time will tell.
Time will take care of that. The dead are nothing
     at all.
     ADMETOS. For God's love, take me, take me with
          you below!
     ALCESTIS. This death is death enough I die for
          you.
     ADMETOS. Detestable Death, to steal a wife so
          dear!
     ALCESTIS. It is quite dark now. My eyes are
          heavy.
     ADMETOS. If you do really leave me, I am lost!
     ALCESTIS. I am nothing. Speak of me as nothing.
     ADMETOS. Turn your face. You can not leave
          your children!
     ALCESTIS. I must. It is not what I wish. Good-bye,
          children.
     ADMETOS. Look at them, look at them!
     ALCESTIS.   No more.
     ADMETOS. What are you doing?
What has happened?
     ALCESTIS. Ah . . .

                         [*She dies. A long pause.*]
     ADMETOS. Oh, I am the most unhappy man that
          ever lived!
     CHORAGOS. She has gone. The King's wife is dead.
     CHILD. Now I am lost. Dearest
Mother has left us, Father,
Gone from the bright day.
I am forsaken.
          Father, look:
Her strange eyes, her fingers
Cold and stiff.
          Oh, Mother,
Can you listen? Here's your little one,
Bending, calling,
Trying to kiss your mouth.
     ADMETOS. She is deaf to us, she is blind. Children,
you and I are struck by the same disaster.
     CHILD. Young to be bereft so,
How can I play now, Father?
Hurt by the whole world.
Oh little sister,
          lonely, too!
And you—your marriage, Father,
All in vain.
          In vain all
Hope of growing old with Mother.
Death came first. Our house is dying,
Desolate in her death.

[ADMETOS *moves slowly towards the central door. The* CHORAGOS *addresses him with remote sternness.*]

CHORAGOS. Admetos, you are not the first man to
    lose a dear wife,
nor will you be the last. Have patience, then, and
    remember
that death comes to all of us.

ADMETOS.   I know it well . . .
This blow fell
not without warning. Long ago I had
foreknowledge, waited anxiously.
                            And now
I must arrange for her funeral.
                        Thessalians:
I command your attendance upon her, I command
that you raise a paean to the deaf King of the
    Dead.
Every man subject to me
shall share in my mourning. Let every man
crop his head and clothe himself in black.
Let horsemen and charioteers
clip their horses' manes. For twelve full months
I forbid the sound of lyre or flute in the city.

For never again shall I bury one more dear to me,
or one more generous. She is worthy of all honor,
since she alone has taken my place in death.

[*He goes into the house. During the singing
of the Funeral Ode the servants raise the litter
and slowly carry* ALCESTIS *within. The door
closes after them. Near the end of the Ode, the*
MAIDSERVANT *comes out, places an urn beside
the door, and retires within.*]

CHORUS. Daughter of Pelias, our love goes with
    you
Under dark earth where you must enter now,
Along the ways of death, the sunless houses.
Even that ancient and gloombearded god,
The Guide of Death, bent to his sad oar,
Let him remember well: no braver woman
Crossed with him ever to the silent shore.

Singers whom the Muse haunts, haunting music
Often shall make to praise you on their strings
Or in bare singing to no instrument,
At Sparta in late summer when the moon
Glows all night long on nights of festival,
Or at rich Athens in the shining noon—
Such loveliness you leave them for their songs.

Would I could save you from the black water,
Bring you to sunlight from that breathless dark!

Dearest of wives, daring alone
To yield your spirit up to death for him,
Light be the earth upon you, lightly rest.
If ever Admetos takes a bride again,
He shall be hateful to me and to your children.

The old ones grudged old bodies to the earth,
Mother and father feared to save their son,
Hugging their lives, hoary and brief.
But you precede your lord; and you are young.
So dear a wife I wish might be my fortune,
So rare a thing, rarest in the world:
Then I would pray she might stay with me ever.

[*Enter* HERAKLES.]

HERAKLES. My good people of Pherai,
is Admetos in his house, and may I see him?

CHORAGOS. He is at home, Heraklês. But tell us,
what brings you to Thessaly and our city here?

HERAKLES. One of those labors of mine for King
    Eurystheus.[12]

CHORAGOS. Where must you go this time?

HERAKLES.   To Thrace.
Diomed's four horses are what I'm after.

CHORAGOS. How will you get them? You don't
    know him, do you?

HERAKLES. I do not. I have never been in his
    country.

CHORAGOS. Then you've a fight on your hands to
    take those horses.

HERAKLES. Maybe. But I've never yet run away
    from a fight.

CHORAGOS. It's either kill Diomed or get killed
    yourself.

HERAKLES. That kind of problem's nothing new
    to me.

CHORAGOS. Suppose you win: what do you get out
    of it?

HERAKLES. Only the horses to drive back to
    Tiryns.

CHORAGOS. Not easy, even to get the bit into their
    mouths.

HERAKLES. Why not?—unless you mean they
    snort fire?

CHORAGOS. No, but they snap and tear men apart
    with their jaws.

HERAKLES. You're thinking of mountain lions,
    friend, not horses.

---

12. The eighth of the Twelve Labors that Heraklês was
obliged to perform for Eurystheus was the capture of the
man-eating mares of Diomedês, a Thracian king. Heraklês
not only stole the mares, but fed their master Diomedês to
them; after which he drove them back as an uncomfortable
gift to Eurystheus.

CHORAGOS. Wait till you see the blood stamped
 in their stalls.

HERAKLES. What does he call himself who reared
 these beauties?

CHORAGOS. The son of Arês. Lord of the Golden
 Shield.

HERAKLES. Then this labor fits my destiny, always
 heavy.

A sheer cliff I keep climbing.
It seems that I must fight all the sons of Arês:
first Lykaôn, then the Swan, so-called,[13]
and now I go to wrestle with the third,
the master of these horses. But I
am Alkmêna's son: no enemy
shall ever see my hand tremble in battle.

[*Enter* ADMETOS *from the house.*]

ADMETOS. Heraklês, son of Zeus, of Perseus' line,
you are welcome to my house.

HERAKLES. Admetos, Prince
of Thessaly, I hope that I find you well.

ADMETOS. I wish . . . But thank you for your
 kind concern.

HERAKLES. Why have you shorn your head? Are
 you in mourning?

ADMETOS. I have a burial to make today.

HERAKLES. God keep all harm away from your
 children!

ADMETOS. My children are alive here in my house.

HERAKLES. If it is your father, why, his time had
 come,

he dies in death's season.

ADMETOS. He and my mother
are both still living, Heraklês.

HERAKLES. The Queen—?
But surely not Alcestis, not your wife?

ADMETOS. There are two answers I might make
 to that.

HERAKLES. Are you saying she is alive, or she is
 dead?

ADMETOS. She is, and she is not. It tortures me.

HERAKLES. What is that supposed to mean? A
 riddle!

ADMETOS. You know the destiny in store for her.

HERAKLES. I certainly know that she promised to
 die for you.

ADMETOS. Then how can I say that she is really
 alive?

HERAKLES. Ah. Don't grieve now, man; wait till
 the time comes.

13. *the Swan:* Kyknos, a son of Arês; the name means
'Swan'.

ADMETOS. Whoever is doomed to death is already
 dead.

HERAKLES. Being and not-being are thought to be
 different things.

ADMETOS. Make the distinction if you like. I can
 not.

HERAKLES. Still, why are you mourning? Who is
 this dead friend?

ADMETOS. A woman. Were we not talking about
 a woman?

HERAKLES. One of your family?

ADMETOS. No; but there were ties between us.

HERAKLES. How did she come to die here in your
 house?

ADMETOS. When her father died she came here to
 live.

HERAKLES. A pity!
I wish I had come when you were not so troubled.

[HERAKLES *turns to go.*]

ADMETOS. What do you mean? What are you
 planning to do?

HERAKLES. I must find lodging with some other
 friend.

ADMETOS. No, no, Lord Heraklês, that must
 never happen!

HERAKLES. A guest is a burden in a house of
 mourning.

ADMETOS. The dead are dead. Come now into my
 house.

HERAKLES. No. It would be painful.

ADMETOS. The guest rooms are apart.

HERAKLES. Let me go, and a thousand blessings.

ADMETOS. No,
you must not go to another house tonight.

[*To a servant*]

Boy, you will show our guest to his rooms.
Open the private ones. Have the servants bring
plenty of food, and shut the main hall doors.
He must not be troubled by the sound of our
 weeping.

[*Exit* HERAKLES.]

CHORAGOS. What are you thinking of, Admetos?
 How can you
entertain a guest, after what has happened here?

ADMETOS. If I turned this traveler away from my
 house,
would you think better of me? Surely not.
What good would it have done?
My sorrow would be no less, and I should have
one friend less;
and this would have been one more calamity,
to have my house called inhospitable.

This man is my good friend when I go to Argos.

CHORAGOS. If he is really as much a friend as that,
how could you keep from telling him your sorrow?

ADMETOS. He would not have wished to stay, if
he had known . . .

I am aware that what I have done will be
misunderstood.

Nevertheless, my house
will always welcome guests and honor them.

[*Exit* ADMETOS.]

CHORUS. It is a gracious house and ever was,
Friendly to strangers, and a home to friends;
The god of Heaven's music loved this place:
Apollo—yet content to be a shepherd,
Down gentle mountains piping
After his flock the bridal songs of the hills.

Joy in that music brought the dappled lynxes
And tawny lions from the Othrys valley,
Following where he led them, without harm;
O Phoibos! from tall pines a spotted doe
Ventured on light hooves, dancing
To the cool tracing of your upland flute.

Along the clear reach of this inland water
Our king has rich lands whitened by his flocks:
Plowland and plain he has: far off his borders,
Westward, where the sun goes down in cloud,
Where Hêlios reins his horses in bright air;
And on the east the sea: no harbors there.

Now he has thrown his doors wide for the stranger,
Weeping, his eyes wet, weeping the new dead.
Here noble courtesy knows no restraining.
I marvel and take heart. Such wisdom guides
The good man that his very recklessness
Becomes high prudence, ordering distress.

[*Enter* ADMETOS *from the house, followed by servants bearing the corpse of* ALCESTIS *on a litter.
This is placed facing the audience, with the head
slightly higher than the feet, so that the face is
clearly visible.*]

ADMETOS. Friends, kindly company: There is
only a
little left for us to do now: my servants have prepared her
for her funeral, for the tomb. But before
we take her away, I would have you salute her as
is customary
for one setting out on this last journey.

CHORAGOS. But look: here is your father coming
in,

and slaves bringing burial ornaments for her.
How old he seems, and how feeble!

[*Enter* PHERES, *slowly, leaning on his staff,
followed by two slaves carrying small gifts.*]

PHERES. I have come to share your grief, son. No
denying,
she was a good wife, and a wise one, and you have
lost her.
Nevertheless, man was born to suffer, to endure,
be the burden never so cruel.

Take them from me
these gifts that I have brought for her adorning,
and let her go in peace to the world below.
So, it is right to honor her, son:
she gave her life to save yours, she did not leave me
childless to drag out my dying day to its close.

Honor of womankind!
Dear audacious girl!
Alcestis, daughter, savior of my son
(and of me also):
even in the house of Death, fare well!

Believe me, son: a marriage like your own
is a blessed thing, a most profitable thing.
Why else should a man take a wife?

ADMETOS. Were you invited here?
You were not. There is no room for you
here, among her friends.

You dare to bring
gifts for her? Take your gifts! She needs
no gifts of yours to be lovely under ground.
You mourn for her?
Did I hear you groan for me when I faced danger?
Then, when I needed you, then—why, then
you stood by and let a stranger die, a young stranger!
And now you squeak for her at the grave's door!

My father!
Or were you my father?
And she, reputed by herself and by
other authorities to be my mother—
was she? Or perhaps I was the brat of a slave girl,
and you graciously gave me your wife's pap to suck
at!
No, you have shown what you are;
I am no son of yours, and I disown you—
you, old, palsied at death's gate, afraid to die,
and with so little life left in you!

Coward! not to
Die for your own son!
Coward! to let a woman die instead!

Well; let her—and her alone—be all
the father and the mother I'll have for ever.

How great you might have been in this, how noble,
dying for your son when your own days were few!
Then we might have lived out all our days,
she and I: I should not now be mourning.

What have you not had that a man might have?
Power in your prime as King, and I to succeed you,
your own son, in your own house: you had in store
no childless death, no partition of your kingdom.

Or was I perhaps a bad son?
You will not say that I was a bad son, either.
I gave you all respect in your old age,
and here is my reward from both of you.
                                        Go,
time is short, go, get more children!
Someone to sit at your death-bed, shroud your
          corpse!
You get no burial from me, this hand of mine
shall be no comfort to you. I am dead,
so far as you could make me dead; and if I live
by grace of another savior—there, I say,
my obligation lies.
                    God, these old men!
How they pray for death! How heavy
they find this life in the slow drag of days!
And yet, when Death comes near them,
you will not find one who will rise and walk with
          him,
not one whose years are still a burden to him.
  CHORAGOS. Let your father alone, Admetos.
There is sorrow enough in this place.
  PHERES. Am I a Lydian slave, or a Phrygian
          slave, son,
that you should abuse me so? Or am I your father,
a Thessalian Thessalian-born, a king, and a free
          man?
This talk of yours is something worse
than a young man's insolence. You will pay for it.
Is it I, who made you heir to my house,
who gave you everything—is it I whose duty it is
to die for you as well? Does your father owe you
          that debt?
That is no law of the Greeks, my father
told me of no such law.

For happiness or unhappiness,
every man is born for himself. I gave you all
you deserved, slaves, subjects, money,
and you'll soon have my lands, as I had them from
          my father.

Then how have I hurt you? How have I cheated
          you?
Die for you—?
Don't you die for me, and I'll not die for you.
You love the daylight: do you think your father
          does not?
Our stay in the world below will be long enough.
Life, I take it, is short: it is none the less agreeable.

And as for dying—
Well, you put up a shameless kind of fight
against death, did you not? Are you dead now?
Have you not found a victim to take your place?
'Coward'! You call me a coward? You,
less brave than a woman? What a pretty-boy hero
          you are!

But you know best.
A gallant road you've found to Immortality!
Marry wife after wife, make sure they'll die for
          you—
that's all.
                    How do you dare insult
your own kin for declining to serve you so?
Hold your tongue, but put your mind on this: You
          love
your own sweet life, but so does every man
on the face of the earth; and if you rail at me,
I'll give you some home truths that will cost you
          dear.
  CHORAGOS. Say no more to your son, old Pherês.
There has been too much bitterness on both sides.
  ADMETOS. Say whatever you like, as I have. If the
          truth
hurts you, that's your fault for blundering here.
  PHERES. The real blunder would have been to die
          for you.
  ADMETOS. Is dying the same thing for a young
          man and an old?
  PHERES. There is one way of breath; there are
          not two.
  ADMETOS. Live on then; live a longer life than
          God!
  PHERES. You curse your parents so, with no cause
          for it?
  ADMETOS. I thought you expressed a wish to go
          on living.
  PHERES. I see Death in this place: but you are
          alive.
  ADMETOS. Proof of your cowardice, you wretched
          old man!
  PHERES. Surely you will not say that she died for
          me?

ADMETOS. Ah,
if only you turn to me for help some day!

PHERES. Take a dozen wives, let a dozen die for
you!

ADMETOS. A double-edged rebuke. You feared to
die.

PHERES. This daylight of God is sweet, I tell you,
sweet!

ADMETOS. And rotten that unmanly soul of yours!

PHERES. Grim, wasn't it, not to cart off the old
man's corpse?

ADMETOS. Oh, you will die some day, and not
with honor.

PHERES. Dishonor will not trouble me, once I am
dead.

ADMETOS. God, God, how shameless these old
men are!

PHERES. This girl was not shameless, was she?
Only demented.

ADMETOS. Leave my house, go! Let me bury my
dead wife.

PHERES. Yes, I will go.
You, being her murderer, should know the best
way to bury her.
But you will also be hearing from her family.
Akástos, I think, is not the man
to let his sister's blood go unavenged.

[*Exit* PHERES.]

ADMETOS. Go back to your woman!
Back, you childless ancestor, and grow older!
You'll not come into my house again.

If heralds and trumpets could cut me off from you,
By God, I'd do it!

—But, friends: our present grief:
come, let us bring her body to burial.

[*During the funeral song the litter is taken
up by the servants and* ALCESTIS *is carried off.
Exit* ADMETOS.]

CHORAGOS. Daughter of Pelias, Alcestis, Queen,
farewell.

CHORUS. Daughter of Pelias, incomparable, O
heart
So daring, and broken in daring: fare well
Even to Hadês' gate!
There, may Hermês greet you, a kindly Angel;
There, may Death be gentle; and if great
Souls, and good, and generous, find favor
Beneath the ground, you shall sit throned beside
The Bride of the Dark King.[14]

14. 'The Bride of the Dark King' is Persephonê, Queen
of Hadês.

[*The stage is empty. Enter a* MANSERVANT *angrily
from the house.*]

MANSERVANT. In my time I've seen plenty of
guests entertained here in Admetos' house, people
from all over Greece, but I'll take my oath that I
never had to look after a worse fellow than this
one, whoever he is! Why, as soon as he got here he
could see that the King was in mourning; but he
had to stay, just the same; and as if this weren't
enough, he felt he must insist upon all the details
of hospitality, ordering us about. I can still see him
hoisting that wine-bowl up in both hands and
pouring the stuff into himself, not a drop of water
in it, until he was flaming drunk; and then he had
to crown himself with myrtle and belch out silly
songs. A pretty bit of counterpoint *that* was! This
man in there bellowing, with never a thought for
all Admetos was suffering, and we in the next
room mourning for our Queen . . . But we had
been told not to let him see us with our eyes wet
. . . And so here I am, waiting on this guest, this
backguard, this bloated burglar, this house-breaker
—And she is gone. The Queen has left her house.
I could not reach out my hand to her, or even say
good-bye to her. She was my dear Lady, my mother,
the mother of all of us. How often she saved us
from punishment when Admetos was angry!—Ah,
this wine-stinking stranger, bursting in on all our
trouble!

[*Enter* HERAKLES, *drunk, crowned with myrtle,
holding a huge cup in both hands.*]

HERAKLES. Hello there. Why so
solemn? Why do you look so
grim?
Is this the correct way for a servant to act,
staring at the guests he serves? It
is not.
You ought to be trotting around with a
smile, like a good
fellow.
Friend,
you behold in me your master's dearest friend.
And what do you do? You look, to say the least,
bilious.
And all for the death of a woman you hardly knew!
Come over here, and grow in wisdom.

[SERVANT *turns away.*]

Do you understand the facts of this mortal life?
You do not. Of course not. Then listen to me:

[*Chanting tunelessly*]

All men have to die, and that's plain fax.
There isn't one knows when he'll get the axe.

Death isn't visible before he comes:
You can't predict your death by doing sums.

There you have it, friend, straight from a first-class
authority. Ponder, rejoice, and have a drink.

Today's today. Tomorrow, we may be
Ourselves gone down the drain of Eternity.

And one other thing:
Aphroditê. Of all your gods and goddesses, your
greater and lesser di-
vinities, Kypris is the sweetest for mortal man.
Honor her, friend. She means well. And
forget whatever it is that's gnawing at you.
Remember what I've been telling you. You
believe me, I hope? I think so. Here, have a
garland, have a drink, have another drink, have
a drink,
          and grief
good-bye!

          O mortal man, think mortal thoughts!

Seriously, friend, this wine will surprise you.
And as for all these sour-faced sigh-blasting belly-
     ache fellows,
what's life to them? Nothing but a catastrophe.
   MANSERVANT. I know all about that. But what we
     are doing today
leaves no room in the house for feasting and laugh-
     ter.
   HERAKLES. Whoever it is that's dead, she's a
stranger, isn't she?
I see no reason for inordinate mourning
since your master and mistress are both well.
   MANSERVANT. Both well? It is possible that even
     now—
   HERAKLES. Has Admetos lied to me?
   MANSERVANT.   Lied to you? No.
He has been too good to you.
   HERAKLES.   Must I go without my dinner
because a stranger has died?
   MANSERVANT.   A stranger . . .
Ah, she was all too close to us!
   HERAKLES.   Is it possible
that Admetos has hidden a real sorrow from me?
   MANSERVANT. Go back to your drinking. Leave
     the suffering to us.
   HERAKLES. This is not the way one speaks of a
casual grief.
   MANSERVANT. If it were that, we should not have
     minded your revelry.

   HERAKLES. Can it be that my friend has made a
     fool of me?
   MANSERVANT. You came at the wrong time, that's
     all.
The house is in mourning. You can see for yourself.
   HERAKLES. Who is it? One of the children? The
     old father?
   MANSERVANT. It is Alcestis, man. The Queen is
     dead.
   [*Long pause.* HERAKLES *throws down his cup
   and slowly removes the garland from his head.*]
   HERAKLES. The Queen.—And you entertained
     me in spite of that?
   MANSERVANT. He would have been ashamed to
     turn you away.
   HERAKLES. Admetos, what a companion you have
     lost!
   MANSERVANT. It's the end of us all, not of the
     Queen alone.
   HERAKLES. I knew it. I felt it. I saw his eyes red
     with weeping,
his hair clipped short, his heavy motion.
But he told me it was all for a stranger, a simple
     death!
And I, blundering my way
into the house of this admirable host, and he
suffering so! Drinking, bawling,
crowning my head with myrtle—But it is not
wholly my fault: you might have told me.

But let that be.
                    Where is he now? Where
shall I find him burying her?
   MANSERVANT.   Go straight out
the Lárissa road, and there,
not far from the town, you'll find the new-cut stone.
                         [*Exit* MANSERVANT.]
   HERAKLES. Now, my brave heart, my good hands
     scarred strong
by many labors,
now you must prove that Alkmêna, Elektryon's
     daughter,
bore Zeus a son indeed.
                    For Admetos' sake
we must bring Alcestis back to her house from the
     dead.
I will follow the blackrobed god,
old Thánatos, to her tomb: for there, I think,
I shall find him drinking the blood of the new vic-
     tims.
If I can take him
from ambush, I will wrestle with death,

I will crack his charnel ribs between my hands
until he lets her go.
                    But if I miss him,
If he leaves the blood of offering untasted,
I will go down into the sad streets of the Dead,
to Persephonê and the dim Lord of Hell, and there
beg for her life.
                    And I
will bring Alcestis back to the good sunlight,
back to my friend who welcomed me in his house
in spite of his hard loss. Oh generous heart!
Where in all Thessaly, where in the whole of
      Greece,
should there be a kindlier, friendlier house than his?
And he must never say
that his effort was wasted upon a scoundrel.
                                    [*Exit* HERAKLES.]

[*Enter* ADMETOS, *from R, accompanied by servants.*
He walks slowly towards the central door, stopping
            at the chanting of the CHORUS.]
    ADMETOS. God, the way home is hateful to me.
the sight of the empty house is hateful.
Where shall I turn? Where can I rest?
What shall I say? What not! Die, and be done
      with it!

My mother was accurst the night she bore me,
and I am faint with envy of all the dead.
How clean they are, who are out of life for ever!
They are beautiful, and I would be with them.

For I shall never be warm in the thick sunlight,
nor walk again as other men walk the earth.
She who was my life has been taken from me,
stolen by Death for his still kingdom.
    CHORUS. Go deep into your house, Admetos: you
      must go in,
Though you are right to weep. We know,
You have walked through bitterness today,
But all your urgency can not move the dead:
You will not see her face again.
    ADMETOS. When you say that, my heart splits
      with the spearhead.
So true a wife lost! What is worse?
Better if she and I had never married,
never lived together in this house.
Men who do not marry, men who have no children,
each of them has one life to live, his own;
and a man can bear the pain of a single life.
He will not see his children sick,
his marriage empty, cold with death;

all his life long he will be safe from this.
    CHORUS. Fate, Fate is a grim wrestler; it is Fate's
      fall,
and yet you will not yield the match to Fate.
More grief than you can bear, and yet you must.
Men have lost their wives before.
Varying shapes of disaster crush us all.
    ADMETOS. Mourning without end, and heartbreak
      here,
and the earth heavy upon the ones we loved!
Why did you hold me back when I would have
      thrown myself
into her grave? I would have lain dead with her,
and now the King of Darkness would have two
instead of one alone.
Together we should have crossed the strange water.
    CHORUS. A relation of mine had a son who died,
      a young man
Full of promise. It was his only son.
Yet he endured this bravely:
Sorrow enough, yet he endured it bravely.
A childless old man, white-haired, and bent to-
      wards death.
    ADMETOS. My strange house! How can I go into it,
how live there, now the evil day has come?
How huge the gap is!
                    I can see,
as if from a great distance,
the evening I came in under the torches,
holding her by the hand, and the music around us,
the singing, and the revel following
to wish her, who is now dead, happiness;
and happiness to me: they said our marriage
joined the magnificence of two lines of kings.
But now instead of songs there is only weeping;
where there were white robes, these in black
beckon me in to sleep in an empty bed.
    CHORUS. You were a stranger to sorrow: therefore
      Fate
Has cursed you. Nevertheless, you have saved your
      life.
The wife you loved is dead;
But is this new, that a wife should leave her love?
Death has dissolved many marriages before this.
    ADMETOS. Friends, Alcestis is happier than I,
whoever may think differently.
Now she will feel no distress, no sorrow ever,
but happiness and peace; and her name is blessed.
But as for me,
I have no right to be living. I've learned that at
      last.
I have begged off dying: now my life is dead.

How can I pass the doorway of this house?
Who will be there to greet me? Who will say
farewell to my going? Going where?—driven
out by the emptiness where once she was:
the bed, and the chairs that were hers, and the floor
covered with dust; and at my knees her children
crying, coming to me day after day, crying,
asking for her . . . And her servants in tears,
remembering what a sweet mistress they have lost.
And in the city there will be weddings, gatherings
with women: How can I bear to meet her friends?
This one who hates me will whisper to another,
'There is the man whose life is a daily shame,
'the man who dared not die, whose cowardice
'let his own wife lay down her life for him.
'What kind of man is he who hates his father
'because he himself is base?' What fame I'll have,
with all my sorrows!
                    I have saved my life?
I have lost my honor. I have lost everything.
  CHORUS. I have found power in the mysteries of
    thought,
Exaltation in the chanting of the Muses;
I have been versed in the reasonings of men;
But Fate is stronger than anything I have known:
Nothing in mortal wisdom can subdue her,
Neither Orphic riddles[15] on Thracian tablets,
Nor the Asklepiad skill that Phoibos taught.
Fate has neither altar nor image, that we may
    kneel to;
She has no bloodstained stone where we can pray.
But let us pray to her now: 'O Goddess, Lady,
'Be never more cruel than you have been this day:
'Though all that God wills you must bring to pass,
'Pitiless and abrupt your ways for ever;
'Though your hand would crumple Chalybéan
    steel.'

Caught by her now, Admetos,
Do you think to escape that grasp?—Rest there,
    friend.
The dead will not hear you crying, you in the day-
    light.
The children of the gods, all the loud heroes,
Where is their bravery now? Thin, drained in
    night.
But she who was dearest among us when she lived,

15. *Orphic riddles*: The legendary poet Orpheus was reputed to have left a collection of mystic writings, some of
them of a medical nature, engraved on tablets and deposited in a shrine of Dionysos, in Thrace. The 'Asklepiad
skill' is the medicine that Phoibos Apollo taught his son
Asklêpios.

She shall be dearest still among the dead.

And not as one dead for ever:
Her tomb is no mere mound above the dead,
But a holy shrine that travelers shall love,
Where, turning from the road, a man may say:
'This woman died for her husband in the old days
'And now lives here, a gracious influence. Lady,
'Your blessing on mine!' So will they pray, and
    pass.
  CHORAGOS. But what is this, Admetos? For some
    reason
Alkmêna's son is coming back to your house.
[*Enter* HERAKLES *with* ALCESTIS, *veiled. During the
ensuing dialogue she is motionless, as though in a
trance, until the moment when her face is disclosed.*]
  HERAKLES. Admetos, a man with a grievance
    against his friend
should speak plainly.
When I came to your house, you were in trouble.
I would have helped you, as a friend should; but
    you,
instead of telling me it was your wife that was dead,
hid the truth from me and made me welcome
here in your sad house.
And I? I crowned myself with myrtle, of course,
and made the usual libations to the gods—
and all the while I was in a house of mourning!
It was wrong of you, Admetos, wrong of you! But I
will not add my reproach to your suffering.

I have come back, and I will tell you why.

You see this woman here: take her, keep her for
    me
until I come again.
                    For I must kill
the Thracian king and bring his horses back . . .
But if I fail—God forbid
that I should fail, though!—, keep her here,
let her serve you in your house.
                              These hands of mine
worked hard to win her. On my way from here
I happened on an athletic contest for all comers
and she was the prize I took. Horses
were awarded to the best runners and jumpers,
herds of oxen for the boxing and wrestling
    champions,
and then this woman. There I was,
and it would have been silly to pass by such a
    prize.

So, as I've said, here is the woman for you.
Take her. I came by her honestly,

418 ALCESTIS

and a time will come when you will thank me for
    her.
    ADMETOS. I had no thought of wronging you,
        friend,
when I hid my wife's unhappy fate from you.
Only, if you had gone to another's house
I should have been hurt twice over. It seemed
    enough
that I should mourn for her.
                            But as for this woman—
Oh, Heraklês, my friend and my lord! if you can
    do so
take her to some other man who has not suffered
and let him keep her for you. Pherai
is full of your friends; you will find someone.

Do not remind me of what I have to bear!
Seeing her here, in my own house,
how could I keep back my tears? I beg you,
do not add grief to grief: I have suffered enough.

A young woman?
Where is there a place here for a young woman?
(For she is young: one can tell by her dress and
    bearing.)
Here, living among men,
do you think she would ever be safe? I tell you,
youth is hot-blooded, youth is hard to restrain!

It is for your own good that I am saying these
    things.

Or perhaps you would have me lead her
to my dead wife's chamber, and install her there?
Could I do that? give her that bed—!
Who would hate me more, the people of my own
    house—
because by tumbling into a new girl's bed
I'd betrayed the memory of her who died for me—
or Alcestis herself? No. It is Alcestis that I
must remember always. She deserves nothing less.

Yet you, woman, whoever you are, you are like
    Alcestis—
did you know it?—the same body, the same—
                                    Heraklês,
Heraklês, for the love of God, take her away!
I am beaten: do not press me any more.
I look at her, and it is Alcestis that I see!
She turns my heart, my eyes
burst with tears.
                    What unspeakable misery!
I taste this torment now for the first time.
    CHORAGOS. I could not call it a happy chance,
        myself.

Nevertheless a man must take what God gives.
    HERAKLES. If only I had a bit of your influence
with Death! Then I could do you the favor
of bringing your wife back to you from the grave.
    ADMETOS. I know you would. But why speak of
        it? The dead
never come back into the sunlight again.
    HERAKLES. You must not be excessive. Try to be
        brave.
    ADMETOS. Easy enough, to say 'be brave'. It is
        harder to do.
    HERAKLES. There is no future in perpetual mourn-
        ing.
    ADMETOS. No future; but my grief is like a
        passion.
    HERAKLES. Love for the dead is strong, I know,
        and bitter.
    ADMETOS. It has destroyed me, more utterly than
        I can say.
    HERAKLES. No man will deny that you have lost
        a devoted wife.
    ADMETOS. And there is no more pleasure for me
        in anything.
    HERAKLES. Time cancels young pain.
    ADMETOS.   Yes, if Time is Death.
    HERAKLES. A new wife will comfort you, a new
        marriage—
    ADMETOS. Not another word! I would not have
        thought this of you.
    HERAKLES. Never take a wife? A cold bed for
        ever?
    ADMETOS. No woman in this world will sleep by
        my side!
    HERAKLES. Do you think this attitude of yours
        will help the dead?
    ADMETOS. I will show her this much honor,
        wherever she is.
    HERAKLES. Good, very good. But some would say
        you're a fool.
    ADMETOS. Let them. They shall never call me a
        bridegroom.
    HERAKLES. I approve of this faithfulness to a
        dead wife.
    ADMETOS. If I betray her, dead, let me die too!
    HERAKLES. And now, friend,
take this woman and keep her in your good house.
    ADMETOS. By the great god who is your father,[16]
        I say No!

16. *the great god who is your father:* Zeus, by Alkmêna,
wife of Amphitryon, a nobleman of Thebes. Nevertheless,
the Heraklês of this play is not to be thought of as a
divine personage.

HERAKLES. You would be terribly wrong to deny me this.

ADMETOS. The shame of it would eat out my heart!

HERAKLES. Come, come,

in a little while you might begin to enjoy it.

ADMETOS. Ah Heraklês,

why did you have to win *her* at the games?

HERAKLES. And yet my victory was a victory for you.

ADMETOS. Very kind of you. But now let the woman go.

HERAKLES. She will go if she must. But must she? Think again.

ADMETOS. She must . . .

Although I would not have you angry with me . . .

HERAKLES. This request of mine has a solid reason behind it.

ADMETOS. Very well, then.

You have won again. But you know what it is costing me.

HERAKLES. Believe me, you'll thank me for this some day.

ADMETOS.   Take her in,

some one of you, since she's to live in our house.

HERAKLES. No. I'll not turn her over to your slaves.

ADMETOS. Then take her in yourself, if you feel that way.

HERAKLES. No. I have given her to you. Here, take her hand.

ADMETOS. I will not touch that woman! She can go in herself.

HERAKLES. I have entrusted her to your hands alone.

ADMETOS. Lord Heraklês, you force me against my will.

HERAKLES. Your hand, then. Stretch out your hand and touch the woman.

ADMETOS. Here it is.

HERAKLES. Looking away, as though you were killing

the Gorgon!17

    —There: you have her hand?

ADMETOS. I have.

HERAKLES. So I see. Then hold it tight! Some day

you will praise the son of Zeus as a good guest.

17. *the Gorgon:* The beautiful face of the Gorgon Medûsa was marred by its power to turn the beholder to stone.

Look at her, Admetos. Do you not see

a resemblance to your wife? Forget your troubles!

    [ALCESTIS *slowly removes her veil.*]

ADMETOS. Oh God, God, God,

what can I say? A miracle, beyond hope!

I see my wife! Is it really she?

or is this a cruel trick that God has played?

HERAKLES. No trick. This lady before you is your own.

ADMETOS. Wait. How do I know she's not a ghost from Hell?

HERAKLES. The guest you honored is not a pimp of ghosts.

ADMETOS. And this is my wife that I laid in her tomb myself?

HERAKLES. Your wife. I understand your finding it strange.

ADMETOS. And I can touch her? Speak to her as though she were alive?

HERAKLES. Speak to her. Everything has come out as you wished.

ADMETOS. Alcestis, Alcestis, my dear, my dearest wife!

You are mine again, and I thought you were lost for ever!

HERAKLES. Yours. And I pray that your happiness bring down

no envious curse from the gods, Admetos.

ADMETOS.   Friend,

great-hearted son of mighty Zeus! May God

keep you and guard you for ever! You alone,

Heraklês, have saved me and my house.

—But tell me: How did you bring her back from the dead?

HERAKLES. Wrestling. I fought the spirit who possessed her.

ADMETOS. Where did you meet this Spirit? Where did you fight him?

HERAKLES. I hid near her tomb, and sprang out and threw him.

ADMETOS. But why is she silent? Can she not speak again?

HERAKLES. It is not permitted you to hear her voice

for three days longer; then she will have washed away

the stain of death and memory of Hell.

So take her in, Admetos, my good friend,

and be a generous host from this time on.

Be happy.

    —As for me, my duty lies

before me, thanks to Sthénelos' royal son.

ADMETOS. Stay with us, Heraklês. All my house
　　is yours.

HERAKLES. Another day, perhaps. Now I must
　　go. 　　　　　　　　　　　　[*Exit* HERAKLES.]

ADMETOS. May every kind of happiness go with
　　you,
and may you soon come back to us.
　　　　　　　　　　　　　　　　—Friends,
I command these things to the whole city, and
the Assembly of the Four Quarters: let groups of
　　dancers
be formed to celebrate the glory of this day;
let the flesh of oxen smoke on every altar
to propitiate the gods. For now
the old life has changed for the new: and I say
that I am the happiest of all men.

　　CHORAGOS.
Destiny has many forms, and Heaven
Works in the dark with riddles and confusion.
　　What seemed must be is not.
　　What could not be, here's brought
　　　　To pass: it is God's way.
This is the meaning of all you have watched today.

The Tempest

BY WILLIAM SHAKESPEARE

Produced at court in 1611 and published in 1623 in the first folio of Shakespeare's plays, *The Tempest* is the last and best-known of the four romances (*Pericles, Cymbeline,* and *The Winter's Tale* are the previous three) with which Shakespeare rounded out his huge and unrivaled vision of life. It is unusual among his dramatic works in having no known literary source, though its opening storm, island setting, and miraculous action indicate his familiarity with the accounts of a contemporary case of shipwreck and deliverance that came to be known as the "Bermuda Pamphlets," as well as his knowledge of other Renaissance travel literature.

The play has long been regarded as Shakespeare's "farewell to the stage." Indeed, in support of that impression, one can cite its artist-magician protagonist, the frequent parallels with the earlier comedies and tragedies, and its theatrically self-conscious epilogue. But the significance of *The Tempest* is not simply personal or biographical, for the play marks the discovery and cultivation of "brave new worlds" in drama and in history—in Shakespeare's imaginative voyage as a playwright and in the actual voyages of Renaissance adventurers to the New World. Prospero's island is anywhere and nowhere; it contains all landscapes and the full range of human (and nonhuman) character. What the cast makes of its experience there parallels what the audience, in turn, can make of the experience of the play. It is not surprising that this most compact and comprehensive of Shakespeare's dramatic visions, both a mirror and a pattern of man's creative capacities, has prompted centuries of wonder and speculation.

Dramatis Personae

ALONSO, *King of Naples*
SEBASTIAN, *his brother*
PROSPERO, *the right Duke of Milan*
ANTONIO, *his brother, the usurping Duke of Milan*
FERDINAND, *son to the King of Naples*
GONZALO, *an honest old councilor*
ADRIAN
FRANCISCO } *lords*
CALIBAN, *a savage and deformed slave*
TRINCULO, *a jester*
STEPHANO, *a drunken butler*
MASTER *of a ship*
BOATSWAIN

MARINERS

MIRANDA, *daughter to Prospero*

ARIEL, *an airy spirit*

IRIS
CERES
JUNO } *presented by spirits*
NYMPHS
REAPERS

OTHER SPIRITS, *attending on Prospero*

SCENE — *A ship at sea: an uninhabited island.*

ACT I

SCENE I. *On a ship at sea. A tempestuous noise of thunder and lightning heard.*°

[*Enter a* SHIPMASTER *and a* BOATSWAIN.]
MAST. Boatswain!
BOATS. Here, master. What cheer?
MAST. Good,° speak to the mariners. Fall to't yarely,° or we run ourselves aground. Bestir, bestir.
[*Exit.*]
[*Enter* MARINERS.]
BOATS. Heigh, my hearts! Cheerly, cheerly, my   6
hearts! Yare, yare! Take in the topsail.° Tend° to the master's whistle. Blow till thou burst thy wind, if room° enough!
[*Enter* ALONSO, SEBASTIAN, ANTONIO, FERDINAND, GONZALO, *and others.*]
ALON. Good boatswain, have care. Where's the master? Play the men.°   11
BOATS. I pray now, keep below.
ANT. Where is the master, boatswain?
BOATS. Do you not hear him? You mar our labor. Keep your cabins. You do assist the storm.   15
GON. Nay, good, be patient.
BOATS. When the sea is. Hence! What cares these roarers for the name of King? To cabin. Silence! Trouble us not.
GON. Good, yet remember whom thou hast aboard.   21

BOATS. None that I more love than myself. You are a councilor. If you can command these elements to silence, and work the peace of the present,° we will not hand a rope more. Use your authority. If you cannot, give thanks you have lived so long, and make yourself ready in your cabin for the mischance of the hour, if it so hap. Cheerly, good hearts!   29
Out of our way, I say.   [*Exit.*]
GON. I have great comfort from this fellow. Methinks he hath no drowning mark upon him, his complexion is perfect gallows.° Stand fast, good Fate, to his hanging. Make the rope of his destiny our cable, for our own doth little advantage. If   35
he be not born to be hanged, our case is miserable.
[*Exeunt.*]
[*Re-enter* BOATSWAIN.]
BOATS. Down with the topmast! Yare! Lower, lower! Bring her to try with main course.° [*A cry within.*] A plague upon this howling! They are louder than the weather or our office.°   40
[*Re-enter* SEBASTIAN, ANTONIO, *and* GONZALO.] Yet again! What do you here? Shall we give o'er, and drown? Have you a mind to sink?
SEB. A pox o' your throat, you bawling, blasphemous, incharitable dog!
BOATS. Work you, then.   45
ANT. Hang, cur! Hang, you whoreson,° insolent noisemaker. We are less afraid to be drowned than thou art.
GON. I'll warrant him for drowning,° though the

Act I, Sc. i: s.d., On . . . heard: The ship is in great danger. The wind is blowing hard from the sea; on the other side lies the rocky island, and between there is too little sea room for her to sail past without being driven ashore by the drift. 3. Good: my good man.   4. yarely: quickly, smartly.   7. Take . . . topsail: i.e., to lessen the drift. Tend: attend.   9. room: sea room.   11. Play . . . men: act like men.

24. work . . . present: bring us peace at once.   32–33. hath . . . gallows: Gonzalo remembers the proverb "He that is born to be hanged will never be drowned," and the boatswain looks like a gallows bird.   38. try . . . course: i.e., use only the mainsail to heave her to. course: sail.   40. office: business.   46. whoreson: bastard.   49. warrant . . . drowning: guarantee him against drowning.

ship were no stronger than a nutshell and as leaky as
an unstanched wench.   51
  BOATS. Lay her ahold,° ahold! Set her two
courses.° Off to sea again, lay her off.

                [*Enter* MARINERS *wet.*]

  MAR. All lost! To prayers, to prayers! All lost!   55
  BOATS. What, must our mouths be cold?°
  GON. The King and Prince at prayers! Let's assist
    them,
For our case is as theirs.
  SEB.   I'm out of patience.
  ANT. We are merely cheated of our lives by
    drunkards.
This wide-chapped° rascal — would thou mightst lie
    drowning
The washing of ten tides!°
  GON.   He'll be hanged yet,   61
Though every drop of water swear against it
And gape at widest to glut° him.

       [*A confused noise within:* "Mercy on us!"
       — "We split, we split!" — "Farewell my
       wife and children!" — "Farewell, brother!"
       — "We split, we split, we split!"]

  ANT. Let's all sink with the King.
  SEB. Let's take leave of him.   68

        [*Exeunt* ANTONIO *and* SEBASTIAN.]

  GON. Now would I give a thousand furlongs of
sea for an acre of barren ground, long heath,° brown
furze,° anything. The wills above be done! But   72
I would fain die a dry death.   [*Exeunt.*]

SCENE II. *The island. Before* PROSPERO'S *cell.*

        [*Enter* PROSPERO *and* MIRANDA.]

  MIRA. If by your art, my dearest father, you have
Put the wild waters in this roar, allay° them.
The sky, it seems, would pour down stinking pitch
But that the sea, mounting to the welkin's° cheek,
Dashes the fire out. Oh, I have suffered   5
With those that I saw suffer! A brave vessel,
Who had no doubt some noble creature in her,
Dashed all to pieces. Oh, the cry did knock
Against my very heart! Poor souls, they perished!
Had I been any god of power, I would   10
Have sunk the sea within the earth or ere
It should the good ship so have swallowed and
The fraughting° souls within her.
  PRO.   Be collected.°

No more amazement. Tell your piteous heart
There's no harm done.
  MIRA.   Oh, woe the day!
  PRO.   No harm.   15
I have done nothing but in care of thee,
Of thee, my dear one, thee, my daughter, who
Art ignorant of what thou art, naught knowing
Of whence I am, nor that I am more better
Than Prospero, master of a full° poor cell,   20
And thy no greater father.
  MIRA.   More to know
Did never meddle° with my thoughts.
  PRO.   'Tis time
I should inform thee farther. Lend thy hand,
And pluck my magic garment from me. — So.

             [*Lays down his mantle.*]

Lie there, my art. Wipe thou thine eyes, have com-
    fort.   25
The direful spectacle of the wreck, which touched
The very virtue of compassion in thee,
I have with such provision° in mine art
So safely ordered that there is no soul,
No, not so much perdition° as a hair,   30
Betid° to any creature in the vessel
Which thou heard'st cry, which thou saw'st sink. Sit
    down,
For thou must now know farther.
  MIRA.   You have often
Begun to tell me what I am, but stopped,
And left me to a bootless inquisition,°   35
Concluding "Stay, not yet."
  PRO.   The hour's now come,
The very minute bids thee ope thine ear.
Obey, and be attentive. Canst thou remember
A time before we came unto this cell?
I do not think thou canst, for then thou wast not   40
Out° three years old.
  MIRA.   Certainly, sir, I can.
  PRO. By what? By any other house or person?
Of anything the image tell me that
Hath kept with thy remembrance.
  MIRA.   'Tis far off,
And rather like a dream than an assurance   45
That my remembrance warrants. Had I not
Four or five women once that tended me?
  PRO. Thou hadst, and more, Miranda. But how
    is it
That this lives in thy mind? What seest thou else
In the dark backward and abysm of time?°   50
If thou remember'st aught ere thou camest here,
How thou camest here thou mayst.
  MIRA.   But that I do not.

---

52. **ahold:** close to the wind.   52–53. **two courses:** two sails; i.e.,
set the foresail as well. The maneuver of heaving-to has failed;
the boatswain now hopes to get the ship moving into the wind
enough to pass the island.   56. **mouths be cold:** Here the boatswain abandons hope and falls to drinking.   60. **wide-chapped:**
large-cheeked, because full of liquor.   61. **washing . . . tides:**
Pirates were hanged on the seashore and left until three high
tides had passed over them.   63. **glut:** swallow.   71. **long
heath:** rough grass.   72. **furze:** a prickly bushy shrub.

  Sc. ii: 2. **allay:** abate.   4. **welkin:** sky.   13. **fraughting:** lit.,
who were her freight. collected: calm.

20. **full:** exceedingly.   22. **meddle:** interfere; i.e., cause to be
curious.   28. **provision:** foresight.   30. **perdition:** loss.
31. **Betid:** befallen.   35. **bootless inquisition:** vain inquiry.
41. **Out:** more than.   50. **abysm of time:** i.e., the past, which is
like a dark abyss.

PRO. Twelve year since, Miranda, twelve year
   since,
Thy father was the Duke of Milan, and
A prince of power.

MIRA.   Sir, are not you my father?   55

PRO. Thy mother was a piece of virtue, and
She said thou wast my daughter, and thy father
Was Duke of Milan, and his only heir
A Princess, no worse issued.

MIRA.   Oh, the Heavens!
What foul play had we that we came from thence?
Or blessèd was't we did?

PRO.   Both, both, my girl.   61
By foul play, as thou say'st, were we heaved thence,
But blessedly holp° hither.

MIRA.   Oh, my heart bleeds
To think o' the teen° that I have turned you to,
Which is from my remembrance! Please you, far-
   ther.   65

PRO. My brother, and thy uncle, called Antonio —
I pray thee mark me — that a brother should
Be so perfidious! — he whom, next thyself,
Of all the world I loved, and to him put
The manage° of my state — as at that time   70
Through all the signories° it was the first,
And Prospero the prime° Duke, being so reputed
In dignity, and for the liberal arts°
Without a parallel, those being all my study —
The government I cast upon my brother,   75
And to my state grew stranger, being transported
And rapt in secret studies. Thy false uncle ——
Dost thou attend me?

MIRA.   Sir, most heedfully.

PRO. Being once perfected° how to grant suits,
How to deny them, who to advance, and who   80
To trash for overtopping,° new-created°
The creatures that were mine, I say, or changed 'em,
Or else new-formed 'em — having both the key°
Of officer and office, set all hearts i' the state
To what tune pleased his ear, that now he was   85
The ivy which had hid my princely trunk,
And sucked my verdure out on't. Thou attend'st
   not.

MIRA. Oh, good sir, I do.

PRO.   I pray thee, mark me.
I, thus neglecting worldly ends, all dedicated
To closeness° and the bettering of my mind   90
With that which, but by being so retired,°
O'erprized all popular rate,° in my false brother

Awaked an evil nature. And my trust,
Like a good parent, did beget of him
A falsehood in its contrary as great   95
As my trust was, which had indeed no limit,
A confidence sans° bound. He being thus lorded,
Not only with what my revenue yielded,
But what my power might else exact, like one
Who having into truth, by telling of it,   100
Made such a sinner of his memory,
To credit his own lie, he did believe
He was indeed the Duke° — out o' the substitution,
And executing the outward face of royalty,
With all prerogative.° — Hence his ambition grow-
   ing ——   105
Dost thou hear?

MIRA.   Your tale, sir, would cure deafness.

PRO. To have no screen between this part he
   played
And him he played it for, he needs will be
Absolute Milan.° Me, poor man, my library
Was dukedom large enough. Of temporal royalties°
He thinks me now incapable; confederates,°   111
So dry° he was for sway, wi' the King of Naples
To give him annual tribute, do him homage,
Subject his coronet to his crown,° and bend
The dukedom, yet unbowed — alas, poor Milan! —
To most ignoble stooping.

MIRA.   Oh, the Heavens!   116

PRO. Mark his condition, and the event,° then tell
   me
If this might be a brother.

MIRA.   I should sin
To think but nobly of my grandmother.
Good wombs have borne bad sons.

PRO.   Now the condition.   120
This King of Naples, being an enemy
To me inveterate, hearkens my brother's suit.
Which was that he, in lieu o' the premises,°
Of homage, and I know not how much tribute,
Should presently° extirpate° me and mine   125
Out of the dukedom, and confer fair Milan,
With all the honors, on my brother. Whereon,
A treacherous army levied, one midnight
Fated to the purpose did Antonio open
The gates of Milan, and, i' the dead of darkness   130
The ministers for the purpose hurried thence
Me and thy crying self.

63. holp: helped.   64. teen: sorrow.   70. manage: management.
71. signories: lordships.   72. prime: leading.   73. liberal arts:
academic learning.   79. perfected: become perfect by practice.
81. trash . . . overtopping: check for running ahead, a metaphor
from training a pack of hounds. new-created: made them new
creatures — by altering their minds.   83. key: tool used for
tuning a stringed instrument.   90. closeness: privacy.   91. but
. . . retired: except that it kept me away from state affairs.
92. O'erprized . . . rate: was worth more than it is commonly
regarded.

97. sans: without.   97–103. He . . . Duke: he, getting such
greatness not only from my wealth but also by abusing my power,
began to believe as he had hitherto pretended, that he was in
truth the Duke.   103–05. out . . . prerogative: from being my
substitute and acting outwardly as Duke with all the rights of a
ruler.   109. Absolute Milan: Duke of Milan in fact.   110. temporal royalties: worldly power.   111. confederates: conspires.
112. dry: thirsty.   114. Subject . . . crown: i.e., pay homage as
to his overlord. The coronet was worn as a symbol by rulers of
lower rank than that of King.   117. event: sequel.   123. in . . .
premises: in return for these conditions.   125. presently: immediately. extirpate: root out.

MIRA.   Alack, for pity!
I, not remembering how I cried out then,
Will cry it o'er again. It is a hint°
That wrings mine eyes to't.
       PRO.   Hear a little further,   135
And then I'll bring thee to the present business
Which now's upon 's, without the which this story
Were most impertinent.
       MIRA.   Wherefore did they not
That hour destroy us?
       PRO.   Well demanded, wench.   139
My tale provokes that question. Dear, they durst not,
So dear the love my people bore me, nor set
A mark so bloody on the business, but
With colors fairer painted their foul ends.
In few,° they hurried us aboard a bark,   144
Bore us some leagues to sea, where they prepared
A rotten carcass of a butt,° not rigged,
Nor tackle, sail, nor mast. The very rats
Instinctively have quit it. There they hoist us,
To cry to the sea that roared to us, to sigh
To the winds, whose pity, sighing back again,   150
Did us but loving wrong.
       MIRA.   Alack, what trouble
Was I then to you!
       PRO.   Oh, a cherubin
Thou wast that did preserve me. Thou didst smile,
Infusèd with a fortitude from Heaven,   154
When I have decked the sea with drops full salt,
Under my burden groaned, which raised in me
An undergoing stomach° to bear up
Against what should ensue.
       MIRA.   How came we ashore?
       PRO. By Providence divine.
Some food we had, and some fresh water, that   160
A noble Neapolitan, Gonzalo,
Out of his charity, who being then appointed
Master of this design, did give us, with
Rich garments, linens, stuffs, and necessaries,
Which since have steaded much.° So, of his gentle-
ness,   165
Knowing I loved my books, he furnished me
From mine own library with volumes that
I prize above my dukedom.
       MIRA.   Would I might
But ever see that man!
       PRO.   Now I arise. [*Resumes his mantle.*]
Sit still, and hear the last of our sea sorrow.   170
Here in this island we arrived, and here
Have I, thy schoolmaster, made thee more profit
Than other princes can that have more time
For vainer hours, and tutors not so careful.
       MIRA. Heavens thank you for't! And now I pray
       you, sir,   175

134. **hint:** occasion.   144. **In few:** in a few words.   146. **butt:** tub.   157. **undergoing stomach:** courage to endure, the stomach being regarded as the seat of valor.   165. **have ... much:** have been of great benefit.

For still 'tis beating° in my mind, your reason
For raising this sea storm?
       PRO.   Know thus far forth.°
By accident most strange, bountiful Fortune,
Now my dear lady,° hath mine enemies
Brought to this shore. And by my prescience°   180
I find my zenith° doth depend upon
A most auspicious star, whose influence
If now I court not,° but omit, my fortunes
Will ever after droop. Here cease more questions.
Thou art inclined to sleep, 'tis a good dullness,   185
And give it way. I know thou canst not choose.
               [MIRANDA *sleeps.*]
Come away, servant, come. I am ready now.
Approach, my Ariel, come.
             [*Enter* ARIEL.]
ARI. All hail, great master! Grave sir, hail! I come
To answer thy best pleasure, be 't to fly,   190
To swim, to dive into the fire, to ride
On the curled clouds, to thy strong bidding task°
Ariel and all his quality.°
       PRO.   Hast thou, spirit,
Performed to point° the tempest that I bade thee?
       ARI. To every article.   195
I boarded the King's ship. Now on the beak,
Now in the waist,° the deck, in every cabin,
I flamed amazement.° Sometime I'd divide,
And burn in many places; on the topmast,   199
The yards and bowsprit, would I flame distinctly,
Then meet and join. Jove's lightnings, the precur-
     sors°
O' the dreadful thunderclaps, more momentary
And sight-outrunning were not. The fire and cracks
Of sulphurous roaring the most mighty Neptune
Seem to besiege, and make his bold waves tremble —
Yea, his dread trident shake.
       PRO.   My brave spirit!   206
Who was so firm, so constant, that this coil°
Would not infect his reason?
       ARI.   Not a soul
But felt a fever of the mad° and played
Some tricks of desperation.° All but mariners   210
Plunged in the foaming brine, and quit the vessel,
Then all afire with me. The King's son, Ferdinand,
With hair upstaring — then like reeds, not hair —
Was the first man that leaped, cried, " Hell is empty,

176. **beating:** throbbing.   177. **Know ... forth:** i.e., I will now tell you more.   179. **Now ... lady:** Fortune (once my foe) is now kind to me.   180. **prescience:** foreknowledge.   181. **zenith:** the highest point of my fortunes.   183. **court not:** do not seek to win.   192. **task:** impose a task on.   193. **quality:** ability.   194. **to point:** in all points, exactly.   197. **waist:** that part of the ship which lies between forecastle and poop. See Pl. 7a and 6a.   198. **flamed amazement:** appeared in the form of fire which caused amazement. This phenomenon, known as Saint Elmo's fire or a corposant, is sometimes seen on ships during a storm.   201. **precursors:** forerunners.   207. **coil:** confusion.   209. **fever ... mad:** fever of madness.   210. **tricks of desperation:** desperate tricks.

And all the devils are here."

PRO.   Why, that's my spirit! 215
But was not this nigh shore?

ARI.   Close by, my master.

PRO. But are they, Ariel, safe?

ARI.   Not a hair perished,
On their sustaining° garments not a blemish,
But fresher than before. And, as thou badest me,
In troops I have dispersed them 'bout the isle.   220
The King's son have I landed by himself,
Whom I left cooling of the air with sighs
In an odd angle° of the isle, and sitting
His arms in this sad knot.°

PRO.   Of the King's ship,
The mariners, say how thou hast disposed,   225
And all the rest o' the fleet.

ARI.   Safely in harbor
Is the King's ship — in the deep nook where once
Thou call'dst me up at midnight to fetch dew
From the still-vexed Bermoothes,° there she's hid.
The mariners all under hatches stowed,   230
Who, with a charm joined to their suffered labor,°
I have left asleep. And for the rest o' the fleet,
Which I dispersed, they all have met again,
And are upon the Mediterranean flote,°
Bound sadly home for Naples,   235
Supposing that they saw the King's ship wrecked
And his great person perish.

PRO.   Ariel, thy charge
Exactly is performed. But there's more work.
What is the time o' the day?

ARI.   Past the midseason.

PRO. At least two glasses.° The time 'twixt six and
now   240
Must by us both be spent most preciously.

ARI. Is there more toil? Since thou dost give me
pains,°
Let me remember° thee what thou hast promisèd,
Which is not yet performed me.

PRO.   How now? Moody?
What is't thou canst demand?

ARI.   My liberty.   245

PRO. Before the time be out? No more!

ARI.   I prithee
Remember I have done thee worthy service,
Told thee no lies, made thee no mistakings, served
Without or grudge or grumblings. Thou didst
promise
To bate° me a full year.

PRO.   Dost thou forget   250
From what a torment I did free thee?

ARI.   No.

PRO. Thou dost, and think'st it much to tread the
ooze
Of the salt deep,
To run upon the sharp wind of the North,
To do me business in the veins o' the earth   255
When it is baked with frost.

ARI.   I do not, sir.

PRO. Thou liest, malignant thing! Hast thou forgot
The foul witch Sycorax, who with age and envy
Was grown into a hoop?° Hast thou forgot her?

ARI. No, sir.

PRO.   Thou hast. Where was she born?
Speak, tell me.   260

ARI. Sir, in Argier.°

PRO.   Oh, was she so? I must
Once in a month recount what thou hast been,
Which thou forget'st. This damned witch Sycorax,
For mischiefs manifold and sorceries terrible
To enter human hearing,° from Argier,   265
Thou know'st, was banished. For one thing she did°
They would not take her life. Is not this true?

ARI. Aye, sir.

PRO. This blue-eyed° hag was hither brought
with child,
And here was left by the sailors. Thou, my slave,
As thou report'st thyself, wast then her servant. 271
And, for thou wast a spirit too delicate
To act her earthy and abhorred commands,
Refusing her grand hests,° she did confine thee,
By help of her more potent ministers   275
And in her most unmitigable° rage,
Into a cloven pine. Within which rift
Imprisoned thou didst painfully remain
A dozen years. Within which space she died,
And left thee there, where thou didst vent thy
groans   280
As fast as mill wheels strike.° Then was this is-
land —
Save for the son that she did litter here,
A freckled whelp hag-born° — not honored with
A human shape.

ARI.   Yes, Caliban her son.

PRO. Dull thing, I say so, he, that Caliban   285
Whom now I keep in service. Thou best know'st
What torment I did find thee in. Thy groans
Did make wolves howl and penetrate the breasts
Of ever-angry bears. It was a torment
To lay upon the damned, which Sycorax   290
Could not again undo. It was mine art,
When I arrived and heard thee, that made gape
The pine and let thee out.

ARI.   I thank thee, master.

---

218. **sustaining:** which bore them up.   223. **angle:** corner.
224. **in . . . knot:** sadly folded. Ariel imitates the posture.
229. **still-vexed Bermoothes:** ever stormy Bermudas. 231. **joined
. . . labor:** as well as the labor they had endured.   234. **flote:**
sea.   240. **glasses:** i.e., hours; turns of the hourglass. 242. **pains:**
toil.   243. **remember:** remind.   250. **bate:** abate, lessen.

259. **grown . . . hoop:** bent double. 261. **Argier:** Algiers. 265. **To
. . . hearing:** for a human being to hear.   266. **one . . . did:** This
good action is not recalled.   269. **blue-eyed:** with dark rings
under the eyes.   274. **hests:** commands.   276. **unmitigable:**
absolute.   281. **mill . . . strike:** i.e., the continuous clack of a
water mill.   283. **hag-born:** child of a hag.

PRO. If thou more murmur'st, I will rend an oak°
And peg thee in his knotty entrails till   295
Thou hast howled away twelve winters.
    ARI.   Pardon, master.
I will be correspondent° to command,
And do my spiriting° gently.
    PRO.   Do so, and after two days
I will discharge thee.
    ARI.   That's my noble master!
What shall I do? Say what. What shall I do?   300
    PRO. Go make thyself like a nymph o' the sea.
Be subject to no sight but thine and mine, invisible
To every eyeball else. Go take this shape,
And hither come in't. Go, hence with diligence!
                    [*Exit* ARIEL.]
Awake, dear heart, awake! Thou hast slept well.
Awake!
    MIRA. The strangeness of your story put   306
Heaviness in me.
    PRO.   Shake it off. Come on,
We'll visit Caliban my slave, who never
Yields us kind answer.
    MIRA.   'Tis a villain, sir,
I do not love to look on.
    PRO.   But, as 'tis,   310
We cannot miss° him. He does make our fire,
Fetch in our wood, and serves in offices
That profit us. What ho! Slave! Caliban!
Thou earth,° thou! Speak.
    CAL. [*Within*]   There's wood enough within.
    PRO. Come forth, I say! There's other business for
    thee.   315
Come, thou tortoise! When?
[*Re-enter* ARIEL *like a water nymph.*] Fine appari-
    tion! My quaint° Ariel,
Hark in thine ear.
    ARI.   My lord, it shall be done. [*Exit.*]
    PRO. Thou poisonous slave, got° by the Devil him-
    self
Upon thy wicked dam,° come forth!   320
             [*Enter* CALIBAN.]
    CAL. As wicked dew as e'er my mother brushed
With raven's feather from unwholesome fen
Drop on you both! A southwest° blow on ye
And blister you all o'er!
    PRO. For this, be sure, tonight thou shalt have
    cramps,   325
Side stitches that shall pen thy breath up. Urchins°
Shall, for that vast° of night that they may work,
All exercise on thee. Thou shalt be pinched
As thick as honeycomb, each pinch more stinging

Than bees that made 'em.
    CAL.   I must eat my dinner.   330
This island's mine, by Sycorax my mother,
Which thou takest from me. When thou camest first,
Thou strokedst me, and madest much of me, wouldst
    give me
Water with berries in't.° And teach me how
To name the bigger light, and how the less,   335
That burn by day and night. And then I loved thee,
And showed thee all the qualities° o' th' isle,
The fresh springs, brine pits, barren place and fer-
    tile.
Cursèd be I that did so! All the charms
Of Sycorax, toads, beetles, bats, light on you!   340
For I am all the subjects that you have,
Which first was mine own king. And here you sty°
    me
In this hard rock whiles you do keep from me
The rest o' th' island.
    PRO.   Thou most lying slave,
Whom stripes° may move, not kindness! I have used
    thee,   345
Filth as thou art, with human care, and lodged thee
In mine own cell till thou didst seek to violate
The honor of my child.
    CAL. Oh ho, oh ho! Would 't had been done!
Thou didst prevent me. I had peopled else   350
This isle with Calibans.
    PRO.   Abhorrèd slave,
Which any print° of goodness wilt not take,
Being capable of all ill! I pitied thee,
Took pains to make thee speak, taught thee each
    hour   354
One thing or other. When thou didst not, savage,
Know thine own meaning, but wouldst gabble like
A thing most brutish, I endowed thy purposes
With words that made them known. But thy vile
    race,
Though thou didst learn, had that in't which good
    natures
Could not abide to be with. Therefore wast thou
Deservedly confined into this rock,   361
Who hadst deserved more than a prison.
    CAL. You taught me language, and my profit on't
Is I know how to curse. The red plague° rid° you
For learning° me your language!
    PRO.   Hagseed,° hence!   365
Fetch us in fuel, and be quick, thou'rt best,
To answer other business. Shrug'st thou, malice?
If thou neglect'st, or dost unwillingly
What I command, I'll rack thee with old° cramps,

---

294. rend an oak: i.e., a far worse torment than imprisonment in a pine. 297. correspondent: agreeable, submissive. 298. spiriting: my work as a spirit. 311. miss: do without. 314. earth: lump of dirt. 317. quaint: elegant. 319. got: begotten. 320. dam: mother. 323. southwest: regarded as an unhealthy wind. 326. Urchins: goblins, or hedgehogs. 327. vast: desolate period.

334. Water . . . in't: Shakespeare apparently took this from Strachey's account, which records that the castaways made a pleasant drink from cedar berries. 337. qualities: good spots. 342. sty: pen. 345. stripes: blows. 352. print: impression. 364. red plague: bubonic plague. rid: destroy. 365. learning: teaching. Hagseed: son of a hag. 369. old: abundant.

Fill all thy bones with aches,° make thee roar   370
That beasts shall tremble at thy din.
    CAL.   No, pray thee.
[*Aside*] I must obey. His art is of such power
It would control my dam's god, Setebos,   373
And make a vassal° of him.
    PRO.   So, slave. Hence!
                           [*Exit* CALIBAN.]
[*Re-enter* ARIEL, *invisible, playing and singing;*
FERDINAND *following.*]
    ARI. [*Sings.*]
      "Come unto these yellow sands,
        And then take hands.
      Curtsied when you have and kissed
        The wild waves whist,°
      Foot it featly° here and there,   380
      And, sweet sprites, the burden° bear."
    BURDEN. [*Dispersedly*]° "Hark, hark!"
                    "Bowwow."
    ARI. "The watchdogs bark."
    BURDEN. [*Dispersedly*]   "Bowwow."
    ARI. "Hark, hark! I hear
      The strain of strutting chanticleer   385
      Cry Cock-a-diddle-dow."
    FER. Where should this music be? I' th' air or th'
      earth?
It sounds no more, and, sure, it waits upon
Some god o' th' island. Sitting on a bank,
Weeping again the King my father's wreck,   390
This music crept by me upon the waters,
Allaying both their fury and my passion°
With its sweet air. Thence I have followed it,
Or it hath drawn me rather. But 'tis gone.   395
No, it begins again.
    ARI. [*Sings.*]
      "Full fathom five thy father lies,
        Of his bones are coral made,
      Those are pearls that were his eyes.
        Nothing of him that doth fade   400
      But doth suffer a sea change
      Into something rich and strange.
      Sea nymphs hourly ring his knell."
    BURDEN.   "Dingdong."
    ARI. "Hark! Now I hear them. — Dingdong,
      bell."
                           404
    FER. The ditty does remember my drowned father.
This is no mortal business, nor no sound
That the earth owes.° — I hear it now above me.
    PRO. The fringèd curtains of thine eye advance,°
And say what thou seest yond.
    MIRA.   What is't? A spirit?
Lord, how it looks about! Believe me, sir,   410

It carries a brave form.° But 'tis a spirit.
    PRO. No, wench, it eats and sleeps and hath such
    senses
As we have, such. This gallant which thou seest
Was in the wreck, and but he's something stained
With grief, that's beauty's canker,° thou mightst
    call him   415
A goodly person. He hath lost his fellows,
And strays about to find 'em.
    MIRA.   I might call him
A thing divine, for nothing natural
I ever saw so noble.
    PRO.   [*Aside*] It goes on,° I see,   419
As my soul prompts it. Spirit, fine spirit! I'll free thee
Within two days for this.
    FER.   Most sure, the goddess
On whom these airs attend!° Vouchsafe my prayer
May know if you remain upon this island,°
And that you will some good instruction give
How I may bear me° here. My prime request,   425
Which I do last pronounce, is, O you wonder!
If you be maid or no?°
    MIRA.   No wonder, sir,
But certainly a maid.
    FER.   My language! Heavens!
I am the best of them° that speak this speech,
Were I but where 'tis spoken.
    PRO.   How? The best?   430
What wert thou if the King of Naples heard thee?
    FER. A single° thing, as I am now, that wonders
To hear thee speak of Naples. He does hear me,
And that he does I weep. Myself am Naples,
Who with mine eyes, never since at ebb,° beheld
The King my father wrecked.
    MIRA.   Alack, for mercy!   436
    FER. Yes, faith, and all his lords, the Duke of
    Milan
And his brave son being twain.°
    PRO.   [*Aside*] The Duke of Milan
And his more braver daughter could control thee,
If now 'twere fit to do't. At the first sight   440
They have changed eyes.° Delicate Ariel,
I'll set thee free for this. [*To* FERDINAND] A word,
    good sir.
I fear you have done yourself some wrong. A word.
    MIRA. Why speaks my father so ungently? This
Is the third man that e'er I saw, the first   445
That e'er I sighed for. Pity move my father
To be inclined my way!

---

370. **aches:** a two-syllable word, pronounced like "h's."
374. **vassal:** slave.   379. **whist:** silent.   380. **featly:** smartly.
381. **burden:** refrain.   382 s.d., **Dispersedly:** from different
sides.   392. **passion:** emotion, sorrow.   407. **owes:** owns, possesses.   408. **advance:** raise.

411. **brave form:** fine shape.   415. **canker:** maggot.   419. **It . . .
on:** i.e., Prospero's plan that Miranda and Ferdinand shall fall in
love.   422. **attend:** wait on.   422–23. **Vouchsafe . . . island:**
grant my prayer, which is to know whether you inhabit this
island.   425. **bear me:** behave myself.   427. **maid or no:** i.e., a
mortal or a goddess.   429. **best of them:** i.e., I am now King of
Naples since my father's death.   432. **single:** lonely.   435. **never
. . . ebb:** i.e., have not ceased to flow.   438. **twain:** i.e., two of
those drowned.   441. **changed eyes:** fallen in love.

FER.   Oh, if a virgin,
And your affection not gone forth,° I'll make you
The Queen of Naples.
     PRO.   Soft, sir! One word more.
[*Aside*] They are both in either's powers. But this
     swift business   450
I must uneasy make, lest too light winning
Make the prize light. [*To* FERDINAND] One word
     more. I charge thee
That thou attend me. Thou dost here usurp
The name thou owest not, and hast put thyself
Upon this island as a spy, to win it   455
From me, the lord on 't.
     FER.   No, as I am a man.
     MIRA. There's nothing ill can dwell in such a
     temple.°
If the ill spirit have so fair a house,
Good things will strive to dwell with 't.
     PRO.   Follow me.
Speak not you for him, he's a traitor. Come,   460
I'll manacle thy neck and feet together.
Sea water shalt thou drink, thy food shall be
The fresh-brook mussels, withered roots, and husks
Wherein the acorn cradled. Follow.
     FER.   No.
I will resist such entertainment till   465
Mine enemy has more power.
          [*Draws, and is charmed from moving.*]
     MIRA.   O dear Father,
Make not too rash a trial of him, for
He's gentle, and not fearful.°
     PRO.   What! I say,
My foot my tutor?° Put thy sword up, traitor,
Who makest a show but darest not strike, thy con-
     science   470
Is so possessed with guilt. Come from thy ward,°
For I can here disarm thee with this stick
And make thy weapon drop.
     MIRA.   Beseech you, Father.
     PRO. Hence! Hang not on my garments.
     MIRA.   Sir, have pity.
I'll be his surety.
     PRO.   Silence! One word more   475
Shall make me chide thee, if not hate thee. What!
An advocate for an impostor! Hush!
Thou think'st there is no more such shapes as he,
Having seen but him and Caliban. Foolish wench!
To the most of men this is a Caliban,   480
And they to him are angels.
     MIRA.   My affections
Are, then, most humble. I have no ambition
To see a goodlier man.

PRO.   Come on, obey.
Thy nerves° are in their infancy again,
And have no vigor in them.
     FER.   So they are.   485
My spirits, as in a dream, are all bound up.
My father's loss, the weakness which I feel,
The wreck of all my friends, nor this man's threats,
To whom I am subdued, are but light to me
Might I but through my prison once a day   490
Behold this maid. All corners else o' th' earth
Let liberty make use of, space enough
Have I in such a prison.
     PRO.   [*Aside*] It works.
                         [*To* FERDINAND] Come on.
Thou hast done well, fine Ariel!
                         [*To* FERDINAND] Follow me.   494
[*To* ARIEL] Hark what thou else shalt do me.
     MIRA.   Be of comfort.
My father's of a better nature, sir,
Than he appears by speech. This is unwonted°
Which now came from him.
     PRO.   Thou shalt be as free
As mountain winds. But then exactly do
All points of my command.
     ARI.   To the syllable.   500
     PRO. Come, follow. Speak not for him. [*Exeunt.*]

ACT II

SCENE I. *Another part of the island.*

[*Enter* ALONSO, SEBASTIAN, ANTONIO, GONZALO,
     ADRIAN, FRANCISCO, *and others.*]
     GON. Beseech you, sir, be merry. You have cause,
So have we all, of joy, for our escape
Is much beyond our loss. Our hint° of woe
Is common. Every day some sailor's wife,   4
The masters of some merchant,° and the merchant,°
Have just our theme of woe. But for the miracle —
I mean our preservation — few in millions
Can speak like us. Then wisely, good sir, weigh
Our sorrow with our comfort.
     ALON.   Prithee, peace.
     SEB. He receives comfort like cold porridge.   10
     ANT. The visitor° will not give him o'er so.
     SEB. Look, he's winding up the watch of his wit.
By and by it will strike.
     GON. Sir ——

---

448. **gone forth:** i.e., been bestowed on someone else. 457. **temple:**
i.e., beautiful body. 468. **fearful:** to be feared. 469. **My . . .
tutor:** The head is the tutor to the body, but Miranda (who is by
nature subordinate and so the foot) is trying to tell her father
what he should do. 471. **ward:** position of defense.

484. **nerves:** sinews. 497. **unwonted:** unusual.
     Act II, Sc. i: 3. hint: occasion. See I.ii.134. 5. **masters . . .
merchant:** captains of merchant ships. **the merchant:** i.e., the
owner. 11. **visitor:** visiting minister. Sebastian means that
Gonzalo will insist on having his say whether Alonso wishes to
hear it or not.

SEB. One. Tell.° 15

GON. When every grief is entertained° that's offered,

Comes to the entertainer ——

SEB. A dollar.

GON. Dolor comes to him, indeed. You have
spoken truer than you purposed. 20

SEB. You have taken it wiselier than I meant you
should.

GON. Therefore, my lord ——

ANT. Fie, what a spendthrift is he of his tongue!

ALON. I prithee, spare. 25

GON. Well, I have done. But yet ——

SEB. He will be talking.

ANT. Which, of he or Adrian, for a good wager,
first begins to crow?

SEB. The old cock. 30

ANT. The cockerel.

SEB. Done. The wager?

ANT. A laughter.°

SEB. A match!

ADR. Though this island seem to be desert ——

SEB. Ha, ha, ha! — So, you're paid.° 36

ADR. Uninhabitable, and almost inaccessible ——

SEB. Yet ——

ADR. Yet ——

ANT. He could not miss 't.° 40

ADR. It must needs be of subtle, tender, and delicate temperance.

ANT. Temperance was a delicate wench.

SEB. Aye, and a subtle, as he most learnedly delivered.° 45

ADR. The air breathes upon us here most sweetly.

SEB. As if it had lungs, and rotten ones.

ANT. Or as 'twere perfumed by a fen.

GON. Here is everything advantageous to life.

ANT. True — save means to live. 50

SEB. Of that there's none, or little.

GON. How lush and lusty the grass looks! How
green!

ANT. The ground indeed is tawny.

SEB. With an eye° of green in't. 55

ANT. He misses not much.

SEB. No, he doth but mistake the truth totally.

GON. But the rarity° of it is — which is indeed almost beyond credit° ——

SEB. As many vouched° rarities are. 60

GON. That our garments, being, as they were,
drenched in the sea, hold notwithstanding their

freshness and glosses, being rather new-dyed than
stained with salt water.

ANT. If but one of his pockets could speak,° would
it not say he lies? 66

SEB. Aye, or very falsely pocket up his report.

GON. Methinks our garments are now as fresh as
when we put them on first in Afric, at the marriage
of the King's fair daughter Claribel to the King of
Tunis. 71

SEB. 'Twas a sweet marriage, and we prosper well
in our return.

ADR. Tunis was never graced° before with such a
paragon to° their Queen. 75

GON. Not since Widow Dido's° time.

ANT. Widow! A pox° o' that! How came that
widow in?° Widow Dido!

SEB. What if he had said " Widower Aeneas " too?
Good Lord, how you take it! 80

ADR. " Widow Dido," said you? You make me
study of that. She was of Carthage, not of Tunis.

GON. This Tunis, sir, was Carthage.

ADR. Carthage?

GON. I assure you, Carthage. 85

ANT. His word is more than the miraculous harp.°

SEB. He hath raised the wall, and houses too.

ANT. What impossible matter will he make easy
next?

SEB. I think he will carry this island home in his
pocket, and give it his son for an apple. 91

ANT. And, sowing the kernels of it in the sea,
bring forth more islands.

GON. Aye.

ANT. Why, in good time. 95

GON. Sir, we were talking that our garments seem
now as fresh as when we were at Tunis at the marriage of your daughter, who is now Queen.

ANT. And the rarest that e'er came there.

SEB. Bate,° I beseech you, Widow Dido. 100

ANT. Oh, Widow Dido! Aye, Widow Dido.

GON. Is not, sir, my doublet° as fresh as the first
day I wore it? I mean, in a sort.°

ANT. That sort was well fished for.°

GON. When I wore it at your daughter's marriage? 105

ALON. You cram these words into mine ears
against

---

65. pockets . . . speak: i.e., his pockets are still wet. 74. graced:
honored. 75. to: for. 76. Widow Dido: Dido was the Queen of
Carthage (near the modern Tunis) who entertained Aeneas on his
way from Troy to Italy. She was a widow and had vowed eternal
fidelity to the memory of her husand, but she fell in love with
Aeneas. When he deserted her, she committed suicide. 77. pox:
plague; lit., venereal disease. 77–78. How . . . in: why do you
call her a widow? 86. His . . . harp: According to the legends
told by Ovid, the walls of Thebes came together at the music of
Amphion's harp. By a like miracle Gonzalo has erected a Carthage at Tunis. 100. Bate: except. 102. doublet: See Pl. 8b
and comment on p. 93a. 103. in a sort: after a fashion. 104. That
. . . for: i.e., he had to add "after a fashion."

---

15. Tell: count. 16. entertained: received. 33. A laughter:
the winner is to have the laugh on the loser, on the principle of
the proverb "He laughs that wins." 36. Ha . . . paid: F1
divides the speech: "Sebastian: Ha, ha, ha. Antonio: So,
you're paid"; i.e., you've had your laugh as winner. 40. He
. . . miss 't: i.e., if he begins the first clause with "though,"
he is sure to follow it up with a "yet." 45. delivered: declared.
55. eye: tinge. 58. rarity: strange thing. 59. credit: belief.
60. vouched: guaranteed.

The stomach of my sense. Would I had never
Married my daughter there! For, coming thence,
My son is lost and, in my rate,° she too
Who is so far from Italy removed   110
I ne'er again shall see her. O thou mine heir
Of Naples and of Milan, what strange fish
Hath made his meal on thee?

FRAN.   Sir, he may live.
I saw him beat the surges° under him,
And ride upon their backs. He trod the water,   115
Whose enmity he flung aside, and breasted
The surge most swoln° that met him. His bold head
'Bove the contentious waves he kept, and oared
Himself with his good arms in lusty stroke
To the shore, that o'er his wave-worn basis bowed,°
As stooping to relieve him. I not doubt   121
He came alive to land.

ALON.   No, no, he's gone.

SEB. Sir, you may thank yourself for this great
    loss,
That would not bless our Europe with your
    daughter,
But rather lose her to an African,   125
Where she, at least, is banished from your eye
Who hath cause to wet° the grief on 't.

ALON.   Prithee, peace.

SEB. You were kneeled to, and importuned other-
    wise,
By all of us, and the fair soul herself   129
Weighed° between loathness° and obedience, at
Which end o' the beam° should bow. We have lost
    your son,
I fear, forever. Milan and Naples have
Mo° widows in them of this business' making
Than we bring men to comfort them.
The fault's your own.

ALON.   So is the dear'st° o' the loss.   135

GON. My lord Sebastian,
The truth you speak doth lack some gentleness,
And time to speak it in. You rub the sore
When you should bring the plaster.

SEB.   Very well.

ANT. And most chirurgeonly.°   140

GON. It is foul weather in us all, good sir,
When you are cloudy.

SEB.   Foul weather?

ANT.   Very foul.

GON. Had I plantation° of this isle, my lord ——

ANT. He'd sow 't with nettle seed.

SEB.   Or docks, or mallows.°

GON. And were the King on 't, what would I do?

SEB. 'Scape being drunk for want of wine.   146

GON. I' the commonwealth I would by con-
    traries°
Execute all things, for no kind of traffic°
Would I admit, no name of magistrate.
Letters° should not be known; riches, poverty,   150
And use of service,° none; contract,° succession,°
Bourn,° bound° of land, tilth,° vineyard, none;
No use of metal,° corn, or wine, or oil;
No occupation° — all men idle, all;
And women too, but innocent and pure;   155
No sovereignty ——

SEB.   Yet he would be King on't.

ANT. The latter end of his commonwealth forgets
the beginning.

GON. All things in common nature should pro-
    duce
Without sweat or endeavor. Treason, felony,   160
Sword, pike, knife, gun, or need of any engine°
Would I not have. But Nature should bring
    forth,
Of it° own kind, all foison,° all abundance,
To feed my innocent people.

SEB. No marrying 'mong his subjects?   165

ANT. None, man — all idle, whores and knaves.

GON. I would with such perfection govern, sir,
To excel the Golden Age.°

SEB.   'Save° His Majesty!

ANT. Long live Gonzalo!

GON.   And — do you mark me, sir?

ALON. Prithee, no more. Thou dost talk nothing to
me.   171

GON. I do well believe your Highness, and did it
to minister occasion° to these gentlemen, who are of
such sensible° and nimble lungs that they always use
to laugh at nothing.   175

ANT. 'Twas you we laughed at.

GON. Who in this kind of merry fooling am nothing to you. So you may continue and laugh at nothing still.

ANT. What a blow was there given!   180

SEB. An° it had not fallen flat-long.°

GON. You are gentlemen of brave mettle,° you
would lift the moon out of her sphere° if she would
continue in it five weeks without changing.

---

109. rate: estimation. 114. surges: waves. 117. swoln: swol-
len. 120. his . . . bowed: hung over its base, which had been
worn away by the sea. 127. wet: weep for. 130. Weighed:
balanced. loathness: reluctance. 131. end . . . beam: which
scale should sink. 133. Mo: more. 135. dear'st: most griev-
ous. 140. chirurgeonly: like a good surgeon. 143. plantation:
colonization, but Antonio pretends to take it literally as "plant-
ing." 144. docks or mallows: common English weeds.

147. by contraries: contrary to the usual plan. 148. traffic:
trade. 150. Letters: learning. 151. use of service: no
one should have servants. contract: legal agreements. succession: right of inheritance. 152. Bourn: boundary. bound:
limit; i.e., private property rights. tilth: tillage. 153. use of
metal: i.e., exchange of money. 154. occupation: manual labor.
161. engine: instrument of warfare. 163. it: its. foison: plenty.
168. Golden Age: the days of perfect innocence at the beginning
of the world. 'Save: God save. 173. minister occasion: provide
opportunity. 174. sensible: sensitive. 181. An: if. flat-long:
on the flat side of the sword. 182. mettle: material, stuff.
183. sphere: course.

[*Enter* ARIEL (*invisible*) *playing solemn music.*]

SEB. We would so, and then go a-batfowling.°

ANT. Nay, good my lord, be not angry.   186

GON. No, I warrant you, I will not adventure my discretion so weakly.° Will you laugh me asleep, for I am very heavy?

ANT. Go sleep, and hear us.   190

[*All sleep except* ALONSO, SEBASTIAN, *and* ANTONIO.]

ALON. What, all so soon asleep! I wish mine eyes Would, with themselves, shut up my thoughts. I find They are inclined to do so.

SEB.   Please you, sir, Do not omit the heavy offer° of it. It seldom visits sorrow. When it doth,   195 It is a comforter.

ANT.   We two, my lord, Will guard your person while you take your rest, And watch your safety.

ALON.   Thank you. — Wondrous heavy.

[ALONSO *sleeps. Exit* ARIEL.]

SEB. What a strange drowsiness possesses them!

ANT. It is the quality° o' the climate.

SEB.   Why   200 Doth it not then our eyelids sink? I find not Myself disposed to sleep.

ANT.   Nor I. My spirits are nimble. They fell together all, as by consent, They dropped as by a thunderstroke. What might, Worthy Sebastian? — Oh, what might? — No more. —   205 And yet methinks I see it in thy face, What thou shouldst be. The occasion speaks thee,° and My strong imagination sees a crown Dropping upon thy head.

SEB.   What, art thou waking?°

ANT. Do you not hear me speak?

SEB.   I do, and surely   210 It is a sleepy language, and thou speak'st Out of thy sleep. What is it thou didst say? This is a strange repose, to be asleep With eyes wide-open — standing, speaking, moving, And yet so fast asleep.

ANT.   Noble Sebastian,   215 Thou let'st thy fortune sleep — die, rather — wink'st Whiles thou art waking.

SEB.   Thou dost snore distinctly. There's meaning in thy snores.

ANT. I am more serious than my custom. You Must be so too, if heed me,° which to do   220

Trebles thee o'er.

SEB.   Well, I am standing water.°

ANT. I'll teach you how to flow.°

SEB.   Do so. To ebb Hereditary sloth instructs me.

ANT.   Oh, If you but knew how you the purpose cherish Whiles thus you mock it! How, in stripping it,   225 You more invest it! Ebbing men, indeed, Most often do so near the bottom run By their own fear or sloth.°

SEB.   Prithee, say on. The setting° of thine eye and cheek proclaim A matter° from thee, and a birth, indeed,   230 Which throes thee much to yield.°

ANT.   Thus, sir. Although this lord of weak remembrance, this,° Who shall be of as little memory When he is earthed, hath here almost persuaded — For he's a spirit of persuasion, only   235 Professes to persuade — the King his son's alive, 'Tis as impossible that he's undrowned As he that sleeps here swims.

SEB.   I have no hope That he's undrowned.

ANT.   Oh, out of that " no hope " What great hope have you! No hope that way is Another way so high a hope that even   241 Ambition cannot pierce a wink beyond, But doubt discovery there.° Will you grant with me That Ferdinand is drowned?

SEB.   He's gone.

ANT.   Then tell me, Who's the next heir of Naples?

SEB.   Claribel.   245

ANT. She that is Queen of Tunis, she that dwells Ten leagues beyond man's life,° she that from Naples Can have no note, unless the sun were post° — The man i' the moon's too slow — till newborn chins Be rough and razorable.° She that from whom   250 We all were sea-swallowed, though some cast° again,

185. batfowling: hunting for birds at night with the aid of torches and sticks or bats.   187–88. adventure . . . weakly: risk my reputation as a discreet man so easily, by showing anger at such as you.   194. omit . . . offer: do not lose this chance of sleeping. 200. quality: nature.   207. occasion . . . thee: opportunity calls you.   209. waking: awake.   220. if . . . me: if you will listen to me.

221. Trebles . . . o'er: makes you three times the man you are. standing water: i.e., at the turning of the tide, which for a while neither ebbs nor flows.   222. flow: advance (like the rising tide). 224–28. If . . . sloth: if you would only realize how much you are moved by the prospect of becoming King, even while you mock it; how in stripping it of its glamour you make it more attractive. *Ebbing men* (i.e., the lazy and unambitious) often run aground through fear or sloth.   229. setting: expression.   230. matter: something serious.   231. throes . . . yield: is very painful to bring forth.   232. this . . . this: i.e., Francisco. See ll. 113–22. 240–43. No . . . there: i.e., your certainty that the true heir is drowned gives you a greater hope in another direction (i.e., of being King yourself), where even your ambition cannot look higher.   247. Ten . . . life: ten leagues farther than a man could travel in his lifetime.   248. post: messenger.   249–50. newborn . . . razorable: i.e., newborn children are grown men.   251. cast: vomited up.

And by that destiny, to perform an act
Whereof what's past is prologue, what to come,
In yours and my discharge.°
   SEB.   What stuff is this! How say you?
'Tis true, my brother's daughter's Queen of Tunis,
So is she heir of Naples, 'twixt which regions   256
There is some space.
   ANT.   A space whose every cubit
Seems to cry out, " How shall that Claribel
Measure us° back to Naples? Keep° in Tunis,
And let Sebastian wake." Say this were death   260
That now hath seized them — why, they were no
     worse
Than now they are. There be that can rule Naples
As well as he that sleeps, lords that can prate
As amply and unnecessarily
As this Gonzalo. I myself could make   265
A chough of as deep chat.° Oh, that you bore
The mind that I do! What a sleep were this
For your advancement! Do you understand me?
   SEB. Methinks I do.
   ANT.   And how does your content
Tender your own good fortune?
   SEB.   I remember   270
You did supplant your brother Prospero.
   ANT.   True.
And look how well my garments sit upon me,
Much feater° than before. My brother's servants
Were then my fellows,° now they are my men.°
   SEB. But — for your conscience.   275
   ANT. Aye, sir, where lies that? If 'twere a kibe,
'Twould put me to my slipper.° But I feel not
This deity in my bosom. Twenty consciences,
That stand 'twixt me and Milan, candied be they,
And melt ere they molest!° Here lies your brother,
No better than the earth he lies upon   281
If he were that which now he's like, that's dead.
Whom I, with this obedient steel, three inches of it,
Can lay to bed forever whiles you, doing thus,
To the perpetual wink° for aye might put   285
This ancient morsel, this Sir Prudence who
Should not upbraid our course. For all the rest,
They'll take suggestion as a cat laps milk,
They'll tell the clock to° any business that
We say befits the hour.
   SEB.   Thy case, dear friend,   290
Shall be my precedent. As thou got'st Milan,
I'll come by Naples. Draw thy sword. One stroke

Shall free thee from the tribute which thou payest,
And I the King shall love thee.
   ANT.   Draw together,
And when I rear my hand, do you the like,   295
To fall° it on Gonzalo.
   SEB.   Oh, but one word. [*They talk apart.*]
             [*Re-enter* ARIEL, *invisible.*]
   ARI. My master through his art foresees the danger
That you, his friend, are in, and sends me forth —
For else his project dies — to keep them living.
             [*Sings in* GONZALO'S *ear.*]
   " While you here do snoring lie,   300
     Open-eyed conspiracy
       His time° doth take.
     If of life you keep a care,
     Shake off slumber, and beware.
      Awake, awake! "   305
   ANT. Then let us both be sudden.
   GON.   Now, good angels
Preserve the King!   [*They wake.*]
   ALON. Why, how now? Ho, awake! — Why are
   you drawn?
Wherefore this ghastly looking?
   GON.   What's the matter?
   SEB. Whiles we stood here securing° your repose,
Even now, we heard a hollow burst of bellowing
Like bulls, or rather lions. Did 't not wake you?   312
It struck mine ear most terribly.
   ALON.   I heard nothing.
   ANT. Oh, 'twas a din to fright a monster's ear,
To make an earthquake! Sure, it was the roar   315
Of a whole herd of lions.
   ALON.   Heard you this, Gonzalo?
   GON. Upon mine honor, sir, I heard a humming,
And that a strange one too, which did awake me.
I shaked you, sir, and cried. As mine eyes opened
I saw their weapons drawn. — There was a noise,
That's verily.° 'Tis best we stand upon our guard,
Or that we quit this place. Let's draw our weapons.
   ALON. Lead off this ground, and let's make further
   search   323
For my poor son.
   GON.   Heavens keep him from these beasts!
For he is sure i' th' island.
   ALON.   Lead away.
   ARI. Prospero my lord shall know what I have
   done.
So, King, go safely on to seek thy son.   [*Exeunt.*]

SCENE II. *Another part of the island.*

[*Enter* CALIBAN *with a burden of wood. A noise of
thunder heard.*]

   CAL. All the infections that the sun sucks up
From bogs, fens, flats, on Prosper fall, and make him

254. discharge: task to be performed.   259. Measure us: retrace her journey after us. Keep: let her remain.   266. chough . . . chat: I could make a jackdaw (*chough*, rhyming with rough) talk as profoundly as he does.   273. feater: more trimly.   274. fellows: equals. men: servants.   276-77. kibe . . . slipper: a chilblain which would make me wear a slipper.   278-80. Twenty . . . molest: i.e., if twenty consciences had stood between me and the dukedom of Milan, I should have let them melt like candy before they would have disturbed me. Other editors take "candied" to mean "frozen."   285. perpetual wink: everlasting sleep.   289. tell . . . to: say it is time for.

296. fall: let fall.   302. time: opportunity.   310. securing: keeping safe.   321. verily: truth.

By inchmeal° a disease! His spirits hear me,
And yet I needs must curse. But they'll nor pinch,
Fright me with urchin shows,° pitch me i' the mire,
Nor lead me, like a firebrand,° in the dark   6
Out of my way, unless he bid 'em. But
For every trifle are they set upon me —
Sometime like apes, that mow° and chatter at me,
And after bite me; then like hedgehogs, which   10
Lie tumbling in my barefoot way and mount°
Their pricks at my footfall. Sometime am I
All wound with adders, who with cloven tongues
Do hiss me into madness.
          [*Enter* TRINCULO.] Lo, now, lo!
Here comes a spirit of his, and to torment me   15
For bringing wood in slowly. I'll fall flat.
Perchance he will not mind me.

TRIN. Here's neither bush nor shrub to bear off
any weather at all, and another storm brewing, I
hear it sing i' the wind. Yond same black cloud,   20
yond huge one, looks like a foul bombard° that
would shed his liquor. If it should thunder as it did
before, I know not where to hide my head. Yond
same cloud cannot choose but fall by pailfuls. What
have we here? A man or a fish? Dead or alive?   25
A fish — he smells like a fish, a very ancient and fish-
like smell, a kind of not of the newest Poor John.° A
strange fish! Were I in England now, as once I was,
and had but this fish painted,° not a holiday fool
there but would give a piece of silver. There would
this monster make a man° — any strange beast   31
there makes a man. When they will not give a doit°
to relieve a lame beggar, they will lay out ten to see
a dead Indian. Legged like a man! And his fins like
arms! Warm, o' my troth! I do now let loose   35
my opinion, hold it no longer — this is no fish, but
an islander that hath lately suffered by a thunderbolt.
[*Thunder.*] Alas, the storm is come again! Best
way is to creep under his gaberdine,° there is no
other shelter hereabout. Misery acquaints a man   40
with strange bedfellows. I will here shroud° till the
dregs of the storm be past.
          [*Enter* STEPHANO, *singing, a bottle in his hand.*]
STE.   " I shall no more to sea, to sea,
               Here shall I die ashore——"   45
This is a very scurvy° tune to sing at a man's funeral.
Well, here's my comfort.   [*Drinks. Sings.*]
" The master, the swabber, the boatswain, and I,
     The gunner, and his mate,
  Loved Mall, Meg, and Marian, and Margery,   50
  But none of us cared for Kate.

For she had a tongue with a tang,°
  Would cry to a sailor, Go hang!
She loved not the savor° of tar nor of pitch,   54
Yet a tailor might scratch her where'er she did itch.
  Then, to sea, boys, and let her go hang! "
This is a scurvy tune too, but here's my comfort.
                              [*Drinks.*]
CAL. Do not torment me. — Oh!   58
STE. What's the matter? Have we devils here? Do
you put tricks upon 's with salvages° and men of
Ind,° ha? I have not 'scaped drowning to be afeard
now of your four legs, for it hath been said,   62
As proper° a man as ever went on four legs cannot
make him give ground. And it shall be said so again
while Stephano breathes at nostrils.
CAL. The spirit torments me. — Oh!   66
STE. This is some monster of the isle with four
legs, who hath got, as I take it, an ague.° Where the
devil should he learn our language? I will give him
some relief, if it be but for that. If I can recover°
him, and keep him tame, and get to Naples with
him, he's a present for any emperor that ever trod on
neat's leather.°   73
CAL. Do not torment me, prithee, I'll bring my
wood home faster.
STE. He's in his fit now, and does not talk after
the wisest. He shall taste of my bottle. If he have
never drunk wine afore, it will go near to remove his
fit. If I can recover him, and keep him tame, I will
not take too much for him.° He shall pay for him
that hath him, and that soundly.   81
CAL. Thou dost me yet but little hurt, thou wilt
anon, I know it by thy trembling.° Now Prosper
works upon thee.   84
STE. Come on your ways. Open your mouth, here
is that which will give language to you, cat. Open
your mouth, this will shake your shaking, I can tell
you, and that soundly. You cannot tell who's your
friend. Open your chaps° again.   89
TRIN. I should know that voice. It should be —
but he is drowned, and these are devils. — Oh, defend me!   92
STE. Four legs and two voices — a most delicate
monster! His forward voice, now, is to speak well of
his friend, his backward voice is to utter foul
speeches and to detract. If all the wine in my bottle
will recover him, I will help his ague. Come. —
Amen! I will pour some in thy other mouth.   99
TRIN. Stephano!
STE. Doth thy other mouth call me? Mercy, mercy!

Sc. ii: 3. inchmeal: by inches.   5. urchin shows: the appearance of goblins. See I.ii.326.   6. firebrand: will-o'-the-wisp.
9. mow: make faces.   11. mount: raise.   21. bombard: large
black leathern jug.   27. Poor John: dried salt hake.   29. had
. . . painted: had a poster of this fish painted.   31. make a
man: i.e., his fortune.   32. doit: a small Dutch coin, a cent.
39. gaberdine: cloak.   41. shroud: cover myself.   46. scurvy:
"lousy."

52. tang: a sharp sound.   54. savor: taste.   60. salvages: savages.   60–61. men of Ind: natives of India.   63. proper: fine.
68. ague: fever, which makes him shiver.   71. recover: cure.
73. neat's leather: i.e., shoes.   79–80. I . . . him: I'll not take
even an excessive price.   83. trembling: Trinculo is the trembler,
for he believes that the voice of Stephano comes from a ghost.
Trinculo is a natural coward.   89. chaps: chops, jaws.

This is a devil and no monster. I will leave him, I
have no long spoon.°   103

TRIN. Stephano! If thou beest Stephano, touch me,
and speak to me, for I am Trinculo — be not afeard
— thy good friend Trinculo.

STE. If thou beest Trinculo, come forth. I'll pull
thee by the lesser legs. If any be Trinculo's legs, these
are they. Thou art very Trinculo indeed! How
camest thou to be the siege° of this mooncalf?° Can
he vent Trinculos?   111

TRIN. I look him to be killed with a thunderstroke. But art thou not drowned, Stephano? I hope,
now, thou art not drowned. Is the storm overblown?
I hid me under the dead mooncalf's gaberdine for
fear of the storm. And art thou living, Stephano? O
Stephano, two Neapolitans 'scaped!   117

STE. Prithee do not turn me about, my stomach is
not constant.°

CAL. [*Aside*] These be fine things, an if they be
    not sprites.
That's a brave god, and bears celestial liquor.
I will kneel to him.   122

STE. How didst thou 'scape? How camest thou
hither? Swear, by this bottle, how thou camest
hither. I escaped upon a butt of sack,° which the
sailors heaved o'erboard, by this bottle, which I made
of the bark of a tree with mine own hands, since I
was cast ashore.   128

CAL. I'll swear upon that bottle to be thy true subject, for the liquor is not earthly.

STE. Here, swear, then, how thou escapedst.

TRIN. Swam ashore, man, like a duck. I can swim
like a duck, I'll be sworn.   133

STE. Here, kiss the book. Though thou canst swim
like a duck, thou art made like a goose.

TRIN. O Stephano, hast any more of this?

STE. The whole butt, man. My cellar is in a rock
by the seaside, where my wine is hid. How now,
mooncalf! How does thine ague?   139

CAL. Hast thou not dropped from Heaven?

STE. Out o' the moon, I do assure thee. I was the
man 'i the moon when time was.°   142

CAL. I have seen thee in her, and I do adore thee.
My mistress showed me thee, and thy dog, and thy
bush.°

STE. Come, swear to that, kiss the book. I will fur-
nish it anon with new contents. Swear.   147

TRIN. By this good light, this is a very shallow
monster! I afeard of him! A very weak monster!
The man i' the moon! A most poor credulous monster! Well drawn,° monster, in good sooth!°   151

CAL. I'll show thee every fertile inch o' th' island,
And I will kiss thy foot. I prithee be my god.

TRIN. By this light, a most perfidious and drunken
monster! When's god's asleep, he'll rob his bottle.

CAL. I'll kiss thy foot, I'll swear myself thy subject.

STE. Come on, then, down, and swear.

TRIN. I shall laugh myself to death at this puppy-
headed monster. A most scurvy monster! I could find
in my heart to beat him ——   160

STE. Come, kiss.

TRIN. But that the poor monster's in drink. An
abominable monster!

CAL. I'll show thee the best springs, I'll pluck thee
    berries,
I'll fish for thee, and get thee wood enough.
A plague upon the tyrant that I serve!
I'll bear him no more sticks, but follow thee,
Thou wondrous man.   168

TRIN. A most ridiculous monster, to make a wonder of a poor drunkard!

CAL. I prithee let me bring thee where crabs°
    grow.   171
And I with my long nails will dig thee pignuts,°
Show thee a jay's nest, and instruct thee how
To snare the nimble marmoset.° I'll bring thee
To clustering filberts, and sometimes I'll get thee
Young scamels° from the rock. Wilt thou go with
    me?   176

STE. I prithee now, lead the way, without any
more talking. Trinculo, the King and all our company else being drowned, we will inherit here. Here,
bear my bottle, fellow Trinculo, we'll fill him by and
by again.   181

CAL. [*Sings drunkenly.*]
    " Farewell, master, farewell, farewell! "

TRIN. A howling monster, a drunken monster!

CAL. " No more dams I'll make for fish.
        Nor fetch in firing   185
        At requiring,
    Nor scrape trencher,° nor wash dish.
    'Ban, 'Ban, Cacaliban
    Has a new master. — Get a new man."
Freedom, heyday! Heyday, freedom! Freedom, heyday, freedom!   191

STE. O brave monster! Lead the way.   [*Exeunt.*]

---

103. I . . . spoon: "He that sups with the Devil needs a long
spoon" — a proverb from the time when men dipped into a common dish. A long spoon was needed, as the Devil's claws were long
and sharp, and his table manners nasty.   110. siege: excrement.
mooncalf: misshapen monster, freak.   119. constant: steady.
Trinculo is pawing him all over, and turning him round in his
excitement.   125. sack: a dry wine from Spain. For Falstaff on
the merits of sack, see *II Hen IV*, IV.iii.   142. when . . .
was: once upon a time.   144–45. thee . . . bush: the man
in the moon had his dog and bush of thorns, as Quince knew.
See *MND*, III.i.

151. drawn: sucked. sooth: truth.   171. crabs: crab apples.
172. pignut: called also earthnut, a plant producing edible
tubers.   174. marmoset: kind of small monkey.   176. scamels:
a much-discussed word which does not occur elsewhere
and so has been variously interpreted or emended, the likeliest guess being seamel: sea gull.   187. trencher: wooden
plate.

ACT III

SCENE I. *Before* PROSPERO's *cell.*

[*Enter* FERDINAND, *bearing a log.*]

FER. There be some sports are painful, and their
labor
Delight in them sets off.° Some kinds of baseness
Are nobly undergone, and most poor matters
Point° to rich ends. This my mean task
Would be as heavy to me as odious, but   5
The mistress which I serve quickens° what's dead
And makes my labors pleasures. Oh, she is
Ten times more gentle than her father's crabbèd,
And he's composed of harshness. I must remove
Some thousands of these logs, and pile them up,   10
Upon a sore injunction.° My sweet mistress
Weeps when she sees me work, and says such base-
ness
Had never like executor.° I forget.
But these sweet thoughts do even refresh my labors,
Most busy lest when I do it.°

[*Enter* MIRANDA, *and* PROSPERO *at a distance,*°
unseen.]

MIRA.   Alas, now, pray you   15
Work not so hard. I would the lightning had
Burned up those logs that you are enjoined to pile!
Pray set it down and rest you. When this burns,
'Twill weep° for having wearied you. My father
Is hard at study, pray now, rest yourself.   20
He's safe for these three hours.

FER.   O most dear mistress,
The sun will set before I shall discharge
What I must strive to do.

MIRA.   If you'll sit down,
I'll bear your logs the while. Pray give me that,
I'll carry it to the pile.

FER.   No, precious creature,   25
I had rather crack my sinews, break my back,
Than you should such dishonor undergo
While I sit lazy by.

MIRA.   It would become me
As well as it does you. And I should do it
With much more ease, for my goodwill is to it,   30
And yours it is against.

PRO.   Poor worm, thou art infected!

Act III, Sc. i: 1–2. their . . . off: the delight which they bring
outweighs the fatigue. 4. Point: lead. 6. quickens: brings to
life. 11. injunction: a command enforced with penalties against
disobedience. 13. executor: performer. 15. Most . . . it: This
line has been much discussed and may be corrupt. It means
apparently "I am most busy when I am idle, for then I think
so many sweet thoughts." lest: least. s.d., and . . . distance: F1
simply reads "Enter Miranda and Prospero." They obviously do
not enter together, and on the Elizabethan stage probably Prospero entered on the balcony above, as later (III.iii.19). The balcony was a most convenient place for eavesdroppers. 19. weep:
i.e., drip with sap when burning.

This visitation° shows it.

MIRA.   You look wearily.

FER. No, noble mistress, 'tis fresh morning with
me
When you are by at night. I do beseech you —
Chiefly that I might set it in my prayers —   35
What is your name?

MIRA.   Miranda. — O my father,
I have broke your hest° to say so!

FER.   Admired Miranda!°
Indeed the top° of admiration! Worth
What's dearest to the world! Full many a lady
I have eyed with best regard, and many a time   40
The harmony of their tongues hath into bondage
Brought my too diligent ear. For several° virtues
Have I liked several women, never any
With so full soul but some defect in her
Did quarrel with the noblest grace she owed,   45
And put it to the foil.° But you, oh, you,
So perfect and so peerless, are created
Of every creature's best!

MIRA.   I do not know
One of my sex, no woman's face remember
Save, from my glass, mine own. Nor have I seen   50
More that I may call men than you, good friend,
And my dear father. How features are abroad,
I am skill-less of.° But, by my modesty,
The jewel in my dower, I would not wish
Any companion in the world but you,   55
Nor can imagination form a shape
Besides yourself to like of. But I prattle
Something too wildly, and my father's precepts
I therein do forget.

FER.   I am, in my condition,
A prince, Miranda, I do think, a king —   60
I would not so! — and would no more endure
This wooden slavery° than to suffer
The flesh fly blow° my mouth. Hear my soul speak.
The very instant that I saw you did
My heart fly to your service, there resides,   65
To make me slave to it, and for your sake
Am I this patient logman.

MIRA.   Do you love me?

FER. O Heaven, O earth, bear witness to this
sound,
And crown what I profess with kind event°
If I speak true! If hollowly, invert   70
What best is boded° me to mischief! I,
Beyond all limit of what else i' the world,

---

32. visitation: visit. 37. hest: command. Admired Miranda: a
play on her name, for *miranda* in Latin means "she who ought to
be wondered at." "Admired" at this time had a stronger meaning
than today. 38. top: summit. 42. several: separate, individual.
46. put . . . foil: bring it to disgrace. 52–53. features . . . of: I
have no experience of how people look elsewhere. 62. wooden
slavery: i.e., task of having to carry wood. 63. blow: lay its eggs
on, foul. 69. event: result. 71. What . . . boded: the best
fate that is prophesied.

Do love, prize, honor you.

MIRA.   I am a fool
To weep at what I am glad of.

PRO.   Fair encounter
Of two most rare affections! Heavens rain grace   75
On that which breeds between 'em!

FER.   Wherefore weep you?

MIRA. At mine unworthiness, that dare not offer
What I desire to give, and much less take
What I shall die to want.° But this is trifling,
And all the more it seeks to hide itself,   80
The bigger bulk it shows. Hence, bashful cunning!
And prompt me, plain and holy innocence!
I am your wife, if you will marry me.
If not, I'll die your maid. To be your fellow°
You may deny me, but I'll be your servant,   85
Whether you will or no.

FER.   My mistress, dearest,
And I thus humble ever.

MIRA.   My husband, then?

FER. Aye, with a heart as willing°
As bondage e'er of freedom. Here's my hand.

MIRA. And mine, with my heart in 't. And now
        farewell   90
Till half an hour hence.

FER.   A thousand thousand!°

[*Exeunt* FERDINAND *and* MIRANDA *severally.*°]

PRO. So glad of this as they I cannot be,
Who° are surprised withal,° but my rejoicing
At nothing can be more. I'll to my book,
For yet ere suppertime must I perform   95
Much business appertaining.   [*Exit.*]

SCENE II. *Another part of the island.*

[*Enter* CALIBAN, STEPHANO, *and* TRINCULO.]

STE. Tell not me. — When the butt is out, we will
drink water, not a drop before. Therefore bear up,°
and board 'em. Servant-monster, drink to me.   4

TRIN. Servant-monster! The folly of this island!°
They say there's but five upon this isle. We are three
of them. If th' other two be brained like us, the state
totters.

STE. Drink, servant-monster, when I bid thee. Thy
eyes are almost set° in thy head.   10

TRIN. Where should they be set else? He were a
brave monster indeed if they were set in his tail.

STE. My man-monster hath drowned his tongue in
sack. For my part, the sea cannot drown me. I swam,

ere I could recover the shore, five-and-thirty leagues°
off and on. By this light, thou shalt be my lieutenant,
monster, or my standard.°   17

TRIN. Your lieutenant, if you list. He's no standard.

STE. We'll not run, Monsieur Monster.

TRIN. Nor go neither, but you'll lie, like dogs, and
yet say nothing neither.

STE. Mooncalf, speak once in thy life, if thou beest
a good mooncalf.   25

CAL. How does thy Honor? Let me lick thy shoe.
I'll not serve him, he is not valiant.

TRIN. Thou liest, most ignorant monster. I am in
case° to jostle a constable. Why, thou deboshed° fish
thou, was there ever man a coward that hath drunk
so much sack as I today? Wilt thou tell a monstrous
lie, being but half a fish and half a monster?   33

CAL. Lo, how he mocks me! Wilt thou let him,
my lord?

TRIN. "Lord," quoth he! That a monster should
be such a natural!°

CAL. Lo, lo, again! Bite him to death, I prithee.

STE. Trinculo, keep a good tongue in your   40
head. If you prove a mutineer — the next tree! The
poor monster's my subject, and he shall not suffer
indignity.

CAL. I thank my noble lord. Wilt thou be pleased
to hearken once again to the suit I made to thee? 45

STE. Marry,° will I. Kneel and repeat it. I will
stand, and so shall Trinculo.

[*Enter* ARIEL, *invisible.*]

CAL. As I told thee before, I am subject to a tyrant,
a sorcerer, that by his cunning hath cheated me of
the island.   50

ARI. Thou liest.

CAL. Thou liest,° thou jesting monkey thou.
I would my valiant master would destroy thee!
I do not lie.

STE. Trinculo, if you trouble him any more in 's
tale, by this hand, I will supplant° some of your
teeth.   57

TRIN. Why, I said nothing.

STE. Mum, then, and no more. Proceed.

CAL. I say, by sorcery he got this isle.   60
From me he got it. If thy greatness will
Revenge it on him — for I know thou darest,
But this thing dare not ——

STE. That's most certain.

CAL. Thou shalt be lord of it, and I'll serve thee.

STE. How now shall this be compassed?° 66
Canst thou bring me to the party?

79. **want:** be without. 84. **fellow:** equal. See II.i.274. 88. **will-ing:** eager. 91. **thousand thousand:** i.e., farewells. **s.d., sever-ally:** by different exits. 93. **Who:** i.e., Ferdinand and Miranda. **withal:** therewith.

Sc. ii: 2. **bear up:** crowd on more sail. 5. **The . . . island:** what a silly place this island is. 10. **set:** closed, dazed with drink.

15. **league:** three miles. 17. **standard:** standard-bearer (or en-sign), the junior officer in the company, the others being the captain and the lieutenant. Caliban is now too unsteady to be a satisfactory *standard*. 29. **in case:** in a condition. **deboshed:** debauched. 38. **natural:** born fool. 46. **Marry:** Mary, by the Virgin. 52. **Thou liest:** Caliban supposes the voice to be Trin-culo's. 56. **supplant:** displace. 66. **compassed:** brought about.

CAL. Yea, yea, my lord. I'll yield him thee asleep,
Where thou mayst knock a nail into his head.
ARI. Thou liest, thou canst not.   70
CAL. What a pied ninny's° this! Thou scurvy
patch!°
I do beseech thy greatness, give him blows,
And take his bottle from him. When that's gone,
He shall drink naught but brine, for I'll not show
him
Where the quick freshes° are.   75
STE. Trinculo, run into no further danger. Inter-
rupt the monster one word further and, by this
hand, I'll turn my mercy out o' doors and make a
stockfish° of thee.
TRIN. Why, what did I? I did nothing. I'll go
farther off.   81
STE. Didst thou not say he lied?
ARI. Thou liest.
STE. Do I so? Take thou that. [Beats him.] As
you like this, give me the lie° another time.   85
TRIN. I did not give the lie. Out o' your wits, and
hearing too? A pox o' your bottle! This can sack
and drinking do. A murrain° on your monster, and
the devil take your fingers!
CAL. Ha, ha, ha!   90
STE. Now, forward with your tale. — Prithee,
stand farther off.
CAL. Beat him enough. After a little time
I'll beat him too.
STE.   Stand farther. — Come, proceed.
CAL. Why, as I told thee, 'tis a custom with him
I' th' afternoon to sleep. There thou mayst brain
him,   96
Having first seized his books, or with a log
Batter his skull, or paunch° him with a stake,
Or cut his weasand° with thy knife. Remember
First to possess his books, for without them   100
He's but a sot, as I am, nor hath not
One spirit to command. They all do hate him
As rootedly° as I. Burn but his books.
He has brave utensils° — for so he calls them —
Which, when he has a house, he'll deck withal.   105
And that most deeply to consider is
The beauty of his daughter. He himself
Calls her a nonpareil.° I never saw a woman
But only Sycorax my dam and she,
But she as far surpasseth Sycorax   110
As great'st does least.
STE.   Is it so brave a lass?
CAL. Aye, lord, she will become thy bed, I warrant,

And bring thee forth brave brood.
STE. Monster, I will kill this man. His daughter
and I will be King and Queen — save our Graces! —
and Trinculo and thyself shall be Viceroys. Dost
thou like the plot, Trinculo?   117
TRIN. Excellent.
STE. Give me thy hand. I am sorry I beat thee, but
while thou livest keep a good tongue in thy head.
CAL. Within this half-hour will he be asleep.
Wilt thou destroy him then?
STE.   Aye, on mine honor.
ARI. This will I tell my master.
CAL. Thou makest me merry, I am full of pleasure.
Let us be jocund. Will you troll° the catch   126
You taught me but whilere?°
STE. At thy request, monster, I will do reason,°
any reason. — Come on, Trinculo, let us sing.
[Sings.]   "Flout° 'em and scout° 'em,
              And scout 'em and flout 'em.   131
              Thought is free."
CAL. That's not the tune.
        [ARIEL plays the tune on a tabor° and pipe.]
STE. What is this same?
TRIN. This is the tune of our catch, played by the
picture of Nobody.°   136
STE. If thou beest a man, show thyself in thy like-
ness. If thou beest a devil, take 't as thou list.
TRIN. Oh, forgive me my sins!
STE. He that dies pays all debts. I defy thee. Mercy
upon us!   141
CAL. Art thou afeard?
STE. No, monster, not I.
CAL. Be not afeard. The isle is full of noises,°
Sounds and sweet airs that give delight and hurt not.
Sometimes a thousand twangling instruments   146
Will hum about mine ears, and sometime voices
That, if I then had waked after long sleep,
Will make me sleep again. And then, in dreaming,
The clouds methought would open and show riches
Ready to drop upon me, that when I waked,   151
I cried to dream again.
STE. This will prove a brave kingdom to me,
where I shall have my music for nothing.
CAL. When Prospero is destroyed.   155
STE. That shall be by and by.° I remember the
story.
TRIN. The sound is going away. Let's follow it,
and after do our work.
STE. Lead, monster, we'll follow. I would I could
see this taborer, he lays it on.   161
TRIN. Wilt come? I'll follow, Stephano. [Exeunt.]

71. pied ninny: patched fool, because Trinculo as a jester wears
motley, the "patched" or particolored dress of his profession.
patch: fool.   75. quick freshes: running springs of fresh
water.   79. stockfish: dried cod, beaten to make it tender.
85. give . . . lie: call me a liar.   88. murrain: plague.   98. paunch:
stab him in the belly.   99. weasand: windpipe.   103. rootedly:
fixedly.   104. utensils: furnishings.   108. nonpareil: without
an equal.

126. troll: sing.   127. whilere: just now.   128. reason:
anything within reason.   130. Flout: mock. scout: deride.
133. s.d., tabor: small drum.   136. picture of Nobody: i.e.,
by an invisible player. There is a picture of Nobody in a play
called Nobody and Some-body, printed 1606. It is all head and
no body, like Humpty Dumpty.   144. noises: music.   156. by
. . . by: in the near future.

SCENE III. *Another part of the island.*

[*Enter* ALONSO, SEBASTIAN, ANTONIO, GONZALO,
ADRIAN, FRANCISCO, *and others.*]

GON. By'r Lakin,° I can go no further, sir,
My old bones ache. Here's a maze trod, indeed,
Through forthrights and meanders!° By your pa-
tience,
I needs must rest me.

ALON.   Old lord, I cannot blame thee,
Who am myself attached with° weariness,   5
To the dulling of my spirits. Sit down and rest.
Even here I will put off my hope, and keep it
No longer for my flatterer. He is drowned
Whom thus we stray to find, and the sea mocks
Our frustrate° search on land. Well, let him go. 10

ANT. [*Aside to* SEBASTIAN] I am right glad that
he's so out of hope.
Do not, for one repulse, forgo the purpose
That you resolved to effect.

SEB. [*Aside to* ANTONIO] The next advantage
Will we take throughly.°

ANT. [*Aside to* SEBASTIAN] Let it be tonight,
For now they are oppressed with travel, they   15
Will not, nor cannot, use such vigilance
As when they are fresh.

SEB. [*Aside to* ANTONIO] I say tonight. No more.
                              [*Solemn and strange music.*]

ALON. What harmony is this? — My good friends,
hark!

GON. Marvelous sweet music!

[*Enter* PROSPERO *above, invisible. Enter several
strange Shapes, bringing in a banquet.° They dance
about it with gentle actions of salutation, and, invit-
ing the King, etc., to eat, they depart.*]

ALON. Give us kind keepers, Heavens! — What
were these?   20

SEB. A living drollery.° Now° I will believe
That there are unicorns, that in Arabia
There is one tree, the phoenix'° throne, one phoenix
At this hour reigning there.

ANT.   I'll believe both,
And what does else want credit,° come to me   25
And I'll be sworn 'tis true. Travelers ne'er did lie,
Though fools at home condemn 'em.

GON.   If in Naples
I should report this now, would they believe me?

If I should say I saw such islanders —
For, certes,° these are people of the island —   30
Who, though they are of monstrous shape, yet note
Their manners are more gentle-kind than of
Our human generation° you shall find
Many — nay, almost any.

PRO.   [*Aside*] Honest lord,   34
Thou hast said well, for some of you there present
Are worse than devils.

ALON.   I cannot too much muse°
Such shapes, such gesture, and such sound, express-
ing —
Although they want the use of tongue — a kind
Of excellent dumb discourse.

PRO.   [*Aside*] Praise in departing.°

FRAN. They vanished strangely.

SEB.   No matter, since   40
They have left their viands behind, for we have
stomachs. —
Will 't please you taste of what is here?

ALON.   Not I.

GON. Faith, sir, you need not fear. When we were
boys,
Who would believe that there were mountaineers
Dewlapped° like bulls, whose throats had hanging
at 'em   45
Wallets of flesh? Or that there were such men
Whose heads stood in their breasts?° Which now
we find
Each putter-out of five for one° will bring us
Good warrant of.

ALON.   I will stand to and feed,
Although my last. No matter, since I feel   50
The best is past. Brother, my lord the Duke,
Stand to, and do as we.

[*Thunder and lightning. Enter* ARIEL, *like a harpy,°
claps his wings upon the table, and, with a quaint
device,° the banquet vanishes.*]

ARI. You are three men of sin, whom Destiny —
That hath to instrument this lower world

---

30. certes: certainly.   **33. generation:** breed.   **36. muse:** wonder at.   **39. Praise in departing:** a proverb meaning "Don't give
thanks for your entertainment until you see how it will end."
45. Dewlapped: having folds of loose skin hanging from the
throat.   **46–47. men . . . breasts:** Sir Walter Raleigh in his account of Guiana (1595) noted "a nation of people whose heads appear not above their shoulders; which though it may be thought a
mere fable, yet for mine own part I am resolved it is true, because
every child in the provinces of Arromaia and Canuri affirms the
same. They are called Ewaipanoma. They are reported to have
their eyes in their shoulders, and their mouths in the middle of
their breasts, and that a long train of hair groweth backward between their shoulders."   **48. putter-out . . . one:** In Shakespeare's time voyages to distant and strange ports were so risky
that the traveler sometimes left a sum of money with a merchant
at home on condition that he should receive five times the amount
if he returned; if he did not, the premium was forfeited.   **52 s.d.,
harpy:** a foul creature, half bird of prey, half woman. This episode
was suggested by an event in Virgil's *Aeneid* when the harpies
seize and foul the food of Aeneas and his followers. **quaint device:**
piece of ingenious stage machinery.

Sc. iii: 1. By'r Lakin: by Our Lady.   **2–3. Here's . . . meanders:** we have wandered as in a maze by straight paths (*forthrights*) and winding paths (*meanders*).   **5. attached with:** overcome by; lit., arrested.   **10. frustrate:** vain.   **14. throughly:**
thoroughly.   **19 s.d., banquet:** light refreshments, such as fruit
and jellies.   **21. drollery:** puppet show.   **21–27. Now . . . 'em:**
i.e., after this we can believe any fantastic traveler's yarn.
23. phoenix: a mythical bird. According to the legend only one
phoenix was alive at a time. It lived for five hundred years. Then
it built itself a nest of spices, which were set alight by the rapid
beating of its wings. From the ashes a new phoenix was born.
25. want credit: is not believed.

And what is in 't° — the never-surfeited° sea   55
Hath caused to belch up you. And on this island,
Where man doth not inhabit — you 'mongst men
Being most unfit to live. I have made you mad,
And even with suchlike valor men hang and drown
Their proper° selves.
          [ALONZO, SEBASTIAN, *etc., draw their swords.*]
                    You fools! I and my fellows   60
Are ministers of Fate. The elements
Of whom your swords are tempered may as well
Wound the loud winds, or with bemocked-at stabs
Kill the still-closing° waters, as diminish
One dowle° that's in my plume.° My fellow minis-
          ters   65
Are like invulnerable. If you could hurt,
Your swords are now too massy° for your strengths,
And will not be uplifted. But remember —
For that's my business to you — that you three
From Milan did supplant good Prospero,   70
Exposed unto the sea, which hath requit° it,
Him and his innocent child. For which foul deed
The powers, delaying not forgetting, have
Incensed the seas and shores — yea, all the crea-
          tures —
Against your peace. Thee of thy son, Alonso,   75
They have bereft, and do pronounce by me
Lingering perdition° — worse than any death
Can be at once — shall step by step attend
You and your ways. Whose wraths to guard you
          from —
Which here, in this most desolate isle, else falls   80
Upon your heads — is nothing but° heart sorrow
And a clear° life ensuing.
[*He vanishes in thunder; then, to soft music, enter
the Shapes again, and dance, with mocks° and
mows,° and carrying out the table.*]
          PRO. Bravely the figure of this harpy hast thou
Performed, my Ariel, a grace it had, devouring.°
Of my instruction hast thou nothing bated°   85
In what thou hadst to say. So, with good life°
And observation° strange,° my meaner ministers°
Their several kinds° have done. My high charms
          work,
And these mine enemies are all knit up°
In their distractions.° They now are in my power,

And in these fits I leave them while I visit   91
Young Ferdinand — whom they suppose is
          drowned —
And his and mine loved darling.   [*Exit above.*]
          GON. I' the name of something holy, sir, why stand
          you
In this strange stare?
          ALON.   Oh, it is monstrous, monstrous!   95
Methought the billows spoke, and told me of it,
The winds did sing it to me, and the thunder,
That deep and dreadful organ pipe, pronounced
The name of Prosper. It did bass my trespass.°
Therefore my son i' th' ooze is bedded, and   100
I'll seek him deeper than e'er plummet° sounded,
And with him there lie mudded.   [*Exit.*]
          SEB.   But one fiend at a time,
I'll fight their legions o'er.
          ANT.   I'll be thy second.
          [*Exeunt* SEBASTIAN *and* ANTONIO.]
          GON. All three of them are desperate. Their great
          guilt,
Like poison given to work a great time after,   105
Now 'gins to bite the spirits. I do beseech you
That are of suppler joints, follow them swiftly,
And hinder them from what this ecstasy°
May now provoke them to.
          ADR.   Follow, I pray you. [*Exeunt.*]

ACT IV

SCENE I. *Before* PROSPERO'S *cell.*

[*Enter* PROSPERO, FERDINAND, *and* MIRANDA.]
          PRO. If I have too austerely punished you,
Your compensation makes amends. For I
Have given you here a third° of mine own life,
Or that for which I live, who once again
I tender° to thy hand. All thy vexations   5
Were but my trials of thy love, and thou
Hast strangely° stood the test. Here, afore Heaven,
I ratify this my rich gift. O Ferdinand,
Do not smile at me that I boast her off,°
For thou shalt find she will outstrip all praise   10
And make it halt° behind her.
          FER.   I do believe it
Against an oracle.°

53–55. **Destiny . . . in 't:** Destiny (Providence), which uses this world below and its powers as its instrument.   55. **never-sur-feited:** never overfull. A surfeit is an excess of food. Even the sea, which can retain most things, cannot stomach Alonso and his fellow sinners.   60. **proper:** own.   64. **still-closing:** always closing up; i.e., which cannot be wounded.   65. **dowle:** downy feather. **plume:** wing.   67. **massy:** heavy.   71. **requit:** paid back.   77. **perdition:** destruction.   81. **is . . . but:** i.e., only repentance will guard you from destruction.   82. **clear:** innocent. **s.d., mocks:** mocking gestures. **mows:** grimaces.   84. **grace . . . devouring:** the action of devouring was splendidly (*bravely*) performed.   85. **bated:** abated, left out.   86. **with . . . life:** realistically.   87. **observation:** obedience. **strange:** unusual. **meaner ministers:** lesser servants.   88. **several kinds:** particular tasks.   89. **knit up:** entangled.   90. **distractions:** fits of madness.

99. **bass my trespass:** proclaim my sin in a deep note.   101. **plummet:** the lead weight at the end of a cord used by sailors to discover the depth of the water.   108. **ecstasy:** mad fit. See *Haml,* III.iv.
Act IV, Sc. i: 3. third: i.e., a great part of.   5. **tender:** hand over.   7. **strangely:** exceptionally.   9. **boast . . . off:** boast about her.   11. **halt:** come limping; i.e., she will excel all praise.   12. **Against an oracle:** i.e., even if a god had said the contrary.

PRO. **Then,** as my gift, and thine own acquisition
Worthily purchased, take my daughter. But
If thou dost break her virgin knot before   15
All sanctimonious° ceremonies may
With full and holy rite be ministered,
No sweet aspersion° shall the Heavens let fall
To make this contract grow;° but barren hate,
Sour-eyed disdain, and discord shall bestrew   20
The union of your bed with weeds so loathly
That you shall hate it both. Therefore take heed,
As Hymen's° lamps shall light you.
FER.   As I hope
For quiet days, fair issue,° and long life,
With such love as 'tis now, the murkiest den,   25
The most opportune place, the strong'st suggestion°
Our worser genius° can, shall never melt
Mine honor into lust, to take away
The edge of that day's celebration
When I shall think or Phoebus' steeds are foundered,
Or Night kept chained below.°
PRO.   Fairly spoke.   31
Sit, then, and talk with her, she is thine own.
What, Ariel! My industrious servant, Ariel!
                    [*Enter* ARIEL.]
ARI. What would my potent master? Here I am.
PRO. Thou and thy meaner fellows your last
    service   35
Did worthily perform, and I must use you
In such another trick. Go bring the rabble,
O'er whom I give thee power, here to this place.
Incite them to quick motion, for I must
Bestow upon the eyes of this young couple   40
Some vanity° of mine art. It is my promise,
And they expect it from me.
ARI.   Presently?°
PRO. Aye, with a twink.°
ARI. Before you can say, " come," and " go,"
And breathe twice and cry, " so, so,"   45
Each one, tripping on his toe,
Will be here with mop° and mow.
Do you love me, master? No?   48
PRO. Dearly, my delicate Ariel. Do not approach
Till thou dost hear me call.
ARI.   Well, I conceive.° [*Exit.*]
PRO. Look thou be true. Do not give dalliance°
Too much the rein. The strongest oaths are straw
To the fire i' the blood. Be more abstemious,
Or else, good night your vow!
FER.   I warrant you, sir,

The white cold virgin snow upon my heart   55
Abates the ardor of my liver.°
PRO.   Well.
Now come, my Ariel! Bring a corollary°
Rather than want° a spirit. Appear, and pertly!°
No tongue! All eyes! Be silent.   [*Soft music.*]
                    [*Enter* IRIS.°]
IRIS. Ceres,° most bounteous lady, thy rich leas°
Of wheat, rye, barley, vetches, oats, and pease;   61
Thy turfy mountains, where live nibbling sheep,
And flat meads° thatched with stover,° them to
    keep;
Thy banks with pioned and twilled brims,°
Which spongy April at thy hest° betrims°   65
To make cold nymphs chaste crowns; and thy
    broom° groves,
Whose shadow the dismissed° bachelor loves,
Being lasslorn;° thy pole-clipped° vineyard;
And thy sea marge,° sterile and rocky-hard,
Where thou thyself dost air — the Queen o' the Sky,°
Whose watery arch° and messenger am I,   71
Bids thee leave these, and with her sovereign grace,
Here on this grassplot, in this very place,
To come and sport. — Her peacocks° fly amain.°
Approach, rich Ceres, her to entertain.   75
                    [*Enter* CERES.]
CER. Hail, many-colored messenger, that ne'er
Dost disobey the wife of Jupiter;
Who, with thy saffron° wings, upon my flowers
Diffusest honey drops, refreshing showers,
And with each end of thy blue bow dost crown   80
My bosky° acres and my unshrubbed down,°
Rich scarf° to my proud earth. — Why hath thy
    Queen
Summoned me hither, to this short-grassed green?
IRIS. A contract of true love to celebrate,
And some donation° freely to estate°   85
On the blest lovers.
CER.   Tell me, heavenly bow,

---

16. **sanctimonious:** religious.   18. **aspersion:** blessing; lit.,
sprinkling.   19. **grow:** prosper.   23. **Hymen:** the god of marriage.   24. **issue:** children.   26. **suggestion:** temptation.
27. **worser genius:** evil angel.   30–31. **or . . . below:** either the
horses of the Sun have fallen or Night has been imprisoned; i.e.,
my wedding day, when night seems never to come.   41. **vanity:**
display.   42. **Presently:** at once.   43. **twink:** the twinkling of
an eye.   47. **mop:** grimace.   50. **conceive:** understand.
51. **dalliance:** fondling.

56. **liver:** passion. The liver was regarded as the seat of passion.
57. **corollary:** excess; i.e., too many rather than too few.
58. **want:** be without. **pertly:** briskly.   59 **s.d., Enter Iris:** Prospero now produces a little wedding masque in honor not
only of the lovers, Ferdinand and Miranda, but as a compliment to the Princess Elizabeth and her bridegroom. **Iris:** the
female messenger of the gods, also the personification of the
rainbow.   60. **Ceres:** goddess of corn and plenty. **leas:** arable
lands.   63. **meads:** meadows. **thatched . . . stover:** covered
over with grass for fodder.   64. **pioned . . . brims:** a difficult
phrase, much disputed and emended. The likeliest explanation
is that *pioned* means dug, and *twilled,* heaped up; i.e., with
high banks.   65. **hest:** command. **betrims:** trims with wild
flowers, especially kingcups, a kind of buttercup that grows
by streams.   66. **broom:** a shrub with yellow flowers.   67. **dismissed:** rejected.   68. **lasslorn:** without his girl. **pole-clipped:**
poles embraced by vines.   69. **sea marge:** seashore.   70. **Queen
. . . Sky:** the goddess Juno, wife of Jupiter.   71. **watery arch:**
i.e., the rainbow.   74. **peacocks:** birds sacred to Juno. **amain:**
swiftly.   78. **saffron:** yellow.   81. **bosky:** wooded. **unshrubbed down:** rolling open country, without shrubs.
82. **scarf:** adornment.   85. **donation:** present. **estate:** donate.

If Venus or her son, as thou dost know,
Do now attend the Queen? Since they did plot
The means that dusky Dis° my daughter got,
Her and her blind boy's° scandaled° company 90
I have forsworn.

  IRIS.   Of her society
Be not afraid. I met Her Deity
Cutting the clouds towards Paphos,° and her son
Dove-drawn° with her. Here thought they to have
  done
Some wanton charm upon this man and maid, 95
Whose vows are, that no bedright shall be paid
Till Hymen's torch° be lighted. But in vain,
Mars's hot minion° is returned again.
Her waspish-headed° son has broke his arrows,
Swears he will shoot no more, but play with spar-
  rows,   100
And be a boy right out.

  CER.   High'st Queen of state,
Great Juno, comes. I know her by her gait.

    [*Enter* JUNO.]

JUNO. How does my bounteous sister? Go with
  me
To bless this twain, that they may prosperous be,
And honored in their issue.   105
[*They sing.*]

  JUNO. " Honor, riches, marriage blessing,
     Long continuance, and increasing,
     Hourly joys be still° upon you!
     Juno sings her blessings on you."

  CER. " Earth's increase, foison° plenty, 110
     Barns and garners never empty,
     Vines with clustering bunches growing,
     Plants with goodly burden bowing,
     Spring come to you at the farthest
     In the very end of harvest!° 115
     Scarcity and want shall shun you,
     Ceres' blessing so is on you."

FER. This is a most majestic vision, and
Harmonious charmingly. May I be bold
To think these spirits?

  PRO.   Spirits which by mine art 120
I have from their confines° called to enact
My present fancies.°

  FER.   Let me live here ever.

So rare a wondered° father and a wise
Makes this place Paradise.

    [JUNO *and* CERES *whisper, and send* IRIS
         on employment.]

  PRO.   Sweet, now silence!
Juno and Ceres whisper seriously, 125
There's something else to do. Hush, and be mute,
Or else our spell is marred.

  IRIS. You nymphs, called Naiads,° of the win-
   dring° brooks,
With your sedged° crowns and ever-harmless looks,
Leave your crisp° channels, and on this green land
Answer your summons. Juno does command. 131
Come, temperate° nymphs, and help to celebrate
A contract of true love. Be not too late.

    [*Enter certain* NYMPHS.]

You sunburned sicklemen,° of August weary,
Come hither from the furrow, and be merry. 135
Make holiday, your rye-straw hats put on,
And these fresh nymphs encounter every one
In country footing.°

[*Enter certain* REAPERS, *properly habited. They join
with the* NYMPHS *in a graceful dance, towards the
end whereof* PROSPERO *starts suddenly, and speaks.
After which, to a strange, hollow, and confused
noise, they heavily° vanish.*]

  PRO. [*Aside*] I had forgot that foul conspiracy
Of the beast Caliban and his confederates 140
Against my life. The minute of their plot
Is almost come. [*To the* SPIRITS] Well done! Avoid,°
  no more!

  FER. This is strange. Your father's in some passion
That works him strongly.

  MIRA.   Never till this day
Saw I him touched with anger so distempered.°

  PRO. You do look, my son, in a movèd sort,° 146
As if you were dismayed. Be cheerful, sir.
Our revels now are ended. These our actors,
As I foretold you, were all spirits, and
Are melted into air, into thin air. 150
And, like the baseless fabric° of this vision,
The cloud-capped towers, the gorgeous palaces,
The solemn temples, the great globe itself —
Yea, all which it inherit — shall dissolve
And, like this insubstantial pageant faded, 155
Leave not a rack° behind. We are such stuff
As dreams are made on, and our little life
Is rounded° with a sleep. Sir, I am vexed.
Bear with my weakness, my old brain is troubled.

---

89. dusky Dis: Pluto, god of the underworld, and so dark. He seized Ceres' daughter Persephone and carried her down to his kingdom. **90. blind boy:** Cupid. **scandaled:** scandalous. **93. Paphos:** in Sicily, a town sacred to Venus. **94. Dove-drawn:** in a chariot drawn by doves. **97. Hymen's torch:** The torches of the wedding god were lit to escort bride and bridegroom to bed. **98. Mars's . . . minion:** Mars' lusty darling; i.e., Venus. **99. waspish-headed:** quick-tempered. **108. still:** always. **110. foison:** bounteous harvest. **114–15. Spring . . . harvest:** may spring follow autumn; i.e., may there be no bitterness of winter in your lives. Cf. *Ant & Cleo,* V.ii. for a similar image. **121. confines:** places of confinement. **122. fancies:** devices of my imagination.

123. wondered: wonderful. **128. Naiads:** water nymphs. **windring:** wandering, winding. **129. sedged:** covered with sedge, a kind of water grass. **130. crisp:** curled, rippling. **132. temperate:** chaste. **134. sicklemen:** reapers, who cut the wheat with sickles. **138. footing:** dancing. **s.d., heavily:** sorrowfully. **142. Avoid:** be gone. **145. distempered:** disturbed. **146. moved sort:** as if you were distressed. **151. baseless fabric:** unreal stuff. **156. rack:** cloud. **158. rounded:** completed; i.e., life is but a moment of consciousness in an everlasting sleep.

Be not disturbed with my infirmity.   160
If you be pleased, retire into my cell,
And there repose. A turn or two I'll walk,
To still my beating° mind.

FER. & MIRA.   We wish your peace.   [*Exeunt.*]

PRO. Come with a thought. I thank thee, Ariel.
Come.

[*Enter* ARIEL.]

ARI. Thy thoughts I cleave to. What's thy pleasure?

PRO.   Spirit,   165
We must prepare to meet with Caliban.

ARI. Aye, my commander. When I presented°
Ceres,
I thought to have told thee of it, but I feared
Lest I might anger thee.

PRO. Say again, where didst thou leave these
varlets?°   170

ARI. I told you, sir, they were red-hot with drinking,
So full of valor that they smote the air
For breathing in their faces, beat the ground
For kissing of their feet, yet always bending°
Toward their project. Then I beat my tabor.   175
At which, like unbacked° colts, they pricked their
ears,
Advanced their eyelids, lifted up their noses
As° they smelt music. So I charmed their ears,
That, calflike, they my lowing followed through
Toothed briers, sharp furzes,° pricking goss,° and
thorns   180
Which entered their frail shins. At last I left them
I' the filthy-mantled° pool beyond your cell,
There dancing up to the chins, that the foul lake
O'erstunk their feet.

PRO.   This was well done, my bird.
Thy shape invisible retain thou still.   185
The trumpery° in my house, go bring it hither,
For stale° to catch these thieves.

ARI.   I go, I go.   [*Exit.*]

PRO. A devil, a born devil, on whose nature
Nurture° can never stick, on whom my pains,
Humanely taken, all, all lost, quite lost.   190
And as with age his body uglier grows,
So his mind cankers.° I will plague them all,
Even to roaring.

[*Re-enter* ARIEL, *loaden with glistering° apparel,
etc.*]

Come, hang them on this line.°

[PROSPERO *and* ARIEL *remain, invisible. Enter*
CALIBAN, STEPHANO, *and* TRINCULO, *all wet.*]

CAL. Pray you, tread softly, that the blind mole
may not
Hear a footfall. We now are near his cell.   195

STE. Monster, your fairy, which you say is a harmless fairy, has done little better than played the jack°
with us.

TRIN. Monster, I do smell all horse piss, at which
my nose is in great indignation.   200

STE. So is mine. Do you hear, monster? If I should
take a displeasure against you, look you ——

TRIN. Thou wert but a lost monster.

CAL. Good my lord, give me thy favor still.
Be patient, for the prize I'll bring thee to   205
Shall hoodwink this mischance.° Therefore speak
softly.
All's hushed as midnight yet.

TRIN. Aye, but to lose our bottles in the pool ——

STE. There is not only disgrace and dishonor in
that, monster, but an infinite loss.   210

TRIN. That's more to me than my wetting. Yet
this is your harmless fairy, monster.

STE. I will fetch off° my bottle, though I be o'er
ears° for my labor.   214

CAL. Prithee, my King, be quiet. See'st thou here,
This is the mouth o' the cell. No noise, and enter.
Do that good mischief which may make this island
Thine own forever, and I, thy Caliban,
For aye thy footlicker.

STE. Give me thy hand. I do begin to have bloody
thoughts.   221

TRIN. O King Stephano!° O peer! O worthy
Stephano! Look what a wardrobe here is for thee!

CAL. Let it alone, thou fool, it is but trash.

TRIN. Oh ho, monster! We know what belongs to
a frippery.° O King Stephano!   226

STE. Put off that gown, Trinculo. By this hand,
I'll have that gown.

TRIN. Thy Grace shall have it.

CAL. The dropsy drown this fool! What do you
mean   230
To dote thus on such luggage?° Let 's alone,
And do the murder first. If he awake
From toe to crown he'll fill our skins with pinches,
Make us strange stuff.   234

STE. Be you quiet, monster. Mistress° line, is not
this my jerkin? Now is the jerkin under the line.
Now, jerkin, you are like to lose your hair and prove
a bald jerkin.

---

163. **beating:** throbbing. Cf. I.ii.176.   167. **presented:** either
introduced the masques or acted the part of Ceres. There is, however, very little time for a change of costume between Ariel's
exit at l. 50 and Ceres' entry at l. 75.   170. **varlets:** knaves.
174. **bending:** inclining.   176. **unbacked:** never saddled.
178. **As:** as if.   180. **furzes:** See I.i.72,n. **goss:** gorse.   182. **filthy-mantled:** covered with scum.   186. **trumpery:** cheap finery.
187. **stale:** bait.   189. **Nurture:** education.   192. **cankers:** grows
malignant.   193 s.d., **glistering:** glittering. **line:** lime tree.

197. **jack:** knave.   206. **hoodwink ... mischance:** blindfold this
misfortune; i.e., make us forget it.   213. **fetch off:** rescue.
214. **o'er ears:** up to my ears in the pond.   222. **O ... Stephano:**
The sight of all the clothes reminds Trinculo of the old ballad
"King Stephen was a worthy peer." See *Oth*, II.iii.   226.
frippery: secondhand-clothes shop.   231. **luggage:** baggage,
which will hinder them.   235–40. **Mistress ... Grace:** These
lines have mystified editors, and indeed elaborate Elizabethan

TRIN. Do, do. We steal by line and level, an 't like your Grace. 240

STE. I thank thee for that jest — here's a garment for 't. Wit shall not go unrewarded while I am King of this country. "Steal by line and level" is an excellent pass of pate° — there's another garment for 't.

TRIN. Monster, come, put some lime° upon 246 your fingers, and away with the rest.

CAL. I will have none on 't. We shall lose our time, And all be turned to barnacles,° or to apes With foreheads villainous low. 250

STE. Monster, lay to your fingers. Help to bear this away where my hogshead of wine is, or I'll turn you out of my kingdom. Go to, carry this.

TRIN. And this.

STE. Aye, and this. 255

[A noise of hunters heard. Enter divers SPIRITS, in shape of dogs and hounds, hunting them about, PROSPERO and ARIEL setting them on.]

PRO. Hey, Mountain, hey!

ARI. Silver! There it goes, Silver!

PRO. Fury, Fury! There, Tyrant,° there! Hark, hark!

[CALIBAN, STEPHANO, and TRINCULO are driven out.]
Go charge my goblins that they grind their joints With dry convulsions. Shorten up their sinews 260 With agèd cramps,° and more pinch-spotted make them Then pard° or cat-o'-mountain.°

ARI. Hark, they roar!

PRO. Let them be hunted soundly. At this hour Lie at my mercy all mine enemies. Shortly shall all my labors end, and thou 265 Shalt have the air at freedom. For a little Follow, and do me service. [Exeunt.]

jokes, especially when made by a half-drunk butler, are not always easy to follow. Stephano begins by addressing the lime tree as "Mistress Line" as if he were talking to the dealer in an old-clothes shop. He appeals to her to decide whether the jerkin is his or Trinculo's. Having taken the jerkin for himself, he then puns on "under the line" (i.e., south of the Equator), where the various skin diseases common to long voyages in the tropics caused hair to fall out. Trinculo caps the remark by a further pun on "line and level"; i.e., "on the square," lit., by the bricklayer's instruments for ensuring perpendicular and horizontal exactness. **245. pass of pate:** sally of wit. **246. lime:** birdlime, to make them sticky, because Caliban disgustedly drops the garments. **249. barnacles:** tree geese. It was believed, even by serious botanists, that from the barnacles, which grow on rotten wood immersed in sea water, emerged creatures which grew into birds like geese. **256-58. Mountain . . . Silver . . . Fury . . . Tyrant:** the names of the hounds. **261. aged cramps:** the cramps which come with old age. **262. pard:** leopard. **cat-o'-mountain:** mountain cat.

ACT V

SCENE I. *Before the cell of* PROSPERO.

[*Enter* PROSPERO *in his magic robes, and* ARIEL.]

PRO. Now does my project gather to a head. My charms crack not,° my spirits obey, and Time Goes upright with his carriage.° How's the day?

ARI. On the sixth hour, at which time, my lord, You said our work should cease.

PRO. I did say so 5 When first I raised the tempest. Say, my spirit, How fares the King and 's followers?

ARI. Confined together In the same fashion as you gave in charge, Just as you left them — all prisoners, sir, In the line grove° which weather-fends° your cell. They cannot budge till your release. The King, 11 His brother, and yours abide all three distracted, And the remainder mourning over them, Brimful of sorrow and dismay. But chiefly Him that you termed, sir, "The good old lord, Gonzalo." 15 His tears run down his beard like winter's drops From eaves of reeds.° Your charm so strongly works 'em That if you now beheld them, your affections Would become tender.

PRO. Dost thou think so, spirit?

ARI. Mine would, sir, were I human.

PRO. And mine shall. 20 Hast thou, which art but air, a touch, a feeling Of their afflictions, and shall not myself, One of their kind, that relish° all as sharply, Passion° as they, be kindlier moved than thou art? Though with their high wrongs I am struck to the quick, 25 Yet with my nobler reason 'gainst my fury Do I take part. The rarer action is In virtue than in vengeance.° They being penitent, The sole drift° of my purpose doth extend Not a frown further. Go release them, Ariel. 30 My charms I'll break, their senses I'll restore, And they shall be themselves.

ARI. I'll fetch them, sir. [Exit.]

PRO. Ye elves of hills, brooks, standing lakes, and groves, And ye that on the sands with printless foot° Do chase the ebbing Neptune° and do fly him 35

Act V, Sc. i: 2. crack not: do not break down. **2-3. Time . . . carriage:** Time bears his burden without stooping, because it has now grown so light. **10. line grove:** grove of lime trees. **weather-fends:** protects from the weather. **17. eaves of reeds:** a thatched roof. **23. relish:** feel. **24. Passion:** suffer emotion. **27-28. rarer . . . vengeance:** it is a finer action to be self-controlled than to take vengeance. **29. drift:** intention. **34. printless foot:** without leaving a footprint. **35. ebbing Neptune:** i.e., the outgoing tide.

When he comes back; you demipuppets° that
By moonshine do the green sour° ringlets° make,
Whereof the ewe not bites; and you whose pastime
Is to make midnight mushrooms° that rejoice
To hear the solemn curfew,° by whose aid —   40
Weak masters though ye be — I have bedimmed
The noontide sun, called forth the mutinous winds,
And 'twixt the green sea and the azured vault°
Set roaring war. To the dread rattling thunder
Have I given fire, and rifted° Jove's stout oak   45
With his own bolt. The strong-based promontory
Have I made shake, and by the spurs° plucked up
The pine and cedar. Graves at my command
Have waked their sleepers, oped, and let 'em forth
By my so potent art. But this rough magic   50
I here abjure, and when I have required
Some heavenly music — which even now I do —
To work mine end upon their senses, that
This airy charm is for, I'll break my staff,
Bury it certain fathoms in the earth,   55
And deeper than did ever plummet° sound
I'll drown my book.°   [*Solemn music.*]
[*Re-enter* ARIEL *before; then* ALONSO, *with a frantic
    gesture, attended by* GONZALO; SEBASTIAN *and*
    ANTONIO *in like manner, attended by* ADRIAN
    and FRANCISCO. *They all enter the circle which*
    PROSPERO *had made, and there stand charmed,
        which* PROSPERO *observing, speaks:*]
A solemn air,° and the best comforter
To an unsettled fancy, cure thy brains,
Now useless, boiled° within thy skull! There stand,
For you are spell-stopped.   61
Holy Gonzalo, honorable man,
Mine eyes, even sociable° to the show of thine,
Fall° fellowly° drops. The charm dissolves apace,°
And as the morning steals upon the night,   65
Melting the darkness, so their rising senses
Begin to chase the ignorant fumes° that mantle°
Their clearer reason. O good Gonzalo,
My true preserver, and a loyal sir
To him thou follow'st! I will pay thy graces   70
Home° both in word and deed. Most cruelly
Didst thou, Alonso, use me and my daughter.
Thy brother was a furtherer in the act.

Thou art pinched for 't now, Sebastian. Flesh and
    blood,
You, brother mine, that entertained ambition,   75
Expelled remorse° and nature, who with Sebas-
    tian —
Whose inward pinches therefore are most strong —
Would here have killed your King, I do forgive thee,
Unnatural though thou art. Their understanding
Begins to swell, and the approaching tide   80
Will shortly fill the reasonable shore°
That now lies foul and muddy. Not one of them
That yet looks on me, or would know me. Ariel,
Fetch me the hat and rapier in my cell.
I will discase° me, and myself present   85
As I was sometime Milan.° Quickly, spirit.
Thou shalt ere long be free.
    ARI. [*Sings and helps to attire him.*]
    "Where the bee sucks, there suck I.
        In a cowslip's bell I lie,
        There I couch° when owls do cry.   90
        On the bat's back I do fly
        After summer merrily.
    Merrily, merrily shall I live now
    Under the blossom that hangs on the bough."
    PRO. Why, that's my dainty Ariel! I shall miss
        thee,   95
But yet thou shalt have freedom. So, so, so.°
To the King's ship, invisible as thou art.
There shalt thou find the mariners asleep
Under the hatches. The master and the boatswain
Being awake, enforce them to this place,   100
And presently, I prithee.
    ARI. I drink the air before me, and return
Or ere your pulse twice beat.   [*Exit.*]
    GON. All torment, trouble, wonder, and amaze-
        ment
Inhabits here. Some heavenly power guide us   105
Out of this fearful country!
    PRO.   Behold, Sir King,
The wrongèd Duke of Milan, Prospero.
For more assurance that a living prince
Does now speak to thee, I embrace thy body,
And to thee and thy company I bid   110
A hearty welcome.
    ALON.   Whether thou be'st he or no,
Or some enchanted trifle° to abuse° me,
As late I have been, I not know. Thy pulse
Beats, as of° flesh and blood, and since I saw thee,
The affliction of my mind amends, with which,   115
I fear, a madness held me. This must crave —

---

36. demipuppets: tiny creatures, half the size of a puppet. **37. sour:** i.e., unacceptable to the cattle. **ringlets:** fairy rings, circles of grass of a darker green often seen in English meadows, supposed to be caused by the fairies dancing in a ring. **39. midnight mushrooms:** As mushrooms grow in a single night, they were thought to be the work of fairies. **40. curfew:** rung at 9 P.M. to warn people to go indoors. Thereafter the fairies can work without interruption. **43. azured vault:** blue sky. **45. rifted:** split. **47. spurs:** roots. **56. plummet:** See III.iii.101,n. **57. book:** i.e., of magic spells. **58. air:** musical air. **60. boiled:** boiling. Cf. *MND*, V.i., "Lovers and madmen have such seething brains." **63. sociable:** of fellow feeling. **64. Fall:** let fall. **fellowly:** in sympathy. **apace:** quickly. **67. ignorant fumes:** mists of ignorance. **mantle:** cloak. **70–71. pay . . . Home:** reward your kind deeds fully.

76. remorse: pity. **81. reasonable shore:** shore of reason; i.e., sanity is beginning to flow back like the incoming tide. **85. discase:** remove my outer garment. Prospero is still in his magic robe and so not recognized by his former associates. **86. As . . . Milan:** as I was when I was Duke of Milan. **90. couch:** lie. **96. So, so, so:** "so," used thus, often indicates movement. Cf. *Lear*, III.vi. **112. enchanted trifle:** hallucination caused by enchantment. **abuse:** deceive. **114. as of:** as if composed of.

An if this be at all° — a most strange story.
Thy dukedom I resign, and do entreat
Thou pardon me my wrongs.° — But how should Prospero
Be living and be here?
    PRO.   First, noble friend,   120
Let me embrace thine age, whose honor cannot
Be measured or confined.
    GON.   Whether this be
Or be not, I'll not swear.
    PRO.   You do yet taste
Some subtilties° o' the isle, that will not let you
Believe things certain. Welcome, my friends all!
[*Aside to* SEBASTIAN *and* ANTONIO] But you, my
    brace of lords, were I so minded,   126
I here could pluck His Highness' frown upon you,
And justify you traitors. At this time
I will tell no tales.
    SEB.   [*Aside*] The Devil speaks in him.
    PRO.   No.
For you, most wicked sir, whom to call brother   130
Would even infect my mouth, I do forgive
Thy rankest fault — all of them — and require
My dukedom of thee, which perforce I know
Thou must restore.
    ALON.   If thou be'st Prospero,
Give us particulars of thy preservation —   135
How thou hast met us here, who three hours since
Were wrecked upon this shore, where I have lost —
How sharp the point of this remembrance is! —
My dear son Ferdinand.
    PRO.   I am woe for't,° sir.
    ALON. Irreparable is the loss, and Patience   140
Says it is past her cure.
    PRO.   I rather think
You have not sought her help of whose soft grace
For the like loss I have her sovereign° aid,
And rest myself content.
    ALON.   You the like loss!
    PRO. As great to me as late, and, supportable   145
To make the dear loss, have I means much weaker
Than you may call to comfort you, for I
Have lost my daughter.
    ALON.   A daughter?
O Heavens, that they were living both in Naples,
The King and Queen there! That they were, I wish
Myself were mudded in that oozy bed   151
Where my son lies. When did you lose your daughter?
    PRO. In this last tempest. I perceive these lords
At this encounter do so much admire°
That they devour their reason, and scarce think   155

Their eyes do offices of truth,° their words
Are natural breath. But howsoe'er you have
Been jostled from your senses, know for certain
That I am Prospero, and that very Duke
Which was thrust forth of Milan, who most strangely
Upon this shore where you were wrecked was landed,   161
To be the lord on 't. No more yet of this,
For 'tis a chronicle of day by day,
Not a relation for a breakfast, nor
Befitting this first meeting. Welcome, sir.   165
This cell's my Court. Here have I few attendants,
And subjects none abroad. Pray you look in.
My dukedom since you have given me again,
I will requite° you with as good a thing,
At least bring forth a wonder to content ye   170
As much as me my dukedom.
[*Here* PROSPERO *discovers*° FERDINAND *and* MIRANDA
    playing at chess.]
    MIRA. Sweet lord, you play me false.
    FER.   No, my dear'st love,
I would not for the world.
    MIRA. Yes, for a score of kingdoms you should wrangle,
And I would call it fair play.
    ALON.   If this prove   175
A vision of the island, one dear son
Shall I twice lose.
    SEB.   A most high miracle!
    FER. Though the seas threaten, they are merciful.
I have cursed them without cause.   [*Kneels.*]
    ALON.   Now all the blessings
Of a glad father compass thee about!   180
Arise, and say how thou camest here.
    MIRA.   Oh, wonder!
How many goodly creatures are there here!
How beauteous mankind is! Oh, brave new world,
That has such people in 't!
    PRO.   'Tis new to thee.
    ALON. What is this maid with whom thou wast at play?   185
Your eld'st° acquaintance cannot be three hours.
Is she the goddess that hath severed us,
And brought us thus together?
    FER.   Sir, she is mortal,
But by immortal Providence she's mine.
I chose her when I could not ask my father   190
For his advice, nor thought I had one. She
Is daughter to this famous Duke of Milan,
Of whom so often I have heard renown
But never saw before, of whom I have
Received a second life, and second father   195
This lady makes him to me.
    ALON.   I am hers.

---

117. **An . . . all:** if this is really true.   119. **my wrongs:** the wrongs which I have committed.   123–24. **You . . . subtilties:** you still have the taste of the magic nature.   139. **woe for't:** sorry for it.   143. **sovereign:** all-powerful.   154. **admire:** wonder.

156. **offices of truth:** true service.   169. **requite:** pay back.   171 **s.d., discovers:** reveals by drawing back the curtain.   186. **eld'st:** longest.

But oh, how oddly will it sound that I
Must ask my child° forgiveness!
    PRO.   There, sir, stop.
Let us not burden our remembrances with
A heaviness that's gone.
    GON.   I have inly wept,   200
Or should have spoke ere this. Look down, you gods,
And on this couple drop a blessèd crown!
For it is you that have chalked forth° the way
Which brought us hither.
    ALON.   I say Amen, Gonzalo!
    GON. Was Milan thrust from Milan, that his issue
Should become Kings of Naples? Oh, rejoice   206
Beyond a common joy! And set it down
With gold on lasting pillars. In one voyage
Did Claribel her husband find at Tunis
And Ferdinand, her brother, found a wife   210
Where he himself was lost, Prospero his dukedom
In a poor isle, and all of us ourselves
When no man was his own.
    ALON. [*To* FERDINAND *and* MIRANDA] Give me your
        hands.
Let grief and sorrow still embrace° his heart
That doth not wish you joy!
    GON.   Be it so! Amen!   215
[*Re-enter* ARIEL, *with the* MASTER *and* BOATSWAIN
        amazedly° *following.*]
Oh, look, sir, look, sir! Here is more of us.
I prophesied if a gallows were on land,
This fellow could not drown.° Now, blasphemy,°
That swear'st grace o'erboard,° not an oath on
    shore?   219
Hast thou no mouth by land? What is the news?
    BOATS. The best news is that we have safely found
Our King and company. The next, our ship —
Which, but three glasses since, we gave out split —
Is tight and yare and bravely rigged as when
We first put out to sea.
    ARI. [*Aside to* PROSPERO] Sir, all this service   225
Have I done since I went.
    PRO. [*Aside to* ARIEL] My tricksy° spirit!
    ALON. These are not natural events, they
        strengthen
From strange to stranger. Say, how came you hither?
    BOATS. If I did think, sir, I were well awake,
I'd strive to tell you. We were dead of sleep,   230
And — how we know not — all clapped° under
    hatches,
Where, but even now, with strange and several
    noises
Of roaring, shrieking, howling, jingling chains,

And mo diversity of sounds, all horrible,
We were awaked, straightway at liberty.   235
Where we, in all her trim, freshly beheld
Our royal, good, and gallant ship, our master
Capering° to eye her. — On a trice, so please you,
Even in a dream, were we divided from them,
And were brought moping hither.
    ARI. [*Aside to* PROSPERO] Was 't well done?   240
    PRO. [*Aside to* ARIEL] Bravely, my diligence. Thou
        shalt be free.
    ALON. This is as strange a maze as e'er men trod,
And there is in this business more than nature
Was ever conduct of. Some oracle
Must rectify° our knowledge.
    PRO.   Sir, my liege,   245
Do not infest your mind with beating on
The strangeness of this business. At picked leisure
Which shall be shortly, single° I'll resolve° you,
Which to you shall seem probable, of every
These happened accidents. Till when, be cheerful,
And think of each thing well. [*Aside to* ARIEL] Come
    hither, spirit.   251
Set Caliban and his companions free,
Untie the spell. [*Exit* ARIEL.] How fares my gracious
    sir?
There are yet missing of your company
Some few odd lads that you remember not.   255
[*Re-enter* ARIEL, *driving in* CALIBAN, STEPHANO, *and*
    TRINCULO, *in their stolen apparel.*]
    STE. Every man shift for all the rest, and let no
man take care for himself, for all is but fortune. —
Coragio,° bully-monster, coragio!
    TRIN. If these be true spies° which I wear in my
head, here's a goodly sight.   260
    CAL. Oh, Setebos, these be brave spirits indeed!
How fine my master is! I am afraid
He will chastise me.
    SEB.   Ha, ha!
What things are these, my lord Antonio?
Will money buy 'em?
    ANT.   Very like. One of them   265
Is a plain fish, and no doubt marketable.
    PRO. Mark but the badges° of these men, my
    lords,
Then say if they be true. This misshapen knave,
His mother was a witch, and one so strong   269
That could control the moon, make flows and ebbs,
And deal in her command,° without her power.°
These three have robbed me, and this demidevil —
For he's a bastard one — had plotted with them
To take my life. Two of these fellows you

---

198. **my child:** i.e., Miranda, who is about to become his daughter-in-law.   203. **chalked forth:** marked out (as with a chalk line).   214. **still embrace:** always cling to.   215 s.d., **amazedly:** in amazement.   217–18. **gallows . . . drown:** see I.i.32–33.   218. **blasphemy:** you blasphemer.   219. **That . . . o'erboard:** that by your swearing drives the grace of God away.   226. **tricksy:** clever.   231. **clapped:** shut in.

238. **Capering:** dancing for joy.   245. **rectify:** prove true.   248. **single:** alone. **resolve:** inform.   258. **Coragio:** courage.   259. **spies:** eyes.   267. **badges:** A nobleman's servant wore a badge displaying his master's coat of arms.   271. **deal . . . command:** i.e., take over the moon's power of controlling the tides. **without . . . power:** without the aid of the moon.

Must know and own, this thing of darkness I   275
Acknowledge mine.
    CAL.   I shall be pinched to death.
    ALON. Is not this Stephano, my drunken butler?
    SEB. He is drunk now. Where had he wine?
    ALON. And Trinculo is reeling ripe. Where should
       they   279
Find this grand liquor that hath gilded 'em?° —
How camest thou in this pickle?
    TRIN. I have been in such a pickle since I saw you
last that I fear me will never out of my bones. I shall
not fear flyblowing.°
    SEB. Why, how now, Stephano!   285
    STE. Oh, touch me not. — I am not Stephano, but
    a cramp.
    PRO. You'd be King o' the isle, sirrah?
    STE. I should have been a sore one, then.
    ALON. This is a strange thing as e'er I looked on.
                 [Pointing to CALIBAN.]
    PRO. He is as disproportioned in his manners°
As in his shape. Go, sirrah, to my cell.   291
Take with you your companions. As you look
To have my pardon, trim° it handsomely.
    CAL. Aye, that I will, and I'll be wise hereafter,
And seek for grace.° What a thrice-double ass   295
Was I to take this drunkard for a god
And worship this dull fool!
    PRO.   Go to, away!
    ALON. Hence, and bestow your luggage where you
    found it.
    SEB. Or stole it, rather.   299
    [Exeunt CALIBAN, STEPHANO, and TRINCULO.]
    PRO. Sir, I invite your Highness and your train
To my poor cell, where you shall take your rest
For this one night. Which, part of it, I'll waste
With such discourse as I not doubt shall make it
Go quick away — the story of my life,
And the particular accidents° gone by   305
Since I came to this isle. And in the morn
I'll bring you to your ship, and so to Naples,
Where I have hope to see the nuptial
Of these our dear-belovèd solemnized,

And thence retire me to my Milan, where   310
Every third thought shall be my grave.
    ALON.   I long
To hear the story of your life, which must
Take the ear strangely.
    PRO.   I'll deliver all,
And promise you calm seas, auspicious° gales,
And sail so expeditious that shall catch   315
Your royal fleet far off. [Aside to ARIEL] My Ariel,
    chick,
That is thy charge. Then to the elements
Be free, and fare thou well! Please you, draw near.
                        [Exeunt.]

EPILOGUE°

SPOKEN BY PROSPERO

Now my charms are all o'erthrown,
And what strength I have's mine own,
Which is most faint. Now, 'tis true,
I must be here confined by you,
Or sent to Naples. Let me not,   5
Since I have my dukedom got,
And pardoned the deceiver, dwell
In this bare island by your spell,
But release me from my bands°
With the help of your good hands.°   10
Gentle breath° of yours my sails
Must fill, or else my project fails,
Which was to please. Now I want°
Spirits to enforce, art to enchant,
And my ending is despair   15
Unless I be relieved by prayer
Which pierces so that it assaults
Mercy itself, and frees all faults.
As you from crimes would pardoned be,
Let your indulgence set me free.   20

314. auspicious: favorable.
    Epilogue: A concluding epilogue is fairly common in Elizabethan plays, especially those performed before a Courtly audience. It is usually a conventional apology for the inadequacies of the performance, and an appeal for applause. Cf. the epilogues in *MND, AYLI,* and *II Hen IV.* **9. bands:** bonds. **10. good hands:** i.e., by clapping. **11. Gentle breath:** kindly criticism. **13. want: lack.**

280. gilded 'em: made them glow. **284. fear flyblowing:** i.e., shall never go bad, for I have been so well pickled. **290. manners:** behavior. **293. trim:** make tidy. **295. grace:** favor. **305. accidents:** events.

The Beggar's Opera

BY JOHN GAY

Gay's ballad opera is probably among the most popular plays of all time. After its first performance in London in 1728, it was produced almost annually for more than a century and continues to be successfully revived up to the present day.

The career of its author all but epitomizes the literary life of the early eighteenth century. A kind of court jester to the wits and nobility of his age, Gay worked in virtually all the fashionable genres—tragedy, comedy, satire, pastoral, fable, essay, lyric—and yet produced nothing of enduring importance in any of them. His personal life was reportedly as varied as his literary career: it shifted several times from near rags to riches and involved him in all levels of Augustan society—from Newgate, where his aunt was imprisoned for debt, to the court, whose patronage he briefly received. This perhaps explains why his friend Jonathan Swift suggested in a letter to their mutual friend Alexander Pope that Gay's multifaceted talent and experience might be applied to "a Newgate pastoral, among the thieves and whores there."

In *The Beggar's Opera* Gay's scattered gifts came together. Although it satirizes the corrupt ministry of the Whig politician Sir Robert Walpole, who appears variously in the figures of Macheath, Mr. Peachum, and Robin of Bagshot, the play is possibly the merriest satire ever written. Apparently, not even Walpole himself took it amiss, for at one performance he loudly echoed the last line of Lockit's song, "That was leveled at me!" Although it parodies the conventions of the popular Italian opera, Gay's play became the chief formative influence on the English musical theater. No other work of satire or parody has more thoroughly transcended its historical topicality and satiric inspiration.

Cast of Characters*

Men	Women

Men

PEACHUM, *a receiver of stolen goods*
LOCKIT, *the jailor at Newgate Prison*
MACHEATH, *a gentleman-highwayman*
FILCH, *a young pickpocket*
JEMMY TWITCHER ⎫
CROOK-FINGERED JACK ⎪
WAT DREARY ⎪
ROBIN OF BAGSHOT ⎬ *Macheath's gang*
NIMMING NED ⎪
HARRY PADINGTON ⎪
MATT OF THE MINT ⎪
BEN BUDGE ⎭
BEGGAR, *who poses in the prologue as the author of the play*
PLAYER, *who is also in the prologue*

Women

MRS. PEACHUM, *Polly's mother*
POLLY PEACHUM, *who is in love with Macheath*
LUCY LOCKIT, *daughter of the jailor; she is also in love with Macheath.*
DIANA TRAPES, *clothier to the ladies of the underworld*
MRS. COAXER ⎫
DOLLY TRULL ⎪
MRS. VIXEN ⎪
BETTY DOXY ⎪
JENNY DIVER ⎬ *Women of the town*
MRS. SLAMMEKIN ⎪
SUKY TAWDRY ⎪
MOLLY BRAZEN ⎭
ALSO *constables, turnkeys, and a group of rabble*

Introduction

BEGGAR, PLAYER

BEGGAR. If poverty be a title to poetry, I am sure nobody can dispute mine. I own myself of the company of beggars, and I make one at their weekly festivals at St. Giles's.[1] I have a small yearly salary for my catches[2] and am welcome to a dinner there whenever I please, which is more than most poets can say.

PLAYER. As we live by the Muses, 'tis but gratitude to us to encourage poetical merit wherever we find it. The Muses, contrary to all other ladies, pay no distinction to dress, and never partially mistake the pertness of embroidery for wit, nor the modesty of want for dulness. Be the author who he will, we push his play as far as it will go. So (though you are in want) I wish you success heartily.

BEGGAR. This piece, I own, was originally writ for the celebrating the marriage of James Chanter and Moll Lay, two most excellent ballad-singers. I have introduced the similes that are in your celebrated operas: the Swallow, the Moth, the Bee, the Ship, the Flower, etc. Besides, I have a prison-scene, which the ladies always reckon charmingly pathetic. As to the parts, I have observed such a nice impartiality to our two ladies, that it is impossible for either of them to take offence. I hope I may be forgiven, that I have not made my opera throughout unnatural, like those in vogue; for I have no recitative; excepting this, as I have consented to have neither prologue nor epilogue, it must be allowed an opera in all its forms. The piece indeed hath been heretofore frequently represented by ourselves in our great room at St. Giles's, so that I cannot too often acknowledge your charity in bringing it now on the stage.

PLAYER. But I see 'tis time for us to withdraw; the actors are preparing to begin. Play away the overture. [*Exeunt.*]

---

* Such label names as Peachum and Lockit are obvious. In thieves' slang a "twitcher" means a pickpocket; "nimming" was stealing; a "budge" was a sneakthief; "trapes" and "slammekin" were names for a slovenly woman; "trull" and "doxy" for a prostitute; "diver" for a pickpocket.

1. The parish of St. Giles-in-the-Fields, near Holborn, was a notorious haunt of thieves and beggars. 2. Songs.

ACT I

SCENE I. PEACHUM's *house*

PEACHUM *sitting at a table with a large book of accounts before him*

PEACHUM.

AIR I—*An old woman clothed in gray, etc.*

Through all the employments of life,
  Each neighbor abuses his brother;
Whore and rogue they call husband and wife:
  All professions be-rogue one another.
The priest calls the lawyer a cheat,
  The lawyer be-knaves the divine;
And the statesman, because he's so great,
  Thinks his trade as honest as mine.

A lawyer is an honest employment; so is mine. Like me, too, he acts in a double capacity, both against rogues and for 'em; for 'tis but fitting that we should protect and encourage cheats, since we live by them.

SCENE II

PEACHUM, FILCH

FILCH. Sir, Black Moll hath sent word her trial comes on in the afternoon, and she hopes you will order matters so as to bring her off.

PEACHUM. Why, she may plead her belly at worst;[1] to my knowledge she hath taken care of that security. But as the wench is very active and industrious, you may satisfy her that I'll soften the evidence.

FILCH. Tom Gagg, sir, is found guilty.

PEACHUM. A lazy dog! When I took him the time before, I told him what he would come to if he did not mend his hand. This is death without reprieve. I may venture to book him. [*Writes.*] For Tom Gagg, forty pounds. Let Betty Sly know that I'll save her from transportation,[2] for I can get more by her staying in England.

FILCH. Betty hath brought more goods into our

lock[3] to-year, than any five of the gang; and in truth, 'tis a pity to lose so good a customer.

PEACHUM. If none of the gang take her off,[4] she may, in the common course of business, live a twelve-month longer. I love to let women 'scape. A good sportsman always lets the hen partridges fly, because the breed of the game depends upon them. Besides, here the law allows us no reward; there is nothing to be got by the death of women —except our wives.

FILCH. Without dispute, she is a fine woman! 'Twas to her I was obliged for my education, and (to say a bold word) she hath trained up more young fellows to the business than the gaming-table.

PEACHUM. Truly, Filch, thy observation is right. We and the surgeons are more beholden to women than all the professions besides.

FILCH.

AIR II—*The bonny gray-eyed morn, etc.*

'Tis woman that seduces all mankind,
  By her we first were taught the wheedling arts;
Her very eyes can cheat; when most she's kind,
  She tricks us of our money with our hearts.
For her, like wolves by night we roam for prey,
  And practise ev'ry fraud to bribe her charms;
For suits of love, like law, are won by pay,
  And beauty must be fee'd into our arms.

PEACHUM. But make haste to Newgate,[5] boy, and let my friends know what I intend; for I love to make them easy one way or other.

FILCH. When a gentleman is long kept in suspense, penitence may break his spirit ever after. Besides, certainty gives a man a good air upon his trial, and makes him risk another without fear or scruple. But I'll away, for 'tis a pleasure to be the messenger of comfort to friends in affliction.

[*Exit.*]

SCENE III

PEACHUM

PEACHUM. But 'tis now high time to look about me for a decent execution against next sessions. I hate a lazy rogue, by whom one can get nothing

---

1. Pregnant women were reprieved.   2. [Deportation] to the colonies.

3. A cant word signifying a warehouse where stolen goods are deposited.   4. Betray her to the authorities.
5. Prison, adjacent to the Old Bailey, the criminal court.

till he is hanged. A register of the gang: [*Reading*] "Crook-fingered Jack. A year and a half in the service." Let me see how much the stock owes to his industry; one, two, three, four, five gold watches, and seven silver ones.—A mighty clean-handed fellow!—Sixteen snuff-boxes, five of them of true gold. Six dozen of handkerchiefs, four silver-hilted swords, half a dozen of shirts, three tie-periwigs, and a piece of broadcloth.—Considering these are only the fruits of his leisure hours, I don't know a prettier fellow, for no man alive hath a more engaging presence of mind upon the road. "Wat Dreary, alias Brown Will"—an irregular dog, who hath an underhand way of disposing of his goods. I'll try him only for a sessions or two longer upon his good behavior. "Harry Padington"—a poor petty-larceny rascal, without the least genius; that fellow, though he were to live these six months, will never come to the gallows with any credit. "Slippery Sam"—he goes off the next sessions, for the villain hath the impudence to have views of following his trade as a tailor, which he calls an honest employment. "Matt of the Mint"—listed[6] not above a month ago, a promising sturdy fellow, and diligent in his way: somewhat too bold and hasty, and may raise good contributions on the public, if he does not cut himself short by murder. "Tom Tipple"—a guzzling, soaking sot, who is always too drunk to stand himself, or to make others stand. A cart is absolutely necessary for him. "Robin of Bagshot, alias Gorgon, alias Bob Bluff, alias Carbuncle, alias Bob Booty!—"[7]

SCENE IV

PEACHUM, MRS. PEACHUM

MRS. PEACHUM. What of Bob Booty, husband? I hope nothing bad hath betided him. You know, my dear, he's a favorite customer of mine. 'Twas he made me a present of this ring.

PEACHUM. I have set his name down in the black list, that's all, my dear; he spends his life among women, and as soon as his money is gone, one or other of the ladies will hang him for the reward, and there's forty pound lost to us forever.

MRS. PEACHUM. You know, my dear, I never

meddle in matters of death; I always leave those affairs to you. Women indeed are bitter bad judges in these cases, for they are so partial to the brave that they think every man handsome who is going to the camp or the gallows.

AIR III—*Cold and raw, etc.*

If any wench Venus's girdle wear,
　Though she be never so ugly;
Lilies and roses will quickly appear,
　And her face look wond'rous smugly.
Beneath the left ear so fit but a cord,
　(A rope so charming a zone is!)
The youth in his cart hath the air of a lord,
　And we cry, There dies an Adonis!

But really, husband, you should not be too hard-hearted, for you never had a finer, braver set of men than at present. We have not had a murder among them all, these seven months. And truly, my dear, that is a great blessing.

PEACHUM. What a dickens is the woman always a-whimp'ring about murder for? No gentleman is ever looked upon the worse for killing a man in his own defence; and if business cannot be carried on without it, what would you have a gentleman do?

MRS. PEACHUM. If I am in the wrong, my dear, you must excuse me, for nobody can help the frailty of an over-scrupulous conscience.

PEACHUM. Murder is as fashionable a crime as a man can be guilty of. How many fine gentlemen have we in Newgate every year, purely upon that article! If they have wherewithal to persuade the jury to bring it in manslaughter, what are they the worse for it? So, my dear, have done upon this subject. Was Captain Macheath here this morning, for the bank-notes he left with you last week?

MRS. PEACHUM. Yes, my dear; and though the bank hath stopped payment, he was so cheerful and so agreeable! Sure there is not a finer gentleman upon the road than the captain! If he comes from Bagshot at any reasonable hour he hath promised to make one with Polly and me, and Bob Booty, at a party of quadrille.[8] Pray, my dear, is the captain rich?

PEACHUM. The captain keeps too good company ever to grow rich. Marybone[9] and the chocolate-houses are his undoing. The man that proposes to get money by play should have the education of

---

6. Enlisted in the gang.　　7. A hit at Robert Walpole.

8. A four-handed card game.　　9. Marylebone, a popular gambling center.

a fine gentleman, and be trained up to it from his youth.

MRS. PEACHUM. Really, I am sorry upon Polly's account the captain hath not more discretion. What business hath he to keep company with lords and gentlemen? he should leave them to prey upon one another.

PEACHUM. Upon Polly's account! What, a plague, does the woman mean?—Upon Polly's account!

MRS. PEACHUM. Captain Macheath is very fond of the girl.

PEACHUM. And what then?

MRS. PEACHUM. If I have any skill in the ways of women, I am sure Polly thinks him a very pretty man.

PEACHUM. And what then? You would not be so mad to have the wench marry him! Gamesters and highwaymen are generally very good to their whores, but they are very devils to their wives.

MRS. PEACHUM. But if Polly should be in love, how should we help her, or how can she help herself? Poor girl, I am in the utmost concern about her.

AIR IV—*Why is your faithful slave disdained? etc.*

> If love the virgin's heart invade,
> How, like a moth, the simple maid
>   Still plays about the flame!
> If soon she be not made a wife,
> Her honor's singed, and then, for life,
> She's—what I dare not name.

PEACHUM. Look ye, wife. A handsome wench in our way of business is as profitable as at the bar of a Temple coffee-house, who looks upon it as her livelihood to grant every liberty but one. You see I would indulge the girl as far as prudently we can —in anything but marriage! After that, my dear, how shall we be safe? Are we not then in her husband's power? For a husband hath the absolute power over all a wife's secrets but her own. If the girl had the discretion of a court lady, who can have a dozen young fellows at her ear without complying with one, I should not matter it; but Polly is tinder, and a spark will at once set her on a flame. Married! If the wench does not know her own profit, sure she knows her own pleasure better than to make herself a property! My daughter to me should be, like a court lady to a minister of state, a key to the whole gang. Married! if the affair is not already done, I'll terrify her from it by the example of our neighbors.

MRS. PEACHUM. Mayhap, my dear, you may injure the girl. She loves to imitate the fine ladies, and she may only allow the captain liberties in the view of interest.

PEACHUM. But 'tis your duty, my dear, to warn the girl against her ruin, and to instruct her how to make the most of her beauty. I'll go to her this moment, and sift her. In the meantime, wife, rip out the coronets and marks of these dozen of cambric handkerchiefs, for I can dispose of them this afternoon to a chap[10] in the city.   [*Exit.*]

SCENE V

MRS. PEACHUM

MRS. PEACHUM. Never was a man more out of the way in an argument than my husband! Why must our Polly, forsooth, differ from her sex, and love only her husband? And why must Polly's marriage, contrary to all observation, make her the less followed by other men? All men are thieves in love, and like a woman the better for being another's property.

AIR V—*Of all the simple things we do, etc.*

> A maid is like the golden ore,
>   Which hath guineas intrinsical in't;
> Whose worth is never known, before
>   It is tried and impressed in the mint.
> A wife's like a guinea in gold,
>   Stamped with the name of her spouse;
> Now here, now there; is bought, or is sold;
>   And is current in every house.

SCENE VI

MRS. PEACHUM, FILCH

MRS. PEACHUM. Come hither, Filch. [*Aside*] I am as fond of this child as though my mind misgave me he were my own. He hath as fine a hand at picking a pocket as a woman, and is as nimble-fingered as a juggler—If an unlucky session does not cut the rope of thy life, I pronounce, boy, thou wilt be a great man in history. Where was your post last night, my boy?

---

10. Chapman, purchaser.

FILCH. I plied at the opera, madam; and considering 'twas neither dark nor rainy, so that there was no great hurry in getting chairs and coaches, made a tolerable hand on't. These seven handkerchiefs, madam.

MRS. PEACHUM. Colored ones, I see. They are of sure sale from our warehouse at Redriff[11] among the seamen.

FILCH. And this snuff-box.

MRS. PEACHUM. Set in gold! A pretty encouragement this to a young beginner.

FILCH. I had a fair tug at a charming gold watch. Pox take the tailors for making the fobs so deep and narrow. It stuck by the way, and I was forced to make my escape under a coach. Really, madam, I fear, I shall be cut off in the flower of my youth, so that every now and then (since I was pumped)[12] I have thoughts of taking up and going to sea.

MRS. PEACHUM. You should go to Hockley-in-the-Hole[13] and to Marybone, child, to learn valor. These are the schools that have bred so many brave men. I thought, boy, by this time, thou hadst lost fear as well as shame.—Poor lad! how little does he know as yet of the Old Bailey! For the first fact I'll insure thee from being hanged; and going to sea, Filch, will come time enough upon a sentence of transportation. But now, since you have nothing better to do, ev'n go to your book, and learn your catechism; for really a man makes but an ill figure in the ordinary's paper,[14] who cannot give a satisfactory answer to his questions. But, hark you, my lad. Don't tell me a lie; for you know I hate a liar. Do you know of anything that hath passed between Captain Macheath and our Polly?

FILCH. I beg you, madam, don't ask me; for I must either tell a lie to you or to Miss Polly—for I promised her I would not tell.

MRS. PEACHUM. But when the honor of our family is concerned—

FILCH. I shall lead a sad life with Miss Polly if ever she come to know that I told you. Besides, I would not willingly forfeit my own honor by betraying anybody.

MRS. PEACHUM. Yonder comes my husband and Polly. Come, Filch, you shall go with me into my own room, and tell me the whole story. I'll give thee a glass of a most delicious cordial that I keep for my own drinking.   [*Exeunt.*]

---

11. Rotherhithe, near the docks.   12. Held under a pump as punishment.   13. North of London, famous for bear gardens and cock fights.   14. The report of the prison chaplain.

SCENE VII

PEACHUM, POLLY

POLLY. I know as well as any of the fine ladies how to make the most of myself and of my man too. A woman knows how to be mercenary, though she hath never been in a court or at any assembly. We have it in our natures, papa. If I allow Captain Macheath some trifling liberties, I have this watch and other visible marks of his favor to show for it. A girl who cannot grant some things, and refuse what is most material, will make but a poor hand of her beauty, and soon be thrown upon the common.

AIR VI—*What shall I do to show how much I love her, etc.*

Virgins are like the fair flower in its luster,
  Which in the garden enamels the ground;
Near it the bees in play flutter and cluster,
  And gaudy butterflies frolic around.
But, when once plucked, 'tis no longer alluring;
  To Covent-garden[15] 'tis sent (as yet sweet),
There fades, and shrinks, and grows past all enduring,
  Rots, stinks, and dies, and is trod under feet.

PEACHUM. You know, Polly, I am not against your toying and trifling with a customer in the way of business, or to get out a secret or so. But if I find out that you have played the fool and are married, you jade you, I'll cut your throat, hussy! Now you know my mind.

SCENE VIII

PEACHUM, POLLY, MRS. PEACHUM

MRS. PEACHUM [*in a very great passion*].

AIR VII—*Oh London is a fine town*

Our Polly is a sad slut! nor heeds what we taught her.
I wonder any man alive will ever rear a daughter!
For she must have both hoods and gowns, and hoops to swell her pride,
With scarfs and stays, and gloves and lace; and she will have men beside;
And when she's dressed with care and cost, all-tempting fine and gay,
As men should serve a cowcumber, she flings herself away.

---

15. London's flower and vegetable market.

You baggage, you hussy! you inconsiderate jade! Had you been hanged, it would not have vexed me, for that might have been your misfortune; but to do such a mad thing by choice! The wench is married, husband.

PEACHUM. Married! The captain is a bold man, and will risk anything for money; to be sure, he believes her a fortune!—Do you think your mother and I should have lived comfortably so long together, if ever we had been married? Baggage!

MRS. PEACHUM. I knew she was always a proud slut; and now the wench has played the fool and married because, forsooth, she would do like the gentry. Can you support the expense of a husband, hussy, in gaming, drinking, and whoring? Have you money enough to carry on the daily quarrels of man and wife about who shall squander most? There are not many husbands and wives who can bear the charges of plaguing one another in a handsome way. If you must be married, could you introduce nobody into our family but a highwayman? Why, thou foolish jade, thou wilt be as ill used, and as much neglected, as if thou hadst married a lord!

PEACHUM. Let not your anger, my dear, break through the rules of decency, for the captain looks upon himself in the military capacity, as a gentleman by his profession. Besides what he hath already, I know he is in a fair way of getting, or of dying; and both these ways, let me tell you, are most excellent chances for a wife.—Tell me, hussy, are you ruined or no?

MRS. PEACHUM. With Polly's fortune, she might very well have gone off to a person of distinction. Yes, that you might, you pouting slut!

PEACHUM. What, is the wench dumb? Speak, or I'll make you plead by squeezing out an answer from you. Are you really bound wife to him, or are you only upon liking?   [Pinches her.]

POLLY [screaming]. Oh!

MRS. PEACHUM. How the mother is to be pitied who hath handsome daughters! Locks, bolts, bars, and lectures of morality are nothing to them; they break through them all. They have as much pleasure in cheating a father and mother as in cheating at cards.

PEACHUM. Why, Polly, I shall soon know if you are married, by Macheath's keeping from our house.

POLLY.

AIR VIII—*Grim king of the ghosts, etc.*

Can love be controlled by advice?
    Will Cupid our mothers obey?
Though my heart were as frozen as ice,
    At his flame 'twould have melted away.
When he kissed me, so closely he pressed,
    'Twas so sweet that I must have complied,
So I thought it both safest and best
    To marry, for fear you should chide.

MRS. PEACHUM. Then all the hopes of our family are gone for ever and ever!

PEACHUM. And Macheath may hang his father- and mother-in-law, in hope to get into their daughter's fortune!

POLLY. I did not marry him (as 'tis the fashion) coolly and deliberately for honor or money—but I love him.

MRS. PEACHUM. Love him! Worse and worse! I thought the girl had been better bred. Oh, husband, husband! her folly makes me mad! my head swims! I'm distracted! I can't support myself— Oh!   [Faints.]

PEACHUM. See, wench, to what a condition you have reduced your poor mother! a glass of cordial, this instant. How the poor woman takes it to heart! [POLLY *goes out and returns with it.*] Ah, hussy, now this is the only comfort your mother has left!

POLLY. Give her another glass, sir; my mama drinks double the quantity whenever she is out of order.—This, you see, fetches her.

MRS. PEACHUM. The girl shows such a readiness, and so much concern, that I could almost find in my heart to forgive her.

AIR IX—*O Jenny, O Jenny, where hast thou been*

O Polly, you might have toyed and kissed;
    By keeping men off, you keep them on.

POLLY.

But he so teased me,
    And he so pleased me,
What I did, you must have done—

MRS. PEACHUM. Not with a highwayman. You sorry slut!

PEACHUM. A word with you, wife. 'Tis no new thing for a wench to take a man without consent of parents. You know 'tis the frailty of woman, my dear.

MRS. PEACHUM. Yes, indeed, the sex is frail. But the first time a woman is frail, she should be somewhat nice, methinks, for then or never is the time to make her fortune. After that, she hath nothing to do but to guard herself from being found out, and she may do what she pleases.

PEACHUM. Make yourself a little easy; I have a thought shall soon set all matters again to rights. Why so melancholy, Polly? Since what is done cannot be undone, we must all endeavor to make the best of it.

MRS. PEACHUM. Well, Polly, as far as one woman can forgive another, I forgive thee.—Your father is too fond of you, hussy.

POLLY. Then all my sorrows are at an end.

MRS. PEACHUM. A mighty likely speech in troth, for a wench who is just married.

POLLY.

AIR X—*Thomas, I cannot, etc.*

I, like a ship in storms, was tossed,
　　Yet afraid to put into land;
For seized in the port, the vessel's lost,
　　Whose treasure is contraband.
　　　　The waves are laid,
　　　　My duty's paid,
　　Oh, joy beyond expression!
　　　　Thus, safe ashore,
　　　　I ask no more,
　　My all is in my possession.

PEACHUM. I hear customers in t'other room. Go, talk with 'em, Polly; but come to us again as soon as they are gone.—But, hark ye, child, if 'tis the gentleman who was here yesterday about the repeating watch, say you believe we can't get intelligence of it till tomorrow—for I lent it to Suky Straddle, to make a figure with it to-night at a tavern in Drury Lane. If t'other gentleman calls for the silver-hilted sword, you know beetle-browed Jemmy hath it on; and he doth not come from Tunbridge till Tuesday night; so that it cannot be had till then. 　　　　　　　　 [*Exit* POLLY.]

SCENE IX

PEACHUM, MRS. PEACHUM

PEACHUM. Dear wife, be a little pacified. Don't let your passion run away with your senses. Polly, I grant you, hath done a rash thing.

MRS. PEACHUM. If she had had only an intrigue with the fellow, why, the very best families have excused and huddled up a frailty of that sort. 'Tis marriage, husband, that makes it a blemish.

PEACHUM. But money, wife, is the true fuller's earth for reputations; there is not a spot or a stain but what it can take out. A rich rogue nowadays is fit company for any gentleman, and the world, my dear, hath not such a contempt for roguery as you imagine. I tell you, wife, I can make this match turn to our advantage.

MRS. PEACHUM. I am very sensible, husband, that Captain Macheath is worth money, but I am in doubt whether he hath not two or three wives already, and then if he should die in a sessions or two, Polly's dower would come into dispute.

PEACHUM. That, indeed, is a point which ought to be considered.

AIR XI—*A soldier and a sailor*

A fox may steal your hens, sir,
A whore your health and pence, sir,
Your daughter rob your chest, sir,
Your wife may steal your rest, sir,
　　A thief your goods and plate.
But this is all but picking;
With rest, pence, chest, and chicken;
It ever was decreed, sir,
If lawyer's hand is fee'd, sir,
　　He steals your whole estate.

The lawyers are bitter enemies to those in our way. They don't care that anybody should get a clandestine livelihood but themselves.

SCENE X

MRS. PEACHUM, PEACHUM, POLLY

POLLY. 'Twas only Nimming Ned. He brought in a damask window-curtain, a hoop petticoat, a pair of silver candlesticks, a periwig, and one silk stocking, from the fire that happened last night.

PEACHUM. There is not a fellow that is cleverer in his way and saves more goods out of the fire, than Ned. But now, Polly, to your affairs; for matters must not be left as they are. You are married then, it seems?

POLLY. Yes, sir.

PEACHUM. And how do you propose to live, child?

POLLY. Like other women, sir,—upon the industry of my husband.

MRS. PEACHUM. What, is the wench turned fool? A highwayman's wife, like a soldier's, hath as little of his pay as of his company.

PEACHUM. And had not you the common views of a gentlewoman in your marriage, Polly?

POLLY. I don't know what you mean, sir.

PEACHUM. Of a jointure, and of being a widow.

POLLY. But I love him, sir; how then could I have thoughts of parting with him?

PEACHUM. Parting with him! Why, that is the whole scheme and intention of all marriage articles. The comfortable estate of widowhood is the only hope that keeps up a wife's spirits. Where is the woman who would scruple to be a wife, if she had it in her power to be a widow whenever she pleased? If you have any views of this sort, Polly, I shall think the match not so very unreasonble.

POLLY. How I dread to hear your advice! Yet I must beg you to explain yourself.

PEACHUM. Secure what he hath got, have him peached[16] the next sessions, and then at once you are made a rich widow.

POLLY. What, murder the man I love! The blood runs cold at my heart with the very thought of it.

PEACHUM. Fie, Polly! What hath murder to do in the affair? Since the thing sooner or later must happen, I dare say the captain himself would like that we should get the reward for his death sooner than a stranger. Why, Polly, the captain knows that as 'tis his employment to rob, so 'tis ours to take robbers; every man in his business. So that there is no malice in the case.

MRS. PEACHUM. Ay, husband, now you have nicked the matter. To have him peached is the only thing could ever make me forgive her.

POLLY.

AIR XII—*Now ponder well, ye parents dear*

Oh, ponder well! be not severe;
    So save a wrenched wife!
For on the rope that hangs my dear
    Depends poor Polly's life.

MRS. PEACHUM. But your duty to your parents, hussy, obliges you to hang him. What would many a wife give for such an opportunity!

POLLY. What is a jointure, what is a widowhood to me? I know my heart. I cannot survive him.

AIR XIII—*Le printemps rappelle aux armes*

The turtle thus with plaintive crying,
    Her lover dying,
The turtle thus with plaintive crying,
    Laments her dove.

16. Indicted.

Down she drops, quite spent with sighing;
    Pair'd in death, as pair'd in love.

Thus, sir, it will happen to your poor Polly.

MRS. PEACHUM. What, is the fool in love in earnest then? I hate thee for being particular. Why, wench, thou art a shame to thy very sex.

POLLY. But hear me, mother,—if you ever loved—

MRS. PEACHUM. Those cursed play-books she reads have been her ruin. One word more, hussy, and I shall knock your brains out, if you have any.

PEACHUM. Keep out of the way, Polly, for fear of mischief, and consider of what is proposed to you.

MRS. PEACHUM. Away, hussy! Hang your husband, and be dutiful.

SCENE XI

MRS. PEACHUM, PEACHUM, POLLY *listening*

MRS. PEACHUM. The thing, husband, must and shall be done. For the sake of intelligence, we must take other measures and have him peached the next sessions without her consent. If she will not know her duty, we know ours.

PEACHUM. But really, my dear, it grieves one's heart to take off a great man. When I consider his personal bravery, his fine stratagem, how much we have already got by him, and how much more we may get, methinks I can't find in my heart to have a hand in his death. I wish you could have made Polly undertake it.

MRS. PEACHUM. But in a case of necessity—our own lives are in danger.

PEACHUM. Then indeed, we must comply with the customs of the world, and make gratitude give way to interest. He shall be taken off.

MRS. PEACHUM. I'll undertake to manage Polly.

PEACHUM. And I'll prepare matters for the Old Bailey.   [*Exeunt.*]

SCENE XII

POLLY

POLLY. Now I'm a wretch, indeed—methinks I see him already in the cart, sweeter and more lovely than the nosegay in his hand!—I hear the crowd extolling his resolution and intrepidity!—

What volleys of sighs are sent from the windows of Holborn, that so comely a youth should be brought to disgrace!—I see him at the tree! The whole circle are in tears!—even butchers weep!—Jack Ketch[17] himself hesitates to perform his duty, and would be glad to lose his fee, by a reprieve. What then will become of Polly? As yet I may inform him of their design, and aid him in his escape. It shall be so!—But then he flies, absents himself, and I bar myself from his dear, dear conversation! That too will distract me. If he keep out of the way, my papa and mama may in time relent, and we may be happy. If he stays, he is hanged, and then he is lost forever! He intended to lie concealed in my room till the dusk of the evening. If they are abroad, I'll this instant let him out, lest some accident should prevent him.

[*Exit, and returns.*]

SCENE XIII

POLLY, MACHEATH

MACHEATH.

AIR XIV—*Pretty Parrot, say*

Pretty Polly, say,
When I was away,
Did your fancy never stray
To some newer lover?

POLLY.

Without disguise,
Heaving sighs,
Doating eyes,
My constant heart discover.
Fondly let me loll!

MACHEATH.

O pretty, pretty Poll.

POLLY. And are *you* as fond as ever, my dear?

MACHEATH. Suspect my honor, my courage—suspect anything but my love. May my pistols miss fire, and my mare slip her shoulder while I am pursued, if I ever forsake thee!

POLLY. Nay, my dear, I have no reason to doubt you, for I find in the romance you lent me, none of the great heroes were ever false in love.

17. A generic name for hangmen, after a famous executioner who died in 1686.

MACHEATH.

AIR XV—*Pray, fair one, be kind*

My heart was so free,
It roved like the bee,
Till Polly my passion requited;
I sipped each flower,
I changed ev'ry hour,
But here ev'ry flower is united.

POLLY. Were you sentenced to transportation, sure, my dear, you could not leave me behind you,—could you?

MACHEATH. Is there any power, any force that could tear me from thee? You might sooner tear a pension out of the hands of a courtier, a fee from a lawyer, a pretty woman from a looking glass, or any woman from quadrille. But to tear me from thee is impossible!

AIR XVI—*Over the hills and far away*

Were I laid on Greenland's coast,
And in my arms embraced my lass;
Warm amidst eternal frost,
Too soon the half year's night would pass.

POLLY.

Were I sold on Indian soil,
Soon as the burning day was closed,
I could mock the sultry toil,
When on my charmer's breast reposed.

MACHEATH. And I would love you all the day,
POLLY. Every night would kiss and play,
MACHEATH. If with me you'd fondly stray
POLLY. Over the hills and far away.

POLLY. Yes, I would go with thee. But oh!—how shall I speak it? I must be torn from thee. We must part.

MACHEATH. How! Part!

POLLY. We must, we must. My papa and mama are set against thy life. They now, even now are in search after thee. They are preparing evidence against thee. Thy life depends upon a moment.

AIR XVII—*'Gin thou wert mine awn thing*

Oh, what pain it is to part!
Can I leave thee, can I leave thee?
Oh, what pain it is to part!
Can thy Polly ever leave thee?
But lest death my love should thwart
And bring thee to the fatal cart,
Thus I tear thee from my bleeding heart!
Fly hence, and let me leave thee.

One kiss and then—one kiss. Begone—farewell.

MACHEATH. My hand, my heart, my dear, is so riveted to thine, that I cannot unloose my hold.

POLLY. But my papa may intercept thee, and then I should lose the very glimmering of hope. A few weeks, perhaps, may reconcile us all. Shall thy Polly hear from thee?

MACHEATH. Must I then go?

POLLY. And will not absence change your love?

MACHEATH. If you doubt it, let me stay—and be hanged.

POLLY. Oh, how I fear! how I tremble!—Go—but when safety will give you leave, you will be sure to see me again; for till then Polly is wretched. [*Parting, and looking back at each other with fondness; he at one door, she at the other*]

MACHEATH.

AIR XVIII—*Oh the broom, etc.*

The miser thus a shilling sees,
   Which he's obliged to pay,
With sighs resigns it by degrees,
   And fears 'tis gone for aye.

POLLY.

The boy, thus, when his sparrow's flown,
   The bird in silence eyes;
But soon as out of sight 'tis gone,
   Whines, whimpers, sobs, and cries.

ACT II

SCENE I. *A tavern near Newgate*

JEREMY TWITCHER, CROOK-FINGERED JACK, WAT DREARY, ROBIN OF BAGSHOT, NIMMING NED, HARRY PADINGTON, MATT OF THE MINT, BEN BUDGE, *and the rest of the gang, at the table, with wine, brandy, and tobacco*

BEN. But prithee, Matt, what is become of thy brother Tom? I have not seen him since my return from transportation.

MATT. Poor brother Tom had an accident this time twelve-month, and so clever a made fellow he was, that I could not save him from those flaying rascals the surgeons; and now, poor man, he is among the anatomies at Surgeons' Hall.

BEN. So, it seems, his time was come.

JEREMY. But the present time is ours, and nobody alive hath more. Why are the laws levelled at us? Are we more dishonest than the rest of mankind? What we win, gentlemen, is our own by the law of arms and the right of conquest.

JACK. Where shall we find such another set of practical philosophers, who to a man are above the fear of death?

WAT. Sound men, and true!

ROBIN. Of tried courage, and indefatigable industry!

NED. Who is there here that would not die for his friend?

HARRY. Who is there here that would betray him for his interest?

MATT. Show me a gang of courtiers that can say as much.

BEN. We are for a just partition of the world, for every man hath a right to enjoy life.

MATT. We retrench the superfluities of mankind. The world is avaricious, and I hate avarice. A covetous fellow, like a jackdaw, steals what he was never able to enjoy, for the sake of hiding it. These are the robbers of mankind, for money was made for the free-hearted and generous; and where is the injury of taking from another, what he hath not the heart to make use of?

JEREMY. Our several stations for the day are fixed. Good luck attend us! Fill the glasses.

MATT.

AIR I—*Fill ev'ry glass, etc.*

Fill ev'ry glass, for wine inspires us,
   And fires us
With courage, love, and joy.
Women and wine should life employ.
Is there aught else on earth desirous?

CHORUS.

Fill ev'ry glass, etc.

SCENE II

To them enter MACHEATH

MACHEATH. Gentlemen, well met. My heart hath been with you this hour, but an unexpected affair hath detained me. No ceremony, I beg you.

MATT. We were just breaking up to go upon duty. Am I to have the honor of taking the air with you, sir, this evening upon the heath? I drink a dram now and then with the stage-coachmen in the way of friendship and intelligence, and I know that about this time there will be passengers upon the Western Road who are worth speaking with.

MACHEATH. I was to have been of that party—but—

MATT. But what, sir?

MACHEATH. Is there any man who suspects my courage?—

MATT. We have all been witnesses of it.—

MACHEATH. My honor and truth to the gang?

MATT. I'll be answerable for it.

MACHEATH. In the division of our booty, have I ever shown the least marks of avarice or injustice?

MATT. By these questions something seems to have ruffled you. Are any of us suspected?

MACHEATH. I have a fixed confidence, gentlemen, in you all, as men of honor, and as such I value and respect you. Peachum is a man that is useful to us.

MATT. Is he about to play us any foul play? I'll shoot him through the head.

MACHEATH. I beg you, gentlemen, act with conduct and discretion. A pistol is your last resort.

MATT. He knows nothing of this meeting.

MACHEATH. Business cannot go on without him. He is a man who knows the world, and is a necessary agent to us. We have had a slight difference, and till it is accommodated I shall be obliged to keep out of his way. Any private dispute of mine shall be of no ill consequence to my friends. You must continue to act under his direction, for the moment we break loose from him, our gang is ruined.

MATT. As a bawd to a whore, I grant you, he is to us of great convenience.

MACHEATH. Make him believe I have quitted the gang, which I can never do but with life. At our private quarters I will continue to meet you. A week or so will probably reconcile us.

MATT. Your instructions shall be observed. 'Tis now high time for us to repair to our several duties; so till the evening at our quarters in Moorfields[1] we bid you farewell.

MACHEATH. I shall wish myself with you. Success attend you. [*Sits down melancholy at the table.*]

MATT.

AIR II—*March in Rinaldo,[2] with drums and trumpets*

Let us take the road.
  Hark! I hear the sound of coaches!
  The hour of attack approaches,
To your arms, brave boys, and load.

    See the ball I hold!
Let the chymists toil like asses,
Our fire their fire surpasses,
    And turns all our lead to gold.

[*The gang, ranged in front of the stage, load their pistols, and stick them under their girdles, then go off singing the first part in chorus.*]

SCENE III

MACHEATH, DRAWER

MACHEATH. What a fool is a fond wench! Polly is most confoundly bit—I love the sex. And a man who loves money might as well be contented with one guinea, as I with one woman. The town perhaps hath been as much obliged to me, for recruiting it with freehearted ladies, as to any recruiting officer in the army. If it were not for us, and the other gentlemen of the sword, Drury Lane[3] would be uninhabited.

AIR III—*Would you have a young virgin, etc.*

If the heart of a man is depressed with cares,
The mist is dispelled when a woman appears;
Like the notes of a fiddle, she sweetly, sweetly
Raises the spirits, and charms our ears.
  Roses and lilies her cheeks disclose,
  But her ripe lips are more sweet than those.
      Press her,
      Caress her
      With blisses,
      Her kisses
Dissolve us in pleasure and soft repose.

I must have women. There is nothing unbends the mind like them. Money is not so strong a cordial for the time. Drawer!
      [*Enter* DRAWER.]
Is the porter gone for all the ladies, according to my directions?

DRAWER. I expect him back every minute. But you know, sir, you sent him as far as Hockley-in-the-Hole for three of the ladies, for one in Vinegar Yard, and for the rest of them somewhere about

---

1. A low district north of London walls.
2. An opera by Handel, 1711.

3. Largely inhabited by prostitutes.

Lewkner's Lane.[4] Sure some of them are below, for I hear the bar bell. As they come I will show them up. Coming! coming!   [*Exit.*]

SCENE IV

MACHEATH, MRS. COAXER, DOLLY TRULL, MRS. VIXEN,
BETTY DOXY, JENNY DIVER, MRS. SLAMMEKIN,
SUKY TAWDRY, *and* MOLLY BRAZEN

MACHEATH. Dear Mrs. Coaxer, you are welcome. You look charmingly to-day. I hope you don't want the repairs of quality, and lay on paint.— Dolly Trull! kiss me, you slut; are you as amorous as ever, hussy? You are always so taken up with stealing hearts, that you don't allow yourself time to steal anything else. Ah Dolly, thou wilt ever be a coquette.—Mrs. Vixen, I'm yours! I always loved a woman of wit and spirit; they make charming mistresses, but plaguy wives.—Betty Doxy! come hither, hussy. Do you drink as hard as ever? You had better stick to good, wholesome beer; for in troth, Betty, strong waters will, in time, ruin your constitution. You should leave those to your betters.—What! and my pretty Jenny Diver too! As prim and demure as ever! There is not any prude, though ever so high bred, hath a more sanctified look, with a more mischievous heart. Ah! thou art a dear artful hypocrite!—Mrs. Slammekin! as careless and genteel as ever! all you fine ladies, who know your own beauty, affect an undress.—But see, here's Suky Tawdry come to contradict what I was saying. Everything she gets one way, she lays out upon her back. Why, Suky, you must keep at least a dozen tallymen.—Molly Brazen! [*She kisses him.*] That's well done. I love a free-hearted wench. Thou hast a most agreeable assurance, girl, and art as willing as a turtle.—But hark! I hear music. The harper is at the door. "If music be the food of love, play on."[5] Ere you seat yourselves, ladies, what think you of a dance? Come in.

[*Enter* HARPER.]

Play the French tune that Mrs. Slammekin was so fond of.

[*A dance à la ronde in the French manner; near the end of it this song and chorus*]

AIR IV—*Cotillion*

Youth's the season made for joys,
     Love is then our duty;
She alone who that employs,
     Well deserves her beauty.
       Let's be gay,
       While we may,
Beauty's a flower despised in decay.

Youth's the season, etc.

Let us drink and sport to-day,
     Ours is not to-morrow.
Love with youth flies swift away,
     Age is nought but sorrow.
       Dance and sing,
       Time's on the wing,
Life never knows the return of spring.

CHORUS.

     Let us drink, etc.

MACHEATH. Now pray, ladies, take your places. Here, fellow. [*Pays the* HARPER.] Bid the drawer bring us more wine. [*Exit* HARPER.] If any of the ladies choose gin, I hope they will be so free to call for it.

JENNY. You look as if you meant me. Wine is strong enough for me. Indeed, sir, I never drink strong waters but when I have the colic.

MACHEATH. Just the excuse of the fine ladies! Why, a lady of quality is never without the colic. I hope, Mrs. Coaxer, you have had good success of late in your visits among the mercers.

MRS. COAXER. We have so many interlopers. Yet, with industry, one may still have a little picking. I carried a silver-flowered lute-string and a piece of black padesoy[6] to Mr. Peachum's lock but last week.

MRS. VIXEN. There's Molly Brazen hath the ogle[7] of a rattlesnake. She riveted a linen-draper's eye so fast upon her, that he was nicked of three pieces of cambric before he could look off.

MOLLY BRAZEN. Oh, dear madam! But sure nothing can come up to your handling of laces! And then you have such a sweet deluding tongue! To cheat a man is nothing; but the woman must have fine parts indeed who cheats a woman!

MRS. VIXEN. Lace, madam, lies in a small compass, and is of easy conveyance. But you are apt, madam, to think too well of your friends.

MRS. COAXER. If any woman hath more art than another, to be sure, 'tis Jenny Diver. Though her

---

4. Famous for pleasure resorts and brothels.   5. The opening line of *Twelfth Night.*

6. Fashionable fabrics.   7. Eyes.

fellow be never so agreeable, she can pick his pocket as cooly as if money were her only pleasure. Now, that is a command of the passions uncommon in a woman!

JENNY. I never go to the tavern with a man but in the view of business. I have other hours, and other sort of men for my pleasure. But had I your address, madam—

MACHEATH. Have done with your compliments, ladies, and drink about. You are not so fond of me, Jenny, as you used to be.

JENNY. 'Tis not convenient, sir, to show my kindness among so many rivals. 'Tis your own choice, and not the warmth of my inclination, that will determine you.

AIR V—*All in a misty morning, etc.*

Before the barn-door crowing,
  The cock by hens attended,
His eyes around him throwing,
  Stands for a while suspended.

Then one he singles from the crew,
  And cheers the happy hen;
With "How do you do," and "How do you do,"
  And "How do you do" again.

MACHEATH. Ah Jenny! thou art a dear slut.

TRULL. Pray, madam, were you ever in keeping?

TAWDRY. I hope, madam, I han't been so long upon the town but I have met with some good fortune as well as my neighbors.

TRULL. Pardon me, madam, I meant no harm by the question; 'twas only in the way of conversation.

TAWDRY. Indeed, madam, if I had not been a fool, I might have lived very handsomely with my last friend. But upon his missing five guineas, he turned me off. Now, I never suspected he had counted them.

SLAMMEKIN. Who do you look upon, madam, as your best sort of keepers?

TRULL. That, madam, is thereafter as they be.

SLAMMEKIN. I, madam, was once kept by a Jew;[8] and bating their religion, to women they are a good sort of people.

TAWDRY. Now for my part, I own I like an old fellow; for we always make them pay for what they can't do.

VIXEN. A spruce prentice, let me tell you, ladies, is no ill thing; they bleed freely. I have sent at least two or three dozen of them in my time to the plantations.

JENNY. But to be sure, sir, with so much good fortune as you have had upon the road, you must be grown immensely rich.

MACHEATH. The road, indeed, hath done me justice, but the gaming-table hath been my ruin.

JENNY.

AIR VI—*When once I lay with another man's wife, etc.*

The gamesters and lawyers are jugglers alike,
  If they meddle, your all is in danger:
Like gypsies, if once they can finger a souse,[9]
  Your pockets they pick, and they pilfer your house,
And give your estate to a stranger.

A man of courage should never put anything to the risk but his life. [*She takes up his pistol.* TAWDRY *takes up the other.*] These are the tools of men of honor. Cards and dice are only fit for cowardly cheats, who prey upon their friends.

TAWDRY. This, sir, is fitter for your hand. Besides your loss of money, 'tis a loss to the ladies. Gaming takes you off from women. How fond could I be of you!—but before company, 'tis ill-bred.

MACHEATH. Wanton hussies!

JENNY. I must and will have a kiss, to give my wine a zest.

[*They take him about the neck, and make signs to* PEACHUM *and* CONSTABLES, *who rush in upon him.*]

SCENE V

To them PEACHUM *and* CONSTABLES

PEACHUM. I seize you, sir, as my prisoner.

MACHEATH. Was this well done, Jenny? Women are decoy ducks: who can trust them? Beasts, jades, jilts, harpies, furies, whores!

PEACHUM. Your case, Mr. Macheath, is not particular. The greatest heroes have been ruined by women. But, to do them justice, I must own they are a pretty sort of creatures, if we could trust them. You must now, sir, take your leave of the ladies, and if they have a mind to make you a visit, they will be sure to find you at home. This gentleman, ladies, lodges in Newgate. Constables, wait upon the captain to his lodgings.

8. [Jews were considered almost synonymous with money-lenders in eighteenth-century London.]

9. A sou.

MACHEATH.

AIR VII—*When first I laid siege to my Chloris, etc.*

> At the tree I shall suffer with pleasure,
> At the tree I shall suffer with pleasure,
>   Let me go where I will,
>   In all kinds of ill,
> I shall find no such furies as these are.

PEACHUM. Ladies, I'll take care the reckoning shall be discharged.

[*Exit* MACHEATH, *guarded, with* PEACHUM *and* CONSTABLES.]

SCENE VI

The WOMEN *remain*

VIXEN. Look ye, Mrs. Jenny; though Mr. Peachum may have made a private bargain with you and Suky Tawdry for betraying the captain, as we were all assisting, we ought all to share alike.

COAXER. I think Mr. Peachum, after so long an acquaintance, might have trusted me as well as Jenny Diver.

SLAMMEKIN. I am sure at least three men of his hanging, and in a year's time too (if he did me justice), should be set down to my account.

TRULL. Mrs. Slammekin, that is not fair. For you know one of them was taken in bed with me.

JENNY. As far as a bowl of punch or a treat, I believe Mrs. Suky will join with me. As for anything else, ladies, you cannot in conscience expect it.

SLAMMEKIN. Dear Madam—

TRULL. I would not for the world—

SLAMMEKIN. 'Tis impossible for me—

TRULL. As I hope to be saved, madam—

SLAMMEKIN. Nay, then I must stay here all night.—

TRULL. Since you command me.

[*Exeunt with great ceremony.*]

SCENE VII. *Newgate*

LOCKIT, TURNKEYS, MACHEATH, CONSTABLES

LOCKIT, Noble captain, you are welcome. You have not been a lodger of mine this year and half. You know the custom, sir. Garnish,[10] captain, garnish! Hand me down those fetters there.

MACHEATH. Those, Mr. Lockit, seem to be the heaviest of the whole set! With your leave, I should like the further pair better.

LOCKIT. Look ye, captain, we know what is fittest for our prisoners. When a gentleman uses me with civility, I always do the best I can to please him.—Hand them down, I say.—We have them of all prices, from one guinea to ten, and 'tis fitting every gentleman should please himself.

MACHEATH. I understand you, sir. [*Gives money.*] The fees here are so many, and so exorbitant, that few fortunes can bear the expense of getting off handsomely, or of dying like a gentleman.

LOCKIT. Those, I see, will fit the captain better. Take down the further pair. Do but examine them, sir,—never was better work. How genteelly they are made! They will fit as easy as a glove, and the nicest man in England might not be ashamed to wear them. [*He puts on the chains.*] If I had the best gentleman in the land in my custody, I could not equip him more handsomely. And so, sir—I now leave you to your private meditations.

SCENE VIII

MACHEATH

MACHEATH.

AIR VIII—*Courtiers, courtiers, think it no harm, etc.*

> Man may escape from rope and gun;
> Nay, some have outlived the doctor's pill;
> Who takes a woman must be undone,
>   The basilisk is sure to kill.
>
> The fly that sips treacle is lost in the sweets,
> So he that tastes woman, woman, woman,
>   He that tastes woman, ruin meets.

To what a woeful plight have I brought myself! Here must I (all day long, till I am hanged) be confined to hear the reproaches of a wench who lays her ruin at my door. I am in the custody of her father, and to be sure if he knows of the matter, I shall have a fine time on't betwixt this and my execution. But I promised the wench marriage. What signifies a promise to a woman? Does not a man in marriage itself promise a hundred

10. Fee me.

things that he never means to perform? Do all we can, women will believe us; for they look upon a promise as an excuse for following their own inclinations.—But here comes Lucy, and I cannot get from her. Would I were deaf!

SCENE IX

MACHEATH, LUCY

LUCY. You base man, you, how can you look me in the face after what hath passed between us?—See here, perfidious wretch, how I am forced to bear about the load of infamy you have laid upon me—Oh, Macheath! thou hast robbed me of my quiet—to see thee tortured would give me pleasure.

AIR IX—*A lovely lass to a friar came, etc.*

Thus when a good housewife sees a rat
    In her trap in the morning taken,
With pleasure her heart goes pit-a-pat
    In revenge for her loss of bacon.
        Then she throws him
        To the dog or cat,
To be worried, crushed, and shaken.

MACHEATH. Have you no bowels, no tenderness, my dear Lucy, to see a husband in these circumstances?

LUCY. A husband!

MACHEATH. In every respect but the form, and that, my dear, may be said over us at any time. Friends should not insist upon ceremonies. From a man of honor, his word is as good as his bond.

LUCY. 'Tis the pleasure of all you fine men to insult the women you have ruined.

AIR X—*'Twas when the sea was roaring, etc.*

How cruel are the traitors
    Who lie and swear in jest,
To cheat unguarded creatures
    Of virtue, fame, and rest!

Whoever steals a shilling
    Through shame the guilt conceals;
In love, the perjured villain
    With boasts the theft reveals.

MACHEATH. The very first opportunity, my dear (have but patience), you shall be my wife in whatever manner you please.

LUCY. Insinuating monster! And so you think I know nothing of the affair of Miss Polly Peachum. I could tear thy eyes out!

MACHEATH. Sure, Lucy, you can't be such a fool as to be jealous of Polly!

LUCY. Are you not married to her, you brute, you?

MACHEATH. Married! Very good. The wench gives it out only to vex thee, and to ruin me in thy good opinion. 'Tis true I go to the house; I chat with the girl, I kiss her, I say a thousand things to her (as all gentlemen do) that mean nothing, to divert myself; and now the silly jade hath set it about that I am married to her, to let me know what she would be at. Indeed, my dear Lucy, these violent passions may be of ill consequence to a woman in your condition.

LUCY. Come, come, captain, for all your assurance, you know that Miss Polly hath put it out of your power to do me the justice you promised me.

MACHEATH. A jealous woman believes everything her passion suggests. To convince you of my sincerity, if we can find the ordinary, I shall have no scruples of making you my wife—and I know the consequence of having two at a time.

LUCY. That you are only to be hanged, and so get rid of them both.

MACHEATH. I am ready, my dear Lucy, to give you satisfaction—if you think there is any in marriage. What can a man of honor say more?

LUCY. So then it seems—you are not married to Miss Polly.

MACHEATH. You know, Lucy, the girl is prodigiously conceited. No man can say a civil thing to her, but (like other fine ladies) her vanity makes her think he's her own for ever and ever.

AIR XI—*The sun had lossed his weary teams, etc.*

The first time at the looking-glass
    The mother sets her daughter,
The image strikes the smiling lass
    With self-love ever after.
Each time she looks, she, fonder grown,
    Thinks ev'ry charm grows stronger.
But alas, vain maid, all eyes but your own
    Can see you are not younger.

When women consider their own beauties, they are all alike unreasonable in their demands; for they expect their lovers should like them as long as they like themselves.

LUCY. Yonder is my father. Perhaps this way

we may light upon the ordinary, who shall try if you will be as good as your word; for I long to be made an honest woman.

[*Exeunt.*]

SCENE X

PEACHUM, LOCKIT *with an account-book*

LOCKIT. In this last affair, brother Peachum, we are agreed. You have consented to go halves in Macheath.

PEACHUM. We shall never fall out about an execution. But as to that article, pray how stands our last year's account?

LOCKIT. If you will run your eye over it, you'll find 'tis fair and clearly stated.

PEACHUM. This long arrear of the government is very hard upon us! Can it be expected that we should hang our acquaintance for nothing, when our betters will hardly save theirs without being paid for it? Unless the people in employment pay better, I promise them for the future, I shall let other rogues live besides their own.

LOCKIT. Perhaps, brother, they are afraid these matters may be carried too far. We are treated, too, by them with contempt, as if our profession were not reputable.

PEACHUM. In one respect, indeed, our employment may be reckoned dishonest, because, like great statesmen, we encourage those who betray their friends.

LOCKIT. Such language, brother, anywhere else might turn to your prejudice. Learn to be more guarded, I beg you.

AIR XII—*How happy are we, etc.*

When you censure the age,
  Be cautious and sage,
Lest the courtiers offended should be.
  If you mention vice or bribe,
  'Tis so pat to all the tribe
Each cries—That was levelled at me.

PEACHUM. Here's poor Ned Clincher's[11] name, I see. Sure, brother Lockit, there was a little unfair proceeding in Ned's case; for he told me in the condemned hold, that for value received, you

11. "Clinch": a canting term for the "condemned hold."

had promised him a sessions or two longer without molestation.

LOCKIT. Mr. Peachum, this is the first time my honor was ever called in question.

PEACHUM. Business is at an end, if once we act dishonorably.

LOCKIT. Who accuses me?

PEACHUM. You are warm, brother.

LOCKIT. He that attacks my honor, attacks my livelihood. And this usage, sir, is not to be borne.

PEACHUM. Since you provoke me to speak, I must tell you too, that Mrs. Coaxer charges you with defrauding her of information-money, for the apprehending of curl-pated Hugh. Indeed, indeed, brother, we must punctually pay our spies, or we shall have no information.

LOCKIT. Is this language to me, sirrah? Who have saved you from the gallows, sirrah!

[*Collaring each other*]

PEACHUM. If I am hanged, it shall be for ridding the world of an arrant rascal.

LOCKIT. This hand shall do the office of the halter you deserve, and throttle you, you dog!

PEACHUM. Brother, brother, we are both in the wrong. We shall be both losers in the dispute— for you know we have it in our power to hang each other. You should not be so passionate.

LOCKIT. Nor you so provoking.

PEACHUM. 'Tis our mutual interest; 'tis for the interest of the world we should agree. If I said anything, brother, to the prejudice of your character, I ask pardon.

LOCKIT. Brother Peachum, I can forgive as well as resent. Give me your hand. Suspicion does not become a friend.

PEACHUM. I only meant to give you occasion to justify yourself. But I must now step home, for I expect the gentleman about this snuff-box that Filch nimmed two nights ago in the park. I appointed him at this hour.   [*Exit.*]

SCENE XI

LOCKIT, LUCY

LOCKIT. Whence come you, hussy?

LUCY. My tears might answer that question.

LOCKIT. You have then been whimpering and

fondling, like a spaniel, over the fellow that hath abused you.

LUCY. One can't help love; one can't cure it. 'Tis not in my power to obey you, and hate him.

LOCKIT. Learn to bear your husband's death like a reasonable woman. 'Tis not the fashion, nowadays, so much as to affect sorrow upon these occasions. No woman would ever marry if she had not the chance of mortality for a release. Act like a woman of spirit, hussy, and thank your father for what he is doing.

LUCY.

AIR XIII—*Of a noble race was Shenkin*

Is then his fate decreed, sir?
　Such a man can I think of quitting?
When first we met, so moves me yet,
　Oh, see how my heart is splitting!

LOCKIT. Look ye, Lucy—there is no saving him —so, I think, you must ev'n do like other widows, buy yourself weeds, and be cheerful.

AIR XIV

You'll think, ere many days ensue,
　This sentence not severe;
I hang your husband, child, 'tis true,
　But with him hang your care.
　　Twang dang dillo dee.

Like a good wife, go moan over your dying husband; that, child, is your duty.—Consider, girl, you can't have the man and the money too—so make yourself as easy as you can by getting all you can from him. [*Exeunt.*]

SCENE XII

LUCY, MACHEATH

LUCY. Though the ordinary was out of the way to-day, I hope, my dear, you will, upon the first opportunity, quiet my scruples.—Oh, sir!—my father's hard heart is not to be softened, and I am in the utmost despair.

MACHEATH. But if you could raise a small sum —would not twenty guineas, think you, move him? Of all are arguments in the way of business, the perquisite is the most prevailing. Your father's perquisites for the escape of prisoners must amount to a considerable sum in the year. Money well timed and properly applied, will do anything.

AIR XV—*London ladies*

If you at an office solicit your due,
　And would not have matters neglected;
You must quicken the clerk with the perquisite too,
　To do what his duty directed.
Or would you the frowns of a lady prevent,
　She too has this palpable failing,
The perquisite softens her into consent;
　That reason with all is prevailing.

LUCY. What love or money can do shall be done, for all my comfort depends upon your safety.

SCENE XIII

LUCY, MACHEATH, POLLY

POLLY. Where is my dear husband?—Was a rope ever intended for this neck? Oh, let me throw my arms about it, and throttle thee with love! Why does thou turn away from me? 'Tis thy Polly—'tis thy wife.

MACHEATH. Was there ever such an unfortunate rascal as I am!

LUCY. Was there ever such another villain!

POLLY. Oh, Macheath! was it for this we parted? Taken! imprisoned! tried! hanged!—cruel reflection! I'll stay with thee till death—no force shall tear thy dear wife from thee now. What means my love?—not one kind word—not one kind look! Think what thy Polly suffers to see thee in this condition.

AIR XVI—*All in the downs, etc.*

Thus when the swallow, seeking prey,
　Within the sash is closely pent,
His consort, with bemoaning lay,
　Without, sits pining for th'event.
Her chattering lovers all around her skim;
She heeds them not (poor bird!)—her soul's with him.

MACHEATH [*aside*]. I must disown her.—The wench is distracted.

LUCY. Am I then bilked of my virtue? Can I have no reparation? Sure, men were born to lie, and women to believe them. Oh, villain! villain!

POLLY. Am I not thy wife? Thy neglect of me, thy aversion to me, too severely proves it.—Look on me. Tell me; am I not thy wife?

LUCY. Perfidious wretch!

POLLY. Barbarous husband!

LUCY. Hadst thou been hanged five months ago, I had been happy.

POLLY. And I too. If you had been kind to me till death, it would not have vexed me—and that's no very unreasonable request (though from a wife) to a man who hath not above seven or eight days to live.

LUCY. Art thou then married to another? Hast thou two wives, monster?

MACHEATH. If women's tongues can cease for an answer—hear me.

LUCY. I won't! Flesh and blood can't bear my usage.

POLLY. Shall I not claim my own? Justice bids me speak.

MACHEATH.

AIR XVII—*Have you heard of a frolicsome ditty, etc.*

> How happy I could be with either,
>   Were t'other dear charmer away!
> But while you thus tease me together,
>   To neither a word will I say;
>   But tol de rol, etc.

POLLY. Sure, my dear, there ought to be some preference shown to a wife! At least she may claim the appearance of it.—He must be distracted with his misfortunes, or he could not use me thus!

LUCY. Oh, villain, villain! thou hast deceived me —I could even inform against thee with pleasure. Not a prude wishes more heartily to have facts against her intimate acquaintance, than I now wish to have facts against thee. I would have her satisfaction, and they should all out.

AIR XVIII—*Irish Trot*

POLLY. I'm bubbled.[12]
LUCY.   —I'm bubbled!
POLLY. Oh how I am troubled!
LUCY. Bamboozled, and bit!
POLLY.   —My distress are doubled.
LUCY.
> When you come to the tree, should the hangman refuse,
> These fingers, with pleasure, could fasten the noose.
POLLY. I'm bubbled, etc.

MACHEATH. Be pacified, my dear Lucy!—This is all a fetch of Polly's to make me desperate with you in case I get off. If I am hanged, she would fain have the credit of being thought my widow. —Really, Polly, this is no time for a dispute of this

12. Cheated.

sort; for whenever you are talking of marriage, I am thinking of hanging.

POLLY. And hast thou the heart to persist in disowning me?

MACHEATH. And hast thou the heart to persist in persuading me that I am married? Why, Polly, dost thou seek to aggravate my misfortunes?

LUCY. Really, Miss Peachum, you but expose yourself. Besides, 'tis barbarous in you to worry a gentleman in his circumstances.

POLLY.

AIR XIX

> Cease your funning,
>   Force or cunning
> Never shall my heart trepan.
>   All these sallies
>   Are but malice
> To seduce my constant man.
>   'Tis most certain,
>   By their flirting,
> Women oft have envy shown;
>   Pleased to ruin
>   Others' wooing
> Never happy in their own!

LUCY. Decency, madam, methinks, might teach you to behave yourself with some reserve with the husband while his wife is present.

MACHEATH. But, seriously, Polly, this is carrying the joke a little too far.

LUCY. If you are determined, madam, to raise a disturbance in the prison, I shall be obliged to send for the turnkey to show you the door. I am sorry, madam, you force me to be so ill-bred.

POLLY. Give me leave to tell you, madam, these forward airs don't become you in the least, madam. And my duty, madam, obliges me to stay with my husband, madam.

LUCY.

AIR XX—*Good morrow, gossip Joan*

> Why, how now, Madam Flirt?
>   If you thus must chatter;
> And are for flinging dirt,
>   Let's try who best can spatter!
>   Madam Flirt!

POLLY.

> Why, how now, saucy jade;
>   Sure the wench is tipsy!
> How can you see me made [*To him*]
>   The scoff of such a gipsy?
>   Saucy jade! [*To her*]

SCENE XIV

LUCY, MACHEATH, POLLY, PEACHUM

PEACHUM. Where's my wench? Ah hussy! hussy! —Come you home, you slut; and when your fellow is hanged, hang yourself, to make your family some amends.

POLLY. Dear, dear father, do not tear me from him; I must speak; I have more to say to him. [*To* MACHEATH] Oh! twist thy fetters about me, that he may not haul me from thee!

PEACHUM. Sure, all women are alike! If ever they commit the folly, they are sure to commit another by exposing themselves.—Away—not a word more —you are my prisoner now, hussy!

POLLY [*holding* MACHEATH, PEACHUM *pulling her*].

AIR XXI—*Irish howl*

No power on earth can e'er divide
The knot that sacred love hath tied.
When parents draw against our mind,
The true-love's knot they faster bind.
    Oh, oh ray, oh amborah—Oh, oh, etc.

[*Exeunt* POLLY *and* PEACHUM.]

SCENE XV

LUCY, MACHEATH

MACHEATH. I am naturally compassionate, wife, so that I could not use the wench as she deserved, which made you at first suspect there was something in what she said.

LUCY. Indeed, my dear, I was strangely puzzled.

MACHEATH. If that had been the case, her father would never have brought me into this circumstance. No, Lucy, I had rather die than be false to thee.

LUCY. How happy am I if you say this from your heart! For I love thee so, that I could sooner bear to see thee hanged than in the arms of another.

MACHEATH. But couldst thou bear to see me hanged?

LUCY. Oh, Macheath, I can never live to see that day.

MACHEATH. You see, Lucy; in the account of love you are in my debt, and you must now be convinced that I rather choose to die than to be another's. Make me, if possible, love thee more, and let me owe my life to thee. If you refuse to assist me, Peachum and your father will immediately put me beyond all means of escape.

LUCY. My father, I know, hath been drinking hard with the prisoners, and I fancy he is now taking his nap in his own room. If I can procure the keys, shall I go off with thee, my dear?

MACHEATH. If we are together, 'twill be impossible to lie concealed. As soon as the search begins to be a little cool, I will send to thee—till then, my heart is thy prisoner.

LUCY. Come then, my dear husband—owe thy life to me—and though you love me not—be grateful. But that Polly runs in my head strangely.

MACHEATH. A moment of time may make us unhappy forever.

LUCY.

AIR XXII—*The lass of Patie's mill, etc.*

I like the fox shall grieve,
    Whose mate hath left her side,
Whom hounds, from morn till eve,
    Chase o'er the country wide,
Where can my lover hide?
    Where cheat the weary pack?
If love be not his guide,
    He never will come back!

ACT III

SCENE I. *Newgate*

LOCKIT, LUCY

LOCKIT. To be sure, wench, you must have been aiding and abetting to help him to this escape.

LUCY. Sir, here hath been Peachum and his daughter Polly, and to be sure they know the ways of Newgate as well as if they had been born and bred in the place all their lives. Why must all your suspicion light upon me?

LOCKIT. Lucy, Lucy, I will have none of these shuffling answers.

LUCY. Well then—if I know anything of him, I wish I may be burnt!

LOCKIT. Keep your temper, Lucy, or I shall pronounce you guilty.

LUCY. Keep yours, sir. I do wish I may be burnt, I do. And what can I say more to convince you?

LOCKIT. Did he tip handsomely? How much did he come down with? Come, hussy, don't cheat your father, and I shall not be angry with you. Perhaps you have made a better bargain with him than I could have done. How much, my good girl?

LUCY. You know, sir, I am fond of him, and would have given money to have kept him with me.

LOCKIT. Ah, Lucy! thy education might have put thee more upon thy guard; for a girl in the bar of an ale-house is always besieged.

LUCY. Dear sir, mention not my education—for 'twas to that I owe my ruin.

AIR I—*If love's a sweet passion, etc.*

When young, at the bar you first taught me to score,
And bid me be free of my lips, and no more.
I was kissed by the parson, the squire, and the sot;
When the guest was departed, the kiss was forgot.
But his kiss was so sweet, and so closely he pressed,
That I languished and pined till I granted the rest.

If you can forgive me, sir, I will make a fair confession, for to be sure he hath been a most barbarous villain to me.

LOCKIT. And so you have let him escape, hussy, have you?

LUCY. When a woman loves, a kind look, a tender word can persuade her to anything, and I could ask no other bribe.

LOCKIT. Thou wilt always be a vulgar slut, Lucy. If you would not be looked upon as a fool, you should never do anything but upon the foot of interest. Those that act otherwise are their own bubbles.

LUCY. But love, sir, is a misfortune that may happen to the most discreet woman, and in love we are all fools alike. Notwithstanding all he swore, I am now fully convinced that Polly Peachum is actually his wife. Did I let him escape (fool that I was!) to go to her? Polly will wheedle herself into his money, and then Peachum will hang him, and cheat us both.

LOCKIT. So I am to be ruined, because, forsooth, you must be in love!—a very pretty excuse!

LUCY. I could murder that impudent happy strumpet! I gave him his life, and that creature enjoys the sweets of it. Ungrateful Macheath!

AIR II—*South-sea Ballad*

My love is all madness and folly,
    Alone I lie,
    Toss, tumble, and cry
What a happy creature is Polly!
Was e'er such a wretch as I!
With rage I redden like scarlet,
That my dear, inconstant varlet,
    Stark blind to my charms,
    Is lost in the arms
Of that jilt, that inveigling harlot!
This, this my resentment alarms.

LOCKIT. And so, after all this mischief, I must stay here to be entertained with your caterwauling, mistress Puss! Out of my sight, wanton strumpet! You shall fast and mortify yourself into reason, with now and then a little handsome discipline to bring you to your senses. Go!   [*Exit* LUCY.]

SCENE II

LOCKIT

LOCKIT. Peachum then intends to outwit me in this affair, but I'll be even with him. The dog is leaky in his liquor; so I'll ply him that way, get the secret from him, and turn this affair to my own advantage. Lions, wolves, and vultures don't live together in herds, droves, or flocks. Of all animals of prey, man is the only sociable one. Every one of us preys upon his neighbor, and yet we herd together. Peachum is my companion, my friend. According to the custom of the world, indeed, he may quote thousands of precedents for cheating me. And shall not I make use of the privilege of friendship to make him a return?

AIR III—*Packington's Pound*

Thus gamesters united in friendship are found,
Though they know that their industry all is a cheat;
They flock to their prey at the dice-box's sound,
And join to promote one another's deceit.
    But if by mishap
    They fail of a chap,
To keep in their hands, they each other entrap.
Like pikes, lank with hunger, who miss of their ends,
They bite their companions, and prey on their friends.

Now, Peachum, you and I, like honest tradesmen, are to have a fair trial which of us two can overreach the other. Lucy!

[*Enter* LUCY.]

Are there any of Peachum's people now in the house?

LUCY. Filch, sir, is drinking a quartern of strong waters in the next room with Black Moll.

LOCKIT. Bid him come to me.   [*Exit* LUCY.]

SCENE III

LOCKIT, FILCH

LOCKIT. Why, boy, thou lookest as if thou wert half starved—like a shotten[1] herring.

FILCH. One had need have the constitution of a horse to go through the business. Since the favorite child-getter was disabled by a mishap, I have picked up a little money by helping the ladies to a pregnancy against their being called down to sentence. But if a man cannot get an honest livelihood any easier way, I am sure 'tis what I can't undertake for another sessions.

LOCKIT. Truly, if that great man should tip off, 'twould be an irreparable loss. The vigor and prowess of a knight-errant never saved half of the ladies in distress that he hath done.—But, boy, canst thou tell me where thy master is to be found?

FILCH. At his lock, sir, at the Crooked Billet.

LOCKIT. Very well. I have nothing more with you. (*Exit* FILCH.) I'll go to him there, for I have many important affairs to settle with him; and in the way of those transactions, I'll artfully get into his secret, so that Macheath shall not remain a day longer out o' my clutches.

SCENE IV. *A gaming-house*

MACHEATH *in a fine tarnished coat,* BEN BUDGE, MATT OF THE MINT

MACHEATH. I am sorry, gentlemen, the road was so barren of money. When my friends are in difficulties, I am always glad that my fortune can be serviceable to them. [*Gives them money.*] You see, gentlemen, I am not a mere court friend, who professes everything and will do nothing.

AIR IV—*Lillibullero*

The modes of the court so common are grown,
    That a true friend can hardly be met;
Friendship for interest is but a loan,
    Which they let out for what they can get.
       'Tis true, you find
       Some friends so kind,
Who will give you good counsel themselves to defend.
      In sorrowful ditty,
      They promise, they pity,
But shift you, for money, from friend to friend.

But we, gentlemen, have still honor enough to break through the corruptions of the world. And while I can serve you, you may command me.

BEN. It grieves my heart that so generous a man should be involved in such difficulties as oblige him to live with such ill company, and herd with gamesters.

MATT. See the partiality of mankind! One man may steal a horse, better than another look over a hedge. Of all mechanics, of all servile handicraftsmen, a gamester is the vilest. But yet, as many of the quality are of the profession, he is admitted amongst the politest company. I wonder we are not more respected.

MACHEATH. There will be deep play tonight at Marybone and consequently money may be picked up upon the road. Meet me there, and I'll give you the hint who is worth setting.

MATT. The fellow with a brown coat with narrow gold binding, I am told, is never without money.

MACHEATH. What do you mean, Matt? Sure you will not think of meddling with him! He's a good honest kind of a fellow, and one of us.

BEN. To be sure, sir, we will put ourselves under your direction.

MACHEATH. Have an eye upon the money-lenders. A rouleau[2] or two would prove a pretty sort of an expedition. I hate extortion.

MATT. These rouleaus are very pretty things. I hate your bank bills. There is such a hazard in putting them off.

MACHEATH. There is a certain man of distinction who in his time hath nicked me out of a great deal of the ready. He is in my cash, Ben. I'll point him out to you this evening, and you shall draw upon him for the debt.—The company are met; I hear the dice-box in the other room. So, gentlemen, your servant! You'll meet me at Marybone.   [*Exeunt.*]

---

1. Thin after spawning.

2. A roll of gold coins.

SCENE V. PEACHUM's *lock. A table with wine, brandy, pipes and tobacco*

PEACHUM, LOCKIT

LOCKIT. The Coronation account,[3] brother Peachum, is of so intricate a nature, that I believe it will never be settled.

PEACHUM. It consists, indeed, of a great variety of articles. It was worth to our people, in fees of different kinds, above ten installments.[4] This is part of the account, brother, that lies open before us.

LOCKIT. A lady's tail[5] of rich brocade—that, I see, is disposed of—

PEACHUM. To Mrs. Diana Trapes, the tally-woman,[6] and she will make a good hand on't in shoes and slippers, to trick out young ladies upon their going into keeping.

LOCKIT. But I don't see any article of the jewels.

PEACHUM. Those are so well known that they must be sent abroad. You'll find them entered under the article of exportation. As for the snuffboxes, watches, swords, etc., I thought it best to enter them under their several heads.

LOCKIT. Seven and twenty women's pockets[7] complete, with the several things therein contained —all sealed, numbered, and entered.

PEACHUM. But, brother, it is impossible for us now to enter upon this affair. We should have the whole day before us. Besides, the account of the last half-year's plate is in a book by itself, which lies at the other office.

LOCKIT. Bring us then more liquor.—Today shall be for pleasure—tomorrow for business.—Ah, brother, those daughters of ours are two slippery hussies. Keep a watchful eye upon Polly, and Macheath in a day or two shall be our own again.

LOCKIT.

AIR V—*Down in the North Country, etc.*

> What gudgeons are we men!
>   Ev'ry woman's easy prey,
> Though we have felt the hook, again
>   We bite and they betray.
> The bird that hath been trapped,
>   When he hears his calling mate,
> To her he flies, again he's clapped
>   Within the wiry grate.

PEACHUM. But what signifies catching the bird if your daughter Lucy will set open the door of the cage?

LOCKIT. If men were answerable for the follies and frailities of their wives and daughters, no friends could keep a good correspondence together for two days. This is unkind of you, brother; for among good friends, what they say or do goes for nothing.

[*Enter a* SERVANT.]

SERVANT. Sir, here's Mrs. Diana Trapes wants to speak with you.

PEACHUM. Shall we admit her, brother Lockit?

LOCKIT. By all means—she's a good customer, and a fine-spoken woman—and a woman who drinks and talks so freely, will enliven the conversation.

PEACHUM. Desire her to walk in.

[*Exit* SERVANT.]

SCENE VI

PEACHUM, LOCKIT, MRS. TRAPES

PEACHUM. Dear Mrs. Dye, your servant—one may know by your kiss, that your gin is excellent.

TRAPES. I was always very curious[8] in my liquors.

LOCKIT. There is no perfumed breath like it. I have been long acquainted with the flavor of those lips—han't I, Mrs. Dye?

TRAPES. Fill it up. I take as large draughts of liquor as I did of love. I hate a flincher in either.

AIR VI— *A shepherd kept sheep, etc.*

> In the days of my youth I could bill like a dove, fa, la, la, etc.
> Like a sparrow at all times was ready for love, fa, la, la, etc.
> The life of all mortals in kissing should pass,
> Lip to lip while we're young—then the lip to the glass, fa, etc.

But now, Mr. Peachum, to our business.—If you have blacks of any kind, brought in of late; mantoes[9]—velvet scarfs—petticoats—let it be what it will, I am your chap[10]—for all my ladies are very fond of mourning.

PEACHUM. Why, look ye, Mrs. Dye—you deal so hard with us, that we can afford to give the gen-

---

3. Account of articles stolen at the coronation of George II, in 1727.   **4.** Annual installations of the Lord Mayors [of London].   **5.** Train.   **6.** A tally-woman sold on credit.   **7.** Pocketbooks.

8. Fastidious.
9. Manteaus [shawls].   **10.** Buyer.

tlemen who venture their lives for the goods, little or nothing.

TRAPES. The hard times oblige me to go very near in my dealing. To be sure, of late years I have been a great sufferer by the parliament. Three thousand pounds would hardly make me amends. The act for destroying the Mint[11] was a severe cut upon our business—till then, if a customer stopped out of the way—we knew where to have her. No doubt you know Mrs. Coaxer—there's a wench now (till to-day) with a good suit of clothes of mine upon her back, and I could never set eyes upon her for three months together. Since the act, too, against imprisonment for small sums, my loss there too hath been very considerable; and it must be so, when a lady can borrow a handsome petticoat, or a clean gown, and I not have the least hank[12] upon her! And, o' my conscience, nowadays most ladies take a delight in cheating, when they can do it with safety!

PEACHUM. Madam, you had a handsome gold watch of us t'other day for seven guineas. Considering we must have our profit—to a gentleman upon the road, a gold watch will be scarce worth the taking.

TRAPES. Consider, Mr. Peachum, that watch was remarkable and not of very safe sale. If you have any black velvet scarfs—they are handsome winter wear, and take with most gentlemen who deal with my customers. 'Tis I that put the ladies upon a good foot. 'Tis not youth or beauty that fixes their price. The gentlemen always pay according to their dress, from half a crown to two guineas; and yet those hussies make nothing of bilking me. Then, too, allowing for accidents—I have eleven fine customers now down under the surgeon's hands; what with fees and other expenses, there are great goings-out, and no comings-in, and not a farthing to pay for at least a month's clothing. We run great risks—great risks, indeed.

PEACHUM. As I remember, you said something just now of Mrs. Coaxer.

TRAPES. Yes, sir. To be sure, I stripped her of a suit of my own clothes about two hours ago, and have left her as she should be, in her shift, with a lover of hers, at my house. She called him upstairs as he was going to Marybone in a hackney coach. And I hope, for her sake and mine, she will persuade the captain to redeem her, for the captain is very generous to the ladies.

11. A district in Southwark, once a refuge for debtors.
12. Hold.

LOCKIT. What captain?

TRAPES. He thought I did not know him—an intimate acquaintance of yours, Mr. Peachum—only Captain Macheath—as fine as a lord.

PEACHUM. To-morrow, dear Mrs. Dye, you shall set your own price upon any of the goods you like. We have at least half a dozen velvet scarfs, and all at your service. Will you give me leave to make you a present of this suit of nightclothes for your own wearing? But are you sure it is Captain Macheath?

TRAPES. Though he thinks I have forgot him, nobody knows him better. I have taken a great deal of the captain's money in my time at second-hand, for he always loved to have his ladies well dressed.

PEACHUM. Mr. Lockit and I have a little business with the captain—you understand me—and we will satisfy you for Mrs. Coaxer's debt.

LOCKIT. Depend upon it—we will deal like men of honor.

TRAPES. I don't enquire after your affairs—so whatever happens, I wash my hands on't. It hath always been my maxim, that one friend should assist another. But if you please, I'll take one of the scarfs home with me. 'Tis always good to have something in hand.

SCENE VII. *Newgate*

LUCY

LUCY. Jealousy, rage, love, and fear are at once tearing me to pieces. How I am weather-beaten and shattered with distresses!

AIR VII—*One evening, having lost my way, etc.*

I'm like a skiff on the ocean tossed,
Now high, now low, with each billow borne;
With her rudder broke, and her anchor lost,
    Deserted and all forlorn.

While thus I lie rolling and tossing all night,
That Polly lies sporting on seas of delight!
    Revenge, revenge, revenge,
Shall appease my restless sprite.

I have the ratsbane ready. I run no risk; for I can lay her death upon the gin, and so many die of that naturally that I shall never be called in question. But say I were to be hanged—I never could be hanged for anything that would give me greater comfort than the poisoning that slut.

[*Enter* FILCH.]

FILCH. Madam, here's our Miss Polly come to wait upon you.

LUCY. Show her in.

SCENE VIII

LUCY, POLLY

LUCY. Dear madam, your servant. I hope you will pardon my passion when I was so happy to see you last. I was so overrun with the spleen,[13] that I was perfectly out of myself. And really when one hath the spleen, everything is to be excused by a friend.

AIR VIII—*Now Roger, I'll tell thee, because thou'rt my son, etc.*

> When a wife's in her pout,
> (As she's sometimes, no doubt);
> The good husband, as meek as a lamb,
>   Her vapors to still,
>   First grants her her will,
> And the quieting draughts is a dram.
> Poor man! And the quieting draught is a dram.

I wish all our quarrels might have so comfortable a reconciliation.

POLLY. I have no excuse for my own behavior, madam, but my misfortunes. And really, madam, I suffer too upon your account.

LUCY. But, Miss Polly—in the way of friendship, will you give me leave to propose a glass of cordial to you?

POLLY. Strong waters are apt to give me the headache; I hope, madam, you will excuse me.

LUCY. Not the greatest lady in the land could have better in her closet, for her own private drinking. You seem mighty low in spirits, my dear.

POLLY. I am sorry, madam, my health will not allow me to accept of your offer. I should not have left you in the rude manner I did when we met last, madam, had not my papa hauled me away so unexpectedly. I was indeed somewhat provoked, and perhaps might use some expressions that were disrespectful. But really, madam, the captain treated me with so much contempt and cruelty,

that I deserved your pity, rather than your resentment.

LUCY. But since his escape, no doubt, all matters are made up again. Ah Polly! Polly! 'tis I am the unhappy wife, and he loves you as if you were only his mistress.

POLLY. Sure, madam, you cannot think me so happy as to be the object of your jealousy! A man is always afraid of a woman who loves him too well—so that I must expect to be neglected and avoided.

LUCY. Then our cases, my dear Polly, are exactly alike. Both of us, indeed, have been too fond.

AIR IX—*O Bessy Bell*

> POLLY. A curse attends that woman's love,
>   Who always would be pleasing.
> LUCY. The pertness of the billing dove,
>   Like ticking, is but teasing.
> POLLY. What then in love can woman do?
> LUCY. If we grow fond they shun us.
> POLLY. And when we fly them, they pursue.
> LUCY. But leave us when they've won us.

LUCY. Love is so very whimsical in both sexes, that it is impossible to be lasting. But my heart is particular, and contradicts my own observation.

POLLY. But really, Mistress Lucy, by his last behavior, I think I ought to envy you. When I was forced from him, he did not shew the least tenderness. But perhaps he hath a heart not capable of it.

AIR X—*Would fate to me Belinda give*

> Among the men, coquets we find,
> Who court by turns all womankind;
> And we grant all their hearts desired,
> When they are flattered and admired.

The coquets of both sexes are self-lovers, and that is a love no other whatever can dispossess. I fear, my dear Lucy, our husband is one of those.

LUCY. Away with these melancholy reflections!— indeed, my dear Polly, we are both of us a cup too low. Let me prevail upon you to accept of my offer.

AIR XI—*Come, sweet lass, etc.*

> Come, sweet lass,
> Let's banish sorrow
> 'Till to-morrow;
> Come, sweet lass,
> Let's take a chirping glass.

13. Spleen, or "vapors": melancholy.

Wine can clear
The vapors of despair;
And make us light as air;
Then drink, and banish care.

I can't bear, child, to see you in such low spirits. And I must persuade you to what I know will do you good. [*Aside*] I shall now soon be even with the hypocritical strumpet.　　　　　[*Exit* LUCY.]

SCENE IX

POLLY

POLLY. All this wheedling of Lucy cannot be for nothing—at this time too, when I know she hates me! The dissembling of a woman is always the forerunner of mischief. By pouring strong waters down my throat, she thinks to pump some secrets out of me. I'll be upon my guard and won't taste a drop of her liquor, I'm resolved.

SCENE X

LUCY, *with strong waters;* POLLY

LUCY. Come, Miss Polly.

POLLY. Indeed, child, you have given yourself trouble to no purpose. You must, my dear, excuse me.

LUCY. Really, Miss Polly, you are as squeamishly affected about taking a cup of strong waters as a lady before company. I vow, Polly, I shall take it monstrously ill if you refuse me. Brandy and men (though women love them never so well) are always taken by us with some reluctance—unless 'tis in private.

POLLY. I protest, madam, it goes against me. What do I see! Macheath again in custody! Now every glimmering of happiness is lost. [*Drops the glass of liquor on the ground.*]

LUCY [*aside*]. Since things are thus, I am glad the wench hath escaped: for by this event, 'tis plain, she was not happy enough to deserve to be poisoned.

SCENE XI

LOCKIT, MACHEATH, PEACHUM, LUCY, POLLY

LOCKIT. Set your heart to rest, captain. You have neither the chance of love or money for another escape; for you are ordered to be called down upon your trial immediately.

PEACHUM. Away, hussies! This is not a time for a man to be hampered with his wives. You see, the gentleman is in chains already.

LUCY. Oh, husband, husband, my heart longed to see thee; but to see thee thus distracts me!

POLLY. Will not my dear husband look upon his Polly? Why hadst thou not flown to me for protection? With me thou hadst been safe.

AIR XII—*The last time I went o'er the moor*

POLLY. Hither, dear husband, turn your eyes.
LUCY. Bestow one glance to cheer me.
POLLY. Think, with that look, thy Polly dies.
LUCY. Oh shun me not—but hear me.
POLLY. 'Tis Polly sues.
LUCY.　　　　　　—'Tis Lucy speaks.
POLLY. Is thus true love requited?
LUCY. My heart is bursting.
POLLY.　　　　　　—Mine too breaks.
LUCY. Must I?
POLLY.　　　—Must I be slighted?

MACHEATH. What would you have me say, ladies? You see, this affair will soon be at an end without my disobliging either of you.

PEACHUM. But the settling this point, captain, might prevent a lawsuit between your two widows.

MACHEATH.

AIR XIII—*Tom Tinker's my true love*

Which way shall I turn me? How can I decide?
Wives, the day of our death, are as fond as a bride.
One wife is too much for most husbands to hear,
But two at a time there's no mortal can bear.
This way, and that way, and which way I will,
What would comfort the one, t'other wife would take
　　ill.

POLLY [*aside*]. But if his own misfortunes have made him insensible to mine—a father sure will be more compassionate—[*to Peachum*] Dear, dear sir, sink the material evidence, and bring him off at his trial! Polly upon her knees begs it of you.

AIR XIV—*I am a poor shepherd undone*

When my hero in court appears,
　　And stands arraigned for his life;
Then think of poor Polly's tears;
　　For ah! poor Polly's his wife.

Like the sailor he holds up his hand,
   Distressed on the dashing wave.
To die a dry death at land,
   Is as bad as a wat'ry grave.
     And alas, poor Polly;
     Alack, and well-a-day!
     Before I was in love,
     Oh, every month was May!

LUCY [*to* LOCKIT]. If Peachum's heart is hardened, sure you, sir, will have more compassion on a daughter. I know the evidence is in your power. How can you be a tyrant to me?   [*Kneeling*]

AIR XV—*Ianthe the lovely, etc.*

When he holds up his hand arrainged for his life,
Oh, think of your daughter, and think I'm his wife!
What are cannons, or bombs, or clashing of swords?
For death is more certain by witnesses' words.
Then nail up their lips; that dread thunder allay;
And each month of my life will hereafter be May.

LOCKIT. Macheath's time is come, Lucy. We know our own affairs; therefore let us have no more whimpering or whining.

AIR—*A cobbler there was, etc.*

Ourselves, like the great, to secure a retreat,
When matters require it, must give up our gang.
     And good reason why,
     Or instead of the fry,
     Ev'n Peachum and I,
Like poor petty rascals, might hang, hang;
Like poor petty rascals might hang.

PEACHUM. Set your heart at rest, Polly. Your husband is to die to-day! therefore, if you are not already provided, 'tis high time to look about for another. There's comfort for you, you slut.

LOCKIT. We are ready, sir, to conduct you to the Old Bailey.

MACHEATH.

AIR XVI—*Bonny Dundee*

The charge is prepared; the lawyers are met,
The judges all ranged (a terrible show!).
I go, undismayed—for death is a debt,
A debt on demand. So, take what I owe.
Then farewell, my love—dear charmers, adieu.
Contented I die— 'tis the better for you.
Here ends all dispute the rest of our lives,
   For this way at once I please all my wives.

Now, gentlemen, I am ready to attend you.
   [*Exeunt* MACHEATH, LOCKIT, *and* PEACHUM.]

SCENE XII

LUCY, POLLY, FILCH

POLLY. Follow them, Filch, to the court; and when the trial is over, bring me a particular account of his behavior, and of everything that happened. You'll find me here with Miss Lucy.
     [*Exit* FILCH.]
But why is all this music?

LUCY. The prisoners whose trials are put off till next sessions are diverting themselves.

POLLY. Sure there is nothing so charming as music! I'm fond of it to distraction! But alas! now, all mirth seems an insult upon my affliction.—Let us retire, my dear Lucy, and indulge our sorrows. The noisy crew, you see, are coming upon us.
     [*Exeunt.*]

[*A dance of prisoners in chains, etc.*]

SCENE XIII. *The condemned hold*

MACHEATH *in a melancholy posture*

MACHEATH.

AIR XVII—*Happy groves*

   O cruel, cruel, cruel case!
   Must I suffer this disgrace?

AIR XVIII—*Of all the girls that are so smart*

Of all the friends in time of grief,
   When threat'ning death looks grimmer,
Not one so sure can bring relief,
   As this best friend, a brimmer.
     [*Drinks.*]

AIR XIX—*Britons, strike home*

Since I must swing, I scorn, I scorn to wince or whine.
     [*Rises.*]

AIR XX—*Chevy Chase*

But now again my spirits sink;
I'll raise them high with wine.
     [*Drinks a glass of wine.*]

AIR XXI—*To old Sir Simon the king*

But valor the stronger grows,
The stronger liquor we're drinking.

And how can we feel our woes,
When we've lost the trouble of thinking?

                         [*Drinks.*]

AIR XXII—*Joy to great Caesar*

     If thus—a man can die,
     Much bolder with brandy.
        [*Pours out a bumper of brandy.*]

AIR XXIII—*There was an old woman*

So I drink off this bumper.—And now I can stand the
     test,
And my comrades shall see that I die as brave as the
     best.

                         [*Drinks.*]

AIR XXIV—*Did you ever hear of a gallant sailor*

     But can I leave my pretty hussies,
     Without one tear, or tender sigh?

AIR XXV—*Why are mine eyes still flowing*

     Their eyes, their lips, their busses,
     Recall my love. Ah, must I die?

AIR XXVI—*Greensleeves*

Since laws were made for ev'ry degree,
To curb vice in others, as well as me,
I wonder we han't better company,
     Upon Tyburn tree!
But gold from law can take out the sting;
And if rich men like us were to swing,
'Twould thin the land, such numbers to string
     Upon Tyburn tree!

          [*Enter a* JAILOR.]

JAILOR. Some friends of yours, captains, desire
to be admitted. I leave you together.   [*Exit.*]

SCENE XIV

MACHEATH, BEN BUDGE, MATT OF THE MINT

MACHEATH. For my having broke prison, you
see, gentlemen, I am ordered immediate execution.
The sheriff's officers, I believe, are now at the
door. That Jenny Twitcher should preach me, I
own, surprised me! 'Tis a plain proof that the
world is all alike, and that even our gang can no
more trust one another than other people. Therefore, I beg you, gentlemen, look well to yourselves, for in all probability you may live some
months longer.

MATT. We are heartily sorry, captain, for your
misfortune. But 'tis what we must all come to.

MACHEATH. Peachum and Lockit, you know, are
infamous scoundrels. Their lives are as much in
your power, as yours are in theirs. Remember your
dying friend!—'Tis my last request. Bring those
villains to the gallows before you, and I am satisfied.

MATT. We'll do't.

          [*Re-enter* JAILOR.]

JAILOR. Miss Polly and Miss Lucy entreat a word
with you.

MACHEATH. Gentlemen, adieu.

        [*Exeunt* BEN, MATT, *and* JAILOR.]

SCENE XV

MACHEATH. My dear Lucy—my dear Polly!
Whatsoever hath passed between us is now at an
end. If you are fond of marrying again, the best
advice I can give you is to ship yourselves off for
the West Indies, where you'll have a fair chance of
getting a husband apiece—or by good luck, two or
three, as you like best.

POLLY. How can I support this sight!

LUCY. There is nothing moves one so much as a
great man in distress.

AIR XXVII—*All you that must take a leap, etc.*

LUCY. Would I might be hanged!

POLLY.   —And I would so too!

LUCY. To be hanged with you.

POLLY.   —My dear, with you.

MACHEATH. Oh, leave me to thought! I fear! I doubt!
I tremble! I droop! See, my courage is out.

         [*Turns up the empty bottle.*]

POLLY. No token of love?

MACHEATH.   See, my courage is out.

         [*Turns up the empty pot.*]

LUCY. No token of love?

POLLY.   Adieu.

LUCY.   Farewell!

MACHEATH. But hark! I hear the toll of the bell!

CHORUS. Tol de rol lol, etc.

[ENTER JAILOR.]

JAILOR. Four women more, captain, with a child
apiece! See, here they come.

        [*Enter* WOMEN *and* CHILDREN.]

MACHEATH. What—four wives more! This is

too much.—Here, tell the Sheriff's officers I am ready.　　　　　　[*Exit* MACHEATH *guarded.*]

SCENE XVI

To them enter PLAYER *and* BEGGAR

PLAYER. But, honest friend, I hope you don't intend that Macheath shall be really executed.

BEGGAR. Most certainly, sir. To make the piece perfect, I was for doing strict poetical justice. Macheath is to be hanged; and for the other personages of the drama, the audience must have supposed they were all either hanged or transported.

PLAYER. Why then, friend, this is a downright deep tragedy. The catastrophe is manifestly wrong, for an opera must end happily.

BEGGAR. Your objection, sir, is very just, and is easily removed; for you must allow that in this kind of drama, 'tis no matter how absurdly things are brought about. So—you rabble there! run and cry a reprieve!—let the prisoner be brought back to his wives in triumph.

PLAYER. All this we must do, to comply with the taste of the town.

BEGGAR. Through the whole piece you may observe such a similitude of manners in high and low life, that it is difficult to determine whether (in the fashionable vices) the fine gentlemen imitate the gentlemen of the road, or the gentlemen of the road the fine gentlemen. Had the play remained as I at first intended, it would have carried a most excellent moral. 'Twould have shown that the lower sort of people have their vices in a degree as well as the rich, and that they are punished for them.

SCENE XVII

To them MACHEATH, *with rabble, etc.*

MACHEATH. So it seems I am not left to my choice, but must have a wife at last.—Look ye, my dears, we will have no controversy now. Let us give this day to mirth, and I am sure she who thinks herself my wife will testify her joy by a dance.

ALL. Come, a dance—a dance!

MACHEATH. Ladies, I hope you will give me leave to present a partner to each of you. And (if I may without offence) for this time, I take Polly for mine. [*To* POLLY] And for life, you slut, for we were really married. As for the rest—but at present keep your own secret.

A Dance

AIR XXVIII—*Lumps of pudding, etc.*

Thus I stand like the Turk, with his doxies around;
From all sides their glances his passion confound:
For black, brown, and fair, his inconstancy burns,
And the different beauties subdue him by turns.
Each calls forth her charms, to provoke his desires;
Though willing to all, with but one he retires.
But think of this maxim, and put off your sorrow,
The wretch of today may be happy to-morrow.

CHORUS. But think of this maxim, etc.

When We Dead Awaken

BY HENRIK IBSEN

TRANSLATED BY WILLIAM ARCHER

When We Dead Awaken (*Når vi døde vågner*), Ibsen's final play, was first published in December 1899, and during the following year it was produced in several major cities of Scandinavia and Germany. Ibsen referred to the play as a "Dramatic Epilogue"; not necessarily an epilogue to his entire dramatic vision, but, as he said in a letter, the culmination of the series of plays that includes *The Master Builder, Little Eyolf,* and *John Gabriel Borkman.* Each of these late plays deals with an overbearing creative personality, the tensions between his domestic or personal life and his imaginative or transcendent self, and his heroic effort to reconcile past guilt with continued aspiration. In their outdoor settings and their incorporation of figures from folklore (the hunter Ulfheim, for example), these plays contrast significantly with the drawing-room settings of Ibsen's problem-plays—notably, *A Doll's House, An Enemy of the People,* and *Ghosts*—and represent a return to the more expansive romantic mode of his earlier poetic dramas, *Brand* and *Peer Gynt.* But as Marjorie Garber points out in her essay written for this collection (see page 231), the notion of break and return is misleading in so far as it ignores the overarching romantic unity of Ibsen's total work within which *When We Dead Awaken* is the capstone. Although the early splurge of production *When We Dead Awaken* enjoyed was perhaps a *succès d'estime*—one that was soon followed by relative eclipse—the play has been revived in recent years with new and broader understanding of its theatrical values.

Characters

PROFESSOR ARNOLD RUBEK, *a sculptor*
MRS. MAIA RUBEK, *his wife*
THE INSPECTOR, *at the Baths*
ULFHEIM, *a landed proprietor*
A STRANGER LADY

A SISTER OF MERCY
SERVANTS, VISITORS *to the Baths, and* CHILDREN

The First Act passes at a bathing establishment on the coast; the Second and Third Acts in the neighborhood of a health resort, high in the mountains.

ACT I

Outside the Bath Hotel. A portion of the main building can be seen to the right. An open, park-like place with a fountain, groups of fine old trees, and shrubbery. To the left, a little pavilion almost covered with ivy and Virginia creeper. A table and chair outside it. At the back a view over the fiord, right out to sea, with headlands and small islands in the distance. It is a calm, warm and sunny summer morning.

PROFESSOR RUBEK *and* MRS. MAIA RUBEK *are sitting in basket chairs beside a covered table on the lawn outside the hotel, having just breakfasted. They have champagne and seltzer water on the table, and each has a newspaper.* PROFESSOR RUBEK *is an elderly man of distinguished appearance, wearing a black velvet jacket, and otherwise in light summer attire.* MAIA *is quite young, with a vivacious expression and lively, mocking eyes, yet with a suggestion of fatigue. She wears an elegant traveling dress.*

MAIA [*sits for some time as though waiting for the* PROFFESSOR *to say something, then lets her paper drop with a deep sigh*]. Oh dear, dear, dear——!

PROFESSOR RUBEK [*looks up from his paper*]. Well, Maia? What is the matter with you?

MAIA. Just listen how silent it is here.

PROFESSOR RUBEK [*smiles indulgently*]. And you can hear that?

MAIA. What?

PROFESSOR RUBEK. The silence?

MAIA. Yes, indeed I can.

PROFESSOR RUBEK. Well, perhaps you are right, *mein Kind*. One can really hear the silence.

MAIA. Heaven knows you can—when it's so absolutely overpowering as it is here——

PROFESSOR RUBEK. Here at the Baths, you mean?

MAIA. Wherever you go at home here, it seems to me. Of course there was noise and bustle enough in the town. But I don't know how it is—even the noise and bustle seemed to have something dead about it.

PROFESSOR RUBEK [*with a searching glance*]. You don't seem particularly glad to be at home again, Maia?

MAIA [*looks at him*]. Are you glad?

PROFESSOR RUBEK [*evasively*]. I——?

MAIA. Yes, you, who have been so much, much farther away than I. Are you entirely happy, now that you are at home again?

PROFESSOR RUBEK. No—to be quite candid—perhaps not entirely happy——

MAIA [*with animation*]. There, you see! Didn't I know it!

PROFESSOR RUBEK. I have perhaps been too long abroad. I have drifted quite away from all this—this home life.

MAIA [*eagerly, drawing her chair nearer him*]. There, you see, Rubek! We had much better get away again! As quickly as ever we can.

PROFESSOR RUBEK [*somewhat impatiently*]. Well, well, that is what we intend to do, my dear Maia. You know that.

MAIA. But why not now—at once? Only think how cozy and comfortable we could be down there, in our lovely new house——

PROFESSOR RUBEK [*smiles indulgently*]. We ought by rights to say: our lovely new home.

MAIA [*shortly*]. I prefer to say house—let us keep to that.

PROFESSOR RUBEK [*his eyes dwelling on her*]. You are really a strange little person.

MAIA. Am I so strange?

PROFESSOR RUBEK. Yes, I think so.

MAIA. But why, pray? Perhaps because I'm not desperately in love with mooning about up here——?

PROFESSOR RUBEK. Which of us was it that was absolutely bent on our coming north this summer?

MAIA. I admit, it was I.

PROFESSOR RUBEK. It was certainly not I, at any rate.

MAIA. But good heavens, who could have dreamed that everything would have altered so terribly at home here? And in so short a time, too! Why, it is only just four years since I went away——

PROFESSOR RUBEK. Since you were married, yes.

MAIA. Married? What has that to do with the matter?

PROFESSOR RUBEK [*continuing*].—since you became the Frau Professor, you found yourself a mistress of a charming home—I beg your pardon—a very handsome house, I ought to say. And a villa on the Lake of Taunitz, just at the point that has become most fashionable, too—— In fact it is all very handsome and distinguished, Maia, there's no denying that. And spacious too. We need not always be getting in each other's way——

MAIA [*lightly*]. No, no, no—there's certainly no lack of house room, and that sort of thing——

PROFESSOR RUBEK. Remember, too, that you have been living in altogether more spacious and distinguished surroundings—in more polished society than you were accustomed to at home.

MAIA [*looking at him*]. Ah, so you think it is *I* that have changed?

PROFESSOR RUBEK. Indeed I do, Maia.

MAIA. I alone? Not the people here?

PROFESSOR RUBEK. Oh, yes, they too—a little perhaps. And not at all in the direction of amiability. That I readily admit.

MAIA. I should think you must admit it, indeed.

PROFESSOR RUBEK [*changing the subject*]. Do you know how it affects me when I look at the life of the people around us here?

MAIA. No. Tell me.

PROFESSOR RUBEK. It makes me think of that night we spent in the train, when we were coming up here——

MAIA. Why, you were sound asleep all the time.

PROFESSOR RUBEK. Not quite. I noticed how silent it became at all the little roadside stations. I heard the silence—like you, Maia——

MAIA. H'm,—like me, yes.

PROFESSOR RUBEK. —and that assured me that we had crossed the frontier—that we were really at home. For the train stopped at all the little stations—although there was nothing doing at all.

MAIA. Then why did it stop—though there was nothing to be done?

PROFESSOR RUBEK. Can't say. No one got out or in; but all the same the train stopped a long, endless time. And at every station I could make out that there were two railway men walking up and down the platform—one with a lantern in his hand—and they said things to each other in the night, low, and toneless, and meaningless.

MAIA. Yes, that is quite true. There are always two men walking up and down, and talking——

PROFESSOR RUBEK. —of nothing. [*Changing to a livelier tone*] But just wait till tomorrow. Then we shall have the great luxurious steamer lying in the harbor. We'll go on board her, and sail all round the coast—northward ho!—right to the polar sea.

MAIA. Yes, but then you will see nothing of the country—and of the people. And that was what you particularly wanted.

PROFESSOR RUBEK [*short and snappishly*]. I have seen more than enough.

MAIA. Do you think a sea voyage will be better for you?

PROFESSOR RUBEK. It is always a change.

MAIA. Well well, if only it is the right thing for you——

PROFESSOR RUBEK. For me? The right thing? There is nothing in the world the matter with me.

MAIA [*rises and goes up to him*]. Yes, there is, Rubek. I am sure you must feel it yourself.

PROFESSOR RUBEK. Why, my dearest Maia—what should be amiss with me?

MAIA [*behind him, bending over the back of his chair*]. That you must tell me. You have begun to wander about without a moment's peace. You cannot rest anywhere—neither at home nor abroad. You have become quite misanthropic of late.

PROFESSOR RUBEK [*with a touch of sarcasm*]. Dear me—have you noticed that?

MAIA. No one that knows you can help noticing it. And then it seems to me so sad that you have lost all pleasure in your work.

PROFESSOR RUBEK. That too, eh?

MAIA. You that used to be so indefatigable—working from morning to night!

PROFESSOR RUBEK [*gloomily*]. Used to be, yes——

MAIA. But ever since you got your great masterpiece out of hand——

PROFESSOR RUREK [*nods thoughtfully*]. "The Ressurection Day"——

MAIA. —the masterpiece that has gone round the whole world, and made you so famous——

PROFESSOR RUBEK. Perhaps that is just the misfortune, Maia.

MAIA. How so?

PROFESSOR RUBEK. When I had finished this masterpiece of mine—[*Makes a passionate movement with his hand.*]—for "The Resurrection Day" is a masterpiece! Or was one in the beginning. No, it is one still. It must, must, must be a masterpiece!

MAIA [*looks at him in astonishment*]. Why, Rubek—all the world knows that.

PROFESSOR RUBEK [*short, repellently*]. All the world knows nothing! Understands nothing!

MAIA. Well, at any rate it can divine something——

PROFESSOR RUBEK. Something that isn't there at all, yes. Something that never was in my mind. Ah, yes, that they can all go into ecstasies over! [*Growling to himself*] What is the good of working oneself to death for the mob and the masses—for "all the world"!

MAIA. Do you think it is better, then—do you think it is worthy of you, to do nothing at all but a portrait bust now and then?

PROFESSOR RUBEK [*with a sly smile*]. They are not exactly portrait busts that I turn out, Maia.

MAIA. Yes, indeed they are—for the last two or three years—ever since you finished your great group and got it out of the house——

PROFESSOR RUBEK. All the same, they are no mere portrait busts, I assure you.

MAIA. What are they, then?

PROFESSOR RUBEK. There is something equivocal, something cryptic, lurking in and behind these busts—a secret something, that the people themselves cannot see——

MAIA. Indeed?

PROFESSOR RUBEK [*decisively*]. I alone can see it. And it amuses me unspeakably—On the surface I give them the "striking likeness," as they call it, that they all stand and gape at in astonishment—[*Lowers his voice.*]—but at bottom they are all respectable, pompous horsefaces, and self-opinionated donkey muzzles, and lop-eared, low-browed dog skulls and fatted swine snouts—and sometimes dull, brutal bull fronts as well—

MAIA [*indifferently*]. All the dear domestic animals, in fact.

PROFESSOR RUBEK. Simply the dear domestic animals, Maia. All the animals which men have bedeviled in their own image—and which have bedeviled men in return. [*Empties his champagne glass and laughs.*] And it is these double-faced works of art that our excellent plutocrats come and order of me. And pay for in all good faith—and in good round figures too—almost their weight in gold, as the saying goes.

MAIA [*fills his glass*]. Come, Rubek! Drink and be happy.

PROFESSOR RUBEK [*passes his hand several times across this forehead and leans back in his chair*]. I am happy, Maia. Really happy—in a way. [*Short silence.*] For after all there is a certain happiness in feeling oneself free and independent on every hand—in having at one's command everything one can possibly wish for—all outward things, that is to say. Do you not agree with me, Maia?

MAIA. Oh yes, I agree. All that is well enough in its way. [*Looking at him.*] But do you remember what you promised me the day we came to an understanding on—on that troublesome point——

PROFESSOR RUBEK [*nods*]. —On the subject of our marriage, yes. It was no easy matter for you, Maia.

MAIA [*continuing unruffled*]. —and agreed that I was to go abroad with you, and live there for good and all—and enjoy myself.—Do you remember what you promised me that day?

PROFESSOR RUBEK [*shaking his head*]. No, I can't say that I do. Well, what did I promise?

MAIA. You said you would take me up to a high mountain and show me all the glory of the world.

PROFESSOR RUBEK [*with a slight start*]. Did I promise you that, too?

MAIA. Me, too? Who else, pray?

PROFESSOR RUBEK [*indifferently*]. No, no, I only meant did I promise to show you——?

MAIA. —all the glory of the world? Yes, you did. And all that glory should be mine, you said.

PROFESSOR RUBEK. That is a sort of figure of speech that I was in the habit of using once upon a time.

MAIA. Only a figure of speech?

PROFESSOR RUBEK. Yes, a schoolboy phrase—the sort of thing I used to say when I wanted to lure the neighbors' children out to play with me, in the woods and on the mountains.

MAIA [*looking hard at him*]. Perhaps you only wanted to lure me out to play, as well?

PROFESSOR RUBEK [*passing it off as a jest*]. Well,

has it not been a tolerably amusing game, Maia?

MAIA [*coldly*]. I did not go with you only to play.

PROFESSOR RUBEK. No, no, I daresay not.

MAIA. And you never took me up with you to any high mountain, or showed me——

PROFESSOR RUBEK [*with irritation*]. —all the glory of the world? No, I did not. For, let me tell you something: you are not really born to be a mountain climber, little Maia.

MAIA [*trying to control herself*]. Yet at one time you seemed to think I was.

PROFESSOR RUBEK. Four or five years ago, yes. [*Stretching himself in his chair.*] Four or five years —it's a long, long time, Maia.

MAIA [*looking at him with a bitter expression*]. Has the time seemed so very long to you, Rubek?

PROFESSOR RUBEK. I am beginning now to find it a trifle long. [*Yawning.*] Now and then, you know.

MAIA [*returning to her place*]. I shall not bore you any longer. [*She resumes her seat, takes up the newspaper, and begins turning over the leaves. Silence on both sides.*]

PROFESSOR RUBEK. [*leaning on his elbows across the table, and looking at her teasingly*]. Is the Frau Professor offended?

MAIA [*coldly, without looking up*]. No, not at all.

[*VISITORS to the baths, most of them ladies, begin to pass, singly and in groups, through the park from the right, and out to the left.*

WAITERS bring refreshments from the hotel, and go off behind the pavilion.

THE INSPECTOR, wearing gloves and carrying a stick, comes from his rounds in the park, meets VISITORS, bows politely, and exchanges a few words with some of them.]

THE INSPECTOR [*advancing to PROFESSOR RUBEK's table and politely taking off his hat*]. I have the honor to wish you good morning, Mrs. Rubek. Good morning, Professor Rubek.

PROFESSOR RUBEK. Good morning, good morning, Inspector.

THE INSPECTOR [*addressing himself to MRS. RUBEK*]. May I venture to ask if you have slept well?

MAIA. Yes, thank you; excellently—for my part. I always sleep like a stone.

THE INSPECTOR. I am delighted to hear it. The first night in a strange place is often rather trying. And the Professor——?

PROFESSOR RUBEK. Oh, my night's rest is never much to boast of—especially of late.

THE INSPECTOR [*with a show of sympathy*]. Oh —that is a pity. But after a few weeks' stay at the Baths—you will quite get over that.

PROFESSOR RUBEK [*looking up at him*]. Tell me, Inspector—are any of your patients in the habit of taking baths during the night?

THE INSPECTOR [*astonished*]. During the night? No, I have never heard of such a thing.

PROFESSOR RUBEK. Have you not?

THE INSPECTOR. No, I don't know of anyone so ill as to require such treatment.

PROFESSOR RUBEK. Well, at any rate there is someone who is in the habit of walking about the park by night?

THE INSPECTOR [*smiling and shaking his head*]. No, Professor—that would be against the rules.

MAIA [*impatiently*]. Good Heavens, Rubek, I told you so this morning—you must have dreamed it.

PROFESSOR RUBEK [*dryly*]. Indeed? Must I? Thank you! [*Turning to THE INSPECTOR.*] The fact is, I got up last night—I couldn't sleep—and I wanted to see what sort of night it was——

THE INSPECTOR [*attentively*]. To be sure—and then——?

PROFESSOR RUBEK. I looked out at the window— and caught sight of a white figure in there among the trees.

MAIA [*smiling to THE INSPECTOR*]. And the Professor declares that the figure was dressed in a bathing costume——

PROFESSOR RUBEK. —Or something like it, I said. Couldn't distinguish very clearly. But I am sure it was something white.

THE INSPECTOR. Most remarkable. Was it a gentleman or a lady?

PROFESSOR RUBEK. I could almost have sworn it was a lady. But then after it came another figure. And that one was quite dark—like a shadow——

THE INSPECTOR [*starting*]. A dark one? Quite black, perhaps?

PROFESSOR RUBEK. Yes, I should almost have said so.

THE INSPECTOR [*a light breaking in upon him*]. And behind the white figure? Following close upon her——?

PROFESSOR RUBEK. Yes—at a little distance——

THE INSPECTOR. Aha! Then I think I can explain the mystery, Professor.

PROFESSOR RUBEK. Well, what was it then?

MAIA [*simultaneously*]. Was the Professor really not dreaming?

THE INSPECTOR [*suddenly whispering, as he directs their attention toward the background on the right*]. Hush, if you please! Look there—— Don't speak loud for a moment.

[*A slender lady, dressed in fine, cream-white cashmere, and followed by a* SISTER OF MERCY *in black, with a silver cross hanging by a chain on her breast, comes forward from behind the hotel and crosses the park toward the pavilion in front on the left. Her face is pale, and its lines seem to have stiffened; the eyelids are drooped and the eyes appear as though they saw nothing. Her dress comes down to her feet and clings to the body in perpendicular folds. Over her head, neck, breast, shoulders and arms she wears a large shawl of white crape. She keeps her arms crossed upon her breast. She carries her body immovably, and her steps are stiff and measured. The* SISTER's *bearing is also measured, and she has the air of a servant. She keeps her brown piercing eyes incessantly fixed upon the lady.* WAITERS, *with napkins on their arms, come forward in the hotel doorway, and cast curious glances at the strangers, who take no notice of anything, and, without looking round, enter the pavilion.*]

PROFESSOR RUBEK [*has risen slowly and involuntarily, and stands staring at the closed door of the pavilion*]. Who was that lady?

THE INSPECTOR. She is a stranger who has rented the little pavilion there.

PROFESSOR RUBEK. A foreigner?

THE INSPECTOR. Presumably. At any rate they both came from abroad—about a week ago. They have never been here before.

PROFESSOR RUBEK [*decidedly; looking at him*]. It was she I saw in the park last night.

THE INSPECTOR. No doubt it must have been. I thought so from the first.

PROFESSOR RUBEK. What is this lady's name, Inspector?

THE INSPECTOR. She has registered herself as "Madame de Satow, with companion." We know nothing more.

PROFESSOR RUBEK [*reflecting*]. Satow? Satow ——?

MAIA [*laughing mockingly*]. Do you know anyone of that name, Rubek? Eh?

PROFESSOR RUBEK [*shaking his head*]. No, no

one. Satow? It sounds Russian—or at all events Slavonic. [*To* THE INSPECTOR] What language does she speak?

THE INSPECTOR. When the two ladies talk to each other, it is in a language I cannot make out at all. But at other times she speaks Norwegian like a native.

PROFESSOR RUBEK [*exclaims with a start*]. Norwegian? You are sure you are not mistaken?

THE INSPECTOR. No, how could I be mistaken in that?

PROFESSOR RUBEK [*looks at him with eager interest*]. You have heard her yourself?

THE INSPECTOR. Yes. I myself have spoken to her —several times.—Only a few words, however; she is far from communicative. But——

PROFESSOR RUBEK. But Norwegian it was?

THE INSPECTOR. Thoroughly good Norwegian— perhaps with a little north country accent.

PROFESSOR RUBEK [*gazing straight before him in amazement, whispers*]. That too!

MAIA [*a little hurt and jarred*]. Perhaps this lady has been one of your models, Rubek? Search your memory.

PROFESSOR RUBEK [*looks cuttingly at her*]. My models!

MAIA [*with a provoking smile*]. In your younger days, I mean. You are said to have had such innumerable models—long ago, of course.

PROFESSOR RUBEK [*in the same tone*]. Oh, no, little Frau Maia. I have in reality had only one single model. One and one only—for everything I have done.

THE INSPECTOR [*who has turned away and stands looking out to the left*]. If you'll excuse me, I think I will take my leave. I see someone coming whom it is not particularly agreeable to meet. Especially in the presence of ladies.

PROFESSOR RUBEK [*looking in the same direction*]. That sportsman there? Who is it?

THE INSPECTOR. It is a certain Mr. Ulfheim, from——

PROFESSOR RUBEK. Oh, Mr. Ulfheim——

THE INSPECTOR. —The bear killer, as they call him——

PROFESSOR RUBEK. I know him.

THE INSPECTOR. Who does not know him?

PROFESSOR RUBEK. Very slightly, however. Is he on your list of patients—at last?

THE INSPECTOR. No, strangely enough—not as yet. He comes here only once a year—on his way up to his hunting grounds.—Excuse me for the moment——[*Makes a movement to go into the hotel.*]

ULFHEIM'S VOICE [*heard outside*]. Stop a moment, man! Devil take it all, can't you stop? Why do you always scuttle away from me?

THE INSPECTOR [*stops*]. I am not scuttling at all, Mr. Ulfheim.

[ULFHEIM *enters from the left followed by a servant with a couple of sporting dogs in leash.* ULFHEIM *is in shooting costume, with high boots and a felt hat with a feather in it. He is a long, lank, sinewy personage, with matted hair and beard, and a loud voice. His appearance gives no precise clue to his age, but he is no longer young.*]

ULFHEIM [*pounces upon* THE INSPECTOR]. Is this a way to receive strangers, hey? You scamper away with your tail between your legs—as if you had the devil at your heels.

THE INSPECTOR [*calmly, without answering him*]. Has Mr. Ulfheim arrived by the steamer?

ULFHEIM [*growls*]. Haven't had the honor of seeing any steamer. [*With his arms akimbo*] Don't you know that *I* sail my own cutter? [*To the* SERVANT] Look well after your fellow creatures, Lars. But take care you keep them ravenous, all the same. Fresh meat bones—but not too much meat on them, do you hear? And be sure it's reeking raw, and bloody. And get something in your own belly while you're about it. [*Aiming a kick at him*] Now then, go to hell with you!

[*The* SERVANT *goes out with the dogs, behind the corner of the hotel.*]

THE INSPECTOR. Would not Mr. Ulfheim like to go into the dining room in the meantime?

ULFHEIM. In among all the half-dead flies and people? No, thank you a thousand times, Mr. Inspector.

THE INSPECTOR. Well, well, as you please.

ULFHEIM. But get the housekeeper to prepare a hamper for me as usual. There must be plenty of provender in it—and lots of brandy——! You can tell her that I or Lars will come and play Old Harry with her if she doesn't——

THE INSPECTOR [*interrupting*]. We know your ways of old. [*Turning.*] Can I give the waiter any orders, Professor? Can I send Mrs. Rubek anything?

PROFESSOR RUBEK. No, thank you; nothing for me.

MAIA. Nor for me.

[THE INSPECTOR *goes into the hotel.*]

ULFHEIM [*stares at them a moment; then lifts his hat*]. Why, blast me if here isn't a country tyke that has strayed into regular tiptop society.

PROFESSOR RUBEK [*looking up*]. What do you mean by that, Mr. Ulfheim?

ULFHEIM [*more quietly and politely*]. I believe I have the honor of addressing no less a person than the great Sculptor Rubek.

PROFESSOR RUBEK [*nods*]. I remember meeting you once or twice—the autumn when I was last at home.

ULFHEIM. That's many years ago now, though. And then you weren't so illustrious as I hear you've since become. At that time even a dirty bear hunter might venture to come near you.

PROFESSOR RUBEK [*smiling*]. I don't bite even now.

MAIA [*looks with interest at* ULFHEIM]. Are you really and truly a bear hunter?

ULFHEIM [*seating himself at the next table, nearer the hotel*]. A bear hunter when I have the chance, madam. But I make the best of any sort of game that comes in my way—eagles, and wolves, and women, and elks, and reindeer—if only it's fresh and juicy and has plenty of blood in it. [*Drinks from his pocket flask.*]

MAIA [*regarding him fixedly*]. But you like bear hunting best?

ULFHEIM. I like it best, yes. For then one can have the knife handy at a pinch. [*With a slight smile*] We both work in a hard material, madam —both your husband and I. He struggles with his marble blocks, I daresay; and I struggle with tense and quivering bear sinews. And we both of us win the fight in the end—subdue and master our material. We never rest till we've got the upper hand of it, though it fight never so hard.

PROFESSOR RUBEK [*deep in thought*]. There's a great deal of truth in what you say.

ULFHEIM. Yes, for I take it the stone has something to fight for too. It is dead, and determined by no manner of means to let itself be hammered into life. Just like the bear when you come and prod him up in his lair.

MAIA. Are you going up into the forests now to hunt?

ULFHEIM. I am going right up into the high mountains.—I suppose you have never been in the high mountains, madam?

MAIA. No, never.

ULFHEIM. Confound it all then, you must be sure and come up there this very summer! I'll take you with me—both you and the Professor, with pleasure.

MAIA. Thanks. But Rubek is thinking of taking a sea trip this summer.

PROFESSOR RUBEK. Round the coast—through the island channels.

ULFHEIM. Ugh—what the devil would you do in those damnable sickly gutters—floundering about in the brackish ditchwater? Dishwater I should rather call it.

MAIA. There, you hear, Rubek!

ULFHEIM. No, much better come up with me to the mountains—away, clean away, from the trail and taint of men. You can't think what that means for me. But such a little lady——

[*The* SISTER OF MERCY *comes out of the pavilion and goes into the hotel.*]

ULFHEIM [*following her with his eyes*]. Just look at her, do! That night crow there!—Who is it that's to be buried?

PROFESSOR RUBEK. I have not heard of anyone——

ULFHEIM. Well, there's someone on the point of giving up the ghost, then—in one corner or another.—People that are sickly and rickety should have the goodness to see about getting themselves buried—the sooner the better.

MAIA. Have you ever been ill yourself, Mr. Ulfheim?

ULFHEIM. Never. If I had, I shouldn't be here. —But my nearest friends—they have been ill, poor things.

MAIA. And what did you do for your nearest friends?

ULFHEIM. Shot them, of course.

PROFESSOR RUBEK [*looking at him*]. Shot them?

MAIA [*moving her chair back*]. Shot them dead?

ULFHEIM [*nods*]. I never miss, madam.

MAIA. But how can you possibly shoot people!

ULFHEIM. I am not speaking of people——

MAIA. You said your nearest friends——

ULFHEIM. Well, who should they be but my dogs?

MAIA. Are your dogs your nearest friends?

ULFHEIM. I have none nearer. My honest, trusty, absolutely loyal comrades—— When one of them turns sick and miserable—bang!—and there's my friend sent packing—to the other world.

[*The* SISTER OF MERCY *comes out of the hotel with a tray on which is bread and milk. She places it on the table outside the pavilion, which she enters.*]

ULFHEIM [*laughs scornfully*]. That stuff there—is that what you call food for human beings! Milk and water and soft, clammy bread. Ah, you should see my comrades feeding. Should you like to see it?

MAIA [*smiling across to the* PROFESSOR *and rising*]. Yes, very much.

ULFHEIM [*also rising*]. Spoken like a woman of spirit, madam! Come with me, then! They swallow whole great thumping meatbones—gulp them up and then gulp them down again. Oh, it's a regular treat to see them. Come along and I'll show you—and while we're about it, we can talk over this trip to the mountains——

[*He goes out by the corner of the hotel,* MAIA *following him.*

Almost at the same moment the STRANGE LADY *comes out of the pavilion and seats herself at the table.*

THE LADY *raises her glass of milk and is about to drink, but stops and looks across at* RUBEK *with vacant, expressionless eyes.*]

PROFESSOR RUBEK [*remains sitting at his table and gazes fixedly and earnestly at her. At last he rises, goes some steps toward her, stops, and says in a low voice*]. I know you quite well, Irene.

THE LADY [*in a toneless voice, setting down her glass*]. You can guess who I am, Arnold?

PROFESSOR RUBEK [*without answering*]. And you recognize me, too, I see.

THE LADY. With you it is quite another matter.

PROFESSOR RUBEK. With me?—How so?

THE LADY. Oh, you are still alive.

PROFESSOR RUBEK [*not understanding*]. Alive—?

THE LADY [*after a short pause*]. Who was the other? The woman you had with you—there at the table?

PROFESSOR RUBEK [*a little reluctantly*]. She? That was my—my wife.

THE LADY [*nods slowly*]. Indeed. That is well, Arnold. Someone, then, who does not concern me——

PROFESSOR RUBEK [*nods*]. No, of course not——

THE LADY. —One whom you have taken to you after my lifetime.

PROFESSOR RUBEK [*suddenly looking hard at her*]. After your——? What do you mean by that, Irene?

IRENE [*without answering*]. And the child? I hear the child is prospering too. Our child survives me—and has come to honor and glory.

PROFESSOR RUBEK [*smiles as at a far-off recollection*]. Our child? Yes, we called it so—then.

IRENE. In my lifetime, yes.

PROFESSOR RUBEK [*trying to take a lighter tone*]. Yes, Irene.—I can assure you "our child" has become famous all the wide world over. I suppose you have read about it.

IRENE [*nods*]. And has made its father famous too.—That was your dream.

PROFESSOR RUBEK [*more softly, with emotion*]. It is to you I owe everything, everything, Irene—and I thank you.

IRENE [*lost in thought for a moment*]. If I had then done what I had a right to do, Arnold——

PROFESSOR RUBEK. Well? What then?

IRENE. I should have killed that child.

PROFESSOR RUBEK. Killed it, you say?

IRENE [*whispering*]. Killed it—before I went away from you. Crushed it—crushed it to dust.

PROFESSOR RUBEK [*shakes his head reproachfully*]. You would never have been able to, Irene. You had not the heart to do it.

IRENE. No, in those days I had not that sort of heart.

PROFESSOR RUBEK. But since then? Afterwards?

IRENE. Since then I have killed it innumerable times. By daylight and in the dark. Killed it in hatred—and in revenge—and in anguish.

PROFESSOR RUBEK [*goes close up to the table and asks softly*]. Irene—tell me now at last—after all these years—why did you go away from me? You disappeared so utterly—left not a trace behind——

IRENE [*shaking her head slowly*]. Oh, Arnold—why should I tell you that now—from the world beyond the grave.

PROFESSOR RUBEK. Was there someone else whom you had come to love?

IRENE. There was one who had no longer any use for my love—any use for my life.

PROFESSOR RUBEK [*changing the subject*]. H'm—don't let us talk any more of the past——

IRENE. No, no—by all means let us not talk of what is beyond the grave—what is now beyond the grave for me.

PROFESSOR RUBEK. Where have you been, Irene? All my inquiries were fruitless—you seemed to have vanished away.

IRENE. I went into the darkness—when the child stood transfigured in the light.

PROFESSOR RUBEK. Have you traveled much about the world?

IRENE. Yes. Traveled in many lands.

PROFESSOR RUBEK [*looks compassionately at her*]. And what have you found to do, Irene?

IRENE [*turning her eyes upon him*]. Wait a moment; let me see— Yes, now I have it. I have posed on the turntable in variety shows. Posed as a naked statue in living pictures. Raked in heaps of money. That was more than I could do with you; for you had none.—And then I turned the heads of all sorts of men. That, too, was more than I could do with you, Arnold. You kept yourself better in hand.

PROFESSOR RUBEK [*hastening to pass the subject by*]. And then you have married, too?

IRENE. Yes; I married one of them.

PROFESSOR RUBEK. Who is your husband?

IRENE. He was a South American. A distinguished diplomatist. [*Looks straight in front of her with a stony smile.*] Him I managed to drive quite out of his mind; mad—incurably mad; inexorably mad.—It was great sport, I can tell you—while it was in the doing. I could have laughed within me all the time—if I had anything within me.

PROFESSOR RUBEK. And where is he now?

IRENE. Oh, in a churchyard somewhere or other. With a fine handsome monument over him. And with a bullet rattling in his skull.

PROFESSOR RUBEK. Did he kill himself?

IRENE. Yes, he was good enough to take that off my hands.

PROFESSOR RUBEK. Do you not lament his loss, Irene?

IRENE [*not understanding*]. Lament? What loss?

PROFESSOR RUBEK. Why, the loss of Herr von Satow, of course.

IRENE. His name was not Satow.

PROFESSOR RUBEK. Was it not?

IRENE. My second husband is called Satow. He is a Russian——

PROFESSOR RUBEK. And where is he?

IRENE. Far away in the Ural Mountains. Among all his gold mines.

PROFESSOR RUBEK. So he lives there?

IRENE [*shrugs her shoulders*]. Lives? Lives? In reality I have killed him——

PROFESSOR RUBEK [*starts*]. Killed——!

IRENE. Killed him with a fine sharp dagger which I always have with me in bed——

PROFESSOR RUBEK [*vehemently*]. I don't believe you, Irene!

IRENE [*with a gentle smile*]. Indeed you may believe it, Arnold.

PROFESSOR RUBEK [*looks compassionately at her*]. Have you never had a child?

IRENE. Yes, I have had many children.

PROFESSOR RUBEK. And where are your children now?

IRENE. I killed them.

PROFESSOR RUBEK [*severely*]. Now you are telling me lies again!

IRENE. I have killed them, I tell you—murdered them pitilessly. As soon as ever they came into the world. Oh, long, long before. One after the other.

PROFESSOR RUBEK [*sadly and earnestly*]. There is something hidden behind everything you say.

IRENE. How can I help that? Every word I say is whispered into my ear.

PROFESSOR RUBEK. I believe I am the only one that can divine your meaning.

IRENE. Surely you ought to be the only one.

PROFESSOR RUBEK [*rests his hands on the table and looks intently at her*]. Some of the strings of your nature have broken.

IRENE [*gently*]. Does not that always happen when a young warm-blooded woman dies?

PROFESSOR RUBEK. Oh, Irene, have done with these wild imaginings——! You are living! Living—living!

IRENE [*rises slowly from her chair and says, quivering*]. I was dead for many years. They came and bound me—laced my arms together behind my back—— Then they lowered me into a grave vault, with iron bars before the loophole. And with padded walls—so that no one on the earth above could hear the grave shrieks—— But now I am beginning, in a way, to rise from the dead. [*She seats herself again.*]

PROFESSOR RUBEK [*after a pause*]. In all this, do you hold me guilty?

IRENE. Yes.

PROFESSOR RUBEK. Guilty of that—your death, as you call it.

IRENE. Guilty of the fact that I had to die. [*Changing her tone to one of indifference*] Why don't you sit down, Arnold?

PROFESSOR RUBEK. May I?

IRENE. Yes.—You need not be afraid of being frozen. I don't think I am quite turned to ice yet.

PROFESSOR RUBEK [*moves a chair and seats himself at her table*]. There, Irene. Now we two are sitting together as in the old days.

IRENE. A little way apart from each other—also as in the old days.

PROFESSOR RUBEK [*moving nearer*]. It had to be so, then.

IRENE. Had it?

PROFESSOR RUBEK [*decisively*]. There had to be a distance between us——

IRENE. Was it absolutely necessary, Arnold?

PROFESSOR RUBEK [*continuing*]. Do you remember what you answered when I asked if you would go with me out into the wide world?

IRENE. I held up three fingers in the air and swore that I would go with you to the world's end and to the end of life. And that I would serve you in all things——

PROFESSOR RUBEK. As the model for my art——

IRENE. —In frank, utter nakedness——

PROFESSOR RUBEK [*with emotion*]. And you did serve me, Irene—so bravely—so gladly and ungrudgingly.

IRENE. Yes, with all the pulsing blood of my youth, I served you!

PROFESSOR RUBEK [*nodding, with a look of gratitude*]. That you have every right to say.

IRENE. I fell down at your feet and served you, Arnold! [*Holding her clenched hand toward him*] But you, you,—you——!

PROFESSOR RUBEK [*defensively*]. I never did you any wrong! Never, Irene!

IRENE. Yes, you did! You did wrong to my innermost, inborn nature——

PROFESSOR RUBEK [*starting back*]. I——!

IRENE. Yes, you! I exposed myself wholly and unreservedly to your gaze—— [*More softly*] And never once did you touch me.

PROFESSOR RUBEK. Irene, did you not understand that many a time I was almost beside myself under the spell of all your loveliness?

IRENE [*continuing undisturbed*]. And yet—if you had touched me, I think I should have killed you on the spot. For I had a sharp needle always upon me—hidden in my hair—— [*Strokes her forehead meditatively.*] But after all—after all—that you could——

PROFESSOR RUBEK [*looks impressively at her*]. I was an artist, Irene.

IRENE [*darkly*]. That is just it. That is just it.

PROFESSOR RUBEK. An artist first of all. And I was sick with the desire to achieve the great work of my life. [*Losing himself in recollection*] It was to be called "The Resurrection Day"—figured in the likeness of a young woman, awakening from the sleep of death——

IRENE. Our child, yes——

PROFESSOR RUBEK [*continuing*]. It was to be the awakening of the noblest, purest, most ideal woman the world ever saw. Then I found you. You were what I required in every respect. And you consented so willingly—so gladly. You renounced home and kindred—and went with me.

IRENE. To go with you meant for me the resurrection of my childhood.

PROFESSOR RUBEK. That was just why I found in you all that I required—in you and in no one else. I came to look on you as a thing hallowed, not to be touched save in adoring thoughts. In those days I was still young, Irene. And the superstition took hold of me that if I touched you, if I desired you with my senses, my soul would be profaned, so that I should be unable to accomplish what I was striving for.—And I still think there was some truth in that.

IRENE [*nods with a touch of scorn*]. The work of art first then the human being.

PROFESSOR RUBEK. You must judge me as you will; but at that time I was utterly dominated by my great task—and exultantly happy in it.

IRENE. And you achieved your great task, Arnold.

PROFESSOR RUBEK. Thanks and praise be to you, I achieved my great task. I wanted to embody the pure woman as I saw her awakening on the Resurrection Day. Not marveling at anything new and unknown and undivined; but filled with a sacred joy at finding herself unchanged—she, the woman of earth—in the higher, freer, happier region—after the long, dreamless sleep of death. [*More softly*] Thus did I fashion her.—I fashioned her in in your image, Irene.

IRENE [*laying her hands flat upon the table and leaning against the back of her chair*]. And then you were done with me——

PROFESSOR RUBEK [*reproachfully*]. Irene!

IRENE. You had no longer any use for me——

PROFESSOR RUBEK. How can you say that!

IRENE. —And began to look about you for other ideals——

PROFESSOR RUBEK. I found none, none after you.

IRENE. And no other models, Arnold?

PROFESSOR RUBEK. You were no model to me. You were the fountainhead of my achievement.

IRENE [*is silent for a short time*]. What poems have you made since? In marble I mean. Since the day I left you.

PROFESSOR RUBEK. I have made no poems since that day—only frittered away my life in modeling.

IRENE. And that woman, whom you are now living with——?

PROFESSOR RUBEK [*interrupting vehemently*]. Do not speak of her now! It makes me tingle with shame.

IRENE. Where are you thinking of going with her?

PROFESSOR RUBEK [*slack and weary*]. Oh, on a tedious coasting voyage to the North, I suppose.

IRENE [*looks at him, smiles almost imperceptibly, and whispers*]. You should rather go high up into the mountains. As high as ever you can. Higher, higher,—always higher, Arnold.

PROFESSOR RUBEK [*with eager expectation*]. Are you going up there?

IRENE. Have you the courage to meet me once again?

PROFESSOR RUBEK [*struggling with himself, uncertainly*]. If we could—oh, if only we could——!

IRENE. Why can we not do what we will? [*Looks at him and whispers beseechingly with folded hands.*] Come, come, Arnold! Oh, come up to me——!

MAIA *enters, glowing with pleasure, from behind the hotel, and goes quickly up to the table where they were previously sitting.*

MAIA [*still at the corner of the hotel, without looking around*]. Oh, you may say what you please, Rubek, but—[*Stops, as she catches sight of* IRENE.]—— Oh, I beg your pardon—I see you have made an acquaintance.

PROFESSOR RUBEK [*curtly*]. Renewed an acquaintance. [*Rises.*] What was it you wanted with me?

MAIA. I only wanted to say this: you may do whatever you please, but *I* am not going with you on that disgusting steamboat.

PROFESSOR RUBEK. Why not?

MAIA. Because I want to go up on the mountains and into the forests—that's what I want. [*Coaxingly*] Oh, you must let me do it, Rubek.—I shall be so good, so good afterwards!

PROFESSOR RUBEK. Who is it that has put these ideas into your head?

MAIA. Why he—that horrid bear killer. Oh you cannot conceive all the marvelous things he has to tell about the mountains. And about life up there! They're ugly, horrid, repulsive, most of the yarns he spins—for I almost believe he's lying—but wonderfully alluring all the same. Oh, won't you let me go with him? Only to see if what he says is true, you understand. May I, Rubek?

PROFESSOR RUBEK. Yes, I have not the slightest objection. Off you go to the mountains—as far and as long as you please. I shall perhaps be going the same way myself.

MAIA [*quickly*]. No, no, no, you needn't do that! Not on my account!

PROFESSOR RUBEK. I want to go to the mountains. I have made up my mind to go.

MAIA. Oh, thanks, thanks! May I tell the bear killer at once?

PROFESSOR RUBEK. Tell the bear killer whatever you please.

MAIA. Oh, thanks, thanks, thanks! [*Is about to take his hand; he repels the movement.*] Oh, how dear and good you are today, Rubek! [*She runs into the hotel.*]

[*At the same time the door of the pavilion is softly and noiselessly set ajar. The* SISTER OF MERCY *stands in the opening, intently on the watch. No one sees her.*]

PROFESSOR RUBEK [*decidedly, turning to* IRENE]. Shall we meet up there then?

IRENE [*rising slowly*]. Yes, we shall certainly meet.—I have sought for you so long.

PROFESSOR RUBEK. When did you begin to seek for me, Irene?

IRENE [*with a touch of jesting bitterness*]. From the moment I realized that I had given away to you something rather indispensable, Arnold. Something one ought never to part with.

PROFESSOR RUBEK [*bowing his head*]. Yes, that is bitterly true. You gave me three or four years of your youth.

IRENE. More, more than that I gave you—spendthrift as I then was.

PROFESSOR RUBEK. Yes, you were prodigal, Irene. You gave me all your naked loveliness——

IRENE. —To gaze upon——

PROFESSOR RUBEK. —And to glorify——

IRENE. Yes, for your own glorification.—And the child's.

PROFESSOR RUBEK. And yours too, Irene.

IRENE. But you have forgotten the most precious gift.

PROFESSOR RUBEK. The most precious——? What gift was that?

IRENE. I gave you my young, living soul. And that gift left me empty within—soulless. [*Looking at him with a fixed stare*] It was that I died of, Arnold.

[*The* SISTER OF MERCY *opens the door wide and makes room for her. She goes into the pavilion.*]

Professor Rubek [*stands and looks after her; then whispers*]. Irene!

ACT II

Near a mountain health resort. The landscape stretches, in the form of an immense treeless upland, toward a long mountain lake. Beyond the lake rises a range of peaks with blue-white snow in the clefts. In the foreground on the left a purling brook falls in severed streamlets down a steep wall of rock, and thence flows smoothly over the upland until it disappears to the right. Dwarf trees, plants, and stones along the course of the brook. In the foreground on the right a hillock, with a stone bench on the top of it. It is a summer afternoon, toward sunset.

At some distance over the upland, on the other side of the brook, a troop of children is singing, dancing, and playing. Some are dressed in peasant costume, others in town-made clothes. Their happy laughter is heard, softened by distance, during the following.

PROFESSOR RUBEK *is sitting on the bench, with a plaid over his shoulders, and looking down at the children's play.*

Presently MAIA *comes forward from among some bushes on the upland to the left, well back, and scans the prospect with her hand, shading her eyes. She wears a flat tourist cap, a short skirt, kilted up, reaching only midway between ankle and knee, and high, stout lace-boots. She has in her hand a long alpenstock.*

MAIA [*at last catches sight of* RUBEK *and calls*]. Hallo! [*She advances over the upland, jumps over the brook, with the aid of her alpenstock, and climbs up the hillock. Panting*] Oh, how I have been rushing around looking for you, Rubek.

PROFESSOR RUBEK [*nods indifferently and asks*]. Have you just come from the hotel?

MAIA. Yes, that was the last place I tried—that flytrap.

PROFESSOR RUBEK [*looking at her for a moment*]. I noticed that you were not at the dinner table.

MAIA. No, we had our dinner in the open air, we two.

PROFESSOR RUBEK. "We two"? What two?

MAIA. Why, I and that horrid bear killer, of course.

PROFESSOR RUBEK. Oh, he.

MAIA. Yes. And first thing tomorrow morning we are going off again.

PROFESSOR RUBEK. After bears?

MAIA. Yes. Off to kill a brown-boy.

PROFESSOR RUBEK. Have you found the tracks of any?

MAIA [*with superiority*]. You don't suppose that bears are to be found in the naked mountains, do you?

PROFESSOR RUBEK. Where, then?

MAIA. Far beneath. On the lower slopes; in the thickest parts of the forest. Places your ordinary townfolk could never get through——

PROFESSOR RUBEK. And you two are going down there tomorrow?

MAIA [*throwing herself down among the heather*]. Yes, so we have arranged.—Or perhaps we may start this evening.—If you have no objection, that's to say?

PROFESSOR RUBEK. I? Far be it from me to——

MAIA [*quickly*]. Of course, Lars goes with us—with the dogs.

PROFESSOR RUBEK. I feel no curiosity as to the movements of Mr. Lars and his dogs. [*Changing the subject*] Would you not rather sit properly on the seat?

MAIA [*drowsily*]. No, thank you. I'm lying so delightfully in the soft heather.

PROFESSOR RUBEK. I can see that you are tired.

MAIA [*yawning*]. I almost think I'm beginning to feel tired.

PROFESSOR RUBEK. You don't notice it till afterwards—when the exitement is over——

MAIA [*in a drowsy tone*]. Just so. I will lie and close my eyes.

[*A short pause.*]

MAIA [*with sudden impatience*]. Ugh, Rubek—how can you endure to sit there listening to these children's screams! And to watch all the capers they are cutting, too!

PROFESSOR RUBEK. There is something harmonious—almost like music—in their movements, now and then; amid all the clumsiness. And it amuses me to sit and watch for these isolated moments—when they come.

MAIA [*with a somewhat scornful laugh*]. Yes, you are always, always an artist.

PROFESSOR RUBEK. And I propose to remain one.

MAIA [*lying on her side, so that her back is turned to him*]. There's not a bit of the artist about him.

PROFESSOR RUBEK [*with attention*]. Who is it that's not an artist?

MAIA [*again in a sleepy tone*]. Why, he—the other one, of course.

PROFESSOR RUBEK. The bear hunter, you mean?

MAIA. Yes. There's not a bit of the artist about him—not the least little bit.

PROFESSOR RUBEK [*smiling*]. No, I believe there's no doubt about that.

MAIA [*vehemently, without moving*]. And so ugly as he is! [*Plucks up a tuft of heather and throws it away.*] So ugly, so ugly! Isch!

PROFESSOR RUBEK. Is that why you are so ready to set off with him—out into the wilds?

MAIA [*curtly*]. I don't know. [*Turning toward him*] You are ugly, too, Rubek.

PROFESSOR RUBEK. Have you only discovered it?

MAIA. No, I have seen it for long.

PROFESSOR RUBEK [*shrugging his shoulders*]. One doesn't grow younger. One doesn't grow younger, Frau Maia.

MAIA. It's not that sort of ugliness that I mean at all. But there has come to be such an expression of fatigue, of utter weariness, in your eyes—when you deign, once in a while, to cast a glance at me.

PROFESSOR RUBEK. Have you noticed that?

MAIA [*nods*]. Little by little this evil look has come into your eyes. It seems almost as though you were nursing some dark plot against me.

PROFESSOR RUBEK. Indeed? [*In a friendly but earnest tone*] Come here and sit beside me, Maia; and let us talk a little.

MAIA [*half rising*]. Then will you let me sit upon your knee? As I used to in the early days?

PROFESSOR RUBEK. No, you musn't—people can see us from the hotel. [*Moves a little.*] But you can sit here on the bench—at my side.

MAIA. No, thank you; in that case I'd rather lie here, where I am. I can hear you quite well here. [*Looks inquiringly at him.*] Well, what is it you want to say to me?

PROFESSOR RUBEK [*begins slowly*]. What do you think was my real reason for agreeing to make this tour?

MAIA. Well—I remember you declared, among other things, that it was going to do me such a tremendous lot of good. But—but——

PROFESSOR RUBEK. But——?

MAIA. But now I don't believe the least little bit that that was the reason——

PROFESSOR RUBEK. Then what is your theory about it now?

MAIA. I think now that it was on account of that pale lady.

PROFESSOR RUBEK. Madame von Satow——!

MAIA. Yes, she who is always hanging at our heels. Yesterday evening she made her appearance up here too.

PROFESSOR RUBEK. But what in all the world——!

MAIA. Oh, I know you knew her very well indeed—long before you knew me.

PROFESSOR RUBEK. And had forgotten her, too—long before I knew you.

MAIA [*sitting upright*]. Can you forget so easily, Rubek?

PROFESSOR RUBEK [*curtly*]. Yes, very easily indeed. [*Adds harshly*] When I want to forget.

MAIA. Even a woman who has been a model to you?

PROFESSOR RUBEK. When I have no more use for her——

MAIA. One who has stood to you undressed?

PROFESSOR RUBEK. That means nothing—nothing for us artists. [*With a change of tone*] And then —may I venture to ask—how was *I* to guess that she was in this country?

MAIA. Oh, you might have seen her name in a Visitors' List—in one of the newspapers.

PROFESSOR RUBEK. But I had no idea of the name she now goes by. I had never heard of any Herr von Satow.

MAIA [*affecting weariness*]. Oh, well then, I suppose it must have been for some other reason that you were so set upon this journey.

PROFESSOR RUBEK [*seriously*]. Yes, Maia—it was for another reason. A quite different reason. And that is what we must sooner or later have a clear explanation about.

MAIA [*in a fit of suppressed laughter*]. Heavens, how solemn you look!

PROFESSOR RUBEK [*suspiciously scrutinizing her*]. Yes, perhaps a little more solemn than necessary.

MAIA. How so——?

PROFESSOR RUBEK. And that is a very good thing for us both.

MAIA. You begin to make me feel curious, Rubek.

PROFESSOR RUBEK. Only curious? Not a little bit uneasy.

MAIA [*shaking her head*]. Not in the least.

PROFESSOR RUBEK. Good. Then listen.—You said that day down at the Baths that it seemed to you I had become very nervous of late——

MAIA. Yes, and you really have.

PROFESSOR RUBEK. And what do you think can be the reason of that?

MAIA. How can I tell——? [*Quickly*] Perhaps you have grown weary of this constant companionship with me.

PROFESSOR RUBEK. Constant——? Why not say "everlasting"?

MAIA. Daily companionship, then. Here have we two solitary people lived down there for four or five mortal years, and scarcely been an hour away from each other.—We two all by ourselves.

PROFESSOR RUBEK [*with interest*]. Well? And then——?

MAIA [*a little oppressed*]. You are not a particularly sociable man, Rubek. You like to keep yourself to yourself and think your own thoughts. And of course I can't talk properly to you about your affairs. I know nothing about art and that sort of thing—— [*With an impatient gesture*] And care very little either, for that matter!

PROFESSOR RUBEK. Well, well; and that's why we generally sit by the fireside, and chat about your affairs.

MAIA. Oh, good gracious—I have no affairs to chat about.

PROFESSOR RUBEK. Well, they are trifles, perhaps; but at any rate the time passes for us in that way as well as another, Maia.

MAIA. Yes, you are right. Time passes. It is passing away from you, Rubek.—And I suppose it is really that that makes you so uneasy——

PROFESSOR RUBEK [*nods vehemently*]. And so restless! [*Writhing in his seat*] No, I shall soon not be able to endure this pitiful life any longer.

MAIA [*rises and stands for a moment looking at him*]. If you want to get rid of me, you have only to say so.

PROFESSOR RUBEK. Why will you use such phrases? Get rid of you?

MAIA. Yes, if you want to have done with me, please say so right out. And I will go that instant.

PROFESSOR RUBEK [*with an almost imperceptible smile*]. Do you intend that as a threat, Maia?

MAIA. There can be no threat for you in what I said.

PROFESSOR RUBEK [*rising*]. No, I confess you are right there. [*Adds after a pause*] You and I cannot possibly go on living together like this——

MAIA. Well? And then——?

PROFESSOR RUBEK. There is no "then" about it.

[*With emphasis on his words*] Because we two cannot go on living together alone—it does not necessarily follow that we must part.

MAIA [*smiles scornfully*]. Only draw away from each other a little, you mean?

PROFESSOR RUBEK [*shakes his head*]. Even that is not necessary.

MAIA. Well then? Come out with what you want to do with me.

PROFESSOR RUBEK [*with some hesitation*]. What I now feel so keenly—and so painfully—that I require, is to have someone about me who really and truly stands close to me——

MAIA [*interrupts him anxiously*]. Don't *I* do that, Rubek?

PROFESSOR RUBEK [*waving her aside*]. Not in that sense. What I need is the companionship of another person who can, as it were, complete me—supply what is wanting in me—be one with me in all my striving.

MAIA [*slowly*]. It's true that things like that are a great deal too hard for me.

PROFESSOR RUBEK. Oh, no, they are not at all in your line, Maia.

MAIA [*with an outburst*]. And heaven knows I don't want them to be, either!

PROFESSOR RUBEK. I know that very well.—And it was with no idea of finding any such help in my lifework that I married you.

MAIA [*observing him closely*]. I can see in your face that you are thinking of someone else.

PROFESSOR RUBEK. Indeed? I have never noticed before that you were a thought reader. But you can see that, can you?

MAIA. Yes, I can. Oh, I know you so well, so well, Rubek.

PROFESSOR RUBEK. Then perhaps you can also see who it is I am thinking of?

MAIA. Yes, indeed I can.

PROFESSOR RUBEK. Well? Have the goodness to——?

MAIA. You are thinking of that—that model you once used for—— [*Suddenly letting slip the train of thought*] Do you know, the people down at the hotel think she's mad.

PROFESSOR RUBEK. Indeed? And pray what do the people down at the hotel think of you and the bear killer?

MAIA. That has nothing to do with the matter. [*Continuing the former train of thought*] But it was this pale lady you were thinking of.

PROFESSOR RUBEK [*calmly*]. Precisely, of her.— When I had no more use for her—and when, besides, she went away from me—vanished without a word——

MAIA. Then you accepted me as a sort of makeshift, I suppose?

PROFESSOR RUBEK [*more unfeelingly*]. Something of the sort, to tell the truth, little Maia. For a year or a year and a half I had lived there lonely and brooding, and had put the last touch—the very last touch, to my work. "The Resurrection Day" went out over the world and brought me fame—and everything else that heart could desire. [*With greater warmth*] But I no longer loved my own work. Men's laurels and incense nauseated me, till I could have rushed away in despair and hidden myself in the depths of the woods. [*Looking at her*] You, who are a thought reader—can you guess what then occurred to me?

MAIA [*lightly*]. Yes, it occurred to you to make portrait busts of gentlemen and ladies.

PROFESSOR RUBEK [*nods*]. To order, yes. With animals' faces behind the masks. Those I threw in gratis—into the bargain, you understand. [*Smiling*] But that was not precisely what I had in my mind.

MAIA. What, then?

PROFESSOR RUBEK [*again serious*]. It was this, that all the talk about the artist's vocation and the artist's mission, and so forth, began to strike me as being very empty, and hollow, and meaningless at bottom.

MAIA. Then what would you put in its place?

PROFESSOR RUBEK. Life, Maia.

MAIA. Life?

PROFESSOR RUBEK. Yes, is not life in sunshine and in beauty a hundred times better worth while than to hang about to the end of your days in a raw, damp hole, and wear yourself out in a perpetual struggle with lumps of clay and blocks of stone?

MAIA [*with a little sigh*]. Yes, I have always thought so, certainly.

PROFESSOR RUBEK. And then I had become rich enough to live in luxury and in indolent, quivering sunshine. I was able to build myself the villa on the Lake of Taunitz, and the palazzo in the capital,—and all the rest of it.

MAIA [*taking up his tone*]. And last but not least, you could afford to treat yourself to me, too. And you gave me leave to share in all your treasures.

PROFESSOR RUBEK [*jesting, so as to turn the conversation*]. Did I not promise to take you up with me to a high mountain and show you all the glory of the world?

MAIA [*with a gentle expression*]. You have perhaps taken me up with you to a high enough mountain, Rubek—but you have not shown me all the glory of the world.

PROFESSOR RUBEK [*with a laugh of irritation*]. How insatiable you are, Maia! Absolutely insatiable! [*With a vehement outburst*] But do you know what is the most hopeless thing of all, Maia? Can you guess that?

MAIA [*with quiet defiance*]. Yes, I suppose it is that you have gone and tied yourself to me—for life.

PROFESSOR RUBEK. I would not have expressed myself so heartlessly.

MAIA. But you would have meant it just as heartlessly.

PROFESSOR RUBEK. You have no clear idea of the inner workings of an artist's nature.

MAIA [*smiling and shaking her head*]. Good heavens, I haven't even a clear idea of the inner workings of my own nature.

PROFESSOR RUBEK [*continuing undisturbed*]. I live at such high speed, Maia. We live so, we artists. I, for my part, have lived through a whole lifetime in the few years we two have known each other. I have come to realize that I am not at all adapted for seeking happiness in indolent enjoyment. Life does not shape itself that way for me and those like me. I must go on working—producing one work after another—right up to my dying day. [*Forcing himself to continue*] That is why I cannot get on with you any longer, Maia—not with you alone.

MAIA [*quietly*]. Does that mean, in plain language, that you have grown tired of me?

PROFESSOR RUBEK [*bursts forth*]. Yes, that is what it means! I have grown tired—intolerably tired and fretted and unstrung—in this life with you! Now you know it. [*Controlling himself*] These are hard, ugly words I am using. I know that very well. And you are not at all to blame in this matter;—that I willingly admit. It is simply and solely I myself, who have once more undergone a revolution—[*Half to himself*]—an awakening to my real life.

MAIA [*involuntarily folding her hands*]. Why in all the world should we not part then?

PROFESSOR RUBEK [*looks at her in astonishment*]. Should you be willing to?

MAIA [*shrugging her shoulders*]. Oh, yes—if there's nothing else for it, then——

PROFESSOR RUBEK [*eagerly*]. But there is something else for it. There is an alternative——

MAIA [*holding up her forefinger*]. Now you are thinking of the pale lady again!

PROFESSOR RUBEK. Yes, to tell the truth, I cannot help constantly thinking of her. Ever since I met her again. [*A step nearer her*] For now I will tell you a secret, Maia.

MAIA. Well?

PROFESSOR RUBEK [*touching his own breast*]. In here, you see—in here I have a little Bramah-locked casket. And in that casket all my sculptor's visions are stored up. But when she disappeared and left no trace, the lock of the casket snapped to. And she had the key—and she took it away with her.—You, little Maia, you had no key; so all that the casket contains must lie unused. And the years pass! And I have no means of getting at the treasure.

MAIA [*trying to repress a subtle smile*]. Then get her to open the casket for you again——

PROFESSOR RUBEK [*not understanding*]. Maia ——?

MAIA. —for here she is, you see. And no doubt it's on account of this casket that she has come.

PROFESSOR RUBEK. I have not said a single word to her on this subject!

MAIA [*looks innocently at him*]. My dear Rubek —is it worth-while to make all this fuss and commotion about so simple a matter?

PROFESSOR RUBEK. Do you think this matter is so absolutely simple?

MAIA. Yes, certainly I think so. Do you attach yourself to whoever you most require. [*Nods to him.*] I shall always manage to find a place for myself.

PROFESSOR RUBEK. Where do you mean?

MAIA [*unconcerned, evasively*]. Well—I need only take myself off to the villa, if it should be necessary. But it won't be; for in town—in all that great house of ours—there must surely, with a little good will, be room enough for three.

PROFESSOR RUBEK [*uncertainly*]. And do you think that would work in the long run?

MAIA [*in a light tone*]. Very well, then—if it won't work, it won't. It is no good talking about it.

PROFESSOR RUBEK. And what shall we do then, Maia—if it does not work?

MAIA [*untroubled*]. Then we two will simply get out of each other's way—part entirely. I shall always find something new for myself, somewhere in the world. Something free! Free! Free!—No need to be anxious about that, Professor Rubek! [*Suddenly points off to the right.*] Look there! There we have her.

PROFESSOR RUBEK [*turning*]. Where?

MAIA. Out on the plain. Striding—like a marble statue. She is coming this way.

PROFESSOR RUBEK [*stands gazing with his hand over his eyes*]. Does not she look like the Resurrection incarnate? [*To himself*] And her I could displace—and move into the shade! Remodel her —— Fool that I was!

MAIA. What do you mean by that?

PROFESSOR RUBEK [*putting the question aside*]. Nothing. Nothing that you would understand.

[IRENE *advances from the right over the upland. The children at their play have already caught sight of her and run to meet her. She is now surrounded by them; some appear confident and at ease, others uneasy and timid. She talks low to them and indicates that they are to go down to the hotel; she herself will rest a little beside the brook. The children run down over the slope to the left, halfway to the back.* IRENE *goes up to the wall of rock, and lets the rillets of the cascade flow over her hands, cooling them.*]

MAIA [*in a low voice*]. Go down and speak to her alone, Rubek.

PROFESSOR RUBEK. And where will you go in the meantime?

MAIA [*looking significantly at him*]. Henceforth I shall go my own ways. [*She descends from the hillock and leaps over the brook, by aid of her alpenstock. She stops beside* IRENE.] Professor Rubek is up there, waiting for you, madam.

IRENE. What does he want?

MAIA. He wants you to help him to open a casket that has snapped to.

IRENE. Can I help him in that?

MAIA. He says you are the only person that can.

IRENE. Then I must try.

MAIA. Yes, you really must, madam. [*She goes down by the path to the hotel.*]

[*In a little while* PROFESSOR RUBEK *comes down to* IRENE, *but stops with the brook between them.*]

IRENE [*after a short pause*]. She—the other one —said that you had been waiting for me.

PROFESSOR RUBEK. I have waited for you year after year—without myself knowing it.

IRENE. I could not come to you, Arnold. I was lying down there, sleeping the long, deep, dreamful sleep.

PROFESSOR RUBEK. But now you have awakened, Irene!

IRENE [*shakes her head*]. I have the heavy, deep sleep still in my eyes.

PROFESSOR RUBEK. You shall see that day will dawn and lighten for us both.

IRENE. Do not believe that.

PROFESSOR RUBEK [*urgently*]. I do believe it! And I know it! Now that I have found you again——

IRENE. Risen from the grave.

PROFESSOR RUBEK. Transfigured!

IRENE. Only risen, Arnold. Not transfigured.

[*He crosses over to her by means of stepping-stones below the cascade.*]

PROFESSOR RUBEK. Where have you been all day, Irene?

IRENE [*pointing*]. Far, far over there, on the great dead waste——

PROFESSOR RUBEK [*turning the conversation*]. You have not your—your friend with you today, I see.

IRENE [*smiling*]. My friend is keeping a close watch on me, none the less.

PROFESSOR RUBEK. Can she?

IRENE [*glancing furtively around*]. You may be sure she can—wherever I may go. She never loses sight of me—— [*Whispering*] Until, one fine sunny morning, I shall kill her.

PROFESSOR RUBEK. Would you do that?

IRENE. With the utmost delight—if only I could manage it.

PROFESSOR RUBEK. Why do you want to?

IRENE. Because she deals in witchcraft. [*Mysteriously*] Only think, Arnold—she has changed herself into my shadow.

PROFESSOR RUBEK [*trying to calm her*]. Well, well, well—a shadow we must all have.

IRENE. I am my own shadow. [*With an outburst*] Do you not understand that!

PROFESSOR RUBEK [*sadly*]. Yes, yes, Irene, I understand it.

[*He seats himself on a stone beside the brook. She stands behind him, leaning against a wall of rock.*]

IRENE [*after a pause*]. Why do you sit there turning your eyes away from me?

PROFESSOR RUBEK [*softly, shaking his head*]. I dare not—I dare not look at you.

IRENE. Why dare you not look at me any more?

PROFESSOR RUBEK. You have a shadow that tortures me. And *I* have the crushing weight of my conscience.

IRENE [*with a glad cry of deliverance*]. At last!

PROFESSOR RUBEK [*springs up*]. Irene—what is it!

IRENE [*motioning him off*]. Keep still, still, still! [*Draws a deep breath and says, as though relieved of a burden*] There! Now they let me go. For this time.—Now we can sit down and talk as we used to—when I was alive.

PROFESSOR RUBEK. Oh, if only we could talk as we used to.

IRENE. Sit there, where you were sitting. I will sit here beside you.

[*He sits down again. She seats herself on another stone, close to him.*]

IRENE [*after a short interval of silence*]. Now I have come back to you from the uttermost regions, Arnold.

PROFESSOR RUBEK. Aye, truly, from an endless journey.

IRENE. Come home to my lord and master——

PROFESSOR RUBEK. To our home;—to our own home, Irene.

IRENE. Have you looked for my coming every single day?

PROFESSOR RUBEK. How dared I look for you?

IRENE [*with a sidelong glance*]. No, I suppose you dared not. For you understood nothing.

PROFESSOR RUBEK. Was it really not for the sake of someone else that you all of a sudden disappeared from me in that way?

IRENE. Might it not quite well be for your sake, Arnold?

PROFESSOR RUBEK [*looks doubtfully at her*]. I don't understand you——?

IRENE. When I had served you with my soul and with my body—when the statue stood there finished—our child as you called it—then I laid at your feet the most precious sacrifice of all—by effacing myself for all time.

PROFESSOR RUBEK [*bows his head*]. And laying my life waste.

IRENE [*suddenly firing up*]. It was just that I wanted! Never, never should you create anything again—after you had created that only child of ours.

PROFESSOR RUBEK. Was it jealousy that moved you, then?

IRENE [*coldly*]. I think it was rather hatred.

PROFESSOR RUBEK. Hatred? Hatred for me?

IRENE [*again vehemently*]. Yes, for you—for the artist who had so lightly and carelessly taken a warm-blooded body, a young human life, and worn the soul out of it—because you needed it for a work of art.

PROFESSOR RUBEK. And you can say that—you who threw yourself into my work with such saintlike passion and such ardent joy?—that work for which we two met together every morning, as for an act of worship.

IRENE [*coldly, as before*]. I will tell you one thing, Arnold.

PROFESSOR RUBEK. Well?

IRENE. I never loved your art, before I met you. —Nor after either.

PROFESSOR RUBECK. But the artist, Irene?

IRENE. The artist I hate.

PROFESSOR RUBEK. The artist in me too?

IRENE. In you most of all. When I unclothed myself and stood for you, then I hated you, Arnold——

PROFESSOR RUBEK [*warmly*]. That you did not, Irene! That is not true!

IRENE. I hated you, because you could stand there so unmoved——

PROFESSOR RUBEK [*laughs*]. Unmoved? Do you think so?

IRENE. —at any rate so intolerably self-controlled. And because you were an artist and an artist only —not a man! [*Changing to a tone fully of warmth and feeling*] But that statue in the wet, living clay, that I loved—as it rose up, a vital human creature, out of those raw, shapeless masses—for that was our creation, our child. Mine and yours.

PROFESSOR RUBEK [*sadly*]. It was so in spirit and in truth.

IRENE. Let me tell you, Arnold—it is for the sake of this child of ours that I have undertaken this long pilgrimage.

PROFESSOR RUBEK [*suddenly alert*]. For the statue's——?

IRENE. Call it what you will. I call it our child.

PROFESSOR RUBEK. And now you want to see it? Finished? In marble, which you always thought so cold? [*Eagerly*] You do not know, perhaps, that it is installed in a great museum somewhere —far out in the world?

IRENE. I have heard a sort of legend about it.

PROFESSOR RUBEK. And museums were always a horror to you. You called them grave vaults——

IRENE. I will make a pilgrimage to the place where my soul and my child's soul lie buried.

PROFESSOR RUBEK [*uneasy and alarmed*]. You must never see that statue again! Do you hear, Irene! I implore you——! Never, never see it again!

IRENE. Perhaps you think it would mean death to me a second time?

PROFESSOR RUBEK [*clenching his hands together*]. Oh, I don't know what I think. But how could I ever imagine that you would fix your mind so immovably on that statue? You, who went away from me—before it was completed.

IRENE. It was completed. That was why I could go away from you—and leave you alone.

PROFESSOR RUBEK [*sits with his elbows upon his knees, rocking his head from side to side, with his hands before his eyes*]. It was not what it afterwards became.

IRENE [*quietly, but quick as lightning, half-unsheathes a narrow-bladed sharp knife which she carries in her breast, and asks in a hoarse whisper*]. Arnold—have you done any evil to our child?

PROFESSOR RUBEK [*evasively*]. Any evil?—How can I be sure what you would call it?

IRENE [*breathless*]. Tell me at once: what have you done to the child?

PROFESSOR RUBEK. I will tell you, if you will sit and listen quietly to what I say.

IRENE [*hides the knife*]. I will listen as quietly as a mother can when she——

PROFESSOR RUBEK [*interrupting*]. And you must not look at me while I am telling you.

IRENE [*moves to a stone behind his back*]. I will sit here, behind you. Now tell me.

PROFESSOR RUBEK [*takes his hands from before his eyes and gazes straight in front of him*]. When I had found you, I knew at once how I should make use of you for my lifework.

IRENE. "The Resurrection Day" you called your lifework.—I call it "our child."

PROFESSOR RUBEK. I was young then—with no knowledge of life. The Resurrection, I thought, would be most beautifully and exquisitely figured as a young unsullied woman—with none of our earth-life's experiences—awakening to light and glory without having to put away from her anything ugly and impure.

IRENE [*quickly*]. Yes—and so I stand there now, in our work?

PROFESSOR RUBEK [*hesitating*]. Not absolutely and entirely so, Irene.

IRENE [*in rising excitement*]. Not absolutely——? Do I not stand as I always stood for you?

PROFESSOR RUBEK [*without answering*]. I learned worldly wisdom in the years that followed, Irene. "The Resurrection Day" became in my mind's eye something more and something—something more complex. The little round plinth on which your figure stood erect and solitary—it no longer afforded room for all the imagery I now wanted to add——

IRENE [*gropes for her knife, but desists*]. What imagery did you add then? Tell me!

PROFESSOR RUBEK. I imaged that which I saw with my eyes around me in the world. I had to include it—I could not help it, Irene. I expanded the plinth—made it wide and spacious. And on it I placed a segment of the curving, bursting earth. And up from the fissures of the soil there now swarm men and women with dimly suggested animal faces. Women and men—as I knew them in real life.

IRENE [*in breathless suspense*]. But in the middle of the rout there stands the young woman radiant with the joy of light? Do I not stand so, Arnold?

PROFESSOR RUBEK [*evasively*]. Not quite in the middle. I had unfortunately to move that figure a little back. For the sake of the general effect, you understand. Otherwise it would have dominated the whole too much.

IRENE. But the joy in the light still transfigures my face?

PROFESSOR RUBEK. Yes, it does, Irene—in a way. A little subdued perhaps—as my altered idea required.

IRENE [*rising noiselessly*]. That design expresses the life you now see, Arnold.

PROFESSOR RUBEK. Yes, I suppose it does.

IRENE. And in that design you have shifted me back, a little toned down—to serve as a background figure—in a group. [*She draws the knife.*]

PROFESSOR RUBEK. Not a background figure. Let us say, at most, a figure not quite in the foreground—or something of that sort.

IRENE [*whispers hoarsely*]. There you uttered your own doom. [*On the point of striking.*]

PROFESSOR RUBEK [*turns and looks up at her*]. Doom?

IRENE [*hastily hides the knife, and says as though choked with agony*]. My whole soul—you and I—

we, we two, and our child were in that solitary figure.

PROFESSOR RUBEK [*eagerly, taking off his hat and drying the drops of sweat upon his brow*]. Yes, but let me tell you, too, how I have placed myself in the group. In front, beside a fountain—as it were here—sits a man weighed down with guilt, who cannot quite free himself from the earth-crust. I call him remorse for a forfeited life. He sits there and dips his fingers in the purling stream—to wash them clean—and he is gnawed and tortured by the thought that never, never will he succeed. Never in all eternity will he attain to freedom and the new life. He will remain forever prisoned in his hell.

IRENE [*hardly and coldly*]. Poet!

PROFESSOR RUBEK. Why poet?

IRENE. Because you are nerveless and sluggish and full of forgiveness for all the sins of your life, in thought and in act. You have killed my soul—so you model yourself in remorse, and self-accusation, and penance—[*Smiling*]—and with that you think your account is cleared.

PROFESSOR RUBEK [*defiantly*]. I am an artist, Irene. And I take no shame to myself for the frailties that perhaps cling to me. For I was born to be an artist, you see. And, do what I may, I shall never be anything else.

IRENE [*looks at him with a lurking evil smile, and says gently and softly*]. You are a poet, Arnold. [*Softly strokes his hair.*] You dear, great, middle-aged child,—is it possible that you cannot see that!

PROFESSOR RUBEK [*annoyed*]. Why do you keep on calling me a poet?

IRENE [*with malign eyes*]. Because there is something apologetic in the word, my friend. Something that suggests forgiveness of sins—and spreads a cloak over all frailty. [*With a sudden change of tone*] But *I* was a human being—then! And I, too, had a life to live,—and a human destiny to fulfill. And all that, look you, I let slip—gave it all up in order to make myself your bondwoman.—Oh, it was self-murder—a deadly sin against myself! [*Half whispering*] And that sin I can never expiate!

[*She seats herself near him beside the brook, keeps close, though unnoticed, watch upon him, and, as though in absence of mind, plucks some flowers from the shrubs around them.*]

IRENE [*with apparent self-control*]. I should have borne children into the world—many children—real children—not such children as are hidden away in grave vaults. That was my vocation. I ought never to have served you—poet.

PROFESSOR RUBEK [*lost in recollection*]. Yet those were beautiful days, Irene. Marvelously beautiful days—as I now look back upon them——

IRENE [*looking at him with a soft expression*]. Can you remember a little word that you said—when you had finished—finished with me and with our child? [*Nods to him.*] Can you remember that little word, Arnold?

PROFESSOR RUBEK [*looks inquiringly at her*]. Did I say a little word then, which you still remember?

IRENE. Yes, you did. Can you not recall it?

PROFESSOR RUBEK [*shaking his head*]. No, I can't say that I do. Not at the present moment, at any rate.

IRENE. You took both my hands and pressed them warmly. And I stood there in breathless expectation. And then you said: "So now, Irene, I thank you from my heart. This," you said, "has been a priceless episode for me."

PROFESSOR RUBEK [*looks doubtfully at her*]. Did I say "episode"? It is not a word I am in the habit of using.

IRENE. You said "episode."

PROFESSOR RUBEK [*with assumed cheerfulness*]. Well, well—after all, it was in reality an episode.

IRENE [*curtly*]. At that word I left you.

PROFESSOR RUBEK. You take everything so painfully to heart, Irene.

IRENE [*drawing her hand over her forehead*]. Perhaps you are right. Let us shake off all the hard things that go to the heart. [*Plucks off the petals of a mountain rose and strews them on the brook.*] Look there, Arnold. There are our birds swimming.

PROFESSOR RUBEK. What birds are they?

IRENE. Can you not see? Of course they are flamingos. Are they not rose red?

PROFESSOR RUBEK. Flamingos do not swim. They only wade.

IRENE. Then they are not flamingos. They are sea gulls.

PROFESSOR RUBEK. They may be sea gulls with red bills, yes. [*Plucks broad green leaves and throws them into the brook.*] Now I send out my ships after them.

IRENE. But there must be no harpoon men on board.

PROFESSOR RUBEK. No, there shall be no harpoon men. [*Smiles to her.*] Can you remember the summer when we used to sit like this outside the little peasant hut on the Lake of Taunitz?

IRENE [*nods*]. On Saturday evenings, yes,—when we had finished our week's work——

PROFESSOR RUBEK. —And taken the train out to the lake—to stay there over Sunday——

IRENE [*with an evil gleam of hatred in her eyes*]. It was an episode, Arnold.

PROFESSOR RUBEK [*as if not hearing*]. Then, too, you used to set birds swimming in the brook. They were water lilies which you——

IRENE. They were white swans.

PROFESSOR RUBEK. I meant swans, yes. And I remember that I fastened a great furry leaf to one of the swans. It looked like a burdock leaf——

IRENE. And then it turned into Lohengrin's boat —with the swan yoked to it.

PROFESSOR RUBEK. How fond you were of that game, Irene.

IRENE. We played it over and over again.

PROFESSOR RUBEK. Every single Saturday, I believe,—all the summer through.

IRENE. You said I was the swan that drew your boat.

PROFESSOR RUBEK. Did I say so? Yes, I daresay I did. [*Absorbed in the game*] Just see how the sea gulls are swimming down the stream!

IRENE [*laughing*]. And all your ships have run ashore.

PROFESSOR RUBEK [*throwing more leaves into the brook*]. I have ships enough in reserve. [*Follows the leaves with his eyes, throws more into the brook, and says after a pause*] Irene,—I have bought the little peasant hut beside the Lake of Taunitz.

IRENE. Have you bought it? You often said you would, if you could afford it.

PROFESSOR RUBEK. The day came when I could afford it easily enough; and so I bought it.

IRENE [*with a sidelong look at him*]. Then do you live out there now—in our old house?

PROFESSOR RUBEK. No, I have had it pulled down long ago. And I have built myself a great, handsome, comfortable villa on the site—with a park around it. It is there that we—[*Stops and corrects himself.*]—there that I usually live during the summer.

IRENE [*mastering herself*]. So you and—and the other one live out there now?

PROFESSOR RUBEK [*with a touch of defiance*]. Yes.

When my wife and I are not traveling—as we are this year.

IRENE [*looking far before her*]. Life was beautiful, beautiful by the Lake of Taunitz.

PROFESSOR RUBEK [*as though looking back into himself*]. And yet, Irene——

IRENE [*completing his thought*]. —Yet we two let slip all that life and its beauty.

PROFESSOR RUBEK [*softly, urgently*]. Does repentance come too late, now?

IRENE [*does not answer, but sits silent for a moment; then she points over the upland*]. Look there, Arnold,—now the sun is going down behind the peaks. See what a red glow the level rays cast over all the heathery knolls out yonder.

PROFESSOR RUBEK [*looks where she is pointing*]. It is long since I have seen a sunset in the mountains.

IRENE. Or a sunrise?

PROFESSOR RUBEK. A sunrise I don't think I have ever seen.

IRENE [*smiles as though lost in recollection*]. I once saw a marvelously lovely sunrise.

PROFESSOR RUBEK. Did you? Where was that?

IRENE. High, high up on a dizzy mountaintop. —You beguiled me up there by promising that I should see all the glory of the world if only I—— [*She stops suddenly.*]

PROFESSOR RUBEK. If only you——? Well?

IRENE. I did as you told me—went with you up to the heights. And there I fell upon my knees, and worshiped you, and served you. [*Is silent for a moment; then says softly*] Then I saw the sunrise.

PROFESSOR RUBEK [*turning the conversation*]. Should you not like to come and live with us in the villa down there?

IRENE [*looks at him with a scornful smile*]. With you—and the other woman?

PROFESSOR RUBEK [*urgently*]. With me—as in our days of creation. You could open all that is locked up in me. Can you not find it in your heart, Irene?

IRENE [*shaking her head*]. I have no longer the key to you, Arnold.

PROFESSOR RUBEK. You have the key! You and you alone possess it! [*Beseechingly*] Help me—that I may be able to live my life over again!

IRENE [*immovable as before*]. Empty dreams! Idle—dead dreams. For the life you and I led there is no resurrection.

PROFESSOR RUBEK [*curtly, breaking off*]. Then let us go on playing.

IRENE. Yes, playing, playing—only playing!

[*They sit and strew leaves and petals over the brook, where they float and sail away.*

Up the slope to the left at the back come ULF-HEIM *and* MAIA *in hunting costume. After them comes the* SERVANT *with the leash of dogs, with which he goes out to the right.*]

PROFESSOR RUBEK [*catching sight of them*]. Ah! there is little Maia, going out with the bear hunter.

IRENE. Your lady, yes.

PROFESSOR RUBEK. Or the other's.

MAIA [*looks around as she is crossing the upland, sees the two sitting by the brook, and calls out*]. Good night, Professor! Dream of me. Now I am going off on my adventures!

PROFESSOR RUBEK [*calls back to her*]. What sort of an adventure is this to be?

MAIA [*approaching*]. I am going to let life take the place of all the rest.

PROFESSOR RUBEK [*mockingly*]. Aha! so you too are going to do that, little Maia?

MAIA. Yes. And I've made a verse about it, and this is how it goes: [*Sings triumphantly*]

I am free! I am free! I am free!
No more life in the prison for me!
I am free as a bird! I am free!
For I believe I have awakened now—at last.

PROFESSOR RUBEK. It almost seems so.

MAIA [*drawing a deep breath*]. Oh—how divinely light one feels on waking!

PROFESSOR RUBEK. Good night, Frau Maia—and good luck to——

ULFHEIM [*calls out, interposing*]. Hush, hush!—for the devil's sake let's have none of your wizard wishes. Don't you see that we are going out to shoot——

PROFESSOR RUBEK. What will you bring me home from the hunting, Maia?

MAIA. You shall have a bird of prey to model. I shall wing one for you.

PROFESSOR RUBEK [*laughs mockingly and bitterly*]. Yes, to wing things—without knowing what you are doing—that has long been quite in your way.

MAIA [*tossing her head*]. Oh, just let me take care of myself for the future, and I wish you then——! [*Nods and laughs roguishly.*] Good-by

—and a good, peaceful summer night on the upland!

PROFESSOR RUBEK [*jestingly*]. Thanks! and all the ill-luck in the world over you and your hunting!

ULFHEIM [*roaring with laughter*]. There now, that is a wish worth having!

MAIA [*laughing*]. Thanks, thanks, thanks, Professor!

[*They have both crossed the visible portion of the upland, and go out through the bushes to the right.*]

PROFESSOR RUBEK [*after a short pause*]. A summer night on the upland! Yes, that would have been life!

IRENE [*suddenly, with a wild expression in her eyes*]. Will you spend a summer night on the upland—with me?

PROFESSOR RUBEK [*stretching his arms wide*]. Yes, yes—come!

IRENE. My adored lord and master!

PROFESSOR RUBEK. Oh, Irene!

IRENE [*hoarsely, smiling and groping in her breast*]. It will be only an episode—— [*Quickly, whispering*] Hush!—do not look around, Arnold!

PROFESSOR RUBEK [*also in a low voice*]. What is it?

IRENE. A face that is staring at me.

PROFESSOR RUBEK [*turns involuntarily*]. Where? [*With a start*] Ah——!

[*The* SISTER OF MERCY's *head is partly visible among the bushes beside the descent to the left. Her eyes are immovably fixed on* IRENE.]

IRENE [*rises and says softly*]. We must part then. No, you must remain sitting. Do you hear? You must not go with me. [*Bends over him and whispers.*] Till we meet again—tonight—on the upland.

PROFESSOR RUBEK. And you will come, Irene?

IRENE. Yes, surely I will come. Wait for me here.

PROFESSOR RUBEK [*repeats dreamily*]. Summer night on the upland. With you. With you. [*His eyes meet hers.*] Oh, Irene—that might have been our life.—And that we have forfeited—we two.

IRENE. We see the irretrievable only when—— [*Breaks off.*]

PROFESSOR RUBEK [*looks inquiringly at her*]. When——?

IRENE. When we dead awaken.

PROFESSOR RUBEK [*shakes his head mournfully*]. What do we really see then?

IRENE. We see that we have never lived. [*She

goes toward the slope and descends.]

[The SISTER OF MERCY *makes way for her and follows her.* PROFESSOR RUBEK *remains sitting motionless beside the brook.*]

MAIA [*is heard singing triumphantly among the hills*].

I am free! I am free! I am free!
No more life in the prison for me!
I am free as a bird! I am free!

ACT III

A wild riven mountainside, with sheer precipices at the back. Snow-clad peaks rise to the right, and lose themselves in drifting mists. To the left, on a stone-scree, stands an old, half-ruined hut. It is early morning. Dawn is breaking. The sun has not yet risen.

MAIA *comes, flushed and irritated, down over the stone-scree on the left.* ULFHEIM *follows, half angry, half laughing, holding her fast by the sleeve.*

MAIA [*trying to tear herself loose*]. Let me go! Let me go, I say!

ULFHEIM. Come, come! are you going to bite now? You're as snappish as a wolf.

MAIA [*striking him over the hand*]. Let me go, I tell you! And be quiet!

ULFHEIM. No, confound me if I will!

MAIA. Then I will not go another step with you. Do you hear?—not a single step!

ULFHEIM. Ho, ho! How can you get away from me, here, on the wild mountainside?

MAIA. I will jump over the precipice yonder, if need be——

ULFHEIM. And mangle and mash yourself up into dogs' meat! A juicy morsel! [*Lets go his hold.*] As you please. Jump over the precipice if you want to. It's a dizzy drop. There's only one narrow footpath down it, and that's almost impassable.

MAIA [*dusts her skirt with her hand, and looks at him with angry eyes*]. Well, you are a nice one to go hunting with!

ULFHEIM. Say, rather, sporting.

MAIA. Oh! So you call this sport, do you?

ULFHEIM. Yes, I venture to take that liberty. It is the sort of sport I like best of all.

MAIA [*tossing her head*]. Well—I must say! [*After a pause; looks searchingly at him.*] Why did you let the dogs loose up there?

ULFHEIM [*blinking his eyes and smiling*]. So that they too might do a little hunting on their own account, don't you see?

MAIA. There's not a word of truth in that! It wasn't for the dogs' sake that you let them go.

ULFHEIM [*still smiling*]. Well, why did I let them go then? Let us hear.

MAIA. You let them go because you wanted to get rid of Lars. He was to run after them and bring them in again, you said. And in the meantime——. Oh, it was a pretty way to behave!

ULFHEIM. In the meantime?

MAIA [*curtly breaking off*]. No matter!

ULFHEIM [*in a confidential tone*]. Lars won't find them. You may safely swear to that. He won't come with them before the time's up.

MAIA [*looking angrily at him*]. No, I daresay not.

ULFHEIM [*catching at her arm*]. For Lars—he knows my—my methods of sport, you see.

MAIA [*eludes him, and measures him with a glance*]. Do you know what you look like, Mr. Ulfheim?

ULFHEIM. I should think I'm probably most like myself.

MAIA. Yes, there you're exactly right. For you're the living image of a faun.

ULFHEIM. A faun?

MAIA. Yes, precisely; a faun.

ULFHEIM. A faun! Isn't that a sort of monster? Or a kind of wood demon, as you might call it?

MAIA. Yes, just the sort of creature you are. A thing with a goat's beard and goat legs. Yes, and the faun has horns too!

ULFHEIM. So, so!—has he horns too?

MAIA. A pair of ugly horns, just like yours, yes.

ULFHEIM. Can you see the poor little horns I have?

MAIA. Yes, I seem to see them quite plainly.

ULFHEIM [*taking the dogs' leash out of his pocket*]. Then I had better see about tying you.

MAIA. Have you gone quite mad? Would you tie me?

ULFHEIM. If I am a demon, let me be a demon! So that's the way of it! You can see the horns, can you?

MAIA [*soothingly*]. There, there, there! Now try to behave nicely, Mr. Ulfheim. [*Breaking off*] But what has become of that hunting castle of yours, that you boasted so much of? You said it lay somewhere hereabouts.

ULFHEIM. [*points with a flourish to the hut*]. There you have it, before your very eyes.

MAIA [*looks at him*]. That old pigsty!

ULFHEIM [*laughing in his beard*]. It has harbored more than one king's daughter, I can tell you.

MAIA. Was it there that that horrid man you told me about came to the king's daughter in the form of a bear?

ULFHEIM. Yes, my fair companion of the chase—this is the scene. [*With a gesture of invitation*] If you would deign to enter——

MAIA. Isch! If ever I set foot in it——! Isch!

ULFHEIM. Oh, two people can doze away a summer night in there comfortably enough. Or a whole summer, if it comes to that.

MAIA. Thanks! One would need to have a pretty strong taste for that kind of thing. [*Impatiently*] But now I am tired both of you and the hunting expedition. Now I am going down to the hotel—before people awaken down there.

ULFHEIM. How do you propose to get down from here?

MAIA. That's your affair. There must be a way down somewhere or other, I suppose.

ULFHEIM [*pointing toward the back*]. Oh, certainly! There is a sort of way—right down the face of the precipice yonder——

MAIA. There, you see. With a little good will——

ULFHEIM. —But just you try if you dare go that way.

MAIA [*doubtfully*]. Do you think I can't?

ULFHEIM. Never in this world—if you don't let me help you.

MAIA [*uneasily*]. Why, then come and help me! What else are you here for?

ULFHEIM. Would you rather I should take you on my back——?

MAIA. Nonsense!

ULFHEIM. —Or carry you in my arms?

MAIA. Now do stop talking that rubbish!

ULFHEIM [*with suppressed exasperation*]. I once took a young girl—lifted her up from the mire of the streets and carried her in my arms. Next my heart I carried her. So I would have borne her all through life—lest haply she should dash her foot against a stone. For her shoes were worn very thin when I found her——

MAIA. And yet you took her up and carried her next your heart?

ULFHEIM. Took her up out of the gutter and carried her as high and as carefully as I could. [*With a growling laugh*] And do you know what I got for my reward?

MAIA. No. What did you get?

ULFHEIM [*looks at her, smiles and nods*]. I got the horns! The horns that you can see so plainly. Is not that a comical story, madam bear murderess?

MAIA. Oh, yes, comical enough! But I know another story that is still more comical.

ULFHEIM. How does that story go?

MAIA. This is how it goes. There was once a stupid girl, who had both a father and a mother—but a rather poverty-stricken home. Then there came a high and mighty seigneur into the midst of all this poverty. And he took the girl in his arms—as you did—and traveled far, far way with her——

ULFHEIM. Was she so anxious to be with him?

MAIA. Yes, for she was stupid, you see.

ULFHEIM. And he, no doubt, was a brilliant and beautiful personage?

MAIA. Oh, no, he wasn't so superlatively beautiful either. But he pretended that he would take her with him to the top of the highest of mountains, where there were light and sunshine without end.

ULFHEIM. So he was a mountaineer, was he, that man?

MAIA. Yes, he was—in his way.

ULFHEIM. And then he took the girl up with him——?

MAIA [*with a toss of the head*]. Took her up with him finely, you may be sure! Oh, no! he beguiled her into a cold, clammy cage, where—as it seemed to her—there was neither sunlight nor fresh air, but only gilding and great petrified ghosts of people all round the walls.

ULFHEIM. Devil take me, but it served her right!

MAIA. Yes, but don't you think it's quite a comical story, all the same?

ULFHEIM [*looks at her a moment*]. Now listen to me, my good companion of the chase——

MAIA. Well, what is it now?

ULFHEIM. Should not we two tack our poor shreds of life together?

MAIA. Is his worship inclined to set up as a patching tailor?

ULFHEIM. Yes, indeed he is. Might not we two try to draw the rags together here and there—so as to make some sort of a human life out of them?

MAIA. And when the poor tatters were quite worn out—what then?

ULFHEIM [*with a large gesture*]. Then there we shall stand, free and serene—as the man and woman we really are!

MAIA [*laughing*]. You with your goat legs, yes!

ULFHEIM. And you with your—— Well, let that pass.

MAIA. Yes, come—let us pass—on.

ULFHEIM. Stop! Whither away, comrade?

MAIA. Down to the hotel, of course.

ULFHEIM. And afterwards?

MAIA. Then we'll take a polite leave of each other, with thanks for pleasant company.

ULFHEIM. Can we part, we two? Do you think we can?

MAIA. Yes, you didn't manage to tie me up, you know.

ULFHEIM. I have a castle to offer you——

MAIA [*pointing to the hut*]. A fellow to that one?

ULFHEIM. It has not fallen to ruin yet.

MAIA. And all the glory of the world, perhaps?

ULFHEIM. A castle, I tell you——

MAIA. Thanks! I have had enough of castles.

ULFHEIM. —With splendid hunting grounds stretching for miles around it.

MAIA. Are there works of art too in this castle?

ULFHEIM [*slowly*]. Well, no—it's true there are no works of art; but——

MAIA [*relieved*]. Ah! that's one good thing, at any rate!

ULFHEIM. Will you go with me, then—as far and as long as I want you?

MAIA. There is a tame bird of prey keeping watch upon me.

ULFHEIM [*wildly*]. We'll put a bullet in his wing, Maia?

MAIA [*looks at him a moment, and says resolutely*]. Come then, and carry me down into the depths.

ULFHEIM [*puts his arm round her waist*]. It is high time! The mist is upon us!

MAIA. Is the way down terribly dangerous?

ULFHEIM. The mountain mist is more dangerous still.

[*She shakes him off, goes to the edge of the precipice and looks over, but starts quickly back.*]

ULFHEIM [*goes toward her, laughing*]. What? Does it make you a little giddy?

MAIA [*faintly*]. Yes, that too. But go and look over. Those two, coming up——

ULFHEIM [*goes and bends over the edge of the precipice*]. It's only your bird of prey—and his strange lady.

MAIA. Can't we get past them—without their seeing us?

ULFHEIM. Impossible! The path is far too narrow. And there's no other way down.

MAIA [*nerving herself*]. Well, well—let us face them here, then!

ULFHEIM. Spoken like a true bear killer, comrade!

[PROFESSOR RUBEK *and* IRENE *appear over the edge of the precipice at the back. He has his plaid over his shoulders; she has a fur cloak thrown loosely over her white dress, and a swansdown hood over her head.*]

PROFESSOR RUBEK [*still only half visible above the edge*]. What, Maia! So we two meet once again?

MAIA [*with assumed coolness*]. At your service. Won't you come up?

[PROFESSOR RUBEK *climbs right up and holds out his hand to* IRENE, *who also comes right to the top.*]

PROFESSOR RUBEK [*coldly to* MAIA]. So you, too, have been all night on the mountain,—as we have?

MAIA. I have been hunting—yes. You gave me permission, you know.

ULFHEIM [*pointing downward*]. Have you come up that path there?

PROFESSOR RUBEK. As you saw.

ULFHEIM. And the strange lady too?

PROFESSOR RUBEK. Yes, of course. [*With a glance at* MAIA] Henceforth the strange lady and I do not intend our ways to part.

ULFHEIM. Don't you know, then, that it is a deadly dangerous way you have come?

PROFESSOR RUBEK. We thought we would try it, nevertheless. For it did not seem particularly hard at first.

ULFHEIM. No, at first nothing seems hard. But presently you may come to a tight place where you can neither get forward nor back. And then you stick fast, Professor! Mountain-fast, as we hunters call it.

PROFESSOR RUBEK [*smiles and looks at him*]. Am I to take these as oracular utterances, Mr. Ulfheim?

ULFHEIM. Lord preserve me from playing the oracle! [*Urgently, pointing up toward the heights.*]

But don't you see that the storm is upon us? Don't you hear the blasts of wind?

PROFESSOR RUBEK [*listening*]. They sound like the prelude to the Resurrection Day.

ULFHEIM. They are storm blasts from the peaks, man! Just look how the clouds are rolling and sinking—soon they'll be all around us like a winding sheet!

IRENE [*with a start and shiver*]. I know that sheet!

MAIA [*drawing* ULFHEIM *away*]. Let us make haste and get down.

ULFHEIM [*to* PROFESSOR RUBEK]. I cannot help more than one. Take refuge in the hut in the meantime—while the storm lasts. Then I shall send people up to fetch the two of you away.

IRENE [*in terror*]. To fetch us away! No, no!

ULFHEIM [*harshly*]. To take you by force if necesesary—for it's a matter of life and death here. Now, you know it. [*To* MAIA.] Come, then—and don't fear to trust yourself in your comrade's hands.

MAIA [*clinging to him*]. Oh, how I shall rejoice and sing, if I get down with a whole skin!

ULFHEIM [*begins the descent and calls to the others*]. You'll wait, then, in the hut, till the men come with ropes, and fetch you away.

[ULFHEIM, *with* MAIA *in his arms, clambers rapidly but warily down the precipice.*]

IRENE [*looks for some time at* PROFESSOR RUBEK *with terror-stricken eyes*]. Did you hear that, Arnold?—men are coming up to fetch me away! Many men will come up here——

PROFESSOR RUBEK. Do not be alarmed, Irene!

IRENE [*in growing terror*]. And she, the woman in black—she will come too. For she must have missed me long ago. And then she will seize me, Arnold! And put me in the strait-waistcoat. Oh, she has it with her, in her box. I have seen it with my own eyes——

PROFESSOR RUBEK. Not a soul shall be suffered to touch you.

IRENE [*with a wild smile*]. Oh, no—I myself have a resource against that.

PROFESSOR RUBEK. What resource do you mean?

IRENE [*drawing out the knife*]. This!

PROFESSOR RUBEK [*tries to seize it*]. Have you a knife?

IRENE. Always, always—both day and night—in bed as well!

PROFESSOR RUBEK. Give me that knife, Irene!

IRENE [*concealing it*]. You shall not have it. I may very likely find a use for it myself.

PROFESSOR RUBEK. What use can you have for it, here?

IRENE [*looks fixedly at him*]. It was intended for you, Arnold.

PROFESSOR RUBEK. For me!

IRENE. As we were sitting by the Lake of Taunitz last evening——

PROFESSOR RUBEK. By the Lake of——

IRENE. Outside the peasant's hut—and playing with swans and water lilies——

PROFESSOR RUBEK. When then—what then?

IRENE. And when I heard you say with such deathly, icy coldness—that I was nothing but an episode in your life——

PROFESSOR RUBEK. It was you that said that, Irene, not I.

IRENE [*continuing*]. —Then I had my knife out. I wanted to stab you in the back with it.

PROFESSOR RUBEK [*darkly*]. And why you hold your hand?

IRENE. Because it flashed upon me with a sudden horror that you were dead already—long ago.

PROFESSOR RUBEK. Dead?

IRENE. Dead. Dead, you as well as I. We sat there by the Lake of Taunitz, we two clay-cold bodies—and played with each other.

PROFESSOR RUBEK. I do not call that being dead. But you do not understand me.

IRENE. Then where is the burning desire for me that you fought and battled against when I stood freely forth before you as the woman arisen from the dead?

PROFESSOR RUBEK. Our love is assuredly not dead, Irene.

IRENE. The love that belongs to the life of earth —the beautiful, miraculous earth life—the inscrutable earth life—that is dead in both of us.

PROFESSOR RUBEK [*passionately*]. And do you know that just that love—it is burning and seething in me as hotly as ever before?

IRENE. And I? Have you forgotten who I now am?

PROFESSOR RUBEK. Be who or what you please, for aught I care! For me, you are the woman I see in my dreams of you.

IRENE. I have stood on the turntable—naked— and made a show of myself to many hundreds of men—after you.

PROFESSOR RUBEK. It was I that drove you to the

turntable—blind as I then was—I, who placed the dead clay image above the happiness of life—of love.

IRENE [*looking down*]. Too late—too late!

PROFESSOR RUBEK. Not by a hairsbreadth has all that has passed in the interval lowered you in my eyes.

IRENE [*with head erect*]. Nor in my own!

PROFESSOR RUBEK. Well, what then! Then we are free—and there is still time for us to live our life, Irene.

IRENE [*looks sadly at him*]. The desire for life is dead in me, Arnold. Now I have arisen. And I look for you. And I find you.—And then I see that you and life lie dead—as I have lain.

PROFESSOR RUBEK. Oh, how utterly you are astray! Both in us and around us life is fermenting and throbbing as fiercely as ever!

IRENE [*smiling and shaking her head*]. The young woman of your Resurrection Day can see all life lying on its bier.

PROFESSOR RUBEK [*throwing his arms violently around her*]. Then let two of the dead—us two—for once live life to its uttermost—before we go down to our graves again!

IRENE [*with a shriek*]. Arnold!

PROFESSOR RUBEK. But not here in the half darkness! Not here with this hideous dank shroud flapping around us——

IRENE [*carried away by passion*]. No, no—up in the light, and in all the glittering glory! Up to the Peak of Promise!

PROFESSOR RUBEK. There we will hold our marriage feast, Irene—oh, my beloved!

IRENE [*proudly*]. The sun may freely look on us, Arnold.

PROFESSOR RUBEK. All the powers of light may freely look on us—and all the powers of darkness, too. [*Seizes her hand.*] Will you then follow me, oh, my grace-given bride?

IRENE [*as though transfigured*]. I follow you, freely and gladly, my lord and master!

PROFESSOR RUBEK [*drawing her along with him*]. We must first pass through the mists, Irene, and then——

IRENE. Yes, through all the mists, and then right up to the summit of the tower that shines in the sunrise.

[*The mist clouds close in over the scene*—PROFESSOR RUBEK *and* IRENE, *hand in hand, climb up over the snow field to the right and soon disappear among the lower clouds. Keen storm gusts hurtle and whistle through the air. The* SISTER OF MERCY *appears upon the stone-scree to the left. She stops and looks around silently and searchingly.*

MAIA *can be heard singing triumphantly far in the depths below.*]

MAIA.
   I am free! I am free! I am free!
   No more life in the prison for me!
   I am free as a bird! I am free!

[*Suddenly a sound like thunder is heard from high up on the snow field, which glides and whirls downwards with headlong speed.* PROFESSOR RUBEK *and* IRENE *can be dimly discerned as they are whirled along with the masses of snow and buried in them.*]

THE SISTER OF MERCY [*gives a shriek, stretches out her arms toward them and cries*]. Irene! [*Stands silent a moment, then makes the sign of the cross before her in the air, and says*] Pax vobiscum!

[MAIA'S *triumphant song sounds from still farther down below.*]

The
Caucasian Chalk Circle

BY BERTOLT BRECHT

TRANSLATED BY ERIC BENTLEY

Brecht's last major play, *The Caucasian Chalk Circle* (*Der kaukasische Kreidekreis*) was written in 1944 and first produced in the present English translation in 1948. Its primary source is an ancient Chinese play called *The Chalk Circle*, which was adapted by the German poet Klabund in 1925, but it also recalls the Biblical story of Solomon (I Kings 3:16–27) in which the wise king by offering to cut a child in half ascertains which of the two disputants is its true mother. In addition *The Caucasian Chalk Circle* also reflects the many fairy tales and pastoral romances in which a lost prince brought up among shepherds or peasants discovers his true identity and regains his birthright. The play radically alters the timeless theme of these works, however, by redefining the child's "real" mother as its *social* guardian rather than its biological parent; in so doing, it replaces proverbial or legalistic "wisdom" with its own vision of social justice.

Brecht's transformation of his sources into a play that has a distinctively modern social meaning is sustained in performance by the theatrical device he called *Verfremdung* or "alienation." This effect, which is repeatedly discussed in his writings on the theater, involves breaking the dramatic illusion by which the audience identifies with the characters and situations on stage and forcing them to contemplate these fabrications with critical and social detachment. Many of the techniques Brecht used to achieve this effect can be found in Elizabethan drama (of which he was a student and adaptor), and in *The Caucasian Chalk Circle* they include: the parabolic nature of the action, the remote Georgian setting, the framing devices of prologue and choric narrator, and the interruptions that result from the play's twelve songs. This play and Brecht's other experiments with episodic or "epic" theater, in which narrative distance replaces dramatic involvement, remain a potent influence on modern drama.

Characters

OLD MAN *on the right*

PEASANT WOMAN *on the right*

YOUNG PEASANT

A VERY YOUNG WORKER

OLD MAN *on the left*

PEASANT WOMAN *on the left*

AGRICULTURIST KATO

GIRL TRACTORIST

WOUNDED SOLDIER

THE DELEGATE *from the capital*

THE SINGER

GEORGI ABASHWILI, *the Governor*

NATELLA, *the Governor's wife*

MICHAEL, *their son*

SHALVA, *an adjutant*

ARSEN KAZBEKI, *a fat prince*

MESSENGER *from the capital*

NIKO MIKADZE *and* MIKA LOLADZE, *doctors*

SIMON SHASHAVA, *a soldier*

GRUSHA VASHNADZE, *a kitchen maid*

OLD PEASANT *with the milk*

CORPORAL *and* PRIVATE

PEASANT *and his wife*

LAVRENTI VASHNADZE, *Grusha's brother*

ANIKO, *his wife*

PEASANT WOMAN, *for a while Grusha's mother-in-law*

JUSSUP, *her son*

MONK

AZDAK, *village recorder*

SHAUWA, *a policeman*

GRAND DUKE

DOCTOR

INVALID

LIMPING MAN

BLACKMAILER

LUDOVICA

INNKEEPER, *her father-in-law*

STABLEBOY

POOR OLD PEASANT WOMAN

IRAKLI, *her brother-in-law, a bandit*

THREE WEALTHY FARMERS

ILLO SHUBOLADZE *and* SANDRO OBOLADZE, *lawyers*

OLD MARRIED COUPLE

Soldiers, Servants, Peasants, Beggars, Musicians, Merchants, Nobles, Architects

The time and the place: After a prologue, set in 1945, we move back perhaps 1000 years.

The action of The Caucasian Chalk Circle *centers on Nuka (or Nukha), a town in Azerbaijan. However, the capital referred to in the prologue is not Baku (capital of Soviet Azerbaijan) but Tiflis (or Tbilisi), capital of Georgia. When Azdak, later, refers to "the capital" he means Nuka itself, though whether Nuka was ever capital of Georgia I do not know: in what reading I have done on the subject I have only found Nuka to be the capital of a Nuka Khanate.*

The word "Georgia" has not been used in this English version because of its American associations; instead, the alternative name "Grusinia" (in Russian, Gruziya) has been used.

The reasons for resettling the old Chinese story in Transcaucasia are not far to seek. The play was written when the Soviet chief of state, Joseph Stalin, was a Georgian, as was his favorite poet, cited in the Prologue, Mayakovsky. And surely there is a point in having this story acted out at the place where Europe and Asia meet, a place incomparably rich in legend and history. Here Jason found the Golden Fleece. Here Noah's Ark touched ground. Here the armies of both Genghis Khan and Tamerlane wrought havoc.

—E.B.

Prologue

Summer, 1945.

Among the ruins of a war-ravaged Caucasian village the members of two Kolkhoz villages, mostly women and older men, are sitting in a circle, smoking and drinking wine. With them is a DELEGATE *of the State Reconstruction Commission from Nuka.*

PEASANT WOMAN, *left [pointing].* In those hills over there we stopped three Nazi tanks, but the apple orchard was already destroyed.

OLD MAN, *right.* Our beautiful dairy farm: a ruin.

GIRL TRACTORIST. I laid the fire, Comrade.

[*Pause.*]

DELEGATE. Nuka, Azerbaijan S.S.R. Delegation received from the goat-breeding Kolkhoz "Rosa Luxemburg." This is a collective farm which moved eastwards on orders from the authorities at the approach of Hitler's armies. They are now planning to return. Their delegates have looked at the village and the land and found a lot of destruction. [*Delegates on the right nod.*] But the neighboring fruit farm—Kolkhoz [*to the left*] "Galinsk"—proposes to use the former grazing land of Kolkhoz "Rosa Luxemburg" for orchards and vineyards. This land lies in a valley where grass doesn't grow very well. As a delegate of the Reconstruction Commission in Nuka I request that the two Kolkhoz villages decide between themselves whether Kolkhoz "Rosa Luxemburg" shall return or not.

OLD MAN, *right.* First of all, I want to protest against the time limit on discussion. We of Kolkhoz "Rosa Luxemburg" have spent three days and three nights getting here. And now discussion is limited to half a day.

WOUNDED SOLDIER, *left.* Comrade, we haven't as many villages as we used to have. We haven't as many hands. We haven't as much time.

GIRL TRACTORIST. All 'pleasures have to be rationed. Tobacco is rationed, and wine. Discussion should be rationed.

OLD MAN, *right [sighing].* Death to the fascists! But I will come to the point and explain why we want our valley back. There are a great many reasons, but I'll begin with one of the simplest. Makinä Abakidze, unpack the goat cheese. [*A peasant woman from right takes from a basket an enormous cheese wrapped in a cloth. Applause and laughter.*] Help yourselves, Comrades, start in!

OLD MAN, *left [suspiciously].* Is this a way of influencing us?

OLD MAN, *right [amid laughter].* How could it be a way of influencing you, Surab, you valley-thief? Everyone knows you'll take the cheese and the valley, too. [*Laughter.*] All I expect from you is an honest answer. Do you like the cheese?

OLD MAN, *left.* The answer is: yes.

OLD MAN, *right.* Really. [*Bitterly*] I ought to have known you know nothing about cheese.

OLD MAN, *left.* Why not? When I tell you I like it?

OLD MAN, *right.* Because you can't like it. Because it's not what it was in the old days. And why not? Because our goats don't like the new grass as they did the old. Cheese is not cheese because grass is not grass, that's the thing. Please put that in your report.

OLD MAN, *left.* But your cheese is excellent.

OLD MAN, *right.* It isn't excellent. It's just passable. The new grazing land is no good, whatever the young people may say. One can't live there. It doesn't even smell of morning in the morning. [*Several people laugh.*]

DELEGATE. Don't mind their laughing: they understand you. Comrades, why does one love one's country? Because the bread tastes better there, the air smells better, voices sound stronger, the sky is higher, the ground is easier to walk on. Isn't that so?

OLD MAN, *right.* The valley has belonged to us from all eternity.

SOLDIER, *left.* What does *that* mean—from all eternity? Nothing belongs to anyone from all eternity. When you were young you didn't even belong to yourself. You belonged to the Kazbeki princes.

OLD MAN, *right.* Doesn't it make a difference, though, what kind of trees stand next to the house you are born in? Or what kind of neighbors you have? Doesn't that make a difference? We want to go back just to have you as our neighbors, valley-thieves! Now you can all laugh again.

OLD MAN, *left [laughing].* Then why don't you listen to what your neighbor, Kato Wachtang, our agriculturist, has to say about the valley?

PEASANT WOMAN, *right.* We've not said all we have to say about our valley. By no means. Not all the houses are destroyed. As for the dairy farm, at least the foundation wall is still standing.

DELEGATE. You can claim State support—here and there—you know that. I have suggestions here in my pocket.

PEASANT WOMAN, *right.* Comrade Specialist, we haven't come here to haggle. I can't take your cap and hand you another, and say "This one's better." The other one might *be* better, but you *like* yours better.

GIRL TRACTORIST. A piece of land is not a cap—not in our country, Comrade.

DELEGATE. Don't get mad. It's true we have to consider a piece of land as a tool to produce something useful, but it's also true that we must recognize love for a particular piece of land. As far as I'm concerned, I'd like to find out more exactly what you [*to those on the left*] want to do with the valley.

OTHERS. Yes, let Kato speak.

KATO [*rising; she's in military uniform*]. Comrades, last winter, while we were fighting in these hills here as Partisans, we discussed how, once the Germans were expelled, we could build up our fruit culture to ten times its original size. I've prepared a plan for an irrigation project. By means of a cofferdam on our mountain lake, 300 hectares of unfertile land can be irrigated. Our Kolkhoz could not only cultivate more fruit, but also have vineyards. The project, however, would pay only if the disputed valley of Kolkhoz "Rosa Luxemburg" were also included. Here are the calculations. [*She hands DELEGATE a briefcase.*]

OLD MAN, *right.* Write into the report that our Kolkhoz plans to start a new stud farm.

GIRL TRACTORIST. Comrades, the project was conceived during days and nights when we had to take cover in the mountains. We were often without ammunition for our half-dozen rifles. Even finding a pencil was difficult. [*Applause from both sides.*]

OLD MAN, *right.* Our thanks to the Comrades of Kolkhoz "Galinsk" and all those who've defended our country! [*They shake hands and embrace.*]

PEASANT WOMAN, *left.* In doing this our thought was that our soldiers—both your men and our men—should return to a still more productive homeland.

GIRL TRACTORIST. As the poet Mayakovsky said: "The home of the Soviet people shall also be the home of Reason"!

[*The delegates excluding the OLD MAN have got up, and with the DELEGATE specified proceed to study the Agriculturist's drawings. Exclamations such as: "Why is the altitude of fall 22 meters?"—"This rock will have to be blown up"—"Actually, all they need is cement and dynamite"—"They force the water to come down here, that's clever!"*]

A VERY YOUNG WORKER, *right* [*to OLD MAN, right*]. They're going to irrigate all the fields between the hills, look at that, Aleko!

OLD MAN, *right.* I'm not going to look. I knew the project would be good. I won't have a pistol pointed at me!

DELEGATE. But they only want to point a pencil at you! [*Laughter.*]

OLD MAN, *right* [*gets up gloomily, and walks over to look at the drawings*]. These valley-thieves know only too well that we in this country are suckers for machines and projects.

PEASANT WOMAN, *right.* Aleko Bereshwili, you have a weakness for new projects. That's well known.

DELEGATE. What about my report? May I write that you will all support the cession of your old valley in the interests of this project when you get back to your Kolkhoz?

PEASANT WOMAN, *right.* I will. What about you, Aleko?

OLD MAN, *right* [*bent over drawings*]. I suggest that you give us copies of the drawings to take along.

PEASANT WOMAN, *right.* Then we can sit down and eat. Once he has the drawings and he's ready to discuss them, the matter is settled. I know him. And it will be the same with the rest of us.

[*Delegates laughingly embrace again.*]

OLD MAN, *left.* Long live the Kolkhoz "Rosa Luxemburg" and much luck to your horse-breeding project!

PEASANT WOMAN, *left.* In honor of the visit of the delegates from Kolkhoz "Rosa Luxemburg" and of the Specialist, the plan is that we all hear a presentation of the Singer Arkadi Tscheidse.

[*Applause. GIRL TRACTORIST has gone off to bring the SINGER.*]

PEASANT WOMAN, *right.* Comrades, your entertainment had better be good. It's going to cost us a valley.

PEASANT WOMAN, *left.* Arkadi Tscheidse knows about our discussion. He's promised to perform something that has a bearing on the problem.

KATO. We wired Tiflis three times. The whole thing nearly fell through at the last minute because his driver had a cold.

PEASANT WOMAN, *left*. Arkadi Tscheidse knows 21,000 lines of verse.

OLD MAN, *left*. He's hard to get. You and the Planning Commission should persuade him to come north more often, Comrade.

DELEGATE. We are more interested in economics, I'm afraid.

OLD MAN, *left* [*smiling*]. You arrange the redistribution of vines and tractors, why not songs?

[*Enter the* SINGER *Arkadi Tscheidse, led by* GIRL TRACTORIST. *He is a well-built man of simple manners, accompanied by* FOUR MUSICIANS *with their instruments. The artists are greeted with applause.*]

GIRL TRACTORIST. This is the Comrade Specialist, Arkadi.

[*The* SINGER *greets them all.*]

DELEGATE. Honored to make your acquaintance. I heard about your songs when I was a boy at school. Will it be one of the old legends?

SINGER. A very old one. It's called "The Chalk Circle" and comes from the Chinese. But we'll do it, of course, in a changed version. Comrades, it's an honor for me to entertain you after a difficult debate. We hope you will find the voice of the old poet also sounds well in the shadow of Soviet tractors. It may be a mistake to mix different wines, but old and new wisdom mix admirably. Now I hope we'll get something to eat before the performance begins—it would certainly help.

VOICES. Surely. Everyone into the Club House!

[*While everyone begins to move,* DELEGATE *turns to* GIRL TRACTORIST.]

DELEGATE. I hope it won't take long. I've got to get back tonight.

GIRL TRACTORIST. How long will it last, Arkadi? The Comrade Specialist must get back to Tiflis tonight.

SINGER [*casually*]. It's actually two stories. An hour or two.

GIRL TRACTORIST [*confidentially*]. Couldn't you make it shorter?

SINGER. No.

VOICE. Arkadi Tscheidse's performance will take place here in the square after the meal.

[*And they all go happily to eat.*]

1

THE NOBLE CHILD

As the lights go up, the SINGER *is seen sitting on the floor, a black sheepskin cloak round his shoulders, and a little, well-thumbed notebook in his hand. A small group of listeners—the chorus —sits with him. The manner of his recitation makes it clear that he has told his story over and over again. He mechanically fingers the pages, seldom looking at them. With appropriate gestures, he gives the signal for each scene to begin.*

SINGER.
In olden times, in a bloody time,
There ruled in a Caucasian city—
Men called it City of the Damned—
A Governor.
His name was Georgi Abashwili.
He was rich as Croesus
He had a beautiful wife
He had a healthy baby.
No other governor in Grusinia
Had so many horses in his stable
So many beggars on his doorstep
So many soldiers in his service
So many petitioners in his courtyard.
Georgi Abashwili—how shall I describe him
    to you?
He enjoyed his life.
On the morning of Easter Sunday
The Governor and his family went to church.

[*At the left a large doorway, at the right an even larger gateway.* BEGGARS *and* PETITIONERS *pour from the gateway, holding up thin* CHILDREN, *crutches and petitions. They are followed by* IRON-SHIRTS, *and then, expensively dressed, the* GOVERNOR'S FAMILY.]

BEGGARS AND PETITIONERS.
—Mercy! Mercy, Your Grace! The taxes are too high.
—I lost my leg in the Persian War, where can I get . . .
—My brother is innocent, Your Grace, a misunderstanding . . .
—The child is starving in my arms!
—Our petition is for our son's discharge from the army, our last remaining son!

—Please, Your Grace, the water inspector takes bribes.

[*One servant collects the petitions. Another distributes coins from a purse. Soldiers push the crowd back, lashing at them with thick leather whips.*]

SOLDIER. Get back! Clear the church door!

[*Behind the* GOVERNOR, *his* WIFE, *and the* ADJUTANT, *the* GOVERNOR'S CHILD *is brought through the gateway in an ornate carriage.*]

CROWD.

—The baby!

—I can't see it, don't shove so hard!

—God bless the child, Your Grace!

SINGER [*while the crowd is driven back with whips*].

> For the first time on that Easter Sunday, the people saw the Governor's heir.
>
> Two doctors never moved from the noble child, apple of the Governor's eye.
>
> Even the mighty Prince Kazbeki bows before him at the church door.

[*The* FAT PRINCE *steps forward and greets the* FAMILY.]

FAT PRINCE. Happy Easter, Natella Abashwili! What a day! When it was raining last night, I thought to myself, gloomy holidays! But this morning the sky was gay. I love a gay sky, a simple heart, Natella Abashwili. And little Michael is a governor from head to foot! Tititi! [*He tickles the* CHILD.]

GOVERNOR'S WIFE. What do you think, Arsen, at last Georgi has decided to start building the east wing. All those wretched slums are to be torn down to make room for the garden.

FAT PRINCE. Good news after so much bad! What's the latest on the war, Brother Georgi? [*The* GOVERNOR *indicates a lack of interest.*] Strategical retreat, I hear. Well, minor reverses are to be expected. Sometimes things go well, sometimes not. Such is war. Doesn't mean a thing, does it?

GOVERNOR'S WIFE. He's coughing. Georgi, did you hear? [*She speaks sharply to the* DOCTORS, *two dignified men standing close to the little carriage.*] He's coughing!

FIRST DOCTOR [*to the* SECOND]. May I remind you, Niko Mikadze, that I was against the lukewarm bath? [*To the* GOVERNOR'S WIFE] There's been a little error over warming the bath water, Your Grace.

SECOND DOCTOR [*equally polite*]. Mika Loladze, I'm afraid I can't agree with you. The temperature of the bath water was exactly what our great, beloved Mishiko Oboladze prescribed. More likely a slight draft during the night, Your Grace.

GOVERNOR'S WIFE. But do pay more attention to him. He looks feverish, Georgi.

FIRST DOCTOR [*bending over the* CHILD]. No cause for alarm, Your Grace. The bath water will be warmer. It won't occur again.

SECOND DOCTOR [*with a venomous glance at the* FIRST]. I won't forget that, my dear Mika Loladze. No cause for concern, Your Grace.

FAT PRINCE. Well, well, well! I always say: "A pain in my liver? Then the doctor gets fifty strokes on the soles of his feet." We live in a decadent age. In the old days one said: "Off with his head!"

GOVERNOR'S WIFE. Let's go into church. Very likely it's the draft here.

[*The procession of* FAMILY *and* SERVANTS *turns into the doorway. The* FAT PRINCE *follows, but the* GOVERNOR *is kept back by the* ADJUTANT, *a handsome young man. When the crowd of* PETITIONERS *has been driven off, a young dust-stained* RIDER, *his arm in a sling, remains behind.*]

ADJUTANT [*pointing at the* RIDER, *who steps forward*]. Won't you hear the messenger from the capital, Your Excellency? He arrived this morning. With confidential papers.

GOVERNOR. Not before Service, Shalva. But did you hear Brother Kazbeki wish me a happy Easter? Which is all very well, but I don't believe it did rain last night.

ADJUTANT [*nodding*]. We must investigate.

GOVERNOR. Yes, at once. Tomorrow.

[*They pass through the doorway. The* RIDER, *who has waited in vain for an audience, turns sharply round and, muttering a curse, goes off. Only one of the palace guards—*SIMON SHASHAVA—*remains at the door.*]

SINGER.

> The city is still.
>
> Pigeons strut in the church square.
>
> A soldier of the Palace Guard
>
> Is joking with a kitchen maid
>
> As she comes up from the river with a bundle.

[*A girl—*GRUSHA VASHNADZE—*comes through the gateway with a bundle made of large green leaves under her arm.*]

SIMON. What, the young lady is not in church? Shirking?

GRUSHA. I was dressed to go. But they needed

another goose for the banquet. And they asked me to get it. I know about geese.

SIMON. A goose? [*He feigns suspicion.*] I'd like to see that goose. [GRUSHA *does not understand.*] One must be on one's guard with women. "I only went for a fish," they tell you, but it turns out to be something else.

GRUSHA [*walking resolutely toward him and showing him the goose*]. There! If it isn't a fifteen-pound goose stuffed full of corn, I'll eat the feathers.

SIMON. A queen of a goose! The Governor himself will eat it. So the young lady has been down to the river again?

GRUSHA. Yes, at the poultry farm.

SIMON. Really? At the poultry farm, down by the river . . . not higher up maybe? Near those willows?

GRUSHA. I only go to the willows to wash the linen.

SIMON [*insinuatingly*]. Exactly.

GRUSHA. Exactly what?

SIMON [*winking*]. Exactly that.

GRUSHA. Why shouldn't I wash the linen by the willows?

SIMON [*with exaggerated laughter*]. "Why shouldn't I wash the linen by the willows!" That's good, really good!

GRUSHA. I don't understand the soldier. What's so good about it?

SIMON [*slyly*]. "If something I know someone learns, she'll grow hot and cold by turns!"

GRUSHA. I don't know what I could learn about those willows.

SIMON. Not even if there was a bush opposite? That one could see everything from? Everything that goes on there when a certain person is— "washing linen"?

GRUSHA. What does go on? Won't the soldier say what he means and have done?

SIMON. Something goes on. Something can be seen.

GRUSHA. Could the soldier mean I dip my toes in the water when it's hot? There's nothing else.

SIMON. There's more. Your toes. And more.

GRUSHA. More what? At most my foot?

SIMON. Your foot. And a little more. [*He laughs heartily.*]

GRUSHA [*angrily*]. Simon Shashava, you ought to be ashamed of yourself! To sit in a bush on a hot day and wait till a girl comes and dips her legs in the river! And I bet you bring a friend along too! [*She runs off.*]

SIMON [*shouting after her*]. I didn't bring any friend along!

[*As the* SINGER *resumes his tale, the* SOLDIER *steps into the doorway as though to listen to the service.*]

SINGER.

The city lies still
But why are there armed men?
The Governor's palace is at peace
But why is it a fortress?
And the Governor returned to his palace
And the fortress was a trap
And the goose was plucked and roasted
But the goose was not eaten this time
And noon was no longer the hour to eat:
Noon was the hour to die.

[*From the doorway at the left the* FAT PRINCE *quickly appears, stands still, looks around. Before the gateway at the right two* IRONSHIRTS *are squatting and playing dice. The* FAT PRINCE *sees them, walks slowly past, making a sign to them. They rise: one goes through the gateway, the other goes off at the right. Muffled voices are heard from various directions in the rear: "To your posts!" The palace is surrounded. The* FAT PRINCE *quickly goes off. Church bells in the distance. Enter, through the doorway, the Governor's family and procession, returning from church.*]

GOVERNOR'S WIFE [*passing the* ADJUTANT]. It's impossible to live in such a slum. But Georgi, of course, will only build for his little Michael. Never for me! Michael is all! All for Michael!

[*The procession turns into the gateway. Again the* ADJUTANT *lingers behind. He waits. Enter the wounded* RIDER *from the doorway. Two* IRONSHIRTS *of the Palace Guard have taken up positions by the gateway.*]

ADJUTANT [*to the* RIDER]. The Governor does not wish to receive military news before dinner—especially if it's depressing, as I assume. In the afternoon His Excellency will confer with prominent architects. They're coming to dinner too. And here they are! [*Enter three gentlemen through the doorway.*] Go to the kitchen and eat, my friend. [*As the* RIDER *goes, the* ADJUTANT *greets the* ARCHITECTS.] Gentlemen, His Excellency expects you at dinner. He will devote all his time to you and your great new plans. Come!

ONE OF THE ARCHITECTS. We marvel that His Excellency intends to build. There are disquieting rumors that the war in Persia has taken a turn for the worse.

ADJUTANT. All the more reason to build! There's nothing to those rumors anyway. Persia is a long way off, and the garrison here would let itself be hacked to bits for its Governor. [*Noise from the palace. The shrill scream of a woman. Someone is shouting orders. Dumbfounded, the* ADJUTANT *moves toward the gateway. An* IRONSHIRT *steps out, points his lance at him.*] What's this? Put down that lance, you dog.

ONE OF THE ARCHITECTS. It's the Princes! Don't you know the Princes met last night in the capital? And they're against the Grand Duke and his Governors? Gentlemen, we'd better make ourselves scarce. [*They rush off. The* ADJUTANT *remains helplessly behind.*]

ADJUTANT [*furiously to the Palace Guard*]. Down with those lances! Don't you see the Governor's life is threatened?

[*The* IRONSHIRTS *of the Palace Guard refuse to obey. They stare coldly and indifferently at the* ADJUTANT *and follow the next events without interest.*]

SINGER.

O blindness of the great!
They go their way like gods,
Great over bent backs,
Sure of hired fists,
Trusting in the power
Which has lasted so long.
But long is not forever.
O change from age to age!
Thou hope of the people!

[*Enter the* GOVERNOR, *through the gateway, between two* SOLDIERS *armed to the teeth. He is in chains. His face is gray.*]

Up, great sir, deign to walk upright!
From your palace the eyes of many foes follow
you!
And now you don't need an architect, a carpenter will do.
You won't be moving into a new palace
But into a little hole in the ground.
Look about you once more, blind man!

[*The arrested man looks round.*]

Does all you had please you?
Between the Easter Mass and the Easter meal
You are walking to a place whence no one
returns.

[*The* GOVERNOR *is led off. A horn sounds an alarm. Noise behind the gateway.*]

When the house of a great one collapses
Many little ones are slain.
Those who had no share in the *good* fortunes of the mighty
Often have a share in their *mis*fortunes.
The plunging wagon
Drags the sweating oxen down with it
Into the abyss.

[*The* SERVANTS *come rushing through the gateway in panic.*]

SERVANTS [*among themselves*].

—The baskets!
—Take them all into the third courtyard! Food for five days!
—The mistress has fainted! Someone must carry her down.
—She must get away.
—What about us? We'll be slaughtered like chickens, as always.
—Goodness, what'll happen? There's bloodshed already in the city, they say.
—Nonsense, the Governor has just been asked to appear at a Princes' meeting. All very correct. Everything'll be ironed out. I heard this on the best authority . . .

[*The two* DOCTORS *rush into the courtyard.*]

FIRST DOCTOR [*trying to restrain the other*]. Niko Mikadze, it is your duty as a doctor to attend Natella Abashwili.

SECOND DOCTOR. My duty! It's yours!

FIRST DOCTOR. Whose turn is it to look after the child today, Niko Mikadze, yours or mine?

SECOND DOCTOR. Do you really think, Mika Loladze, I'm going to stay a minute longer in this accursed house on that little brat's account? [*They start fighting. All one hears is:* "You neglect your duty!" *and* "Duty, my foot!" *Then the* SECOND DOCTOR *knocks the* FIRST *down.*] Go to hell! [Exit.]

[*Enter the soldier,* SIMON SHASHAVA. *He searches in the crowd for* GRUSHA.]

SIMON. Grusha! There you are at last! What are you going to do?

GRUSHA. Nothing. If worst comes to worst, I've a brother in the mountains. How about you?

SIMON. Forget about me. [*Formally again*] Grusha Vashnadze, your wish to know my plans fills me with satisfaction. I've been ordered to accompany Madam Abashwili as her guard.

GRUSHA. But hasn't the Palace Guard mutinied?

SIMON [*seriously*]. That's a fact.

GRUSHA. Isn't it dangerous to go with her?

SIMON. In Tiflis, they say: Isn't the stabbing dangerous for the knife?

GRUSHA. You're not a knife, you're a man, Simon Shashava, what has that woman to do with you?

SIMON. That woman has nothing to do with me. I have my orders, and I go.

GRUSHA. The soldier is pigheaded: he is running into danger for nothing—nothing at all. I must get into the third courtyard, I'm in a hurry.

SIMON. Since we're both in a hurry we shouldn't quarrel. You need time for a good quarrel. May I ask if the young lady still has parents?

GRUSHA. No, just a brother.

SIMON. As time is short—my second question is this: Is the young lady as healthy as a fish in water?

GRUSHA. I may have a pain in the right shoulder once in a while. Otherwise I'm strong enough for my job. No one has complained. So far.

SIMON. That's well known. When it's Easter Sunday, and the question arises who'll run for the goose all the same, she'll be the one. My third question is this: Is the young lady impatient? Does she want apples in winter?

GRUSHA. Impatient? No. But if a man goes to war without any reason and then no message comes—that's bad.

SIMON. A message will come. And now my final question . . .

GRUSHA. Simon Shashava, I must get to the third courtyard at once. My answer is yes.

SIMON [*very embarrassed*]. Haste, they say, is the wind that blows down the scaffolding. But they also say: The rich don't know what haste is. I'm from . . .

GRUSHA. Kutsk . . .

SIMON. The young lady has been inquiring about me? I'm healthy, I have no dependents, I make ten piasters a month, as paymaster twenty piasters, and I'm asking—very sincerely—for your hand.

GRUSHA. Simon Shashava, it suits me well.

SIMON [*taking from his neck a thin chain with a little cross on it*]. My mother gave me this cross, Grusha Vashnadze. The chain is silver. Please wear it.

GRUSHA. Many thanks, Simon.

SIMON [*hangs it round her neck*]. It would be better to go to the third courtyard now. Or there'll be difficulties. Anyway, I must harness the horses. The young lady will understand?

GRUSHA. Yes, Simon.

[*They stand undecided.*]

SIMON. I'll just take the mistress to the troops that have stayed loyal. When the war's over, I'll be back. In two weeks. Or three. I hope my intended won't get tired, awaiting my return.

GRUSHA.
Simon Shashava, I shall wait for you.
Go calmly into battle, soldier
The bloody battle, the bitter battle
From which not everyone returns:
When you return I shall be there.
I shall be waiting for you under the green elm
I shall be waiting for you under the bare elm
I shall wait until the last soldier has returned
And longer
When you come back from the battle
No boots will stand at my door
The pillow beside mine will be empty
And my mouth will be unkissed.
When you return, when you return
You will be able to say: It is just as it was.

SIMON. I thank you, Grusha Vashnadze. And good-bye!

[*He bows low before her. She does the same before him. Then she runs quickly off without looking round. Enter the* ADJUTANT *from the gateway.*]

ADJUTANT [*harshly*]. Harness the horses to the carriage! Don't stand there doing nothing, scum!

[SIMON SHASHAVA *stands to attention and goes off. Two* SERVANTS *crowd from the gateway, bent low under huge trunks. Behind them, supported by her women, stumbles* NATELLA ABASHWILI. *She is followed by a* WOMAN *carrying the* CHILD.]

GOVERNOR'S WIFE. I hardly know if my head's still on. Where's Michael? Don't hold him so clumsily. Pile the trunks onto the carriage. No news from the city, Shalva?

ADJUTANT. None. All's quiet so far, but there's not a minute to lose. No room for all those trunks in the carriage. Pick out what you need. [*Exit quickly.*]

GOVERNOR'S WIFE. Only essentials! Quick, open the trunks! I'll tell you what I need. [*The trunks are lowered and opened. She points at some brocade dresses.*] The green one! And, of course, the one with the fur trimming. Where are Niko Mikadze and Mika Loladze? I've suddenly got the most terrible migraine again. It always starts in the temples. [*Enter* GRUSHA.] Taking your time, eh? Go and get the hot water bottles this minute! [GRUSHA *runs off, returns later with hot water bottles; the* GOVERNOR'S WIFE *orders her about by signs.*] Don't tear the sleeves.

A YOUNG WOMAN. Pardon, madam, no harm has come to the dress.

GOVERNOR'S WIFE. Because I stopped you. I've been watching you for a long time. Nothing in your head but making eyes at Shalva Tzereteli. I'll kill you, you bitch! [*She beats the* YOUNG WOMAN.]

ADJUTANT [*appearing in the gateway*]. Please make haste, Natella Abashwili. Firing has broken out in the city. [*Exit.*]

GOVERNOR'S WIFE [*letting go of the* YOUNG WOMAN]. Oh dear, do you think they'll lay hands on us? Why should they? Why? [*She herself begins to rummage in the trunks.*] How's Michael? Asleep?

WOMAN WITH THE CHILD. Yes, madam.

GOVERNOR'S WIFE. Then put him down a moment and get my little saffron-colored boots from the bedroom. I need them for the green dress. [*The* WOMAN *puts down the* CHILD *and goes off.*] Just look how these things have been packed! No love! No understanding! If you don't give them every order yourself . . . At such moments you realize what kind of servants you have! They gorge themselves at your expense, and never a word of gratitude! I'll remember this.

ADJUTANT [*entering, very excited*]. Natella, you must leave at once!

GOVERNOR'S WIFE. Why? I've got to take this silver dress—it cost a thousand piasters. And that one there, and where's the wine-colored one?

ADJUTANT [*trying to pull her away*]. Riots have broken out! We must leave at once. Where's the baby?

GOVERNOR'S WIFE [*calling to the* YOUNG WOMAN *who was holding the baby*]. Maro, get the baby ready! Where on earth are you?

ADJUTANT [*leaving*]. We'll probably have to leave the carriage behind and go ahead on horse-back.

[*The* GOVERNOR'S WIFE *rummages again among her dresses, throws some onto the heap of chosen clothes, then takes them off again. Noises, drums are heard. The* YOUNG WOMAN *who was beaten creeps away. The sky begins to grow red.*]

GOVERNOR'S WIFE [*rummaging desperately*]. I simply cannot find the wine-colored dress. Take the whole pile to the carriage. Where's Asja? And why hasn't Maro come back? Have you all gone crazy?

ADJUTANT [*returning*]. Quick! Quick!

GOVERNOR'S WIFE [*to the* FIRST WOMAN]. Run! Just throw them into the carriage!

ADJUTANT. We're not taking the carriage. And if you don't come now, I'll ride off on my own.

GOVERNOR'S WIFE [*as the* FIRST WOMAN *can't carry everything*]. Where's that bitch Asja? [*The* ADJUTANT *pulls her away.*] Maro, bring the baby! [*To the* FIRST WOMAN] Go and look for Masha. No, first take the dresses to the carriage. Such nonsense! I wouldn't dream of going on horseback!

[*Turning round, she sees the red sky, and starts back rigid. The fire burns. She is pulled out by the* ADJUTANT. *Shaking, the* FIRST WOMAN *follows with the dresses.*]

MARO [*from the doorway with the boots*]. Madam! [*She sees the trunks and dresses and runs toward the* CHILD, *picks it up, and holds it a moment.*] They left it behind, the beasts. [*She hands it to* GRUSHA.] Hold it a moment. [*She runs off, following the* GOVERNOR'S WIFE.]

[*Enter* SERVANTS *from the gateway.*]

COOK. Well, so they've actually gone. Without the food wagons, and not a minute too early. It's time for us to clear out.

GROOM. This'll be an unhealthy neighborhood for quite a while. [*To one of the* WOMEN] Suliko, take a few blankets and wait for me in the foal stables.

GRUSHA. What have they done with the Governor?

GROOM [*gesturing throat cutting*]. Fffft.

A FAT WOMAN [*seeing the gesture and becoming hysterical*]. Oh dear, oh dear, oh dear, oh dear! Our master Georgi Abashwili! A picture of health he was, at the morning Mass—and now! Oh, take me away, we're all lost, we must die in sin like our master, Georgi Abashwili!

OTHER WOMAN [*soothing her*]. Calm down, Nina! You'll be taken to safety. You've never hurt a fly.

FAT WOMAN [*being led out*]. Oh dear, oh dear, oh dear! Quick! Let's all get out before they come, before they come!

A YOUNG WOMAN. Nina takes it more to heart than the mistress, that's a fact. They even have to have their weeping done for them.

COOK. We'd better get out, all of us.

ANOTHER WOMAN [*glancing back*]. That must be the East Gate burning.

YOUNG WOMAN [*seeing the* CHILD *in* GRUSHA's *arms*]. The baby! What are you doing with it?

GRUSHA. It got left behind.

YOUNG WOMAN. She simply left it there. Michael, who was kept out of all the drafts!

[*The* SERVANTS *gather round the* CHILD.]

GRUSHA. He's waking up.

GROOM. Better put him down, I tell you. I'd rather not think what'd happen to anybody who was found with that baby.

COOK. That's right. Once they get started, they'll kill each other off, whole families at a time. Let's go.

[*Exeunt all but* GRUSHA, *with the* CHILD *on her arm, and* TWO WOMEN.]

TWO WOMEN. Didn't you hear? Better put him down.

GRUSHA. The nurse asked me to hold him a moment.

OLDER WOMAN. She's not coming back, you simpleton.

YOUNGER WOMAN. Keep your hands off it.

OLDER WOMAN [*amiably*]. Grusha, you're a good soul, but you're not very bright, and you know it. I tell you, if he had the plague he couldn't be more dangerous.

GRUSHA [*stubbornly*]. He hasn't got the plague. He looks at me! He's human!

OLDER WOMAN. Don't look at *him*. You're a fool —the kind that always gets put upon. A person need only say, "Run for the salad, you have the longest legs," and you run. My husband has an ox cart—you can come with us if you hurry! Lord, by now the whole neighborhood must be in flames.

[*Both women leave, sighing. After some hesitation,* GRUSHA *puts the sleeping* CHILD *down, looks at it for a moment, then takes a brocade blanket from the heap of clothes and covers it. Then both women return, dragging bundles.* GRUSHA *starts guiltily away from the* CHILD *and walks a few steps to one side.*]

YOUNGER WOMAN. Haven't you packed anything yet? There isn't much time, you know. The Iron-shirts will be here from the barracks.

GRUSHA. Coming!

[*She runs through the doorway. Both women go to the gateway and wait. The sound of horses is heard. They flee, screaming. Enter the* FAT PRINCE *with drunken* IRONSHIRTS. *One of them carries the Governor's head on a lance.*]

FAT PRINCE. Here! In the middle! [*One soldier climbs onto the other's back, takes the head, holds it tentatively over the door.*] That's not the middle. Farther to the right. That's it. What I do, my friends, I do well. [*While with hammer and nail, the soldier fastens the head to the wall by its hair*] This morning at the church door I said to Georgi Abashwili: "I love a gay sky." Actually, I prefer the lightning that comes out of a gay sky. Yes, indeed. It's a pity they took the brat along, though, I need him, urgently.

[*Exit with* IRONSHIRTS *through the gateway. Trampling of horses again. Enter* GRUSHA *through the doorway looking cautiously about her. Clearly she has waited for the* IRONSHIRTS *to go. Carrying a bundle, she walks toward the gateway. At the last moment, she turns to see if the* CHILD *is still there. Catching sight of the head over the doorway, she screams. Horrified, she picks up her bundle again, and is about to leave when the* SINGER *starts to speak. She stands rooted to the spot.*]

SINGER.

As she was standing between courtyard and gate,

She heard or she thought she heard a low voice calling.

The child called to her,

Not whining, but calling quite sensibly,

Or so it seemed to her.

"Woman," it said, "help me."

And it went on, not whining, but saying quite sensibly:

"Know, woman, he who hears not a cry for help

But passes by with troubled ears will never hear

The gentle call of a lover nor the blackbird at dawn

Nor the happy sigh of the tired grape-picker as the Angelus rings."

[*She walks a few steps toward the* CHILD *and bends over it.*]

Hearing this she went back for one more look at the child:

Only to sit with him for a moment or two,

Only till someone should come,

His mother, or anyone.

[*Leaning on a trunk, she sits facing the* CHILD.]

Only till she would have to leave, for the danger was too great,

The city was full of flame and crying.

[*The light grows dimmer, as though evening and night were coming on.*]

Fearful is the seductive power of goodness!

[GRUSHA *now settles down to watch over the* CHILD *through the night. Once, she lights a small lamp to look at it. Once, she tucks it in with a coat. From time to time she listens and looks to see whether someone is coming.*]

> And she sat with the child a long time,
> Till evening came, till night came, till dawn came.
> She sat too long, too long she saw
> The soft breathing, the small clenched fists,
> Till toward morning the seduction was complete
> ~~And she rose, and bent down and, sighing, took the child~~
> And carried it away.

[*She does what the* SINGER *says as he describes it.*]

> As if it was stolen goods she picked it up.
> As if she was a thief she crept away.

2

THE FLIGHT INTO THE NORTHERN MOUNTAINS

SINGER.
> When Grusha Vashnadze left the city
> On the Grusinian highway
> On the way to the Northern Mountains
> She sang a song, she bought some milk.

CHORUS.
> How will this human child escape
> The bloodhounds, the trap-setters?
> Into the deserted mountains she journeyed
> Along the Grusinian highway she journeyed
> She sang a song, she bought some milk.

[GRUSHA VASHNADZE *walks on. On her back she carries the* CHILD *in a sack, in one hand is a large stick, in the other a bundle. She sings.*]

THE SONG OF THE FOUR GENERALS

> Four generals
> Set out for Iran.
> With the first one, war did not agree.
> The second never won a victory.
> For the third the weather never was right.
> For the fourth the men would never fight.
> Four generals
> And not a single man!

> Sosso Robakidse
> Went marching to Iran
> With him the war did so agree
> He soon had won a victory.
> For him the weather was always right.
> For him the men would always fight.
> Sosso Robakidse,
> He is our man!

[*A peasant's cottage appears.*]

GRUSHA [*to the* CHILD]. Noontime is meal time. Now we'll sit hopefully in the grass, while the good Grusha goes and buys a little pitcher of milk. [*She lays the* CHILD *down and knocks at the cottage door. An* OLD MAN *opens it.*] Grandfather, could I have a little pitcher of milk? And a corn cake, maybe?

OLD MAN. Milk? We have no milk. The soldiers from the city have our goats. Go to the soldiers if you want milk.

GRUSHA. But grandfather, you must have a little pitcher of milk for a baby?

OLD MAN. And for a God-bless-you, eh?

GRUSHA. Who said anything about a God-bless-you? [*She shows her purse.*] We'll pay like princes. "Head in the clouds, backside in the water." [*The peasant goes off, grumbling, for milk.*] How much for the milk?

OLD MAN. Three piasters. Milk has gone up.

GRUSHA. Three piasters for this little drop? [*Without a word the* OLD MAN *shuts the door in her face.*] Michael, did you hear that? Three piasters! We can't afford it! [*She goes back, sits down again, and gives the* CHILD *her breast.*] Suck. Think of the three piasters. There's nothing there, but you *think* you're drinking, and that's something. [*Shaking her head, she sees that the* CHILD *isn't sucking any more. She gets up, walks back to the door, and knocks again.*] Open, grandfather, we'll pay. [*Softly*] May lightning strike you! [*When the* OLD MAN *appears*] I thought it would be half a piaster. But the baby must be fed. How about one piaster for that little drop?

OLD MAN. Two.

GRUSHA. Don't shut the door again. [*She fishes a long time in her bag.*] Here are two piasters. The milk better be good. I still have two days' journey ahead of me. It's a murderous business you have here—and sinful, too!

OLD MAN. Kill the soldiers if you want milk.

GRUSHA [*giving the* CHILD *some milk*]. This is an expensive joke. Take a sip, Michael, it's a week's pay. Around here they think we earned our money just sitting on our behinds. Oh, Michael, Michael, you're a nice little load for a girl to take on! [*Uneasy, she gets up, puts the* CHILD *on her back, and walks on. The* OLD MAN, *grumbling, picks up the pitcher and looks after her unmoved.*]

SINGER.

As Grusha Vashnadze went northward
The Princes' Ironshirts went after her.

CHORUS.

How will the barefoot girl escape the Iron-shirts,
The bloodhounds, the trap-setters?
They hunt even by night.
Pursuers never tire.
Butchers sleep little.

[*Two* IRONSHIRTS *are trudging along the highway.*]

CORPORAL. You'll never amount to anything, blockhead, your heart's not in it. Your senior officer sees this in little things. Yesterday, when I made the fat gal, yes, you grabbed her husband as I commanded, and you did kick him in the belly, at my request, but did you *enjoy* it, like a loyal Private, or were you just doing your duty? I've kept an eye on you blockhead, you're a hollow reed and a tinkling cymbal, you won't get promoted. [*They walk a while in silence.*] Don't think I've forgotten how insubordinate you are, either. Stop limping! I forbid you to limp! You limp because I sold the horses, and I sold the horses because I'd never have got that price again. You limp to show me you don't like marching. I know you. It won't help. You wait. Sing!

TWO IRONSHIRTS [*singing*].

Sadly to war I went my way
Leaving my loved one at her door.
My friends will keep her honor safe
Till from the war I'm back once more.

CORPORAL. Louder!

TWO IRONSHIRTS [*singing*].

When 'neath a headstone I shall be
My love a little earth will bring:
"Here rest the feet that oft would run to me
And here the arms that oft to me would cling."

[*They begin to walk again in silence.*]

CORPORAL. A good soldier has his heart and soul in it. When he receives an order, he gets a hard-on, and when he drives his lance into the enemy's guts, he comes. [*He shouts for joy.*] He lets himself be torn to bits for his superior officer, and as he lies dying he takes note that his corporal is nodding approval, and that is reward enough, it's his dearest wish. *You* won't get any nod of approval, but you'll croak all right. Christ, how'm I to get my hands on the Governor's bastard with the help of a fool like you! [*They stay on stage behind.*]

SINGER.

When Grusha Vashnadze came to the River Sirra

Flight grew too much for her, the helpless child too heavy.
In the cornfields the rosy dawn
Is cold to the sleepless one, only cold.
The gay clatter of the milk cans in the farm-yard where the smoke rises
Is only a threat to the fugitive.
She who carries the child feels its weight and little more.

[GRUSHA *stops in front of a farm. A fat* PEASANT WOMAN *is carrying a milk can through the door.* GRUSHA *waits until she has gone in, then approaches the house cautiously.*]

GRUSHA [*to the* CHILD]. Now you've wet yourself again, and you know I've no linen. Michael, this is where we part company. It's far enough from the city. They wouldn't want you *so* much that they'd follow you all *this* way, little good-for-nothing. The peasant woman is kind, and can't you just smell the milk? (*She bends down to lay the* CHILD *on the threshold.*) So farewell, Michael, I'll forget how you kicked me in the back all night to make me walk faster. And you can forget the meager fare—it was meant well. I'd like to have kept you—your nose is so tiny—but it can't be. I'd have shown you your first rabbit, I'd have trained you to keep dry, but now I must turn around. My sweetheart the soldier might be back soon, and suppose he didn't find me? You can't ask that, can you? [*She creeps up to the door and lays the* CHILD *on the threshold. Then, hiding behind a tree, she waits until the* PEASANT WOMAN *opens the door and sees the bundle.*]

PEASANT WOMAN. Good heavens, what's this? Husband!

PEASANT. What is it? Let me finish my soup.

PEASANT WOMAN [*to the* CHILD]. Where's your mother then? Haven't you got one? It's a boy. Fine linen. He's from a good family, you can see that. And they just leave him on our doorstep. Oh, these are times!

PEASANT. If they think we're going to feed it,

they're wrong. You can take it to the priest in the village. That's the best we can do.

PEASANT WOMAN. What'll the priest do with him? He needs a mother. There, he's waking up. Don't you think we could keep him, though?

PEASANT [*shouting*]. No!

PEASANT WOMAN. I could lay him in the corner by the armchair. All I need is a crib. I can take him into the fields with me. See him laughing? Husband, we have a roof over our heads. We can do it. Not another word out of you!

[*She carries the* CHILD *into the house. The* PEASANT *follows protesting.* GRUSHA *steps out from behind the tree, laughs, and hurries off in the opposite direction.*]

SINGER.
    Why so cheerful, making for home?
CHORUS.
    Because the child has won new parents with
        a laugh,
    Because I'm rid of the little one, I'm cheerful.
SINGER.
    And why so sad?
CHORUS.
    Because I'm single and free, I'm sad
    Like someone who's been robbed
    Someone who's newly poor.

[*She walks for a short while, then meets the two* IRONSHIRTS *who point their lances at her.*]

CORPORAL. Lady, you are running straight into the arms of the Armed Forces. Where are you coming from? And when? Are you having illicit relations with the enemy? Where is he hiding? What movements is he making in your rear? How about the hills? How about the valleys? How are your stockings held in position? [GRUSHA *stands there frightened.*] Don't be scared, we always withdraw, if necessary . . . what, blockhead? I always withdraw. In that respect at least, I can be relied on. Why are you staring like that at my lance? In the field no soldier drops his lance, that's a rule. Learn it by heart, blockhead. Now, lady, where are you headed?

GRUSHA. To meet my intended, one Simon Shashava, of the Palace Guard in Nuka.

CORPORAL. Simon Shashava? Sure, I know him. He gave me the key so I could look you up once in a while. Blockhead, we are getting to be unpopular. We must make her realize we have honorable intentions. Lady, behind apparent frivolity I conceal a serious nature, so let me tell you officially: I want a child from you. [GRUSHA *utters a little*

scream.] Blockhead, she understands me. Uh-huh, isn't it a sweet shock? "Then first I must take the noodles out of the oven, Officer. Then first I must change my torn shirt, Colonel." But away with jokes, away with my lance! We are looking for a baby. A baby from a good family. Have you heard of such a baby, from the city, dressed in fine linen, and suddenly turning up here?

GRUSHA. No, I haven't heard a thing. [*Suddenly she turns round and runs back, panic-stricken. The* IRONSHIRTS *glance at each other, then follow her, cursing.*]

SINGER.
    Run, kind girl! The killers are coming!
    Help the helpless babe, helpless girl!
    And so she runs!
CHORUS.
    In the bloodiest times
    There are kind people.

[*As* GRUSHA *rushes into the cottage, the* PEASANT WOMAN *is bending over the* CHILD'*s crib.*]

GRUSHA. Hide him. Quick! The Ironshirts are coming! I laid him on your doorstep. But he isn't mine. He's from a good family.

PEASANT WOMAN. Who's coming? What Ironshirts?

GRUSHA. Don't ask questions. The Ironshirts that are looking for it.

PEASANT WOMAN. They've no business in my house. But I must have a little talk with you, it seems.

GRUSHA. Take off the fine linen. It'll give us away.

PEASANT WOMAN. Linen, my foot! In this house I make the decisions! "*You* can't vomit in *my* room!" Why did you abandon it? It's a sin.

GRUSHA [*looking out of the window*]. Look, they're coming out from behind those trees! I shouldn't have run away, it made them angry. Oh, what shall I do?

PEASANT WOMAN [*looking out of the window and suddenly starting with fear*]. Gracious! Ironshirts!

GRUSHA. They're after the baby.

PEASANT WOMAN. Suppose they come in!

GRUSHA. You mustn't give him to them. Say he's yours.

PEASANT WOMAN. Yes.

GRUSHA. They'll run him through if you hand him over.

PEASANT WOMAN. But suppose they ask for it? The silver for the harvest is in the house.

GRUSHA. If you let them have him, they'll run him through, right here in this room! You've got to say he's yours!

PEASANT WOMAN. Yes. But what if they don't believe me?

GRUSHA. You must be firm.

PEASANT WOMAN. They'll burn the roof over our heads.

GRUSHA. That's why you must say he's yours. His name's Michael. But I shouldn't have told you. [The PEASANT WOMAN nods.] Don't nod like that. And don't tremble—they'll notice.

PEASANT WOMAN. Yes.

GRUSHA. And stop saying yes, I can't stand it. [She shakes the WOMAN.] Don't you have any children?

PEASANT WOMAN [muttering]. He's in the war.

GRUSHA. Then maybe he's an Ironshirt? Do you want him to run children through with a lance? You'd bawl him out. "No fooling with lances in my house!" you'd shout, "is that what I've reared you for? Wash your neck before you speak to your mother!"

PEASANT WOMAN. That's true, he couldn't get away with anything around here!

GRUSHA. So you'll say he's yours?

PEASANT WOMAN. Yes.

GRUSHA. Look! They're coming!

[There is a knocking at the door. The women don't answer. Enter IRONSHIRTS. The PEASANT WOMAN bows low.]

CORPORAL. Well, here she is. What did I tell you? What a nose I have! I smelt her. Lady, I have a question for you. Why did you run away? What did you think I would do to you? I'll bet it was something unchaste. Confess!

GRUSHA [while the PEASANT WOMAN bows again and again]. I'd left some milk on the stove, and I suddenly remembered it.

CORPORAL. Or maybe you imagined I looked at you unchastely? Like there could be something between us? A carnal glance, know what I mean?

GRUSHA. I didn't see it.

CORPORAL. But it's possible, huh? You admit that much. After all, I might be a pig. I'll be frank with you: I could think of all sorts of things if we were alone. [To the PEASANT WOMAN] Shouldn't you be busy in the yard? Feeding the hens?

PEASANT WOMAN [falling suddenly to her knees]. Soldier, I didn't know a thing about it. Please don't burn the roof over our heads.

CORPORAL. What are you talking about?

PEASANT WOMAN. I had nothing to do with it. She left it on my doorstep, I swear it.

CORPORAL [suddenly seeing the CHILD and whistling]. Ah, so there's a little something in the crib! Blockhead, I smell a thousand piasters. Take the girl outside and hold on to her. It looks like I have a little cross-examining to do. [The PEASANT WOMAN lets herself be led out by the PRIVATE, without a word.] So, you've got the child I wanted from you! [He walks toward the crib.]

GRUSHA. Officer, he's mine. He's not the one you're after.

CORPORAL. I'll just take a look. [He bends over the crib. GRUSHA looks round in despair.]

GRUSHA. He's mine! He's mine!

CORPORAL. Fine linen!

[GRUSHA dashes at him to pull him away. He throws her off and again bends over the crib. Again looking round in despair, she sees a log of wood, seizes it, and hits the CORPORAL over the head from behind. The CORPORAL collapses. She quickly picks up the CHILD and rushes off.]

SINGER.

> And in her flight from the Ironshirts
> After twenty-two days of journeying
> At the foot of the Janga-Tau Glacier
> Grusha Vashnadze decided to adopt the child.

CHORUS.

> The helpless girl adopted the helpless child.

[GRUSHA squats over a half-frozen stream to get the CHILD water in the hollow of her hand.]

GRUSHA.

> Since no one else will take you, son,
> I must take you.
> Since no one else will take you, son,
> You must take me.
> O black day in a lean, lean year,
> The trip was long, the milk was dear,
> My legs are tired, my feet are sore:
> But I wouldn't be without you any more.
> I'll throw your silken shirt away
> And wrap you in rags and tatters.
> I'll wash you, son, and christen you in glacier
>   water.
> We'll see it through together.

[She has taken off the CHILD's fine linen and wrapped it in a rag.]

SINGER.

> When Grusha Vashnadze
> Pursued by the Ironshirts
> Came to the bridge on the glacier
> Leading to the villages of the Eastern Slope

She sang the Song of the Rotten Bridge
And risked two lives.

[*A wind has risen. The bridge on the glacier is visible in the dark. One rope is broken and half the bridge is hanging down the abyss.* MERCHANTS, *two men and a woman, stand undecided before the bridge as* GRUSHA *and the* CHILD *arrive. One man is trying to catch the hanging rope with a stick.*]

FIRST MAN. Take your time, young woman. You won't get across here anyway.

GRUSHA. But I *have* to get the baby to the east side. To my brother's place.

MERCHANT WOMAN. Have to? How d'you mean, "have to"? I have to get there, too—because I have to buy carpets in Atum—carpets a woman had to sell because her husband had to die. But can *I* do what I have to? Can she? Andrei's been fishing for that rope for hours. And I ask you, how are we going to fasten it, even if he gets it up?

FIRST MAN [*listening*]. Hush, I think I hear something.

GRUSHA. The bridge isn't quite rotted through. I think I'll try it.

MERCHANT WOMAN. *I* wouldn't—if the devil himself were after me. It's suicide.

FIRST MAN [*shouting*]. Hi!

GRUSHA. Don't shout! [*To the* MERCHANT WOMAN] Tell him not to shout.

FIRST MAN. But there's someone down there calling. Maybe they've lost their way.

MERCHANT WOMAN. Why shouldn't he shout? Is there something funny about you? Are they after you?

GRUSHA. All right, I'll tell. The Ironshirts are after me. I knocked one down.

SECOND MAN. Hide our merchandise!

[*The* WOMAN *hides a sack behind a rock.*]

FIRST MAN. Why didn't you say so right away? [*To the others*] If they catch her they'll make mincemeat out of her!

GRUSHA. Get out of my way. I've got to cross that bridge.

SECOND MAN. You can't. The precipice is two thousand feet deep.

FIRST MAN. Even with the rope it'd be of no use. We could hold it up with our hands. But then we'd have to do the same for the Ironshirts.

GRUSHA. Go away.

[*There are calls from the distance:* "Hi, up there!"]

MERCHANT WOMAN. They're getting near. But you can't take the child on that bridge. It's sure to break. And look!

[GRUSHA *looks down into the abyss. The* IRONSHIRTS *are heard calling again from below.*]

SECOND MAN. Two thousand feet!

GRUSHA. But those men are worse.

FIRST MAN. You can't do it. Think of the baby. Risk your life but not a child's.

SECOND MAN. With the child she's that much heavier!

MERCHANT WOMAN. Maybe she's *really* got to get across. Give *me* the baby. I'll hide it. Cross the bridge alone!

GRUSHA. I won't. We belong together. [*To the* CHILD] "Live together, die together." [*She sings.*]

THE SONG OF THE ROTTEN BRIDGE

> Deep is the abyss, son,
> I see the weak bridge sway
> But it's not for us, son,
> To choose the way.
>
> The way I know
> Is the one you must tread,
> And all you will eat
> Is my bit of bread.
>
> Of every four pieces
> You shall have three.
> Would that I knew
> How big they will be!

Get out of my way, I'll try it without the rope.

MERCHANT WOMAN. You are tempting God!

[*There are shouts from below.*]

GRUSHA. Please throw that stick away, or they'll get the rope and follow me. [*Pressing the* CHILD *to her, she steps onto the swaying bridge. The* MERCHANT WOMAN *screams when it looks as though the bridge is about to collapse. But* GRUSHA *walks on and reaches the far side.*]

FIRST MAN. She made it!

MERCHANT WOMAN [*who has fallen on her knees and begun to pray, angrily*]. I still think it was a sin.

[*The* IRONSHIRTS *appear; the* CORPORAL's *head is bandaged.*]

CORPORAL. Seen a woman with a child?

FIRST MAN [*while the* SECOND MAN *throws the stick into the abyss*]. Yes, there! but the bridge won't carry you!

CORPORAL. You'll pay for this, blockhead!

[GRUSHA, *from the far bank, laughs and shows*

the CHILD *to the* IRONSHIRTS. *She walks on. The wind blows.*]

GRUSHA [*turning to the* CHILD]. You mustn't be afraid of the wind. He's a poor thing too. He has to push the clouds along and he gets quite cold doing it. [*Snow starts falling.*] And the snow isn't so bad, either, Michael. It covers the little fir trees so they won't die in winter. Let me sing you a little song. [*She sings.*]

THE SONG OF THE CHILD

Your father is a bandit
A harlot the mother who bore you.
Yet honorable men
Shall kneel down before you.
Food to the baby horses
The tiger's son will take.
The mothers will get milk
From the son of the snake.

3

IN THE NORTHERN MOUNTAINS

SINGER.

Seven days the sister, Grusha Vashnadze,
Journeyed across the glacier
And down the slopes she journeyed.
"When I enter my brother's house," she thought,
"He will rise and embrace me."
"Is that you, sister?" he will say,
"I have long expected you.
This is my dear wife,
And this is my farm, come to me by marriage,
With eleven horses and thirty-one cows. Sit down.
Sit down with your child at our table and eat."
The brother's house was in a lovely valley.
When the sister came to the brother,
She was ill from walking.
The brother rose from the table.

[*A fat peasant couple rise from the table.* LAVRENTI VASHNADZE *still has a napkin round his neck, as* GRUSHA, *pale and supported by a* SERVANT, *enters with the* CHILD.]

LAVRENTI. Where've *you* come from, Grusha?

GRUSHA [*feebly*]. Across the Janga-Tu Pass, Lavrenti.

SERVANT. I found her in front of the hay barn. She has a baby with her.

SISTER-IN-LAW. Go and groom the mare.

[*Exit the* SERVANT.]

LAVRENTI. This is my wife Aniko.

SISTER-IN-LAW. I thought you were in service in Nuka.

GRUSHA [*barely able to stand*]. Yes, I was.

SISTER-IN-LAW. Wasn't it a good job? We were told it was.

GRUSHA. The Governor got killed.

LAVRENTI. Yes, we heard there were riots. Your aunt told us. Remember, Aniko?

SISTER-IN-LAW. Here with us, it's very quiet. City people always want something going on. [*She walks toward the door, calling*] Sosso, Sosso, don't take the cake out of the oven yet, d'you hear? Where on earth are you? [*Exit, calling.*]

LAVRENTI [*quietly, quickly*]. Is there a father? [*As she shakes her head*] I thought not. We must think up something. She's religious.

SISTER-IN-LAW [*returning*]. Those servants! [*To* GRUSHA] You have a child.

GRUSHA: It's mine. [*She collapses.* LAVRENTI *rushes to her assistance.*]

SISTER-IN-LAW. Heavens, she's ill—what are we going to do?

LAVRENTI [*escorting her to a bench near the stove*]. Sit down, sit. I think it's just weakness, Aniko.

SISTER-IN-LAW. As long as it's not scarlet fever!

LAVRENTI. She'd have spots if it was. It's only weakness. Don't worry, Aniko. [*To* GRUSHA] Better, sitting down?

SISTER-IN-LAW. Is the child hers?

GRUSHA. Yes, mine.

LAVRENTI. She's on her way to her husband.

SISTER-IN-LAW. I see. Your meat's getting cold. [LAVRENTI *sits down and begins to eat.*] Cold food's not good for you, the fat mustn't get cold, you know your stomach's your weak spot. [*To* GRUSHA] If your husband's not in the city, where is he?

LAVRENTI. She got married on the other side of the mountain, she says.

SISTER-IN-LAW. On the other side of the mountain. I see. [*She also sits down to eat.*]

GRUSHA. I think I should lie down somewhere, Lavrenti.

SISTER-IN-LAW. If it's consumption we'll all get it. [*She goes on cross-examining her.*] Has your husband got a farm?

GRUSHA. He's a soldier.

LAVRENTI. But he's coming into a farm—a small one—from his father.

SISTER-IN-LAW. Isn't he in the war? Why not?

GRUSHA [with effort]. Yes, he's in the war.

SISTER-IN-LAW. Then why d'you want to go to the farm?

LAVRENTI. When he comes back from the war, he'll return to his farm.

SISTER-IN-LAW. But you're going there now?

LAVRENTI. Yes, to wait for him.

SISTER-IN-LAW [calling shrilly]. Sosso, the cake!

GRUSHA [murmuring feverishly]. A farm—a soldier—waiting—sit down, eat.

SISTER-IN-LAW. It's scarlet fever.

GRUSHA [starting up]. Yes, he's got a farm!

LAVRENTI. I think it's just weakness, Aniko. Would you look after the cake yourself, dear?

SISTER-IN-LAW. But when will he come back if war's broken out again as people say? [She waddles off, shouting] Sosso! Where on earth are you? Sosso!

LAVRENTI [getting up quickly and going to GRUSHA]. You'll get a bed in a minute. She has a good heart. But wait till after supper.

GRUSHA [holding out the CHILD to him]. Take him.

LAVRENTI [taking it and looking around]. But you can't stay here long with the child. She's religious, you see.

[GRUSHA collapses. LAVRENTI catches her.]

SINGER.

The sister was so ill,
The cowardly brother had to give her shelter.
Summer departed, winter came.
The winter was long, the winter was short.
People mustn't know anything.
Rats mustn't bite.
Spring mustn't come.

[GRUSHA sits over the weaving loom in a workroom. She and the CHILD, who is squatting on the floor, are wrapped in blankets. She sings.]

THE SONG OF THE CENTER

And the lover started to leave
And his betrothed ran pleading after him
Pleading and weeping, weeping and teaching:
"Dearest mine, dearest mine
When you go to war as now you do
When you fight the foe as soon you will
Don't lead with the front line

And don't push with the rear line
At the front is red fire
In the rear is red smoke
Stay in the war's center
Stay near the standard bearer
The first always die
The last are also hit
Those in the center come home."

Michael, we must be clever. If we make ourselves as small as cockroaches, the sister-in-law will forget we're in the house, and then we can stay till the snow melts.

[Enter LAVRENTI. He sits down beside his sister.]

LAVRENTI. Why are you sitting there muffled up like coachmen, you two? Is it too cold in the room?

GRUSHA [hastily removing one shawl]. It's not too cold, Lavrenti.

LAVRENTI. If it's too cold, you shouldn't be sitting here with the child. Aniko would never forgive herself! [Pause.] I hope our priest didn't question you about the child?

GRUSHA. He did, but I didn't tell him anything.

LAVRENTI. That's good. I wanted to speak to you about Aniko. She has a good heart but she's very, very sensitive. People need only mention our farm and she's worried. She takes everything hard, you see. One time our milkmaid went to church with a hole in her stocking. Ever since, Aniko has worn two pairs of stockings in church. It's the old family in her. [He listens.] Are you sure there are no rats around? If there are rats, you couldn't live here. [There are sounds as of dripping from the roof.] What's that, dripping?

GRUSHA. It must be a barrel leaking.

LAVRENTI. Yes, it must be a barrel. You've been here six months, haven't you? Was I talking about Aniko? [They listen again to the snow melting.] You can't imagine how worried she gets about your soldier-husband. "Suppose he comes back and can't find her!" she says and lies awake. "He can't come before the spring," I tell her. The dear woman! [The drops begin to fall faster.] When d'you think he'll come? What do you think? [GRUSHA is silent.] Not before the spring, you agree? [GRUSHA is silent.] You don't believe he'll come at all? [GRUSHA is silent.] But when the spring comes and the snow melts here and on the passes, you can't stay on. They may come and look for you. There's already talk of an illegitimate child. [The "glockenspiel" of the falling drops has *grown faster and steadier.*] Grusha, the snow is melting on the roof. Spring is here.

GRUSHA. Yes.

LAVRENTI [*eagerly*]. I'll tell you what we'll do. You need a place to go, and, because of the child [*he sighs*], you have to have a husband, so people won't talk. Now I've made cautious inquiries to see if we can find you a husband. Grusha, I *have* one. I talked to a peasant woman who has a son. Just the other side of the mountain. A small farm. And she's willing.

GRUSHA. But I *can't* marry! I must wait for Simon Shashava.

LAVRENTI. Of course. That's all been taken care of. You don't need a man in bed—you need a man on paper. And I've found you one. The son of this peasant woman is going to die. Isn't that wonderful? He's at his last gasp. And all in line with our story—a husband from the other side of the mountain! And when you met him he was at the last gasp. So you're a widow. What do you say?

GRUSHA. It's true I could use a document with stamps on it for Michael.

LAVRENTI. Stamps make all the difference. Without something in writing the Shah couldn't prove he's a Shah. And you'll have a place to live.

GRUSHA. How much does the peasant woman want?

LAVRENTI. Four hundred piasters.

GRUSHA. Where will you find it?

LAVRENTI [*guiltily*]. Aniko's milk money.

GRUSHA. No one would know us there. I'll do it.

LAVRENTI [*getting up*]. I'll let the peasant woman know.

[*Quick exit.*]

GRUSHA. Michael, you make a lot of work. I came by you as the pear tree comes by sparrows. And because a Christian bends down and picks up a crust of bread so nothing will go to waste. Michael, it would have been better had I walked quickly away on that Easter Sunday in Nuka in the second courtyard. Now I *am* a fool.

SINGER.

> The bridegroom was on his deathbed when the bride arrived.
> The bridegroom's mother was waiting at the door, telling her to hurry.
> The bride brought a child along.
> The witness hid it during the wedding.

[*On one side the bed. Under the mosquito net lies a very sick man.* GRUSHA *is pulled in at a run by her future mother-in-law. They are followed by* LAVRENTI *and the* CHILD.]

MOTHER-IN-LAW. Quick! Quick! Or he'll die on us before the wedding. [*To* LAVRENTI]I was never told she had a child already.

LAVRENTI. What difference does it make? [*Pointing toward the dying man*] It can't matter to him —in his condition.

MOTHER-IN-LAW. To him? But I'll never survive the shame! We are honest people. [*She begins to weep.*] My Jussup doesn't have to marry a girl with a child!

LAVRENTI. All right, make it another two hundred piasters. You'll have it in writing that the farm will go to you: but she'll have the right to live here for two years.

MOTHER-IN-LAW [*drying her tears*]. It'll hardly cover the funeral expenses. I hope she'll really lend a hand with the work. And what's happened to the monk? He must have slipped out through the kitchen window. We'll have the whole village on our necks when they hear Jussup's end is come! Oh dear, I'll go get the monk. But he musn't see the child!

LAVRENTI. I'll take care he doesn't. But why only a monk? Why not a priest?

MOTHER-IN-LAW. Oh, he's just as good. I only made one mistake. I paid half his fee in advance. Enough to send him to the tavern. I only hope . . . [*She runs off.*]

LAVRENTI. She saved on the priest, the wretch! Hired a cheap monk.

GRUSHA. You *will* send Simon Shashava to see me if he turns up after all?

LAVRENTI. Yes. [*Pointing at the* SICK PEASANT] Won't you take a look at him? [GRUSHA, *taking* MICHAEL *to her, shakes her head.*] He's not moving an eyelid. I hope we aren't too late.

[*They listen. On the opposite side enter neighbors who look around and take up positions against the walls, thus forming another wall near the bed, yet leaving an opening so that the bed can be seen. They start murmuring prayers. Enter the* MOTHER-IN-LAW *with a* MONK. *Showing some annoyance and surprise, she bows to the guests.*]

MOTHER-IN-LAW. I hope you don't mind waiting a few moments? My son's bride has just arrived from the city. An emergency wedding is about to be celebrated. [*To the* MONK *in the bedroom*] I might have known you couldn't keep your trap shut. [*To* GRUSHA] The wedding can take place at once. Here's the license. Me and the bride's brother [LAVRENTI *tries to hide in the background, after having quietly taken* MICHAEL *back from* GRUSHA. *The* MOTHER-IN-LAW *waves him away.*] are the witnesses.

[GRUSHA *has bowed to the* MONK. *They go to the bed. The* MOTHER-IN-LAW *lifts the mosquito net. The* MONK *starts reeling off the marriage ceremony in Latin. Meanwhile the* MOTHER-IN-LAW *beckons to* LAVRENTI *to get rid of the* CHILD, *but fearing that it will cry he draws its attention to the ceremony,* GRUSHA *glances once at the* CHILD, *and* LAVRENTI *waves the* CHILD's *hand in a greeting.*]

MONK. Are you prepared to be a faithful, obedient, and good wife to this man, and to cleave to him until death do you part?

GRUSHA [*looking at the* CHILD]. I am.

MONK [*to the* SICK PEASANT]. Are you prepared to be a good and loving husband to your wife until death you do part? [*As the* SICK PEASANT *does not answer, the* MONK *looks inquiringly around.*]

MOTHER-IN-LAW. Of course he is! Didn't you hear him say yes?

MONK. All right. We declare the marriage contracted! How about extreme unction?

MOTHER-IN-LAW. Nothing doing! The wedding cost quite enough. Now I must take care of the mourners. [*To* LAVRENTI] Did we say seven hundred?

LAVRENTI. Six hundred. [*He pays.*] Now I don't want to sit with the guests and get to know people. So farewell, Grusha, and if my widowed sister comes to visit me, she'll get a welcome from my wife, or I'll show my teeth. [*Nods, gives the* CHILD *to* GRUSHA, *and leaves. The mourners glance after him without interest.*]

MONK. May one ask where this child comes from?

MOTHER-IN-LAW. Is there a child? I don't see a child. And you don't see a child either—you understand? Or it may turn out I saw all sorts of things in the tavern! Now come on.

[*After* GRUSHA *has put the* CHILD *down and told him to be quiet, they move over left.* GRUSHA *is introduced to the neighbors.*] This is my daughter-in-law. She arrived just in time to find dear Jussup still alive.

ONE WOMAN. He's been ill now a whole year, hasn't he? When our Vassili was drafted he was there to say good-bye.

ANOTHER WOMAN. Such things are terrible for a farm. The corn all ripe and the farmer in bed!

It'll really be a blessing if he doesn't suffer too long, I say.

FIRST WOMAN [*confidentially*]. You know why we thought he'd taken to his bed? Because of the draft! And now his end is come!

MOTHER-IN-LAW. Sit yourselves down, please! And have some cakes!

[*She beckons to* GRUSHA *and both women go into the bedroom, where they pick up the cake pans off the floor. The guests, among them the* MONK, *sit on the floor and begin conversing in subdued voices.*]

ONE PEASANT [*to whom the* MONK *has handed the bottle which he has taken from his soutane*]. There's a child, you say! How can that have happened to Jussup?

A WOMAN. She was certainly lucky to get herself married, with him so sick!

MOTHER-IN-LAW. They're gossiping already. And wolfing down the funeral cakes at the same time! If he doesn't die today, I'll have to bake some more tomorrow!

GRUSHA. I'll bake them for you.

MOTHER-IN-LAW. Yesterday some horsemen rode by, and I went out to see who it was. When I came in again he was lying there like a corpse! So I sent for you. It can't take much longer. [*She listens.*]

MONK. Dear wedding and funeral guests! Deeply touched, we stand before a bed of death and marriage. The bride gets a veil; the groom, a shroud: how varied, my children, are the fates of men! Alas! One man dies and has a roof over his head, and the other is married and the flesh turns to dust from which it was made. Amen.

MOTHER-IN-LAW. He's getting his own back. I shouldn't have hired such a cheap one. It's what you'd expect. A more expensive monk would behave himself. In Sura there's one with a real air of sanctity about him, but of course he charges a fortune. A fifty piaster monk like that has no dignity, and as for piety, just fifty piasters' worth and no more! When I came to get him in the tavern he'd just made a speech, and he was shouting: "The war is over, beware of the peace!" We must go in.

GRUSHA [*giving* MICHAEL *a cake*]. Eat this cake, and keep nice and still, Michael.

[*The two women offer cakes to the guests. The dying man sits up in bed. He puts his head out from under the mosquito net, stares at the two women, then sinks back again. The* MONK *takes two bottles from his soutane and offers them to the peas-*

ant beside him. Enter three MUSICIANS *who are greeted with a sly wink by the* MONK.]

MOTHER-IN-LAW [*to the* MUSICIANS]. What are you doing here? With instruments?

ONE MUSICIAN. Brother Anastasius here [*pointing at the* MONK] told us there was a wedding on.

MOTHER-IN-LAW. What? You brought them? Three more on my neck! Don't you know there's a dying man in the next room?

MONK. A very tempting assignment for a musician: something that could be either a subdued Wedding March or a spirited Funeral Dance.

MOTHER-IN-LAW. Well, you might as well play. Nobody can stop you eating in any case.

[*The musicians play a potpourri. The women serve cakes.*]

MONK. The trumpet sounds like a whining baby. And you, little drum, what have you got to tell the world?

DRUNKEN PEASANT [*beside the* MONK, *sings*].
There was a young woman who said:
I thought I'd be happier, wed.
But my husband is old
And remarkably cold
So I sleep with a candle instead.

[*The* MOTHER-IN-LAW *throws the* DRUNKEN PEASANT *out. The music stops. The guests are embarrassed.*]

GUESTS [*loudly*]:
—Have you heard? The Grand Duke is back! But the Princes are against him.
—They say the Shah of Persia has lent him a great army to restore order in Grusinia.
—But how is that possible? The Shah of Persia is the enemy . . .
—The enemy of Grusinia, you donkey, not the enemy of the Grand Duke!
—In any case, the war's over, so our soldiers are coming back.

[GRUSHA *drops a cake pan.* GUESTS *help her pick up the cake.*]

AN OLD WOMAN [*to* GRUSHA]. Are you feeling bad? It's just excitement about dear Jussup. Sit down and rest a while, my dear. [GRUSHA *staggers.*]

GUESTS. Now everything'll be the way it was. Only the taxes'll go up because now we'll have to pay for the war.

GRUSHA [*weakly*]. Did someone say the soldiers are back?

A MAN. I did.

GRUSHA. It can't be true.

FIRST MAN [*to a woman*]. Show her the shawl. We bought it from a soldier. It's from Persia.

GRUSHA [*looking at the shawl*]. They are here. [*She gets up, takes a step, kneels down in prayer, takes the silver cross and chain out of her blouse, and kisses it.*]

MOTHER-IN-LAW [*while the guests silently watch* GRUSHA]. What's the matter with you? Aren't you going to look after our guests? What's all this city nonsense got to do with us?

GUESTS [*resuming conversation while* GRUSHA *remains in prayer*].
—You can buy Persian saddles from the soldiers too. Though many want crutches in exchange for them.
—The leaders on one side can win a war, the soldiers on both sides lose it.
—Anyway, the war's over. It's something they can't draft you any more.

[*The dying man sits bolt upright in bed. He listens.*]
—What we need is two weeks of good weather.
—Our pear trees are hardly bearing a thing this year.

MOTHER-IN-LAW [*offering cakes*]. Have some more cakes and welcome! There are more!

[*The* MOTHER-IN-LAW *goes to the bedroom with the empty cake pans. Unaware of the dying man, she is bending down to pick up another tray when he begins to talk in a hoarse voice.*]

PEASANT. How many more cakes are you going to stuff down their throats? D'you think I can shit money?

[*The* MOTHER-IN-LAW *starts, stares at him aghast, while he climbs out from behind the mosquito net.*]

FIRST WOMAN [*talking kindly to* GRUSHA *in the next room*]. Has the young wife got someone at the front?

A MAN. It's good news that they're on their way home, huh?

PEASANT. Don't stare at me like that! Where's this wife you've saddled me with?

[*Receiving no answer, he climbs out of bed and in his nightshirt staggers into the other room. Trembling, she follows him with the cake pan.*]

GUESTS [*seeing him and shrieking*]. Good God! Jussup!

[*Everyone leaps up in alarm. The women rush to the door.* GRUSHA, *still on her knees, turns round and stares at the man.*]

PEASANT. A funeral supper! You'd enjoy that,

wouldn't you? Get out before I throw you out!
[*As the guests stampede from the house, gloomily
to* GRUSHA] I've upset the apple cart, huh? [*Receiving no answer, he turns round and takes a cake
from the pan which his mother is holding.*]

SINGER.

> O confusion! The wife discovers she has a
> husband.
> By day there's the child, by night there's the
> husband.
> The lover is on his way both day and night.
> Husband and wife look at each other.
> The bedroom is small.

[*Near the bed the* PEASANT *is sitting in a high
wooden bathtub, naked, the* MOTHER-IN-LAW *is
pouring water from a pitcher. Opposite* GRUSHA
cowers with MICHAEL, *who is playing at mending
straw mats.*]

PEASANT [*to his mother*]. That's her work, not
yours. Where's she hiding out now?

MOTHER-IN-LAW [*calling*]. Grusha! the peasant
wants you!

GRUSHA [*to* MICHAEL]. There are still two holes
to mend.

PEASANT [*when* GRUSHA *approaches*]. Scrub my
back!

GRUSHA. Can't the peasant do it himself?

PEASANT. "Can't the peasant do it himself?" Get
the brush! To hell with you! Are you the wife
here? Or are you a visitor? [*To the* MOTHER-IN-
LAW] It's too cold!

MOTHER-IN-LAW. I'll run for hot water.

GRUSHA. Let me go.

PEASANT. You stay here. [*The* MOTHER-IN-LAW
exits.] Rub harder. And no shirking. You've seen
a naked fellow before. That child didn't come out
of thin air.

GRUSHA. The child was not conceived in joy, if
that's what the peasant means.

PEASANT [*turning and grinning*]. You don't look
the type. [GRUSHA *stops scrubbing him, starts back.
Enter the* MOTHER-IN-LAW.]

PEASANT. A nice thing you've saddled me with!
A simpleton for a wife!

MOTHER-IN-LAW. She just isn't cooperative.

PEASANT. Pour—but go easy! Ow! Go easy, I
said. [*To* GRUSHA] Maybe you did something
wrong in the city . . . I wouldn't be surprised.
Why else should you be here? But I won't talk
about that. I've not said a word about the illegitimate object you brought into my house either.
But my patience has limits! It's against nature. [*To

the* MOTHER-IN-LAW] More! [*To* GRUSHA] And even
if your soldier does come back, you're married.

GRUSHA. Yes.

PEASANT. But your soldier won't come back.
Don't you believe it.

GRUSHA. No.

PEASANT. You're cheating me. You're my wife
and you're not my wife. Where you lie, nothing
lies, and yet no other woman can lie there. When
I go to work in the morning I'm tired—when I lie
down at night I'm awake as the devil. God has
given you sex—and what d'you do? I don't have
ten piasters to buy myself a woman in the city.
Besides, it's a long way. Woman weeds the fields
and opens up her legs, that's what our calendar
says. D'you hear?

GRUSHA [*quietly*]. Yes. I didn't mean to cheat
you out of it.

PEASANT. She didn't mean to cheat me out of it!
Pour some more water! [*The* MOTHER-IN-LAW
pours.] Ow!

SINGER.

> As she sat by the stream to wash the linen
> She saw his image in the water
> And his face grew dimmer with the passing
> moons.
> As she raised herself to wring the linen
> She heard his voice from the murmuring
> maple
> And his voice grew fainter with the passing
> moons.
> Evasions and sighs grew more numerous,
> Tears and sweat flowed.
> With the passing moons the child grew up.

[GRUSHA *sits by a stream, dipping linen into the
water. In the rear, a few children are standing.*]

GRUSHA [*to* MICHAEL]. You can play with them,
Michael, but don't let them boss you around just
because you're the littlest. [MICHAEL *nods and joins
the children. They start playing.*]

BIGGEST BOY. Today it's the Heads-Off Game.
[*To a* FAT BOY] You're the Prince and you laugh.
[*To* MICHAEL] You're the Governor. [*To a* GIRL]
You're the Governor's wife and you cry when his
head's cut off. And I do the cutting. [*He shows
his wooden sword.*] With this. First, they lead the
Governor into the yard. The Prince walks in front.
The Governor's wife comes last.

[*They form a procession. The* FAT BOY *is first
and laughs. Then comes* MICHAEL, *then the* BIGGEST
BOY, *and then the* GIRL, *who weeps.*]

MICHAEL [*standing still*]. Me cut off head!

BIGGEST BOY. That's my job. You're the littlest. The Governor's the easy part. All you do is kneel down and get your head cut off—simple.

MICHAEL. Me want sword!

BIGGEST BOY. It's mine! [*He gives* MICHAEL *a kick.*]

GIRL [*shouting to* GRUSHA]. He won't play his part!

GRUSHA [*laughing*]. Even the little duck is a swimmer, they say.

BIGGEST BOY. You can be the Prince if you can laugh. [MICHAEL *shakes his head.*]

FAT BOY. I laugh best. Let him cut off the head just once. Then you do it, then me.

[*Reluctantly, the* BIGGEST BOY *hands* MICHAEL *the wooden sword and kneels down. The* FAT BOY *sits down, slaps his thigh, and laughs with all his might. The* GIRL *weeps loudly.* MICHAEL *swings the big sword and "cuts off" the head. In doing so, he topples over.*]

BIGGEST BOY. Hey! I'll show you how to cut heads off!

[MICHAEL *runs away. The children run after him.* GRUSHA *laughs, following them with her eyes. On looking back, she sees* SIMON SHASHAVA *standing on the opposite bank. He wears a shabby uniform.*]

GRUSHA. Simon!

SIMON. Is that Grusha Vashnadze?

GRUSHA. Simon!

SIMON [*formally*]. A good morning to the young lady. I hope she is well.

GRUSHA [*getting up gaily and bowing low*]. A good morning to the soldier. God be thanked he has returned in good health.

SIMON. They found better fish, so they didn't eat me, said the haddock.

GRUSHA. Courage, said the kitchen boy. Good luck, said the hero.

SIMON. How are things here? Was the winter bearable? The neighbor considerate?

GRUSHA. The winter was a trifle rough, the neighbor as usual, Simon.

SIMON. May one ask if a certain person still dips her toes in the water when rinsing the linen?

GRUSHA. The answer is no. Because of the eyes in the bushes.

SIMON. The young lady is speaking of soldiers. Here stands a paymaster.

GRUSHA. A job worth twenty piasters?

SIMON. And lodgings.

GRUSHA [*with tears in her eyes*]. Behind the barracks under the date trees.

SIMON. Yes, there. A certain person has kept her eyes open.

GRUSHA. She has, Simon.

SIMON. And has not forgotten? [GRUSHA *shakes her head.*] So the door is still on its hinges as they say? [GRUSHA *looks at him in silence and shakes her head again.*] What's this? Is anything not as it should be?

GRUSHA. Simon Shashava, I can never return to Nuka. Something has happened.

SIMON. What can have happened?

GRUSHA. For one thing, I knocked an Ironshirt down.

SIMON. Grusha Vashnadze must have had her reasons for that.

GRUSHA. Simon Shashava, I am no longer called what I used to be called.

SIMON [*after a pause*]. I do not understand.

GRUSHA. When do women change their names, Simon? Let me explain. Nothing stands between us. Everything is just as it was. You must believe that.

SIMON. Nothing stands between us and yet there's something?

GRUSHA. How can I explain it so fast and with the stream between us? Couldn't you cross the bridge there?

SIMON. Maybe it's no longer necessary.

GRUSHA. It is very necessary. Come over on this side, Simon, Quick!

SIMON. Does the young lady wish to say someone has come too late?

[GRUSHA *looks up at him in despair, her face streaming with tears.* SIMON *stares before him. He picks up a piece of wood and starts cutting it.*]

SINGER.

So many words are said, so many left unsaid.
The soldier has come.
Where he comes from, he does not say.
Hear what he thought and did not say:
"The battle began, gray at dawn, grew bloody at noon.
The first man fell in front of me, the second behind me, the third at my side.
I trod on the first, left the second behind, the third was run through by the captain.
One of my brothers died by steel, the other by smoke.
My neck caught fire, my hands froze in my gloves, my toes in my socks.
I fed on aspen buds, I drank maple juice, I slept on stone, in water."

SIMON. I see a cap in the grass. Is there a little one already?

GRUSHA. There is, Simon. There's no keeping *that* from you. But please don't worry, it is not mine.

SIMON. When the wind once starts to blow, they say, it blows through every cranny. The wife need say no more. [GRUSHA *looks into her lap and is silent.*]

SINGER.
>There was yearning but there was no waiting.
>The oath is broken. Neither could say why.
>Hear what she thought but did not say:
>"While you fought in the battle, soldier,
>The bloody battle, the bitter battle
>I found a helpless infant
>I had not the heart to destroy him
>I had to care for a creature that was lost
>I had to stoop for breadcrumbs on the floor
>I had to break myself for that which was not
>   mine
>That which was other people's.
>Someone must help!
>For the little tree needs water
>The lamb loses its way when the shepherd is
>   asleep
>And its cry is unheard!"

SIMON. Give me back the cross I gave you. Better still, throw it in the stream. [*He turns to go.*]

GRUSHA [*getting up*]. Simon Shashava, don't go away! He isn't mine! He isn't mine! [*She hears the children calling.*] What's the matter, children?

VOICES. Soldiers! And they're taking Michael away!

[GRUSHA *stands aghast as two* IRONSHIRTS, *with* MICHAEL *between them, come toward her.*]

ONE OF THE IRONSHIRTS. Are you Grusha? [*She nods.*] Is this your child?

GRUSHA. Yes. [SIMON *goes.*] Simon!

IRONSHIRT. We have orders, in the name of the law, to take this child, found in your custody, back to the city. It is suspected that the child is Michael Abashwili, son and heir of the late Governor Georgi Abashwili, and his wife, Natella Abashwili. Here is the document and the seal. [*They lead the* CHILD *away.*]

GRUSHA [*running after them, shouting*]. Leave him here. Please! He's mine!

SINGER.
>The Ironshirts took the child, the beloved
>   child.

The unhappy girl followed them to the city,
>   the dreaded city.
>She who had borne him demanded the child.
>She who had raised him faced trial.
>Who will decide the case?
>To whom will the child be assigned?
>Who will the judge be? A good judge? A
>   bad?
>The city was in flames.
>In the judge's seat sat Azdak.*

4

THE STORY OF THE JUDGE

SINGER.
>Hear the story of the judge
>How he turned judge, how he passed judg-
>   ment, what kind of judge he was.
>On that Easter Sunday of the great revolt,
>   when the Grand Duke was overthrown
>And his Governor Abashwili, father of our
>   child, lost his head
>The Village Scrivener Azdak found a fugitive
>   in the woods and hid him in his hut.

[AZDAK, *in rags and slightly drunk, is helping an old beggar into his cottage.*]

AZDAK. Stop snorting, you're not a horse. And it won't do you any good with the police to run like a snotty nose in April. Stand still, I say. [*He catches the* OLD MAN, *who has marched into the cottage as if he'd like to go through the walls.*] Sit down. Feed. Here's a hunk of cheese. [*From under some rags, in a chest, he fishes out some cheese, and the* OLD MAN *greedily begins to eat.*] Haven't eaten in a long time, huh? [*The* OLD MAN *growls.*] Why were you running like that, asshole? The cop wouldn't even have seen you.

OLD MAN. Had to! Had to!

AZDAK. Blue funk? [*The* OLD MAN *stares, uncomprehending.*] Cold feet? Panic? Don't lick your chops like a Grand Duke. Or an old sow. I can't stand it. We have to accept respectable stinkers as God made them, but not you! I once heard of a senior judge who farted at a public dinner to show an independent spirit! Watching you eat like that gives me the most awful ideas. Why don't

---

* The name Azdak should be accented on the second syllable.—E. B.

you say something? [*Sharply*] Show me your hand. Can't you hear? [*The* OLD MAN *slowly puts out his hand.*] White! So you're not a beggar at all! A fraud, a walking swindle! And I'm hiding you from the cops like you were an honest man! Why were you running like that if you're a landowner? For that's what you are. Don't deny it! I see it in your guilty face! [*He gets up.*] Get out! [*The* OLD MAN *looks at him uncertainly.*] What are you waiting for, peasant-flogger?

OLD MAN. Pursued. Need undivided attention. Make proposition . . .

AZDAK. Make what? A proposition? Well, if that isn't the height of insolence. He's making me a proposition! The bitten man scratches his fingers bloody, and the leech that's biting him makes him a proposition! Get out, I tell you!

OLD MAN. Understand point of view! Persuasion! Pay hundred thousand piasters one night! Yes?

AZDAK. What, you think you can buy me? For a hundred thousand piasters? Let's say a hundred and fifty thousand. Where are they?

OLD MAN. Have not them here. Of course. Will be sent. Hope do not doubt.

AZDAK. Doubt very much. Get out!

[*The* OLD MAN *gets up, waddles to the door. A* VOICE *is heard offstage.*]

VOICE. Azdak!

[*The* OLD MAN *turns, waddles to the opposite corner, stands still.*]

AZDAK [*calling out*]. I'm not in! [*He walks to door.*] So *you're* sniffing around here again, Shauwa?

SHAUWA [*reproachfully*]. You caught another rabbit, Azdak. And you'd promised me it wouldn't happen again!

AZDAK [*severely*]. Shauwa, don't talk about things you don't understand. The rabbit is a dangerous and destructive beast. It feeds on plants, especially on the species of plants known as weeds. It must therefore be exterminated.

SHAUWA. Azdak, don't be so hard on me. I'll lose my job if I don't arrest you. I know you have a good heart.

AZDAK. I do not have a good heart! How often must I tell you I'm a man of intellect?

SHAUWA [*slyly*]. I know, Azdak. You're a superior person. You say so yourself. I'm just a Christian and an ignoramus. So I ask you: When one of the Prince's rabbits is stolen, and I'm a policeman, what should I do with the offending party?

AZDAK. Shauwa, Shauwa, shame on you. You stand and ask me a question, than which nothing could be more seductive. It's like you were a woman—let's say that bad girl Nunowna, and you showed me your thigh—Nunowna's thigh, that would be—and asked me: "What shall I do with my thigh, it itches?" Is she as innocent as she pretends? Of course not. I catch a rabbit, but you catch a man. Man is made in God's image. Not so a rabbit, you know that. I'm a rabbit-eater, but you're a man-eater, Shauwa. And God will pass judgment on you. Shauwa, go home and repent. No, stop, there's something . . . [*He looks at the* OLD MAN *who stands trembling in the corner.*] No, it's nothing. Go home and repent. [*He slams the door behind* SHAUWA.] Now you're surprised, huh? Surprised I didn't hand you over? I couldn't hand over a bedbug to that animal. It goes against the grain. Now don't tremble because of a cop! So old and still so scared? Finish your cheese, but eat it like a poor man, or else they'll still catch you. Must I even explain how a poor man behaves? [*He pushes him down, and then gives him back the cheese.*] That box is the table. Lay your elbows on the table. Now, encircle the cheese on the plate like it might be snatched from you at any moment —what right have you to be safe, huh?—now, hold your knife like an undersized sickle, and give your cheese a troubled look because, like all beautiful things, it's already fading away. [AZDAK *watches him.*] They're after you, which speaks in your favor, but how can we be sure they're not mistaken about you? In Tiflis one time they hanged a landowner, a Turk, who could prove he quartered his peasants instead of merely cutting them in half, as is the custom, and he squeezed twice the usual amount of taxes out of them, his zeal was above suspicion. And yet they hanged him like a common criminal—because he was a Turk—a thing he couldn't do much about. What injustice! He got onto the gallows by a sheer fluke. In short, I don't trust you.

SINGER.

Thus Azdak gave the old beggar a bed,
And learned that old beggar was the old butcher, the Grand Duke himself,
And was ashamed.
He denounced himself and ordered the policeman to take him to Nuka, to court, to be judged.

[*In the court of justice three* IRONSHIRTS *sit*

drinking. From a beam hangs a man in judge's robes. Enter AZDAK, *in chains, dragging* SHAUWA *behind him.*]

AZDAK [*shouting*]. I've helped the Grand Duke, the Grand Thief, the Grand Butcher, to escape! In the name of justice I ask to be severely judged in public trial!

FIRST IRONSHIRT. Who's this queer bird?

SHAUWA. That's our Village Scrivener, Azdak.

AZDAK. I am contemptible! I am a traitor! A branded criminal! Tell them, flatfoot, how I insisted on being tied up and brought to the capital. Because I sheltered the Grand Duke, the Grand Swindler, by mistake. And how I found out afterwards. See the marked man denounce himself! Tell them how I forced you to walk half the night with me to clear the whole thing up.

SHAUWA. And all by threats. That wasn't nice of you, Azdak.

AZDAK. Shut your mouth, Shauwa. You don't understand. A new age is upon us! It'll go thundering over you. You're finished. The police will be wiped out—poof! Everything will be gone into, everything will be brought into the open. The guilty will give themselves up. Why? They couldn't escape the people in any case. [*To* SHAUWA] Tell them how I shouted all along Shoemaker Street [*with big gestures, looking at the* IRONSHIRTS] "In my ignorance I let the Grand Swindler escape! So tear me to pieces, brothers!" I wanted to get it in first.

FIRST IRONSHIRT. And what did your brothers answer?

SHAUWA. They comforted him in Butcher Street, and they laughed themselves sick in Shoemaker Street. That's all.

AZDAK. But with you it's different. I can see you're men of iron. Brothers, where's the judge? I must be tried.

FIRST IRONSHIRT [*pointing at the hanged man*]. There's the judge. And please stop "brothering" us. It's rather a sore spot this evening.

AZDAK. "There's the judge." An answer never heard in Grusinia before. Townsman, where's His Excellency the Governor? [*Pointing to the ground*] There's His Excellency, stranger. Where's the Chief Tax Collector? Where's the official Recruiting Officer? The Patriarch? The Chief of Police? There, there, there—all there. Brothers, I expected no less of you.

SECOND IRONSHIRT. What? *What* was it you expected, funny man?

AZDAK. What happened in Persia, brother, what happened in Persia?

SECOND IRONSHIRT. What did happen in Persia?

AZDAK. Everybody was hanged. Viziers, tax collectors. Everybody. Forty years ago now. My grandfather, a remarkable man by the way, saw it all. For three whole days. Everywhere.

SECOND IRONSHIRT. And who ruled when the Vizier was hanged?

AZDAK. A peasant ruled when the Vizier was hanged.

SECOND IRONSHIRT. And who commanded the army?

AZDAK. A soldier, a soldier.

SECOND IRONSHIRT. And who paid the wages?

AZDAK. A dyer. A dyer paid the wages.

SECOND IRONSHIRT. Wasn't it a weaver, maybe?

FIRST IRONSHIRT. And why did all this happen, Persian?

AZDAK. Why did all this happen? Must there be a special reason? Why do you scratch yourself, brother? War! Too long a war! And no justice! My grandfather brought back a song that tells how it was. I will sing it for you. With my friend the policeman. [*To* SHAUWA] And hold the rope tight. It's very suitable. [*He sings, with* SHAUWA *holding the rope tight around him.*]

THE SONG OF INJUSTICE IN PERSIA

Why don't our sons bleed any more? Why don't our daughters weep?
Why do only the slaughterhouse cattle have blood in their veins?
Why do only the willows shed tears on Lake Urmia?
The king must have a new province, the peasant must give up his savings.
That the roof of the world might be conquered, the roof of the cottage is torn down.
Our men are carried to the ends of the earth, so that great ones can eat at home.
The soldiers kill each other, the marshals salute each other.
They bite the widow's tax money to see if it's good, their swords break.
The battle was lost, the helmets were paid for.
Refrain: Is it so? Is it so?

SHAUWA [*refrain*].

Yes, yes, yes, yes, yes it's so.

AZDAK. Want to hear the rest of it? [*The* FIRST IRONSHIRT *nods.*]

SECOND IRONSHIRT [*to* SHAUWA]. Did he teach you that song?

SHAUWA. Yes, only my voice isn't very good.

SECOND IRONSHIRT. No. [*To* AZDAK] Go on singing.

AZDAK. The second verse is about the peace. [*He sings.*]

The offices are packed, the streets overflow with officials.
The rivers jump their banks and ravage the fields.
Those who cannot let down their own trousers rule countries.
They can't count up to four, but they devour eight courses.
The corn farmers, looking round for buyers, see only the starving.
The weavers go home from their looms in rags.
Refrain: Is it so? Is it so?

SHAUWA [*refrain*].

Yes, yes, yes, yes, yes it's so.

AZDAK.

That's why our sons don't bleed any more, that's why our daughters don't weep.
That's why only the slaughterhouse cattle have blood in their veins,
And only the willows shed tears on Lake Urmia toward morning.

FIRST IRONSHIRT. Are you going to sing that song here in town?

AZDAK. Sure. What's wrong with it?

FIRST IRONSHIRT. Have you noticed that the sky's getting red? [*Turning round,* AZDAK *sees the sky red with fire.*] It's the people's quarters on the outskirts of town. The carpet weavers have caught the "Persian Sickness," too. And they've been asking if Prince Kazbeki isn't eating too many courses. This morning they strung up the city judge. As for us we beat them to pulp. We were paid one hundred piasters per man, you understand?

AZDAK [*after a pause*]. I understand. [*He glances shyly round and, creeping away, sits down in a corner, his head in his hands.*]

IRONSHIRTS [*to each other*]. If there ever was a troublemaker it's him.

—He must've come to the capital to fish in the troubled waters.

SHAUWA. Oh, I don't think he's a really bad character, gentlemen. Steals a few chickens here and there. And maybe a rabbit.

SECOND IRONSHIRT [*approaching* AZDAK]. Came to fish in the troubled waters, huh?

AZDAK [*looking up*]. I don't know why I came.

SECOND IRONSHIRT. Are you in with the carpet weavers maybe? [AZDAK *shakes his head.*] How about that song?

AZDAK. From my grandfather. A silly and ignorant man.

SECOND IRONSHIRT. Right. And how about the dyer who paid the wages?

AZDAK [*muttering*]. That was in Persia.

FIRST IRONSHIRT. And this denouncing of yourself? Because you didn't hang the Grand Duke with your own hands?

AZDAK. Didn't I tell you I let him run? [*He creeps farther away and sits on the floor.*]

SHAUWA. I can swear to that: he let him run.

[*The* IRONSHIRTS *burst out laughing and slap* SHAUWA *on the back.* AZDAK *laughs loudest. They slap* AZDAK *too, and unchain him. They all start drinking as the* FAT PRINCE *enters with a young man.*]

FIRST IRONSHIRT [*to* AZDAK, *pointing at the* FAT PRINCE]. There's your "new age" for you! [*More laughter.*]

FAT PRINCE. Well, my friends, what is there to laugh about? Permit me a serious word. Yesterday morning the Princes of Grusinia overthrew the warmongering government of the Grand Duke and did away with his Governors. Unfortunately the Grand Duke himself escaped. In this fateful hour our carpet weavers, those eternal troublemakers, had the effrontery to stir up a rebellion and hang the universally loved city judge, our dear Illo Orbeliani. Ts—ts—ts. My friends, we need peace, peace, peace in Grusinia! And justice! So I've brought along my dear nephew Bizergan Kazbeki. He'll be the new judge, hm? A very gifted fellow. What do you say? I want your opinion. Let the people decide!

SECOND IRONSHIRT. Does this mean *we* elect the judge?

FAT PRINCE. Precisely. Let the people propose some very gifted fellow! Confer among yourselves, my friends. [*The* IRONSHIRTS *confer.*] Don't worry, my little fox. The job's yours. And when we catch the Grand Duke we won't have to kiss this rabble's ass any longer.

IRONSHIRTS [*among themselves*].

—Very funny: they're wetting their pants because they haven't caught the Grand Duke.

—When the outlook isn't so bright, they say: "My friends!" and "Let the people decide!"

—Now he even wants justice for Grusinia! But fun is fun as long as it lasts! [*Pointing at* AZDAK] *He* knows all about justice. Hey, rascal, would you like this nephew fellow to be the judge?

AZDAK. Are you asking me? You're not asking *me?!*

FIRST IRONSHIRT. Why not? Anything for a laugh!

AZDAK. You'd like to test him to the marrow, correct? Have you a criminal on hand? An experienced one? So the candidate can show what he knows?

SECOND IRONSHIRT. Let's see. We do have a couple of doctors downstairs. Let's use them.

AZDAK. Oh, no, that's no good, we can't take real criminals till we're sure the judge will be appointed. He may be dumb, but he must be appointed, or the law is violated. And the law is a sensitive organ. It's like the spleen, you mustn't hit it—that would be fatal. Of course you can hang those two without violating the law, because there was no judge in the vicinity. But judgment, when pronounced, must be pronounced with absolute gravity—it's all such nonsense. Suppose, for instance, a judge jails a woman—let's say she's stolen a corn cake to feed her child—and this judge isn't wearing his robes—or maybe he's scratching himself while passing sentence and half his body is uncovered—a man's thigh *will* itch once in a while —the sentence this judge passes is a disgrace and the law is violated. In short it would be easier for a judge's robe and a judge's hat to pass judgment than for a man with no robe and no hat. If you don't treat it with respect, the law just disappears on you. Now you don't try out a bottle of wine by offering it to a dog; you'd only lose your wine.

FIRST IRONSHIRT. Then what do you suggest, hairsplitter?

AZDAK. I'll be the defendant.

FIRST IRONSHIRT. You? [*He bursts out laughing.*]

FAT PRINCE. What have you decided?

FIRST IRONSHIRT. We've decided to stage a rehearsal. Our friend here will be the defendant. Let the candidate be the judge and sit there.

FAT PRINCE. It isn't customary, but why not? [*To the* NEPHEW] A mere formality, my little fox. What have I taught you? Who got there first—the slow runner or the fast?

NEPHEW. The silent runner, Uncle Arsen.

[*The* NEPHEW *takes the chair. The* IRONSHIRTS *and the* FAT PRINCE *sit on the steps. Enter* AZDAK, *mimicking the gait of the Grand Duke.*]

AZDAK [*in the Grand Duke's accent*]. Is any here knows me? Am Grand Duke.

IRONSHIRTS.

—*What* is he?

—The Grand Duke. He knows him, too.

—Fine. So get on with the trial.

AZDAK. Listen! Am accused instigating war? Ridiculous! Am saying ridiculous! That enough? If not, have brought lawyers. Believe five hundred. [*He points behind him, pretending to be surrounded by lawyers.*] Requisition all available seats for lawyers! [*The* IRONSHIRTS *laugh; the* FAT PRINCE *joins in.*]

NEPHEW [*to the* IRONSHIRTS]. You really wish me to try this case? I find it rather unusual. From the taste angle, I mean.

FIRST IRONSHIRT. Let's go!

FAT PRINCE [*smiling*]. Let him have it, my little fox!

NEPHEW. All right. People of Grusinia versus Grand Duke. Defendant, what have you got to say for yourself?

AZDAK. Plenty. Naturally, have read war lost. Only started on the advice of patriots. Like Uncle Arsen Kazbeki. Call Uncle Arsen as witness.

FAT PRINCE [*to the* IRONSHIRTS, *delightedly*]. What a madcap!

NEPHEW. Motion rejected. One cannot be arraigned for declaring a war, which every ruler has to do once in a while, but only for running a war badly.

AZDAK. Rubbish! Did not run it at all! Had it run! Had it run by Princes! Naturally, they messed it up.

NEPHEW. Do you by any chance deny having been commander-in-chief?

AZDAK. Not at all! Always *was* commander-in-chief. At birth shouted at wet nurse. Was trained drop turds in toilet, grew accustomed to command. Always commanded officials rob my cash box. Officers flog soldiers only on command. Landowners sleep with peasants' wives only on strictest command. Uncle Arsen here grew his belly at *my* command!

IRONSHIRTS [*clapping*]. He's good! Long live the Grand Duke!

FAT PRINCE. Answer him, my little fox: I'm with you.

NEPHEW. I shall answer him according to the dignity of the law. Defendant, preserve the dignity of the law!

AZDAK. Agreed. Command you proceed with trial!

NEPHEW. It is not your place to command me.

You claim that the Princes forced you to declare war. How can you claim, then, that they—er—"messed it up"?

AZDAK. Did not send enough people. Embezzled funds. Sent sick horses. During attack, drinking in whorehouse. Call Uncle Arsen as witness.

NEPHEW. Are you making the outrageous suggestion that the Princes of this country did not fight?

AZDAK. No. Princes fought. Fought for war contracts.

FAT PRINCE [*jumping up*]. That's too much! This man talks like a carpet weaver!

AZDAK. Really? Told nothing but truth.

FAT PRINCE. Hang him! Hang him!

FIRST IRONSHIRT [*pulling the* PRINCE *down*]. Keep quiet! Go on, Excellency!

NEPHEW. Quiet! I now render a verdict: You must be hanged! By the neck! Having lost war!

AZDAK. Young man, seriously advise not fall publicly into jerky clipped speech. Cannot be watchdog if howl like wolf. Got it? If people realize Princes speak same language as Grand Duke, may hang Grand Duke *and Princes,* huh? By the way, must overrule verdict. Reason? War lost, but not for Princes. Princes won their war. Got 3,863,000 piasters for horses not delivered, 8,240,000 piasters for food supplies not produced. Are therefore victors. War lost only for Grusinia, which is not present in this court.

FAT PRINCE. I think that will do, my friends. [*To* AZDAK] You can withdraw, funny man. [*To the* IRONSHIRTS] You may now ratify the new judge's appointment, my friends.

FIRST IRONSHIRT. Yes, we can. Take down the judge's gown. [*One* IRONSHIRT *climbs on the back of the other, pulls the gown off the hanged man.*] [*To the* NEPHEW] Now you run away so the right ass can get on the right chair. [*To* AZDAK] Step forward! Go to the judge's seat! Now sit in it! [AZDAK *steps up, bows, and sits down.*] The judge was always a rascal! Now the rascal shall be a judge! [*The judge's gown is placed round his shoulders, the hat on his head.*] And what a judge!

SINGER.

And there was civil war in the land.
The mighty were not safe.
And Azdak was made a judge by the Ironshirts.
And Azdak remained a judge for two years.

SINGER AND CHORUS.

When the towns were set afire

And rivers of blood rose higher and higher,
Cockroaches crawled out of every crack.
And the court was full of schemers
And the church of foul blasphemers.
In the judge's cassock sat Azdak.

[AZDAK *sits in the judge's chair, peeling on apple.* SHAUWA *is sweeping out the hall. On one side an* INVALID *in a wheelchair. Opposite, a young man accused of blackmail. An* IRONSHIRT *stands guard, holding the Ironshirts' banner.*]

AZDAK. In consideration of the large number of cases, the Court today will hear two cases at a time. Before I open the proceedings, a short announcement—I accept. [*He stretches out his hand. The* BLACKMAILER *is the only one to produce any money. He hands it to* AZDAK.] I reserve the right to punish one of the parties for contempt of court. [*He glances at the* INVALID.] You [*to the* DOCTOR] are a doctor, and you [*to the* INVALID] are bringing a complaint against him. Is the doctor responsible for your condition?

INVALID. Yes. I had a stroke on his account.

AZDAK. That would be professional negligence.

INVALID. Worse than negligence. I gave this man money for his studies. So far, he hasn't paid me back a cent. It was when I heard he was treating a patient free that I had my stroke.

AZDAK. Rightly. [*To a* LIMPING MAN] And what are *you* doing here?

LIMPING MAN. I'm the patient, Your Honor.

AZDAK. He treated your leg for nothing?

LIMPING MAN. The wrong leg! My rheumatism was in the left leg, he operated on the right. That's why I limp.

AZDAK. And you were treated free?

INVALID. A five-hundred-piaster operation free! For nothing! For a God-bless-you! And I paid for this man's studies! [*To the* DOCTOR] Did they teach you to operate free?

DOCTOR. Your Honor, it is the custom to demand the fee before the operation, as the patient is more willing to pay before an operation than after. Which is only human. In the case in question I was convinced, when I started the operation, that my servant had already received the fee. In this I was mistaken.

INVALID. He was mistaken! A good doctor doesn't make mistakes! He examines before he operates!

AZDAK. That's right: [*To* SHAUWA] Public Prosecutor, what's the other case about?

SHAUWA [*busily sweeping*]. Blackmail.

BLACKMAILER. High Court of Justice, I'm innocent. I only wanted to find out from the land-owner concerned if he really *had* raped his niece. He informed me very politely that this was not the case, and gave me the money only so I could pay for my uncle's studies.

AZDAK. Hm. [*To the* DOCTOR] You, on the other hand, can cite no extenuating circumstances for your offense, huh?

DOCTOR. Except that to err is human.

AZDAK. And you are aware that in money matters a good doctor is a highly responsible person? I once heard of a doctor who got a thousand piasters for a sprained finger by remarking that sprains have something to do with blood circulation, which after all a less good doctor might have overlooked, and who, on another occasion made a real gold mine out of a somewhat disordered gall bladder, he treated it with such loving care. You have no excuse, Doctor. The corn merchant Uxu had his son study medicine to get some knowledge of trade, our medical schools are so good. [*To the* BLACK-MAILER] What's the landowner's name?

SHAUWA. He doesn't want it mentioned.

AZDAK. In that case I will pass judgment. The Court considers the blackmail proved. And you [*to the* INVALID] are sentenced to a fine of one thousand piasters. If you have a second stroke, the doctor will have to treat you free. Even if he has to amputate. [*To the* LIMPING MAN] As compensation, you will receive a bottle of rubbing alcohol. [*To the* BLACKMAILER] You are sentenced to hand over half the proceeds of your deal to the Public Prosecutor to keep the landowner's name secret. You are advised, moreover, to study medicine—you seem well suited to that calling. [*To the* DOC-TOR] You have perpetrated an unpardonable error in the practice of your profession: you are acquitted. Next cases!

SINGER AND CHORUS.
Men won't do much for a shilling.
For a pound they may be willing.
For twenty pounds the verdict's in the sack.
As for the many, all too many,
Those who've only got a penny—
They've one single, sole recourse: Azdak.

[*Enter* AZDAK *from the caravansary on the high-road, followed by an old bearded* INNKEEPER. *The judge's chair is carried by a stableman and* SHAUWA. *An* IRONSHIRT, *with a banner, takes up his position.*]

AZDAK. Put me down. Then we'll get some air,

maybe even a good stiff breeze from the lemon grove there. It does justice good to be done in the open: the wind blows her skirts up and you can see what she's got. Shauwa, we've been eating too much. These official journeys are exhausting. [*To the* INNKEEPER] It's a question of your daughter-in-law?

INNKEEPER. Your Worship, it's a question of the family honor. I wish to bring an action on behalf of my son, who's away on business on the other side the mountain. This is the offending stable-man, and here's my daughter-in-law.

[*Enter the* DAUGHTER-IN-LAW, *a voluptuous wench. She is veiled.*]

AZDAK [*sitting down*]. I accept. [*Sighing, the* INNKEEPER *hands him some money.*] Good. Now the formalities are disposed of. This is a case of rape?

INNKEEPER. Your Honor, I caught the fellow in the act. Ludovica was in the straw on the stable floor.

AZDAK. Quite right, the stable. Lovely horses! I specially liked the little roan.

INNKEEPER. The first thing I did, of course, was to question Ludovica. On my son's behalf.

AZDAK [*seriously*]. I said I specially liked the little roan.

INNKEEPER [*coldly*]. Really? Ludovica confessed the stableman took her against her will.

AZDAK. Take your veil off, Ludovica. [*She does so.*] Ludovica, you please the Court. Tell us how it happened.

LUDOVICA [*well schooled*]. When I entered the stable to see the new foal the stableman said to me on his own accord: "It's hot today!" and laid his hand on my left breast. I said to him: "Don't do that!" But he continued to handle me indecently, which provoked my anger. Before I realized his sinful intentions, he got much closer. It was all over when my father-in-law entered and accidentally trod on me.

INNKEEPER [*explaining*]. On my son's behalf.

AZDAK [*to the* STABLEMAN]. You admit you started it?

STABLEMAN. Yes.

AZDAK. Ludovica, you like to eat sweet things?

LUDOVICA. Yes, sunflower seeds!

AZDAK. You like to lie a long time in the bathtub?

LUDOVICA. Half an hour or so.

AZDAK. Public Prosecutor, drop your knife—there on the ground. [SHAUWA *does so.*] Ludovica, pick up that knife. [LUDOVICA, *swaying her hips, does so.*] See that? [*He points at her.*] The way it moves? The rape is now proven. By eating too much—sweet things, especially—by lying too long in warm water, by laziness and too soft a skin, you have raped that unfortunate man. Think you can run around with a behind like that and get away with it in court? This is a case of intentional assault with a dangerous weapon! You are sentenced to hand over to the Court the little roan which your father liked to ride "on his son's behalf." And now, come with me to the stables, so the Court can inspect the scene of the crime, Ludovica.

SINGER AND CHORUS.
When the sharks the sharks devour
Little fishes have their hour.
For a while the load is off their back.
On Grusinia's highways faring
Fixed-up scales of justice bearing
Strode the poor man's magistrate: Azdak.

And he gave to the forsaken
All that from the rich he'd taken.
And a bodyguard of roughnecks was Azdak's.
And our good and evil man, he
Smiled upon Grusinia's Granny.
His emblem was a tear in sealing wax.

All mankind should love each other
But when visiting your brother
Take an ax along and hold it fast.
Not in theory but in practice
Miracles are wrought with axes
And the age of miracles is not past.

[AZDAK's *judge's chair is in a tavern. Three rich* FARMERS *stand before* AZDAK. SHAUWA *brings him wine. In a corner stands an* OLD PEASANT WOMAN. *In the open doorway, and outside, stand villagers looking on. An* IRONSHIRT *stands guard with a banner.*]

AZDAK. The Public Prosecutor has the floor.

SHAUWA. It concerns a cow. For five weeks, the defendant has had a cow in her stable, the property of the farmer Suru. She was also found to be in possession of a stolen ham, and a number of cows belonging to Shutoff were killed after he asked the defendant to pay the rent on a piece of land.

FARMERS.
—It's a matter of my ham, Your Honor.
—It's a matter of my cow, Your Honor.
—It's a matter of my land, Your Honor.

AZDAK. Well, Granny, what have *you* got to say to all this?

OLD WOMAN. Your Honor, one night toward morning, five weeks ago, there was a knock at my door, and outside stood a bearded man with a cow. "My dear woman," he said, "I am the miracle-working Saint Banditus and because your son has been killed in the war, I bring you this cow as a souvenir. Take good care of it."

FARMERS.
—The robber, Irakli, Your Honor!
—Her brother-in-law, Your Honor!
—The cow-thief!
—The incendiary!
—He must be beheaded!

[*Outside, a woman screams. The crowd grows restless, retreats. Enter the* BANDIT *Irakli with a huge ax.*]

BANDIT. A very good evening, dear friends! A glass of vodka!

FARMERS [*crossing themselves*]. Irakli!

AZDAK. Public Prosecutor, a glass of vodka for our guest. And who are you?

BANDIT. I'm a wandering hermit, Your Honor. Thanks for the gracious gift. [*He empties the glass which* SHAUWA *has brought.*] Another!

AZDAK. I am Azdak. [*He gets up and bows. The* BANDIT *also bows.*] The Court welcomes the foreign hermit. Go on with your story, Granny.

OLD WOMAN. Your Honor, that first night I didn't yet know Saint Banditus could work miracles, it was only the cow. But one night, a few days later, the farmer's servants came to take the cow away again. Then they turned round in front of my door and went off without the cow. And bumps as big as a fist sprouted on their heads. So I knew that Saint Banditus had changed their hearts and turned them into friendly people.

[*The* BANDIT *roars with laughter.*]

FIRST FARMER. I know what changed them.

AZDAK. That's fine. You can tell us later. Continue.

OLD WOMAN. Your Honor, the next one to become a good man was the farmer Shutoff—a devil, as everyone knows. But Saint Banditus arranged it so he let me off the rent on the little piece of land.

SECOND FARMER. Because my cows were killed in the field.

[*The* BANDIT *laughs.*]

OLD WOMAN [*answering* AZDAK's *sign to continue*]. Then one morning the ham came flying in at my window. It hit me in the small of the back. I'm still lame, Your Honor, look. [*She limps a few steps. The* BANDIT *laughs.*] Your Honor, was there ever a time when a poor old woman could get a ham *without* a miracle?

[*The* BANDIT *starts sobbing.*]

AZDAK [*rising from his chair*]. Granny, that's a question that strikes straight at the Court's heart. Be so kind as to sit here. [*The* OLD WOMAN, *hesitating, sits in the judge's chair.*]

AZDAK [*sits on the floor, glass in hand, reciting*].
Granny
We could almost call you Granny Grusinia
The Woebegone
The Bereaved Mother
Whose sons have gone to war.
Receiving the present of a cow
She bursts out crying.
When she is beaten
She remains hopeful.
When she's not beaten
She's surprised.
On us
Who are already damned
May you render a merciful verdict
Granny Grusinia!

[*Bellowing at the* FARMERS] Admit you don't believe in miracles, you atheists! Each of you is sentenced to pay five hundred piasters! For godlessness! Get out! [*The* FARMERS *slink out.*] And you Granny, and you [*to the* BANDIT] pious man, empty a pitcher of wine with the Public Prosecutor and Azdak!

SINGER AND CHORUS.
And he broke the rules to save them.
Broken law like bread he gave them,
Brought them to shore upon his crooked back.
At long last the poor and lowly
Had someone who was not too holy
To be bribed by empty hands: Azdak.

For two years it was his pleasure
To give the beasts of prey short measure:
He became a wolf to fight the pack.
From All Hallows to All Hallows
On his chair beside the gallows
Dispensing justice in his fashion sat Azdak.

SINGER.
But the era of disorder came to an end.
The Grand Duke returned.
The Governor's wife returned.

A trial was held.
Many died.
The people's quarters burned anew.
And fear seized Azdak.

[AZDAK'S *judge's chair stands again in the court of justice.* AZDAK *sits on the floor, shaving and talking to* SHAUWA. *Noises outside. In the rear the* FAT PRINCE'S *head is carried by on a lance.*]

AZDAK. Shauwa, the days of your slavery are numbered, maybe even the minutes. For a long time now I have held you in the iron curb of reason, and it has torn your mouth till it bleeds. I have lashed you with reasonable arguments, I have manhandled you with logic. You are by nature a weak man, and if one slyly throws an argument in your path, you *have* to snap it up, you can't resist. It is your nature to lick the hand of some superior being. But superior beings can be of very different kinds. And now, with your liberation, you will soon be able to follow your natural inclinations, which are low. You will be able to follow your infallible instinct, which teaches you to plant your fat heel on the faces of men. Gone is the era of confusion and disorder, which I find described in the Song of Chaos. Let us now sing that song together in memory of those terrible days. Sit down and don't do violence to the music. Don't be afraid. It sounds all right. And it has a fine refrain. [*He sings.*]

THE SONG OF CHAOS

Sister, hide your face! Brother, take your knife!
The times are out of joint!
Big men are full of complaint
And small men full of joy.
The city says:
"Let us drive the mighty from our midst!"
Offices are raided. Lists of serfs are destroyed.
They have set Master's nose to the grindstone.
They who lived in the dark have seen the light.
The ebony poor box is broken.
Sesnem* wood is sawed up for beds.
Who had no bread have full barns.
Who begged for alms of corn now mete it out.

* I do not know what kind of wood this is, so I have left the word exactly as it stands in the German original. The song is based on an Egyptian papyrus which Brecht cites as such in his essay, "Five Difficulties in the Writing of the Truth." I should think he must have come across it in Adolf Erman's *Die Literatur der Aegypter*, 1923, p. 130 ff. Erman too gives the word as Sesnem. The same papyrus is quoted in Karl Jaspers' *Man in the Modern Age* (Anchor edition, pp. 18–19) but without the sentence about the Sesnem wood.—E.B.

SHAUWA [*refrain*].

> Oh, oh, oh, oh.

AZDAK [*refrain*].

> Where are you, General, where are you?
> Please, please, please, restore order!

> The nobleman's son can no longer be recognized;
> The lady's child becomes the son of her slave-girl
> The councilors meet in a shed.
> Once, this man was barely allowed to sleep on the wall;
> Now, he stretches his limbs in a bed.
> Once, this man rowed a boat; now, he owns ships.
> Their owner looks for them, but they're his no longer.
> Five men are sent on a journey by their master.
> "Go yourself," they say, "we have arrived."

SHAUWA [*refrain*].

> Oh, oh, oh, oh.

AZDAK [*refrain*].

> Where are you, General, where are you?
> Please, please, please, restore order!

Yes, so it might have been, had order been neglected much longer. But now the Grand Duke has returned to the capital, and the Persians have lent him an army to restore order with. The people's quarters are already aflame. Go and get me the big book I always sit on. [SHAUWA *brings the big book from the judge's chair.* AZDAK *opens it.*] This is the Statute Book and I've always used it, as you can testify. Now I'd better look in this book and see what they can do to me. I've let the down-and-outs get away with murder, and I'll have to pay for it. I helped poverty onto its skinny legs, so they'll hang me for drunkenness. I peeped into the rich man's pocket, which is bad taste. And I can't hide anywhere—everybody knows me because I've helped everybody.

SHAUWA. Someone's coming!

AZDAK [*in panic, he walks trembling to the chair*]. It's the end. And now they'd enjoy seeing what a Great Man I am. I'll deprive them of that pleasure. I'll beg on my knees for mercy. Spittle will slobber down my chin. The fear of death is in me.

[*Enter Natella Abashwili, the* GOVERNOR'S WIFE, *followed by the* ADJUTANT *and an* IRONSHIRT.]

GOVERNOR'S WIFE. What sort of a creature is that, Shalva?

AZDAK. A willing one, Your Highness, a man ready to oblige.

ADJUTANT. Natella Abashwili, wife of the late Governor, has just returned. She is looking for her two-year-old son, Michael. She has been informed that the child was carried off to the mountains by a former servant.

AZDAK. The child will be brought back, Your Highness, at your service.

ADJUTANT. They say that the person in question is passing it off as her own.

AZDAK. She will be beheaded, Your Highness, at your service.

ADJUTANT. That is all.

GOVERNOR'S WIFE [*leaving*]. I don't like that man.

AZDAK [*following her to door, bowing*]. At your service, Your Highness, it will all be arranged.

5

THE CHALK CIRCLE

SINGER.

> Hear now the story of the trial
> Concerning Governor Abashwili's child
> And the determination of the true mother
> By the famous test of the Chalk Circle.

[*Law court in Nuka.* IRONSHIRTS *lead* MICHAEL *across stage and out at the back.* IRONSHIRTS *hold* GRUSHA *back with their lances under the gateway until the* CHILD *has been led through. Then she is admitted. She is accompanied by the former Governor's* COOK. *Distant noises and a fire-red sky.*]

GRUSHA [*trying to hide*]. He's brave, he can wash himself now.

COOK. You're lucky. It's not a real judge. It's Azdak, a drunk who doesn't know what he's doing. The biggest thieves have got by through him. Because he gets everything mixed up and the rich never offer him big enough bribes, the like of us sometimes do pretty well.

GRUSHA. I *need* luck right now.

COOK. Touch wood. [*She crosses herself.*] I'd better offer up another prayer that the judge may be drunk. [*She prays with motionless lips, while*

GRUSHA *looks around, in vain, for the* CHILD.] Why must you hold on to it at any price if it isn't yours? In days like these?

GRUSHA. He's mine. I brought him up.

COOK. Have you never thought what'd happen when she came back?

GRUSHA. At first I thought I'd give him to her. Then I thought she wouldn't come back.

COOK. And even a borrowed coat keeps a man warm, hm? [GRUSHA *nods.*] I'll swear to anything for you. You're a decent girl. [*She sees the soldier* SIMON SHASHAVA *approaching.*] You've done wrong by Simon, though. I've been talking with him. He just can't understand.

GRUSHA [*unaware of* SIMON's *presence*]. Right now I can't be bothered whether he understands or not!

COOK. He knows the child isn't yours, but you married and not free "till death you do part"—he can't understand *that*.

[GRUSHA *sees* SIMON *and greets him.*]

SIMON [*gloomily*]. I wish the lady to know I will swear I am the father of the child.

GRUSHA [*low*]. Thank you, Simon.

SIMON. At the same time I wish the lady to know my hands are not tied—nor are hers.

COOK. You needn't have said that. You know she's married.

SIMON. And it needs no rubbing in.

[*Enter an* IRONSHIRT.]

IRONSHIRT. Where's the judge? Has anyone seen the judge?

ANOTHER IRONSHIRT [*stepping forward*]. The judge isn't here yet. Nothing but a bed and a pitcher in the whole house!

[*Exeunt* IRONSHIRTS.]

COOK. I hope nothing has happened to him. With any other judge you'd have as much chance as a chicken has teeth.

GRUSHA [*who has turned away and covered her face*]. Stand in front of me. I shouldn't have come to Nuka. If I run into the Ironshirt, the one I hit over the head . . .

[*She screams. An* IRONSHIRT *had stopped and, turning his back, had been listening to her. He now wheels around. It is the* CORPORAL, *and he has a huge scar across his face.*]

IRONSHIRT [*in the gateway*]. What's the matter, Shotta? Do you know her?

CORPORAL [*after staring for some time*]. No.

IRONSHIRT. She's the one who stole the Abashwili child, or so they say. If you know anything about it you can make some money, Shotta.

[*Exit the* CORPORAL, *cursing.*]

COOK. Was it him? [GRUSHA *nods.*] I think he'll keep his mouth shut, or he'd be admitting he was after the child.

GRUSHA. I'd almost forgotten him.

[*Enter the* GOVERNOR's WIFE, *followed by the* ADJUTANT *and two* LAWYERS.]

GOVERNOR's WIFE. At least there are no common people here, thank God. I can't stand their smell. It always gives me migraine.

FIRST LAWYER. Madam, I must ask you to be careful what you say until we have another judge.

GOVERNOR's WIFE. But I didn't say anything, Illo Shuboladze. I love the people with their simple straight-forward minds. It's only that their smell brings on my migraine.

SECOND LAWYER. There won't be many spectators. The whole population is sitting at home behind locked doors because of the riots in the people's quarters.

GOVERNOR's WIFE [*looking at* GRUSHA]. Is that the creature?

FIRST LAWYER. Please, most gracious Natella Abashwili, abstain from invective until it is certain the Grand Duke has appointed a new judge and we're rid of the present one, who's about the lowest fellow ever seen in judge's gown. Things are all set to move, you see.

[*Enter* IRONSHIRTS *from the courtyard.*]

COOK. Her Grace would pull your hair out on the spot if she didn't know Azdak is for the poor. He goes by the face.

[IRONSHIRTS *begin fastening a rope to a beam.* AZDAK, *in chains, is led in, followed by* SHAUWA, *also in chains. The three* FARMERS *bring up the rear.*]

AN IRONSHIRT. Trying to run away, were you? [*He strikes* AZDAK.]

ONE FARMER. Off with his judge's gown before we string him up!

[IRONSHIRTS *and* FARMERS *tear off* AZDAK's *gown. His torn underwear is visible. Then someone kicks him.*]

AN IRONSHIRT [*pushing him into someone else*]. Want a load of justice? Here it is!

[*Accompanied by shouts of* "You take it!" *and* "Let me have him, Brother!" *they throw* AZDAK *back and forth until he collapses. Then he is lifted up and dragged under the noose.*]

GOVERNOR'S WIFE [*who, during this "ballgame,"* *has clapped her hands hysterically*]. I disliked that man from the moment I first saw him.

AZDAK [*covered with blood, panting*]. I can't see. Give me a rag.

AN IRONSHIRT. What is it you want to see?

AZDAK. You, you dogs! [*He wipes the blood out* *of his eyes with his shirt.*] Good morning, dogs! How goes it, dogs! How's the dog world? Does it smell good? Got another boot for me to lick? Are you back at each other's throats, dogs?

[*Accompanied by a* CORPORAL, *a dust-covered* RIDER *enters. He takes some documents from a* *leather case, looks at them, then interrupts.*]

RIDER. Stop! I bring a dispatch from the Grand Duke, containing the latest appointments.

CORPORAL [*bellowing*]. Atten—shun!

RIDER. Of the new judge it says: "We appoint a man whom we have to thank for saving a life indispensable to the country's welfare—a certain Azdak of Nuka." Which is he?

SHAUWA [*pointing*]. That's him, Your Excellency.

CORPORAL [*bellowing*]. What's going on here?

AN IRONSHIRT. I beg to report that His Honor Azdak was already His Honor Azdak, but on these farmers' denunciation was pronounced the Grand Duke's enemy.

CORPORAL [*pointing at the* FARMERS]. March them off! [*They are marched off. They bow all the* *time.*] See to it that His Honor Azdak is exposed to no more violence.

[*Exeunt* RIDER *and* CORPORAL.]

COOK [*to* SHAUWA]. She clapped her hands! I hope he saw it!

FIRST LAWYER. It's a catastrophe.

[AZDAK *has fainted. Coming to, he is dressed* *again in judge's robes. He walks, swaying, toward* *the* IRONSHIRTS.]

AN IRONSHIRT. What does Your Honor desire?

AZDAK. Nothing, fellow dogs, or just an occasional boot to lick. [*To* SHAUWA] I pardon you. [*He is unchained.*] Get me some red wine, the sweet kind. [SHAUWA *stumbles off.*] Get out of here, I've got to judge a case. [*Exeunt* IRONSHIRTS. SHAUWA *returns with a pitcher of wine.* AZDAK *gulps it down.*] Something for my backside. [SHAUWA *brings the Statute Book, puts it on the* *judge's chair.* AZDAK *sits on it.*] I accept.

[*The Prosecutors, among whom a worried coun-* *cil has been held, smile with relief. They whisper.*]

COOK. Oh dear!

SIMON. A well can't be filled with dew, they say.

LAWYERS [*approaching* AZDAK, *who stands up,* *expectantly*]. A quite ridiculous case, Your Honor. The accused has abducted a child and refuses to hand it over.

AZDAK [*stretching out his hand, glancing at* GRUSHA]. A most attractive person. [*He fingers the* *money, then sits down, satisfied.*] I declare the proceedings open and demand the whole truth. [*To* GRUSHA] Especially from you.

FIRST LAWYER. High Court of Justice! Blood, as the popular saying goes, is thicker than water. This old adage . . .

AZDAK [*interrupting*]. The Court wants to know the lawyer's fee.

FIRST LAWYER [*surprised*]. I beg your pardon? [AZDAK, *smiling, rubs his thumb and index finger.*] Oh, I see. Five hundred piasters, Your Honor, to answer the Court's somewhat unusual question.

AZDAK. Did you hear? The question is unusual. I ask it because I listen in quite a different way when I know you're good.

FIRST LAWYER [*bowing*]. Thank you, Your Honor. High Court of Justice, of all ties the ties of blood are strongest. Mother and child—is there a more intimate relationship? Can one tear a child from its mother? High Court of Justice, she has conceived it in the holy ecstasies of love. She has carried it in her womb. She has fed it with her blood. She has borne it with pain. High Court of Justice, it has been observed that the wild tigress, robbed of her young, roams restless through the mountains, shrunk to a shadow. Nature herself . . .

AZDAK [*interrupting, to* GRUSHA]. What's your answer to all this and anything else that lawyer might have to say?

GRUSHA. He's mine.

AZDAK. Is that all? I hope you can prove it. Why should I assign the child to you in any case?

GRUSHA. I brought him up like the priest says "according to my best knowledge and conscience." I always found him something to eat. Most of the time he had a roof over his head. And I went to such trouble for him. I had expenses too. I didn't look out for my own comfort. I brought the child up to be friendly with everyone, and from the beginning taught him to work. As well as he could, that is. He's still very little.

FIRST LAWYER. Your Honor, it is significant that

the girl herself doesn't claim any tie of blood between her and the child.

AZDAK. The Court takes note of that.

FIRST LAWYER. Thank you, Your Honor. And now permit a woman bowed in sorrow—who has already lost her husband and now has also to fear the loss of her child—to address a few words to you. The gracious Natella Abashwili is . . .

GOVERNOR'S WIFE [*quietly*]. A most cruel fate, sir, forces me to describe to you the tortures of a bereaved mother's soul, the anxiety, the sleepless nights, the . . .

SECOND LAWYER [*bursting out*]. It's outrageous the way this woman is being treated! Her husband's palace is closed to her! The revenue of her estates is blocked, and she is cold-bloodedly told that it's tied to the heir. She can't do a thing without that child. She can't even pay her lawyers!! [*To the* FIRST LAWYER, *who, desperate about this outburst, makes frantic gestures to keep him from speaking*] Dear Illo Shuboladze, surely it can be divulged now that the Abashwili estates are at stake?

FIRST LAWYER. Please, Honored Sandro Oboladze! We agreed . . . [*To* AZDAK] Of course it is correct that the trial will also decide if our noble client can take over the Abashwili estates, which are rather extensive. I say "also" advisedly, for in the foreground stands the human tragedy of a mother, as Natella Abashwili very properly explained in the first words of her moving statement. Even if Michael Abashwili were not heir to the estates, he would still be the dearly beloved child of my client.

AZDAK. Stop! The Court is touched by the mention of estates. It's a proof of human feeling.

SECOND LAWYER. Thanks, Your Honor. Dear Illo Shuboladze, we can prove in any case that the woman who took the child is not the child's mother. Permit me to lay before the Court the bare facts. High Court of Justice, by an unfortunate chain of circumstances, Michael Abashwili was left behind on that Easter Sunday while his mother was making her escape. Grusha, a palace kitchen maid, was seen with the baby . . .

COOK. All her mistress was thinking of was what dresses she'd take along!

SECOND LAWYER [*unmoved*]. Nearly a year later Grusha turned up in a mountain village with a baby and there entered into the state of matrimony with . . .

AZDAK. How'd you get to that mountain village?

GRUSHA. On foot, Your Honor. And he was mine.

SIMON. I'm the father, Your Honor.

COOK. I used to look after it for them, Your Honor. For five piasters.

SECOND LAWYER. This man is engaged to Grusha, High Court of Justice: his testimony is suspect.

AZDAK. Are you the man she married in the mountain village?

SIMON. No, Your Honor, she married a peasant.

AZDAK [*to* GRUSHA]. Why? [*Pointing at* SIMON] Is he no good in bed? Tell the truth.

GRUSHA. We didn't get that far. I married because of the baby. So he'd have a roof over his head. [*Pointing at* SIMON] He was in the war, Your Honor.

AZDAK. And now he wants you back again, huh?

SIMON. I wish to state in evidence . . .

GRUSHA [*angrily*]. I am no longer free, Your Honor.

AZDAK. And the child, you claim, comes from whoring? [GRUSHA *doesn't answer.*] I'm going to ask you a question: What kind of child is he? A ragged little bastard? Or from a good family?

GRUSHA [*angrily*]. He's an ordinary child.

AZDAK. I mean—did he have refined features from the beginning?

GRUSHA. He had a nose on his face.

AZDAK. A very significant comment! It has been said of me that I went out one time and sniffed at a rosebush before rendering a verdict—tricks like that are needed nowadays. Well, I'll make it short, and not listen to any more lies. [*To* GRUSHA] Especially not yours. [*To all the accused*] I can imagine what you've cooked up to cheat me! I know you people. You're swindlers.

GRUSHA [*suddenly*]. I can understand your wanting to cut it short, now I've seen what you accepted!

AZDAK. Shut up! Did I accept anything from you?

GRUSHA [*while the* COOK *tries to restrain her*]. I haven't got anything.

AZDAK. True. Quite true. From starvelings I never get a thing. I might just as well starve, myself. You want justice, but do you want to pay for it, hm? When you go to a butcher you know you have to pay, but you people go to a judge as if you were off to a funeral supper.

SIMON [*loudly*]. When the horse was shod, the

horsefly held out its leg, as the saying is.

AZDAK [*eagerly accepting the challenge*]. Better a treasure in manure than a stone in a mountain stream.

SIMON. A fine day. Let's go fishing said the angler to the worm.

AZDAK. I'm my own master, said the servant, and cut off his foot.

SIMON. I love you as a father, said the Czar to the peasants, and had the Czarevitch's head chopped off.

AZDAK. A fool's worst enemy is himself.

SIMON. However, a fart has no nose.

AZDAK. Fined ten piasters for indecent language in court! That'll teach you what justice is.

GRUSHA [*furiously*]. A fine kind of justice! You play fast and loose with us because we don't talk as refined as that crowd with their lawyers.

AZDAK. That's true. You people are too dumb. It's only right you should get it in the neck.

GRUSHA. You want to hand the child over to her, and she wouldn't even know how to keep it dry, she's so "refined"! You know about as much about justice as I do!

AZDAK. There's something in that. I'm an ignorant man. Haven't even a decent pair of pants on under this gown. Look! With me, everything goes on food and drink—I was educated in a convent. Incidentally, I'll fine you ten piasters for contempt of court. And you're a very silly girl, to turn me against you, instead of making eyes at me and wiggling your backside a little to keep me in a good temper. Twenty piasters!

GRUSHA. Even if it was thirty, I'd tell you what I think of your justice, you drunken onion! [*Incoherently*] How dare you talk to me like the cracked Isaiah on the church window? As if you were somebody? For you weren't born to this. You weren't born to rap your own mother on the knuckles if she swipes a little bowl of salt someplace. Aren't you ashamed of yourself when you see how I tremble before you? You've made yourself their servant so no one will take their houses from them—houses they had stolen! Since when have houses belonged to the bedbugs? But you're on the watch, or they couldn't drag our men into their wars! You bribetaker!

[AZDAK *half gets up, starts beaming. With his little hammer he halfheartedly knocks on the table as if to get silence. As* GRUSHA's *scolding continues, he only beats time with his hammer.*]

GRUSHA. I've no respect for you. No more than for a thief or a bandit with a knife! You can do what you want. You can take the child away from me, a hundred against one, but I tell you one thing: only extortioners should be chosen for a profession like yours, and men who rape children! As punishment! Yes, let *them* sit in judgment on their fellow creatures. It is worse than to hang from the gallows.

AZDAK [*sitting down*]. Now it'll be thirty! And I won't go on squabbling with you—we're not in a tavern. What'd happen to my dignity as a judge? Anyway, I've lost interest in your case. Where's the couple who wanted a divorce? [*To* SHAUWA] Bring 'em in. This case is adjourned for fifteen minutes.

FIRST LAWYER [*To the* GOVERNOR'S WIFE]. Even without using the rest of the evidence, Madam, we have the verdict in the bag.

COOK [*to* GRUSHA]. You've gone and spoiled your chances with him. You won't get the child now.

GOVERNOR'S WIFE. Shalva, my smelling salts!

[*Enter a very old couple.*]

AZDAK. I accept. [*The old couple don't understand.*] I hear you want to be divorced. How long have you been together?

OLD WOMAN. Forty years, Your Honor.

AZDAK. And why do you want a divorce?

OLD MAN. We don't like each other, Your Honor.

AZDAK. Since when?

OLD WOMAN. Oh, from the very beginning, Your Honor.

AZDAK. I'll think about your request and render my verdict when I'm through with the other case. [SHAUWA *leads them back.*] I need the child. [*He beckons* GRUSHA *to him and bends not unkindly toward her.*] I've noticed you have a soft spot for justice. I don't believe he's your child, but if he *were* yours, woman, wouldn't you want him to be rich? You'd only have to say he wasn't yours, and he'd have a palace and many horses in his stable and many beggars on his doorstep and many soldiers in his service and many petitioners in his courtyard, wouldn't he? What do you say—don't you want him to be rich?

[GRUSHA *is silent.*]

SINGER.

Hear now what the angry girl thought but did not say:
Had he golden shoes to wear

He'd be as cruel as a bear
Evil would his life disgrace.
He'd laugh in my face.

Carrying a heart of flint
Is too troublesome a stint.
Being powerful and bad
Is hard on a lad.

Then let hunger be his foe!
Hungry men and women, no.
Let him fear the darksome night
But not daylight!

AZDAK. I think I understand you, woman.

GRUSHA [suddenly and loudly]. I won't give him up. I've raised him, and he knows me.

[Enter SHAUWA with the CHILD.]

GOVERNOR'S WIFE. He's in rags!

GRUSHA. That's not true. But I wasn't given time to put his good shirt on.

GOVERNOR'S WIFE. He must have been in a pigsty.

GRUSHA [furiously]. I'm not a pig, but there are some who are! Where did you leave your baby?

GOVERNOR'S WIFE. I'll show you, you vulgar creature! [She is about to throw herself on GRUSHA, but is restrained by her lawyers.] She's a criminal, she must be whipped. Immediately!

SECOND LAWYER [holding his hand over her mouth]. Natella Abashwili, you promised . . . Your Honor, the plaintiff's nerves . . .

AZDAK. Plaintiff and defendant! The Court has listened to your case, and has come to no decision as to who the real mother is; therefore, I, the judge, am obliged to choose a mother for the child. I'll make a test. Shauwa, get a piece of chalk and draw a circle on the floor. [SHAUWA does so.] Now place the child in the center. [SHAUWA puts MICHAEL, who smiles at GRUSHA, in the center of the circle.] Stand near the circle, both of you. [The GOVERNOR'S WIFE and GRUSHA step up to the circle.] Now each of you take the child by one hand. [They do so.] The true mother is she who can pull the child out of the circle.

SECOND LAWYER [quickly]. High Court of Justice, I object! The fate of the great Abashwili estates, which are tied to the child, as the heir, should not be made dependent on such a doubtful duel. In addition, my client does not command the strength of this person, who is accustomed to physical work.

AZDAK. She looks pretty well fed to me. Pull! [The GOVERNOR'S WIFE pulls the CHILD out of the circle on her side; GRUSHA has let go and stands aghast.] What's the matter with you? You didn't pull.

GRUSHA. I didn't hold on to him.

FIRST LAWYER [congratulating the GOVERNOR'S WIFE]. What did I say! The ties of blood!

GRUSHA [running to AZDAK]. Your Honor, I take back everything I said against you. I ask your forgiveness. But could I keep him till he can speak all the words? He knows a few.

AZDAK. Don't influence the Court. I bet you only know about twenty words yourself. All right, I'll make the test once more, just to be certain. [The two women take up their positions again.] Pull! [Again GRUSHA lets go of the CHILD.]

GRUSHA [in despair]. I brought him up! Shall I also tear him to bits? I can't!

AZDAK [rising]. And in this manner the Court has determined the true mother. [To GRUSHA] Take your child and be off. I advise you not to stay in the city with him. [To the GOVERNOR'S WIFE] And you disappear before I fine you for fraud. Your estates fall to the city. They'll be converted into a playground for the children. They need one, and I've decided it'll be called after me: Azdak's Garden.

[The GOVERNOR'S WIFE has fainted and is carried out by the LAWYERS and the ADJUTANT. GRUSHA stands motionless. SHAUWA leads the CHILD toward her.]

AZDAK. Now I'll take off this judge's gown—it's too hot for me. I'm not cut out for a hero. In token of farewell I invite you all to a little dance in the meadow outside. Oh, I'd almost forgotten something in my excitement . . . to sign the divorce decree. [Using the judge's chair as a table, he writes something on a piece of paper, and prepares to leave. Dance music has started.]

SHAUWA [having read what is on the paper]. But that's not right. You've not divorced the old people. You've divorced Grusha!

AZDAK. Divorced the wrong couple? What a pity! And I never retract! If I did, how could we keep order in the land? [To the old couple] I'll invite you to my party instead. You don't mind dancing with each other, do you? [To GRUSHA and SIMON] I've got forty piasters coming from you.

SIMON [pulling out his purse]. Cheap at the price, Your Honor. And many thanks.

AZDAK [*pocketing the cash*]. I'll be needing this.

GRUSHA [*to* MICHAEL]. So we'd better leave the city tonight, Michael? [*To* SIMON] You like him?

SIMON. With my respects, I like him.

GRUSHA. Now I can tell you: I took him because on that Easter Sunday I got engaged to you. So he's a child of love. Michael, let's dance.

[*She dances with* MICHAEL, SIMON *dances with the* COOK, *the old couple with each other.* AZDAK *stands lost in thought. The dancers soon hide him from view. Occasionally he is seen, but less and less as more couples join the dance.*]

SINGER.

And after that evening Azdak vanished and was never seen again.

The people of Grusinia did not forget him but long remembered

The period of his judging as a brief golden age,

Almost an age of justice.

[*All the couples dance off.* AZDAK *has disappeared.*]

But you, you who have listened to the Story of the Chalk Circle,

Take note what men of old concluded:

That what there is shall go to those who are good for it,

Children to the motherly, that they prosper,

Carts to good drivers, that they be driven well,

The valley to the waterers, that it yield fruit.

The
Cocktail Party

BY T. S. ELIOT

The possibility of creating an English poetic drama in the twentieth century has engaged the attention of two of its foremost lyric poets, W. B. Yeats and T. S. Eliot. They approached their common task from opposite directions, however: whereas Yeats adapted to Irish myth and legend the techniques of French symbolist and Japanese *noh* drama, Eliot superimposed on the stuff of contemporary English life the characteristic forms of Greek, medieval, and Elizabethan drama. Thus, while Yeats's plays cultivate the "remote, spiritual, and ideal," and are increasingly considered a coterie drama, Eliot's seem naturalistic, urbane, almost prosaic by contrast, and have achieved a popular appeal beyond their author's expectations.

Nonetheless the underlying method and purpose of Eliot's plays, as of Yeats's, is to penetrate the appearances of life and reveal its hidden pattern—that is, for Eliot, a Christian pattern of regeneration. In *The Cocktail Party,* however, that pattern is not simply, or simplistically, Christian. While Celia experiences Christian conversion and martyrdom, the Chamberlaynes undergo the less apocalyptic but no less romantic experience of a revitalized marriage within a secular context. Eliot himself called attention to the ways in which the play parallels Euripides' *Alcestis* (see the essay by Robert B. Heilman that appears on pages 244–51), but *The Cocktail Party* also owes much to *The Tempest;* the efforts of the modern psychiatrist have simply replaced those of the Renaissance magician in the movement toward personal, marital, and social harmony. Shakespeare's final romances, in fact, became a resting point of Eliot's consciousness toward the end of his career. He called them "the work of a dramatist who has seen through the dramatic action of men into a spiritual action which transcends it," Eliot's own objective.

The Cocktail Party was first produced in 1949 at the Edinburgh Festival and shortly thereafter was successfully staged in both London and New York. With this printing, it is anthologized for the first time.

Persons

EDWARD CHAMBERLAYNE

JULIA (MRS. SHUTTLETHWAITE)

CELIA COPLESTONE

ALEXANDER MACCOLGIE GIBBS

PETER QUILPE

AN UNIDENTIFIED GUEST, *later identified as*

  SIR HENRY HARCOURT-REILLY

LAVINIA CHAMBERLAYNE

A NURSE-SECRETARY

CATERER'S MAN

The scene is laid in London

ACT I

SCENE I

The drawing room of the Chamberlaynes' London flat. Early evening. EDWARD CHAMBERLAYNE, JULIA SHUTTLETHWAITE, CELIA COPLESTONE, PETER QUILPE, ALEXANDER MACCOLGIE GIBBS, *and an* UNIDENTIFIED GUEST.

ALEX. You've missed the point completely, Julia:
There *were* no tigers. *That* was the point.

JULIA. Then what were you doing, up in a tree:
You and the Maharaja?

ALEX. My dear Julia!
It's perfectly hopeless. You haven't been listening.

PETER. You'll have to tell us all over again, Alex.

ALEX. I never tell the same story twice.

JULIA. But I'm still waiting to know what happened.
I know it started as a story about tigers.

ALEX. I said there were no tigers.

CELIA. Oh do stop wrangling,
Both of you. It's your turn, Julia.
Do tell us that story you told the other day, about
  Lady Klootz and the wedding cake.

PETER. And how the butler found her in the pantry, rinsing her mouth out with champagne.
I like that story.

CELIA. I love that story.

ALEX. *I'm* never tired of hearing that story.

JULIA. Well, you all seem to know it.

CELIA. Do we all know it?
But we're never tired of hearing *you* tell it.
I don't believe everyone here knows it.

[*To the* UNIDENTIFIED GUEST]
You don't know it, do you?

UNIDENTIFIED GUEST. No, I've never heard it.

CELIA. Here's one new listener for you, Julia;
And I don't believe that Edward knows it.

EDWARD. I may have heard it, but I don't remember it.

CELIA. And Julia's the only person to tell it.
She's such a good mimic.

JULIA. Am I a good mimic?

PETER. You *are* a good mimic. You never miss anything.

ALEX. She never misses anything unless she wants to.

CELIA. Especially the Lithuanian accent.

JULIA. Lithuanian? Lady Klootz?

PETER. I thought she was Belgian.

ALEX. Her father belonged to a Baltic family—
One of the *oldest* Baltic families
With a branch in Sweden and one in Denmark.
There were several very lovely daughters:
I wonder what's become of them now.

JULIA. Lady Klootz was very lovely, once upon a time.
What a life she led! I used to say to her: 'Greta!
You have too much vitality.' But she enjoyed herself.

[*To the* UNIDENTIFIED GUEST]
Did *you* know Lady Klootz?

UNIDENTIFIED GUEST. No, I never met her.

CELIA. Go on with the story about the wedding cake.

JULIA. Well, but it really isn't my story.
I heard it first from Delia Verinder
Who was there when it happened.

[*To the* UNIDENTIFIED GUEST]
Do *you* know Delia Verinder?

UNIDENTIFIED GUEST. No, I don't know her.

JULIA.   Well, one can't be too careful
Before one tells a story.

ALEX.   Delia Verinder?
Was she the one who had three brothers?

JULIA. How many brothers? Two, I think.

ALEX. No, there were three, but you wouldn't
know the third one:
They kept him rather quiet.

JULIA.   Oh, you mean *that* one.

ALEX. He was feeble-minded.

JULIA.   Oh, not feeble-minded:
He was only harmless.

ALEX.   Well then, harmless.

JULIA. He was very clever at repairing clocks;
And he had a remarkable sense of hearing—
The only man I ever met who could hear the cry
of bats.

PETER. Hear the cry of bats?

JULIA.   He could hear the cry of bats.

CELIA. But how do you know he could hear the
cry of bats?

JULIA. Because he said so. And I believed him.

CELIA. But if he was so . . . harmless, how
could you believe him?
He might have imagined it.

JULIA.   My darling Celia,
You needn't be so sceptical. I stayed there once
At their castle in the North. How he suffered!
They had to find an island for him
Where there were no bats.

ALEX.   And is he still there?
Julia is really a mine of information.

CELIA. There isn't much that Julia doesn't know.

PETER. Go on with the story about the wedding
cake.

[EDWARD *leaves the room.*]

JULIA. No, we'll wait until Edward comes back
into the room.
Now I want to relax. Are there any more cocktails?

PETER. But do go on. Edward wasn't listening
anyway.

JULIA. No, he wasn't listening, but he's such a
strain—
Edward without Lavinia! He's quite impossible!
Leaving it to me to keep things going.
What a host! And nothing fit to eat!
The only reason for a cocktail party
For a gluttonous old woman like me
Is a really nice tit-bit. I can drink at home.

[EDWARD *returns with a tray.*]

Edward, give me another of those delicious olives.

What's that? Potato crisps? No, I can't endure
them.
Well, I started to tell you about Lady Klootz.
It was at the Vincewell wedding. Oh, so many
years ago!

[*To the* UNIDENTIFIED GUEST]

Did *you* know the Vincewells?

UNIDENTIFIED GUEST. No, I don't know the Vincewells.

JULIA. Oh, they're both dead now. But I wanted
to know.
If they'd been friends of yours, I couldn't tell the
story.

PETER. Were they the parents of Tony Vincewell?

JULIA. Yes. Tony was the product, but not the
solution.
He only made the situation more difficult.
You know Tony Vincewell? You knew him at
Oxford?

PETER. No, I never knew him at Oxford:
I came across him last year in California.

JULIA. I've always wanted to go to California.
Do tell us what you were doing in California.

CELIA. Making a film.

PETER.   Trying to make a film.

JULIA. Oh, what film was it? I wonder if I've
seen it.

PETER. No, you wouldn't have seen it. As a mat-
ter of fact
It was never produced. They did a film
But they used a different scenario.

JULIA. Not the one you wrote?

PETER.   Not the one I wrote:
But I had a very enjoyable time.

CELIA. Go on with the story about the wedding
cake.

JULIA. Edward, do sit down for a moment.
I know you're always the perfect host,
But just try to pretend you're another guest
At Lavinia's party. There are so many questions
I want to ask you. It's a golden opportunity
Now Lavinia's away. I've always said:
'If I could only get Edward alone
And have a really *serious* conversation!'
I said so to Lavinia. She agreed with me.
She said: 'I wish you'd try.' And this is the first
time
I've ever seen you without Lavinia
Except for the time she got locked in the lavatory
And couldn't get out. I know what you're think-
ing!

I know you think I'm a silly old woman
But I'm really very serious. Lavinia takes me se-
riously.
I believe that's the reason why she went away—
So that I could make you talk. Perhaps she's in
the pantry
Listening to all we say!

EDWARD.   No, she's not in the pantry.

CELIA. Will she be away for some time, Edward?

EDWARD. I really don't know until I hear from
her.

If her aunt is very ill, she may be gone some time.

CELIA. And how will you manage while she is
away?

EDWARD. I really don't know. I may go away
myself.

CELIA. Go away yourself!

JULIA.   Have you an aunt too?

EDWARD. No, I haven't any aunt. But I might go
away.

CELIA. But, Edward . . . what was I going to
say?

It's dreadful for old ladies alone in the country,
And almost impossible to get a nurse.

JULIA. Is that her Aunt Laura?

EDWARD.   No; another aunt
Whom you wouldn't know. Her mother's sister
And rather a recluse.

JULIA.   Her favourite aunt?

EDWARD. Her aunt's favourite niece. And she's
rather difficult.
When she's ill, she insists on having Lavinia.

JULIA. I never heard of her being ill before.

EDWARD. No, she's always very strong. That's
why when she's ill
She gets into a panic.

JULIA.   And sends for Lavinia.
I quite understand. Are there any prospects?

EDWARD. No, I think she put it all into an annuity.

JULIA. So it's very unselfish of Lavinia
Yet very like her. But really, Edward,
Lavinia may be away for weeks,
Or she may come back and be called away again.
I understand these tough old women—
I'm one myself. I feel as if I knew
All about that aunt in Hampshire.

EDWARD.   Hampshire?

JULIA. Didn't you say Hampshire?

EDWARD.   No, I didn't say Hampshire.

JULIA. Did you say Hampstead?

EDWARD.   No, I didn't say Hampstead.

JULIA. But she must live somewhere.

EDWARD.   She lives in Essex.

JULIA. Anywhere near Colchester? Lavinia loves
oysters.

EDWARD. No. In the *depths* of Essex.

JULIA.   Well, we won't probe into it.
You have the address, and the telephone number?
I might run down and see Lavinia
On my way to Cornwall. But let's be sensible:
Now you must let me be *your* maiden aunt—
Living on an annuity, of course.
I am going to make you dine alone with me
On Friday, and talk to me about everything.

EDWARD. Everything?

JULIA.   Oh, you know what I mean.
The next election. And the secrets of your cases.

EDWARD. Most of my secrets are quite uninteresting.

JULIA. Well, you shan't escape. You dine with
me on Friday.
I've already chosen the people you're to meet.

EDWARD. But you asked me to dine with you
alone.

JULIA.   Yes, alone!
Without Lavinia! You'll like the other people—
But you're to talk to me. So that's all settled.
And now I must be going.

EDWARD.   Must you be going?

PETER. But won't you tell the story about Lady
Klootz?

JULIA. What Lady Klootz?

CELIA.   And the wedding cake.

JULIA. Wedding cake? I wasn't at her wedding.
Edward, it's been a delightful evening:
The potato crisps were really excellent.
Now let me see. Have I got everything?
It's such a nice party, I hate to leave it.
It's such a nice party, I'd like to repeat it.
Why don't you *all* come to dinner on Friday?
No, I'm afraid my good Mrs. Batten
Would give me notice. And now I must be going.

ALEX. I'm afraid *I* ought to be going.

PETER.   Celia—
May I walk along with you?

CELIA.   No, I'm sorry, Peter;
I've got to take a taxi.

JULIA.   You come with me, Peter:
You can get *me* a taxi, and then I can drop you.
I expect you on Friday, Edward. And Celia—
I must see you very soon. Now don't all go
Just because I'm going. Good-bye, Edward.

EDWARD. Good-bye, Julia.

[*Exeunt* JULIA *and* PETER.]

CELIA.   Good-bye, Edward.
Shall I see you soon?

EDWARD.   Perhaps. I don't know.

CELIA. Perhaps you don't know? Very well,
    good-bye.

EDWARD. Good-bye, Celia.

ALEX.   Good-bye, Edward I do hope
You'll have better news of Lavinia's aunt.

EDWARD. Oh . . . yes . . . thank you. Good-bye,
    Alex,
It was nice of you to come.

[*Exeunt* ALEX *and* CELIA.]

[*To the* UNIDENTIFIED GUEST]

                        Don't go yet.
Don't go yet. We'll finish the cocktails.
Or would you rather have whisky?

UNIDENTIFIED GUEST.   Gin.

EDWARD. Anything in it?

UNIDENTIFIED GUEST.   A drop of water.

EDWARD. I want to apologise for this evening.
The fact is, I tried to put off this party:
These were only the people I couldn't put off
Because I couldn't get at them in time;
And I didn't know that *you* were coming.
I thought that Lavinia had told me the names
Of all the people she said she'd invited.
But it's only that dreadful old woman who mat-
    tered—
I shouldn't have minded anyone else,

[*The bell rings.* EDWARD *goes to the door, saying*]

But she always turns up when she's least wanted.
    [*Opens the door*]
Julia!

[*Enter* JULIA.]

JULIA. Edward! How lucky that it's raining!
It made me remember my umbrella,
And there it is! Now what are you two plotting?
How very lucky it was my umbrella,
And not Alexander's—*he's* so inquisitive!
But *I* never poke into other people's business.
Well, good-bye again. I'm off at last.

[*Exit.*]

EDWARD. I'm sorry. I'm afraid I don't know your
    name.

UNIDENTIFIED GUEST. I ought to be going.

EDWARD.   Don't go yet.
I very much want to talk to somebody;
And it's easier to talk to a person you don't know.
The fact is, that Lavinia has left me.

UNIDENTIFIED GUEST. Your wife has left you?

EDWARD.   Without warning, of course;
Just when she'd arranged a cocktail party.
She'd gone when I came in, this afternoon.
She left a note to say that she was leaving me;
But I don't know where she's gone.

UNIDENTIFIED GUEST.   This is an occasion.
May I take another drink?

EDWARD.   Whisky?

UNIDENTIFIED GUEST.   Gin.

EDWARD. Anything in it?

UNIDENTIFIED GUEST.   Nothing but water.
And I recommend you the same prescription . . .
Let me prepare it for you, if I may . . .
Strong . . . but sip it slowly . . . and drink it
    sitting down.
Breathe deeply, and adopt a relaxed position.
There we are. Now for a few questions.
How long married?

EDWARD.   Five years.

UNIDENTIFIED GUEST.   Children?

EDWARD. No.

UNIDENTIFIED GUEST. Then look on the brighter
    side.
You say you don't know where she's gone?

EDWARD.   No, I do not.

UNIDENTIFIED GUEST. Do you know who the man
    is?

EDWARD.   There was no other man—
None that I know of.

UNIDENTIFIED GUEST. Or another woman
Of whom she thought she had cause to be jealous?

EDWARD. She had nothing to complain of in my
    behaviour.

UNIDENTIFIED GUEST. Then no doubt it's all for
    the best.
With another man, she might have made a mis-
    take
And want to come back to you. If another woman,
She might decide to be forgiving
And gain an advantage. If there's no other woman
And no other man, then the reason may be deeper
And you've ground for hope that she won't come
    back at all.
If another man, then you'd want to re-marry
To prove to the world that somebody wanted you;
If another woman, you might have to marry her—
You might even imagine that you wanted to marry
    her.

EDWARD. But I want my wife back.

UNIDENTIFIED GUEST. That's the natural reaction.
It's embarrassing, and inconvenient.
It was inconvenient, having to lie about it

Because you can't tell the truth on the telephone.
It will all take time that you can't well spare;
But I put it to you . . .

EDWARD.   Don't put it to me.
UNIDENTIFIED GUEST. Then I suggest . . .
EDWARD.   And please don't suggest.

I have often used these terms in examining wit-
nesses,
So I don't like them. May I put it to *you*?
I know that I invited this conversation:
But I don't know who you are. This is not what
I expected.
I only wanted to relieve my mind
By telling someone what I'd been concealing.
I don't think I want to know who you are;
But, at the same time, unless you know my wife
A good deal better than I thought, or unless you
know
A good deal more about us than appears—
I think your speculations rather offensive.

UNIDENTIFIED GUEST. I know you as well as I
know your wife;

And I knew that all you wanted was the luxury
Of an intimate disclosure to a stranger.
Let me, therefore, remain the stranger.
But let me tell you, that to approach the stranger
Is to invite the unexpected, release a new force,
Or let the genie out of the bottle.
It is to start a train of events
Beyond your control. So let me continue.
I will say then, you experience some relief
Of which you're not aware. It will come to you
slowly:
When you wake in the morning, when you go to
bed at night,
That you are beginning to enjoy your indepen-
dence;
Finding your life becoming cosier and cosier
Without the consistent critic, the patient misunder-
stander
Arranging life a little better than you like it,
Preferring not quite the same friends as yourself,
Or making your friends like her better than you;
And, turning the past over and over,
You'll wonder only that you endured it for so long.
And perhaps at times you will feel a little jealous
That she saw it first, and had the courage to break
it—
Thus giving herself a permanent advantage.

EDWARD. It might turn out so, yet . . .

UNIDENTIFIED GUEST. Are you going to say, you
love her?

EDWARD. Why, I thought we took each other for
granted.
I never thought I should be any happier
With another person. Why speak of love?
We were used to each other. So her going away
At a moment's notice, without explanation,
Only a note to say that she had gone
And was not coming back—well, I can't under-
stand it.
Nobody likes to be left with a mystery:
It's so . . . unfinished.

UNIDENTIFIED GUEST. Yes, it's unfinished;

And nobody likes to be left with a mystery.
But there's more to it than that. There's a loss of
personality;
Or rather, you've lost touch with the person
You thought you were. You no longer feel quite
human.
You're suddenly reduced to the status of an ob-
ject—
A living object, but no longer a person.
It's always happening, because one is an object
As well as a person. But we forget about it
As quickly as we can. When you've dressed for a
party
And are going downstairs, with everything about
you
Arranged to support you in the role you have
chosen,
Then sometimes, when you come to the bottom
step
There is one step more than your feet expected
And you come down with a jolt. Just for a mo-
ment
You have the experience of being an object
At the mercy of a malevolent staircase.
Or, take a surgical operation.
In consultation with the doctor and the surgeon,
In going to bed in the nursing home,
In talking to the matron, you are still the subject,
The centre of reality. But, stretched on the table,
You are a piece of furniture in a repair shop
For those who surround you, the masked actors;
All there is of you is your body
And the 'you' is withdrawn. May I replenish?

EDWARD. Oh, I'm sorry. What were you drinking?
Whisky?

UNIDENTIFIED GUEST. Gin.

EDWARD.   Anything with it?
UNIDENTIFIED GUEST.   Water.
EDWARD. To what does this lead?

UNIDENTIFIED GUEST.   To finding out
What you really are. What you really feel.
What you really are among other people.
Most of the time we take ourselves for granted,
As we have to, and live on a little knowledge
About ourselves as we were. Who are you now?
You don't know any more than I do,
But rather less. You are nothing but a set
Of obsolete responses. The one thing to do
Is to do nothing. Wait.
    EDWARD.   Wait!
But waiting is the one thing impossible.
Besides, don't you see that it makes me ridiculous?
    UNIDENTIFIED GUEST. It will do you no harm to
    find yourself ridiculous.
Resign yourself to be the fool you are.
That's the best advice that *I* can give you.
    EDWARD. But how can I wait, not knowing what
    I'm waiting for?
Shall I say to my friends, 'My wife has gone
    away'?
And they answer 'Where?' and I say 'I don't
    know';
And they say 'But when will she be back?'
And I reply 'I don't know that she *is* coming
    back.'
And they ask 'But what are you going to do?'
And I answer 'Nothing.' They will think me mad
Or simply contemptible.
    UNIDENTIFIED GUEST. All to the good.
You will find that you survive humiliation.
And that's an experience of incalculable value.
    EDWARD. Stop! I agree that much of what you've
    said
Is true enough. But that is not all.
Since I saw her this morning when we had break-
    fast
I no longer remember what my wife is like.
I am not quite sure that I could describe her
If I had to ask the police to search for her.
I'm sure I don't know what she was wearing
When I saw her last. And yet I want her back.
And I *must* get her back, to find out what has
    happened
During the five years that we've been married.
I must find out who she is, to find out who I am.
And what is the use of all your analysis
If I am to remain always lost in the dark?
    UNIDENTIFIED GUEST. There is certainly no pur-
    pose in remaining in the dark
Except long enough to clear from the mind
The illusion of having ever been in the light.

The fact that you can't give a reason for wanting
    her
Is the best reason for believing that you want her.
    EDWARD. I want to see her again—here.
    UNIDENTIFIED GUEST.   You shall
    see her again—here.
    EDWARD. Do you mean to say that you know
    where she is?
    UNIDENTIFIED GUEST. That question is not worth
    the trouble of an answer.
But if I bring her back it must be on one condi-
    tion:
That you promise to ask her no questions
Of where she has been.
    EDWARD.   I will not ask them.
And yet—it seems to me—when we began to talk
I was not sure I wanted her; and now I want her.
Do I want her? Or is it merely your suggestion?
    UNIDENTIFIED GUEST. We do not know yet. In
    twenty-four hours
She will come to you here. You will be here to
    meet her.
[*The doorbell rings.*]
    EDWARD. I must answer the door.
[EDWARD *goes to the door.*]
                 So, it's you again, Julia!
    [*Enter* JULIA *and* PETER.]
    JULIA. Edward, I'm so glad to find you.
Do you know, I must have left my glasses here,
And I simply can't see a thing without them.
I've been dragging Peter all over town
Looking for them everywhere I've been.
Has anybody found them? You can tell if they're
    mine—
Some kind of a plastic sort of frame—
I'm afraid I don't remember the colour,
But I'd know them, because one lens is missing.
    UNIDENTIFIED GUEST [*sings*].

    As I was drinkin' gin and water,
      And me bein' the One Eyed Riley,
    Who came in but the landlord's daughter
      And she took my heart entirely.

You will keep our appointment?
    EDWARD.   I shall keep it.
    UNIDENTIFIED GUEST [*sings*].

    Tooryooly toory-iley,
      What's the matter with One Eyed Riley?

                         [*Exit.*]
    JULIA. Edward, who *is* that dreadful man?
I've never been so insulted in my life.

It's very lucky that I left my spectacles:
This is what I call an adventure!
Tell me about him. You've been *drinking* together!
So this is the kind of friend you have
When Lavinia is out of the way! Who is he?

EDWARD. *I* don't know.

JULIA.   *You* don't know?

EDWARD.   I never saw him before in my life.

JULIA. But how did he come here?

EDWARD.   *I* don't know.

JULIA. *You* don't know! And what's his name?
Did I hear him say his name was Riley?

EDWARD. I don't know his name.

JULIA.   You don't know his *name*?

EDWARD. I tell you I've no idea who he is
Or how he got here.

JULIA.   But what did you talk about?
Or were you singing songs all the time?
There's altogether too much mystery
About this place today.

EDWARD.   I'm very sorry.

JULIA. No, I love it. But that reminds me
About my glasses. That's the greatest mystery.
Peter! Why aren't you looking for them?
Look on the mantelpiece. Where was I sitting?
Just turn out the bottom of that sofa—
No, this chair. Look under the cushion.

EDWARD. Are you quite sure they're not in your
    bag?

JULIA. Why no, of course not: that's where I
    keep them.

Oh, here they are! Thank you, Edward;
That really was very clever of you;
I'd never have found them but for you.
The next time I lose *anything,* Edward,
I'll come straight to you, instead of to St. Anthony.
And now I must fly. I've kept the taxi waiting.
Come along, Peter.

PETER.   I hope you won't mind
If I don't come with you, Julia? On the way back
I remembered something I had to say to Ed-
    ward . . .

JULIA. Oh, about Lavinia?

PETER.   No, not about Lavinia.
It's something I want to consult him about,
And I could do it now.

JULIA.   Of course I don't mind.

PETER. Well, at least you must let me take you
    down in the lift.

JULIA. No, you stop and talk to Edward. I'm not
    helpless yet.

And besides, I like to manage the machine my-
    self—
In a lift I can meditate. Good-bye then.
And thank you—both of you—very much.

[*Exit.*]

PETER. I hope I'm not disturbing you, Edward.

EDWARD. I seem to have been disturbed already;
And I did rather want to be alone.
But what's it all about?

PETER.   I want your help.
I was going to telephone and try to see you later;
But this seemed an opportunity.

EDWARD.   And what's your trouble?

PETER. This evening I felt I could bear it no
    longer.
That awful party! I'm sorry, Edward;
Of course it was really a very nice party
For everyone but me. And that wasn't your fault.
I don't suppose you noticed the situation.

EDWARD. I did think I noticed one or two things;
But I don't pretend I was aware of everything.

PETER. Oh, I'm very glad that you didn't notice:
I must have behaved rather better than I thought.
If you didn't notice, I don't suppose the others did,
Though I'm rather afraid of Julia Shuttlethwaite.

EDWARD. Julia is certainly observant,
But I think she had some other matter on her
    mind.

PETER. It's about Celia. Myself and Celia.

EDWARD. Why, what could there be about your-
    self and Celia?
Have you anything in common, do you think?

PETER. It seemed to me we had a great deal in
    common.
We're both of us artists.

EDWARD.   I never thought of that,
What arts do you practise?

PETER.   You won't have seen my novel,
Though it had some very good reviews.
But it's more the cinema that interests both of us.

EDWARD. A common interest in the moving pic-
    tures
Frequently brings young people together.

PETER. Now you're only being sarcastic:
Celia was interested in the art of the film.

EDWARD. As a possible profession?

PETER.   She might make it a profession;
Though she had her poetry.

EDWARD.   Yes, I've seen her poetry—
Interesting if one is interested in Celia.
Apart, of course, from its literary merit

Which I don't pretend to judge.

PETER.   Well, I can judge it,
And I think it's very good. But that's not the
 point.
The point is, I thought we had a great deal in
 common
And I think she thought so too.

EDWARD.   How did you come to know her?
        [Enter ALEX.]

ALEX. Ah, there you are, Edward! Do you know
 why *I've* looked in?

EDWARD. I'd like to know first how you *got* in,
 Alex.

ALEX. Why, I came and found that the door was
 open
And so I thought I'd slip in and see if anyone
 was with you.

PETER. Julia must have left it open.

EDWARD.   Never mind;
So long as you both shut it when you go out.

ALEX. Ah, but you're coming with me, Edward.
I thought, Edward may be all alone this evening,
And I know that he hates to spend an evening
 alone,
So you're going to come out and have dinner with
 me.

EDWARD. That's very thoughtful of you, Alex,
 I'm sure;
But I rather *want* to be alone, this evening.

ALEX. But you've got to have some dinner. Are
 you going out?
Is there anyone here to get dinner for you?

EDWARD. No, I shan't want much, and I'll get it
 myself.

ALEX. Ah, in that case I know what I'll do.
I'm going to give you a little surprise:
You know, I'm rather a famous cook.
I'm going straight to your kitchen now
And I shall prepare you a nice little dinner
Which you can have alone. And then we'll leave
 you.
Meanwhile, you and Peter can go on talking
And I shan't disturb you.

EDWARD.   My dear Alex,
There'll be nothing in the larder worthy of your
 cooking.
I couldn't think of it.

ALEX.   Ah, but that's my special gift—
Concocting a toothsome meal out of nothing.
Any scraps you have will do. I learned that in the
 East.

With a handful of rice and a little dried fish
I can make half a dozen dishes. Don't say a word.
I shall begin at once.
        [Exit to kitchen.]

EDWARD.   Well, where did you leave off?

PETER. You asked me how I came to know
 Celia.
I met her here, about a year ago.

EDWARD. At one of Lavinia's amateur Thursdays?

PETER. A Thursday. Why do you say amateur?

EDWARD. Lavinia's attempts at starting a salon.
Where I entertained the minor guests
And dealt with the misfits, Lavinia's mistakes.
But you were one of the minor successes
For a time at least.

PETER.   I wouldn't say that.
But Lavinia was awfully kind to me
And I owe her a great deal. And then I met Celia.
She was different from any girl I'd ever known
And not easy to talk to, on that occasion.

EDWARD. Did you see her often?

ALEX'S VOICE. Edward, have you a double boiler?

EDWARD. I suppose there must be a double boiler:
Isn't there one in every kitchen?

ALEX'S VOICE.   I can't find it.
There goes *that* surprise. I must think of another.

PETER.   Not very often.
And when I did, I got no chance to talk to her.

EDWARD. You and Celia were asked for different
 purposes.
Your role was to be one of Lavinia's discoveries;
Celia's, to provide society and fashion.
Lavinia always had the ambition
To establish herself in two worlds at once—
But she herself had to be the link between them.
That is why, I think, her Thursdays were a fail-
 ure.

PETER. You speak as if everything was finished.

EDWARD. Oh no, no, everything is left unfinished.
But you haven't told me how you came to know
 Celia.

PETER. I saw her again a few days later
Alone at a concert. And I was alone.
I've always gone to concerts alone—
At first, because I knew no one to go with,
And later, I found I preferred to go alone.
But a girl like Celia, it seemed very strange,
Because I had thought of her merely as a name
In a society column, to find her there alone.
Anyway, we got into conversation

And I found that she went to concerts alone
And to look at pictures. So we often met
In the same way, and sometimes went together.
And to be with Celia, that was something different
From company or solitude. And we sometimes had
    tea
And once or twice dined together.

EDWARD.   And after that
Did she ever introduce you to her family
Or to any of her friends?

PETER. No, but once or twice she spoke of them
And about their lack of intellectual interests.

EDWARD. And what happened after that?

PETER.   Oh, nothing happened.
But I thought that she really cared about me.
And I was so happy when we were together—
So . . . contented, so . . . at peace: I can't ex-
    press it;
I had never imagined such quiet happiness.
I had only experienced excitement, delirium,
Desire for possession. It was not like that at all.
It was something very strange. There was such
    . . . tranquillity . . .

EDWARD. And what interrupted this interesting
    affair?
    [Enter ALEX in shirtsleeves and an apron.]

ALEX. Edward, I can't find any curry powder.

EDWARD. There isn't any curry powder. Lavinia
    hates curry.

ALEX. There goes another surprise, then. I must
    think.
I didn't expect to find any mangoes,
But I did count upon curry powder.
                                    [Exit.]

PETER. That is exactly what I want to know.
She has simply faded—into some other picture—
Like a film effect. She doesn't want to see me;
Makes excuses, not very plausible,
And when I do see her, she seems preoccupied
With some secret excitement which I cannot share.

EDWARD. Do you think she has simply lost in-
    terest in you?

PETER. You put it just wrong. I think of it dif-
    ferently.
It is not her interest in me that I miss—
But those moments in which we seemed to share
    some perception,
Some feeling, some indefinable experience
In which we were both unaware of ourselves.
In your terms, perhaps, she's lost interest in me.

EDWARD. That is all very normal. If you could
    only know

How lucky you are. In a little while
This might have become an ordinary affair
Like any other. As the fever cooled
You would have found that she was another
    woman
And that you were another man. I congratulate
    you
On a timely escape.

PETER.   I should prefer to be spared
Your congratulations. I had to talk to someone.
And I have been telling you of something real—
My first experience of reality
And perhaps it is the last. And you don't under-
    stand.

EDWARD. My dear Peter, I have only been telling
    you
What would have happened to you with Celia
In another six months' time. There it is.
You can take it or leave it.

PETER.   But what am I to do?

EDWARD. Nothing. Wait. Go back to California.

PETER. But I must see Celia.

EDWARD.   Will it be the same Celia?
Better be content with the Celia you remember.
Remember! I say it's already a memory.

PETER. But I must see Celia at least to make her
    tell me
What has happened, in her terms. Until I know
    that
I shan't know the truth about even the memory.
Did we really share these interests? Did we really
    feel the same
When we heard certain music? Or looked at cer-
    tain pictures?
There was something real. But what is the re-
    ality . . .
    [The telephone rings.]

EDWARD. Excuse me a moment.
[Into telephone] Hello! . . . I can't talk now . . .
Yes, there is . . . Well then, I'll ring you
As soon as I can.
                    I'm sorry. You were saying?

PETER. I was saying, what is the reality
Of experience between two unreal people?
If I can only hold to the memory
I can bear any future. But I must find out
The truth about the past, for the sake of the
    memory.

EDWARD. There's no memory you can wrap in
    camphor
But the moths will get in. So you want to see
    Celia.

I don't know why I should be taking all this
     trouble
To protect you from the fool you are.
What do you want me to do?

     PETER.   See Celia for me.
You know her in a different way from me
And you are so much older.

     EDWARD.   So much older?

     PETER. Yes, I'm sure that she would listen to you
As someone disinterested.

     EDWARD.   Well, I will see Celia.

     PETER. Thank you, Edward. It's very good of
     you.
         [*Enter* ALEX, *with his jacket on.*]

     ALEX. Oh, Edward! I've prepared you such a
     treat!
I really think that of all my triumphs
This is the greatest. To make something out of
     nothing!
Never, even when travelling in Albania,
Have I made such a supper out of so few materials
As I found in your refrigerator. But of course
I was lucky to find a half-a-dozen eggs.

     EDWARD. What! You used all those eggs! La-
     vinia's aunt
Has just sent them from the country.

     ALEX.   Ah, so the aunt
Really exists. A substantial proof.

     EDWARD. No, no . . . I mean, this is another
     aunt.

     ALEX. I understand. The real aunt. But you'll be
     grateful.
There are very few peasants in Montenegro
Who can have the dish that you'll be eating, now-
     adays.

     EDWARD. But what about my breakfast?

     ALEX.   Don't worry about breakfast.
All you should want is a cup of black coffee
And a little dry toast. I've left it simmering.
Don't leave it longer than another ten minutes.
Now I'll be going, and I'll take Peter with me.

     PETER. Edward, I've taken too much of your
     time,
And you want to be alone. Give my love to La-
     vinia
When she comes back . . . but, if you don't mind,
I'd rather you didn't tell *her* what I've told you.

     EDWARD. I shall not say anything about it to
     Lavinia.

     PETER. Thank you, Edward. Good night.

     EDWARD.   Good night, Peter,
And good night, Alex. Oh, and if you don't mind,

Please *shut the door after you,* so it latches.

     ALEX. Remember, Edward, not more than ten
     minutes.
Twenty minutes, and my work will be ruined.
            [*Exeunt* ALEX *and* PETER.]
[EDWARD *picks up the telephone, and dials a
number. There is no reply.*]

CURTAIN

ACT I

SCENE II

The same room a quarter of an hour later. ED-
WARD *is alone, playing Patience. The doorbell rings,
and he answers it.*

     CELIA'S VOICE. Are you alone?
         [EDWARD *returns with* CELIA.]

     EDWARD.   Celia! Why have you come back?
I said I would telephone as soon as I could:
And I tried to get you a moment ago.

     CELIA. If there had happened to be anyone with
     you
I was going to say I'd come back for my um-
     brella. . . .
I must say you don't seem very pleased to see me.
Edward, I understand what has happened
But I could not understand your manner on the
     telephone.
It did not seem like you. So I felt I must see you.
Tell me it's all right, and then I'll go.

     EDWARD. But how can you say you understand
     what has happened?
I don't know what has happened, or what is going
     to happen;
And to try to understand it, I want to be alone.

     CELIA. I should have thought it was perfectly
     simple.
Lavinia has left you.

     EDWARD.   Yes, that *was* the situation.
I suppose it was pretty obvious to everyone.

     CELIA. It was obvious that the aunt was a pure
     invention
On the spur of the moment, and not a very good
     one.
You should have been prepared with something
     better, for Julia;

But it doesn't really matter. They will know soon
    enough.
Doesn't that settle all our difficulties?
    EDWARD. It has only brought to light the real
        difficulties.
    CELIA. But surely, these are only temporary.
You know I accepted the situation
Because a divorce would ruin your career;
And we thought that Lavinia would never want to
    leave you.
Surely you don't hold to that silly convention
That the husband must always be the one to be
    divorced?
And if she chooses to give *you* the grounds . . .
    EDWARD. I see. But it is not like that at all.
Lavinia is coming back.
    CELIA.   Lavinia coming back!
Do you mean to say that she's laid a trap for us?
    EDWARD. No. If there is a trap, we are all in the
        trap,
We have set it for ourselves. But I do not know
What kind of a trap it is.
    CELIA.   Then what has happened?
    [*The telephone rings.*]
    EDWARD. Damn the telephone. I suppose I must
        answer it.
Hello . . . oh, hello! . . . No. I mean yes, Alex;
Yes, of course . . . it was marvellous.
I've never tasted anything like it . . .
Yes, that's very interesting. But I just wondered
Whether it mightn't be rather indigestible? . . .
Oh, no, Alex, don't bring me any cheese;
I've got some cheese . . . No, not Norwegian;
But I don't really want cheese . . . Slipper
    what? . . .
Oh, from Jugoslavia . . . prunes and alcohol?
No, really Alex, I don't want anything.
I'm very tired. Thanks awfully, Alex.
Good night.
    CELIA.   What on earth was that about?
    EDWARD. That was Alex.
    CELIA.   I know it was Alex.
But what was he talking of?
    EDWARD.   I had quite forgotten.
He made his way in, a little while ago,
And insisted on cooking me something for supper;
And he said I must eat it within ten minutes.
I suppose it's still cooking.
    CELIA.   You suppose it's still cooking!
I thought I noticed a peculiar smell:
Of course it's still cooking—or doing *something*.
I must go and investigate.
    [*Starts to leave the room*]
    EDWARD.   For heaven's sake, don't bother!
                    [*Exit* CELIA.]
Suppose someone came and found you in the
    kitchen?
    [EDWARD *goes over to the table and inspects his
    game of Patience. He moves a card. The doorbell
    rings repeatedly. Re-enter* CELIA, *in an apron.*]
    CELIA. You'd better answer the door, Edward.
It's the best thing to do. Don't lose your head.
You see, I really did leave my umbrella;
And I'll say I found you here starving and helpless
And had to do something. Anyway, I'm *staying*
And I'm not going to hide.
    [*Returns to kitchen. The bell rings again.*]
    EDWARD. [*goes to front door, and is heard to say*]
                    Julia!
What have you come back for?
                    [*Enter* JULIA.]
    JULIA.   I've had an inspiration!
    [*Enter* CELIA *with saucepan.*]
    CELIA. Edward, it's ruined!
    EDWARD.   What a good thing.
    CELIA. But it's ruined the saucepan too.
    EDWARD.   *And* half-a-dozen eggs.
I wanted one for breakfast. A boiled egg.
It's the only thing I know how to cook.
    JULIA. Celia! I see you've had the same inspira-
        tion
That I had. Edward must be fed.
He's under such a strain. We must keep his
    strength up.
Edward! Don't you realise how lucky you are
To have *two* Good Samaritans? I never heard of
    that before.
    EDWARD. The man who fell among thieves was
        luckier than I:
He was left at an inn.
    JULIA.   Edward, how ungrateful!
What's in that saucepan?
    CELIA.   Nobody knows.
    EDWARD. It's something that Alex came and pre-
        pared for me.
He *would* do it. Three Good Samaritans.
I forgot all about it.
    JULIA.   But you mustn't touch it.
    EDWARD. Of course I shan't touch it.
    JULIA.   My dear, I should have warned you:
Anything that Alex makes is absolutely deadly.
I could tell such tales of his poisoning people.
Now, my dear, you give me that apron
And we'll see what I can do. You stay and talk to

Edward.

          [*Exit* JULIA.]

CELIA. But what has happened, Edward? What
  has happened?

EDWARD. Lavinia is coming back, I think.

CELIA. You think! don't you know?

EDWARD. No, but I believe it. That man who was
  here—

CELIA. Yes, who was that man? I was rather
  afraid of him;

He has some sort of power.

  EDWARD.   I don't know who he is.

But I had some talk with him, when the rest of
  you had left,

And he said he would bring Lavinia back, tomorrow.

  CELIA. But why should that man want to bring
  her back—

Unless he is the Devil! I could believe he was.

  EDWARD. Because I asked him to.

  CELIA.   Because you asked him to!

Then he *must* be the Devil! He must have be-
  witched you.

How did he persuade you to want her back?

[*A popping noise is heard from the kitchen.*]

  EDWARD. What the devil's that?

[*Re-enter* JULIA, *in apron, with a tray and three
  glasses.*]

  JULIA.   I've had an inspiration!

There's nothing in the place fit to eat:

I've looked high and low. But I found some champagne—

Only a half bottle, to be sure,

And of course it isn't chilled. But it's so refreshing;

And I thought, we are all in need of a stimulant

After this disaster. Now I'll propose a health.

Can you guess whose health I'm going to propose?

  EDWARD. No, I can't. But I won't drink to Alex's.

  JULIA. Oh, it isn't Alex's. Come, I give you

Lavinia's aunt! You might have guessed it.

  EDWARD *and* CELIA. Lavinia's aunt.

  JULIA.   Now, the next question

Is, what's to be done. That's very simple.

It's too late, or too early, to go to a restaurant.

You must both come home with me.

  EDWARD.   No, I'm sorry, Julia.

I'm too tired to go out, and I'm not at all hungry.

I shall have a few biscuits.

  JULIA.   But you, Celia?

You must come and have a light supper with me—

Something very light.

  CELIA.   Thank you, Julia.

I think I will, if I may follow you

In about ten minutes? Before I go, there's something

I want to say to Edward.

  JULIA.   About Lavinia?

Well, come on quickly. And take a taxi.

You know, you're looking absolutely famished.

Good night, Edward.

          [*Exit* JULIA.]

  CELIA.   Well, how did he persuade you?

  EDWARD. How did he persuade me? Did he persuade me?

I have a very clear impression

That he tried to persuade me it was all for the best

That Lavinia had gone; that I ought to be thankful.

He talked as if he thought he knew all about it;

And yet, the effect of all his argument

Was to make me see that I wanted her back.

  CELIA. That's the Devil's method! So you want
  Lavinia back!

Lavinia! So the one thing you care about

Is to avoid a break—anything unpleasant!

No, it can't be that. I won't think it's that.

I think it is just a moment of surrender

To fatigue. And panic. You can't face the trouble.

  EDWARD. No, it is not that. It is not only that.

  CELIA. It cannot be simply a question of vanity:

That you think the world will laugh at you

Because your wife has left you for another man?

I shall soon put that right, Edward,

When you are free.

  EDWARD.   No, it is not that.

And all these reasons were suggested to me

By the man I call Riley—though his name is not
  Riley;

It was just a name in a song he sang . . .

  CELIA. He sang you a song about a man named
  Riley!

Really, Edward, I think you are mad—

I mean, you're on the edge of a nervous breakdown.

Edward, if I go away now

Will you promise me to see a very great doctor

Whom I have heard of—and his name *is* Reilly!

  EDWARD. It would need someone greater than the
  greatest doctor

To cure *this* illness.

  CELIA.   Edward, if I go now,

Will you assure me that everything is right,

That you do not mean to have Lavinia back

And that you do mean to gain your freedom,

And that everything is all right between us?
That's all that matters. Truly, Edward,
If that is right, everything else will be,
I promise you.

    EDWARD.   No, Celia.
It has been very wonderful, and I'm very grateful,
And I think you are a very rare person.
But it was too late. And I should have known
That it wasn't fair to you.

    CELIA.   It wasn't fair to *me!*
You can stand there and talk about being fair to
    me!

    EDWARD. But for Lavinia leaving, this would
    never have arisen.
What future had you ever thought there could be?

    CELIA. What had I thought that the future could
    be?
I abandoned the future before we began,
And after that I lived in a present
Where time was meaningless, a private world of
    ours,
Where the word 'happiness' had a different mean-
    ing
Or so it seemed.

    EDWARD.   I have heard of that experience.

    CELIA. A dream. I was happy in it till today,
And then, when Julia asked about Lavinia
And it came to me that Lavinia had left you
And that you would be free—then I suddenly dis-
    covered
That the dream was not enough; that I wanted
    something more
And I waited, and wanted to run to tell you.
Perhaps the dream was better. It seemed the real
    reality,
And if this is reality, it is very like a dream.
Perhaps it was I who betrayed my own dream
All the while; and to find I wanted
This world as well as that . . . well, it's humiliat-
    ing.

    EDWARD. There is no reason why you should feel
    humiliated . . .

    CELIA. Oh, don't think that *you* can humiliate
    me!
Humiliation—it's something I've done to myself.
I am not sure even that you seem real enough
To humiliate me. I suppose that most women
Would feel degraded to find that a man
With whom they thought they had shared some-
    thing wonderful
Had taken them only as a passing diversion.

Oh, I dare say that you deceived yourself;
But that's what it was, no doubt.

    EDWARD. I *didn't* take you as a passing diversion!
If you want to speak of passing diversions
How did you take Peter?

    CELIA.   Peter? Peter who?

    EDWARD. Peter Quilpe, who was here this eve-
    ning. *He* was in a dream
And now he is simply unhappy and bewildered.

    CELIA. I simply don't know what you are talking
    about.
Edward, this is really too crude a subterfuge
To justify yourself. There was never anything
Between me and Peter.

    EDWARD.   Wasn't there? *He* thought so.
He came back this evening to talk to me about it.

    CELIA. But this is ridiculous! I never gave Peter
Any reason to suppose I cared for him.
I thought he had talent; I saw that he was lonely;
I thought that I could help him. I took him to
    concerts.
But then, as he came to make more acquaintances,
I found him less interesting, and rather conceited.
But why should we talk about Peter? All that mat-
    ters
Is, that you think you want Lavinia.
And if that is the sort of person you are—
Well, you had better have her.

    EDWARD.   It's not like that.
It is not that I am in love with Lavinia.
I don't think I was ever really in love with her.
If I have ever been in love—and I think that I
    have—
I have never been in love with anyone but you,
And perhaps I still am. But this can't go on.
It never could have been . . . a permanent thing:
You should have a man . . . nearer your own age.

    CELIA. I don't think I care for advice from you,
    Edward.
You are not entitled to take any interest
Now, in *my* future. I only hope you're competent
To manage your own. But if you are not in love
And never have been in love with Lavinia,
What is it that you want?

    EDWARD.   I am not sure.
The one thing of which I am relatively certain
Is, that only since this morning
I have met myself as a middle-aged man
Beginning to know what it is to feel old.
That is the worst moment, when you feel that you
    have lost

The desire for all that was most desirable,
And before you are contented with what you can
    desire;
Before you know what is left to be desired;
And you go on wishing that you could desire
What desire has left behind. But you cannot under-
    stand.
How could *you* understand what it is to feel old?
    CELIA. But I want to understand you. I could
    understand.
And, Edward, please believe that whatever happens
I shall not loathe you. I shall only feel sorry for
    you.
It's only myself I am in danger of hating.
But what will your life be? I cannot bear to think
    of it.
Oh, Edward! Can you be happy with Lavinia?
    EDWARD. No—not happy: or, if there is any hap-
    piness,
Only the happiness of knowing
That the misery does not feed on the ruin of
    loveliness,
That the tedium is not the residue of ecstasy.
I see that my life was determined long ago
And that the struggle to escape from it
Is only a make-believe, a pretence
That what is, is not, or could be changed.
The self that can say 'I want this—or want that'—
The self that wills—he is a feeble creature;
He has to come to terms in the end
With the obstinate, the tougher self; who does not
    speak,
Who never talks, who cannot argue;
And who in some men may be the *guardian*—
But in men like me, the dull, the implacable,
The indomitable spirit of mediocrity.
The willing self can contrive the disaster
Of this unwilling partnership—but can only flour-
    ish
In submission to the rule of the stronger partner.
    CELIA. I am not sure, Edward, that I understand
    you;
And yet I understand as I never did before.
I think—I believe—you are being yourself
As you never were before, with me.
Twice you have changed since I have been looking
    at you.
I looked at your face: and I thought that I knew
And loved every contour; and as I looked
It withered, as if I had unwrapped a mummy.
I listened to your voice, that had always thrilled
    me,

And it became another voice—no, not a voice:
What I heard was only the noise of an insect,
Dry, endless, meaningless, inhuman—
You might have made it by scraping your legs
    together—
Or however grasshoppers do it. I looked,
And listened for your heart, your blood;
And saw only a beetle the size of a man
With nothing more inside it than what comes out
When you tread on a beetle.
    EDWARD.   Perhaps that is what I am.
Tread on me, if you like.
    CELIA.   No, I won't tread on you.
That is not what you are. It is only what was left
Of what I had thought you were. I see another
    person,
I see you as a person whom I never saw before.
The man I saw before, he was only a projection—
I see that now—of something that I wanted—
No, not *wanted*—something I aspired to—
Something that I desperately wanted to exist.
It must happen somewhere—but what, and where
    is it?
And I ask you to forgive me.
    EDWARD.   You . . . ask me to forgive *you!*
    CELIA. Yes, for two things. First . . .
    [*The telephone rings.*]
    EDWARD.   Damn the telephone.
I suppose I had better answer it.
    CELIA.   Yes, better answer it.
    EDWARD. Hello! . . . Oh, Julia: what is it now?
Your spectacles again . . . where did you leave
    them?
Or have we . . . have I got to hunt all over?
Have you looked in your bag? . . . Well, don't
    snap my head off . . .
You're sure, in the kitchen? Beside the cham-
    pagne bottle?
You're quite sure? . . . Very well, hold on if you
    like;
We . . . I'll look for them.
    CELIA.   Yes, you look for them.
I shall never go into your kitchen again.
    [*Exit* EDWARD. *He returns with the spectacles
and a bottle.*]
    EDWARD. She was right for once.
    CELIA.   She is always right.
But why bring an empty champagne bottle?
    EDWARD. It isn't empty. It may be a little flat—
But why did she say that it was a half bottle?
It's one of my best: and I have no half bottles.

Well, I hoped that you would drink a final glass
     with me.
CELIA. What should we drink to?
EDWARD.   Whom shall we drink to?
CELIA. To the Guardians.
EDWARD.   To the Guardians?
CELIA. To the Guardians. It was you who spoke
     of guardians.
     [*They drink.*]
It may be that even Julia is a guardian.
Perhaps she is *my* guardian. Give me the spec-
     tacles.
Good night, Edward.
     EDWARD.   Good night . . . Celia.
                                   [*Exit* CELIA.]
                                          Oh!

[*He snatches up the receiver.*]
Hello, Julia! are you there? . . .
Well, I'm awfully sorry to have kept you waiting;
But we . . . I had to hunt for them . . . No, I
     found them.
. . . Yes, she's bringing them now . . . Good
     night.

                    CURTAIN

ACT I

SCENE III

The same room: late afternoon of the next day.
EDWARD *alone. He goes to the door.*

     EDWARD. Oh . . . good evening.
          [*Enter the* UNIDENTIFIED GUEST.]
     UNIDENTIFIED GUEST.   Good evening, Mr.
          Chamberlayne.
     EDWARD. Well. May I offer you some gin and
          water?
     UNIDENTIFIED GUEST. No, thank you. This is a
          different occasion.
     EDWARD. I take it that as you have come alone
You have been unsuccessful.
     UNIDENTIFIED GUEST.   Not at all.
I have come to remind you—you have made a
     decision.
     EDWARD. Are you thinking that I may have
          changed my mind?

UNIDENTIFIED GUEST. No. You will not be ready
     to change your mind
Until you recover from having made a decision.
No. I have come to tell you that you will change
     your mind,
But that it will not matter. It will be too late.
     EDWARD. I have half a mind to change my mind
          now
To show you that I am free to change it.
     UNIDENTIFIED GUEST. You will change your mind,
          but you are not free.
Your moment of freedom was yesterday.
You made a decision. You set in motion
Forces in your life and in the lives of others
Which cannot be reversed. That is one considera-
     tion.
And another is this: it is a serious matter
To bring someone back from the dead.
     EDWARD.   From the dead?
That figure of speech is somewhat . . . dramatic,
As it was only yesterday that my wife left me.
     UNIDENTIFIED GUEST. Ah, but we die to each
          other daily.
What we know of other people
Is only our memory of the moments
During which we knew them. And they have
     changed since then.
To pretend that they and we are the same
Is a useful and convenient social convention
Which must sometimes be broken. We must also
     remember
That at every meeting we are meeting a stranger.
     EDWARD. So you want me to greet my wife as a
          stranger?
That will not be easy.
     UNIDENTIFIED GUEST. It is very difficult.
But it is perhaps still more difficult
To keep up the pretence that you are not strangers.
The affectionate ghosts: the grandmother,
The lively bachelor uncle at the Christmas party,
The beloved nursemaid—those who enfolded
Your childhood years in comfort, mirth, security—
If they returned, would it not be embarrassing?
What would you say to them, or they to you
After the first ten minutes? You would find it
     difficult
To treat them as strangers, but still more difficult
To pretend that you were not strange to each
     other.
     EDWARD. You can hardly expect me to obliterate
The last five years.

UNIDENTIFIED GUEST. I ask you to forget nothing.
To try to forget is to try to conceal.

    EDWARD. There are certainly things I should like
      to forget.

    UNIDENTIFIED GUEST. And persons also. But you
      must not forget them.
You must face them all, but meet them as stran-
    gers.

    EDWARD. Then I myself must also be a stranger.

    UNIDENTIFIED GUEST. And to yourself as well. But
      remember,
When you see your wife, you must ask no ques-
    tions
And give no explanations. I have said the same to
    her.
Don't strangle each other with knotted memories.
Now I shall go.

    EDWARD.   Stop! Will you come back with her?

    UNIDENTIFIED GUEST. No, I shall not come with
      her.

    EDWARD.   I don't know why,
But I think I should like you to bring her yourself.

    UNIDENTIFIED GUEST. Yes, I know you would.
      And for definite reasons
Which I am not prepared to explain to you
I must ask you not to speak of me to her;
And she will not mention me to you.

    EDWARD. I promise.

    UNIDENTIFIED GUEST. And now you must await
      your visitors.

    EDWARD. Visitors? What visitors?

                     Whoever comes.
    The strangers.
As for myself, I shall take the precaution
Of leaving by the service staircase.

    EDWARD. May I ask one question?

    UNIDENTIFIED GUEST.   You may ask it.

    EDWARD. Who are you?

    UNIDENTIFIED GUEST.   I also am a stranger.

    [*Exit. A pause.* EDWARD *moves about restlessly.*
The bell rings, and he goes to the front door.]

    EDWARD. Celia!

    CELIA.   Has Lavinia arrived?

    EDWARD.   Celia! Why have you come?
I expect Lavinia at any moment.
You must not be here. Why have you come here?

    CELIA. Because Lavinia asked me.

    EDWARD.   Because Lavinia asked you!

    CELIA. Well, not directly. Julia had a telegram
Asking her to come, and to bring me with her.
Julia was delayed, and sent me on ahead.

    EDWARD. It seems very odd. And not like Lavinia.
I suppose there is nothing to do but wait.
Won't you sit down?

    CELIA.   Thank you.

    [*Pause*]

    EDWARD. Oh, my God, what shall we talk about?
We can't sit here in silence.

    CELIA.   Oh, I could.
Just looking at you. Edward, forgive my laughing.
You look like a little boy who's been sent for
To the headmaster's study; and is not quite sure
What he's been found out in. I never saw you so
    before.
This is really a ludicrous situation.

    EDWARD. I'm afraid I can't see the humorous side
      of it.

    CELIA. I'm not really laughing at *you*, Edward.
I couldn't have laughed at anything, yesterday;
But I've learnt a lot in twenty-four hours.
It wasn't a very pleasant experience.
Oh, I'm glad I came!
I can see you at last as a human being.
Can't you see me that way too, and laugh about it?

    EDWARD. I wish I could. I wish I understood any-
      thing.
I'm completely in the dark.

    CELIA.   But it's all so simple.
Can't you see that . . .

    [*The doorbell rings.*]

    EDWARD.   There's Lavinia.

    [*Goes to front door.*]

                           Peter!

                 [*Enter* PETER.]

    PETER. Where's Lavinia?

    EDWARD.   Don't tell me that Lavinia
Sent you a telegram . . .

    PETER.   No, not to me,
But to Alex. She told him to come here
And to bring me with him. He'll be here in a
    minute.
Celia! Have you heard from Lavinia too?
Or am I interrupting?

    CELIA.   I've just explained to Edward—
I only got here this moment myself—
That she telegraphed to Julia to come and bring
    me with her.

    EDWARD. I wonder whom else Lavinia has in-
      vited.

    PETER. Why, I got the impression that Lavinia
      intended
To have yesterday's cocktail party today.
So I don't suppose her aunt can have died.

    EDWARD. What aunt?

PETER.   The aunt you told us about.
But Edward—you remember our conversation
    yesterday?
    EDWARD. Of course.
    PETER.   I hope you've done nothing about it.
    EDWARD. No, I've done nothing.
    PETER.   I'm so glad.
Because I've changed my mind. I mean, I've de-
    cided
That it's all no use. I'm going to California.
    CELIA. You're going to California!
    PETER.   Yes, I have a new job.
    EDWARD. And how did that happen, overnight?
    PETER. Why, it's a man Alex put me in touch
    with
And we settled everything this morning.
Alex is a wonderful person to know,
Because, you see, he knows everybody, everywhere.
So what I've really come for is to say good-bye.
    CELIA. Well, Peter, I'm awfully glad, for your
    sake,
Though of course we . . . I shall miss you;
You know how I depended on you for concerts,
And picture exhibitions—more than you realised.
It *was* fun, wasn't it! But now you'll have a chance,
I hope, to realise your ambitions.
I shall miss you.
    PETER.   It's nice of you to say so;
But you'll find someone better, to go about with.
    CELIA. I don't think that I shall be going to con-
    certs.
I am going away too.
    [LAVINIA *lets herself in with a latch-key.*]
    PETER.   You're going abroad?
    CELIA. I don't know. Perhaps.
    EDWARD.   You're both going away!
            [*Enter* LAVINIA.]
    LAVINIA. Who's going away? Well, Celia. Well,
    Peter.
I didn't expect to find either of you here.
    PETER *and* CELIA. But the telegram!
    LAVINIA.   What telegram?
    CELIA.   The one you sent to Julia.
    PETER. And the one you sent to Alex.
    LAVINIA.   I don't know what you mean.
Edward, have you been sending telegrams?
    EDWARD. Of course I haven't sent any telegrams.
    LAVINIA. This is some of Julia's mischief.
And is *she* coming?
    PETER.   Yes, and Alex.
    LAVINIA. Then I shall ask *them* for an explana-
    tion.

Meanwhile, I suppose we might as well sit down.
What shall we talk about?
    EDWARD.   Peter's going to America.
    PETER. Yes, and I would have rung you up
    tomorrow
And come in to say good-bye before I left.
    LAVINIA. And Celia's going too? Was that what
    I heard?
I congratulate you both. To Hollywood, of course?
How exciting for you, Celia! Now you'll have a
    chance
At last, to realise your ambitions.
You're going together?
    PETER.   We're not going together.
Celia told us she was going away,
But I don't know where.
    LAVINIA.   You don't know where?
And do you know where you are going, yourself?
    PETER. Yes, of course, I'm going to California.
    LAVINIA. Well, Celia, why don't *you* go to Cali-
    fornia?
Everyone says it's a wonderful climate:
The people who go there never want to leave it.
    CELIA. Lavinia, I think I understand about Peter
    . . .
    LAVINIA. I have no doubt you do.
    CELIA.   And why he is going . . .
    LAVINIA. I don't doubt that either.
    CELIA.   And I believe he is right to go.
    LAVINIA. Oh, so you advised him?
    PETER.   She knew nothing about it.
    CELIA. But now that I may be going away—
    somewhere—
I should like to say good-bye—as friends.
    LAVINIA. Why, Celia, but haven't we always been
    friends?
I thought you were one of my dearest friends—
At least, in so far as a girl *can* be a friend
Of a woman so much older than herself.
    CELIA.   Lavinia,
Don't put me off. I may not see you again.
What I want to say is this: I should like you to
    remember me
As someone who wants you and Edward to be
    happy.
    LAVINIA. You are very kind, but very mysterious.
I'm sure that we shall manage somehow, thank
    you,
As we have in the past.
    CELIA.   Oh, not as in the past!
    [*The doorbell rings, and* EDWARD *goes to answer
it.*]

Oh, I'm afraid that all this sounds rather silly!
But . . .

[EDWARD *re-enters with* JULIA.]

JULIA. There you are, Lavinia! I'm sorry to be
late.

But your telegram was a bit unexpected.
I dropped everything to come. And how is the dear
aunt?

LAVINIA. So far as I know, she is very well,
thank you.

JULIA. She must have made a marvellous recovery.

I said so to myself, when I got your telegram.

LAVINIA. But where, may I ask, was this telegram
sent from?

JULIA. Why, from Essex, of course.

LAVINIA. And why from Essex?

JULIA. Because you've been in Essex.

LAVINIA. Because I've been in Essex!

JULIA. Lavinia! Don't say you've had a lapse of
memory!

Then that accounts for the aunt—and the telegram.

LAVINIA. Well, perhaps I was in Essex. I really
don't know.

JULIA. You don't know where you were? Lavinia!

Don't tell me you were abducted! Tell us;
I'm thrilled . . .

[*The doorbell rings.* EDWARD *goes to answer it.
Enter* ALEX.]

ALEX. Has Lavinia arrived?

EDWARD. Yes.

ALEX. Welcome back, Lavinia!
When I got your telegram . . .

LAVINIA. Where from?

ALEX. Dedham.

LAVINIA. Dedham is in Essex. So it was from
Dedham.

Edward, have *you* any friends in Dedham?

EDWARD. No, *I* have no connections in Dedham.

JULIA. Well, it's all delightfully mysterious.

ALEX. But what is the mystery?

JULIA. Alex, *don't* be inquisitive.
Lavinia has had a lapse of memory,
And so, of course, she sent us telegrams:
And now I don't believe she really wants us.
I can see that she is quite worn out
After her anxiety about her aunt—
Who, you'll be glad to hear, has quite recovered,
Alex—
And after that long journey on the old Great East-
ern,

Waiting at junctions. And I suppose she's famished.

ALEX. Ah, in that case I know what I'll do . . .

JULIA. No, Alex.
We must leave them alone, and let Lavinia rest.
Now we'll all go back to *my* house. Peter, call a
taxi.

[*Exit* PETER.]

We'll have a cocktail party at *my* house today.

CELIA. Well, I'll go now. Good-bye, Lavinia.
Good-bye, Edward.

EDWARD. Good-bye, Celia.

CELIA. Good-bye, Lavinia.

LAVINIA. Good-bye, Celia.

[*Exit* CELIA.]

JULIA. And now, Alex, you and I should be
going.

EDWARD. Are you sure you haven't left anything, Julia?

JULIA. Left anything? Oh, you mean my spec-
tacles.
No, they're here. Besides, they're no use to me.
I'm not coming back again *this* evening.

LAVINIA. Stop! I want you to explain the telegram.

JULIA. Explain the telegram? What do you
think, Alex?

ALEX. No, Julia, *we* can't explain the telegram.

LAVINIA. I am sure that you could explain the
telegram.
I don't know why. But it seems to me that yester-
day
I started some machine, that goes on working,
And I cannot stop it; no, it's not like a machine—
Or if it's a machine, someone else is running it.
But who? Somebody is always interfering . . .
I don't feel free . . . and yet I started it . . .

JULIA. Alex, do you think we could explain *anything?*

ALEX. I think not, Julia. She must find out for
herself:
That's the only way.

JULIA. How right you are!
Well, my dears, I shall see you very soon.

EDWARD. *When* shall we see you?

JULIA. Did I say you'd see me?
Good-bye. I believe . . . I haven't left anything.

[*Enter* PETER.]

PETER. I've got a taxi, Julia.

JULIA. Splendid! Good-bye!

[*Exeunt* JULIA, ALEX *and* PETER.]

LAVINIA. I must say, you don't seem very pleased
to see me.

EDWARD. I can't say that I've had much opportunity
To seem anything. But of course I'm glad to see
you.

LAVINIA. Yes, that was a silly thing to say.
Like a schoolgirl. Like Celia. I don't know why
I said it.
Well, here I am.

EDWARD.   I am to ask no questions.

LAVINIA. And I know I am to give no explanations.

EDWARD. And I am to give no explanations.

LAVINIA. And I am to ask no questions. And
yet . . . why not?

EDWARD. I don't know why not. So what are we
to talk about?

LAVINIA. There is one thing I ought to know,
because of other people
And what to do about them. It's about that party.
I suppose you won't believe I forgot all about it!
I let you down badly. What did you do about it?
I only remembered after I had left.

EDWARD. I telephoned to everyone I knew was
coming
But I couldn't get everyone. And so a few came.

LAVINIA. Who came?

EDWARD.   Just those who were here
this evening . . .

LAVINIA. That's odd.

EDWARD. . . . and one other. I don't know who
he was,
But you ought to know.

LAVINIA.   Yes, I think I know.
But I'm puzzled by Julia. That woman is the devil.
She knows by instinct when something's going to
happen.
Trust her not to miss any awkward situation!
And what did you tell them!

EDWARD.   I invented an aunt
Who was ill in the country, and had sent for you.

LAVINIA. Really, Edward! You had better have
told the truth:
Nothing less than the truth could deceive Julia.
But how did the aunt come to live in Essex?

EDWARD. Julia compelled me to make her live
somewhere.

LAVINIA. I see. So Julia made her live in Essex;
And made the telegrams come from Essex.
Well, I shall have to tell Julia the truth.
I shall always tell the truth now.

We have wasted such a lot of time in lying.

EDWARD. I don't quite know what you mean.

LAVINIA.   Oh, Edward!
The point is, that since I've been away
I see that I've taken you much too seriously.
And now I can see how absurd you are.

EDWARD. That is a very serious conclusion
To have arrived at in . . . how many? . . .
thirty-two hours.

LAVINIA. Yes, a very important discovery,
Finding that you've spent five years of your life
With a man who has no sense of humour;
And that the effect upon me was
That I lost all sense of humour myself.
That's what came of always giving in to you.

EDWARD. I was unaware that you'd always given
in to me.
It struck me very differently. As we're on the subject,
I thought that it was I who had given in to you.

LAVINIA. I know what you mean by giving in to
me:
You mean, leaving all the practical decisions
That you should have made yourself. I remem-
ber—
Oh, I ought to have realised what was coming—
When we were planning our honeymoon,
I couldn't make you say where you wanted to
go . . .

EDWARD. But I wanted you to make that decision.

LAVINIA. But how could I tell where I wanted to
go
Unless you suggested some other place first?
And I remember that finally in desperation
I said: 'I suppose you'd as soon go to Peace-
haven'—
And you said 'I don't mind.'

EDWARD.   Of course I didn't mind.
I meant it as a compliment.

LAVINIA.   You meant it as a compliment!

EDWARD. It's just that way of taking things that
makes you so exasperating.

LAVINIA. You were so considerate, people said;
And you thought you were unselfish. It was only
passivity;
You only wanted to be bolstered, encouraged . . .

EDWARD. Encouraged? To what?

LAVINIA.   To think well of yourself.
You know it was I who made you work at the
Bar . . .

EDWARD. You nagged me because I didn't get
enough work

And said that I ought to meet more people:
But when the briefs began to come in—
And they didn't come through any of *your*
   friends—
You suddenly found it inconvenient
That I should always be too busy or too tired
To be of use to you socially . . .
   LAVINIA.   I *never* complained.
   EDWARD. No; and it was perfectly infuriating,
The way you *didn't* complain . . .
   LAVINIA.   It was you who complained
Of seeing nobody but solicitors and clients . . .
   EDWARD. And you were never very sympathetic.
   LAVINIA. Well, but I tried to do something about
   it.
That was why I took so much trouble
To have those Thursdays, to give you the chance
Of talking to intellectual people . . .
   EDWARD. You would have given me about as
      much opportunity
If you had hired me as your butler:
Some of your guests may have thought I *was* the
   butler.
   LAVINIA. And on several occasions, when some-
      body was coming
Whom I particularly wanted you to meet,
You didn't arrive until just as they were leaving.
   EDWARD. Well, at least, *they* can't have thought
      I was the butler.
   LAVINIA. Everything I tried only made matters
      worse,
And the moment you were offered something that
   you wanted
You wanted something else. I shall treat you very
   differently
In future.
   EDWARD. Thank you for the warning. But tell
      me,
Since this is how you see me, why did you come
   back?
   LAVINIA. Frankly, I don't know. I was warned
      of the danger,
Yet something, or somebody, compelled me to
   come.
And why did you want me?
   EDWARD.   I don't know either.
You say you were trying to 'encourage' me:
Then why did you always make me feel insig-
   nificant?
I may not have known what life I wanted,
But it wasn't the life you chose for me.
You wanted your husband to be *successful,*

You wanted me to supply a public background
For your kind of public life. You wished to be a
   hostess
For whom my career would be a support.
Well, I tried to be accommodating. But in future,
I shall behave, I assure you, very differently.
   LAVINIA. Bravo! This is surprising.
Now who could have taught you to answer back
   like that?
   EDWARD. I have had quite enough humiliation
Lately, to bring me to the point
At which humiliation ceases to humiliate.
You get to the point at which you cease to feel
And then you speak your mind.
   LAVINIA.   That will be a novelty
To find that you have a mind to speak.
Anyway, I'm prepared to take you as you are.
   EDWARD. You mean, you are prepared to take me
As I was, or as you think I am.
But what do you think I am?
   LAVINIA.   Oh, what you always were.
As for me, I'm rather a different person
Whom you must get to know.
   EDWARD.   This is very interesting:
But you seem to assume that you've done all the
   changing—
Though I haven't yet found it a change for the
   better.
But doesn't it occur to you that possibly
I may have changed too?
   LAVINIA. Oh, Edward, when you were a little
      boy,
I'm sure you were always getting yourself mea-
   sured
To prove how you had grown since the last holi-
   days.
You were always intensely concerned with your-
   self;
And if other people grow, well, you want to
   grow too.
In what way have you changed?
   EDWARD.   The change that comes
From seeing oneself through the eyes of other
   people.
   LAVINIA. That must have been very shattering
      for you.
But never mind, you'll soon get over it
And find yourself another little part to play,
With another face, to take people in.
   EDWARD. One of the most infuriating things
      about you
Has always been your perfect assurance

That you understood me better than I understood
    myself.
    LAVINIA. And the most infuriating thing about
    you
Has always been your placid assumption
That I wasn't worth the trouble of understanding.
    EDWARD. So here we are again. Back in the
    trap,
With only one difference, perhaps—we can fight
    each other,
Instead of each taking his corner of the cage.
Well, it's a better way of passing the evening
Than listening to the gramophone.
    LAVINIA.   We have very good records;
But I always suspected that you really hated music
And that the gramophone was only your escape
From talking to me when we had to be alone.
    EDWARD. I've often wondered why you married
    me.
    LAVINIA. Well, you really were rather attractive,
    you know;
And you kept on *saying* that you were in love
    with me—
I believe you were trying to persuade yourself you
    were.
I seemed always on the verge of some wonderful
    experience
And then it never happened. I wonder now
How you could have thought you were in love
    with me.
    EDWARD. Everybody told me that I was;
And they told me how well suited we were.
    LAVINIA. It's a pity that you had no opinion of
    your own.
Oh, Edward, I should like to be good to you—
Or if that's impossible, at least be horrid to you—
Anything but nothing, which is all you seem to
    want of me.
But I'm sorry for you . . .
    EDWARD.   Don't say you are sorry for me!
I have had enough of people being sorry for me.
    LAVINIA. Yes, because they can never be so sorry
    for you
As you are for yourself. And that's hard to bear.
I thought that there might be some way out for you
If I went away. I thought that if I died
To you, I who had been only a ghost to you,
You might be able to find the road back
To a time when you were real—for you must have
    been real
At some time or other, before you ever knew me.

Perhaps only when you were a child.
    EDWARD. I don't want you to make yourself re-
    sponsible for me:
It's only another kind of contempt.
And I do not want you to explain me to myself.
You're still trying to invent a personality for me
Which will only keep me away from myself.
    LAVINIA. You're complicating what is in fact
    very simple.
But there is one point which I see clearly:
We are not to relapse into the kind of life we led
Until yesterday morning.
    EDWARD.   There was a door
And I could not open it. I could not touch the
    handle.
Why could I not walk out of my prison?
What is hell? Hell is oneself,
Hell is alone, the other figures in it
Merely projections. There is nothing to escape
    from
And nothing to escape to. One is always alone.
    LAVINIA. Edward, what *are* you talking about?
Talking to yourself. Could you bear, for a moment,
To think about *me*?
    EDWARD.   It was only yesterday
That damnation took place. And now I must live
    with it
Day by day, hour by hour, forever and ever.
    LAVINIA. I think you're on the edge of a nervous
    breakdown!
    EDWARD. Don't say that!
    LAVINIA.   I must say it.
I know . . . of a doctor who I think could help
    you.
    EDWARD. If I go to a doctor, I shall make my
    own choice;
Not take one whom you choose. How do I know
That you wouldn't see him first, and tell him all
    about me
From *your* point of view? But I don't need a
    doctor.
I am simply in hell. Where there are no doctors—
At least, not in a professional capacity.
    LAVINIA. One can be practical, even in hell:
And you know I am much more practical than you
    are.
    EDWARD. I ought to know by now what you con-
    sider practical.
Practical! I remember, on our honeymoon,
You were always wrapping things up in tissue
    paper

And then had to unwrap everything again
To find what you wanted. And I never could
  teach you
How to put the cap on a tube of tooth-paste.
  LAVINIA. Very well then, I shall not try to press
    you.
You're much too divided to know what you want.
But, being divided, you will tend to compromise,
And your sort of compromise will be the old one.
  EDWARD. You don't understand me. Have I not
    made it clear
That in future you will find me a different person?
  LAVINIA. Indeed. And has the difference nothing
    to do
With Celia going off to California?
  EDWARD. Celia? Going to California?
  LAVINIA.   Yes, with Peter.
Really, Edward, if you were human
You would burst out laughing. But you won't.
  EDWARD. O God, O God, if I could return to
    yesterday
Before I thought that I had made a decision.
What devil left the door on the latch
For these doubts to enter? And then you came
  back, you
The angel of destruction—just as I felt sure.
In a moment, at your touch, there is nothing but
  ruin.
O God, what have I done? The python. The oc-
  topus.
Must I become after all what you would make me?
  LAVINIA. Well, Edward, as I am unable to make
    you laugh,
And as I can't persuade you to see a doctor,
There's nothing else at present that I can do about
  it.
I ought to go and have a look in the kitchen.
I know there are some eggs. But we must go out
  for dinner.
Meanwhile, my luggage is in the hall downstairs:
Will you get the porter to fetch it up for me?

CURTAIN

ACT II

SIR HENRY HARCOURT-REILLY's *consulting room in
London. Morning: several weeks later.* SIR HENRY
*alone at his desk. He presses an electric button.
The* NURSE-SECRETARY *enters, with Appointment
Book.*

  REILLY. About those three appointments this morn-
    ing, Miss Barraway:
I should like to run over my instructions again.
You understand, of course, that it is important
To avoid any meeting?
  NURSE-SECRETARY.   You made that clear, Sir
    Henry:
The first appointment at eleven o'clock.
He is to be shown into the small waiting room;
And you will see him almost at once.
  REILLY. I shall see him at once. And the second?
  NURSE-SECRETARY. The second to be shown into
    the other room.
Just as usual. She arrives at a quarter past;
But you may keep her waiting.
  REILLY.   Or she may keep me waiting;
But I think she will be punctual.
  NURSE-SECRETARY.   I telephone through
The moment she arrives. I leave her there
Until you ring three times.
  REILLY.   And the third patient?
  NURSE-SECRETARY. The third one to be shown
    into the small room;
And I need not let you know that she has ar-
  rived.
Then, when you ring, I show the others out;
And only after they have left the house . . .
  REILLY. Quite right, Miss Barraway. That's all
    for the moment.
  NURSE-SECRETARY. Mr. Gibbs is here, Sir Henry.
  REILLY.   Ask him to come straight in.
                    [*Exit* NURSE-SECRETARY.]
        [ALEX *enters almost immediately.*]
  ALEX. When is Chamberlayne's appointment?
  REILLY.   At eleven o'clock,
The conventional hour. We have not much time.
Tell me now, did you have any difficulty
In convincing him I was the man for his case?
  ALEX. Difficulty? No! He was only impatient
At having to wait four days for the appointment.
  REILLY. It was necessary to delay his appointment
To lower his resistance. But what I mean is,
Does he trust your judgment?
  ALEX.   Yes, implicitly.
It's not that he regards me as very intelligent,
But he thinks I'm well informed: the sort of per-
  son

Who would know the right doctor, as well as the
    right shops.
Besides, he was ready to consult any doctor
Recommended by anyone except his wife.
    REILLY. I had already impressed upon her
That she was not to mention my name to him.
    ALEX. With your usual foresight. Now, he's quite
    triumphant
Because he thinks he's stolen a march on her.
And when you've sent him to a sanatorium
Where she can't get at him—then, he believes,
She will be very penitent. He's enjoying his illness.
    REILLY. Illness offers him a double advantage:
To escape from himself—and get the better of his
    wife.
    ALEX. Not to escape from her?
    REILLY.   He doesn't want to escape from her.
    ALEX. He is staying at his club.
    REILLY.   Yes, that is where he wrote from.
    [The house-telephone rings.]
Hello! yes, show him up.
    ALEX.   You will have a busy morning!
I will go out by the service staircase
And come back when they've gone.
    REILLY.   Yes, when they've gone.
        [Exit ALEX by side door.]
    [EDWARD is shown in by NURSE-SECRETARY.]
    EDWARD. Sir Henry Harcourt-Reilly—
    [Stops and stares at REILLY]
    REILLY [without looking up from his papers].
            Good morning, Mr. Chamberlayne.
Please sit down. I won't keep you a moment.
—Now, Mr. Chamberlayne?
    EDWARD.   It came into my mind
Before I entered the door, that you might be the
    same person:
And I dismissed that as just another symptom.
Well, I should have known better than to come
    here
On the recommendation of a man who did not
    know you.
But Alex is so plausible. And his recommendations
Of shops have always been satisfactory.
I beg your pardon. But he is a blunderer.
I should like to know . . . but what is the use!
I suppose I might as well go away at once.
    REILLY. No. If you please, sit down, Mr. Cham-
    berlayne.
You are not going away, so you might as well sit
    down.
You were going to ask a question.

    EDWARD.   When you came to my flat
Had you been invited by my wife as a guest
As I supposed? . . . Or did she send you?
    REILLY. I cannot say that I had been invited,
And Mrs. Chamberlayne did not know that I was
    coming.
But I knew you would be there, and whom I
    should find with you.
    EDWARD. But you had seen my wife?
    REILLY.   Oh yes, I had seen her.
    EDWARD. So this is a trap!
    REILLY.   Let's not call it a trap.
But if it is a trap, then you cannot escape from it:
And so . . . you might as well sit down.
I think you will find that chair comfortable.
    EDWARD.   You knew,
Before I began to tell you, what had happened?
    REILLY. That is so, that is so. But all in good
    time.
Let us dismiss that question for the moment.
Tell me first, about the difficulties
On which you want my professional opinion.
    EDWARD. It's not for me to blame you for bring-
    ing my wife back,
I suppose. You seemed to be trying to persuade
    me
That I was better off without her. But didn't you
    realise
That I was in no state to make a decision?
    REILLY. If I had not brought your wife back,
    Mr. Chamberlayne,
Do you suppose that things would be any better—
    now?
    EDWARD. I don't know, I'm sure. They could
    hardly be worse.
    REILLY. They might be much worse. You might
    have ruined three lives
By your indecision. Now there are only two—
Which you still have the chance of redeeming from
    ruin.
    EDWARD. You talk as if I was capable of action:
If I were, I should not need to consult you
Or anyone else. I came here as a patient.
If you take no interest in my case, I can go else-
    where.
    REILLY. You have reason to believe that you are
    very ill?
    EDWARD. I should have thought a doctor could
    see that for himself.
Or at least that he would enquire about the symp-
    toms.

Two people advised me recently,
Almost in the same words, that I ought to see a
    doctor.
They said—again, in almost the same words—
That I was on the edge of a nervous breakdown.
I didn't know it then myself—but if they saw it
I should have thought that a doctor could see it.
    REILLY. 'Nervous breakdown' is a term I never
      use:
It can mean almost anything.
    EDWARD.   And since then, I have realised
That mine is a very unusual case.
    REILLY. All cases are unique, and very similar
      to others.
    EDWARD. Is there a sanitorium to which you send
      such patients
As myself, under your personal observation?
    REILLY. You are very impetuous, Mr. Chamber-
      layne.
There are several kinds of sanatoria
For several kinds of patient. And there are also
    patients
For whom a sanatorium is the worst place possible.
We must first find out what is wrong with you
Before we decide what to do with you.
    EDWARD. I doubt if you have ever had a case like
      mine:
I have ceased to believe in my own personality.
    REILLY. Oh, dear yes; this is serious. A very
      common malady.
Very prevalent indeed.
    EDWARD.   I remember, in my childhood . . .
    REILLY. I always begin from the immediate sit-
      uation
And then go back as far as I find necessary.
You see, your memories of childhood—
I mean, in your present state of mind—
Would be largely fictitious; and as for your
    dreams,
You would produce amazing dreams, to oblige me.
I could make you dream any kind of dream I
    suggested,
And it would only go to flatter your vanity
With the temporary stimulus of feeling interesting.
    EDWARD. But I am obsessed by the thought of my
      own insignificance.
    REILLY. Precisely. And I could make you feel
      important,
And you would imagine it a marvellous cure;
And you would go on, doing such amount of
    mischief

As lay within your power—until you came to grief.
Half of the harm that is done in this world
Is due to people who want to feel important.
They don't mean to do harm—but the harm does
    not interest them.
Or they do not see it, or they justify it
Because they are absorbed in the endless struggle
To think well of themselves.
    EDWARD.   If I am like that
I must have done a great deal of harm.
    REILLY. Oh, not so much as you would like to
      think.
Only, shall we say, within your modest capacity.
Try to explain what has happened since I left you.
    EDWARD. I see now why I wanted my wife to
      come back.
It was because of what she had made me into.
We had not been alone again for fifteen minutes
Before I felt, and still more acutely—
Indeed, acutely, perhaps, for the first time,
The whole oppression, the unreality
Of the role she had always imposed upon me
With the obstinate, unconscious, sub-human
    strength
That some women have. Without her, it was va-
    cancy.
When I thought she had left me, I began to dis-
    solve,
To cease to exist. That was what she had done to
    me!
I cannot live with her—that is now intolerable;
I cannot live without her, for she has made me
    incapable
Of having any existence of my own.
That is what she has done to me in five years to-
    gether!
She has made the world a place I cannot live in
Except on her terms. I must be alone,
But not in the same world. So I want you to put
    me
Into your sanatorium. I could be alone there?
    [*House-telephone rings.*]
    REILLY [*into telephone*]. Yes.
    [*To* EDWARD]
              Yes, you could be alone there.
    EDWARD.   I wonder
If you have understood a word of what I have been
    saying.
    REILLY. You must have patience with me, Mr.
      Chamberlayne:
I learn a good deal by merely observing you,

And letting you talk as long as you please,
And taking note of what you do not say.

   EDWARD. I once experienced the extreme of
    physical pain,

And now I know there is suffering worse than
that.
It is surprising, if one had time to be surprised:
I am not afraid of the death of the body,
But this death is terrifying. The death of the
spirit—
Can you understand what I suffer?

   REILLY.   I understand what you mean.

   EDWARD. I can no longer act for myself.

Coming to see you—that's the last decision
I was capable of making. I am in your hands.
I cannot take any further responsibility.

   REILLY. Many patients come in that belief.

   EDWARD. And now will you send me to the sana-
    torium?

   REILLY. You have nothing else to tell me?

   EDWARD.   What else can I tell you?

You don't want to hear about my early history.

   REILLY. No, I did not want to hear about your
    early history.

   EDWARD. And so will you send me to the sana-
    torium?

I can't go home again. And at my club
They won't let you keep a room for more than
seven days;
I haven't the courage to go to a hotel,
And besides, I need more shirts—you can get my
wife
To have my things sent on: whatever I shall need.
But of course you mustn't tell her where I am.
Is it far to go?

   REILLY.   You might say, a long journey.

But before I treat a patient like yourself
I need to know a great deal more about him,
Than the patient himself can always tell me.
Indeed, it is often the case that my patients
Are only pieces of a total situation
Which I have to explore. The single patient
Who is ill by himself, is rather the exception.
I have recently had another patient
Whose situation is much the same as your own.

   [*Presses the bell on his desk three times*]

You must accept a rather unusual procedure:
I propose to introduce you to the other patient.

   EDWARD. What do you mean? Who is this other
    patient?

I consider this very unprofessional conduct—
I will not discuss my case before another patient.

   REILLY. On the contrary. That is the only way

In which it can be discussed. You have told me
nothing.
You have had the opportunity, and you have said
enough
To convince me that you have been making up
your case
So to speak, as you went along. A barrister
Ought to know his brief before he enters the
court.

   EDWARD. I am at least free to leave. And I pro-
    pose to do so.

My mind is made up. I shall go to a hotel.

   REILLY. It is just because you are not free, Mr.
    Chamberlayne,

That you have come to me. It is for me to give you
that—
Your freedom. That is my affair.

   [LAVINIA *is shown in by the* NURSE-SECRETARY.]

But here is the other patient.

   EDWARD.   Lavinia!

   LAVINIA.   Well, Sir Henry!

I said I would come to talk about my husband:
I didn't say I was prepared to meet him.

   EDWARD. And I did not expect to meet *you*, La-
    vinia.

I call this a very dishonourable trick.

   REILLY. Honesty before honour, Mr. Chamber-
    layne.

Sit down, please, both of you. Mrs. Chamberlayne,
Your husband wishes to enter a sanatorium,
And that is a question which naturally concerns
you.

   EDWARD. I am not going to any sanatorium.

I am going to a hotel. And I shall ask you, Lavinia,
To be so good as to send me on some clothes.

   LAVINIA. Oh, to what hotel?

   EDWARD.   I don't know—I mean to say,

That doesn't concern you.

   LAVINIA.   In that case, Edward,

I don't think your clothes concern me either.

   [*To* REILLY]

I presume you will send him to the same sanatorium
To which you sent me? Well, he needs it more
than I did.

   REILLY. I am glad that you have come to see it
    in that light—

At least, for the moment. But, Mrs. Chamberlayne,
You have never visited my sanatorium.

LAVINIA. What do you mean? I asked to be sent
And you took me there. If that was not a sana-
torium
What was it?

REILLY.   A kind of hotel. A retreat
For people who imagine that they need a respite
From everyday life. They return refreshed;
And if they believe it to be a sanatorium
That is good reason for not sending them to one.
The people who need my sort of sanatorium
Are not easily deceived.

LAVINIA.   Are you a devil
Or merely a lunatic practical joker?

EDWARD. I incline to the second explanation
Without the qualification 'lunatic.'
Why should *you* go to a sanatorium?
I have never known anyone in my life
With fewer mental complications than you;
You're stronger than a . . . battleship. That's
     what drove me mad.
I am the one who needs a sanatorium—
But I'm not going there.

REILLY.   You are right, Mr. Chamberlayne.
You are no case for my sanatorium:
You are much too ill.

EDWARD.   Much too ill?
Then I'll go and be ill in a suburban boarding-
     house.

LAVINIA. That would never suit you, Edward.
     Now I know of a hotel
In the New Forest . . .

EDWARD.   How like you, Lavinia.
You always know of something better.

LAVINIA. It's only that I have a more practical
     mind
Than you have, Edward. You do know that.

EDWARD. Only because you've told me so often.
I'd like to see *you* filling up an income-tax form.

LAVINIA. Don't be silly, Edward. When I say
     practical,
I mean practical in the things that really matter.

REILLY. May I interrupt this interesting discus-
     sion?
I say you are both too ill. There are several symp-
     toms
Which must occur together, and to a marked de-
     gree,
To qualify a patient for *my* sanatorium:
And one of them is an honest mind.
That is one of the causes of their suffering.

LAVINIA. No one can say my husband has an
     honest mind.

EDWARD. And I could not honestly say that of
     you, Lavinia.

REILLY. I congratulate you both on your perspi-
     cacity,
But this does not bring us to the heart of the
     matter.
I do not trouble myself with the common cheat,
Or with the insuperably, innocently dull:
My patients such as you are the self-deceivers
Taking infinite pains, exhausting their energy,
Yet never quite successful. You have both of you
     pretended
To be consulting me; both, tried to impose upon
     me
Your own diagnosis, and prescribe your own cure.
But when you put yourselves into hands like mine
You surrender a great deal more than you meant
     to.
This is the consequence of trying to lie to me.

LAVINIA. I did not come here to be insulted.

REILLY. You have come where the word 'insult'
     has no meaning;
And you must put up with that. All that you have
     told me—
Both of you—was true enough; you described your
     feelings—
Or some of them—omitting the important facts.
Let me take your husband first.
     [*To* EDWARD]
                  You were lying to me
By concealing your relations with Miss Coplestone.

EDWARD. This is monstrous! My wife knew noth-
     ing about it.

LAVINIA. Really, Edward! Even if I'd been blind
There were plenty of people to let me know about
     it.
I wonder if there was anyone who didn't know.

REILLY. There was one, in fact. But you, Mrs.
     Chamberlayne,
Tried to make me believe that it was this dis-
     covery
Precipitated what you called your nervous break-
     down.

LAVINIA. But it's true! I was completely pros-
     trated;
Even if I have made a partial recovery.

REILLY. Certainly, you were completely pros-
     trated,
And certainly, you have somewhat recovered.
But you failed to mention that the cause of your
     distress
Was the defection of your lover—who suddenly

For the first time in his life, fell in love with
      someone,
And with someone of whom you had reason to be
      jealous.

EDWARD. Really, Lavinia! This is very interesting.
You seem to have been much more successful at
      concealment
Than I was. Now I wonder who it could have
      been.

LAVINIA. Well, tell him if you like.

REILLY.   A young man named Peter.

EDWARD. Peter? Peter who?

REILLY.   Mr. Peter Quilpe
Was a frequent guest.

EDWARD.   Peter Quilpe!
Peter Quilpe! Really Lavinia!
I congratulate you. You could not have chosen
Anyone I was less likely to suspect.
And then he came to *me* to confide about Celia!
I have never heard anything so utterly ludicrous:
This is the best joke that ever happened.

LAVINIA. I never knew you had such a sense
      of humour.

REILLY. It is the first more hopeful symptom.

LAVINIA. How did you know all this?

REILLY.   That I cannot disclose.
I have my own method of collecting information
About my patients. You must not ask me to reveal
      it—
That is a matter of professional etiquette.

LAVINIA. I have not noticed much professional
      etiquette
About your behaviour today.

REILLY.   A point well taken.
But permit me to remark that my revelations
About each of you, to one another,
Have not been of anything that you confided to
      me.
The information I have exchanged between you
Was all obtained from outside sources.
Mrs. Chamberlayne, when you came to me two
      months ago
I was dissatisfied with your explanation
Of your obvious symptoms of emotional strain
And so I made enquiries.

EDWARD.   It was two months ago
That your breakdown began! And I never noticed
      it.

LAVINIA. You wouldn't notice anything. You
      never noticed *me*.

REILLY. Now, I want to point out to both of you

How much you have in common. Indeed, I con-
      sider
That you are exceptionally well-suited to each
      other.
Mr. Chamberlayne, when you thought your wife
      had left you,
You discovered, to your surprise and consterna-
      tion,
That you were not really in love with Miss Cop-
      lestone . . .

LAVINIA. My husband has never been in love
      with anybody.

REILLY. And were not prepared to make the least
      sacrifice
On her account. This injured your vanity.
You liked to think of yourself as a passionate
      lover.
Then you realised, what your wife has justly re-
      marked,
That you had never been in love with anybody;
Which made you suspect that you were incapable
Of loving. To men of a certain type
The suspicion that they are incapable of loving
Is as disturbing to their self-esteem
As, in cruder men, the fear of impotence.

LAVINIA. You *are* cold-hearted, Edward.

REILLY.   So you say, Mrs. Chamberlayne.
And now, let us turn to your side of the problem.
When you discovered that your young friend
(Though you knew, in your heart, that he was
      not in love with you,
And were always humiliated by the awareness
That you had forced him into this position)—
When, I say, you discovered that your young friend
Had actually fallen in love with Miss Coplestone,
It took you some time, I have no doubt,
Before you would admit it. Though perhaps you
      knew it
Before he did. You pretended to yourself,
I suspect, and for as long as you could,
That he was aiming at a higher social distinction
Than the honour conferred by being *your* lover.
When you had to face the fact that his feelings
      towards her
Were different from any you had aroused in him—
It was a shock. You had wanted to be loved;
You had come to see that no one had ever loved
      you.
Then you began to fear that no one *could* love you.

EDWARD. I'm beginning to feel very sorry for you,
      Lavinia.

You know, you really are exceptionally unlovable,
And I never quite knew why. I thought it was *my*
    fault.

    REILLY. And now you begin to see, I hope,
How much you have in common. The same iso-
    lation.
A man who finds himself incapable of loving
And a woman who finds that no man can love her.

    LAVINIA. It seems to me that what we have in
    common
Might be just enough to make us loathe one an-
    other.

    REILLY. See it rather as the bond which holds you
    together.
While still in a state of unenlightenment,
You could always say: 'He could not love any
    woman';
You could always say: 'No man could love her.'
You could accuse each other of your own faults,
And so could avoid understanding each other.
Now, you have only to reverse the propositions
And put them together.

    LAVINIA.   Is that possible?

    REILLY. If I had sent either of you to the sana-
    torium
In the state in which you came to me—I tell you
    this:
It would have been a horror beyond your imagin-
    ing,
For you would have been left with what you
    brought with you:
The shadow of desires of desires. A prey
To the devils who arrive at their plenitude of
    power
When they have you to themselves.

    LAVINIA.   Then what can we do
When we can go neither back nor forward? Ed-
    ward!
What can we do?

    REILLY. You have answered your own question,
Though you do not know the meaning of what
    you have said.

    EDWARD. Lavinia, we must make the best of a
    bad job.
That is what he means.

    REILLY.   When you find, Mr. Chamberlayne,
The best of a bad job is all any of us make of it—
Except of course, the saints—such as those who go
To the sanatorium—you will forget this phrase,
And in forgetting it will alter the condition.

    LAVINIA. Edward, there *is* that hotel in the New
    Forest
If you want to go there. The proprietor
Who has just taken over, is a friend of Alex's.
I could go down with you, and then leave you
    there
If you want to be alone . . .

    EDWARD.   But I can't go away!
I have a case coming on next Monday.

    LAVINIA. Then will you stop at your club?

    EDWARD.   No, they won't let me.
I must leave tomorrow—but how did you know
I was staying at the club?

    LAVINIA.   Really, Edward!
I have *some* sense of responsibility.
I was going to leave some shirts there for you.

    EDWARD. It seems to me that I might as well go
    home.

    LAVINIA. Then we can share a taxi, and be eco-
    nomical.
Edward, have you anything else to ask him
Before we go?

    EDWARD.   Yes, I have.
But it's difficult to say.

    LAVINIA.   But I wish you would say it.
At least, there is something I would like you to
    ask.

    EDWARD. It's about the future of . . . the others.
I don't want to build on other people's ruins.

    LAVINIA. Exactly. And I have a question too.
Sir Henry, was it you who sent those telegrams?

    REILLY. I think I will dispose of your husband's
    problem.

    [*To* EDWARD]
Your business is not to clear your conscience
But to learn how to bear the burdens on your con-
    science.
With the future of the others you are not con-
    cerned.

    LAVINIA. I think you have answered my question
    too.
They had to tell us, themselves, that they had
    made their decision.

    EDWARD. Have you anything else to say to us, Sir
    Henry?

    REILLY. No. Not in this capacity.

    [EDWARD *takes out his cheque-book.* REILLY
raises his hand.]
My secretary will send you my account.
Go in peace. And work out your salvation with
    diligence.

[*Exeunt* EDWARD *and* LAVINIA.]
[REILLY *goes to the couch and lies down. The house-telephone rings. He gets up and answers it.*]
REILLY. Yes? . . . Yes. Come in.
[*Enter* JULIA *by side door.*]
She's waiting downstairs.
JULIA. I know that, Henry. I brought her here myself.
REILLY. Oh? You didn't let her know you were seeing me first?
JULIA. Of course not. I dropped her at the door
And went on in the taxi, round the corner;
Waited a moment, and slipped in by the back way.
I only came to tell you, I am sure she is ready
To make a decision.
REILLY. Was she reluctant?
Was that why you brought her?
JULIA. Oh no, not reluctant:
Only diffident. She cannot believe
That you will take her seriously.
REILLY. That is not uncommon.
JULIA. Or that she deserves to be taken seriously.
REILLY. That is most uncommon.
JULIA. Henry, get up. You can't be as tired as that. I shall wait in the next room,
And come back when she's gone.
REILLY. Yes, when she's gone.
JULIA. Will Alex be here?
REILLY. Yes, he'll be here.
[*Exit* JULIA *by side door.*]
[REILLY *presses button.* NURSE-SECRETARY *shows in* CELIA.]
REILLY. Miss Celia Coplestone? . . . Won't you sit down?
I believe you are a friend of Mrs. Shuttlethwaite.
CELIA. Yes, it was Julia . . . Mrs. Shuttlethwaite
Who advised me to come to you.—But I've met you before,
Haven't I, somewhere? . . . Oh, of course.
But I didn't know . . .
REILLY. There is nothing you need to know.
I was there at the instance of Mrs. Shuttlethwaite.
CELIA. That makes it even more perplexing. However,
I don't want to waste your time. And I'm awfully afraid
That you'll think that I am wasting it anyway.
I suppose most people, when they come to see you,
Are obviously ill, or can give good reasons
For wanting to see you. Well, I can't.
I just came in desperation. And I shan't be offended

If you simply tell me to go away again.
REILLY. Most of my patients begin, Miss Coplestone,
By telling me exactly what is the matter with them,
And what I am to do about it. They are quite sure
They have had a nervous breakdown—that is what they call it—
And usually they think that someone else is to blame.
CELIA. I at least have no one to blame but myself.
REILLY. And after that, the prologue to my treatment
Is to try to show them that they are mistaken
About the nature of their illness, and lead them to see
That it's not so interesting as they had imagined.
When I get as far as that, there is something to be done.
CELIA. Well, I can't pretend that my trouble is interesting;
But I shan't begin that way. I feel perfectly well.
I could lead an active life—if there's anything to work for;
I don't imagine that I am being persecuted;
I don't hear any voices, I have no delusions—
Except that the world I live in seems all a delusion!
But oughtn't I first to tell you the circumstances?
I'd forgotten that you know nothing about me;
And with what I've been going through, these last weeks,
I somehow took it for granted that I needn't explain myself.
REILLY. I know quite enough about you for the moment:
Try first to describe your present state of mind.
CELIA. Well, there are two things I can't understand,
Which you might consider symptoms. But first I must tell you
That I should really *like* to think there's something wrong with me—
Because, if there isn't, then there's something wrong,
Or at least, very different from what it seemed to be,
With the world itself—and that's much more frightening!
That would be terrible. So I'd rather believe
There is something wrong with me, that could be put right.

I'd do anything you told me, to get back to nor-
    mality.
    REILLY. We must find out about you, before we
      decide
What *is* normality. You say there are two things:
What is the first?
    CELIA.   An awareness of solitude.
But that sounds so flat. I don't mean simply
That there's been a crash: though indeed there has
    been.
It isn't simply the end of an illusion
In the ordinary way, or being ditched.
Of course that's something that's always happening
To all sorts of people, and they get over it
More or less, or at least they carry on.
No. I mean that what has happened has made me
    aware
That I've always been alone. That one always is
    alone.
Not simply the ending of one relationship,
Not even simply finding that it never existed—
But a revelation about my relationship
With *everybody*. Do you know—
It no longer seems worth while to *speak* to anyone!
    REILLY. And what about your parents?
    CELIA.   Oh, they live in the country,
Now they can't afford to have a place in town.
It's all they can do to keep the country house
    going:
But it's been in the family so long, they won't
    leave it.
    REILLY. And you live in London?
    CELIA.   I share a flat
With a cousin: but she's abroad at the moment,
And my family want me to come down and stay
    with them.
But I just can't face it.
    REILLY.   So you want to see no one?
    CELIA. No . . . it isn't that I *want* to be alone,
But that everyone's alone—or so it seems to me.
They make noises, and think they are talking to
    each other;
They make faces, and think they understand each
    other.
And I'm sure that they don't. Is that a delusion?
    REILLY. A delusion is something we must return
      from.
There are other states of mind, which we take to
    be delusion,
But which we have to accept and go on from.
And the second symptom?
    CELIA.   That's stranger still.

It sounds ridiculous—but the only word for it
That I can find, is a sense of sin.
    REILLY. You suffer from a sense of sin, Miss
      Coplestone?
This is most unusual.
    CELIA.   It seemed to *me* abnormal.
    REILLY. We have yet to find what would be
      normal
For *you*, before we use the term 'abnormal.'
Tell me what you mean by a sense of sin.
    CELIA. It's much easier to tell you what I don't
      mean:
I don't mean sin in the ordinary sense.
    REILLY. And what, in your opinion, is the ordi-
      nary sense?
    CELIA. Well . . . I suppose it's being immoral—
And I don't feel as if I was immoral:
In fact, aren't the people one thinks of as immoral
Just the people who we say have no moral sense?
I've never noticed that immorality
Was accompanied by a sense of sin:
At least, I have never come across it.
I suppose it is wicked to hurt other people
If you know that you're hurting them. I haven't
    hurt *her*.
I wasn't taking anything away from her—
Anything she wanted. I may have been a fool:
But I don't mind at all having been a fool.
    REILLY. And what is the point of view of your
      family?
    CELIA. Well, my bringing up was pretty conven-
      tional—
I had always been taught to disbelieve in sin.
Oh, I don't mean that it was ever mentioned!
But anything wrong, from our point of view,
Was either bad form, or was psychological.
And bad form always led to disaster
Because the people one knew disapproved of it.
I don't worry much about form, myself—
But when everything's bad form, or mental kinks,
You either become bad form, and cease to care,
Or else, if you care, you must be kinky.
    REILLY. And so you suppose you have what you
      call a 'kink'?
    CELIA. But everything seemed so right, at the
      time!
I've been thinking about it, over and over;
I can see now, it was all a mistake:
But I don't see why mistakes should make one
    feel sinful!
And yet I can't find any other word for it.
It must be some kind of hallucination;

Yet, at the same time, I'm frightened by the fear
That it is more real than anything I believed in.

   REILLY. What is more real than anything you believed in?

   CELIA. It's not the feeling of anything I've ever *done,*

Which I might get away from, or of anything in me
I could get rid of—but of emptiness, of failure
Towards someone, or something, outside of myself;
And I feel I must . . . *atone*—is that the word?
Can you treat a patient for such a state of mind?

   REILLY. What had you believed were your relations with this man?

   CELIA. Oh, you'd guessed that, had you? That's clever of you.

No, perhaps I made it obvious. You don't need to know
About him, do you?

   REILLY.   No.

   CELIA.   Perhaps I'm only typical.

   REILLY. There are different types. Some are rarer than others.

   CELIA. Oh, I thought that I was giving him so much!

And he to me—and the giving and the taking
Seemed so right: not in terms of calculation
Of what was good for the persons we had been
But for the new person, *us.* If I could feel
As I did then, even now it would seem right.
And then I found we were only strangers
And that there had been neither giving nor taking
But that we had merely made use of each other
Each for his purpose. That's horrible. Can we only love
Something created by our own imagination?
Are we all in fact unloving and unlovable?
Then one *is* alone, and if one is alone
Then lover and belovèd are equally unreal
And the dreamer is no more real than his dreams.

   REILLY. And this man. What does he now seem like, to you?

   CELIA. Like a child who has wandered into a forest

Playing with an imaginary playmate
And suddenly discovers he is only a child
Lost in a forest, wanting to go home.

   REILLY. Compassion may be already a clue
Towards finding your own way out of the forest.

   CELIA. But even if I find my way out of the forest

I shall be left with the inconsolable memory
Of the treasure I went into the forest to find
And never found, and which was not there
And perhaps is not anywhere? But if not anywhere,
Why do I feel guilty at not having found it?

   REILLY. Disillusion can become itself an illusion
If we rest in it.

   CELIA.   I cannot argue.

It's not that I'm afraid of being hurt again:
Nothing again can either hurt or heal.
I have thought at moments that the ecstasy is real
Although those who experience it may have no reality.
For what happened is remembered like a dream
In which one is exalted by intensity of loving
In the spirit, a vibration of delight
Without desire, for desire is fulfilled
In the delight of loving. A state one does not know
When awake. But what, or whom I loved,
Or what in me was loving, I do not know.
And if that is all meaningless, I want to be cured
Of a craving for something I cannot find
And of the shame of never finding it.
Can you cure me?

   REILLY.   The condition is curable.

But the form of treatment must be your own choice:
I cannot choose for you. If that is what you wish,
I can reconcile you to the human condition,
The condition to which some who have gone as far as you
Have succeeded in returning. They may remember
The vision they have had, but they cease to regret it,
Maintain themselves by the common routine,
Learn to avoid excessive expectation,
Become tolerant of themselves and others,
Giving and taking, in the usual actions
What there is to give and take. They do not repine;
Are contented with the morning that separates
And with the evening that brings together
For casual talk before the fire
Two people who know they do not understand each other,
Breeding children whom they do not understand
And who will never understand them.

   CELIA.   Is that the best life?

   REILLY. It is a good life. Though you will not know how good

Till you come to the end. But you will want noth-
ing else,
And the other life will be only like a book
You have read once, and lost. In a world of lunacy,
Violence, stupidity, greed . . . it is a good life.
    CELIA. I know I ought to be able to accept that
If I might still have it. Yet it leaves me cold.
Perhaps that's just a part of my illness,
But I feel it would be a kind of surrender—
No, not a surrender—more like a betrayal.
You see, I think I really had a vision of something
Though I don't know what it is. I don't want to
forget it.
I want to live with it. I could do without every-
thing,
Put up with anything, if I might cherish it.
In fact, I think it would really be dishonest
For me, now, to try to make a life with *any*body!
I couldn't give anyone the kind of love—
I wish I could—which belongs to that life.
Oh, I'm afraid this sounds like raving!
Or just cantankerousness . . . still,
If there's no other way . . . then I feel just hope-
less.
    REILLY. There *is* another way, if you have the
courage.
The first I could describe in familiar terms
Because you have seen it, as we all have seen it,
Illustrated, more or less, in lives of those about us.
The second is unknown, and so requires faith—
The kind of faith that issues from despair.
The destination cannot be described;
You will know very little until you get there;
You will journey blind. But the way leads towards
possession
Of what you have sought for in the wrong place.
    CELIA. That sounds like what I want. But what
is my duty?
    REILLY. Whichever way you choose will prescribe
its own duty.
    CELIA. Which way is better?
    REILLY.   Neither way is better.
Both ways are necessary. It is also necessary
To make a choice between them.
    CELIA.   Then I choose the second.
    REILLY. It is a terrifying journey.
    CELIA.   I am not frightened
But glad. I suppose it is a lonely way?
    REILLY. No lonelier than the other. But those
who take the other
Can forget their loneliness. You will not forget
yours.

Each way means loneliness—and communion.
Both ways avoid the final desolation
Of solitude in the phantasmal world
Of imagination, shuffling memories and desires.
    CELIA. That is the hell I have been in.
    REILLY.   It isn't hell
Till you become incapable of anything else.
Now—do you feel quite sure?
    CELIA.   I want your second way.
So what am I to do?
    REILLY.   You will go to the sanatorium.
    CELIA. Oh, what an anti-climax! I have known
people
Who have been to your sanatorium, and come back
again—
I don't mean to say they weren't much better for
it—
That's why I came to you. But they returned as
. . . normal people.
    REILLY. True. But the friends you have in mind
Cannot have been to this sanatorium.
I am very careful whom I send there:
Those who go do not come back as these did.
    CELIA. It sounds like a prison. But they can't *all*
stay there!
I mean, it would make the place so over-crowded.
    REILLY. Not very many go. But I said they did
not come back
In the sense in which your friends came back.
I did not say they stayed there.
    CELIA.   What became of them?
    REILLY. They choose, Miss Coplestone. Nothing
is forced on them.
Some of them return, in a physical sense;
No one disappears. They lead very active lives
Very often, in the world.
    CELIA.   How soon will you send me there?
    REILLY. How soon will you be ready?
    CELIA.   Tonight, by nine o'clock.
    REILLY. Go home then, and make your prepara-
tions.
Here is the address for you to give your friends;
[*Writes on a slip of paper.*]
You had better let your family know at once.
I will send a car for you at nine o'clock.
    CELIA. What do I need to take with me?
    REILLY.   Nothing.
Everything you need will be provided for you.
And you will have no expenses at the sanatorium.
    CELIA. I don't in the least know what I am doing
Or why I am doing it. There is nothing else to do:
That is the only reason.

REILLY.   It is the best reason.

CELIA. But I know it is I who have made the decision:

I must tell you that. Oh, I almost forgot—

May I ask what your fee is?

REILLY.   I have told my secretary

That there is no fee.

CELIA.   But . . .

REILLY.   For a case like yours

There is no fee.

[*Presses button.*]

CELIA.   You have been very kind.

REILLY. Go in peace, my daughter.

Work out your salvation with diligence.

[NURSE-SECRETARY *appears at door. Exit* CELIA. REILLY *dials on house-telephone.*]

REILLY. [*into telephone*]. It is finished. You can come in now.

          [*Enter* JULIA *by side door.*]

She will go far, that one.

JULIA.   Very far, I think.

You do not need to tell me. I knew from the beginning.

REILLY. It's the other ones I am worried about.

JULIA. Nonsense, Henry. *I* shall keep an eye on them.

REILLY. To send them back: what have they to go back to?

To the stale food mouldering in the larder,

The stale thoughts mouldering in their minds.

Each unable to disguise his own meanness

From himself, because it is known to the other.

It's not the knowledge of the mutual treachery

But the knowledge that the other understands the motive—

Mirror to mirror, reflecting vanity.

I have taken a great risk.

JULIA.   We must always take risks.

That is our destiny. Since you question the decision

What possible alternative can you imagine?

REILLY. None.

JULIA.   Very well then. We must take the risk.

All we could do was to give them the chance.

And now, when they are stripped naked to their souls

And can choose, whether to put on proper costumes

Or huddle quickly into new disguises,

They have, for the first time, somewhere to start from.

Oh, of course, they might just murder each other!

But I don't think they will do that. We shall see.

It's the thought of Celia that weighs upon my mind.

REILLY. Of Celia?

JULIA.   Of Celia.

REILLY.   But when I said just now

That she would go far, you agreed with me.

JULIA. Oh yes, she will go far. And we know where she is going.

But what do we know of the terrors of the journey?

You and I don't know the process by which the human is

Transhumanised: what do we know

Of the kind of suffering they must undergo

On the way of illumination?

REILLY.   Will she be frightened

By the first appearance of projected spirits?

JULIA. Henry, you simply do not understand innocence.

She will be afraid of nothing; she will not even know

That there is anything there to be afraid of.

She is too humble. She will pass between the scolding hills,

Through the valley of derision, like a child sent on an errand

In eagerness and patience. Yet she must suffer.

REILLY. When I express confidence in anything

You always raise doubts; when I am apprehensive

Then you see no reason for anything but confidence.

JULIA. That's one way in which I am so useful to you.

You ought to be grateful.

REILLY.   And when I say to one like her,

'Work out your salvation with diligence,' I do not understand

What I myself am saying.

JULIA.   You must accept your limitations.

—But how much longer will Alex keep us waiting?

REILLY. He should be here by now. I'll speak to Miss Barraway.

[*Takes up house-telephone.*]

Miss Barraway, when Mr. Gibbs arrives . . .

Oh, very good.

[*To* JULIA]

          He's on his way up.

[*Into telephone*]

You may bring the tray in now, Miss Barraway.

[*Enter* ALEX.]

ALEX. Well! Well! and how have we got on?

JULIA.   Everything is in order.

ALEX. The Chamberlaynes have chosen?

REILLY.   They accept their destiny.

ALEX. And *she* has made the choice?

REILLY.   She will be fetched this evening.

[NURSE-SECRETARY *enters with a tray, a decanter and three glasses, and exits.* REILLY *pours drinks.*]

And now we are ready to proceed to the libation.

ALEX. The words for the building of the hearth.

[*They raise their glasses.*]

REILLY. Let them build the hearth
Under the protection of the stars.

ALEX. Let them place a chair each side of it.

JULIA. May the holy ones watch over the roof,
May the Moon herself influence the bed.

[*They drink.*]

ALEX. The words for those who go upon a
    journey.

REILLY. Protector of travellers
Bless the road.

ALEX. Watch over her in the desert
Watch over her in the mountain
Watch over her in the labyrinth
Watch over her by the quicksand.

JULIA. Protect her from the Voices
Protect her from the Visions
Protect her in the tumult
Protect her in the silence.

[*They drink.*]

REILLY. There is one for whom the words can-
    not be spoken.

ALEX. They cannot be spoken yet.

JULIA.   You mean Peter Quilpe.

REILLY. He has not yet come to where the words
    are valid.

JULIA. Shall we ever speak them?

ALEX.   Others, perhaps, will speak them.
You know, I have connections—even in California.

CURTAIN

ACT III

*The drawing room of the Chamberlaynes' Lon-
don flat. Two years later. A late afternoon in July.
A* CATERER'S MAN *is arranging a buffet table.*
LAVINIA *enters from side door.*

CATERER'S MAN. Have you any further orders for
    us, Madam?

LAVINIA. You could bring in the trolley with the
    glasses
And leave them ready.

CATERER'S MAN.   Very good, Madam.

[*Exit.*]

[LAVINIA *looks about the room critically and
moves a bowl of flowers. Re-enter* CATERER'S MAN
with trolley.]

LAVINIA. There, in that corner. That's the most
    convenient;
You can get in and out. Is there anything you need
That you can't find in the kitchen?

CATERER'S MAN.   Nothing, Madam.
Will there be anything more you require?

LAVINIA. Nothing more, I think, till half past six.

[*Exit* CATERER'S MAN.]

[EDWARD *lets himself in at the front door.*]

EDWARD. I'm in good time, I think. I hope you've
    not been worrying.

LAVINIA. Oh no. I did in fact ring up your cham-
    bers,
And your clerk told me you had already left.
But all I rang up for was to reassure you . . .

EDWARD [*smiling*]. That you hadn't run away?

LAVINIA.   Now Edward, that's unfair!
You know that we've given *several* parties
In the last two years. And I've attended *all* of
    them.
I hope you're not too tired?

EDWARD.   Oh no, a quiet day.
Two consultations with solicitors
On quite straightforward cases. It's you who
    should be tired.

LAVINIA. I'm not tired yet. But I know that I'll
    be glad
When it's all over.

EDWARD.   I like the dress you're wearing:
I'm glad you put on that one.

LAVINIA.   Well, Edward!
Do you know it's the first time you've paid me a
    compliment
Before a party? And that's when one needs them.

EDWARD. Well, you deserve it.—We asked too
    many people.

LAVINIA. It's true, a great many more accepted
Than we thought would want to come. But what
    can you do?
There's usually a lot who don't want to come
But all the same would be bitterly offended

To hear we'd given a party without asking them.

EDWARD. Perhaps we ought to have arranged to have two parties
Instead of one.

LAVINIA.   That's never satisfactory.
Everyone who's asked to either party
Suspects that the other one was more important.

EDWARD. That's true. You have a very practical mind.

LAVINIA. But you know, I don't think that you need worry:
They won't all come, out of those who accepted.
You know we said, 'We can ask twenty more
Because they will be going to the Gunnings instead.'

EDWARD. I know, that's what we said at the time;
But I'd forgotten what the Gunnings' parties were like.
Their guests will get just enough to make them thirsty;
They'll come on to us later, roaring for drink.
Well, let's hope that those who come to us early
Will be going on to the Gunnings afterwards,
To make room for those who come from the Gunnings.

LAVINIA. And if it's very crowded, they can't get at the cocktails,
And the man won't be able to take the tray about,
So they'll go away again. Anyway, at that stage
There's nothing whatever you can do about it:
And everyone likes to be seen at a party
Where everybody else is, to show they've been invited.
That's what makes it a success. Is that picture straight?

EDWARD. Yes, it is.

LAVINIA.   No, it isn't. Do please straighten it.

EDWARD. Is it straight now?

LAVINIA.   Too much to the left.

EDWARD. How's that now?

LAVINIA.   No, I meant the right.
That will do. I'm too tired to bother.

EDWARD. After they're all gone, we will have some champagne,
Just ourselves. You lie down now, Lavinia.
No one will be coming for at least half an hour;
So just stretch out.

LAVINIA.   You must sit beside me,
Then I can relax.

EDWARD.   This is the best moment
Of the whole party.

LAVINIA.   Oh no, Edward.
The best moment is the moment it's over;
And then to remember, it's the end of the season
And no more parties.

EDWARD.   And no more committees.

LAVINIA. Can we get away soon?

EDWARD.   By the end of next week
I shall be quite free.

LAVINIA.   And we can be alone.
I love that house being so remote.

EDWARD. That's why we took it. And I'm really thankful
To have that excuse for not seeing people;
And you do need to rest now.

[The doorbell rings.]

LAVINIA.   Oh, bother!
Now who would come so early? I simply *can't* get up.

CATERER'S MAN. Mrs. Shuttlethwaite!

LAVINIA.   Oh, it's Julia!

[Enter JULIA. ALEX *is seen to enter with her and pass back-stage towards the kitchen.*]

JULIA. Well, my dears, and here I am!
I seem *literally* to have caught you napping!
I know I'm much too early; but the fact is, my dears,
That I have to go on to the Gunnings' party—
And you know what *they* offer in the way of food and drink!
And I've had to miss my tea, and I'm simply ravenous
And dying of thirst. What can Parkinson's do for me?
Oh yes, I know this is a Parkinson party;
I recognised one of their men at the door—
An old friend of mine, in fact. But I'm forgetting!
I've got a surprise: I've brought Alex with me!
He only got back this morning from somewhere—
One of his mysterious expeditions,
And we're going to get him to tell us all about it.
But what's become of him?

[Enter ALEX.]

                        Alex, where have you been?

ALEX. I thought I would give them a little surprise
And come in unannounced.

EDWARD.   Well, Alex!
Where on earth do you turn up from?

ALEX. Where on earth? From the East. From Kinkanja—
An island that you won't have heard of

Yet. Got back this morning. I heard about your
 party
And, as I thought you might be leaving for the
 country,
I said, I must not miss the opportunity
To see Edward and Lavinia.
   LAVINIA.   How are you, Alex?
   ALEX. I did try to get you on the telephone
After lunch, but my secretary couldn't get through
 to you.
Never mind, I said—to myself, not to her—
Never mind: the unexpected guest
Is the one to whom they give the warmest wel-
 come.
I know them well enough for that.
   JULIA.   But tell us, Alex.
What were you doing in this strange place—
What's it called?
   ALEX.   Kinkanja.
   JULIA.   What were you doing
In Kinkanja? Visiting some Sultan?
You were shooting tigers?
   ALEX.   There are no tigers, Julia,
In Kinkanja. And there are no sultans.
I have been staying with the Governor.
Three of us have been out on a tour of inspection
Of local conditions.
   JULIA.   What about? Monkey nuts?
   ALEX. That was a nearer guess than you think.
No, not monkey nuts. But it had to do with mon-
 keys—
Though whether the monkeys are the core of the
 problem
Or merely a symptom, I am not so sure.
At least, the monkeys have become the pretext
For general unrest amongst the natives.
   EDWARD. But how do the monkeys create unrest?
   ALEX. To begin with, the monkeys are very de-
 structive . . .
   JULIA. You don't need to tell me that monkeys
 are destructive.
I shall never forget Mary Mallington's monkey,
The horrid little beast—stole my ticket to Mentone
And I had to travel in a very slow train
And in a *couchette*. She was very angry
When I told her the creature ought to be destroyed.
   LAVINIA. But can't they exterminate these mon-
 keys
If they are a pest?
   ALEX.   Unfortunately,
The majority of the natives are heathen:

They hold these monkeys in peculiar veneration
And do not want them killed. So they blame the
 Government
For the damage that the monkeys do.
   EDWARD. That seems unreasonable.
   ALEX.   It is unreasonable,
But characteristic. And that's not the worst of it.
Some of the tribes are Christian converts,
And, naturally, take a different view.
They trap the monkeys. And they eat them.
The young monkeys are extremely palatable:
I've cooked them myself . . .
   EDWARD.   And did anybody eat them
When you cooked them?
   ALEX.   Oh yes, indeed.
I invented for the natives several new recipes.
But you see, what with eating the monkeys
And what with protecting their crops from the
 monkeys
The Christian natives prosper exceedingly:
And that creates friction between them and the
 others.
And that's the real problem. I hope I'm not boring
 you?
   EDWARD. No indeed: we are anxious to learn the
 solution.
   ALEX. I'm not sure that there *is* any solution.
But even this does not bring us to the heart of the
 matter.
There are also foreign agitators,
Stirring up trouble . . .
   LAVINIA.   Why don't you expel them?
   ALEX. They are citizens of a friendly neighbour-
 ing state
Which we have just recognised. You see, Lavinia,
There are very deep waters.
   EDWARD.   And the agitators;
How do they agitate?
   ALEX.   By convincing the heathen
That the slaughter of monkeys has put a curse on
 them
Which can only be removed by slaughtering the
 Christians.
They have even been persuading some of the con-
 verts—
Who, after all, prefer not to be slaughtered—
To relapse into heathendom. So, instead of eating
 monkeys
They are eating Christians.
   JULIA.   Who have eaten monkeys.
   ALEX. The native is not, I fear, very logical.

JULIA. I wondered where you were taking us, with your monkeys.
I thought I was going to dine out on those monkeys:
But one can't dine out on eating Christians—
Even among pagans!

ALEX.   Not on the *whole* story.

EDWARD. And have any of the English residents been murdered?

ALEX. Yes, but they are not usually eaten.
When these people have done with a European
He is, as a rule, no longer fit to eat.

EDWARD. And what has your commission accomplished?

ALEX. We have just drawn up an interim report.

EDWARD. Will it be made public?

ALEX.   It cannot be, at present:
There are too many international complications.
Eventually, there may be an official publication.

EDWARD. But when?

ALEX.   In a year or two.

EDWARD.   And meanwhile?

ALEX. Meanwhile the monkeys multiply.

LAVINIA.   And the Christians?

ALEX. Ah, the Christians! Now, I think I ought to tell you
About someone you know—or knew . . .

JULIA.   Edward!
Somebody must have walked over my grave:
I'm feeling so chilly. Give me some gin.
Not a cocktail. I'm freezing—in July!

CATERER'S MAN. Mr. Quilpe!

EDWARD.   Now who . . .

[*Enter* PETER.]

                    Why, it's Peter!

LAVINIA. Peter!

PETER.   Hullo, everybody!

LAVINIA.   When did you arrive?

PETER. I flew over from New York last night—
I left Los Angeles three days ago.
I saw Sheila Paisley at lunch today
And she told me you were giving a party—
She's coming on later, after the Gunnings—
So I said, I really must crash in:
It's my only chance to see Edward and Lavinia.
I'm only over for a week, you see,
And I'm driving down to the country this evening,
So I knew you wouldn't mind my looking in so early.
It does seem ages since I last saw any of you!
And how are you, Alex? And dear old Julia!

LAVINIA. So you've just come from New York.

PETER.   Yeah, from New York.
The Bologolomskys saw me off.
You remember Princess Bologolomsky
In the old days? We dined the other night
At the Saffron Monkey. That's the place to go now.

ALEX. How very odd. *My* monkeys are saffron.

PETER. Your monkeys, Alex? I always said
That Alex knew everybody. But I didn't know
That he knew any monkeys.

JULIA.   But give us your news;
Give us your news of the world, Peter.
We lead such a quiet life, here in London.

PETER. You always did enjoy a leg-pull, Julia:
But you all know I'm working for Pan-Am-Eagle?

EDWARD. No, Tell us, what is Pan-Am-Eagle?

PETER. You must have been living a quiet life!
Don't you go to the movies?

LAVINIA.   Occasionally.

PETER.   Alex knows.
Did you see my last picture, Alex?

ALEX. I knew about it, but I didn't see it.
There is no cinema in Kinkanja.

PETER. Kinkanja? Where's that? They don't have pictures?
Pan-Am-Eagle must look into this.
Perhaps it would be a good place to make one.
—Alex knows all about Pan-Am-Eagle:
It was he who introduced me to the great Bela.

JULIA. And who is the great Bela?

PETER.   Why, Bela Szogody—
He's my boss. I thought everyone knew *his* name.

JULIA. Is he your connection in California, Alex?

ALEX. Yes, we have sometimes obliged each other.

PETER. Well, it was Bela sent me over
Just for a week. And I have my hands full.
I'm going down tonight, to Boltwell.

JULIA. To stay with the Duke?

PETER.   And do him a good turn.
We're making a film of English life
And we want to use Boltwell.

JULIA.   But I understood that Boltwell
Is in a very decayed condition.

PETER. Exactly. It is. And that's why we're interested.
The most decayed noble mansion in England!
At least, of any that are still inhabited.
We've got a team of experts over
To study the decay, so as to reproduce it.
Then we build another Boltwell in California.

JULIA. But what is your position, Peter?
Have you become an expert on decaying houses?

PETER. Oh dear no! I've written the script of this film,
And Bela is very pleased with it.
He thought I should see the original Boltwell;
And besides, he thought that as I'm English
I ought to know the best way to handle a duke.
Besides that, we've got the casting director:
He's looking for some typical English faces—
Of course, only for minor parts—
And I'll help him decide what faces are typical.

JULIA. Peter, I've thought of a wonderful idea!
I've always wanted to go to California:
Couldn't you persuade your casting director
To take us all over? We're all very typical.

PETER. No, I'm afraid . . .

CATERER'S MAN.   Sir Henry Harcourt-Reilly!

JULIA. Oh, I forgot! I'd another surprise for you.

[Enter REILLY.]

I want you to meet Sir Henry Harcourt-Reilly—

EDWARD. We're delighted to see him. But we *have* met before.

JULIA. Then if you know him already, you won't be afraid of him.
You know, I was afraid of him at first:
He looks so forbidding . . .

REILLY.   My dear Julia,
You are giving me a very bad introduction—
Supposing that an introduction was necessary.

JULIA. My dear Henry, you are interrupting me.

LAVINIA. If you can interrupt Julia, Sir Henry,
You are the perfect guest we've been waiting for.

REILLY. I should not dream of trying to interrupt Julia . . .

JULIA. But you're both interrupting!

REILLY.   Who is interrupting now?

JULIA. Now my head's fairly spinning. I must have a cocktail.

EDWARD [To REILLY]. And will you have a cocktail?

REILLY.   Might I have a glass of water?

EDWARD. Anything with it?

REILLY.   Nothing, thank you.

LAVINIA. May I introduce Mr. Peter Quilpe?
Sir Henry Harcourt-Reilly. Peter's an old friend
Of my husband and myself. Oh, I forgot—
[Turning to ALEX]
I rather assumed that you knew each other—
I don't know why I should. Mr. MacColgie Gibbs.

ALEX. Indeed, yes, we have met.

REILLY.   On several commissions.

JULIA. We've been having such an interesting conversation.
Peter's just over from California
Where he's something very important in films.
He's making a film of English life
And he's going to find parts for all of us. Think of it!

PETER. But, Julia, I was just about to explain—
I'm afraid I can't find parts for anybody
In *this* film—it's not my business;
And that's not the way we do it.

JULIA.   But, Peter;
If you're taking Boltwell to California
Why can't you take me? It's very much cheaper.

PETER. We're not taking Boltwell. We reconstruct a Boltwell.

JULIA. Well, why can't you reconstruct *me?* Oh, dear,
I can see you're determined not to have me:
So good-bye to my hopes of seeing California.

PETER. You know you'd never come if we invited you.
But there's someone I wanted to ask about,
Who did really want to get into films,
And I always thought she could make a success of it
If she only got the chance. It's Celia Coplestone.
She always wanted to. And now I could help her.
I've already spoken to Bela about her,
And I want to introduce her to our casting director.
I've got an idea for another film.
Can you tell me where she is? I couldn't find her
In the telephone directory.

JULIA.   Not in the directory,
Or in any directory. You can tell them now, Alex.

LAVINIA. What does Julia mean?

ALEX.   I was about to speak of her
When you came in, Peter. I'm afraid you can't have Celia.

PETER. Oh . . . Is she married?

ALEX.   Not married, but dead.

LAVINIA. Celia?

ALEX.   Dead.

PETER. Dead. That knocks the bottom out of it.

EDWARD. Celia dead.

JULIA.   You had better tell them, Alex,
The news that you bring back from Kinkanja.

LAVINIA. Kinkanja? What was Celia doing in Kinkanja?

We heard that she had joined some nursing order . . .

  ALEX. She had joined an order. A very austere
  one.

And as she already had experience of nursing . . .

  LAVINIA. Yes, she had been a V.A.D. I remember.

  ALEX. She was directed to Kinkanja,

Where there are various endemic diseases

Besides, of course, those brought by Europeans,

And where the conditions are favourable to plague.

  EDWARD. Go on.

  ALEX. It seems that there were three of them—

Three sisters at this station, in a Christian village;

And half the natives were dying of pestilence.

They must have been overworked for weeks.

  EDWARD. And then?

  ALEX.   And then, the insurrection broke out

Among the heathen, of which I was telling you.

They knew of it, but would not leave the dying
  natives.

Eventually, two of them escaped:

One died in the jungle, and the other

Will never be fit for normal life again.

But Celia Coplestone, she was taken.

When our people got there, they questioned the
  villagers—

Those who survived. And then they found her
  body,

Or at least, they found traces of it.

  EDWARD. But before that . . .

  ALEX.   It was difficult to tell.

But from what we know of local practices

It would seem that she must have been crucified

Very near an ant-hill.

  LAVINIA.   But Celia! . . . of all people . . .

  EDWARD. And just for a handful of plague-
  stricken natives

Who would have died anyway.

  ALEX.   Yes, the patients died anyway;

Being tainted with the plague, they were not
  eaten.

  LAVINIA. Oh, Edward, I'm so sorry—what a
  feeble thing to say!

But you know what I mean.

  EDWARD.   And you know what I'm thinking.

  PETER. I don't understand at all. But then I've
  been away

For two years and don't know what happened

To Celia, during those two years.

Two years! Thinking about Celia.

  EDWARD. It's the waste that I resent.

  PETER.   You know more than I do:

For me, it's everything else that's a waste.

Two years! And it was all a mistake.

Julia! Why don't you say anything?

  JULIA. You gave her those two years, as best you
  could.

  PETER. When did she . . . take up this career?

  JULIA.   Two years ago.

  PETER. Two years ago! I tried to forget about
  her,

Until I began to think myself a success

And got a little more self-confidence;

And then I thought about her again. More and
  more.

At first I did not want to know about Celia

And so I never asked. Then I wanted to know

And did not dare to ask. It took all my courage

To ask you about her just now; but I never
  thought

Of anything like this. I suppose I didn't know her,

I didn't understand her. I understand nothing.

  REILLY. You understand your metier, Mr.
  Quilpe—

Which is the most that any of us can ask for.

  PETER. And what a metier! I've tried to believe
  in it

So that I might believe in myself.

I thought I had ideas to make a revolution

In the cinema, that no one could ignore—

And here I am, making a second-rate film!

But I thought it was going to lead to something
  better,

And that seemed possible, while Celia was alive.

I wanted it, believed in it, for Celia.

And, of course, I wanted to do something for
  Celia—

But what mattered was, that Celia was alive.

And now it's all worthless. Celia's not alive.

  LAVINIA. No, it's not all worthless, Peter. You've
  only just begun.

I mean, this only brings you to the point

At which you must begin. You were saying just
  now

That you never knew Celia. We none of us did.

What you've been living on is an image of Celia

Which you made for yourself, to meet your own
  needs.

Peter, please don't think I'm being unkind . . .

  PETER. No, I don't think you're being unkind,
  Lavinia:

You're telling me what I ought to know about
  myself.

LAVINIA. No, but what I'm saying is something
  I've been learning.
That's how I know that your picture of Celia
Was only a substitute for another picture—
That of yourself as a famous novelist.
It was bound to come a crash—better sooner than
  later!
I'm not very clever at explaining . . .
  PETER. But I know that you're right.
  LAVINIA.   And perhaps what I've been saying
Will seem less unkind if I can make you under-
  stand
That in fact I've been talking about myself.
  EDWARD. Lavinia is right. This is where you start
    from.
If you find out now, Peter, things about yourself
That you don't like to face: well, just remember
That some men have to learn much worse things
About themselves, and learn them later
When it's harder to recover, and make a new be-
  ginning.
It's not so hard for you. You're naturally good.
  PETER. I'm sorry. I don't believe I've taken in
All that you've been saying. But I'm grateful all
  the same.
You know, all the time that you've been talking,
One thought has been going round and round in
  my head—
That I've only been interested in myself:
And that isn't good enough for Celia.
  JULIA. You must have learned how to look at
    people, Peter,
When you look at them with an eye for the films:
That is, when you're not concerned with yourself
But just being an eye. You will come to think of
  Celia
Like that, some day. And then you'll understand
  her
And be reconciled, and be happy in the thought of
  her.
And now I'm going to change the subject.
Celia chose a road that led her to Kinkanja;
You have chosen one that leads you to Boltwell—
And you've got to go there.
  PETER.   Oh. I'm glad you reminded me.
The car will be waiting. I mustn't keep them.
Yes, I'm off to Boltwell—with a team of experts.
So now I'll be going.
  EDWARD.   Shall we see you again, Peter,
Before you leave England?
  LAVINIA.   Do try to come to see us.
You know, I think it would do us all good—

You and me and Edward . . . to talk about Celia.
  PETER. Thanks very much. But not this time—
I simply shan't be able to.
  EDWARD.   But on your next visit?
  PETER. The next time I come to England, I
  promise you.
I really do want to see you both, very much.
Good-bye, Julia. Good-bye, Alex. Good-bye, Sir
  Henry.
                                   [*Exit.*]
  LAVINIA. Sir Henry, there is something I want
    to say to you
Now that Peter's left us.
  REILLY.   That young man
Is very intelligent. He should go far—
Along his own lines.
  ALEX.   Yes, I was well advised
To put him in the hands of Bela Szogody.
  LAVINIA. It came to me, when Alex told about
    Celia
And I looked at your face. It seemed to convey to
  me
That the way in which she died was not important
Or the fact that she died because she would not
  leave
A few dying natives.
  REILLY.   Who knows, Mrs. Chamberlayne,
The difference that made to the natives who were
  dying
Or the state of mind in which they died?
  LAVINIA. I'm willing to grant that. What struck
    me, though,
Was that your face showed no surprise or horror
At the way in which she died. I don't know if you
  knew her.
I suspect you did. In any case you know *about* her.
Yet I thought your expression was one of . . .
  satisfaction!
Interest, yes, but not in the details.
  ALEX. There's one detail which is rather inter-
    esting
And rather touching, too. We found that the na-
  tives,
After we'd re-occupied the village
Had erected a sort of shrine for Celia
Where they brought offerings of fruit and flowers,
Fowls, and even sucking pigs.
They seemed to think that by propitiating Celia
They might insure themselves against further
  misfortune.
We left *that* problem for the Bishop to wrestle
  with.

REILLY. Yes, the Bishop's problem is certainly a detail.

—Mrs. Chamberlayne, I must be very transparent
Or else you are very perceptive.

JULIA. Oh, Henry!

Lavinia is much more observant than you think.
I believe, Henry, if I may put it vulgarly,
That Lavinia has forced you to a show-down.

REILLY. You state the position correctly, Julia.
Do you mind if I quote poetry, Mrs. Chamberlayne?

LAVINIA. Oh no, I should love to hear you speaking poetry . . .

JULIA. She has made a point, Henry.

LAVINIA. . . . if it answers my question.

REILLY.

                    *Ere Babylon was dust
The magus Zoroaster, my dead child,
Met his own image walking in the garden.
That apparition, sole of men, he saw.
For know there are two worlds of life and death:
One that which thou beholdest; but the other
Is underneath the grave, where do inhabit
The shadows of all forms that think and live
Till death unite them and they part no more.*

—When I first met Miss Coplestone, in this room,
I saw the image, standing behind her chair,
Of a Celia Coplestone whose face showed the astonishment
Of the first five minutes after a violent death.
If this strains your credulity, Mrs. Chamberlayne,
I ask you only to entertain the suggestion
That a sudden intuition, in certain minds,
May tend to express itself at once in a picture.
That happens to me, sometimes. So it was obvious
That here was a woman under sentence of death.
That was her destiny. The only question
Then was, what sort of death? *I* could not know;
Because it was for her to choose the way of life
To lead to death, and, without knowing the end
Yet choose the form of death. We know the death she chose.
I did not know that she would die in this way;
She did not know. So all that I could do
Was to direct her in the way of preparation.
That way, which she accepted, led to this death.
And if that is not a happy death, what death is happy?

* Quoted from Percy Bysshe Shelley's lyrical drama, *Prometheus Unbound*, I, 191–99. [Editor's note.]

EDWARD. Do you mean that having chosen this form of death
She did not suffer as ordinary people suffer?

REILLY. Not at all what I mean. Rather the contrary.
I'd say that she suffered all that we should suffer
In fear and pain and loathing—all these together—
And reluctance of the body to become a *thing*.
I'd say she suffered more, because more conscious
Than the rest of us. She paid the highest price
In suffering. That is part of the design.

LAVINIA. Perhaps she had been through greater agony beforehand.
I mean—I know nothing of her last two years.

REILLY. That shows some insight on your part, Mrs. Chamberlayne;
But such experience can only be hinted at
In myths and images. To speak about it
We talk of darkness, labyrinths, Minotaur terrors.
But that world does not take the place of this one.
Do you imagine that the Saint in the desert
With spiritual evil always at his shoulder
Suffered any less from hunger, damp, exposure,
Bowel trouble, and the fear of lions,
Cold of the night and heat of the day, than we should?

EDWARD. Sir Henry, you only make the horrible more horrible;
Yet I think I begin to see your point of view.
But if this was right—if this was right for Celia—
There must be something else that is terribly wrong,
And the rest of us are somehow involved in the wrong.
I should only speak for myself. I'm sure that *I* am.

REILLY. Let me free your mind from one impediment:
You must try to detach yourself from what you still feel
As your responsibility.

EDWARD. I cannot help the feeling
That, in some way, my responsibility
Is greater than that of a band of half-crazed savages.

LAVINIA. Oh, Edward, I knew! I knew what you were thinking!
Doesn't it help you, that I feel guilty too?

REILLY. If we all were judged according to the consequences
Of all our words and deeds, beyond the intention

And beyond our limited understanding
Of ourselves and others, we should all be con-
demned.
Mrs. Chamberlayne, I often have to make a de-
cision
Which may mean restoration or ruin to a patient—
And sometimes I have made the wrong decision.
As for Miss Coplestone, because you think her
death was waste
You blame yourselves, and because you blame
yourselves
You think her life was wasted. It was triumphant.
But I am no more responsible for the triumph—
And just as responsible for her death as you are.

LAVINIA. Yet I know I shall go on blaming my-
self
For being so unkind to her . . . so spiteful.
I shall go on seeing her at the moment
When she said good-bye to us, two years ago.

EDWARD. Your responsibility is nothing to mine,
Lavinia.

LAVINIA. I'm not sure about that. If I had understood you
Then I might not have misunderstood Celia.

REILLY. You will have to live with these mem-
ories and make them
Into something new. Only by acceptance
Of the past will you alter its meaning.

JULIA. Henry, I think it is time that *I* said
something:
So please don't interrupt.

REILLY.   I won't interrupt you.

JULIA. Everyone makes a choice, of one kind or
another,
And then must take the consequences. Celia chose
A way of which the consequence was crucifixion;
Peter Quilpe chose a way that takes him to Bolt-
well;
And now the consequence of the Chamberlaynes'
choice
Is a cocktail party. They must be ready for it.
Their guests may be arriving at any moment.
                    [ALEX *leaves the room.*]

REILLY. Julia, you are right. It is also right
That the Chamberlaynes should now be giving a
party.

LAVINIA. And I have been thinking, for these
last five minutes,
How I could face my guests. I wish it was over.
I mean . . . I am glad you came . . . I am glad
Alex told us . . .

And Peter had to know . . .

EDWARD.   Now I think I understand . . .

LAVINIA. Then I hope you will explain it to me!

EDWARD.   Oh, it isn't much
That I understand yet! But Sir Henry has been
saying,
I think, that every moment is a fresh beginning;
And Julia, that life is only keeping on;
And somehow, the two ideas seem to fit together.

LAVINIA. But all the same . . . I don't want to
see these people.

REILLY. It is your appointed burden. And as for
the party,
I am sure it will be a success.
                    [*Re-enter* ALEX.]

JULIA.   And I think, Henry,
That we should leave before the party begins.
They will get on better without us. You too, Alex.

ALEX. Just a moment, Julia. There is one brief
ceremony
Before we go . . .
[*Enter* CATERER'S MAN *with a tray and five glasses.*]
                    I took the liberty
Of bringing a bottle of my own champagne—
I thought it should be mine, for this occasion—
And giving instructions at the door as I came in.
I wish to propose a toast.
    [*They all rise.*]
EDWARD [*absently*].
                    To the Guardians.

ALEX. To one particular Guardian, whom you
have forgotten.
I give you—Lavinia's Aunt!

ALL.   Lavinia's Aunt!
[*They drink, and the* CATERER'S MAN *takes out
the tray.*]

JULIA. Now, Henry. Now, Alex.

JULIA, REILLY *and* ALEX.
                    We're going to the Gunnings'.
            [*Exeunt* JULIA, REILLY *and* ALEX.]

LAVINIA. Edward, how am I looking?

EDWARD.   Very well.
I might almost say, your best. But you always look
your best.

LAVINIA. Oh, Edward, that spoils it. No woman
can believe
That she always looks her best. You're rather
transparent,
You know, when you're trying to cheer me up.
To say I always look my best can only mean the
worst.

EDWARD. I never shall learn how to pay a compliment.

LAVINIA. What you should have done was to admire my dress.

EDWARD. But I've already told you how much I
like it.

LAVINIA. But so much has happened since then.
And besides,
One sometimes likes to hear the same compliment
twice.

EDWARD. And now for the party.

LAVINIA.   Now for the party.

EDWARD. It will soon be over.

LAVINIA.   I wish it would begin.

EDWARD. There's the doorbell.

LAVINIA.   Oh, I'm glad. It's begun.

CURTAIN

II

THEORY

The Theatre

BY W. B. YEATS

I

I remember, some years ago, advising a distinguished, though too little recognized, writer of poetical plays to write a play as unlike ordinary plays as possible, that it might be judged with a fresh mind, and to put it on the stage in some small suburban theatre, where a small audience would pay its expenses. I said that he should follow it the year after, at the same time of the year, with another play, and so on from year to year; and that the people who read books, and do not go to the theatre, would gradually find out about him. I suggested that he should begin with a pastoral play, because nobody would expect from a pastoral play the succession of nervous tremours which the plays of commerce, like the novels of commerce, have substituted for the purification that comes with pity and terror to the imagination and intellect. He followed my advice in part, and had a small but perfect success, filling his small theatre for twice the number of performances he had announced; but instead of being content with the praise of his equals, and waiting to win their praise another year, he hired immediately a big London theatre, and put his pastoral play and a new play before a meagre and unintelligent audience. I still remember his pastoral play with delight, because, if not always of high excellence, it was always poetical; but I remember it at the small theatre, where my pleasure was magnified by the pleasure of those about me, and not at the big

theatre, where it made me uncomfortable, as an unwelcome guest always makes one uncomfortable.

Why should we thrust our works, which we have written with imaginative sincerity and filled with spiritual desire, before those quite excellent people who think that Rossetti's women are 'guys,' that Rodin's women are 'ugly,' and that Ibsen is 'immoral,' and who only want to be left at peace to enjoy the works so many clever men have made especially to suit them? We must make a theatre for ourselves and our friends, and for a few simple people who understand from sheer simplicity what we understand from scholarship and thought. We have planned the Irish Literary Theatre with this hospitable emotion, and, that the right people may find out about us, we hope to act a play or two in the spring of every year; and that the right people may escape the stupefying memory of the theatre of commerce which clings even to them, our plays will be for the most part remote, spiritual, and ideal.

A common opinion is that the poetic drama has come to an end, because modern poets have no dramatic power; . . . I find it easier to believe that audiences, who have learned, as I think, from the life of crowded cities to live upon the surface of life, and actors and managers, who study to please them, have changed, than that imagination, which is the voice of what is eternal in man, has changed. The arts are but one Art; and why should all intense painting and all intense poetry have become not merely unintelligible but hateful to the greater number of men and women, and intense drama move them to pleasure? The audiences of Sophocles and of Shakespeare and of Calderon were not unlike the audiences I have heard listening in Irish cabins to songs in Gaelic about 'an old poet telling his sins,' and about 'the five young men who were drowned last year,' and about 'the lovers that were drowned going to America,' or to some tale of Oisin and his three hundred years in *Tir nan Oge.* . . .

Blake has said that all Art is a labour to bring again the Golden Age, and all culture is certainly a labour to bring again the simplicity of the first ages, with knowledge of good and evil added to it. The drama has need of cities that it may find men in sufficient numbers, and cities destroy the emotions to which it appeals, and therefore the days of the drama are brief and come but seldom. It has one day when the emotions of the cities still remember the emotions of sailors and husbandmen and shepherds and users of the spear and the bow; as the houses and furniture and earthen vessels of cities, before the coming of machinery, remember the rocks and the woods and the hillside; and it has another day, now beginning, when thought and scholarship discover their desire. In the first day, it is the Art of the people; and in the second day, like the dramas acted of old times in the hidden places of temples, it is the preparation of a Priesthood. It may be, though the world is not old enough to show us any example, that this Priesthood will spread their Religion everywhere, and make their Art the Art of the people.

When the first day of the drama had passed by, actors found that an always larger number of people were more easily moved through the eyes than through the ears. The emotion that comes with the music of words is exhausting, like all intellectual emotions, and few people like exhausting emotions; and therefore actors began to speak as if they were reading something out of the newspapers. They forgot the noble art of oratory, and gave all their thought to the poor art of acting, that is content with the sympathy of our nerves; until at last those who love poetry found it better to read alone in their rooms what they had once delighted to

hear sitting friend by friend, lover by beloved. . . .

As audiences and actors changed, managers learned to substitute meretricious landscapes, painted upon wood and canvas, for the descriptions of poetry, until the painted scenery, which had in Greece been a charming explanation of what was least important in the story, became as important as the story. It needed some imagination, some gift for day-dreams, to see the horses and the fields and flowers of Colonus as one listened to the elders gathered about Œdipus, or to see 'the pendent bed and procreant cradle' of the 'martlet' as one listened to Duncan before the castle of Macbeth; but it needs no imagination to admire a painting of one of the more obvious effects of nature painted by somebody who understands how to show everything to the most hurried glance. At the same time the managers made the costumes of the actors more and more magnificent, that the mind might sleep in peace, while the eye took pleasure in the magnificence of velvet and silk and in the physical beauty of women. These changes gradually perfected the theatre of commerce, the masterpiece of that movement towards externality in life and thought and Art, against which the criticism of our day is learning to protest.

Even if poetry were spoken as poetry, it would still seem out of place in many of its highest moments upon a stage, where the superficial appearances of nature are so closely copied; for poetry is founded upon convention, and becomes incredible the moment painting or gesture remind us that people do not speak verse when they meet upon the highway. The theatre of Art, when it comes to exist, must therefore discover grave and decorative gestures, . . . and grave and decorative scenery, that will be forgotten the moment an actor has said 'It is dawn,' or 'It is raining,' or 'The wind is shaking the trees'; and dresses of so little irrelevant magnificence that the mortal actors and actresses may change without much labour into the immortal people of romance. The theatre began in ritual, and it cannot come to its greatness again without recalling words to their ancient sovereignty.

It will take a generation, and perhaps generations, to restore the theatre of Art; for one must get one's actors, and perhaps one's scenery, from the theatre of commerce, until new actors and new painters have come to help one; and until many failures and imperfect successes have made a new tradition, and perfected in detail the ideal that is beginning to float before our eyes. If one could call one's painters and one's actors from where one would, how easy it would be. I know some painters, who have never painted scenery, who could paint the scenery I want, but they have their own work to do; and in Ireland I have heard a red-haired orator repeat some bad political verses with a voice that went through one like flame, and made them seem the most beautiful verses in the world; but he has no practical knowledge of the stage, and probably despises it.

(May 1899)

II

Dionysius, the Areopagite, wrote that 'He has set the borders of the nations according to His angels.' It is these angels, each one the genius of some race about to be unfolded, that are the founders of intellectual traditions; and as lovers understand in their first glance all that is to befall them, and as poets and musicians see the whole work in its first impulse, so races prophesy at their awakening whatever the generations that are to prolong their traditions shall accomplish in detail. It is only at the awakening— as in ancient Greece, or in Elizabethan England, or in contemporary Scandinavia—that great numbers of men understand that a right understanding of life and of destiny is more important than amusement. In London, where all the intellectual traditions gather to die, men hate a play if they are told it is literature, for they will not endure a spiritual superiority; but in Athens, where so many intellectual traditions were born, Euripides once changed hostility to enthusiasm by asking his playgoers whether it was his business to teach them, or their business to teach him. New races understand instinctively, because the future cries in their ears, that the old revelations are insufficient, and that all life is revelation beginning in miracle and enthusiasm, and dying out as it unfolds itself in what we have mistaken for progress. It is one of our illusions, as I think, that education, the softening of manners, the perfecting of law— countless images of a fading light—can create nobleness and beauty, and that life moves slowly and evenly towards some perfection. Progress is miracle, and it is sudden, because miracles are the work of an all-powerful energy, and nature in herself has no power except to die and to forget. If one studies one's own mind, one comes to think with Blake, that 'every time less than a pulsation of the artery is equal to six thousand years, for in this period the poet's work is done; and all the great events of time start forth and are conceived in such a period, within a pulsation of the artery.'

(February 1900)

The Mythos of Summer: Romance

BY NORTHROP FRYE

The romance is nearest of all literary forms to the wish-fulfillment dream, and for that reason it has socially a curiously paradoxical role. In every age the ruling social or intellectual class tends to project its ideals in some form of romance, where the virtuous heroes and beautiful heroines represent the ideals and the villains the threats to their ascendancy. This is the general character of chivalric romance in the Middle Ages, aristocratic romance in the Renaissance, bourgeois romance since the eighteenth century, and revolutionary romance in contemporary Russia. Yet there is a genuinely "proletarian" element in romance too which is never satisfied with its various incarnations, and in fact the incarnations themselves indicate that no matter how great a change may take place in society, romance will turn up again, as hungry as ever, looking for new hopes and desires to feed on. The perennially child-like quality of romance is marked by its extraordinarily persistent nostalgia, its search for some kind of imaginative golden age in time or space. There has never to my knowledge been any period of Gothic English literature, but the list of Gothic revivalists stretches completely across its entire history, from the *Beowulf* poet to writers of our own day.

The essential element of plot in romance is adventure, which means that romance is naturally a sequential and processional form, hence we know it better from fiction than from drama. At its most naive it is an endless form in which

THE MYTHOS OF SUMMER: ROMANCE From "Theory of Myths" in Northrop Frye, *Anatomy of Criticism* (copyright © 1957 by Princeton University Press; Princeton Paperback, 1971), pp. 186 through 206. Reprinted by permission of Princeton University Press.

a central character who never develops or ages goes through one adventure after another until the author himself collapses. We see this form in comic strips, where the central characters persist for years in a state of refrigerated deathlessness. However, no book can rival the continuity of the newspaper, and as soon as romance achieves a literary form, it tends to limit itself to a sequence of minor adventures leading up to a major or climactic adventure, usually announced from the beginning, the completion of which rounds off the story. We may call this major adventure, the element that gives literary form to the romance, the quest.

The complete form of the romance is clearly the successful quest, and such a completed form has three main stages: the stage of the perilous journey and the preliminary minor adventures; the crucial struggle, usually some kind of battle in which either the hero or his foe, or both, must die; and the exaltation of the hero. We may call these three stages respectively, using Greek terms, the *agon* or conflict, the *pathos* or death-struggle, and the *anagnorisis* or discovery, the recognition of the hero, who has clearly proved himself to be a hero even if he does not survive the conflict. Thus the romance expresses more clearly the passage from struggle through a point of ritual death to a recognition scene that we discovered in comedy. A threefold structure is repeated in many features of romance—in the frequency, for instance, with which the successful hero is a third son, or the third to undertake the quest, or successful on his third attempt. It is shown more directly in the three-day rhythm of death, disappearance and revival which is found in the myth of Attis and other dying gods, and has been incorporated in our Easter.

A quest involving conflict assumes two main characters, a protagonist or hero, and an antagonist or enemy. (No doubt I should add, for the benefit of some readers, that I have read the article "Protagonist" in Fowler's *Modern English Usage*.) The enemy may be an ordinary human being, but the nearer the romance is to myth, the more attributes of divinity will cling to the hero and the more the enemy will take on demonic mythical qualities. The central form of romance is dialectical: everything is focussed on a conflict between the hero and his enemy, and all the reader's values are bound up with the hero. Hence the hero of romance is analogous to the mythical Messiah or deliverer who comes from an upper world, and his enemy is analogous to the demonic powers of a lower world. The conflict however takes place in, or at any rate primarily concerns, *our* world, which is in the middle, and which is characterized by the cyclical movement of nature. Hence the opposite poles of the cycles of nature are assimilated to the opposition of the hero and his enemy. The enemy is associated with winter, darkness, confusion, sterility, moribund life, and old age, and the hero with spring, dawn, order, fertility, vigor, and youth. As all the cyclical phenomena can be readily associated or identified, it follows that any attempt to prove that a romantic story does or does not resemble, say, a solar myth, or that its hero does or does not resemble a sungod, is likely to be a waste of time. If it is a story within this general area, cyclical imagery is likely to be present, and solar imagery is normally prominent among cyclical images. If the hero of a romance returns from a quest disguised, flings off his beggar's rags, and stands forth in the resplendent scarlet cloak of the prince, we do not have a theme which has necessarily descended from a solar myth; we have the literary device of displacement. The hero does something which we may or may not, as we like, associate with the myth of the sun returning at dawn. If we are reading the story as critics, with an eye to structural principles, we shall make the association, because the solar analogy explains why the hero's

act is an effective and conventional incident. If we are reading the story for fun, we need not bother; that is, some murky "subconscious" factor in our response will take care of the association.

We have distinguished myth from romance by the hero's power of action: in the myth proper he is divine, in the romance proper he is human. This distinction is much sharper theologically than it is poetically, and myth and romance both belong in the general category of mythopoeic literature. The attributing of divinity to the chief characters of myth, however, tends to give myth a further distinction, already referred to, of occupying a central *canonical* position. Most cultures regard certain stories with more reverence than others, either because they are thought of as historically true or because they have come to bear a heavier weight of conceptual meaning. The story of Adam and Eve in Eden has thus a canonical position for poets in our tradition whether they believe in its historicity or not. The reason for the greater profundity of canonical myth is not solely tradition, but the result of the greater degree of metaphorical identification that is possible in myth. In literary criticism the myth is normally the metaphorical key to the displacements of romance, hence the importance of the quest-myth of the Bible in what follows. But because of the tendency to expurgate and moralize in canonical myth, the less inhibited area of legend and folk tale often contains an equally great concentration of mythical meaning.

The central form of quest-romance is the dragon-killing theme exemplified in the stories of St. George and Perseus, already referred to. A land ruled by a helpless old king is laid waste by a sea-monster, to whom one young person after another is offered to be devoured, until the lot falls upon the king's daughter: at that point the hero arrives, kills the dragon, marries the daughter, and succeeds to the kingdom. Again, as with comedy, we have a simple pattern with many complex elements. The ritual analogies of the myth suggest that the monster *is* the sterility of the land itself, and that the sterility of the land is present in the age and impotence of the king, who is sometimes suffering from an incurable malady or wound, like Amfortas in Wagner. His position is that of Adonis overcome by the boar of winter, Adonis's traditional thigh-wound being as close to castration symbolically as it is anatomically.

In the Bible we have a sea-monster usually named leviathan, who is described as the enemy of the Messiah, and whom the Messiah is destined to kill in the "day of the Lord." The leviathan is the source of social sterility, for it is identified with Egypt and Babylon, the oppressors of Israel, and is described in the Book of Job as "king over all the children of pride." It also seems closely associated with the natural sterility of the fallen world, with the blasted world of struggle and poverty and disease into which Job is hurled by Satan and Adam by the serpent in Eden. In the Book of Job God's revelation to Job consists largely of descriptions of the leviathan and a slightly less sinister land cousin named behemoth. These monsters thus apparently represent the fallen order of nature over which Satan has some control. (I am trying to make sense of the meaning of the Book of Job as we now have it, on the assumption that whoever was responsible for its present version had some reason for producing that version. Guesswork about what the poem may originally have been or meant is useless, as it is only the version we know that has had any influence on our literature.) In the Book of Revelation the leviathan, Satan, and the Edenic serpent are all identified. This identification is the basis for an elaborate dragon-killing metaphor in Christian symbolism in which the hero is Christ (often represented in art standing on a prostrate monster), the dragon Satan, the impotent old king Adam, whose son Christ becomes, and the rescued bride the Church.

Now if the leviathan is the whole fallen world of sin and death and tyranny into which Adam fell, it follows that Adam's children are born, live, and die inside his belly. Hence if the Messiah is to deliver us by killing the leviathan, he releases us. In the folk tale versions of dragon-killing stories we notice how frequently the previous victims of the dragon come out of him

alive after he is killed. Again, if we are inside the dragon, and the hero comes to help us, the image is suggested of the hero going down the monster's open throat, like Jonah (whom Jesus accepted as a prototype of himself), and returning with his redeemed behind him. Hence the symbolism of the Harrowing of Hell, hell being regularly represented in iconography by the "toothed gullet of an aged shark," to quote a modern reference to it. Secular versions of journeys inside monsters occur from Lucian to our day, and perhaps even the Trojan horse had originally some links with the same theme. The image of the dark winding labyrinth for the monster's belly is a natural one, and one that frequently appears in heroic quests, notably that of Theseus. A less displaced version of the story of Theseus would have shown him emerging from the labyrinth at the head of a procession of the Athenian youths and maidens previously sacrificed to the Minotaur. In many solar myths, too, the hero travels perilously through a dark labyrinthine underworld full of monsters between sunset and sunrise. This theme may become a structural principle of fiction on any level of sophistication. One would expect to find it in fairy tales or children's stories, and in fact if we "stand back" from *Tom Sawyer* we can see a youth with no father or mother emerging with a maiden from a labyrinthine cave, leaving a bat-eating demon imprisoned behind him. But in the most complex and elusive of the later stories of Henry James, *The Sense of the Past,* the same theme is used, the labyrinthine underworld being in this case a period of past time from which the hero is released by the sacrifice of a heroine, an Ariadne figure. In this story, as in many folktales, the motif of the two brothers connected by sympathetic magic of some sort is also employed.

In the Old Testament the Messiah-figure of Moses leads his people out of Egypt. The Pharaoh of Egypt is identified with the leviathan by Ezekiel, and the fact that the infant Moses was rescued by Pharaoh's daughter gives to the Pharaoh something of the role of the cruel father-figure who seeks the hero's death, a role also taken by the raging Herod of the miracle plays.

Moses and the Israelites wander through a labyrinthine desert, after which the reign of the law ends and the conquest of the Promised Land is achieved by Joshua, whose name is the same as that of Jesus. Thus when the angel Gabriel tells the Virgin to call her son Jesus, the typological meaning is that the era of the law is over, and the assault on the Promised Land is about to begin. There are thus two concentric quest-myths in the Bible, a Genesis-apocalypse myth and an Exodus-millennium myth. In the former Adam is cast out of Eden, loses the river of life and the tree of life, and wanders in the labyrinth of human history until he is restored to his original state by the Messiah. In the latter Israel is cast out of his inheritance and wanders in the labyrinths of Egyptian and Babylonian captivity until he is restored to his original state in the Promised Land. Eden and the Promised Land, therefore, are typologically identical, as are the tyrannies of Egypt and Babylon and the wilderness of the law. *Paradise Regained* deals with the temptation of Christ by Satan, which is, Michael tells us in *Paradise Lost,* the true form of the dragon-killing myth assigned to the Messiah. Christ is in the situation of Israel under the law, wandering in the wilderness: his victory is at once the conquest of the Promised Land typified by his namesake Joshua and the raising of Eden in the wilderness.

The leviathan is usually a sea-monster, which means metaphorically that he *is* the sea, and the prophecy that the Lord will hook and land the leviathan in Ezekiel is identical with the prophecy in Revelation that there shall be no more sea. As denizens of his belly, therefore, we are also metaphorically under water. Hence the importance of fishing in the Gospels, the apostles being "fishers of men" who cast their nets into the sea of this world. Hence, too, the later development, referred to in *The Waste Land,* of Adam or the impotent king as an ineffectual "fisher king." In the same poem the appropriate link is also made with Prospero's rescuing of a society out of the sea in *The Tempest.* In other comedies, too, ranging from *Sakuntala* to *Rudens,* something indispensable to the action or the *cognitio* is fished out of the sea, and many quest heroes, including Beowulf, achieve their greatest feats under water. The insistence on Christ's ability to command the sea belongs to the same aspect of symbolism. And as the leviathan, in his aspect as the fallen world, contains all forms of life imprisoned within himself, so as the sea he contains the imprisoned life-giving rain waters whose coming marks the spring. The monstrous animal who swallows all the water in the world and is then teased or tricked or forced into disgorging it is a favorite of folk tales, and a Mesopotamian version lies close behind the story of Creation in Genesis. In many solar myths the sun god is represented as sailing in a boat on the surface of our world.

Lastly, if the leviathan is death, and the hero has to enter the body of death, the hero has to die, and if his quest is completed the final stage of it is, cyclically, rebirth, and, dialectically, resurrection. In the St. George plays the hero dies in his dragon-fight and is brought to life by a doctor, and the same symbolism runs through all the dying-god myths. There are thus not three but four distinguishable aspects to the quest-myth. First, the *agon* or conflict itself. Second, the *pathos* or death, often the mutual death of hero and monster. Third, the disappearance of the hero, a theme which often takes the form of *sparagmos* or tearing to pieces. Sometimes the hero's body is divided among his followers, as in Eucharist symbolism: sometimes it is distributed around the natural world, as in the stories of Orpheus and more especially Osiris. Fourth, the reappearance and recognition of the hero, where sacramental Christianity follows the metaphorical logic: those who in the fallen world have partaken of their redeemer's divided body are united with his risen body.

The four *mythoi* that we are dealing with, comedy, romance, tragedy, and irony, may now be seen as four aspects of a central unifying myth. *Agon* or conflict is the basis or archetypal theme of romance, the radical of romance being a sequence of marvellous adventures. *Pathos* or catastrophe, whether in triumph or in defeat, is the archetypal theme of tragedy. *Sparagmos,* or the sense that heroism and effective action are absent, disorganized or foredoomed to defeat, and that confusion and anarchy reign over the world, is the archetypal theme of irony and satire. *Anagnorisis,* or recognition of a newborn society rising in triumph around a still somewhat mysterious hero and his bride, is the archetypal theme of comedy.

We have spoken of the Messianic hero as a redeemer of society, but in the secular quest-romances more obvious motives and rewards for the quest are more common. Often the dragon guards a hoard: the quest for buried treasure has been a central theme of romance from the Siegfried cycle to *Nostromo,* and is unlikely to be exhausted yet. Treasure means wealth, which in mythopoeic romance often means wealth in its ideal forms, power and wisdom. The lower world, the world inside or behind the guarding dragon, is often inhabited by a prophetic sybil, and is a place of oracles and secrets, such as Woden was willing to mutilate himself to obtain. Mutilation or physical handicap, which combines the themes of *sparagmos* and ritual death, is often the price of unusual wisdom or power, as it is in the figure of the crippled smith Weyland or Hephaistos, and in the story of the blessing of Jacob. The Arabian Nights are full of stories of what may be called the etiology of mutilation. Again, the reward of the quest usually is or includes a bride. This bride-figure is ambiguous: her psychological connection with the mother in an Oedipus fantasy is more insistent than in comedy. She is often to be found in a perilous, forbidden, or tabooed place, like Brunnhilde's wall of fire or the sleeping beauty's wall of thorns, and she is, of course, often rescued from the unwelcome embraces of another and generally older male, or from giants or bandits or other usurpers. The removal of some stigma from the heroine figures prominently in romance as in comedy, and ranges from the "loathly lady" theme of Chaucer's *Wife of Bath's Tale* to the forgiven harlot of the Book of Hosea. The "black but comely" bride of the Song of Songs belongs in the same complex.

The quest-romance has analogies to both rituals and dreams, and the rituals examined by Frazer and the dreams examined by Jung show the remarkable similarity in form that we should expect of two symbolic structures analogous to the same thing. Translated into dream terms, the quest-romance is the search of the libido or desiring self for a fulfilment that will deliver it from the anxieties of reality but will still contain that reality. The antagonists of the quest are often sinister figures, giants, ogres, witches and magicians, that clearly have a parental origin; and yet redeemed and emancipated paternal figures are involved too, as they are in the psychological quests of both Freud and Jung. Translated into ritual terms, the quest-romance is the victory of fertility over the waste land. Fertility means food and drink, bread and wine, body and blood, the union of male and female. The precious objects brought back from the quest, or seen or obtained as a result of it, sometimes combine the ritual and the psychological associations. The Holy Grail, for instance, is connected with Christian Eucharist symbolism; it is related to or descended from a miraculous food-provider like the cornucopia, and, like other cups and hollow vessels, it has female sexual affinities, its masculine counterpart being, we are told, the bleeding lance. The pairing of solid food and liquid refreshment recurs in the edible tree and the water of life in the Biblical apocalypse.

We may take the first book of *The Faerie Queene* as representing perhaps the closest following of the Biblical quest-romance theme in English literature: it is closer even than *The Pilgrim's Progress,* which resembles it because they both resemble the Bible. Attempts to compare Bunyan and Spenser without reference to the Bible, or to trace their similarities to a common origin in *secular* romance, are more or less perverse. In Spenser's account of the quest of St. George, the patron saint of England, the protagonist represents the Christian Church in England, and hence his quest is an imitation of that of Christ. Spenser's Redcross Knight is led by the lady Una (who is veiled in black) to the kingdom of her parents, which is being laid waste by a dragon. The dragon is of somewhat unusual size, at least allegorically. We are told that Una's parents held "all the world" in their control until the dragon "Forwasted all their land, and them expelled." Una's parents are Adam and Eve; their kingdom is Eden or the unfallen world, and the dragon, who is the entire fallen world, is identified with the leviathan, the serpent of Eden, Satan, and the beast of Revelation. Thus St. George's mission, a repetition of that of Christ, is by killing the dragon to raise Eden in the wilderness and restore England to the status of Eden. The association of an ideal England with Eden, assisted by legends of a happy island in the western ocean and by the similarity of the Hesperides story to that of Eden, runs through English literature at least from the end of Greene's *Friar Bacon* to Blake's "Jerusalem" hymn. St. George's wanderings with Una, or without her, are parallel to the wandering of the Israelites in the wilderness, between Egypt and the Promised Land, bearing the veiled ark of the covenant and yet ready to worship a golden calf.

The battle with the dragon lasts, of course, three days: at the end of each of the first two days St. George is beaten back and is strengthened, first by the water of life, then by the tree of life. These represent the two sacraments which the reformed church accepted; they are the two features of the garden of Eden to be restored to man in the apocalypse, and they have also a more general Eucharist connection. St. George's emblem is a red cross on a white ground, which is the flag borne by Christ in traditional iconography when he returns in triumph from the prostrate dragon of hell. The red and white symbolize the two aspects of the risen body, flesh and blood, bread and wine, and in Spenser they have a historical connection with the union of red and white roses in the reigning head of the church. The link between the sacramental and the sexual aspects of the red and white symbolism is indicated in alchemy, with which Spenser was clearly acquainted, in which a crucial phase of the production of the elixir of immortality is known as the union of the red king and the white queen.

The characterization of romance follows its general dialectic structure, which means that

subtlety and complexity are not much favored. Characters tend to be either for or against the quest. If they assist it they are idealized as simply gallant or pure; if they obstruct it they are caricatured as simply villainous or cowardly. Hence every typical character in romance tends to have his moral opposite confronting him, like black and white pieces in a chess game. In romance the "white" pieces who strive for the quest correspond to the *eiron* group in comedy, though the word is no longer appropriate, as irony has little place in romance. Romance has a counterpart to the benevolent retreating *eiron* of comedy in its figure of the "old wise man," as Jung calls him, like Prospero, Merlin, or the palmer of Spenser's second quest, often a magician who affects the action he watches over. The Arthur of *The Faerie Queene*, though not an old man, has this function. He has a feminine counterpart in the sybilline wise mother-figure, often a potential bride like Solveig in *Peer Gynt*, who sits quietly at home waiting for the hero to finish his wanderings and come back to her. This latter figure is often the lady for whose sake or at whose bidding the quest is performed: she is represented by the Faerie Queene in Spenser and by Athene in the Perseus story. These are the king and queen of the white pieces, though their power of movement is of course reversed in actual chess. The disadvantage of making the queen-figure the hero's mistress, in anything more than a political sense, is that she spoils his fun with the distressed damsels he meets on his journey, who are often enticingly tied naked to rocks or trees, like Andromeda or Angelica in Ariosto. A polarization may thus be set up between the lady of duty and the lady of pleasure—we have already glanced at a late development of this in the light and dark heroines of Victorian romance. One simple way out is to make the former the latter's mother-in-law: a theme of reconciliation after enmity and jealousy most commonly results, as in the relations of Psyche and Venus in Apuleius. Where there is no reconciliation, the older female remains sinister, the cruel stepmother of folk tale.

The evil magician and the witch, Spenser's

Archimago and Duessa, are the black king and queen. The latter is appropriately called by Jung the "terrible mother," and he associates her with the fear of incest and with such hags as Medusa who seem to have a suggestion of erotic perversion about them. The redeemed figures, apart from the bride, are generally too weak to be strongly characterized. The faithful companion or shadow figure of the hero has his opposite in the traitor, the heroine her opposite in the siren or beautiful witch, the dragon his opposite in the friendly or helping animals that are so conspicuous in romance, among which the horse who gets the hero to his quest has naturally a central place. The conflict of son and father that we noted in comedy recurs in romance: in the Bible the second Adam comes to the rescue of the first one, and in the Grail cycle the pure son Galahad accomplishes what his impure father Lancelot failed in.

The characters who elude the moral antithesis of heroism and villainy generally are or suggest spirits of nature. They represent partly the moral neutrality of the intermediate world of nature and partly a world of mystery which is glimpsed but never seen, and which retreats when approached. Among female characters of this type are the shy nymphs of Classical legends and the elusive half-wild creatures who might be called daughter-figures, and include Spenser's Florimell, Hawthorne's Pearl, Wagner's Kundry, and Hudson's Rima. Their male counterparts have a little more variety. Kipling's Mowgli is the best known of the wild boys; a green man lurked in the forests of medieval England, appearing as Robin Hood and as the knight of Gawain's adventure; the "salvage man," represented in Spenser by Satyrane, is a Renaissance favorite, and the awkward but faithful giant with unkempt hair has shambled amiably through romance for centuries.

Such characters are, more or less, children of nature, who can be brought to serve the hero, like Crusoe's Friday, but retain the inscrutability of their origin. As servants or friends of the hero, they impart the mysterious rapport with nature that so often marks the central figure of

romance. The paradox that many of these children of nature are "supernatural" beings is not as distressing in romance as in logic. The helpful fairy, the grateful dead man, the wonderful servant who has just the abilities the hero needs in a crisis, are all folk tale commonplaces. They are romantic intensifications of the comic tricky slave, the author's *architectus*. In James Thurber's *The Thirteen Clocks* this character type is called the "Golux," and there is no reason why the word should not be adopted as a critical term.

In romance, as in comedy, there seem to be four poles of characterization. The struggle of the hero with his enemy corresponds to the comic contest of *eiron* and *alazon*. In the nature-spirits just referred to we find the parallel in romance to the buffoon or master of ceremonies in comedy: that is, their function is to intensify and provide a focus for the romantic mood. It remains to be seen if there is a character in romance corresponding to the *agroikos* type in comedy, the refuser of festivity or rustic clown.

Such a character would call attention to realistic aspects of life, like fear in the presence of danger, which threaten the unity of the romantic mood. St. George and Una in Spenser are accompanied by a dwarf who carries a bag of "needments." He is not a traitor, like the other bag-carrier Judas Iscariot, but he is "fearful," and urges retreat when the going is difficult. This dwarf with his needments represents, in the dream world of romance, the shrunken and wizened form of practical waking reality: the more realistic the story, the more important such a figure would become, until, when we reach the opposite pole in *Don Quixote,* he achieves his apotheosis as Sancho Panza. In other romances we find fools and jesters who are licensed to show fear or make realistic comments, and who provide a localized safety valve for realism without allowing it to disrupt the conventions of romance. In Malory a similar role is assumed by Sir Dinadan, who, it is carefully explained, is really a gallant knight as well as a jester: hence when he makes jokes "the king and Launcelot laughed that they might not sit"—the suggestion of excessive and hysterical laughter being psychologically very much to the point.

Romance, like comedy, has six isolatable phases, and as it moves from the tragic to the comic area, the first three are parallel to the first three phases of tragedy and the second three to the second three phases of comedy, already examined from the comic point of view. The phases form a cyclical sequence in a romantic hero's life.

The first phase is the myth of the birth of the hero, the morphology of which has been studied in some detail in folklore. This myth is often associated with a flood, the regular symbol of the beginning and the end of a cycle. The infant hero is often placed in an ark or chest floating on the sea, as in the story of Perseus; from there he drifts to land, as in the exordium to *Beowulf*, or is rescued from among reeds and bulrushes on a river bank, as in the story of Moses. A landscape of water, boat, and reeds appears at the beginning of Dante's journey up the mount of Purgatory, where there are many suggestions that the soul is in that stage a newborn infant. On dry land the infant may be rescued either from or by an animal, and many heroes are nurtured by animals in a forest during their nonage. When Goethe's Faust begins to look for his Helena, he searches in the reeds of the Peneus, and then finds a centaur who carried her to safety on his back when she was a child.

Psychologically, this image is related to the embryo in the womb, the world of the unborn often being thought of as liquid; anthropologically, it is related to the image of seeds of new life buried in a dead world of snow or swamp. The dragon's treasure hoard is closely linked with this mysterious infant life enclosed in a chest. The fact that the real source of wealth is potential fertility or new life, vegetable or human, has run through romance from ancient myths to Ruskin's *King of the Golden River*, Ruskin's treatment of wealth in his economic works being essentially a commentary on this fairy tale. A similar association of treasure hoard

and infant life appears in more plausible guise in *Silas Marner*. The long literary history of the theme of mysterious parentage from Euripides to Dickens has already been mentioned.

In the Bible the end of a historical cycle and the birth of a new one is marked by parallel symbols. First we have a universal deluge and an ark, with the potency of all future life contained in it, floating on the waters; then we have the story of the Egyptian host drowned in the Red Sea and the Israelites set free to carry their ark through the wilderness, an image adopted by Dante as the basis of his purgatorial symbolism. The New Testament begins with an infant in a manger, and the tradition of depicting the world outside as sunk in snow relates the Nativity to the same archetypal phase. Images of returning spring soon follow: the rainbow in the Noah story, the bringing of water out of a rock by Moses, the baptism of Christ, all show the turning of the cycle from the wintry water of death to the reviving waters of life. The providential birds, the raven and dove in the Noah story, the ravens feeding Elijah in the wilderness, the dove hovering over Jesus, belong to the same complex.

Often, too, there is a search for the child, who has to be hidden away in a secret place. The hero being of mysterious origin, his true paternity is often concealed, and a false father appears who seeks the child's death. This is the role of Acrisius in the Perseus story, of the Cronos of Hesiodic myth who tries to swallow his children, of the child-killing Pharaoh in the Old Testament, and of Herod in the New. In later fiction he often modulates to the usurping wicked uncle who appears several times in Shakespeare. The mother is thus often the victim of jealousy, persecuted or calumniated like the mother of Perseus or like Constance in the *Man of Law's Tale*. This version is very close psychologically to the theme of the rivalry of the son and a hateful father for possession of the mother. The theme of the calumniated girl ordered out of the house with her child by a cruel father, generally into the snow, still drew tears from audiences of Victorian melodramas, and literary developments of the theme of the hunted mother in the same period extend from Eliza crossing the ice in *Uncle Tom's Cabin* to *Adam Bede* and *Far from the Madding Crowd*. The false mother, the celebrated cruel stepmother, is also common: her victim is of course usually female, and the resulting conflict is portrayed in many ballads and folktales of the Cinderella type. The true father is sometimes represented by a wise old man or teacher: this is the relation of Prospero to Ferdinand, as well as of Chiron the centaur to Achilles. The double of the true mother appears in the daughter of Pharaoh who adopts Moses. In more realistic modes the cruel parent speaks with the voice of, or takes the form of, a narrow-minded public opinion.

The second phase brings us to the innocent youth of the hero, a phase most familiar to us from the story of Adam and Eve in Eden before the Fall. In literature this phase presents a pastoral and Arcadian world, generally a pleasant wooded landscape, full of glades, shaded valleys, murmuring brooks, the moon, and other images closely linked with the female or maternal aspect of sexual imagery. Its heraldic colors are green and gold, traditionally the colors of vanishing youth: one thinks of Sandburg's poem *Between Two Worlds*. It is often a world of magic or desirable law, and it tends to center on a youthful hero, still overshadowed by parents, surrounded by youthful companions. The archetype of erotic innocence is less commonly marriage than the kind of "chaste" love that precedes marriage; the love of brother for sister, or of two boys for each other. Hence, though in later phases it is often recalled as a lost happy time or Golden Age, the sense of being close to a moral taboo is very frequent, as it is of course in the Eden story itself. Johnson's *Rasselas*, Poe's *Eleanora*, and Blake's *Book of Thel* introduce us to a kind of prison-Paradise or unborn world from which the central characters long to escape to a lower world, and the same feeling of malaise and longing to enter a world of action recurs in the most exhaustive treatment of the phase in English literature, Keats's *Endymion*.

The theme of the sexual barrier in this phase takes many forms: the serpent of the Eden story recurs in *Green Mansions*, and a barrier of fire separates Amoret in Spenser from her lover Scudamour. At the end of the *Purgatorio* the soul reaches again its unfallen childhood or lost Golden Age, and Dante consequently finds himself in the garden of Eden, separated from the young girl Matelda by the river Lethe. The dividing river recurs in William Morris's curious story *The Sundering Flood*, where an arrow shot over it has to do for the symbol of sexual contact. In *Kubla Khan*, which is closely related both to the Eden story in *Paradise Lost* and to *Rasselas*, a "sacred river" is closely followed by the distant vision of a singing damsel. Melville's *Pierre* opens with a sardonic parody of this phase, the hero still dominated by his mother but calling her his sister. A good deal of the imagery of this world may be found in the sixth book of *The Faerie Queene*, especially in the stories of Tristram and Pastorella.

The third phase is the normal quest theme that we have been discussing, and needs no further comment at this point. The fourth phase corresponds to the fourth phase of comedy, in which the happier society is more or less visible throughout the action instead of emerging only in the last few moments. In romance the central theme of this phase is that of the maintaining of the integrity of the innocent world against the assault of experience. It thus often takes the form of a moral allegory, such as we have in Milton's *Comus*, Bunyan's *Holy War*, and many morality plays, including *The Castell of Perseveraunce*. The much simpler scheme of the *Canterbury Tales*, where the only conflict is to preserve the mood of holiday and festivity against bickering, seems for some reason to be less frequent.

The integrated body to be defended may be individual or social, or both. The individual aspect of it is presented in the allegory of temperance in the second book of *The Faerie Queene*, which forms a natural sequel to the first book, dealing as it does with the more difficult theme of consolidating heroic innocence in this world after the first great quest has been completed. Guyon, the knight of temperance, has as his main antagonists Acrasia, the mistress of the Bower of Bliss, and Mammon. These represent "Beauty and money," in their aspects as instrumental goods perverted into external goals. The temperate mind contains its good within itself, continence being its prerequisite, hence it belongs to what we have called the innocent world. The intemperate mind seeks its good in the external object of the world of experience. Both temperance and intemperance could be called natural, but one belongs to nature as an order and the other to nature as a fallen world. Comus's temptation of the Lady is based on a similar ambiguity in the meaning of nature. A central image in this phase of romance is that of the beleaguered castle, represented in Spenser by the House of Alma, which is described in terms of the economy of the human body.

The social aspect of the same phase is treated in the fifth book of *The Faerie Queene*, the legend of justice, where power is the prerequisite of justice, corresponding to continence in relation to temperance. Here we meet, in the vision of Isis and Osiris, the fourth-phase image of the monster tamed and controlled by the virgin, an image which appears episodically in Book One in connection with Una, who tames satyrs and a lion. The Classical prototype of it is the Gorgon's head on the shield of Athene. The theme of invincible innocence or virginity is associated with similar images in literature from the child leading the beasts of prey in Isaiah to Marina in the brothel in *Pericles*, and it reappears in later fictions in which an unusually truculent hero is brought to heel by the heroine. An ironic parody of the same theme forms the basis of Aristophanes' *Lysistrata*.

The fifth phase corresponds to the fifth phase of comedy, and like it is a reflective, idyllic view of experience from above, in which the movement of the natural cycle has usually a prominent place. It deals with a world very similar to that of the second phase except that the mood is a contemplative withdrawal from or sequel to action rather than a youthful preparation for it. It is, like the second phase, an erotic world, but

it presents experience as comprehended and not as a mystery. This is the world of most of Morris's romances, of Hawthorne's *Blithedale Romance*, of the mature innocent wisdom of *The Franklin's Tale*, and of most of the imagery of the third book of *The Faerie Queene*. In this last, as well as in the late Shakespearean romances, notably *Pericles*, and even *The Tempest*, we notice a tendency to the moral stratification of characters. The true lovers are on top of a hierarchy of what might be called erotic imitations, going down through the various grades of lust and passion to perversion (Argante and Oliphant in Spenser; Antiochus and his daughter in *Pericles*). Such an arrangement of characters is consistent with the detached and contemplative view of society taken in this phase.

The sixth or *penseroso* phase is the last phase of romance as of comedy. In comedy it shows the comic society breaking up into small units or individuals; in romance it marks the end of a movement from active to contemplative adventure. A central image of this phase, a favorite of Yeats, is that of the old man in the tower, the lonely hermit absorbed in occult or magical studies. On a more popular and social level it takes in what might be called cuddle fiction: the romance that is physically associated with comfortable beds or chairs around fireplaces or warm and cosy spots generally. A characteristic feature of this phase is the tale in quotation marks, where we have an opening setting with a small group of congenial people, and then the real story told by one of the members. In *The Turn of the Screw* a large party is telling ghost stories in a country house; then some people leave, and a much smaller and more intimate circle gathers around the crucial tale. The opening dismissal of catechumens is thoroughly in the spirit and conventions of this phase. The effect of such devices is to present the story through a relaxed and contemplative haze as something that entertains us without, so to speak, confronting us, as direct tragedy confronts us.

Collections of tales based on a symposium device like the *Decameron* belong here. Morris's

Earthly Paradise is a very pure example of the same phase: there a number of the great archetypal myths of Greek and Northern culture are personified as a group of old men who forsook the world during the Middle Ages, refusing to be made either kings or gods, and who now interchange their myths in an ineffectual land of dreams. Here the themes of the lonely old men, the intimate group, and the reported tale are linked. The calendar arrangement of the tales links it also with the symbolism of the natural cycle. Another and very concentrated treatment of the phase is Virginia Woolf's *Between the Acts,* where a play representing the history of English life is acted before a group. The history is conceived not only as a progression but as a cycle of which the audience is the end, and, as the last page indicates, the beginning as well.

From Wagner's *Ring* to science fiction, we may notice an increasing popularity of the flood archetype. This usually takes the form of some cosmic disaster destroying the whole fictional society except a small group, which begins life anew in some sheltered spot. The affinities of this theme to that of the cosy group which has managed to shut the rest of the world out are clear enough, and it brings us around again to the image of the mysterious newborn infant floating on the sea.

One important detail in poetic symbolism remains to be considered. This is the symbolic presentation of the point at which the undisplaced apocalyptic world and the cyclical world of nature come into alignment, and which we propose to call the point of epiphany. Its most common settings are the mountain-top, the island, the tower, the lighthouse, and the ladder or staircase. Folk tales and mythologies are full of stories of an original connection between heaven or the sun and earth. We have ladders of arrows, ropes pecked in two by mischievous birds, and the like: such stories are often analogues of the Biblical stories of the Fall, and survive in Jack's beanstalk, Rapunzel's hair, and even the curious bit of floating folklore known as the Indian rope trick. The movement from one world to the other may be symbolized by the golden fire that descends from the sun, as in the mythical basis of the Danae story, and by its human response, the fire kindled on the sacrificial altar. The "gold bug" in Poe's story, which reminds us that the Egyptian scarab was a solar emblem, is dropped from above on the end of a string through the eyehole of a skull on a tree and falls on top of a buried treasure: the archetype here is closely related to the complex of images we are dealing with, especially to some alchemical versions of it.

In the Bible we have Jacob's ladder, which in *Paradise Lost* is associated with Milton's cosmological diagram of a spherical cosmos hanging from heaven with a hole in the top. There are several mountain-top epiphanies in the Bible, the Transfiguration being the most notable, and the mountain vision of Pisgah, the end of the road through the wilderness from which Moses saw the distant Promised Land, is typologically linked. As long as poets accepted the Ptolemaic universe, the natural place for the point of epiphany was a mountain-top just under the moon, the lowest heavenly body. Purgatory in Dante is an enormous mountain with a path ascending spirally around it, on top of which, as the pilgrim gradually recovers his lost innocence and casts off his original sin, is the garden of Eden. It is at this point that the prodigious apocalyptic epiphany of the closing cantos of the *Purgatorio* is achieved. The sense of being between an apocalyptic world above and a cyclical world below is present too, as from the garden of Eden all seeds of vegetable life fall back into the world, while human life passes on.

In *The Faerie Queene* there is a Pisgah vision in the first book, when St. George climbs the mountain of contemplation and sees the heavenly city from a distance. As the dragon he has to kill is the fallen world, there is a level of the allegory in which his dragon is the space between himself and the distant city. In the corresponding episode of Ariosto the link between the mountain-top and the sphere of the moon is clearer. But Spenser's fullest treatment of the theme is the brilliant metaphysical comedy known as the *Mutabilitie Cantoes,* where the conflict of being and becoming, Jove and Mutability, order and change, is resolved at the sphere of the moon. Mutability's evidence consists of the cyclical movements of nature, but this evidence is turned against her and proved to be a principle of order in nature instead of mere change. In this poem the relation of the heavenly bodies to the apocalyptic world is not metaphorical identification, as it is, at least as a poetic convention, in Dante's *Paradiso,* but likeness: they are still within nature, and only in the final stanza of the poem does the real apocalyptic world appear.

The distinction of levels here implies that there may be analogous forms of the point of epiphany. For instance, it may be presented in erotic terms as a place of sexual fulfilment, where there is no apocalyptic vision but simply a sense of arriving at the summit of experience in nature. This natural form of the point of epiphany is called in Spenser the Gardens of Adonis. It recurs under that name in Keats's *Endymion* and is the world entered by the lovers at the end of Shelley's *Revolt of Islam.* The Gardens of Adonis, like Eden in Dante, are a place of seed, into which everything subject to the cyclical order of nature enters at death and proceeds from at birth. Milton's early poems are, like the *Mutabilitie Cantoes,* full of the sense of a distinction between nature as a divinely sanctioned order, the nature of the music of the spheres, and nature as a fallen and largely chaotic world. The former is symbolized by the Gardens of Adonis in *Comus,* from whence the attendant spirit descends to watch over the Lady. The central image of this archetype, Venus watching over Adonis, is (to use a modern distinction) the analogue in terms of Eros to the Madonna and Son in the context of Agape.

Milton picks up the theme of the Pisgah vision in *Paradise Regained,* which assumes an elementary principle of Biblical typology in which the events of Christ's life repeat those of the history of Israel. Israel goes to Egypt, brought down by Joseph, escapes a slaughter of innocents, is cut off from Egypt by the Red Sea, organizes into twelve tribes, wanders forty years in the wilderness, receives the law from Sinai, is saved by a brazen serpent on a pole, crosses the Jordan, and enters the Promised Land under "Joshua, whom the Gentiles Jesus call." Jesus goes to Egypt in infancy, led by Joseph, escapes a slaughter of innocents, is baptized and recognized as the Messiah, wanders forty days in the wilderness, gathers twelve followers, preaches the Sermon on the Mount, saves mankind by dying on a pole, and thereby conquers the Promised Land as the real Joshua. In Milton the temptation corresponds to the Pisgah vision of Moses, except that the gaze is turned in the opposite direction. It marks the climax of Jesus' obedience to the law, just before his active redemption of the world begins, and the sequence of temptations consolidates the world, flesh, and devil into the single form of Satan. The point of epiphany is here represented by the pinnacle of the temple, from which Satan falls away as Jesus remains motionless on top of it. The fall of Satan reminds us that the point of epiphany is also the top of the wheel of fortune, the point from which the tragic hero falls. This ironic use of the point of epiphany occurs in the Bible in the story of the Tower of Babel.

The Ptolemaic cosmos eventually disappeared, but the point of epiphany did not, though in more recent literature it is often ironically reversed, or brought to terms with greater demands for credibility. Allowing for this, one may still see the same archetype in the final mountain-top scene of Ibsen's *When We Dead Awaken* and in the central image of Virginia Woolf's *To the Lighthouse.* In the later poetry of Yeats and Eliot it becomes a central unifying image. Such titles as *The Tower* and *The Winding Stair* indicate its importance for Yeats, and the lunar symbolism and the apocalyptic imagery of *The Tower* and *Sailing to Byzantium* are both thoroughly consistent. In Eliot it is the flame reached in the fire sermon of *The Waste Land,* in contrast to the natural cycle which is symbolized by water, and it is also the "multifoliate rose" of *The Hollow Men. Ash*

Wednesday brings us back again to the purgatorial winding stair, and *Little Gidding* to the burning rose, where there is a descending movement of fire symbolized by the Pentecostal tongues of flame and an ascending one symbolized by Hercules' pyre and "shirt of flame."

The Internalization of Quest-Romance

BY HAROLD BLOOM

Freud, in an essay written sixty years ago on the relation of the poet to daydreaming, made the surmise that all aesthetic pleasure is forepleasure, an "incitement premium" or narcissistic fantasy. The deepest satisfactions of literature, on this view, come from a release of tensions in the psyche. That Freud had found, as almost always, either part of the truth or at least a way to it, is clear enough, even if a student of Blake or Wordsworth finds, as probably he must, this Freudian view to be partial, reductive, and a kind of mirror-image of the imagination's truth. The deepest satisfactions of reading Blake or Wordsworth come from the realization of new ranges of tensions in the mind, but Blake and Wordsworth both believed, in different ways, that the pleasures of poetry were only forepleasures, in the sense that poems, finally, were scaffoldings for a more imaginative vision, and not ends in themselves. I think that what Blake and Wordsworth do for their readers, or can do, is closely related to what Freud does or can do for his, which is to provide both a map of the mind and a profound faith that the map can be put to a saving use. Not that the uses agree, or that the maps quite agree either, but the enterprise is a humanizing one in all three of these discoverers. The humanisms do not agree either; Blake's is apocalyptic, Freud's is naturalistic, and Wordsworth's is—sometimes sublimely, sometimes uneasily—blended of elements that dominate in the other two.

Freud thought that even romance, with its element of play, probably commenced in some actual experience whose "strong impression on the writer had stirred up a memory of an earlier experience, generally belonging to childhood, which then arouses a wish that finds a fulfillment in the work in question, and in which elements of the recent event and the old memory should be discernible." Though this is a brilliant and comprehensive thought, it seems inadequate to the complexity of romance, particularly in the period during which romance as a genre, however displaced, became again the dominant form, which is to say the age of Romanticism. For English-speaking readers, this age may be defined as extending from the childhood of Blake and Wordsworth to the present moment. Convenience dictates that we distinguish the High Romantic period proper, during which a half-dozen major English poets did their work, from the generations that have come after them, but the distinction is difficult to justify critically.

Freud's embryonic theory of romance contains within it the potential for an adequate account of Romanticism, particularly if we interpret his "memory of an earlier experience" to mean also the recall of an earlier insight, or yearning, that may not have been experiential. The immortal longings of the child, rather variously interpreted by Freud, Blake, and Wordsworth, may not be at the roots of romance, historically speaking, since those roots go back to a psychology very different from ours, but they do seem to be at the sources of the mid-eighteenth-century revival of a romance consciousness, out of which nineteenth-century Romanticism largely came. . . .

Behind Continental Romanticism there lay very little in the way of a congenial native tradition of major poets writing in an ancestral mode, particularly when compared to the English Romantic heritage of Spenser, Shakespeare, and Milton. What allies Blake and Wordsworth, Shelley and Keats, is their strong mutual conviction that they are reviving the true English tradition of poetry, which they thought had vanished after the death of Milton, and had reappeared in diminished form, mostly after the death of Pope, in admirable but doomed poets like Chatterton, Cowper, and Collins, victims of circumstance and of their own false dawn of Sensibility. It is in this highly individual sense that English Romanticism legitimately can be called, as traditionally it has been, a revival of romance. More than a revival, it is an internalization of romance, particularly of the quest variety, an internalization made for more than therapeutic purposes, because made in the name of a humanizing hope that approaches apocalyptic intensity. The poet takes the patterns of quest-romance and transposes them into his own imaginative life, so that the entire rhythm of the quest is heard again in the movement of the poet himself from poem to poem. . . .

The movement of quest-romance, before its internalization by the High Romantics, was from nature to redeemed nature, the sanction of redemption being the gift of some external spiritual authority, sometimes magical. The Romantic movement is from nature to the imagination's freedom (sometimes a reluctant freedom), and the imagination's freedom is frequently purgatorial, redemptive in direction but destructive of the social self. The high cost of Romantic internalization, that is, of finding paradises within a renovated man, tends to manifest itself in the arena of self-consciousness. The quest is to widen consciousness as well as intensify it, but the quest is shadowed by a spirit that tends to narrow consciousness to an acute

preoccupation with self. This shadow of imagination is solipsism, what Shelley calls the Spirit of Solitude or *Alastor,* the avenging daimon who is a baffled residue of the self, determined to be compensated for its loss of natural assurance, for having been awakened from the merely given condition that to Shelley, as to Blake, was but the sleep of death-in-life. Blake calls this spirit of solitude a Spectre, or the genuine Satan, the Thanatos or death-impulse in every natural man. Modernist poetry in English organized itself, to an excessive extent, as a supposed revolt against Romanticism, in the mistaken hope of escaping this inwardness (though it was unconscious that this was its prime motive). . . .

Wordsworth's Copernican revolution in poetry is marked by the evanescence of any subject but subjectivity, the loss of what a poem is "about." If . . . one rejects a poetry that is not "about" something, one has little use for (or understanding of) Wordsworth. But . . . one can understand and love Wordsworth, and still ask of his radical subjectivity: was it necessary? Without hoping to find an answer, one can explore the question so as to come again on the central problem of Romantic (and post-Romantic) poetry: what, for men without belief and even without credulity, is the spiritual form of romance? How can a poet's (or any man's) life be one of continuous allegory (as Keats thought Shakespeare's must have been) in a reductive universe of death, a separated realm of atomized meanings, each discrete from the next? Though all men are questers, even the least, what is the relevance of quest in a gray world of continuities and homogenized enterprises? Or, in Wordsworth's own terms, which are valid for every major Romantic, what knowledge might yet be purchased except by the loss of power?

Frye, in his theory of myths, explores the analogue between quest-romance and the dream: "Translated into dream terms, the quest-romance is the search of the libido or desiring self for a fulfillment that will deliver it from the anxieties of reality but will still contain that reality." Internalized romance, and *The Prelude* and *Jerusalem* can be taken as the greatest examples of this kind, traces a Promethean and revolutionary quest, and cannot be translated into dream terms, for in it the libido turns inward into the self. Shelley's *Prometheus Unbound* is the most drastic High Romantic version of internalized quest, but there are more drastic versions still in our own age, though they present themselves as parodistic, as in the series of marvelous interior quests by Stevens, that go from *The Comedian As the Letter C* to the climactic *Notes Toward a Supreme Fiction*. The hero of internalized quest is the poet himself, the antagonists of quest are everything in the self that blocks imaginative work, and the fulfillment is never the poem itself but the poem beyond that is made possible by the apocalypse of imagination. "A timely utterance gave that thought relief" is the Wordsworthian formula for the momentary redemption of the poet's sanity by the poem already written, and might stand as a motto for the history of the modern lyric from Wordsworth to Hart Crane.

The Romantics tended to take Milton's Satan as the archetype of the heroically defeated Promethean quester, a choice in which modern criticism has not followed them. But they had a genuine insight into the affinity between an element in their selves and an element in Milton that he would externalize only in a demonic form. What *is* heroic about Milton's Satan is a real Prometheanism and a thoroughly internalized one; he can steal only his own fire in the poem, since God can appear as fire, again in the poem, only when he directs it against Satan. In Romantic quest the Promethean hero stands finally, quite alone, upon a tower that is only himself, and his stance is all the fire there is. This realization leads neither to nihilism nor to solipsism, though Byron plays with the former and all fear the latter.

The dangers of idealizing the libido are of course constant in the life of the individual, and such idealizations are dreadful for whole societies, but the internalization of quest-romance had to accept these dangers. The creative process is the hero of Romantic poetry, and imaginative inhibitions, of every kind, necessarily must be the antagonists of the poetic quest. The special

puzzle of Romanticism is the dialectical role that nature had to take in the revival of the mode of romance. Most simply, Romantic nature poetry, despite a long critical history of misrepresentation, was an antinature poetry, even in Wordsworth who sought a reciprocity or even a dialogue with nature, but found it only in flashes. . . .

. . . Romantic or internalized romance, especially in its purest version of the quest form, the poems of symbolic voyaging that move in a continuous tradition from Shelley's *Alastor* to Yeats' *The Wanderings of Oisin,* tends to see the context of nature as a trap for the mature imagination. This point requires much laboring, as the influence of older views of Romanticism is very hard to slough off. Even Northrop Frye, the leading romance theorist we have had at least since Ruskin, Pater, and Yeats, says that "in Romanticism the main direction of the quest of identity tends increasingly to be downward and inward, toward a hidden basis or ground of identity between man and nature." The directional part of this statement is true, but the stated goal I think is not. Frye still speaks of the Romantics as seeking a final unity between man and his nature, but Blake and Shelley do not accept such a unity as a goal, unless a total transformation of man and nature can precede unity. . . . If the goal of Romantic internalization of the quest was a wider consciousness that would be free of the excesses of self-consciousness, a consideration of the rigors of experimental psychology will show, quite rapidly, why nature could not provide adequate context. The program of Romanticism, and not just in Blake, demands something more than a natural man to carry it through. Enlarged and more numerous senses are necessary, an enormous virtue of Romantic poetry clearly being that it not only demands such expansion but begins to make it possible, or at least attempts to do so. . . .

Only the Selfhood, for the Romantics as for such Christian visionaries as Eckhart before them, burns in Hell. The Selfhood is not the erotic principle, but precisely that part of the erotic that cannot be released in the dialectic of love, whether between man and man, or man and nature. Here the Romantics, all of them, I think, even Keats, part company with Freud's dialectics of human nature. Freud's beautiful sentence on marriage is a formula against which the Romantic Eros can be tested: "A man shall leave father and mother—according to the Biblical precept—and cleave to his wife; then are tenderness and sensuality united." By the canons of internalized romance, that translates: a poet shall leave his Great Original (Milton, for the Romantics) and nature—according to the precept of Poetic Genius—and cleave to his Muse or Imagination; then are the generous and solitary halves united. But, so translated, the formula has ceased to be Freudian and has become High Romantic. In Freud, part of the ego's own self-love is projected onto an outward object, but part always remains in the ego, and even the projected portion can find its way back again. Somewhere Freud has a splendid sentence that anyone unhappy in love can take to heart: "Object-libido was at first ego-libido and can be again transformed into ego-libido," which is to say that a certain degree of narcissistic mobility is rather a good thing. Somewhere else Freud remarks that all romance is really a form of what he calls "family-romance"; one could as justly say, in his terms, that all romance is necessarily a mode of ego-romance. This may be true, and in its humane gloom it echoes a great line of realists who culminate in Freud, but the popular notion that High Romanticism takes a very different view of love is a sounder insight into the Romantics than most scholarly critics ever achieve (or at least state). All romance, literary and human, is founded upon enchantment; Freud and the Romantics differ principally in their judgment as to what it is in us that resists enchantment, and what the value of resistance is. For Freud it is the reality-principle, working through the great disenchanter, reason, the scientific attitude, and without it no civilized values are possible. For the Romantics, this is again a dialectical matter, as two principles intertwine in the resistance to enchantment, one "organic," an anxiety-principle masquerading as a reality-principle and

identical to the ego's self-love that never ventures out to others, and the other "creative," which resists enchantment in the name of a higher mode than the sympathetic imagination. . . .

The internalization of quest-romance made of the poet-hero not a seeker after nature but after his own mature powers, and so the Romantic poet turned away, not from society to nature, but from nature to what was more integral than nature, within himself. The widened consciousness of the poet did not give him intimations of a former union with nature or the Divine, but rather of his former selfless self. One thinks of Yeats's Blakean declaration: "I'm looking for the face I had/Before the world was made." Different as the major Romantics were in their attitudes toward religion, they were united (except for Coleridge) in *not* striving for unity with anything but what might be called their Tharmas or id component, Tharmas being the Zoa or Giant Form in Blake's mythology who was the unfallen human potential for realizing instinctual desires, and so was the regent of Innocence. Tharmas is a shepherd-figure, his equivalent in Wordsworth being a number of visions of man against the sky, of actual shepherds Wordsworth had seen in his boyhood. This Romantic pastoral vision (its pictorial aspect can be studied in the woodcuts of Blake's Virgil series, and in the work done by Palmer, Calvert, and Richmond while under Blake's influence) is biblical pastoralism, but not at all of a traditional kind. Blake's Tharmas is inchoate when fallen, as the id or appetite is inchoate, desperately starved and uneasily allied to the Spectre of Urthona, the passive ego he has projected outward to meet an object-world from which he has been severed so unwillingly. Wordsworth's Tharmas, besides being the shepherd image of human divinity, is present in the poet himself as a desperate desire for continuity in the self, a desperation that at its worst sacrifices the living moment, but at its best produces a saving urgency that protects the imagination from the strong enchantments of nature. . . .

There are thus two main elements in the major phase of Romantic quest, the first being the

inward overcoming of the Selfhood's temptation, and the second the outward turning of the
triumphant Imagination, free of further in-
ternalizations, though "outward" and "inward"
become cloven fictions or false conceptual distinctions in this triumph, which must complete
a dialectic of love by uniting the Imagination
with its bride, a transformed, ongoing creation
of the Imagination rather than a redeemed nature. Blake and Wordsworth had long lives,
and each contemplated his version of this dialectic. Coleridge gave up the quest, and became
only an occasional poet, while Byron's quest,
even had he lived into middle age, would have
become increasingly ironic. Keats died at
twenty-five, and Shelley at twenty-nine; despite
their fecundity, they did not complete their development, but their death-fragments, *The Fall
of Hyperion* and *The Triumph of Life,* prophesy
the final phase of the quest in them. Each work
breaks off with the Selfhood subdued, and there
is profound despair in each, particularly in
Shelley's, but there are still hints of what the
Imagination's triumph would have been in
Keats. In Shelley, the final despair may be total,
but a man who had believed so fervently that
the good time would come, had already given a
vision of imaginative completion in the closing
act of *Prometheus Unbound,* and we can go
back to it and see what is deliberately lacking in
The Triumph of Life. . . .

Dreams, to Shelley and Keats, are not wish-
fulfillments. It is not Keats but Moneta, the passionate and wrong-headed Muse in *The Fall of
Hyperion,* who first confounds poets and dreamers as one tribe, and then overreacts by insisting
that they are totally distinct, and even sheer
opposites, antipodes. Freud is again a clear-
headed guide; the manifest and latent content of
the dream can be distinct, even opposite, but
in the poem they come together. The younger
Romantics do not seek to render life a dream,
but to recover the dream for the health of life.
What is called real is too often an exhausted
phantasmagoria, and the reality-principle can
too easily be debased into a principle of surrender, an accommodation with death-in-life. . . .

Whatever else the love that the full Romantic
quest aims at may be, it cannot be a therapy. It
must make all things new, and then marry what
it has made. Less urgently, it seeks to define
itself through the analogue of each man's creative potential. But it learns, through its poets,
that it cannot define what it is, but only what it
will be. The man prophesied by the Romantics
is a central man who is always in the process of
becoming his own begetter, and though his major poems perhaps have been written, he as yet
has not fleshed out his prophecy, nor proved the
final form of his love.

III

CRITICISM

Undream'd Shores: *The Tempest*

BY HOWARD FELPERIN

When Gonzalo in the second act of *The Tempest* confounds ancient Carthage in modern Tunis, Antonio compares the old man's lapse of memory to the poet Amphion's "miraculous harp," at whose sound stones took their places within the wall of Thebes. "What impossible matter," Antonio jibes, "will he make easy next?" (II.i.85) It is easy to imagine Ben Jonson, who had jibed at Shakespeare for giving Bohemia a seacoast in *The Winter's Tale,* asking the same question on his way to see *The Tempest* for the first time. For if Gonzalo is comically unlike Amphion, the Shakespeare of the last romances, and of *The Tempest* in particular, is not. By a similar poetic magic, Shakespeare contains an action that stretches from "the dark backward and abysm of time" to the dramatic present, from a lost Golden Age to a future Apocalypse, and that spans the Mediterranean from Italy to North Africa, and the Atlantic from the Old World to the New, to a single afternoon and a single place, an island brought forth from the sea by the kind of spontaneous generation Antonio goes on to ridicule. The raw material of his three earlier romances now takes its place within the neo-classical architecture of *The Tempest* like the stones of the wall of Thebes. Not only does Shakespeare "make easy" his impossible matter, but he departs from his usual practice and makes it up. The absence of a literary source for *The Tempest* only reinforces the already strong sense, arising from the fantastic nature of its island setting and of its native inhabitants, of

UNDREAM'D SHORES: THE TEMPEST From Howard Felperin, *Shakespearean Romance* (Princeton University Press, 1972). Reprinted by permission of Princeton University Press.

creation out of nothing. If the Shakespeare of *The Winter's Tale* is like Julio Romano, the painstaking carver whose art is indistinguishable from nature itself, the Shakespeare of *The Tempest* is more like Amphion, the poet-magician who calls into being a second nature, like and unlike nature, at the touch of a miraculous harp. . . .

If this most "allegorical" of Shakespeare's plays does not have a literary source in the usual sense, it does have historical sources: William Strachey's *A True Reportory of the Wreck and Redemption of Sir Thomas Gates, Knight* and Silvester Jourdain's *A Discovery in the Bermudas*. Although their titles promise a documentary fidelity to fact, the "Bermuda pamphlets" are anything but mundane reportage of contemporary history. Both accounts consistently allegorize the events they purport merely to describe:

It pleased God out of His most gracious and merciful providence so as to direct and guide our ship (being left to the mercy of the sea) for her most advantage . . . . Every man bustled up and gathered his strength and feeble spirits together to perform as much as their weak force would permit him; through which weak means it pleased God to work so strongly as the water was stayed for that little time . . . and the ship kept from present sinking . . . .

And there neither did our ship sink, but more fortunately in so great a misfortune, fell in between two rocks, where she was fast lodged and locked for further budging . . . . But our delivery was not more strange, in falling so opportunely and happily upon the land, as our feeding and preservation was beyond our hopes and all men's expectations most admirable.

215

Both Strachey and Jourdain, in their readiness to see the miraculous at work, to moralize on the conduct of the crew, and to discern the hand of providence in every turn of events, take what may be called Gonzalo's view of their experience. . . .

For to the minds of the early voyagers, the New World was as much a moral and mythological landscape as a physical and geographical one. In both its benign and sinister aspects it was described as if it existed outside of time and space, more like the settings of Dante and Spenser than anything on the known map of Europe. Columbus, as everyone knows, thought he had discovered the terrestrial paradise, and Amerigo Vespucci similarly described the South America he had almost certainly never seen, compiling his idealized account of the place, like many who had seen it, out of earlier literature. To Peter Martyr, the natives of Cuba "seem to live in the golden world, without toil, living in open gardens, not entrenched with dikes, divided with hedges, or defended with walls . . . without laws, without books, and without judges." Arthur Barlow characterizes the Indians of Virginia as a people "most gentle, loving, and faithful, void of all guile and treason and such as lived after the manner of the Golden Age," and their land as productive of "all things in abundance as in the first creation, without toil or labour." The classical myth of a primordial Golden Age and the Christian myth of a lost paradise were repeatedly invoked to describe a contemporary reality. Michael Drayton, eulogizing the Virginia voyage of 1607, styles the English plantation "Earth's onely paradise" where "the golden age / Still natures law does give." Such hyperbolic accounts of the New World of course invited parody, such as the description of Virginia in Johnson's *Eastward Ho!*, where it is said that even the chamberpots of Virginia are made of pure gold—an instance of conspicuous consumption borrowed from More's *Utopia*. . . .

The Renaissance voyagers, . . . in their casting about for classical and Christian analogues to their experience, in their eagerness to see the miraculous at work and the special providence

of God in all that happens, to see hope in disaster and lessons in trials, remind us more than a little of Gonzalo. From his comments on the breakdown of shipboard discipline during the opening storm to his wishful celebration of everyone's self-recovery near the end, Gonzalo tries, like the Renaissance voyagers behind him, to see a providential design in the experience of the play, to moralize that experience into what the Renaissance would call an "allegory." In doing so, although he does not "mistake the truth totally," as Antonio claims, he does have to bend reality ever so slightly to the desires of his mind and to that extent falsify it; not quite everyone, for example, has found himself by the end of the play as Gonzalo would like to think. His allusions to Carthage and "widow Dido" do distort Virgil in the strenuous effort to hammer out the parallel, and are representative of his efforts at perception throughout. One such effort is his benevolent vision of an island utopia:

GONZALO. Had I plantation of this isle, my lord,—
ANTONIO. He'd sow't with nettle seed.
SEBASTIAN.   Or docks, or mallows,
GONZALO. And were the King on't, what would I do?
SEBASTIAN. 'Scape being drunk for want of wine.
GONZALO. I'th'commonwealth I would by contraries
Execute all things; for no kind of traffic
Would I admit; no name of magistrate;
Letters should not be known; riches, poverty,
And use of service, none; contract, succession,
Bourn, bound of land, tilth, vineyard, none;
No use of metal, corn, or wine, or oil;
No occupation; all men idle, all;
And women too, but innocent and pure;
No sovereignty;—
SEBASTIAN. Yet he would be King on't
ANTONIO. The latter end of his commonwealth forgets the beginning.
GONZALO. All things in common Nature should produce
Without sweat or endeavor: treason, felony,
Sword, pike, knife, gun, or need of any engine,
Would I not have; but Nature should bring forth,
Of it own kind, all foison, all abundance,
To feed my innocent people.
SEBASTIAN. No marrying 'mong his subjects?

ANTONIO. None, man; all idle; whores and
  knaves.
  GONZALO. I would with such perfection govern,
  sir,
T'excel the Golden Age.   (II.i.139–63)

Whether the island is in fact "lush and lusty"
with grass, as Gonzalo earlier says, or "tawny
. . . With an eye of green in 't," as Antonio
and Sebastian contend, is less important than
the state of mind of the speaker, which the
island, like a mirror, reflects. . . . Gonzalo proceeds to imagine not simply a reformed micro-
cosm of the court but a brave new world
founded on revolutionary principles, one that
not merely equals but actually excels the Golden
Age.

The similarities between his daydream of an
island utopia and the voyagers' dreams of the
New World quoted above are obvious. Gonzalo's speech is in fact lifted in its entirety from
the supposedly firsthand account of the New
World which Montaigne reports in "Of the
Cannibals." But if Montaigne glorifies pristine
America mainly to indict degenerate Europe, his
irony undergoes a seachange in Shakespeare's
hands. Gonzalo's ideal commonwealth presup-
poses the benignity of nature and the instantane-
ous perfectibility of man, highly questionable assumptions in view of the natural disaster which
has left them stranded on the island in the first
place and to the cynical banter of Antonio and
Sebastian, whose capacity for redemption is
still in doubt even at the end of the play and
whose very presence to that extent invalidates
Gonzalo's ideal. The speech is not simply the
fancy of an old innocent (Ferdinand and Miranda are the voices of real innocence within the
play), for Gonzalo should know better. His
banishment of "treason" from his vision of the
good and natural life represents a spurious attempt to escape from the burden of history into
a timeless realm of romance, when he himself
is at least implicated in the treasons which drove
Prospero from his dukedom twelve years before
and which are about to be reenacted, this time
directed against Alonso. . . . The jibes of Antonio and Sebastian that frame Gonzalo's monologue no doubt damage their speakers more

than their target, but they also serve to remind
us that there is no escape from history, that
Gonzalo envisions a commonwealth not simply
of "contraries" but of contradictions, and that
life offers real resistance to the fiats of the
idealizing imagination.

The fact is that Gonzalo's "allegorical" reading of events is repeatedly qualified by the
events themselves. . . . Similarly, *The Tempest* itself is not so much a straight reflection of
earlier Renaissance travel literature as an ironic
commentary on it. Consider, for example, the
scene in which Ariel and the other spirits present the starving courtiers with a banquet. Even
the skepticism of Antonio and Sebastian breaks
down, and they momentarily suspend their dis-
belief: "Now I will believe / That there are
unicorns," says Sebastian, "that in Arabia /
There is one tree, the phoenix' throne; one
phoenix / At this hour reigning there." And
Antonio echoes: "travellers ne'er did lie, /
Though fools at home condemn 'em." (III.iii.21–
7) Gonzalo characteristically goes even further
in not accepting the reality of these "strange
shapes" but assuming their benevolence:

> If in Naples
> I should report this now, would they believe
>   me?
> If I should say I saw such islanders—
> For, certes, these are people of the island,—
> Who, though they are of monstrous shape,
>   yet, note,
> Their manners are more gentle, kind,
>   than of
> Our human generation you shall find
> Many, nay, almost any.   (III.iii.27–34)

The speech illustrates once again Gonzalo's
readiness to find good in everything and, with
its flattering contrast of native with European
manners, reflects the reports of numerous Renaissance "soft primitivists," notably Montaigne.
But Gonzalo's generous sentiments once again
prove misplaced as Ariel reenters "like a
Harpy," claps his wings over the banquet which
disappears, and pronounces his sentence of
"ling'ring perdition" on the three men of sin
present. Of course Gonzalo's trust, as Prospero
standing on the upper stage reminds us, is not

ultimately misplaced, for the spirits are in his service and the play in which they appear does turn out after all to be a romance. But at this stage in the development of the play his instinctive goodwill is sentimental, untested and unconfirmed by experience.

Or consider the savage of *The Tempest*. Rather than the rough diamond of Renaissance pastoral romance or his counterpart in Renaissance travel literature, the noble savage of the New World, Caliban is, as Prospero never tires of insisting, "a born devil, on whose nature / Nurture can never stick." (IV.i.188–9) It is only too easy, in our post-Enlightenment bias toward the primitive and the natural, to sentimentalize Caliban, to point to his sensitivity to the sounds and "qualities" of the island, to his poignant dream-life, and to his harsh treatment at Prospero's hands. But it is wiser to take our cue from Prospero than from Gonzalo. For Prospero has himself tried the enlightened approach to Caliban, had presumed the educability of the creature and treated him kindly, with near-disastrous results. Caliban's romantic and idealized prototype may be the noble American Indian then on exhibit in England, where according to Trinculo, such a "monster would make a man" (II.ii.31), but Caliban is a degraded version of this figure. As Trinculo's quibble implies, Caliban represents not human nature without nurture but subhuman nature incapable of receiving nurture. . . .

. . . But if Prospero's treatment of Caliban is understandable, what are we to make of his similar treatment of Ferdinand? Prospero's management of the "romance" plot proper within *The Tempest* is, like his handling of everything else, curiously anti-romantic. After brainwashing Ferdinand through Ariel's dirge into accepting his father's death, Prospero further afflicts and humiliates him during the first strange and fatal interview with Miranda. Prospero's harshness cannot be written off as parental tyranny . . . nor, as is sometimes said, as that nervous tension which accompanies the magician's role, for Prospero reveals himself fully conscious of what he is about. Lest their love "too light winning / Make the prize light"

(I.ii.454–5), he tells us in one of several asides, Prospero embarks on a program for trying Ferdinand that includes subjection to Caliban's labors and a coarsened version of his diet: "Seawater shalt thou drink; thy food shall be / The fresh-brook mussels, wither'd roots, and husks / Wherein the acorn cradled." (I.ii.463–6) Behind these lines lies not only the natural fare the Bermudan castaways had found so appetizing but the traditional menu of milk, honey, and acorns "where-with licentious Poesie hath proudly imbellished the golden age."

For Prospero's program stands on their heads not only the romantic diet but most of the other romantic myths and motifs of love in the Golden Age. Recall that Gonzalo, as well as abolishing all labor and decreeing hearty means for everyone in his utopia, had also abolished marriage. Yet he would have everyone "innocent and pure.". . . Prospero, however, will have no part of golden-age sexual ethics, nor is his standard of innocence and purity in the least ambiguous:

> If thou dost break her virgin-knot before
> All sanctimonious ceremonies may
> With full and holy rite be minister'd,
> No sweet aspersion shall the heavens let fall
> To make this contract grow.   (IV.i.15–19)

Prospero also executes all things by contraries, but without contradiction. Behind Ferdinand's labor of love is the logic of Dante's *Purgatorio*. By subjection to Caliban's diet and drudgery, Ferdinand is to be purged of the Caliban within, of the impulse to bow down in idolatry at the first sight of Miranda (as Caliban does to Stephano, and Amerindians did to European voyagers), and of the memory of those ladies at the Neapolitan court, the harmony of whose "tongues hath into bondage / Brought my too diligent ear." (III.i.41–2) In so far as Ferdinand regards his servitude as the condition of his freedom, however, it begins to resemble Ariel's labor more than Caliban's: that labor which Yeats calls "blossoming or dancing" and which represents the fulfillment of human nature rather than its curse.

The betrothal masque Prospero stages for

the couple is a figuration on Gonzalo's utopia and enacts on a mythological level the human action of the play. Now it is Prospero's turn to try his hand at making allegories, and the product is more sophisticated in every sense than that of Gonzalo:

> Earth's increase, foison plenty,
> Barns and garners never empty;
> Vines with clust'ring bunches growing;
> Plants with goodly burthen bowing;
> Spring come to you at the farthest
> In the very end of harvest!
> Scarcity and want shall shun you;
> Ceres' blessing so is on you. (IV.i.110–17)

In what amounts to a revision of Gonzalo's earlier vision, Prospero has made some significant changes. Whereas Gonzalo had simply banished by fiat all the nastier aspects of civilization, Prospero's working principle in the masque is that of inclusion. The traditional golden motif of eternal spring has been added, and the bans on "tilth" and vineyards have been lifted. The "foison" of Gonzalo's speech stands, but it is now seen as the fruit of tilth, of labor, of agri*culture*. The blessing that Ceres comes "to estate / On the blest lovers" (IV.i.85–6) is not a piece of choice real estate like Bermuda or Gonzalo's island plantation but an estate of the spirit; not the result of a pagan or primitivist subversion of European customs but of their fulfillment; not the spontaneous generation of nature but a collaboration of nature with nurture; not a paradise needless of moral and physical effort but one dependent on both. The "evils" of labor, vineyards, marriage are all present in a redeemed form. . . . When Ferdinand remarks, "Let me live here ever; / So rare a wonder'd father and a wife / Makes this place Paradise," he is quickly silenced by Prospero. Ferdinand cannot live "ever" with his wife in the seeming paradise of their father's making, but . . . must return from this ideal vision to historical reality, to the continuing labor of governing Naples and himself. The spirit Ariel may sport endlessly after summer in an ideal landscape at the end of the play, but its human beings may not.

For even though Prospero's vision is a more full and comprehensive model of the redeemed world than Gonzalo's, it too is based on some rather arbitrary exclusions: the enforced absence of Venus and Cupid, who thought "to have done / some wanton charm upon this man and maid" (IV.i.94–5) being one. As its banishment of lust suggests, not even the masque of Ceres is to be taken at face value, so mistrustful is *The Tempest,* is this "ideal" drama, of the endeavors of the idealizing imagination, of Prospero's as well as Gonzalo's attempts to allegorize experience. While there are no cynical courtiers present to mock Prospero's vision of the good and natural life, as there were at Gonzalo's, there is a Caliban plotting at that very moment to destroy it. And Prospero is aware of his own limitations as a utopist, serves as his own severest critic. The masque of Ceres is framed by his own commentary on it as a "vanity of mine Art" (IV.i.41) and as an "insubstantial pageant faded." (IV.i.155) Prospero has good reason to be aware of the "vanity," the frivolousness and pride and self-indulgence, of artistic endeavor, for it was by overdoing his passion for the liberal arts that he lost his dukedom in the first place. By indulging his desire to luxuriate in the paradise of his books, a desire very close to Ferdinand's during the masque, and "neglecting worldly ends" (I.ii.89), Prospero created a power-vacuum in Milan into which Antonio stepped. In Prospero's description of the Milanese coup d'état, his passion for the contemplative life amounts to nothing less than a hedonist idyll—"my library / Was dukedom large enough." (I.ii.109–10)—an escape from the public responsibilities of office into a private and insular world of art.

While Prospero studied an art wholly benign but completely out of this world, dedicated himself to "closeness and the bett'ring of my mind" (I.ii.90), Antonio was busily exercising an art altogether this-worldly: the Machiavellian art of the player-king:

> Being once perfected how to grant suits,
> How to deny them, who t'advance, and who
> To trash for over-topping, new created

The creatures that were mine, I say, or
    chang'd 'em,
Or else new form'd 'em; having both the key
Of officer and office, set all hearts i' th' state
To what tune pleas'd his ear. . . .
                                        like one
Who having into truth, by telling of it,
Made such a sinner of his memory,
To credit his own lie, he did believe
He was indeed the duke; out o' th'
    substitution,
And executing th' outward face of royalty,
With all prerogative;—hence his ambition
    growing, . . .
To have no screen between this part he play'd
And him he play'd it for, he needs will be
Absolute Milan.   (I.ii.79–85, 99–109)

Musical and dramatic talent seems to run in the family, for Antonio apparently possesses the theatrical gifts of setting a score, creating character, managing plots, and playing roles that Prospero displays on the island, but all to perverted ends. We see in action Antonio's talent for envisioning and casting scenes when he tempts Sebastian to play the same part with respect to his brother Alonso that he himself had played toward his brother twelve years earlier: "My strong imagination sees a crown," he tells Sebastian, "Dropping upon thy head" (II.i.202–3) —a vision of royalty that aligns him with other visionaries and dreamers in the play, Prospero, Gonzalo, and as we shall see, Caliban. The episode of the Milanese coup illustrates, among other things, how easily that art which is uncontrolled by ethical and social concern collapses into egocentricity, at best the self-indulgence of a Prospero and at worse the self-aggrandizement of an Antonio. The two brothers divide the libertine potentialities of the imagination between them.

There is an important sense, then, in which Prospero himself stands in need of redemption at the outset of the play as much as the others, whose guilt is more blatant. And he does seem to have changed during his twelve-year exile, both in his attitude toward his dukedom and in his attitude toward his art. Whereas he had previously neglected the former as a result of his total absorption in the latter—"My library /

Was dukedom large enough"—he now directs his art outward onto the world. The art that had been an end in itself is now the means, not only of recovering his dukedom, but of exercising his function as governor. The art of power and the power of art have become in Prospero's hands, not divided and distinguished worlds as they were before, but one and the same thing. The first requirement, in Renaissance terms, for the prince and the theurgist alike is self-discipline, and this Prospero would seem to have achieved. Having learned the hard way to discipline himself, to keep his own aesthetic passion in its proper place, he now bends his efforts to redressing the disorder of the Milanese court and the inward disorder of the individuals who compose it, that disorder revealed in the opening storm scene, where Antonio and Sebastian see the Boatswain's honest efforts to save them as an act of social insubordination worthy of hanging, while the real subversives are the courtiers themselves; or, closer to home, the spiritual anarchy within Caliban that causes him to claim kingship of the island "by Sycorax my mother" (I.ii.333) and just as rashly to resign his claim to the besotted Stephano.

To restore spiritual and social order Prospero employs his "so potent art.". . . Ferdinand is led by Ariel's music into love at first sight of Miranda, and after his ordeal as log-bearer, both are treated to the vision of the betrothal masque. Prospero has Ariel present the starving and exhausted courtiers, after their vain wandering in search of Ferdinand, with a tantalizing banquet only to have it vanish like a mirage and leave them tormented by their own frustrated appetite. The banquet, whatever its significance as an allegorical emblem, works dramatically to mirror their own grasping natures, as does the Harpy form in which Ariel appears to pronounce his sentence on the "men of sin" present. That sentence, with its language of surfeit and regurgitation, arises from the physical image of the banquet and reflects the almost cannibalistic appetite of men "'mongst men unfit to live," men who in a phrase of Shelley's have "made the world their prey" and who are actually about to prey on one another. Prospero has Ariel lead Caliban and his drunken crew on a penal trek through the nastier spots on the island:

> I beat my tabor;
> At which, like unback'd colts, they prick'd
>   their ears,
> Advanc'd their eyelids, lifted up their noses
> As they smelt music: so I charm'd their ears,
> That, calf-life, they my lowing follow'd,
>   through
> Tooth'd briers, sharp furzes, pricking goss,
>   and thorns,
> Which enter'd their frail shins: at last I left
>   them
> I' th' filthy-mantled pool beyond your cell.
>
> (IV.i.175–82)

These men (and one not-quite-man) of more than average sensuality are misled and tormented by the mutiny of their own senses, which land them in the slimy element appropriate to their gross and brutal natures. Prospero then proceeds to deceive their eyes with illusory wealth in a kind of parody of Caliban's recurrent wish-dream of "riches / Ready to drop upon me." (III.ii.139–40) When Trinculo and Stephano linger over the "trumpery" laid out to distract them from their scheme, "divers Spirits, in shape of dogs and hounds" (IV.i.254. S.D.) drive them off, the same spirits that appeared to the courtiers as a Harpy and "strange shapes" and to the lovers as goddesses and nymphs. . . . In his capacity as master illusionist, and to that extent "god o' th' island" (I.ii. 392), Prospero sends a rare vision or a maddening hallucination to each of the principles according to his ability and need, an idealized projection or a grotesque parody of the spiritual condition of each, their basest obsessions or highest aspirations made flesh. . . .

But as I have tried to show, *The Tempest* is finally intolerant of all attempts to allegorize or idealize experience, whether they be ours or those of the characters within the play. Prospero's scenario is a noble one to be sure, born of the loftiest ideals and aspirations of the Renaissance mind, and if he could successfully stage it, he would no doubt deserve the titles of god and superman, philosopher-king, and ideal

Christian prince that critics have bestowed on him. But *The Tempest* is as much about the limitations of the idealizing imagination as it is about its power, and of this Prospero seems to grow increasingly aware. Why, for example, does Prospero persist in referring to his art as a "vanity" and a "rough magic?" Why does he feel that he has to abandon it at all? And finally, just how successful is his art in producing his stated objectives?

Something that Prospero . . . has to learn for himself is that any attempt to manipulate human life artistically, even in a good cause, has its attendant dangers. . . . Throughout Shakespeare's work we find a healthy mistrust of characters who turn the world into a stage on which to mount their histrionic or directorial fancies, the "good" characters (Friar Lawrence, Henry IV, Duke Vincentio), as well as the "bad" (Richard III, Richard II, Iago). Only in *The Winter's Tale* is the power of art in human life seen as wholly positive, and there Shakespeare takes pains to establish that the art employed by Camillo and Paulina is "an art," as Polixenes unwittingly puts it, "Which does mend nature—change it rather—but / The art itself is nature." Paulina expressly disclaims all magical art in her unveiling of Hermione's "statue," and Leontes says then that "If this be magic, let it be an art / Lawful as eating," which of course it is, since she uses no art at all. The same cannot be said of Prospero's art. "This is no mortal business, nor no sound / That the earth owes" (I.ii.409–10):

> Full fadom five thy father lies;
>   Of his bones are coral made;
> Those are pearls that were his eyes:
>   Nothing of him that doth fade,
> But doth suffer a sea-change
>   Into something rich and strange.
>
> (I.ii.399–404)

The exquisite dirge presages the spiritual transformation Prospero's art does work on Alonso, but in so doing suggests the ambivalent moral status of that art. For the sea change it describes (imagine a coral and pearl Alonso) is unnatural and artificial in the extreme. . . . Ariel's song also conjures up the kind of transformation that medieval and Renaissance alchemists, highly suspect artificers, attempted to perform, the transmutation of base substances into pure and precious ones. (Prospero associates his art with alchemy in the opening lines of the last act, and with astrology, a sister-science of doubtful repute, during his exposition to Miranda in the first.) My point is not that Prospero's art is downright wicked (Shakespeare makes clear that it is "white-magic" he practices as opposed to the "black-magic" practiced by Sycorax) but that associations of dark and prideful learning still cling to it, despite the fact that it is now directed toward a good end. For in Prospero's artistic manipulation of human life lies a danger that besets the modern psychotherapist as much as the Renaissance magician: the danger of playing God. . . . It is necessary, not so much to render the ending of *The Tempest* one of unalloyed joy, for it is not that, but to dramatize Prospero's reform of himself, that he repudiate his art and return to the ranks of humanity. To do so is to renounce the total success of his "project," to make himself vulnerable again. But it is also to renounce once and for all that untransmuted residue of self-dramatization and self-aggrandizement inherent in any effort to recreate the world after one's desires and in one's own image. So far as Prospero is concerned, his renunciation *is* his real triumph. When he resolves to "drown my book," he redeems the belated promise of an earlier magician of the Elizabethan stage to "burn my books." He redeems the Faustus in himself. The "mercy" he finally exercises and asks the audience to exercise on him is the mature and social equivalent of the adolescent and histrionic "magic" he had formerly indulged.

The "brave new world" that emerges in the final scene is neither so brave nor so new as Prospero himself could have wished, neither the paradise regained Ferdinand had seen in the betrothal masque nor the golden age restored of Gonzalo's fancy. Presented with the son he believed dead, Alonso questions whether this too is not merely one more "vision of the island." (v.i.176) But the vision of Ferdinand and Miranda at chess is made "of flesh and blood," like the man (as Alonso is amazed to discover) who made it possible. So too the "blessed crown" Gonzalo calls down in prayer on the couple is, or soon will be, literal fact, the reality of Antonio's and Caliban's delusions of royalty and riches are mere parodies. Even Sebastian exclaims: "A most high miracle!" (v.i.177) He is referring . . . to the working out of Providence and to the old plays in which that working out was portrayed. But the pattern of the miracle play fits only Alonso's family, despite the efforts of Gonzalo to squeeze everyone into it. In his last great monologue on the renunciation of his art, Prospero speaks scornfully of that art as "this rough magic," and it is rough indeed compared with the creative activity of God—the divinity who alone, as Hamlet says in his final act, "shapes our ends, / Rough-hew them how we will."

In his appropriation and secularization of the forms of the medieval religious drama for his final romances, Shakespeare reassigns the role once played by the grace of God to the art of man: the role of raising and reforming mere nature. In the romances art is still closely associated with grace. But just as the private imaginative visions of Gonzalo, Antonio, and Caliban all fade before Prospero's higher and more comprehensive vision, so too, it is strongly hinted, Prospero's own vision fades before that of God. There is a point at which artistic transformation ends and divine transubstantiation begins, as in the Mass or the Apocalypse, and *The Tempest* stops this side of it. Intimations of Apocalypse are at hand in Prospero's speech on the ending of the revels, in which cloud-capped towers, gorgeous palaces, solemn temples, and the great globe itself—man's noblest artifacts and the material world of which they are made—are condemned to demolition to make room, in the Christian scheme of things, for the eternal art and architecture of the New Jerusalem, suggested perhaps in Gonzalo's summarial speech by the "lasting pillars" (v.i.208) on which this marvelous episode of human history is to be set down in gold. That brave new world will be built on a firmer base and of a more substantial fabric than was Prospero's vision in the bethrothal masque. . . . Prospero's vision was dispelled because "the beast Caliban" had literally been forgotten in its making, that hunk of brute nature that Prospero has to "acknowledge" in the end but cannot reform. Also outside the magic circle of raised human nature at the end is Antonio, who willfully defies any art, however transcendent, to reform him. Both figures perhaps suggest in different ways the ultimate resistance that life throws up against being transmuted into art at all, and especially into romance; that renders any human art finally no better than the world it works with and on; and that makes Prospero's efforts at once so potent and so limited, so fully and so merely human.

But if Prospero is not God, to what extent or in what sense may we legitimately think of him as Shakespeare? They are clearly analogous figures up to a point, not simply because they share a talent for putting on shows and because the epilogue fits the stage manager and the magician alike, but because both are directly concerned with the creation of brave new worlds, or more precisely with transmuting old worlds into new, brazen into golden. *The Tempest* is a definition in action of the poetics of romance, a kind of commentary on the imagination that created it, for Prospero goes about his project in much the same way that Shakespeare goes about his. . . . The creation of brave new worlds, whether in literature or in life, is achieved not by despising or ignoring the imperfections of this old one (as Gonzalo does in his vision of the island or Prospero had done before his deposition), but by repairing them. Wine is a grace of civilization which may be abused by a Stephano, Trinculo, or Caliban, but which finds a place in Prospero's vision of abundance. The "letters," which Gonzalo would prohibit along with wine, may be profaned by a Caliban or over-indulged by an immature Prospero, but it is the power conferred by his book

that enables the Christian Platonist to reorder his society and redeem at least one guilty soul. Any brave new world is merely an old one rehabilitated. Our initial impression of *The Tempest* as the product of spontaneous generation, of Shakespeare's own magical imagination, is finally inadequate. Prospero and Shakespeare do not, as Gonzalo and Antonio do, create out of nothing or out of themselves. Just as Prospero attempts to build a new Milan out of the ruins of its original social structure, so Shakespeare builds the play itself out of imperfect literary structures—travelers' tales, moldy old morality plays, pastoral romances—some of it second hand and shabby stuff, but capable of renovation. Even a miraculous harp like Amphion's needs stones to work on.

But here the analogy between Prospero and Shakespeare breaks down, and Shakespeare becomes . . . a greater magician than his own Prospero. For the vision of the play as a whole is greater than any single vision it contains, including that of Prospero. While Prospero labors, finally with only partial success, to create a brave new world, Shakespeare is creating his own, with complete success, in the form of the play itself. And Prospero's partial failure becomes the condition of Shakespeare's total triumph, for as we have seen, the ultimate validity of any romance world depends on an implicit recognition that romance is all but impossible to achieve while remaining faithful to life. To the extent that Gonzalo's word is more than the miraculous harp, that he can effortlessly bring forth utopian islands from the sea, he is an untrustworthy romancer; to the extent that Prospero's word is finally less than the miraculous harp, he is an unsuccessful one. Shakespeare's is the harp itself. For in the making of the play Shakespeare begins where Prospero ends: with the awareness that there is a fatal gap between the ideal world of romance and the real world of history, and that no act of magic can ever make them one.

The Beggar's Opera:

Mock-Pastoral as the Cult of Independence

BY WILLIAM EMPSON

Some queer forces often at work in literature can be seen there unusually clearly; its casualness and inclusiveness allow it to collect into it things that had been floating in tradition. It is both mock-heroic and mock-pastoral, but these take Heroic and Pastoral for granted; they must be used as conventions and so as ways of feeling if they are even to be denied. It would be as reasonable to say that human nature is exalted as that it is debased by this process; it makes Macheath seem like the heroes and swains no less than the heroes and swains like Macheath. If the joke against him is that he is vain to adopt the grand manner of the genteel rakes he at least stands their own final test; he has the courage to sustain it: 'What would you have me say, ladies? You see this affair will soon be at an end, without my disobliging either of you.' Indeed the audience did not want to despise heroic and pastoral but to enjoy them without feeling cheated; to turn them directly onto Marlborough and the contemporary ploughboy did make it feel cheated. The main joke is not against the characters of the play at all, nor does any one in the discussions about its morality seem to have taken it as against the appalling penal code and prison system; it is against the important people who are *like* the characters; the main thing is the political attack and the principles behind it. But pastoral usually works like that; it describes the lives of 'simple' low

THE BEGGAR'S OPERA: MOCK-PASTORAL AS THE CULT OF INDEPENDENCE From William Empson, *Some Versions of Pastoral* (New York: New Directions, 1960). All rights reserved. Reprinted by permission of New Directions Publishing Corporation and of Chatto and Windus Ltd.

people to an audience of defined wealthy people, so as to make them think first 'this is true about everyone' and then 'this is specially true about us.' So far as that goes the play is Swift's first conception of it—the pastoral method applied to Newgate.

There is a natural connection between heroic and pastoral before they are parodied, and this gives extra force to the comic mixture. Both when in their full form assume or preach what the parody need not laugh at, a proper or beautiful relation between rich and poor. Hence they belong to the same play—they are the two stock halves of the double plot. It is felt that you cannot have a proper hero without a proper people, even if the book only gives him an implied or magical relation to it; one takes this so much for granted in Sydney's *Arcadia* that the eventual labour trouble over a revolt of Helots seems oddly out of place. . . .

. . . Clearly it is important for a nation with a strong class-system to have an art-form that not merely evades but breaks through it, that makes the classes feel part of a larger unity or simply at home with each other. This may be done in odd ways, and as well by mockery as admiration. The half-conscious purpose behind the magical ideas of heroic and pastoral was being finely secured by the *Beggar's Opera* when the mob roared its applause both against and with the applause of Walpole.

One of the traditional ideas at the back of the hero was that he was half outside morality, because he must be half outside his tribe in order to mediate between it and God, or it and Nature. (In the same way the swain of pastoral is half Man half 'natural.' The corresponding idea in religion is that Christ is the scapegoat.) This in a queer way was still alive in the theatre; no perversion of human feeling might not be justified in the Restoration tragic hero, because he was so ideal, and the Restoration comic hero was a rogue because he was an aristocrat. The process of fixing these forms into conventions, the Tragedy of Admiration and the comedy of the predatory wit, undertaken because the forms had come to seem unreal, for some reason brought out their primitive ideas more sharply. Now on the one hand, this half-magical view seemed to the Augustans wicked as well as ridiculous; all men were men; they had just put down the witch-burnings; to a rational pacificism Marlborough and Alexander were bullies glorified by toadies. On the other hand, they were Tory poets, and the heroic tradition, always royalist (the king's divine right made the best magical symbol), had died on their hands. The only way to use the heroic convention was to turn it onto the mock-hero, the rogue, the man half-justified by pastoral, and the only romance to be extracted from the Whig government was to satirise it as the rogue. The two contradictory feelings were satisfied by the same attitude.

The rogue so conceived is not merely an object of satire; he is like the hero because he is strong enough to be independent of society (in some sense), and can therefore be the critic of it. There was a feeling that the unity of society had become somehow fishy—Hobbes' arguments in its favour, for instance, themselves products of civil war, only affected one the other way—and that the independent individual—the monad, the gravitating particle—was now the only real unit. Hence the 'rogue become judge' formula, with its obscure Christian connections, is used by a long series of writers for almost any purpose in hand. That is why the merchant-pioneer Robinson Crusoe was such a hero and yet must apologise for his life. The interest of the Noble Savage (Dryden's phrase) was that he was another myth about the politically and intellectually free man. Macheath

means laird of the open ground where he robs people; he is king of the Waste Land. Dullness to Pope and Dryden is a goddess, so that the theme of human folly is not trivial; she is a hideous danger to civilisation; both she and the hero her representative can tell us with authority who is dull. Moll Flanders in her second robbery is tempted to murder the child robbed, for greater safety; to escape from a moment of horror at herself she becomes indignant with the child's parents, explains how it ought to be looked after, and hopes the robbery will teach them to take better care of it; this makes her touching and competent. All Jonathan Wild's acts, according to himself in Fielding, might be excused in a hero; a denunciation of heroes; it makes him intolerable. Gay has many uses for the formula; a typical joke, that always delights a modern audience, gives its application to marriage, when Peachum says on discovering the marriage of Polly:

Married! the captain is a bold man, and will risk anything for money; to be sure he thinks her a fortune. Do you think your mother and I should have lived comfortably so long together if we had been married? Baggage!

The point of this is that it is a defence of marriage by one who thinks he is attacking it; marriage is not exalted (one can accept the mockery of the comedies), but it is more stable than its laws. The rogue has only to free it from the offensive approval of society to find it natural.

It may be said that there is no real cult of independence in this, because the irony admits that the hero is not really independent or should not be admired for it. Certainly the irony is necessary; later versions like the raggle-taggle-gypsy business which merely admire the apparently free man obviously leave out part of the truth. But though one may be puzzled by what the *Opera* means, certainly the turns of phrase it uses are pro-independent. The irony may well say that at a higher level the idea of independence is all nonsense; everything is one, all men are dependent on society, man can only be happy through generosity and a good conscience, or what not. But this does not annul the feeling for independence because one is made to feel that at so high a level the common rules of society are nonsense too. (This talk of levels seems evasive; the parallel with extreme pacificism may make it less vague. Granted that it is true that the right thing is for no man to resist another under any circumstances, a man who lives the life of a religious mendicant has or nearly has the right to appeal to it. But a man who allows the police to protect his property, however passively, is already not living by that rule and cannot appeal to it, only to the lower-level idea of justice. Which level is being used is thus a matter of logical consistency.) The feeling of universality given by this ironical method is due to the reader's sense that 'levels' are implied one above another. Not that this is the only way of giving a feeling of universality, which has been done, I suppose, more strongly by works whose thought and feeling seem straightforward, but it gives a clear case open to analysis. . . .

I should say then that the essential process behind the *Opera* was a resolution of heroic and pastoral into a cult of independence. But the word is capable of great shifts of meaning, chiefly because nobody can be independent altogether; Gay meant Peachum to be the villain, and there is a case for thinking him more independent than Macheath. The animus against him seems not only that due to a traitor; Gay dislikes him as a successful member of the shopkeeping middle class, whereas Macheath is either from a high class or a low one. . . .

One cannot go far into the play without insisting on the distinction between the two sorts of rogues, which is made very clearly and gives a rich material for irony. The thieves and whores parody the aristocratic ideal, the dishonest prison-keeper and thief-catcher and their families parody the bourgeois ideal (though the divine Polly has a foot in both camps); these two ideals are naturally at war, and the rise to power of the bourgeois had made the war important. Their most obvious difference is in the form of Independence that they idealise; thus the Peachums' chief objection to Macheath as a son-in-law is that he is a hanger-on of the aristocracy.

MRS. P. Really, I am sorry, upon Polly's account, the captain hath not more discretion. What business hath he to keep company with lords and gentlemen? He should leave them to prey upon each other.

P. Upon Polly's account? What the plague does the woman mean?

The discovery follows. The puzzle is that both Peachums feel dicing with the aristocracy might involve independence in their sense as well as his.

MRS. P. I knew she was always a proud slut, and now the wench hath played the fool and married, because, forsooth, she would do like the gentry! Can you support the expense of a husband, hussy, in gaming, drinking, and whoring? . . . If you must be married, could you introduce nobody into our family but a highwayman? Why, thou foolish jade, thou wilt be as ill-used and as much neglected as if thou hadst married a lord.

P. Let not your anger, my dear, break through the rules of decency; for the captain looks upon himself in the military capacity as a gentleman by his profession. Besides what he hath already, I know he is in a fair way of getting or dying, and both these, let me tell you, are most excellent chances for a wife. Tell me, hussy, are you ruined or no?

MRS. P. With Polly's fortune she might very well have gone off to a person of distinction; yes, that you might, you pouting slut.

Decency is the polite tone the bourgeois should keep up towards the wasteful aristocrat he half despises, so it is not clear whether *ruined* means 'married' or 'unmarried'; he is merely, with bourgeois primness, getting the situation clear. But who is a *person of distinction?* Mrs. Peachum is muddled enough to mean a real lord. (First joke; they will marry anything for money.) But she may mean a wealthy merchant or the squire he could become. (Second joke; this gets at the squires by classing them as bourgeois and at the lords by preferring the squires.) Squire Western, a generation later, was indignant in just this way at the idea of marrying his daughter to a lord.

Gay forced this clash onto his material by splitting up the real Jonathan Wild into Peachum and Macheath, who appear in the story as villain and hero. Swift complained that Gay had wasted a chance of good mock-heroic in Macheath's last speech to the gang; he should have said 'let my empire be to the worthiest' like Alexander. Gay was busy with his real feelings, and Macheath says, 'Bring those villains to the gallows before you, and I am satisfied.' But though he hates Peachum he makes him the parody of a real sort of dignity, that of the man making an independent income in his own line of business, and seems to have been puzzled between the two ideals in his own life. In the play the conflict is hardly made real except in the character of Polly; the fact that both parties are compared to Walpole serves to weaken it to the tone of comedy.

The ironies of the two parties are naturally of different intentions.

JEMMY. . . . Why are the laws leveled at us? Are we more dishonest than the rest of mankind? What we win, gentlemen, is our own, by the law of arms and the right of conquest.

[This specially heroic member preached.]

CROOK. Where shall we find such another set of practical philosophers, who, to a man, are above the fear of death?

WAT. Sound men, and true.

ROBIN. Of tried courage, and indefatigable industry.

NED. Who is there here that would not die for his friend?

HARRY. Who is there here that would betray him for his interest?

MAT. Show me a gang of courtiers that can say as much.

BEN. We are for a just partition of the world, for every man hath a right to enjoy life.

The main effect of this mutual comparison, of the assumption of a heroic manner here, is to make the aristocrats seem wicked and the thieves vain. But even for this purpose it must act the other way, and make both charming by exchanging their virtues; that the aristocrats can be satirised like this partly justifies the thieves, and to extend to Walpole's government the sort of sympathy it was generous to feel for the thieves was strong satire precisely because it was gay. The author means the passage hardly less than the thieves do as a statement of an attitude admittedly heroic; . . . and in people like thieves, in whom heroism does so much less harm than politicians, Gay is ready enough for an irresponsible sort of admiration. . . .

The political ironies of Peachum and Lockit are of a different sort. The difficulty in saying whether they mean their ironies does not arise because they are simple-minded but because they are indifferent; they bring out the justification that they are necessary to the state and partake of its dignity firmly and steadily, as a habitual politeness, and this goes on till we see them as portentous figures with the whole idea of the state, sometimes a cloud that's dragonish, dissolving in their hands.

PEACHUM. In one respect indeed we may be reckoned dishonest, because, like great statesmen, we encourage those who betray their friends.

LOCKIT. Such language, brother, anywhere else might turn to your prejudice. Learn to be more guarded, I beg you.

Either 'it is not safe to accuse the great' or 'it is bad for any man's credit to admit that in anything he is as bad as they are.' But there is no sense of surprise in this double meaning; the primness of caution is merely indistinguishable from the primness of superior virtue.

PEACHUM. 'Tis for our mutual interest, 'tis for the interest of the world that we should agree. If I said anything, brother, to the prejudice of your credit, I ask pardon.

Credit is used both about business and glory—'that fellow, though he were to live these six months, will never come to the gallows with any credit.' The world may be the whole of society or Society, the only people who are 'anybody,' the rich who alone receive the benefits of civilisation. The traditional hero has a magical effect on everything; the Whig politicians act like tradesmen but affect the whole country; Lockit and Peachum have the heroic dignity of the great because they too have a calculating indifference to other men's lives. The point of the joke is that the villains are right, not that they are wrong; 'the root of the normal order of society is a mean injustice; it is ludicrous to be complacent about this; but one cannot conceive its being otherwise.' The conclusion is not that society should be altered but that only the individual can be admired.

This double-irony method, out of which the jokes are constructed, is inherent in the whole movement of the story. We feel that Macheath's death is not 'downright deep tragedy,' nor his reprieve—a sort of insult to the audience not made real in the world of the play—a happy ending, because, after all, the characters, from their extraordinary way of life, are all going to die soon anyway; then this turns back and we feel that we are all going to die soon anyway. One of the splendid plain phrases of Macheath brings out the feeling very sharply:

A moment of time may make us unhappy for ever.

The antithesis might make *for ever* 'in the life of eternity' from a speaker who expected such a thing, or as derived from heaven 'in one of those moments whose value seems outside time.' His life seems the more dazzlingly brief because 'for ever' assumes it is unending.

That Jemmy Twitcher should peach me I own surprised me. 'Tis a plain proof that the world is all alike, and that even our gang can no more trust one another than other people; therefore, I beg you, gentlemen, to look well to yourselves, for, in all probability, you may live some months longer.

'And no more; take care because you are in danger' is the plain sense; but the turn of the phrase suggests 'You may live as long as several months, so it is worth taking trouble. If you were dying soon like me you might be at peace.' It is by these faint double meanings that he gets genuine dignity out of his ironical and genteel calm.

An odd trick is used to drive this home; as most literature uses the idea of our eventual death as a sort of frame or test for its conception of happiness, so this play uses hanging.

LUCY. How happy am I, if you say this from your heart! For I love thee so, that I could sooner bear to see thee hanged than in the arms of another.

It is true enough, but she means merely 'dead' by *hanged;* no other form of death occurs to her.

MRS. P. Away, hussy. Hang your husband, and be dutiful.

Hang here has its real sense crossed with the light use in swearing—'don't trouble about him; he's a nuisance; be dutiful to your parents.'

POLLY. And will absence change your love?

MACH. If you doubt it, let me stay—and be hanged.

'Whatever happens' or even 'and be hanged to you,' but he really would be hanged.

MACHEATH (in prison). To what a woeful plight have I brought myself! Here must I (all day long, till I am hanged) be confined to hear the reproaches of a wench who lays her ruin at my door.

His natural courage, and the joke that the scolding woman is a terror to which all others are as nothing, give 'till I am hanged' the force of 'for the rest of my life,' as if he was merely married to her. Finally as a clear light use:

PEACHUM. Come home, you slut, and when your fellow is hanged, hang yourself, to make your family some amends.

Hanging in the songs may even become a sort of covert metaphor for true love. 'Oh twist thy fetters about me, that he may not haul me from thee,' cries Polly very gracefully, but her song while her father is hauling carries a different suggestion.

> No power on earth can e'er divide
> The knot that sacred love hath joined.
> When parents draw against our mind
> The true love's knot they faster bind.

It is the hangman's knot, and the irony goes on echoing through the play. The songs can afford to be metaphysical poetry in spite of their date because they are intended to be comically 'low'; only an age of reason could put so much beauty into burlesque or would feel it needed the protection; they take on the vigour of thought which does not fear to be absurd. This excellence depends on the same ironical generosity—a feeling that life is fresh among these people—as lies behind Gay's whole attitude to his characters. (The point that genuine pastoral could then only be reached through burlesque was indeed made clearly by Johnson about Gay's own admirable *Pastorals*.) . . .

. . . (On the face of things a prostitute is unlike other women in only wanting money. In this satire a prostitute is an independent woman who wants all the nobility included in the idea of freedom, and a chaste genteel woman only wants a rich marriage. If you hate Jenny for betraying the hero then she is actually as bad as a good woman, but Mrs. Coaxer assumes that she obviously can't be, and therefore that her behaviour on the crucial issue of money shows nobility; she is faithful to her sorority when she acts like this. Jenny's reply shows the humility of a truly heroic soul.)

MACHEATH. Have done with your compliments, ladies, and drink about. You are not so fond of me, Jenny, as you used to be.

JENNY. 'Tis not convenient, sir, to show my fondness before so many rivals. 'Tis your own choice, and not my inclination, that will determine you.

He cannot say she has deceived him. 'What,' he says as she enters:

And my pretty Jenny Diver too! as prim and demure as ever! There is not any prude, however high bred, hath a more sanctified look, with a more mischievous heart: ah, thou art a dear artful hypocrite!

He loves her for having the power to act as she so soon acts to him (there is a bitter gentility in it which he too feels to be heroic) both as a walking satire on the claims to delicacy of the fine ladies and as justified in her way of life by her likeness to the fine ladies, whose superiority he half admits.

MACHEATH. . . . If any of the ladies choose gin, I hope they will be so free as to call for it.

JENNY. You look as if you meant me. Wine is strong enough for me. Indeed, sir, I never drink strong waters but when I have the colic.

MACHEATH. Just the excuse of the fine ladies! why, a lady of quality is never without the colic.

The colic as a justification for drinking is a dis-

ease like the spleen, half-mental, caused by a life of extreme refinement, especially as expressed by tight-lacing. It is because he so fully understands and appreciates her half-absurd charm that he is so deeply shocked by what should have been obvious, that it is a weapon frankly used against himself.

His respect for her is very near the general respect for independence; the main conflict in his question is that between individualism and the need for loyalty. In being a 'beast of prey,' the play repeats, she is like all humanity except in her self-knowledge and candour, which make her better. She is the test and therefore somehow the sacrifice of her philosophy; quasi-heroic because she takes a theory to its extreme; if wrong then because she was 'loyal' to it. Macheath's question becomes 'It is a fine thing when individuals like us can sustain themselves against society. But for that very reason we ought to hold together; surely it is not well done of you to prey upon *me*'—with the idea 'I thought I could make her love me so much that I could disarm her.' Jenny's answer is supplied by Mrs. Slammekin in her complaint at not sharing in the profits; 'I think Mr. Peachum, after so long an acquaintance, might have trusted me as well as Jenny Diver'; she owes as much faith to the professional betrayer as to Macheath in his capacity of genteel rake, 'martyr to the fair.' . . .

Poor man. He is a martyr to the fair, so that his weaknesses are due to his modish greatness of spirit; when a man takes this tone about himself he means that he considers himself very successful with women, and pays them out. Lucy is boasting of the strength of the spleen as a weapon against him. Poor man, more generally, because of the fundamental human contradictions that are displayed; he is a beast of prey forced to be sociable. And 'poor man, in the end he kills her, and is no doubt hanged'—for the force of *and*, prominent and repeated, is to make giving a quieting draught something quite different from, and later than, the attempt to 'give her will'—it might be only drink she willed for, and the attempt to give it once for all was anyway hopeless. The comparison of the dramatic and condemned thing—murder by poison—to the dull and almost universal one—quieting by drink—is used to show that the dramatic incident is a symbol or analysis of something universal. Afterwards (the double irony trick) this both refutes itself and insists on its point more suggestively (appears analysis not symbol) by making us feel that the dramatic thing is itself universal—the good meek husband, whether by poison or plain gin, is as much a murderer as Lucy. From whatever cause there is a queer note of triumph in the line.

The attempted murder is called a 'comfort' chiefly because it is no more; to kill Polly won't get her back Macheath. And it fails because she finds Polly is not happy enough to deserve it; at the crucial moment Macheath is brought back in chains. There is no more need for murder in Lucy, because Macheath seems to have despised Polly's help, and anyway is separated from her. There is no more hope of 'comfort' for Polly; she tosses gin and death together to the floor. So both women are left to poison his last moments. The playwright then refuses to kill Macheath, from the same cheerful piercing contempt; he is not dignified enough, he tells the audience, 'though you think he is,' to be made a tragic hero. Lucy's attempt is useless except for its ill-nature, which makes it seem a 'typically human' and therefore pathetic piece of folly; she takes up an enthusiasm for murder because otherwise she would have to admit the facts (which the human creature can never afford to do) and give way to the 'spleen' and despair —the spleen which is the despair of the most innocent and highly refined characters because to such characters this existence is essentially inadequate. Lucy's comic vanity in taking this tone (as in Macheath's different use of the device) is displayed only to be justified; 'what better right has anyone else to it?'; it is not

denied, such is the pathos of the effect, that the refined ladies may well take this tone, but they must not think it a specially exalted one. (To the Freudian, indeed, it is the human infant to whose desires this life is essentially inadequate; King Lear found a mystical pathos in the fact that the human infant, alone among the young of the creatures, is subject to impotent fits of fury.) It is this clash and identification of the refined, the universal, and the low that is the whole point of pastoral.

For the final meaning of this play, whose glory it is to give itself so wholeheartedly to vulgarisation, I can only list a few approaches to its irony. 'I feel quite grateful to these fools; they make me feel sure I am right because they are so obviously wrong' (in this hopeful form satire is widely used to 'keep people going' after loss of faith); . . . 'low as these men are, the old heroes were like them, and one may well feel the stronger for them; life was never dignified, and is still spirited.' (The good spirits of Fielding making a Homeric parody of a village scuffle.) 'The old heroes were much more like the modern thief than the modern aristocrat; the present order of society is based on an inversion of real values' (Pope sometimes made rather fussy local satire out of this); 'this is always likely to happen; everything spiritual and valuable has a gross and revolting parody, very similar to it, with same name; only unremitting effort can distinguish between them' (Swift); 'this always happens; no human distinction between high and low can be accepted for a moment; Christ on earth found no fit company but the thieves' (none of them accepted the full weight of the anarchy of this, but none of them forgot it; perhaps the mere easiness of Gay makes one feel it in him most easily). It is a fine thing that the play is still popular, however stupidly it is enjoyed.

The Generic Context of
When We Dead Awaken

BY MARJORIE B. GARBER

Ibsen is not generally regarded as a mythological playwright. His reputation is rather that of a demythologizer, a dismantler of systems of belief, ardent in his sponsorship of the individual. Yet he is also the poet of a secular religion which finds its ultimate object, as well as its concrete expression, in the figure of the maker: the crusading priest Brand, the architect Solness, the sculptor Rubek. *When We Dead Awaken,* his last play and self-designated "dramatic epilogue," is an explicit and compelling statement of this will to art. But the pattern of this final play is present in the earlier works as well; the fundamental design of Ibsen's plays remains constant over a career of fifty years. At the center of them, when stripped of the accidents of time and place, lies the romantic myth of the secular—a myth which may be conveniently exemplified in the omnipresent figure of the Promethean hero.

Shelley's *Prometheus Unbound* had appeared in 1820, and its continental cousin, Goethe's *Faust,* in 1808 (Part I) and 1832 (Part II). Both works exhibit the Prometheanism of the romantic movement at its most energetic and unabashed. In each a central figure, heroic but mortal, caught in the dialectical struggle between the will to knowledge and the will to belief, strives to usurp the place of God and turn the world to a Utopian and egalitarian society. This portrait of the artist as a young god, the placing of the human creator at the center of the turning world, is accomplished in the two dramas with remarkable similarity, by building the romantic quest around a woman so idealized as to become a first principle, at once lover and Muse. Faust, whose first experience with love has been with the Northern peasant girl Gretchen, significantly transfers his affections south and east, toward the classical lands which are the traditional well-springs of poetry. His infatuation with Helen of Troy is overtly an art-quest, an attempt to synthesize, in the serio-comic image of the medieval castle in Greece, the German Romantic tradition with the timeless Arcadian literature of antiquity. But Helen vanishes—the modern world is seen to be time-bound and devoid of redemptive power—and Faust is left holding her robe, the cloak of the poetic spirit, for Goethe as for Shakespeare's Prospero the tangible sign of election in art. The play's final vision, that of the "eternal feminine," is a still further abstraction of the principle of the "other," the quested-for. Eternal womanhood leads the male quester on high, yet his own resolution is carefully placed within the sphere of the fallen world; Care and Death seize his body, though his soul is saved.

A very similar situation is found in *Prometheus Unbound.* Here the Titan, literally as well as figuratively bound to the earth, is aided in his quest by his spouse Asia, with whom he has once roamed free in an Arcadian landscape of "rock-embosomed lawns, and snow-fed streams" (I,120). Asia, whose name once more suggests the magical east as the "other" of poetic inspiration, becomes a tutelary spirit of place, a naturalized quest object, analogous to such earlier female place-figures as the Shulamite in *The Song of Solomon,* or Shakespeare's Cleopatra (generally addressed as "Egypt"). Asia explicitly indicates her preference for the "weak yet beautiful" mortal creator (II.iii.15), and the play as a whole, like *Faust,* becomes essentially an art-fable, in which the quest of the time-bound mortal hero is simultaneously for love and for poetry, both seen as aspects of the creative female principle. We might note that in both cases the feminine spirit is not passive but active, "drawing on" Faust or undertaking a journey to the cave of Demogorgon to free Prometheus, and that the male questers both confront their enemy, Time, from the traditional vantage point of vision, the pinnacle or mountaintop. Both of these motifs will appear in a strongly marked way in *When We Dead Awaken.*

The hero of high romantic drama is a superman of sorts, the form of the play is episodic and dreamlike (neither *Faust* nor *Prometheus Unbound* was written to be performed), unlimited by "realistic" expectations about space and time, and the central quest is that of the protagonist for his lost faith. The romantic quester typically finds himself in conflict with time, which is to say with the fact of his own mortality. His solution, and the secular answer to religious transcendence, is *ekphrasis,* transmutation into art; hence the tendency to turn into a statue, or some other permanent work of art, as in Prometheus' vision of a cave in which he and Asia will be visited by "the progeny immortal/Of Painting, Sculpture, and rapt Poesy,/And arts, though unimagined, yet to be" (III.iii.54–56). The tendency to *ekphrasis* is central to the quest-romance; it appears conspicuously in Renaissance romances like *The Winter's Tale,* and is significantly approached from the perspective of the nineteenth century in *When We Dead Awaken.* For the quester it is a replica of transcendence—it does not replace the transcendence of the hero, and indeed the price of aesthetic awareness is an acknowledgement of human mortality. It is fully appropriate that the statue sculpted by Rubek in *When We Dead Awaken* should be called "The Day of Resurrection," a phrase which was also Ibsen's original title for the play.

The characteristic pattern of romantic drama, then, is closely related to the pattern of all quest-romance—the striving of men toward godhead. In the modern theatre, of which Ibsen is often considered the founder, this is importantly a reflexive tendency, the dramatist looking at himself. And like so many romantic artists, Ibsen sought this pattern not only as the functional core of his plays—it is equally true of *Peer Gynt, A Doll's House,* and *When We Dead Awaken*—but also in his life. Like so many of his contemporaries and successors, he spent a large part of his life in self-chosen exile. Born in Norway in 1828, he enjoyed his first artistic success, the epic drama *Brand,* immediately after emigrating to Italy at the age of 36. For the next twenty-seven years he remained in exile, living successively in Rome, Dresden, and Munich, returning to Norway only in 1891 to spend the last fifteen years of his life. Nor was this displacement for Ibsen merely a geographical exodus, but rather an interior journey self-consciously perceived. Upon his return to Norway, he wrote to his long-time friend, Georg Brandes,

> Oh, dear Brandes, it is not without its consequences that a man lives for twenty-seven years in the wider, emancipated and emancipating spiritual conditions of the great world. Up here, by the fjords, is my native land. But—but—but! Where am I to find my home-land?

His antidote for displacement, self-prescribed, is art.

> In my loneliness here [he writes] I am employing myself in planning something new of the nature of a drama. But I have no distinct idea yet what it will be.

In fact the drama, when it finally appeared, was to be *When We Dead Awaken.*

"Where am I to find my home-land?"—this cry of romantic displacement is Rubek's cry too. Rubek has two spiritual homes: the little cottage on the Taunitzer Zee, where he and Irene used to play at being gods, transforming leaves and petals dropped in a stream to swans and boats; and the mountain top from which he expects to see and show "all the glory of the world." Yet he has bought the Taunitzer Zee cottage only to tear it down, replacing it with a "handsome house" which Maja refuses to call a "home," and the journey to the top of the mountain, the archetypal Pisgah vision become the quest of the romantic artist, is one he is afraid to venture. It will take the reunion with Irene, the "eternal feminine" as quest-object, to lead him up the mountain to death.

Rubek, like Ibsen, is a man who has passed through many stages of an artistic career at once public and private. And in the sculptor, as in the playwright, we can perceive what is a crux of artistic self-examination, a reflexiveness so total as to be almost self-annihilating. Rubek's career (like Ibsen's) is divided into three major phases: a period of innocent idealism, in which he creates the original "Day of Resurrection," the "child" of an unfallen imaginative world; a subsequent period of growing social awareness which forces him to modify his vision, oppressing him with a consciousness of the "domestic animals" who surround and inhabit the world of ideals; finally, a period of synthesis, in which he regains a sense of his initial dedication, restoring Irene to the world of his statue, and acknowledging—to himself and to her—his dual role as creator and victim.

This triple pattern finds its counterpart in the dramatic career of Ibsen, whose literary consistency, despite apparently changing modes, deserves more attention than it has received. The central period of his dramatic productiveness, the period which includes *A Doll's House* (1879), *Ghosts* (1881), and *An Enemy of the People* (1882), has all too often been considered as a period of intense social realism and social criticism; Ibsen thus emerges as the prophetic champion of women's rights and the progressive antagonist of venereal disease and water pollution. But this emphasis on social reform is in Ibsen a matter of the subjugation of subject matter to artistic form. Syphilis and the oppression of women become for him the accidental materials of a greater romantic vision, obstacles to the achievement of selfhood, the dominant theme of his plays from first to last.

Ibsen began his mature career with epic dramas of a scope so broad that, until our own age, they were rarely performed—plays which, like *Brand* and *Peer Gynt,* examined the emergence of the self and the nature of the will. Brand and Peer are essentially supermen of the imagination, romantic products of the constant dialectic between will and nature, art or craft and love. It is no accident that both involve northern landscapes, though both were written in Italy; Ibsen shares with much of Scandinavian and German literature the concept that the north is the land of the real, the south that of the classical or ideal, just as in *Faust* the action of the play is split between Faust's gothic chambers in the north and the person and artistic spirit of the divinely southern Helen of Troy. The playwright, caught in the dialectic out of which he made dramatic tension, fluctuates constantly from a critique of the idealist to a critique of the realist.

The idealistic hero of *Brand,* his first mature work, is a preacher whose motto is "All or Nothing" ("Brand is myself in my best moments," Ibsen wrote to a friend); living and working in a village among the fjords and mountains, he stubbornly subjects both his wife and his child to a climate so harsh that they weaken and die, despite the advice of a physician and the implorings of his wife Agnes that they move to the magic south. Brand himself comes to his death as he climbs a mountain in search of the natural Ice Church, a gigantic structure strongly contrasted to the tiny and ordinary church in the village. As he climbs, urged on by a mad peasant girl, he is caught in an avalanche and dies. Over him a nameless voice murmurs in what may be reproach or benediction, "He is the God of Love." The similarities to *When We Dead Awaken* are evident: the mountainous landscape, the avalanche, the mysterious final pronouncement, the ghostly and unreal women, wife and waif, the murdered child, the obsessive and messianic character of the hero. In his earliest heroic dramas Ibsen is already employing themes and materials which will appear in his final play. In fact, writing in a letter of the character Brand, he says "I could have constructed the same syllogism just as easily on the subject of a sculptor or a politician, as of a priest." The "sculptor" latent in Brand was to emerge thirty years later in the artist-hero Rubek.

Where Brand is all will, Peer Gynt is will-less. The other side of the Hegelian dialectic of character and personality, Peer is all public image, no inner conviction. Himself the supreme opportunist, he adapts himself to all situations; Brand's motto was "All or Nothing," Peer's is "go round"—not straight through. Yet he, like Brand, is "led on" by the power of an almost superhuman woman; we hear that he is strong because he has "women behind him," and the deliberate confusion between the two women in his life, Aase his mother and Solveig his bride, follows the now-familiar Faustian pattern of the eternal feminine as quest-object and Muse. Structurally, then, it is with *Brand* and *Peer Gynt,* the early epics of creative imagination, that *When We Dead Awaken* has its greatest affinities. Yet Ibsen's works are, as has been said, essentially homogeneous in character, despite apparent formal differences. There is a fundamental consistency, both thematic and structural, linking the early romantic epics of the self, the naturalistic middle period of plays of social concern, and the late expressionist plays like *When We Dead Awaken* and *Little Eyolf,* which combine the prophetic romanticism of his youth with the classical restraint of the middle period. "People believe that I have changed my views in the course of time," Ibsen said at the end of his career; "This is a great mistake. My development has, as a matter of fact, been absolutely consistent. I myself can distinctly follow and indicate the thread of its whole course—the unity of my ideas and their gradual development." His plays are for him, then, analogous to Rubek's statue—in essence a single work which has changed through time. The statue changes from an ideal figure of redemption—parallel to the epics of self, *Brand* and *Peer Gynt*—to a multiple structure, crowded with ordinary people who look like domestic animals, a social vision much like that of Ibsen's middle plays. Brooding over all, holding the pieces of the composition together, is the figure of the artist himself:

In the foreground, beside a spring, as it might be here, there sits a man weighed down by guilt; he cannot free himself from the earth's crust. I call him remorse—remorse for a forfeited life. He sits there dipping his fingers in the rippling water, to wash them clean; and he is gnawed and tormented by the knowledge that he will never, never succeed. He will never, in all eternity, free himself, and be granted resurrection. He must stay forever in his Hell.

Ibsen died in 1906, murmuring the phrase "on the contrary." The modern drama of dialectic and confrontation is vividly figured in his work, in a constant oscillation between real and ideal, epic and domestic, optimist and cynic, and *When We Dead Awaken* presents this dialectic in its purest and yet its most romantic form, in the conflict between the paired characters—Rubek and Ulfheim, artist and bear hunter; Maja and Irene, wife and model. The play's full title is *When We Dead Awaken: A Dramatic Epilogue,* and there is something in it of the self-conscious summing-up, the dramatic farewell. An epilogue is normally spoken by one person, and the play may well be read as a kind of interior dialectical drama within the mind of Rubek; the other characters, deliberately stylized and idiosyncratic, function at least in part as aspects of his psychology and history. The impulse to palinode is not absent from his mind, nor from Ibsen's; both playwright and hero are in the position of looking back over a lifetime of creative vision. For Rubek the universe of his work is not wholly distinct from the visible external universe—the play, that is, is a symbolist document, formally closer in many ways to Strindberg and Maeterlinck than to *An Enemy of the People.* Had Ibsen continued to write, he would almost surely have moved even further toward symbolism and expressionism, as he himself acknowledged in a comment on the play: by "epilogue," he said, he meant an epilogue to the cycle of plays which began twenty years earlier with *A Doll's House.* "I shall not be able to absent myself long from the old battlefields. But if I return, I shall come forward with new weapons, and with new equipment." *When We Dead Awaken* thus stands on the brink of a new mode of theatrical expression, and this novelty is figured in its entire management of plot and character.

Rubek dominates the play as his image dominates the statue. He is in a way a Faustian figure, successful in his work, personally conscious of lack of fulfillment—but as the play opens he, unlike Faust, has ceased to strive. Significantly, he is called "Rubek" by his wife—his last name, his artist's name in the world, as we might say "Rembrandt" or "Cezanne." It is only Irene, whose claim is on his bond with humanity rather than his professional role, who calls him "Arnold." Rubek sees the world as populated by "domestic animals"—both the portrait busts he now produces for profit and the incremental figures added to his great masterpiece are nominally likenesses of men, but secretly those of beasts.

Deep within [he says], I have sculpted the righteous and estimable faces of horses, the opinionated muzzles of donkeys, the lop ears and low brows of dogs, the overgorged chaps of swine, and the dull and brutalized fronts of oxen.

All these, he says, are the animals "which man has corrupted in his own image, and which have corrupted him in return." And so saying, he empties his champagne glass, and smiles.

In sharp contrast to these domestic animals stand the wild and vicious animals hunted by Ulfheim. "Bear for choice," he says. "But if they're not to be had, I'll take any wild thing that crosses my path . . . as long as it's fresh and juicy and has good red blood in its veins." The prey he ultimately stalks, of course, is Maja, Rubek's wife, who has composed for herself a song which she cries over and over again: "I am free as a bird—I am free." Ulfheim thus stands in direct contrast to the cultivated and artistic Rubek, as a man of direct speech and action whose best friends are his pack of hunting dogs. Yet there are salient points of similarity between the two men, emphasizing the mirroring structure of the play. Both men have

been drawn to Maja by her vitality and force; both climb the mountain. Maja, who returns their passion in some measure, nonetheless finds both of them sensually "ugly."

MAJA. . . . he's so ugly! [*Picks a tuft of heather, and throws it away.*] So ugly, so ugly! Ugh!

RUBEK. Is that why you're so delighted to be going off with him into the forests?

MAJA, [*curtly*]. I don't know. [*Turns toward him.*] You're ugly too, Rubek.

RUBEK. Have you only just discovered that?

MAJA. No, I've noticed it for a long time.

Opposites here become identities: the realist and the idealist, the hunter and the artist, the man of instinct and the man of civilization. Ulfheim's quest as an aspect of Rubek's, and its alternative. The neglected persona of natural man, Maja's "faun . . . with a beard like a goat and legs like a goat," animates a landscape in process of coming to terms with its own mortality.

In this context, Ulfheim is a doppleganger quest figure, and Maja and Irene aspects of the quest-object, articulated and deliberately attenuated elements of Rubek's interior consciousness. Maja's name suggests spring and the promise of earthly renewal; she is part of the joyful fallenness of the quotidian world, "free as a bird," prudent of her life and conscious of its ineluctable boundaries. Irene, by contrast, belongs to the world of art. Her name means peace, a concept and a state of mind rather than a season. Yet in place of transcendence she has achieved only negation, a soulless death-in-life forced upon her by Rubek. "I stripped myself naked for you to gaze at me," she reproaches him, "and you never once touched me." She has in effect forgot herself to stone.

I have stood like a statue, naked on a revolving platform, in music halls. I made a lot of money. . . . I've been with men, whom I could drive crazy. That was something I'd never been able to do to you, Arnold. You had such self control.

The transformation here is a reversal of the Galatea myth which so fascinated Ibsen's contemporary, Shaw. Irene exchanges identities with Rubek's statue, the "Day of Resurrection." In the act of posing she has lost her own connection with humanity; museums for her, as for the younger Rubek, are only "tombs." This exchange of identity between the art object and its model is in a way a perfect expression of the romantic dilemma—the self split into image and essence, the operation of time and humanity affecting the artifact and not the model, who has become an empty shell. Rubek's statue turns from an image of redemptive optimism, "a pure young girl, unstained by life, awakening to light and glory without having to free herself from anything ugly or unclean," to a complex cluster of animal-headed bourgeoisie in which the young girl becomes "a background figure, in a crowd." The progress is from innocence to experience.

Irene is immobilized in time, frozen into death-in-life by Rubek's excessive and displacing self-consciousness. Her diminishment reverses the pattern of Galatea, and also, interestingly, that of Pandora, the classical ancestress of all women. Pandora had opened a forbidden casket, and set loose upon the world the evils and diseases which are the common lot of mortal men; like Eve, her counterpart in the Christian tradition, she thus precipitates the fall, rendering impossible the dream of a timeless golden age, and confronting man with his own mortality. In Ibsen's deliberate inversion of the myth, Irene has the key to the casket, but Rubek cannot find it. The casket is a metaphor for his creative power, "a small casket, with a lock that cannot be picked." In it, he says, "all my visions lie. But when she left me, and vanished from my life, the lock of that casket snapped shut. She had the key, and she took it with her." The rejection of Irene by Rubek is a denial of his humanity, made overt by his refusal to touch her, the pathetic fact that the statue is their only "child," her final despairing rebellion against being treated as an object. While the secular redemption of Prometheus and Faust had come through a recognition of their intrinsic bond with humanity, the striving of the artist toward godhead reconciled with an acknowledgement of mortality and pain, for Ru-

bek this realization comes late, and is only possible through reunion with Irene. She is for him at once the human element he omits from his own contacts with the world, and the source of inspiration that makes his art possible—an expressionistic extension of his mind and art as well as an independent character in the world of the play. The realism of *When We Dead Awaken* is a poetic realism of symbol rather than a pictorial realism of fact. Irene is seen clearly as an idea toward which Rubek is striving, a quest-object directly parallel to Asia, or Helen, Ibsen's earlier Solveig and Agnes.

Ibsen's expressionism admits of a dual reality. Irene exists as a character in a landscape at the same time that she is clearly discernible as an aspect of Rubek's centrifugal consciousness. Maja, the voice of a more rationalizing vision, suggests to Rubek that her ghostly figure is only an illusion. "You've been dreaming," is her practical and limited response to his description of the mysterious "figure dressed in white." But the dream is also reality—the existence of the nocturnal stroller is verified, for the audience as for Maja, by the spa inspector, whose evidence is unimpeachable because he is a man of no imagination. Irene exists for Rubek as both a memory and a reality—her white dress, like the light of transfiguration into which Rubek wishes to lead her, is appropriate to both her present resigned purity and her symbolic associations with light and enlightenment. By contrast the nun, her constant attendant, is clothed in traditional black. She has been suggestively identified with the spirit of the past, which imprisons both Irene and Rubek. At the same time, however, she seems to embody the rigid system of belief against which Rubek, like Faust and Prometheus, is constantly struggling: the old religion, a falsely comforting exterior standard against which to measure the redemptive energy of man. The nun is the secret arbiter of the lovers' climb to the mountain peak. Her cry, "Pax vobiscum," is the benediction of the uncomprehending world, apposite less for its doctrinal comfort than for the gratifying accident that "pax" and "irene" are synonymous. The chosen death of Rubek and Irene becomes their affirmation of value in a mortal universe.

At this moment Irene achieves her full power as the "eternal feminine"—the creative principle toward which the romantic hero-as-artist is constantly journeying. The machinery of religion is here, in the nun, the Latin benediction, the image of the Day of Resurrection. But Ibsen employs it in a profoundly secular way, as a means of illuminating the necessary freedom of the spirit from systems which comfort and restrain. The lovers do not hear the nun's final cry.

The characters of *When We Dead Awaken* are deliberately stylized, aspects of a single dominating consciousness; the setting is literally unstageable—a mountain, an avalanche, a coastal plain. In fact, the true terrain of the play is the fertile ground of the imagination. The epiphany on the mountaintop, and the power of the spectral Irene, at once woman and Muse, recapitulate in uncompromising terms the fundamental tenets of romantic Prometheanism. At the same time, the consistency with Ibsen's total dramatic work is frank and full. The consciousness of the artist Rubek, which in this expressionist drama includes and subsumes the entire cast of characters, remains dominant and compelling, the fullest articulation of a striving for immortality-in-the-mortal which began more than thirty years earlier with *Brand* and *Peer Gynt*.

The Caucasian Chalk Circle

BY ERIC BENTLEY

In the prologue to *The Caucasian Chalk Circle*, the people of two collective farms in Georgia debate their respective titles to the ownership of a piece of land. Up to now it has belonged to one farm, but now the other claims to be able to make better use of it. Who should own *anything*? Should possession be nine-tenths of the law? Or should law and possession be open to review? That is the question Brecht raises. In the first draft of the play, the date of this bit of action was in the 1930s. Later, Brecht shifted to 1945 for two reasons: so that the land can be approached as a new problem, in that the farmers on it had all been ordered east at the approach of Hitler's armies; and so that the farmers newly claiming it can have partially earned it by having fought as partisans against the invader.

The Prologue is a bit of shock for American audiences. Here are all these Communists—

Russians at that—calling each other Comrades, and so on. That is why, until recently, the Prologue was always omitted from American productions. In 1965, however, it was included in the Minnesota Theatre Company's production without untoward incidents or, so far as I know, outraged comment. With the years the Prologue had not changed, but the world had. America had. The existence of the U.S.S.R. is now generally conceded in the U.S.A. That Communists do use the title "Comrades" is taken in stride. There is even understanding for the fact that the playwright Bertolt Brecht sympathized with communism in those days, even more consistently than Jean-Paul Sartre and Peter Weiss do today.

However, disapproval of the Prologue is not caused merely by the labels. A deeper malaise is caused by the *mode* of the dispute over the land. Land has always been fought over, often with guns. The expectation that some individual should pull a gun, or threaten to, is part of our stock response to the situation, but in the pro-

THE CAUCASIAN CHALK CIRCLE From *Theatre of War* by Eric Bentley. Copyright © 1966 by Eric Bentley. All rights reserved. Reprinted by permission of the Viking Press, Inc.

logue, this expectation receives a calculated disappointment. The conflict is, or has been, real, but a new way of resolving it has been found, a new attitude to antagonists has been found. Not to mention the new solution: the land goes to the "interlopers," the impostors, because they offer convincing evidence that they will be able to make better use of it. Both the conclusion and the road by which it is reached imply a complete reversal of the values by which our civilization has been living.

And Soviet civilization? Were we to visit Georgia, should we actually witness such decisions being made, and being arrived at in Brecht's way? It is certainly open to doubt, even in 1966, while, in 1945, nothing could have been more misleading than Brecht's Prologue, if it was intended to give an accurate picture of Stalin's Russia. We hear that Soviet citizens have themselves complained that, quite apart from the political point, they find nothing recognizably Russian in this German scene.

Is it thereby invalidated? "The home of the Soviet people shall also be the home of Reason!" That is certainly a key line in the Prologue, but the verb is "shall be," not "is." That Brecht aligned himself with socialism, and saw the Soviet Union as the chief champion of socialism, is clear, yet is only to say that he saw Russia as on the right path, not by any means as having arrived at the goal. Let the worried reader of the Prologue to *The Caucasian Chalk Circle* also read Brecht's poem "Are the People Infallible?"* in which the poet speaks in this vein of the death in 1939 of the Soviet playwright Tretyakov: "My teacher who was great and kind has been shot, sentenced to death by a People's Court as a spy. Suppose he is innocent? The sons of the people have found him guilty. On the supposition that he is innocent, what will he be thinking as he goes to his death?" In any case, to prove Brecht wrong about Russia would not necessarily be to prove him wrong about socialism.

A socialist play, is this a play for Socialists only? That, ultimately, is for non-Socialists to

* Full text in *Tulane Drama Review*, Summer 1966, and *Nation*, April 18, 1966.

decide. From Brecht's viewpoint, a lot of people are potential Socialists who might—at this time, in this place—be very surprised to hear it. In principle it is a play for all who are not identified with those it shows to be the common enemy, and in actuality it may turn out to be a play even for some of those who *are* identified with the enemy, since they may not recognize the identification, preferring a life-illusion. French aristocrats applauded *Figaro. The Threepenny Opera* must have been enjoyed by many who, very shortly afterward, voted for Hitler.

The Prologue shows a country (forget it is Russia, if that offends you) where Reason has made inroads upon Unreason. Unreason, in *The Caucasian Chalk Circle,* takes the form of private property, and the laws that guarantee it. "Property is theft," and, by paradox, a private person who steals another private person's property, infringing the law, only re-enacts the original rape of the earth, and confirms the law—of private property. The characters in *Chalk Circle* who most firmly believe in private property are most actively engaged in fighting over private property—whether to cling to it or grab it.

Where is private property's most sensitive spot? One learns the answer whenever a businessman announces that his son will be taking over the business or whenever a spokesman for all things holy comes to his favorite theme of mother and child.

. . . of all ties, the ties of blood are strongest. Mother and child, is there a more intimate relationship? Can one tear a child from its mother? High Court of Justice, she has conceived it in the holy ecstasies of love, she has carried it in her womb, she has fed it with her blood, she has borne it with pain. . . .

This is the voice of one of the spokesmen for all things holy in *The Caucasian Chalk Circle,* and so, when the possession of a child has been in dispute, whether at the court of Solomon in Israel, or before a Chinese magistrate in the year 1000 A.D., the question asked has been only: Which womb did it come out of? Which loins begat it? The ultimate *locus* of private property is in the private parts.

Plato had other plans. He knew that a given parent may in fact be the worst person to bring up his or her child. Our concern, he assumes, should be to produce the best human beings, the best society, not to sacrifice these ends to an, after all, arbitrary notion of "natural" right. The point about an umbilical cord is that it has to be cut. Children should be assigned to those best qualified to bring them up. . . . Plato's Republic *is* "the home of Reason."

The Georgia of *The Caucasian Chalk Circle* is not. After a Prologue which provides a hint of what it would mean to begin to create a home for Reason on this earth, the play transports us to a world which, for all its exotic externals, is nothing other than the world we live in, *our* world, the world of Unreason, of Disorder, of Injustice. Those who are upset by the idealizations of the Prologue, by its "utopianism," need not fret. The play itself provides an image of life in its customary mode, soiled, stinking, cruel, and outrageous.

Even in a jungle, lovely flowers will spring up here and there, such being the fecundity of nature, and however badly our pastors and masters run our society, however much they pull to pieces that which they claim to be keeping intact, nature remains fecund, human beings are born with human traits, sometimes human strength outweighs human weakness, and human grace shows itself amid human ugliness. "In the bloodiest times," as our play has it, "there are kind people." Their kindness is arbitrary. No sociologist could deduce it from the historical process. Just the contrary. It represents the brute refusal of nature to be submerged in history and therefore, arguably (and this *is* Brecht's argument), the possibility that the creature should, at some future point, subdue history.

For the present, though—a present that has spread itself out through the whole course of historical time—the sociologists win, and man is not the master but the slave of society. History is the history of power struggles conducted (behind the moralistic rhetoric familiar to us all from the mass media) with minimum scrupulousness and maximum violence. To give way

to the promptings of nature, to natural sympathy, to the natural love of the Good, is to be a Sucker. America invented that expressive word, and America's most articulate comedian, W. C. Fields, called one of his films *Never Give a Sucker an Even Break*. Which is the credo of Western civilization as depicted in the works of Bertolt Brecht.

In *The Caucasian Chalk Circle* a sucker gets an even break. That seems contradictory, and in the contradiction—or contradictiousness—lies the whole interest of the story. Or rather of its second part. In the first part, we see the inevitable working itself out. The sucker—the good girl who gives way to her goodness—is not given any breaks at all. She is punished for her non-sin, her anti-sin. She loses everything, both the child she has saved and adopted, and the soldier-fiancé whom she has loyally loved and waited for. She is abandoned, isolated, stripped, torn apart, like other people in Brecht's plays and our world who persist in the practice of active goodness.

> The Ironshirts took the child, the beloved
> child.
> The unhappy girl followed them to the city,
> the dreaded city.
> She who had borne him demanded the child.
> She who had raised him faced trial.

So ends Part One: a complete Brecht play in itself. In Part Two Brecht was determined to put the question: Suppose the inevitable did not continue to work itself out? Now how could he do this? By having a Socialist revolution destroy private property and establish the rule of Reason? That is what he would have done, had he been as narrow and doctrinaire as some readers of his Prologue assume. But what is in the Prologue is not in the play itself. For the second half of his play Brecht invented a new version of the Chalk Circle legend, which is also a new version of another idea from literary tradition, the idea that the powers that be can sometimes be temporarily overthrown and a brief Golden Age ensue.

> Who will decide the case?
> To whom will the child be assigned?

Who will the judge be? A good judge? A bad?
The city was in flames.
In the judge's seat sat—Azdak.

Inevitably, necessarily, a judge in the society depicted in *The Caucasian Chalk Circle* must assign a child to its actual mother. In that proposition, the law of private property seems to receive the sanction of Mother Nature herself —that is to say, the owners of private property are able to appeal to nature without conscious irony. Such an event, however, would give Brecht at best a brief epilogue to Part One. What gives him a second part to his play, and one which enables him in the end to pick up the loose ends left by the Prologue, is that the judge is Azdak, and that Azdak is a mock king, an Abbot of Unreason, a Lord of Misrule, who introduces "a brief Golden Age, almost an age of justice."

The reign of Zeus [says F. M. Cornford in *The Origin of Attic Comedy*] stood in the Greek mind for the existing moral and social order; its overthrow, which is the theme of so many of the comedies, might be taken to symbolise . . . the breaking up of all ordinary restraints, or again . . . the restoration of the Golden Age of Justice and Loving-kindness, that Age of Kronos which lingered in the imagination of poets, like the afterglow of a sun that had set below the horizon of the Age of Iron. The seasonal festivals of a Saturnalian character celebrated the return, for a brief interregnum, of a primitive innocence that knew not shame, and a liberty that at any other time would have been licentious. Social ranks were inverted, the slave exercising authority over the master. At Rome each household became a miniature republic, the slaves being invested with the dignities of office. A mock king was chosen to bear rule during the festival, like the mediaeval Abbot of Unreason or Lord of Misrule.

In this case, how is the play any different from the Prologue, except in the temporariness of Azdak's project? Its temporariness is of a piece with its precariousness, its freakishness, its skittishness, its semiaccidental character. Only with a touch of irony can one say that Azdak establishes a Golden Age or even that he is a good judge. The age remains far from

golden, and his judging is often outrageous enough. But his *extra*ordinary outrages call our attention to the ordinary outrages of ordinary times—to the fact that outrage *is* ordinary, is the usual thing, and that we are shocked, not by injustice per se, but only by injustice that favors the poor and the weak. Azdak did not rebuild a society, nor even start a movement that had such an end in view. He only provided Georgia with something to think about and us with a legend, a memory, an image.

So much for the ideological *schema*. The play would be too rigidly schematic if Brecht had just brought together the Good Girl with the Appropriate Judge, using both characters simply as mouthpieces for a position. There is more to both of them than that. Azdak is one of the most complex figures in modern drama.

Discussing the role of the Ironical Man in ancient comedy, F. M. Cornford remarks that "the special kind of irony" he practices is

feigned stupidity. The word Ironist itself in the fifth century appears to mean "cunning" or (more exactly) "sly." Especially it meant the man who masks his batteries of deceit behind a show of ordinary good nature or indulges a secret pride and conceit of wisdom, while he affects ignorance and self-depreciation, but lets you see all the while that he could enlighten you if he chose, and so makes a mock of you. It was for putting on these airs that Socrates was accused of "irony" by his enemies.

This passage sets forth what I take to be the preliminary design of Azdak's character, but then Brecht complicates the design. Azdak is not simply an embodiment of an ironical viewpoint, he is a person with a particular history, who needs irony for a particular reason—and not all the time. It is through the chinks in the ironical armor that we descry the man. *Azdak is not being ironical when he tells us he wanted to denounce himself for letting the Grand Duke escape.* He supposed, it seems, that, while the Grand Duke and his Governors were busy fighting the Princes, the carpet weavers had brought off a popular revolution, and, as a revolutionary, he wished to denounce himself for a counter-revolutionary act.

What kind of revolutionary was he? A very modern kind: a disenchanted one. Those who like to compare Azdak the Judge to Robin Hood should not fail to compare Azdak the Politician to Arthur Koestler. Before the present revolt of the carpet weavers, decades earlier, there had been another popular uprising. Azdak maintains, or pretends, that this was in his grandfather's time, forty years ago, and not in Georgia, but in Persia. His two songs—which lie at the very heart of our play—tell both of the conditions that produced the uprising and of the uprising itself.* The pretense is that revolution represents disorder, and the suppression of revolutions, order; and that Azdak is appealing to the Generals to restore order. This last item is not a hollow pretense or a single irony, for Azdak has not championed revolt. He has withdrawn into his shell. His job as a "village scrivener" is the outward token of the fact. In a note, Brecht advises the actor of the role not to imagine that Azdak's rags directly indicate his character. He wears them, Brecht says, as a Shakespearean wears the motley of a fool. Azdak is not lacking in wisdom. Only it is the bitter wisdom of the disillusioned intellectual, and, in Brecht's view, a partly false wisdom

* Azdak's "Song of Chaos" is adapted from a translation of an ancient Egyptian lament, brought to notice in 1903, but dating back to about 2500 B.C. The document describes a state of social disintegration and revolt, appeals to the King and other authorities to take action. Brecht reverses the point of view, as his custom is, but since he does so ironically, he is able to stay close to such words of the original as the following:

Nay, but the highborn are full of lamentations, and the poor are full of joy. Every town saith: 'Let us drive out the powerful from our midst.'
Nay, but the son of the highborn man is no longer to be recognized. The child of his lady is become [no more than] the son of his handmaid.
Nay, but the boxes of ebony are broken up. Precious sesnem [sic] wood is out in pieces for beds.
Nay, but the public offices are opened and their lists [of serfs] are taken away. Serfs become lords of serfs.
Behold, ladies lie on cushions [in lieu of beds] and magistrates in the storehouse. He that could not sleep upon walls now possesseth a bed.
Behold, he that never build for himself a boat now possesseth ships. He that possessed the same looketh at them, but they are no longer his.
(Translated from the Egyptian by A. M. Blackman, and published in *The Literature of the Ancient Egyptians* by Adolf Erman. London, 1927.)

prompted not alone by objective facts but quite as much by the "wise" man's own limitations.

Azdak has the characteristic limitation of the Brechtian rogue: cowardice. Or at any rate: courage insufficient to the occasion. He is Brecht's Herr Keuner saying no to tyranny only after the tyrant is safely dead. At least, this is how Azdak is, if left to himself. Yet, like other human beings, he is not a fixed quantity but influenceable by the flow of things, and especially by the people he meets. A passive sort of fellow, he acts less than he *re*acts. Our play describes his reaction to a new and unforeseen situation, and especially, in the end, to a single person: Grusha. Which gives the last section of the play its organic movement.

Azdak needs drawing out, and what Brecht does is expose him to a series of persons and situations that do draw him out. (That he also brings with him into the Golden Age his unregenerate self creates the comic contradictions. It is hard, through all the little trial scenes, to tell where selfishness leaves off and generosity begins: this is a source of amusement, and also enables Brecht to question accepted assumptions on the relation of social and antisocial impulses.) The Test of the Chalk Circle with which the action culminates does not follow automatically from the philosophy of Azdak but is a product of a dramatic development. At the outset he is in no mood to be so good or so wise. He has just been mercilessly beaten, but then he reacts in his especially sensitive way to all that ensues, and above all to the big speech in which Grusha denounces him:

AZDAK. Fined twenty piasters!
GRUSHA. Even if it was thirty, I'd tell you what I think of your justice, you drunken onion! How dare you talk to me like the cracked Isaiah on the church window? As if you were somebody. You weren't born to this. You weren't born to rap your own mother on the knuckles if she swipes a little bowl of salt someplace. Aren't you ashamed when you see how I tremble before you? You've made yourself their servant so they won't get their houses stolen out from under them—houses they themselves stole! Since when did a house belong to its bedbugs? But you're their watchdog, or how would they get our men into their wars? Bribe

taker! I don't respect you. No more than a thief or a bandit with a knife. Do what you like. You can all do what you like, a hundred against one, but do you know who should be chosen for a profession like yours? Extortioners! Men who rape children! Let it be their punishment to sit in judgment on their fellow men! Which is worse than to hang from the gallows.

AZDAK. Now it is thirty.

She could hardly know how she got under his skin. Her denunciation, quite guileless and spontaneous, happens to be couched in just the terms that come home to him. For she is representing him as a traitor to his class. Who does he think he is, who is now setting himself up as a Lord over his own people? Well, in his own view, Azdak *was* something of a traitor to his class, but he has been busy for a year or two trying to make it up to them, and now Grusha is providing him with the happiest of all occasions to prove this. His decision to give her the child grows out of his sense of guilt and out of his delight in opportunities to make good.

One could say, too, that his earlier confrontation with Granny Grusinia prepares the way for the later one with Grusha. Here, too, he has to be drawn out, partly by threats, but even more by finding again his original identification with the cause of the people. Between them, Granny Grusinia and Grusha are the Marxian, Brechtian version of the "eternal feminine" whom our blundering, uncourageous Faust needs, if he is to move "onwards and upwards." Hence, although the Chalk Circle incident occupies only a minute or two at the end of a long play, it is rightly used for the title of the whole.

The incident not only clarifies the meaning of Azdak, it also brings together the various thematic threads of the play. In the first instance, there is the stated conclusion:

Take note of what men of old concluded:
That what there is shall go to those who
    are good for it, thus:
Children to the motherly, that they prosper,
Carts to good drivers, that they be driven well,
The valley to the waterers, that it yield fruit.

But this was never in doubt. Any spectator who has spent the evening hoping for a surprise at the end courted disappointment. He should have been warned by the Prologue. In an early draft Brecht planned to let the decision on the collective farms wait till the Chalk Circle story has been told. That, however, is politically ludicrous, if it means, as it would have to, that Soviet planners depend on folksingers in the way that some other leaders depend upon astrologers. And an infringement of a main principle of Brechtian drama would have occurred. In this type of play there should be no doubt as to what is going to happen, only as to how and why.

The valley is assigned to the waterers already in the Prologue, and already in the first scenes that follow we see that Michael has a bad mother but has been befriended by a better one. What remains to be said? On what grounds can we be asked to stay another couple of hours in the theatre? One sufficient reason would be: to see Grusha *become* the mother. This is not Plato's Republic, and Grusha is no trained educator in a Platonic crèche. In the first phase of the action her purpose is only to rescue the child, not keep it: she is going to leave it on a peasant's doorstep and return home. We see the child becoming hers by stages, so that when Azdak reaches his verdict in the final scene, he is not having a brainstorm ("Grusha would be a splendid mother for this child") but recognizing an accomplished fact ("She *is* the mother of this child"). Another paradox: in this play that says possession is not nine-tenths of the law we learn that (in another sense) possession is ten-tenths of the law.

It should not escape notice that, in the end, the child becomes Simon Shashava's too:

GRUSHA. You like him?

SIMON. With my respects, I like him.

GRUSHA. Now I can tell you: I took him because on that Easter Sunday I got engaged to you. So he's a child of love.

Michael had been a child of the loveliness of his actual mother and the lifelessness of his actual father, but now it turns out that he will have a father who has been spared death in war and is very much alive, and a mother who did not love him at his conception, nor yet at his delivery, but who loves him *now*. The term "lovechild" is applied to bastards, and Michael, who was legitimate in the legal sense, however illegitimate humanly and morally, will now become a bastard in a sense which the story . . . legitimizes.

> Your father is a bandit
> A harlot the mother who bore you
> Yet honorable men
> Shall kneel before you.
>
> Food to the baby horses
> The tiger's son will take.
> The mothers will get milk
> From the son of the snake.

Brecht's play broadens out into myth, and we hear many echoes—from the Bible, from Pirandello—but it is more relevant to see the phenomenon the other way around: not that Brecht lets his story spread outward toward other stories, but that he uses other stories, and mythical patterns, and pulls them in, brings them, as we say, "down to earth," in concrete, modern meanings. Most important, in this regard, is Brecht's use of what a recent scholar has called festive comedy. *The Caucasian Chalk Circle* is not an *inquiry* into the dispute over ownership presented in the Prologue but a *celebration* of the assignment of the land to "those who are good for it."

A main preoccupation of this oldest form of comedy in Western tradition was with Impostors. The point of comedy was, and has remained, to expose the imposture. *The Caucasian Chalk Circle* does this, for what could be a more gross imposture than the claims to either rulership or parenthood of the Abashwili couple? But Brecht does not leave the ancient patterns alone. Even as he turns around the old tale of the Chalk Circle, so also he plays his ironic, dialectical game with the patterns. *For Azdak and Grusha are imposters too.* That is what makes them brother and sister under the

skin. In the imposter-mother, the imposter-judge recognizes his own.

> As if it was stolen goods she picked it up.
> As if she was a thief she sneaked away.

Thus the Singer, describing how Grusha got the baby. He is too generous. Legally, she *is* a thief; the child *is* stolen goods; and Azdak has "stolen" the judgeship, though, characteristically, not on his own initiative: he is, if you will, a receiver of stolen goods. The special pleasure for Azdak in his Chalk Circle verdict is that, at the moment when he will return his own "stolen" goods to their "rightful" owners, he is able to give Grusha and Simon "their" child in (what they can hope is) perpetuity.

I have called the irony a game, for art is a game, but this is not to say that Brecht's playfulness is capricious. In the inversion lies the meaning, and it is simply our good fortune that there is fun in such things, that, potentially at least, there is fun in *all* human contradictions and oppositions. The old patterns have, indeed, no meaning for Brecht *until* they are inverted. For instance, this important pattern: the return to the Age of Gold. We, the modern audience, Russian or American, *return* to the Age of Gold when we see Azdak inverting our rules and laws. Azdak *returns* to an Age of Gold when he nostalgically recalls the popular revolt of a former generation. On the other hand, the Age of Azdak is not, literally, an Age of Gold at all. It is an age of war and internecine strife in which just a little justice can, by a fluke, be done. Nor is the traditional image of a Golden Age anything like a revolutionary's happy memories of days on the barricades: just the reverse. Finally, Brecht repudiates our hankering after past Ages of Gold altogether. That revolutions, for Azdak, are identified with the past is precisely what is wrong with him. In *The Caucasian Chalk Circle* we move back in order to move forward. The era of Azdak has the transitory character of the Saturnalia and so is properly identified with it. After the interregnum is over, the mock king goes back into anonymity, like Azdak. But the Prologue suggests a *regnum* that is not accidental and shortlived but deliberate and perhaps not *inter.* And then there is the ultimate inversion: that the Golden Age should be envisaged not in the past but in the future, and not in fairyland or heaven, but in Georgia.

The Russian Georgia. But ours is included, at least in the sense that the play is about our twentieth century world, and in a specific way. As Brecht saw things, this century came in on a wave of democratic hope. A new age was dawning, or seemed to be. So universally was this felt that the most powerful of counterrevolutionary movements, the Hitler movement, had to represent itself as Socialist and announce, in its turn, the dawn of a new 'age. It could bring in no dawn of its own, of course, but in Germany it certainly prevented the arrival of the dawn that had seemed imminent.

This grouping of forces is what we have in *The Caucasian Chalk Circle.* A true dawn is promised by the rebellious carpet weavers. It never arrives, because the Ironshirts are paid to cut the weavers to pieces. At this point, when a triumphant Fat Prince enters, very much in the likeness of Marshal Goering, Azdak points at him with the comment: There's your new age all right! The thought of the new age, the longing for a new age, hovers over *The Caucasian Chalk Circle* from beginning to end, and any good production would seem haunted by it.

The Prologue will say different things to different people as to what has already been achieved and where, but to all it conveys Brecht's belief that the new age is possible. What his audience is to be haunted by is not a memory, a fantasy, or a dream, but a possibility.   (*1966*)

Alcestis and *The Cocktail Party*

BY ROBERT B. HEILMAN

In revealing, in 1951, the affinity between his *Cocktail Party* and Euripides' *Alcestis,* T. S. Eliot permitted himself a hint of triumph that this relationship had not yet (two years after the first performance of his play) been detected. Mr. Eliot had had the very human satisfaction of keeping his secret, and in keeping it he had incidentally insured that the immediate criticism of *The Cocktail Party* would not be, like that of *The Family Reunion,* confused by observations upon its genealogy.

After the pleasure of keeping silent, there was the pleasure of breaking the silence and of proclaiming the unsuspected truth. But this pleasure, with its legitimate histrionic ingredient,

ALCESTIS AND THE COCKTAIL PARTY From *Comparative Literature,* V (1953). Reprinted by permission of the author and of the publisher.

must have been compounded by the fact that the hidden history now brought to light was really not quite credible. Mr. Eliot admitted that it took "detailed explanation" to convince his acquaintance of the "genuineness of the inspiration." For the public, his unelaborated assertion of the kinship remains almost shocking; surely one of the minor Greek dramas, very much less than a tragedy though considerably more than a satyr play, seems the unlikeliest source for a "sophisticated" contemporary play, with its dominant comedy of manners, its intimation of tragedy, its reminiscences of parable, and its ambiguity. The bafflingness which hangs over *The Cocktail Party* is the least conspicuous trait of *Alcestis.* Nor did Eliot cushion his shock by outlining parallels that would compel recognition and assent.

Rather his public statement had the effect of retaining, at the moment of revelation, something of the mystery, for he noted only a single resemblance—that of the eccentric guest who drinks and sings. But in *The Cocktail Party* the Unidentified Guest's partiality to gin and song is so incidental that one is scarcely aware of it except at the level of theatrical gag; that it may have been suggested by Heracles' conduct at Admetus's palace is of no help whatsoever in assessing the serious role of Sir Henry Harcourt-Reilly. Perhaps Mr. Eliot believed that further elaboration would be uninteresting; or perhaps his tip was partly playful, embodying the incomplete confession of a devoted entertainer carrying a little further the theatrical game to which he had committed himself. Or there's another possibility; Mr. Eliot's apparent joke may be a pedagogical joke, and his meager clue to what he has done an invitation to seek out the heart of his performance.

About the intention of his announcement we need not speculate; but the fact is that to look at *The Cocktail Party* steadily in the light of *Alcestis* is to see some of its lineaments a little more clearly (and, conversely, the Eliot play provides a perspective from which one can discern potentialities, perhaps unsuspected, in the Euripides play). Again, one need not inquire into the formal intention of the playwright, which at best is likely to be more complex or fluid than some students of literature may be predisposed to admit or than the author himself may be aware—and which, as the work itself assumes autonomy, may undergo progressive and radical modifications until, in the end, the "intention" realized in the completed work may be quite different from the "intention" which presided over the first strokes of composition. We might say, for instance, that Eliot intended to "imitate" *Alcestis* or to write a "creative revision" (cf. Dryden's "regulative revision" of *Antony and Cleopatra*) or a "dramatic analogue" of it, but all of these formulations would be loose. I would rather say, going on the evidence of the plays, that *The Cocktail Party* seizes upon thematic material latent in *Alcestis* and dramatically explores it further, reinter-

prets it, and enlarges it. As Raymond Radiguet has said, "A creative writer runs no risk in 'copying' a work, since this is impossible to him. The creative mind will instinctively discard the model, and use it only as a fulcrum."

Eliot may even have got a hint from the tone of *Alcestis* and then, as with theme and character, gone markedly beyond his original. *Alcestis* is, in our terms, romantic comedy; but its distinction lies in its almost daring flirtation with tragedy. From one point of view, Admetus is like a Molière butt; from another, he is almost the tragic hero—the "good man" with a flaw that leads to disaster, and with some capacity for self-recognition. Admetus comes very close to the soul searching of an Oedipus or an Othello: "O my friends, what then avails it that I live, if I must live in misery and shame?" But his facing of the situation he has brought about, his facing of himself, his facing of guilt —all this is cut short by a miraculous intervention which, in restoring Alcestis to him, accomplishes that adjustment of circumstance which is at the heart of the comic mode. Eliot calls his play "a comedy," and in its wit, in its agile use of incongruity, and in its espousal of accommodation as a value its comic quality is plain. But Edward and Lavinia Chamberlayne are both treated like Admetus in being compelled to undergo moral introspection; indeed, theirs is very much more severe and penetrating than his, and to that extent *The Cocktail Party* goes further toward the tone of tragedy. Besides, there is Celia, who alone of the dramatis personae is capable of living tragically. But her derivation from *Alcestis,* if indeed she does derive from it, is a problem of character to which we return later.

The way in which Eliot has imaginatively worked out from *Alcestis* in his own direction will be most clear if we first notice the parallels in plot, the anatomical resemblances, between the two plays. These are astonishingly frequent. The action of *Alcestis* takes place on the day on which Alcestis dies for Admetus, the action of *The Cocktail Party* begins on the day Lavinia leaves Edward. Admetus is grief-stricken, Edward is chagrined and even seriously disturbed. However, Admetus is most hospitable to Heracles, and Edward carries on with the cocktail party, trying to be a good host to his guests. Admetus minimizes the seriousness of the situation by concealing the fact that it is his wife who has died; likewise Edward tries to pass off Lavinia's desertion as something less serious, a visit to a sick aunt. By giving Edward not one but many guests to contend with, Eliot has enlarged the social situation created for Admetus by the arrival of Heracles.

But if Heracles in one sense becomes many guests, the parallel between him and the Unidentified Guest is not given up but is rather carefully elaborated. Heracles' arrival is unscheduled, the Guest appears to have "crashed" the cocktail party. Immediately on Heracles' arrival, his courage and resourcefulness are established for us by his telling the Chorus about his adventures; as soon as the Guest talks to Edward alone, he exhibits confidence and authority. Heracles' questioning of Admetus is exactly paralleled by the Guest's blunt interrogation of Edward. As Eliot has told us, Heracles gets drunk and uproarious, and the Guest drinks and sings. The Servant reproves Heracles for his conduct; Julia mockingly reproaches Edward,

> You've been *drinking* together!
> So this is the kind of friend you have
> When Lavinia is out of the way! Who is he?

Heracles promises to "bring back" Alcestis to Admetus; the Guest, referring to Lavinia, uses the phrase, "If I bring her back," and then assures Edward, "In twenty-four hours/She will come to you here." Heracles makes a game of urging Admetus to give up his grief and find consolation in a new marriage, and similarly the Guest enjoys pointing out to Edward the advantages of independence from his wife; both husbands, of course, want their wives back, and in each story the wife is brought back by the tormentor. Heracles' sudden unveiling of Alcestis is paralleled by Sir Henry's surprise confrontation of Edward and Lavinia in his office; although Lavinia has come back to Edward physically, Sir Henry now takes on the major task of restoring them to each other morally. And, to complete this catalogue of surface likenesses, Death has come literally to Admetus's palace to snatch Alcestis, a fact surely alluded to, humorously, in Julia's exclamation to the newly returned Lavinia, "Don't tell me you were abducted!"

Eliot's variations are plain enough to dispose of any idle supposition that he is simply rephrasing, as it were, an original, just as the evident substance of his own work makes impossible a suspicion of mere virtuoso ingenuity. The ingenuity—even the virtuosity—is there, of course; but having in a sense paid tribute to it by noting the systematic affiliations of play to play, we need to go ahead and see what end it serves. Eliot's underlying performance is the perception and the amplification of certain meanings which inhere in Euripides' plot and characters—in the myth which he took over and in the skillful entertainment which he made of it. When Heracles, reproved by the Servant, makes a lively, imaged promise that he will leap upon Death, wrestle with him, wound him, and compel him to yield up Alcestis, he gives us the background for the Guest's sober statement to Edward: ". . . it is a serious matter/To bring someone back from the dead." From the original action Eliot has distilled an "idea" which he proceeds to work up. Edward replies:

> From the dead?
> That figure of speech is somewhat . . . dramatic,
> As it was only yesterday that my wife left me.

By "dramatic" Edward doubtless means theatrical, improbable—a judgment that might almost seem to have point if we did not see that the metaphor is drawn from the literal story in Euripides. Now, since Eliot has said that he wished the origin of his plot to remain unknown, the reinterpretation of a wife's dying for her husband as a desertion of her husband may seem a dextrous trick of concealment. But it is clearly more than a tour de force; rather, Eliot is taking the literal story and uncovering its symbolic possibilities, or, in other terms, both naturalizing and universalizing the folk mystery. The result—the definition of desertion as death, and, by extension, of the rupture of the marriage as itself a death (rather than, say, a convenience or a casual legality or quest for integrity)—is to compel a reconsideration of the nature of the relationship of Edward and Lavinia, that is of husbands and wives generally, and a profounder sense of what it entails. Husbands and wives are "alive" to each other when their relationship, even a halting one, goes on; in this sense marriage itself is "life." But Eliot is not content to halt at this recognition; he characteristically pushes on to the paradox that must be assimilated. The Guest replies to Edward:

> Ah, but we die to each other daily.
> What we know of other people
> Is only our memory of the moments
> During which we knew them.*

In the more obvious sense death is departure, separation, rupture; but in a profounder sense, death is ever present, inevitable, the unbridgeable separateness of men and women even in their most intimate relationship. Marriage is life, but this life must be understood to include death. The doctrine does not propose despair, however, but looks toward conquering the death of separation by a reunion grounded in the acknowledgement of imperfect actuality. Through "death" they gain not eternal, but temporal, life, which must include something of death. This "moralizing" of the literal death in Euripides is one source of the relative spaciousness of Eliot's drama. Another source is Eliot's working out of the potentialities of Euripides' characters.

The treatment of Edward and Lavinia in Acts II and III of *The Cocktail Party* leaves us with so strong a sense, first, of the need of both of them to understand themselves and to

work toward making "the best of a bad job," as Edward calls it, and then, of their reciprocal efforts to achieve what Reilly calls "a good life," that we are likely to forget the situation in Act I, when the picture we are given is not of a blowup caused by equal failure on both sides, but of Lavinia's precipitating the break through motives which she at least regards as generous and helpful. She tells Edward:

> I thought that if I died
> To you, I who had been only a ghost to you,
> You might be able to find the road back
> To a time when you were real—

Again the double value of death: death as a breaking of their life, and death as a concomitant of their life—though here, in Lavinia's view, it has gone beyond the "normal" alienation of individuals implied in the earlier speeches of Reilly (the Guest). In the fine paradox of the "ghost" who can "die" Eliot has amplified the Euripides story, just as he has subtly varied it by the minute change of *die for* to *die to*. In granting to Lavinia an element of unselfishness (and in this instance she is hardly to be read as a victim of self-deception), Eliot retains the center of Alcestis's character, but at the same time he alters the proportions. In Alcestis the over-all emphasis is on the spirit of sacrifice, with the self-regarding emotions coming in secondly and secondarily—some self-righteousness, some resentment against Admetus's parents, and a bargaining sense and fondness for power which lead her to proscribe remarriage for Admetus. In Lavinia we have only a glimpse of generosity, and see her mainly (before the new self-discipline and insight of Act III) as an agile combatant in marriage, opposing her husband with a selfishness that complements his own, and with a managerial tendency derived from Alcestis but greatly expanded.

This change of proportions, however, is less important than another difference; Eliot has really seen two characters in Alcestis—the ordinary woman and the saint—and has boldly split Alcestis into Lavinia and Celia (whose name, we may suppose, is not an accident). On the face of it such a split looks like a reduction of one complex

---

* Several lesser details in this scene involve, despite the ironic seriousness of tone, a kind of joking reminder of *Alcestis.* When Edward asks, "So you want me to greet my wife as a stranger?", and the Guest prescribes, "When you see your wife, you must ask no questions", we can hardly fail to see a recasting of Euripides' final scene, in which the veiled Alcestis is a "stranger" to Admetus and in which Admetus is told Alcestis must preserve a three-day silence. The ritual requirement is translated into a psychiatric stratagem.

person (the woman not completely submerged in the nun, as Lowes said of Chaucer's Prioress) into two simpler ones—the housewife and the *religieuse.* But Eliot is very careful to leave neither wife nor saint at a level of allegorical simplicity. He endows Lavinia with some trace of the self-abnegatory and with a capacity for understanding herself and others and for feeling a general moral responsibility in the world— just as he compels Celia to earn her sainthood by the trial and error of an affair with Edward, by the "desperation" of a sense of aloneness and sin, and by the rigors of her "journey." The fact that he makes the split shows the influence of his belief upon the form of the materials in which his play originates; world and spirit are different realities, and must be represented in different dramatic actions (since Lavinia—and with her, Edward—is granted a kind of "salvation" within their ordinary, secular world, we can see Eliot's development from *The Family Reunion,* in which, so to speak, salvation was possible only to spirit and the world was simply condemned for not being spirit). As the possessor of a rare capacity for spiritual achievement, Celia appears in a dramatic movement which in effect reverses that of Alcestis. Alcestis has performed her great act of spirit before the play opens, and a considerable part of her own actions on the stage show her dwindling into a wife, whereas Celia grows, having to discover the inadequacy for her of the mere wifely, so to speak (she sees that she had created Edward, her lover and possible husband, out of her own aspiration), before she can make her great choice of the "second way." Yet at that it is remarkable how much of the Alcestis story remains in the treatment of Celia—for instance, the suffering and horror of the final experience, as both dramatists instinctively guard against the cloying effect of the Griselda motif. Alcestis cries out, "What a path must I travel,/O most hapless of women!" and Reilly acknowledges to Celia "It is a terrifying journey" and says after her death,

I'd say she suffered all that we should suffer
In fear and pain and loathing—all those
    together—

And reluctance of the body to become a *thing.*
I'd say she suffered more, because more
    conscious
Than the rest of us. She paid the highest price
In suffering. That is part of the design.

Euripides' story is virtually made for Christian readaptation—a human being dying that another may live and then rising from the dead. Eliot omits the resurrection, except symbolically, perhaps, in the impact of the Celia story on others, but he does heighten the Christian analogy by having Celia die by crucifixion. At this point, unfortunately, the drama of Celia has trailed off into an undramatic post mortem.

Eliot has drawn heavily upon Admetus, not only in such details of the action as we have mentioned, but in the general outlines of the moral experience. As soon as Alcestis actually leaves him, Admetus begins to realize her value to him; he tells Heracles that he does not want another wife. Likewise Edward realizes his need for Lavinia and rejects Celia, whom now he might have. In fact, when Eliot makes Edward say both "I cannot live with her" and "I cannot live without her," he is echoing Admetus's situation, with a very ironic twist in meaning. For both men the sense of loss and the following scenes of recrimination lead to a fairly thorough experience of self-recognition, and after the self-recognition each gets his wife back (for Edward, the recognition and the return have several phases). At the end each play leaves the impression of a successfully continuing marriage, though Eliot has made a major point of studying the impact upon their relationship of the exploration of self which each participant has undergone, whereas Euripides entirely excludes consideration of the quality of the postre-union marriage.

While it would be easy to pass over the story of Admetus as simply another fantasy or popular tale of wonder, as many readers are probably inclined to do, Eliot has plainly seen that it has great symbolic possibilities and has modeled on Admetus a character who embodies a great deal of the ordinary man moving toward middle age and even of ordinary humanity generally. One can imagine Eliot consciously refusing to regard Admetus as simply a stock figure in a romantic drama, replaceable by any other stock figure who could be called a husband, but instead taking him seriously as a character and asking, "What kind of man would ask others to die for him? What is the meaning of the situation that he has worked himself into?" Perhaps he read Admetus as a precursor of the Struldbrugs, as an early instance in the tradition of human beings who want to live forever; for the play makes some inquiry into the human discontent with the limitations of the human condition. The man who has fallen out with his fate is "a middle-aged man/Beginning to know what it is to feel old" and unassured and disenchanted. He is not without intelligence and imagination, but he is limited in both (Edward speaks of his "dull . . . spirit of mediocrity"). Again, he "has no sense of humour," as Lavinia says of Edward, who makes a good target for her wit and fails to join Celia and Lavinia in humorous recognition of their joint plight. He is given to feeling sorry for himself. When Edward says, "I have had enough of people being sorry for me," he opens himself up to Lavinia's riposte, "Yes, because they can never be so sorry for you/As you are for yourself. And that's hard to bear." He is a self-deceiver, as is Lavinia; Reilly says to them, "My patients such as you are the self-deceivers." Edward is vastly self-centered; the phase of self-discovery which goes on after Lavinia's return is a lamentation on the theme, "Hell is oneself," so painfully carried on that Lavinia's reply has justice, "Could you bear, for a moment,/To think about *me?*" To be self-centered is to be lacking in love; Lavinia says that Edward "has never been in love with anybody." He lives not understandingly but mechanically; Reilly says that he is "a set/Of obsolete responses." Edward wants to be "bolstered, encouraged/ . . . To think well of yourself," as Lavinia sharply tells him.

In all this, Eliot has shrewdly amplified Admetus or actualized what is latent in him. What is more—and what is not so immediately apparent—Edward's affair with Celia is certainly to be understood as a version of Admetus's wanting someone to die for him; in each case

what is at stake is self-esteem, and the heart of the action is a testing for loyalties and flattering responses. We see this unmistakably in Edward, who comes to realize that Celia has been a psychological utility rather than an object of love; and Eliot's keen analysis of Edward enables us to perceive that Admetus's quest for a substitute die-er proceeds, not only from obvious love of life, but also from some self-doubt, some sense of inadequacy to role. Perhaps we might claim as a general truth that excessive love of life is a function of a feared, or sensed, or actual mediocrity in life. Admetus, then, cannot be disposed of simply as a ridiculous or incredible figure. Rather his poll of life-giving alternates, with its expressionistic immediacy that is initially shocking, exhibits a familiar human need—the need to have reassurance about one's own significance and power in the world. Wanting an additional life and wanting an additional love come to much the same thing. Both heroes are Everyman wrestling with the problem which at some time in his life he must face —the problem of knowing that he is not Superman. To Edward one might even apply the familiar modern term "Little Man." But Eliot neither sentimentalizes nor idealizes the Little Man; rather he bids him recognize himself, have no illusions about himself, and come to terms with himself. Further, he unmistakably generalizes the case of Edward, when he has him say, "But I am obsessed by the thought of my own insignificance," as a clear preparation for Reilly's reply:

Half of the harm that is done in this world
Is due to people who want to feel important.
They don't mean to do harm—but the harm
    does not interest them
Or they do not see it, or they justify it
Because they are absorbed in the endless
    struggle
To think well of themselves.

A little later Eliot throws us right back into Euripides when he has Edward say, "I am not afraid of the death of the body,/But this death is terrifying. The death of the spirit—" Here is the death theme again, but now with a variation that sums up the present point. Admetus was afraid of the death of the body, true, but in his fear we have seen a symbolic expression of a sense of spiritual inadequacy, the same sense that, at first unrecognized, determined much of Edward's action. The self-recognition to which Admetus progressed took, as we have seen, this form: ". . . what then avails it that I live, if I just live in misery and shame?" Like Admetus, Edward learns that the real issue is not quantity (of life or love), but quality of life (i.e., "death of the spirit"). But Euripides, who has already pushed the satyr drama as far as it will go, cannot go on to make Admetus act upon his recognition; whereas Edward must still learn that he cannot prescribe the conditions for the life of the spirit but must discover, and make do, whatever potentialities of life lie right there where "death of the spirit" has seemed inevitable.

Edward's mentor, Dr. Reilly, who as "psychiatrist" may seem incontrovertibly modern, also has his roots in the Euripides play. In him, indeed, Eliot combines the functions of two characters in *Alcestis*—of Heracles, as he has indicated, and, almost as importantly, of Pheres. Pheres is the source whom we are likely to miss, because he is easiest to remember as a hurt and bad-tempered father. But Pheres' abuse of Admetus is not only a response to Admetus's attack upon him; it is also in part a painfully accurate analysis of Admetus and in effect a summons to him to see himself as he is: "You were born to live your own life, whether miserable or fortunate; . . . But you . . . you shirked your fate by killing her! . . . You, the worst of cowards, surpassed by a woman who died for you . . ." The shock of this denunciation, as well as his own grief, leads Admetus to face the issue, instead of disguising it by blaming others and blaming Fate, and to achieve a measure of self-understanding. As a professional man and as one who is not on the defensive, Reilly is different from Pheres; but he has the same role of telling unpleasant truths the shock of which drives Edward (and later Lavinia) to a new self-recognition. "Resign yourself to be the fool you are." "You might have ruined three lives/. . . Now there are only two—" ". . . you

have been making up your case/So to speak, as you went along." "You were lying to me . . ."

Since Reilly's chief business is helping human beings to see the truth and find their destiny, it may seem that he is largely explicable as an ingenious version of the angry truth teller, Pheres, and that his resemblance to Heracles—the only resemblance to which Eliot has publicly called attention—stops at certain incidents of conduct, such as conviviality in the midst of distress. To this we might add that Heracles and Reilly both enter the situation at the right time, both show great power, and both effect rescues—the one from Death, the other from death of the spirit. But there is a little more to it than that. Surely to Euripides' audience Heracles must have been an ambivalent figure—to some a boisterous strong man, to others a devoted servant of duty, bringing more than brute force into play. Likewise Reilly can be read as simply an ingenious psychiatrist, but the more alert will have to see in him something more. (Incidentally, it is an easy phonetic leap from *Heracles* or *Hercules* to *Harcourt-Reilly*.)

Eliot would of course sense the doubleness of Heracles, and it is difficult to resist the conclusion that he found in him the suggestion for the thematic basis of his own play—the dualism of world and spirit, and the interpenetration of world by spirit. For Heracles, as the son of Alcmena and Zeus, is half human, half divine; and in Reilly there is an ambiguity which makes a limited naturalistic view of him seem continually inadequate. Not that Reilly is wholly "transhumanized," to use the word applied by Julia to the experience undergone by Celia in her "journey"; just as Heracles, in the words of a recent handbook, "erred occasionally, being half-mortal," so Reilly "must always take risks," and, as he himself says, ". . . sometimes I have made the wrong decision." Nor is he omniscient; Julia reminds him, "You must accept your limitations." But he has remarkable insight and exercises a special power affecting human destiny. And, although his actions may virtually all be accounted for in naturalistic terms, Eliot has been most successful in creating an air, if not of the inexplicable, at least of the unexplained, of the quizzically irregular, of the modestly elusive, of the herculean at once urbane and devoted; from the time when Reilly tells Edward that he (i.e., Edward) has started "a train of events/Beyond your control," and Lavinia confesses (in terms that Alcestis might have used), "Yet something, or somebody, compelled me to come," until the end of the play, we are given continual impressions of mysterious forces in action. With his benedictions, Reilly could be the priest; with his emphasis on free will, on the choice which is uncompelled but which has its consequences, the theologian; yet in his concern with salvation there is another suggestion that is made most sharply when he says, after dismissing Celia, "It is finished." Since the words on the Cross impose a little more weight than the immediate dramatic situation, which is not primarily an ordeal for Reilly, can bear, we are not wholly comfortable with them here. Yet, as a part of the over-all strategy of suggestion, they enlarge the possibilities before us. For the man who died on the Cross was the "Son of God" but born of a mortal mother—just like Heracles; and the death on the Cross was a mode of bringing life to others, just as Heracles brought back Alcestis from Death, and as Reilly rescues his patients from something which both they and we see as a kind of death. To this extent at least we have another hint of the myth of Christ to which we have already seen parallels in the stories of Alcestis and Celia.

Reilly, it thus becomes clear, is considerably more than the psychiatrist whom in so many details he resembles. He is less the psychological repair man than the soul healer. Psychiatry takes on a spiritual dimension. Out of a couple of interlocking triangles in which the participants are at best half alive come four new lives grounded in the recognition and choice of destiny—that of the artist, that of the ordinary, imperfect, but tolerable and even saving marriage, and that of the saint. These transformations appear as more than standardized "adjustment," as, indeed, the product of great labors by a bringer of life who has both an extraordinary personality and special resources, not wholly identified, to draw upon. The situation which Eliot dramatizes is described with notable accuracy in the final chorus of Euripides, which, in the Aldington translation, even "sounds like" Eliot:

Spirits have many shapes,
Many strange things are performed by the
  Gods.
The expected does not always happen.
And God makes a way for the unexpected.
So ends this action.

SUGGESTIONS
FOR FURTHER READING

Suggestions for Further Reading

I. OTHER ROMANCES BY THE SIX PLAYWRIGHTS

Although the *Helen, Ion, and Iphigenia in Tauris* of Euripides are less well-known than his *Alcestis*, each is an equally beautiful example of the romance mode. Similarly, among Shakespeare's four final romances, *The Winter's Tale* is less familiar than its companion piece *The Tempest*, though some consider it richer and more vital. Among the early plays of Shakespeare, *A Midsummer Night's Dream, As You Like It*, and *Twelfth Night*, all romantic comedies, can be fruitfully studied in relation to the playwright's late romances proper. John Gay wrote a sequel to *The Beggar's Opera* called *Polly*, set on a colonial plantation, and another pastoral opera entitled *Acis and Galatea*.

Both are far inferior to his masterpiece, but the student may benefit from reading them and considering why they are less effective. As with Shakespeare, the other late plays of Ibsen, *The Master Builder, Little Eyolf*, and *John Gabriel Borkman*, can be revealingly compared with his earlier romantic plays, *Brand* and *Peer Gynt*. Bertolt Brecht is only rarely and problematically a romantic playwright, but his *Threepenny Opera* does offer a sharp and suggestive contrast with the Gay play on which it is based. Eliot's other romantic comedies in verse are *The Confidential Clerk* and *The Elder Statesman*, the former based on Euripides' *Ion* and the latter, one suspects, on Sophocles' *Oedipus at Colonus*.

II. ROMANCES BY OTHER PLAYWRIGHTS

The late plays of Euripides' older rival Sophocles, *Philoctetes* and *Oedipus at Colonus*, represent a distinct turning toward romance, perhaps in emulation of Euripides. Dramatic romance surrounds Shakespeare on all sides, in the popular extravagances of Thomas Heywood's *Fair Maid of the West* and Robert Greene's *Friar Bacon and Friar Bungay* (a dim prefiguration of *The Tempest*), as well as in the more sophisticated sentimentalities of John Lyly's *Endimion*, George Peele's *Arraignment of Paris*, John Fletcher's *Faithful Shepherdess*, and Beaumont and Fletcher's *Philaster* and *A King and No King*. The Elizabethans also produced two skillful and hilarious parodies of their popular romances: Peele's *Old Wives' Tale* and Francis Beaumont's *Knight of the Burning Pestle*. Outside of England, Italian Renaissance pastoral drama, notably Torquato Tasso's *Aminta* and

Giambattista Guarini's *Il Pastor Fido*, are interesting both in themselves and as influences on Shakespeare and other Elizabethans.

The classicism that intervened between Renaissance and Romantic literature was not congenial to vernacular romance; nevertheless, in its French and English forms, seventeenth-century heroic drama has selective affinities with romance. (When suppressed, romance has always had a way of popping up in unexpected places and guises.) *The Cid* by Pierre Corneille and *The Conquest of Granada* by John Dryden are good examples. It is with Romanticism proper, what Harold Bloom has described as "a renaissance of the Renaissance" in the late eighteenth and early nineteenth century in Germany and England, that dramatic romance again comes to the fore, albeit more in the form of lyrical dramas than stageable plays. The two greatest dramatic products of high Romanticism, Goethe's *Faust* and Shelley's *Prometheus Unbound,* fall into this category and for that reason are not included in this collection. They are absolutely indispensible, however, to a full understanding of such later developments of Romanticism as symbolism and expressionism.

Both of these turn-of-the-century movements concentrate on the lyrical expression of inner states at the expense of action and characterization, thus limiting their theatrical potential. But the serious student of dramatic romance cannot afford to ignore the music-dramas of Richard Wagner, often called the father of symbolist drama, his *Tristan and Isolde* and *Parsifal* being two among a welter of masterpieces. Among symbolist dramas the plays of the Belgian writer Maurice Maeterlinck, notably *Pelléas and Mélisande,* deserve attention. In Germany, Hugo von Hofmannsthal wrote a number of symbolist plays and an adaptation of *Alcestis,* but perhaps his greatest contributions to dramatic romance are his brilliant librettos to the operas of Richard Strauss, *Helen of Egypt* (based on Euripides' romantic version of the myth) and *The Woman Without a Shadow.* The plays with which W. B. Yeats helped to establish an Irish national theater and revive poetic drama in English bear deep affinities with symbolism. *The Shadowy Waters, At the Hawk's Well,* and *The Resurrection* are representative of his ritualized, anti-naturalistic treatments of the legends of the Irish hero Cuchulain and Christ.

The related modern movement of expressionism is noteworthy for two playwrights of enduring importance: August Strindberg, Ibsen's younger contemporary and Swedish rival, and Eugene O'Neill, the dominant genius of the American theater. Strindberg's *A Dream Play, To Damascus,* and *The Ghost Sonata* illustrate the dramatic transformation of the world by and through a central authorial consciousness, the defining principle of expressionism. His *Easter* is closer to the last plays of Ibsen in its skillful combination of expressionism and naturalism. Eugene O'Neill adapted the expressionist technique of Strindberg and several German playwrights to the American stage in a series of experimental plays written during the 1920s. *The Great God Brown, Lazarus Laughed, Days Without End,* and *Marco Millions* are closest in theme and technique to the concerns of this collection. O'Neill is best known for his later tragic and naturalistic plays, but even these, particularly *A Touch of the Poet,* reflect and continue the romantic, or in his term, "super-naturalistic" interest of his youth. It is worth noting that another twentieth-century master, George Bernard Shaw, though not involved with the expressionist movement and working primarily within a naturalistic tradition, did write a few plays of a utopian and romantic cast, notably *The Simpleton of the Unexpected Isles* and *Back to Methuselah.* His more successful *Pygmalion* reworks an age-old theme of romantic transformation in a naturalistic manner.

III. NON-DRAMATIC ROMANCE

The fictional mode of romance obviously is not confined to the drama, and the student may wish to pursue it into the area of narrative verse and prose. Homer's *Odyssey,* the fountainhead of romance tradition, is the place to start. Derived from Homer are several late classical prose romances, Heliodorus' *Aethiopica,* Longus' *Daphnis and Chloe,* and Xenophon's *Ephesiaca;* the latter two are available in *Three Greek Romances,* trans. Moses Hadas (New York, 1953). During the Middle Ages chivalric romance was the dominant mode of secular literature, and any suggested readings are bound to be less than representative. Among the hundreds of medieval romances, Chrétien de Troyes' *Lancelot* and *Perceval,* Gottfried von Strassburg's *Tristan and Isolt,* and Wolfram von Eschenbach's *Parzival* stand out. A useful selection can be found in *Medieval Romances,* eds. R. S. and L. H. Loomis (New York, 1957). In England, Geoffrey Chaucer's *Troilus and Criseyde, Knight's Tale,* and *Franklin's Tale,* as well as the brilliant *Sir Ga-*

wain and the Green Knight, by an unidentified northern contemporary, are the culmination of this medieval tradition. Sir Thomas Malory's *Morte Darthur* is the late medieval source of all subsequent Arthurian romance in English. Classical and chivalric romance combined in the Renaissance to produce a distinguished succession of romantic epics. In Italy, Lodovico Ariosto's *Orlando Furioso* was followed by Torquato Tasso's *Gerusalemme Liberata.* Both exerted a profound influence in England, particularly on Edmund Spenser's *Faerie Queene* and Sir Philip Sidney's *Arcadia,* which influenced, in turn, Shakespeare's final romances.

The Romantic movement in England was, among other things, a revival of romance as a dominant mode, and offers a number of outstanding verse romances to compare with their medieval and Renaissance prototypes: Coleridge's *Rime of the Ancient Mariner* and *Christabel;* Keats's *Endymion* and *Eve of St. Agnes;* Shelley's *Alastor.* Each of the major Victorian poets also continued and modified the work of the Romantics: Tennyson in the *Idylls of the King,* Matthew Arnold in *The Scholar Gypsy,*

and Robert Browning in "Childe Roland to the Dark Tower Came," a dazzling elaboration on Keats's "La Belle Dame Sans Merci."

Although the novel begins in the antiromance of *Don Quixote* and develops its characteristic realism throughout the eighteenth and nineteenth centuries, there are nonetheless a number of works that are more prose romance than novel. The historical romances of Sir Walter Scott, such as *Ivanhoe* and *Rob Roy,* and the adventure stories of Robert Louis Stevenson, notably *Treasure Island,* are more serious than their relegation to children's bookshelves suggests. And in the novels of Joseph Conrad, *Heart of Darkness, Lord Jim,* and *Victory,* among others, romance is raised to its highest power. The tradition of the American novel is especially rich in the pastoral and visionary motifs of romance, from James Fenimore Cooper's *The Prairie* through Mark Twain's *Huckleberry Finn,* Nathaniel Hawthorne's *Blithedale Romance* and *The Marble Faun,* and Herman Melville's *Moby Dick,* to F. Scott Fitzgerald's *The Great Gatsby.*

IV. CRITICISM

In addition to the critical essays reprinted here, the student may wish to consult a number of works that deal with one or more of the six plays and authors from a related point of view. Kenneth Muir's *Last Periods of Shakespeare, Racine, and Ibsen* (Detroit, 1961) and David Grene's *Reality and the Heroic Pattern* (Chicago, 1967) treat the last plays of Shakespeare and Ibsen as mature recapitulations of their authors' careers. The essay by Bernard Knox, "Euripidean Comedy," in *The Rarer Action,* eds. Alan Cheuse and Richard Koffler (New Brunswick, N.J., 1970), points out suggestive parallels between the late plays of Euripides and Shakespeare. A provocative contrast between *Alcestis* and *The Cocktail Party* can be found in William Arrowsmith's "The Comedy of T. S. Eliot," in *English Stage Comedy,* ed. W. K. Wimsatt, Jr. (New York, 1955). *Twentieth*

Century Interpretations of Euripides' Alcestis, ed. John R. Wilson (Englewood Cliffs, N.J., 1968) brings together several essays on that play. *The Tempest* has inspired a vast critical literature, but Northrop Frye's *A Natural Perspective* (New York, 1965) stands out. For a discussion of the romantic dimension of Brecht, see Keith Sagar, "Brecht in Neverneverland: *The Caucasian Chalk Circle,*" in *Modern Drama,* Vol. 9, No. 1 (May, 1966), 11-17. An excellent study of *The Cocktail Party* appears in C. H. Smith, *T. S. Eliot's Dramatic Theory and Practice* (Princeton, 1963).

The critical literature on romance in general is much less extensive than that on tragedy or comedy and is consequently more easily managed by the interested student. A recent introduction to the entire field of romance, *The Romance* by Gillian Beer (London, 1972), is helpful, as are two collections of essays: *Pastoral and Romance: Modern Essays in Criticism,* ed. Eleanor Terry Lincoln (Englewood Cliffs, N.J., 1969), and *Four Essays on Romance,* ed. Herschel Baker (Cambridge, Mass., 1971). More specialized works dealing with one or another aspect of this fictional mode are numerous, and only a few of them can be listed here. On medieval romance, W. P. Ker's *Epic and Romance* (London, 1908) is still useful, as is Jessie Weston's *From Ritual to Romance* (Cambridge, 1920). Charles Muscatine's *Chaucer and the French Tradition* (Berkeley, 1957) deals with Chaucer's use of the mode. On the relation between medieval and Renaissance romance, see Rosamond Tuve, *Allegorical Imagery: Some Medieval Books and their Posterity* (Princeton, 1966), and R. S. Crane, *The Vogue of Medieval Chivalric Romance during the English Renaissance* (Menasha, Wis., 1919). Works on the romantic epics of Ariosto, Tasso, and Spenser and their medieval forerunners include John Arthos, *On the Poetry of Spenser and the Form of Romances* (London, 1956), C. S. Lewis, *The Allegory of Love* (New York, 1958), and A. Bartlett Giamatti, *The Earthly Paradise and the Renaissance Epic* (Princeton, 1966). Of related interest are Samuel Lee Wolff, *The Greek Romances in Elizabethan Prose Fiction* (New York, 1912), and Carol Gesner, *Shakespeare and Greek Romance* (Lexington, Ky., 1970). On the tradition and conventions of pastoral, the student should consult W. W. Greg, *Pastoral Poetry and Pastoral Drama* (London, 1905), Peter Marinelli, *Pastoral* (London, 1972), and David Young, *The Heart's Forest: A Study of Shakespeare's Pastoral Plays* (New Haven, 1972). The continuity of Romanticism with earlier romance is discussed in several of the essays in Geoffrey Hartman's *Beyond Formalism* (New Haven, 1970). Relations between romance and the novel are examined in Ian Watt, *The Rise of the Novel* (London, 1957); Harry Levin, *The Gates of Horn* (New York, 1967); and Robert Kiely, *The Romantic Novel in England* (Cambridge, Mass., 1972). The American prose romance is studied by Richard Chase, *The American Novel and Its Tradition* (New York, 1957), and by Joel Porte, *The Romance in America* (Middletown, 1969). Romantic, or what he terms "messianic," tendencies in modern drama are persuasively traced by Robert Brustein in *The Theatre of Revolt* (Boston, 1964).